"Janine Roberts is that rare individual who unflinchingly speaks truth to power. She battles her way past all the obstacles and provides us a glimpse of those who are in the innermost circles of global power. But instead of being seduced by their power and wealth, she exposes what they do and how they do it and how it comes to hurt us all.

I count myself among the privileged in this world to know Janine and her work. In *Glitter and Greed* she graphically reveals the brutality of those who orchestrate the diamond wars that continue to wreck Africa today. She gave testimony for me at a hearing in Congress that was shocking in its revelations, but thorough in its documentation.

She has hunted down the shady dealers of the diamond cartel and of De Beers, itself. She reveals here for the first time the disturbing secrets of the individuals, governments, and corporations that have ruled the diamond world for the past one hundred years.

Read and get ready to defy conventional wisdom that no one really cares enough to challenge business as usual in the diamond world. For after reading *Glitter and Greed*, you will be compelled to act. Africans should mine, cut, polish, market, distribute, manufacture, and export the jewelry that originates upon its shores in much the same way that France controls its wine production and the United States controls its defense technology."

Former Congresswoman Cynthia McKinney

GLITTER & GREED

The Secret World of the Diamond Empire
by Janine Roberts

disinformation

There are many victims of blood diamonds:

The farmers crippled by landmines bought with diamonds

The children who lose limbs to diamond-mining terrorists

The African miners who dig diamonds for
a pittance under dangerous conditions

The children and young people cutting gem diamonds
in conditions the UN defines as slavery...

... And the customers who buy diamonds without knowing
what they are supporting

Contents

Contents

Preface

Diamonds are crystallized carbon, forged in the interior of volcanoes.

Their raw material is the remains of the early living creatures of this planet deeply buried many eons ago. They breathed or gave off methane gas, which by a strange alchemy became diamonds.

They were not the only crystals created thus. A wealth of other gems surrounded them. They were not the rarest – just the hardest. This hardness made them a symbol of virility worn by men in ancient India. Today pure raw diamonds can be forged by a much more mundane alchemy. I have watched scientists grow flawless diamond gems,

Diamond mineworkers at home.

the "ones in a million," with oxyacetylene torches, creating them out of the methane in Washington, DC sewage gas. De Beers uses a similar process in secretive factories on the Isle of Man and in South Africa – and I know the Russians do likewise.

There are many secrets in the diamond world – many worlds waiting to be discovered as we trace the way diamonds have been manipulated, shaped and used. They are a gift of nature but not the rarest of gems. They are commonly mined for between $2 and $20 a carat – and are cut for less than $1 each. At the end of the 20th century there were still horrific working conditions in De Beers mines in Africa. In India young children still cut diamonds in conditions of slavery.

In order to conceal this alchemy of greed, the companies most involved set up a world-wide system whereby diamonds are secretively shipped with their origins changed or concealed, diamond production suppressed and prices set sky-high. This international, secretive and lucrative system made it possible for diamonds to fund terrorism.

Diamonds also provide a window into an outside world exposed to Americans by the terror of September 11th. They reveal what lies behind the hype and spin that weaved the web that created vast profits out of the misery of others.

This book is not just an indictment of a corrupt world of glitter but an account that reflects on how we can use these crystals to build a better world.

THE DIAMOND TRADE AND REFORM

I should like to stress that, despite all the abuses documented within this book, reform of the diamond trade is possible and highly desirable. Human frailties and greed will never let it be perfect – but it could relatively easily be reformed in a manner that would greatly benefit small-scale local producers, cutters and jewelry makers. I look forward to a diamond world where there are excellent codes of conduct agreed for both mining companies and cutters, in which diamonds are sold with certificates guaranteeing that these standards were followed. It is not only conflict diamonds that need to be removed from the market. It is also those produced by scandalously ill-paid African miners and child labor working in very unsafe conditions. I look forward also to a world where the developing nations with diamond resources cut many of their own diamonds and set them into jewelry that embodies local art and talent – thus giving customers a richer choice. Such a diamond world would no longer be run by a cartel. I hope this book helps create this better cut of diamond world.

ACKNOWLEDGEMENTS

With many thanks to Mandy Rogers and Allison Hall for their help with proof-reading my early drafts, to all the many friends and family who helped with the research and production of *The Diamond Empire* and this book, to Gary Baddeley, Russ Kick and everyone at The Disinformation Company, Graham Taylor and Browns, and Peter Greenwood for the jacket photograph.

Introduction

Blood Diamonds and Terrorists: An Overview

Diamonds have helped arm many terrorists, according to United Nations reports. Osama Bin Laden reportedly bought diamonds to protect the wealth of al-Qaeda. African children were brutally maimed by thugs who funded themselves with uncut diamonds. Their victims appeared on television worldwide.

The horror of this trade of diamonds for arms has created an international campaign now supported by over 40 countries and across political parties. In the first years of the 21st century, President Bush, Republicans, Democrats, De Beers and the diamond industry gave overwhelming support to the "Clean Diamond Trade Act," designed to ban diamonds used to fund conflict from the shores of America. Similar bills were planned around the world.

Senator Dick Durbin, a Democrat from Illinois, said at a Capitol Hill press conference that, "the diamond – a symbol of love in America – should not be paid for by the blood of Africans... The brutal wars in African nations may be thousands of miles away, but the source of the funds that buy the weapons may be as close as your ring finger. Our legislation says 'if you can't prove to US Customs agents that your diamonds are legitimate, take your business and your diamonds elsewhere.' " Durbin added that it was essential to "start tracking rough diamonds soon after they are mined and ensure that 'conflict diamonds' – gems mined and sold by terrorists to fund their operations – never enter the stream of legitimate commerce."[1]

Eli Izhakoff, chairman of the World Diamond Council, said his industry was "committed to the enactment of strong legislation that will help establish an international system to ensure that only legitimate diamonds are traded." He added: "Our goal is to stop the abhorrent practices of rebel movements in Africa that use illegal diamond sales to finance their brutal insurgencies."

But what substance is there to this campaign? How sure are governments that it will work? The BBC's prestigious *Correspondent* program investigated and concluded that the conflict diamond campaign "is reduced to a Public Relations exercise to pacify consumers and the international community."[2]

At first it seemed that the claim that bin Laden traded blood diamonds had little substance – for the only sources given were unnamed secret service officials. The only other evidence was that the price of black market diamonds went up some months before the September 11th, 2001 attack on the World Trade Center and the Pentagon. Many observers remained highly skeptical. UN sources responded scathingly, saying their experts found no sign of al-Qaeda in the diamond trade – and the Sierra Leonean rebels who had supposedly supplied al-Qaeda responded by denying these allegations vehemently.

But then I obtained an unpublished report by UN experts[3] that described an economic web spun between the war-torn diamond-producing states of Africa and the United Arab Emirates on the Persian Gulf, along whose threads arms merchants traveled to sell their wares in Afghanistan and Pakistan. Al-Qaeda operatives were at the same time operating on this web, using the United Arab Emirates while planning their attack on New York.[4]

According to the report, diamonds were used to pay for arms supplied by Victor Bout, who,

> oversees a complex network of over fifty planes and multiple cargo charter and freight-forwarding companies, many of which are involved in shipping illicit cargo … operating mainly out of the United Arab Emirates [whose] Sharjah Airport is used as an "airport of convenience" for planes registered in many other countries. Bout's Ilyushin 76 cargo plane shipped arms deliveries from Eastern Europe to Liberia [through which many Sierra Leonean blood diamonds are traded]. This aircraft and an Antonov made 4 deliveries, on July 4 and 27, and on August 1 and 23, 2000. The cargo included military helicopters, spare rotors, anti-tank and anti-aircraft systems, missiles, armored vehicles, machine guns and ammunition.[5]

It seemed also that this arms network was directly involved in the arming of al-Qaeda in Afghanistan.

Bout's planes allegedly had multiple registrations that he could change at a moment's notice. Thus a plane could take off with a Liberian registration and mid-flight change to a Gambian registration. They also flew out of airports in West Africa without radar where flights could not be easily monitored. Thus Liberian officials swore they only had nine planes on their country's register, while the UN noted another fifteen that claimed to have Liberian registration. Planes were secretly and regularly flying in and out of a dozen or more countries where diamonds were being traded for arms.

The UN told how key bin Laden aides came to West Africa to 1998 to discuss the purchase of diamonds. Among them were Ahmed Khalifan Guailani, wanted for his alleged role in providing the truck used to bomb the US embassy in Tanzania, Fazul Abdullah Mohammed, allegedly the head of al-Qaeda in Kenya, and Abdullah Ahmed Abdulla of whom the FBI called "a top bin Laden advisor who helped plan a number of al-Qaeda's operations." Allegedly, these men met Sam "Mosquito" Bockerie, a senior commander of Sierra Leone's Revolutionary United Front (RUF) and discussed with him a regular purchase of Sierra Leonean blood diamonds. Apparently $100,000 changed hands for the first purchase.

The UN named two Antwerp-based Lebanese diamond dealers who allegedly brought these diamonds into Europe. They were Aziz Nassur and Samih Ossailly Hezballah, men also accused by the *Washington Post* of dealing in conflict diamonds in the Congo.[6] Both men strongly protested their innocence, suggesting that business rivals were trying to destroy them by leaking false information. The press allegations were vague in their detail and may have been exaggerated or untrue.[7]

But the UN report named Americans as well as Arabs. These were a retired US Army General, Robert A. Yerks, and Fred Rindel, a former US military attaché, who allegedly helped train members of the RUF. The retired US General "was involved with ITC [International Trust Company] and is currently a senior official in LISCR [Liberian International Ship and Corporate Registry]". LISCR is allegedly an American company, registered in Tyson's Corner, Virginia.[8] Congressman Frank Wolf of Virginia, a member of the House Armed Services Committee, has testified that this "US based ... Liberian flag registry has been implicated in contributing to the continued reign of Charles Taylor, the leader one of the most brutal, murderous and dangerous regimes in the world. In short, there is blood on the flag."[9] These companies were also suspected of being both major traders in blood diamonds from the Sierra Leonean rebels[10] and the major funder of the Liberian Government, as well as having links to Bout's private air network.

Bout was born in the Soviet Union and served in Afghanistan. When the Soviet Union collapsed, he found himself well positioned to sell the torrent of surplus weapons that then came onto the international market. He served customers in weak states riven by old Cold War conflicts in Asia and Africa on the behalf of wealthy weapons traders in both the West and Russia.[11]

A UN Report to the Security Council in late 2001 noted the major role also played by Israelis in the conflict diamond trade. They were trading these tainted diamonds in the Democratic Republic of the Congo, Angola and Sierra Leone: "In all cases, the pattern is the same. Conflict diamonds are exchanged for money, weapons and military training. These diamonds are shifted to Tel Aviv by former Israeli Air Force pilots whose numbers have significantly increased both in UNITA-held territory in Angola and in the Democratic Republic of the Congo. In Israel these diamonds are cut and sold at the Ramat Gan Diamond Center."[12]

Another UN report spoke of the presence in the Angolan diamond industry of retired Israeli General Ze'ev Zahrine and of the influence of Danny Yatom, former head of MOSSAD, the Israeli intelligence service.[13] These Israelis competed against Lebanese merchants. It thus seemed that diamonds were used to fund Middle Eastern and African conflicts from well before al-Qaeda came into being after the 1991 Gulf War. I had also met Lebanese diamond dealers with Hezbollah sympathies in 1989 in Antwerp – the same year that a manager of a diamond cutting works in Israel told me he would never employ Arab Israelis for, "Arabs have oil. Israelis have diamonds."

The RUF began its rebellion in protest against corruption in the Sierra Leonean government. It captured the country's major diamond fields and used these to fund the expansion of its militia into a well-equipped force of thousands. These troops were guilty of many acts of great brutality. Although this war came to an end in 2002, this did not prevent the continuing smuggling of diamonds. Many parties were implicated in this illicit trade – including corrupt government officers, the RUF, peacekeeping troops and various diamond merchants.

Nor were acts of brutality committed only by the RUF. Human Rights Watch noted in 2001 that pro-government militia had killed 20 or more civilians in just one of many incidents. A woman told them "I tried to protect my neck with my left hand but they slashed it. They said in the Kono language: 'You'll be dead – all of you are RUF wives.' After cutting me, I lie still, pretending to be dead. I was bleeding so much."[14]

But the UN focused on the ill deeds of the RUF, as did much of the American press, and thus targeted only the diamonds sold by the rebels – if these stones could be traced. This proved a nearly impossible task.

In Angola, the brutal diamond-funded war between the Government and the UNITA rebels also came to an end in 2002, after the death of UNITA's leader, Jonas Savimbi. Initially the CIA had sustained UNITA's war to undermine Angola's socialist government. After CIA support was withdrawn, UNITA continued to fight, using revenue from captured diamond mines. Hundreds of thousands died. Then came a peace deal and an internationally supervised election. But when UNITA lost this election, it did not accept the result: launching the 1993 "War of the Cities," which caused in five months another 182,000 casualties.

Between 1992 and 1998 UNITA made over $4 billion from stolen diamonds – enough to import military aircraft and very sophisticated weaponry. It sold its diamonds to De Beers' buyers. De Beers ran much of the world's diamond trade and it made no secret of buying up these UNITA-produced diamonds in order to keep the price of diamonds from falling. It was De Beers' glowing reports about these purchases that eventually alerted the international human rights bodies and in 1999 created the "conflict diamond" campaign.

But it took time for this campaign to have much effect. Two years later, in 2001, the UN reported: "UNITA has revived its terrorist attacks on innocent civilians. It has attacked schools, buses and trains. It has shot at World Food program planes."[15] That year UNITA killed over 250 people in just one attack on a train – and sold over $100 million dollars worth of diamonds. Most of these ended up in American jewelry.

The campaign against blood diamonds gained widespread governmental support when the human rights organization Global Witness, operating out of North London, had the inspired idea of sending mock diamond jewelry, made from cut glass, in plush velvet cases, to newspaper editors along with a brief report on how romantic diamonds were funding murder and mayhem in Angola. Other similarly minded groups in Canada and the Netherlands joined forces – and together they managed to gain the attention of the British Foreign Office, the UN Security Council and the White House.

Their revelations deserved this support. But I was surprised when they gained the support of De Beers, the firm that dominates the world's diamond trade, which had assiduously resisted over decades the labeling of diamonds by origin, and which treated its own miners appallingly. This was an amazing success. But when a leading Canadian campaigner told me on the phone that he had "nothing against De Beers,"[16] it caused me much disquiet. It made me wonder if he had realized how much De Beers was responsible for the system that now made the trade in "blood diamonds" so difficult to prevent?

I had first become involved with diamonds in 1979 when I tried to help Aboriginal women protect a place they held sacred in the desert mountains of Northwest Australia. It was their Dreaming Site, a place of special ritual. Their ancestors had probably worshiped there for thousands of years. Unfortunately, it also contained diamonds, and the women had no legal right to protect their tribal land from the greed of mining companies. The company that gained possession, CRA Limited,[17] subsequently part-funded a national campaign against Aboriginal civil rights.

Since then I had traveled around the world to investigate the diamond trade – and witnessed much that has horrified me. In southern Africa De Beers tried to prevent me gaining access to its diamond mines. The Mineworkers' Union told me I was the first person De Beers had banned since the Emergency of the 1980s. When I nevertheless gained entry, I witnessed and photographed the horrific conditions in which many black miners lived within barbed wire compounds, without proper beds, without kitchens, with the absolute minimum of survival rations and no safety equipment, paid only a third of the union's then minimum agreed rate of $200 a month[18] – and this under the rule of the ANC.

In 1994 my feature length documentary *The Diamond Empire* appeared on US and Canadian television, with a two-part BBC version shown at peak times in the UK. This revealed, among other things, how De Beers' interests allegedly employed terrorists in Sierra Leone. I continued to campaign after the film came out, with meetings attended by those who were to begin the Global Witness campaign.[19]

One of my interviews was with a former chief executive of Selection Trust, a company that once managed the diamond mines of Sierra Leone, selling all that country's diamonds to De Beers. He told me De Beers had invented prices without even inspecting the diamonds.[20] His company won compensation from De Beers for many under-valued shipments. This deceit and fraud was carried out with little regard for the local people whose impoverishment helped create much of the current strife and misery. In the Congo, De Beers was reported to be "the company which Zairians blame more than any other foreign firm for helping Mobutu suck his country dry."[21]

I also visited cutting workshops in India. These cut nine out of ten of the world's gem diamonds. In these shops I found children as young as eight working in what the UN recognized as a form of slavery, sleeping by their diamond cutting wheels, in hazardous conditions, breathing diamond dust. They were recruited from agricultural villages because sharp eyes were needed to cut the smallest diamonds. After the documenting of this abuse in my film, *The Diamond Empire*, the number of children employed was sharply cut. But otherwise things did not improve. The wages paid to the adult cutters were slashed in January 2001 from 40 cents to just 20 cents for cutting and polishing a diamond, giving an adult take-home pay, after deductions, of just 60 cents a day. This was for cutting and polishing seven diamonds.

Representative Tony Hall, the instigator of the Clean Diamond Trade Act, stated during a White House Press Conference, "1999 was a very good year for the diamond industry. De Beers, the monopoly that controls 65 percent of the market, posted profits nearly 90 percent higher than in 1998. Lazare Kaplan, the largest American player in the industry, earned nearly 40 percent more."[22] The last named company was that of Maurice Tempelsman, a frequent visitor to the White House of whom we will hear more later.

What else? I knew that De Beers ran off with the fantastically rich state diamond stockpile of South Africa just before Nelson Mandela came to power – and refused to return it. I knew how and where it hid its superfluous diamond deposits so no others would gain access. I knew of its techniques to make flawless diamonds from methane gas – while they sold identical gems as the "ones in a million." I knew that Tempelsman, a diamond merchant they supplied, was a key supporter of the dictator Mobutu Sese Seko from just after the murder of Patrice Lumumba, the elected Prime Minister of the Congo. And I knew the secret trading routes used by De Beers that now made the trade in blood diamonds so difficult to prevent.

CAN CONFLICT DIAMONDS BE BANNED?

Could the Clean Diamond Trade Act really do what its sponsors wanted – and what President Bush said he wanted? Would it guarantee that the diamonds sold to romantic couples had a history of which they could be proud?

A UN report issued in 2001 told how the ban imposed on Sierra Leonean diamonds resulted in practically its entire diamond production moving over the borders to be exported under different national labels – effectively wrecking all controls on blood diamonds in West Africa.[23] The BBC *Correspondent* report told how government "officers are bribed and many of the diamond traders are unlicensed, happy to buy stones – no questions asked."[24]

Most of these diamonds were no longer conflict diamonds because the conflict was coming to an end. Nevertheless they were still outlawed by the proposed sanctions and laws on "clean diamonds," laws drawn up to stop trade in "blood diamonds," diamonds used to fund wars. The diamonds still banned were now in practice mostly illicit diamonds, diamonds sold without paying government taxes, quite another thing.

A UN expert described how the new certificates would not be able to prevent diamond merchants from mixing blood diamonds with legitimate stones and thus concealing them: "the new certificates of origin deal, made with Antwerp's HRD (Diamond Council) on 27th April 2001, is an entirely superficial system as conflict diamonds enter official routes at the same points as non-conflict artisan diamonds, long before tamper proof certificates with water marks and sequential numbers are relevant."[25]

As for Congolese blood diamonds, the UN had not imposed sanctions on them, so companies such as Arslanian Freres could legally import them into Europe even if they had been mined by militia in rebel areas and used to fund weapons and ammunition.

What of Angola, the other main source of "blood diamonds"? The UN thought in 2001 that the Angolan government's diamond agency, Angolan Selling Corporation or "Ascorp," could recognize diamonds produced by UNITA terrorists, as they looked "different" – and come in "bigger parcels."[26] This was palpably nonsense. UNITA mined its diamonds in close proximity to legitimate mines so its diamonds would be identical – and of course they could be packed into smaller parcels if needed to avoid sanctions.

De Beers claimed that it never bought UNITA's diamonds. A leading South African newspaper, the *Mail and Guardian,* investigated and said this was an attempt to "airbrush history." The UN Experts Panel named a prominent diamond firm, De Decker Diamonds, as trading in UNITA diamonds. This company allegedly admitted to the *Mail and Guardian* that "we brokered diamonds for UNITA." It said it sold these diamonds on in large parcels, worth $4-5 million each, to a De Beers subsidiary in Antwerp and Tel Aviv.[27]

The UN also reported in 2001: "To date not a single parcel of illicit Angolan diamonds has been intercepted anywhere, to the knowledge of the Mechanism [the UN monitoring body on Angolan Diamonds] ... No dealer has ... witnessed Angolan gems being sold by trader or by bourse. The gems seem to vanish into thin air after leaving Angola. How is this possible, given the magnitude of the trade, which is close to the value of Australia or Namibia ... more importantly, why is it possible for diamonds to vanish?"[28]

The UN discovered an answer. De Beers had long operated a system that concealed the diamond production of nations – and still had this system up and running. Originally, this served different purposes. For example, it made it impossible for diamond miners to discover the profit De Beers made when it sold their diamonds for them. It also prevented sanctions being effectively imposed on diamond production from apartheid South Africa – and protected Russian diamonds from an import tax imposed by the US only on Russian stones.

The UN found the De Beers system made it very difficult to track blood diamonds. When it investigated, it found that the UK had officially exported one year to Switzerland over 40 million carats of diamonds (De Beers diamonds – given that De Beers was practically the only major diamond exporter in the UK) while Switzerland said it had received only about 1,500 carats of diamonds. The UN investigators were stunned. A priceless shipment of literally tonnes of diamonds had seemingly vanished into the air.

On further investigation, they found that De Beers maintained a warehouse in the Free Trade Zone at Zurich airport. Diamonds arriving there were not counted officially as arriving in Switzerland. Here De Beers could mix and sort its diamonds before it sent them on to their final destinations. But there was also another twist. If De Beers did the paperwork to export a parcel of, say, Congolese diamonds from this Free Trade Zone to, say, Russia, it could then legally import them into Switzerland as Russian gems – even if they had not left the Free Trade Zone since they arrived. This created a major problem for the UN in the tracking of blood diamonds, for diamonds arriving at the Free Port were "losing their identity."[29] They could arrive from Africa and by the morning be transformed into Australian or Russian gems.

As the UN dug, more layers of deception were revealed. Despite the UK and Switzerland having no diamond mines of their own, their customs authorities were constantly reporting that that they were supplying millions of diamonds to each other while not receiving many diamonds from the other. In 2000, the UK Foreign Secretary gave his forthright support for blood diamond sanctions – yet a year later, when the UK Customs Authority was asked if it checked rough diamond imports to ensure none were blood diamonds, it answered that it did not. Instead it was sending the imported parcels of diamonds unchecked and unopened (nearly entirely to De Beers) as the contents of such parcels were "commercially confidential."[30] De Beers evidently was simply being trusted by the UK not to import blood diamonds.

UK Customs officially said it was recording the origin of diamonds as they arrived – but usually all it recorded was that the diamonds were of "undeclared origin." It even put down imports from Belgium as of "undeclared origin" when the diamonds came with certificates giving their origin![31]

Once De Beers received its diamonds, it used a system of patronage to distribute them that made sure few questions would be asked about their origin. It picked between 150 and 200 of its favorite diamond merchants from around the world and invited them every five weeks to London to pick up a box of diamonds at what was called a "Sight." The merchants had to pay for their boxes before they opened them. De Beers stated that no blood diamonds were in the boxes – but produced no proof. If a diamond merchant rejected his assigned box, he might never be invited again – and thus lose his diamond supplies. But if he had kept to cartel rules or otherwise helped De Beers, then he might find particularly fine diamonds in his box. If he had not, then he might find diamonds that would lose him money. The merchants need not be overly concerned if any of the stones were "conflict" or "blood" diamonds, they knew that once the diamonds were cut, no one would be able to tell if any came from regions likely to produce blood diamonds. De Beers' staff disdainfully called this system "feeding the ducks."[32]

Since the UN had named Liberia as a major conduit for the secret movement of blood diamonds – and had banned Liberian diamonds – I was surprised to find that the leaders of the diamond world took advantage of Liberia's secrecy and lack of taxation. The Oppenheimer family used a Liberian company to control De Beers but in 2003 declared itself "proudly South African."[33]

Belgium has long been a major center of the world bulk rough diamond trade. In 1999 its government was stung by accusations that its diamond merchants freely imported blood diamonds – so put in place seemingly rigorous controls. But these were bypassed when the local merchants decided not to use a Belgian airport but to bring in their diamonds through Schipol airport in The Netherlands – where in 2001 there was only one customs official with any knowledge of diamonds – and practically no checking for blood diamonds.[34]

The UN Panel of Experts reported:

Belgium has recently changed the data requirements on the import licenses that it requires for each shipment. It now requires that each import shipment state the country of provenance, as well as the country of origin. A review of selected Company "A" import licenses, however, showed that diamonds far in excess of the quality or quantity available in Liberia had been imported [into Belgium] as Liberian in provenance and origin. Invoices from "Liberian" firms – none on the list of licensees provided by the Liberian government – accompanied the Belgian import license. A physical check of the Monrovia street addresses given by most of these firms revealed that there were no such companies, and no such addresses.[35]

The report continued, "They would have transited Liberia and become 'Liberian,' just as other diamonds transit Switzerland, Belgium or the UK, becoming 'Swiss,' 'Belgian' or 'British.'"

A report by the NGO Fatal Transactions noted other strange anomalies. In 1999 Belgium officially imported 150 million carats of rough diamonds while exporting 173 million carats of rough diamonds, seemingly without drawing down on Belgium's stockpiles. Belgium also reported that its exports were worth less than its imports. This suggested massive undeclared profits.[36]

Belgium provided import statistics that revealed where its diamonds were mined. These revealed more inconsistencies. For example, it was discovered: "Belgium appears to import almost double the volume that is exported from Guinea, and the per carat value is almost 75 percent higher than what leaves Guinea."[37] Belgium said it imported $117 million worth of rough diamonds from Congo in September-December 2000 while the Congo reported it had only supplied Belgium during that period with $72 million worth of diamonds.[38] The UN noted that Belgium said it imported "6 million carats between 1994 and 1999" from the Ivory Coast, "about 13 times more than was apparently produced" by the Ivory Coast. This suggested that vast numbers of diamonds were leaving Africa undeclared, without paying local taxes.

So what then of the United States? Can its Customs Service sort out and stop imports of blood diamonds? The answer is that it cannot, for it has not hired the experts needed to do so. Since the Cold War, when customs duty was imposed on diamonds produced in Russia, Russian diamonds have arrived in the United States pre-labeled as British or as Swiss. The US admitted in 2002 that its Customs could not distinguish or keep out conflict diamonds.[39]

When the UN analyzed the numbers of diamonds flowing uncontrolled into the world market, it found that some 20 percent of the world diamond trade was "illicit" – meaning traded without government certificates and without government authorization. As De Beers controlled some 65 percent of the world's production, and the Russians and Australians controlled and reported much of the rest, the UN concluded that De Beers itself was probably trading part of this illicit production.[40]

It should be noted that conflict diamonds are not new. The reality is that for decades diamonds have been traded to fund wars and dictatorships – including by the CIA and the White House.

For example: when the first elected President of Ghana, Kwame Nkrumah, set up an alternative system for selling diamonds, his security officials discovered, through bugging the phone of a leading American customer of De Beers, that a coup had been organized against him with CIA involvement. When Patrice Lumumba, the Congo's first and only truly elected President, was murdered, again by or at the behest of the CIA, a deal was immediately arranged by the same American diamond merchant to help fund his unelected replacement.

De Beers headquarters in Kimberley, South Africa.

For decades, De Beers retained control over diamond pricing by buying up the entire production of black Africa. But by the 1990s it was finding this very costly. It was thus fortunate for De Beers when another, cheaper solution presented itself: the blood diamond campaign tainted the diamonds produced by Angola, the Congo and West Africa to De Beers' benefit.

De Beers announced it would stop buying even the certificated diamond production of Angola, Sierra Leone and the Congo – stones guaranteed not to be "blood diamonds" – on the grounds that it wanted to be completely sure it was not dealing in blood diamonds. This decision should have both solved one of De Beers' problems and devastated the economies of these wartorn states – but De Beers had miscalculated.

Waiting in the wings were wealthy independent diamond merchants prepared to replace De Beers. Within a very short time they had helped the Congolese and Angolan governments set up their own diamond marketing schemes.[41]

The Angolan government's scheme was backed by Lev Leviev, a powerful diamond merchant with high connections in Israel and Russia, whose companies had a diamond income of over $1.5 billion a year. This plan reportedly initially doubled the Angolan government's revenues from diamonds. He also helped to bring in Russian diamond mining expertise to provide Angola with a new diamond mine.

The Congolese government had a marketing scheme organized for it by a company called IDI, headed by the well-connected Dan Gertler whose uncle, Shmuel Schnitza, was the President of the Israel Diamond Exchange and Vice President of the World Diamond Council. Their scheme also reportedly doubled the Congo Government's tax income from diamonds. Despite this, the scheme came under heavy attack from others within the diamond trade, and eventually broke down. It was then rumored that some of those involved had also traded in conflict diamonds.

When the UN investigated it found that the trade was not in conflict stones but in illicit stones. In other words, diamonds were being smuggled solely for reasons of profit, not to finance war. This was also true in Angola where, in 2001, of the 250 million carats that did not go through the official system, two thirds were diamonds sold on the black market rather than to the government monopoly in order to get better prices. It was also found that 20 million carats were smuggled out of the Democratic Republic of the Congo to Congo-Brazzaville – principally because merchants there could afford to pay higher prices as they were less taxed – not because the stones were blood diamonds. Illicit diamonds were also mixed with real conflict diamonds traded by Rwandan troops who had invaded the DRC. It was thus impossible to tell illicit diamonds from conflict.[42]

The UN soon was to conclude: "It became obvious to the Panel that there is a very large trade in illicit diamonds, and that conflict diamonds are only a part of this trade. They are, in essence, illicit diamonds that have gone septic."[43]

This should not have been surprising. By 2002, UNITA's illegal diamond exports from Angola had sharply diminished as it was suffering military defeat. In Sierra Leone the civil war had come to an end. This should have meant that there were fewer conflict diamonds on the market.

But then a major change was introduced into the "conflict" diamond campaign. Its target was extended by the UN and government negotiators to include the "illicit" diamonds as if they were "conflict" stones. In future most of the so-called "conflict diamonds" will be entirely innocent of any association with terrorism. This greatly extended ban was excellent news for De Beers for it had eliminated much unwelcome competition. It meant effectively the removal of some 14 percent of the international trade, rather than 4 percent.

But this manipulated the pledges made by President Bush and by the legislators who had supported laws to ban blood diamonds from the US. They had backed a system of international certificates to exclude conflict diamonds. They had ended up unwittingly banning many more.

Thus, the scheme supposedly set up in the hope of eliminating conflict diamonds came to target perhaps five times more diamonds than those used to support wars. All that these stones had in common was that they were sold on the "free market" without proper government certificates, perhaps to avoid taxes, perhaps to avoid government monopolies, or the exclusive contracts some made with De Beers, in order to obtain the higher prices of the free market. They were thus a trade a government would want to stop. But stopping tax evasion and protecting De Beers' contracts were not the reasons why sanctions were introduced and backed by so many nations around the world. They had thought they were fighting terrorism.

The diamond control system negotiated was named the "Kimberley Process." This created certificates that governments could place on parcels of diamonds to formally guarantee that they contained no stones previously used to fund terrorism or non-state endorsed wars. But despite these words, the reality was that the process had gone well beyond its original mandate and the intent of the American "Clean Diamond Trade Act." It entailed a guarantee that said one thing and did something else entirely.

And, even when issued, these Kimberley Process certificates could still not guarantee that the diamonds in the packages were untainted by terrorism.

For example: The UN experts in 2001 judged that Ascorp, the Angolan government agency that would issue these certificates, would buy up blood diamonds whenever they were offered them – and once it did, it would issue certificates for them as it would for others. The UN reasoned: "If it refuses certain stones or deters intermediaries dealing with UNITA, these diamonds would be sold across Angola's borders [cutting the government's revenues]. The result is that Angola's certificate of origin is a public relations tool that may not correspond to realities in Angola's diamond fields."[44]

This might be unduly suspicious. Ascorp cancelled the registration of 40 diamond traders suspected of dealing with UNITA in 2001 – but the de-registered dealers could find other ways to sell their diamonds, such as by putting them into parcels sold by other dealers. It was impossible for Ascorp to physically tell a UNITA traded stone from a legally mined stone.

The revenues from certified stones might still be used for weapons purchase. The certification system offered no guarantee that justice would be on the government's side. The DRC government was quite open about using revenues from its MIBA diamond mine to buy weapons. It even sometimes asked MIBA to handle the deals.

The Indians who cut over 70 percent of the world's diamonds had other complaints against the Kimberley system. Nilesh Shah said:

"Many in the Indian diamond industry feel that the entire conflict diamonds issue and the Kimberley Process are more about finding scapegoats than anything else. Many feel that India is being specifically targeted… At the first Kimberley Process meeting, there was no one to represent India. At that meeting, representatives from other centers claimed that all the conflict rough in the world was processed in India. It was only at the second meeting, when we were present, along with an Indian government officer, that we were able to set the record straight. This statement underscores a strong sense of resentment against the Kimberley Process. As one diamond dealer put it: "The countries that are sponsoring this whole process are the ones who are selling arms and ammunition to these people. Now they're trying to blame everybody else for it. Diamonds are easy to smuggle; arms and ammunition are not."[45]

In February 2002, the US General Accounting Office concluded an investigation into the effectiveness of the proposed Clean Diamonds Trade Act by pointing out that diamonds "are virtually untraceable back to the original source … Diamonds are a high value commodity that is easily concealed and transported. These conditions allow diamonds to be used in lieu of currency in arms deals, money laundering and crime. Lack of transparency in industry operations also facilitates illegal activity."[46] It also noted "the nature of diamonds make them attractive to criminal elements. … Smuggling routes are well established by those who have done so for decades to evade taxes … Once mixed they have become virtually untraceable … Apparently, any conflict diamond could be claimed as a stockpiled diamond." The GAO went on to say the proposed scheme was flawed, for it had no independent auditing, only voluntary enforcement. It also noted how Belgium had claimed to send $355 million worth of diamonds to the US – while only $192 million worth arrived. It finally concluded: "Under the current import system, the US cannot determine the true origin of diamond imports to ensure that conflict diamonds do not enter the country" and that much work remained to be done to make the proposed system work.

But despite these flaws, many highly reputed international human rights organizations saw great advantage in the Kimberley Process, as long as it could be extended to more widely covered human rights abuses. Thus in 2002-3 Survival International appealed for Botswana's diamonds to be banned as conflict diamonds, for as long as that nation endangered the survival of the Bushmen as a people.

Likewise, in 2002 Amnesty International begged De Beers and other diamond companies to help put an end to human rights violations at diamond mines in the Congo. It wrote: "Dozens of people are being shot dead every year in the diamond fields of Mbuji-Mayi." In October 2002 a UN panel called for the Security Council to impose sanctions against the companies and individuals plundering the resources of the Congo. It said the plundering was by "elite networks" running a self-financing war, deriving "financial benefit … through a variety of criminal activities, including theft, embezzlement, diversion of public funds, under-valuation of goods, smuggling, false invoicing, non-payment of taxes, kickbacks to public officials and bribery." It listed several companies as violating ethical guidelines, including Anglo American and De Beers.

As Amnesty International has pointed out, the diamonds involved were exempt from sanctions under the Kimberley Process. They were thus being certified as "conflict-free" by the diamond industry, and sold as such to consumers worldwide.

Despite the reservations of the GAO, The Clean Diamond Trade Act was signed into law by President Bush on April 23, 2003. It mandated that all rough diamonds entering the United States had to have Kimberley Process Certificates, but it had been modified since it went through the House of Representatives. It now contained no mention of excluding diamond jewelry, no matter if these contained diamonds cut from conflict stones. Since few uncut diamonds are imported into the United States, this new law would affect few diamonds.

But, despite its limited range, there were two major advantages to the new law: firstly, it meant ethical issues had become of foremost importance in the diamond trade, and secondly the opportunity was created for an extended Kimberley System that could eliminate many cases of human rights abuses in the diamond industry around the world.

What can be done?

There is a growing demand for an extension of the Kimberley Process, and perhaps, if this cannot be done readily, for a parallel system, enabling at least some diamonds to be marketed with certificates guaranteeing that they are not contaminated by human rights abuses. I believe such a scheme is feasible and could be based on internationally agreed standards for diamond mines and cutting workshops. It could even give the stones it certified a marketing edge. It would not need to work by trying to certify every diamond, as attempted by the Kimberley Process, but by building a market for certified stones among those who want their diamond to have a truly flawless pedigree.

1 Quoted by Jim Fisher-Thompson, *Washington File.* June 21st, 2001.
2 BBC2 *Correspondent,* October 21st, 2001.
3 *Report by the Panel of Experts to the United Nations on Sierra Leone.* Unauthorized copy provided by the Netherlands Institute of South Africa. October 2001.
4 See Dan Eggan and Kathleen Day. "U.S. Probe Of Sept. 11 Financing Wraps Up Terror Money Traced Via ATM, Credit Card Usage." *Washington Post.* January 7th, 2002, p. A1.
5 *United Nations Panel of Experts Report Sierra Leone.* Para. 27.
6 Douglas Farrah. "Digging Up Congo's Dirty Gems Officials Say Diamond Trade Funds Radical Islamic Groups." *Washington Post.* December 30th, 2001, p. A1.
7 Farrah, p. A1.
8 Rapaport News October 24th, 2001.
9 Congressman Wolf in a speech delivered on June 13, 2002 before the House Armed Services Committee Special Oversight Panel on the Merchant Marine.
10 *United Nations Panel of Experts on Sierra Leone.* Para. 127.
11 See 2002 investigation by the Center for Public Integrity in Washington, DC.
12 Report for the United Nations Security Council. *Addendum to the report of the Panel of Experts on the Illegal Exploitation of Natural Resources and Other Forms of Wealth of the Democratic Republic of the Congo.* November 13th, 2001.
13 *United Nations Panel of Experts on Sierra Leone.*
14 "Sierra Leone: Most Serious Attacks in Months." *Human Rights Watch Interviews: Victims and Witnesses.* July 24th, 2001.
15 *United Nations Monitoring Mechanism on Sanctions Against UNITA.* Supplementary Report, October 23rd, 2001.
16 Private conversation with a principal organizer of the Canadian Partnership in Africa group.
17 CRA Limited merged with The RTZ Corporation PLC in December 1995 to form Rio Tinto Limited and Rio Tinto plc, respectively, operating as a single entity. They are generally referred to herein as RTZ.
18 The National Union of Mineworkers negotiated an increase to a minimum of $250 a month for diamond mineworkers in 2002.
19 Alex Yearsley of Global Witness told me at a meeting on conflict diamonds in 2002: "You know you started this. My colleague was at a meeting you spoke at [around 1996] when you were trying to raise funds for a campaign." Until then I did not realize that there was this link.
20 Edward Wharton-Tigar. *Burning Bright: The Autobiography of Edward Wharton- Tigar.* Metal Bulletin Books, 1997.
21 *Mail and Guardian,* South Africa, April 18th, 1997.

22 Press Release distributed by the US Mission to Botswana, September 15th, 2000.
23 *United Nations Panel of Experts on Sierra Leone.*
24 BBC *Correspondent* report, October 21st, 2001.
25 Charles Dietrich; Report for the International Peace Information Service, Antwerp, 2001.
26 UN report. Addendum to the Final Report of the Monitoring Mechanism on Sanctions Against UNITA, S/2001/363, April 18th, 2001, paragraph 71.
27 *Mail and Guardian,* March 24th, 2000.
28 *Report of the Panel of Experts on the Illegal Exploitation of Natural Resources and Other Forms of Wealth of the Democratic Republic of the Congo.* April 21st, 2001.
29 Ibid.
30 *Fatal Transactions: Conflict diamonds crossing European Borders.* Amsterdam, August 2001.
31 Ibid.
32 Wake-Walker, former De Beers executive, quoted in Eric Burton, *Diamonds* 3rd ed. London: N.A.G. Press, 1976, p. 133.
33 Speech made by Nicky Oppenheimer, Chairman of De Beers, on April 29th, 2003.
34 *Fatal Transactions*, 2001.
35 *United Nations Panel of Experts on Sierra Leone.* Para. 126 and 127.
36 *Fatal Transactions*, 2001.
37 *United Nations Panel of Experts on Sierra Leone.* Para. 136.
38 There is a small discrepancy here. The Congo statistics are for between October-January 2000-2001 – the Belgian from September to December 2000-2001.
39 "International Trade. Significant challenges remain in deterring trade in Conflict Diamonds" GAO-02-425ST February 13th, 2002.
40 *United Nations Panel of Experts on Sierra Leone.* Para. 149.
41 B. Stanley, "Diamond monopoly hands obscure Israeli firm the key to Congo's economy." Associated Press, March 18th, 2001.
42 *UN Report on the Congo to the Security Council.* 2001.
43 UN Panel of Experts on Sierra Leone Report, Para. 150.
44 *UN Mechanism on Angola.*
45 Vinod Kuriyan, "No Problems Here: Success, Complacency and Suspicion in the Indian Diamond Industry." 2002. An Occasional Paper of the Diamonds and Human Security project, a joint initiative of Partnership Africa Canada (Ottawa), International Peace Information Services (Antwerp) and Network Movement for Justice and Development (Freetown).
46 "International Trade. Significant challenges remain in deterring trade in Conflict Diamonds" GAO-02-425ST. February 13th, 2002.

Chapter 1 – The Diamond Hunt

My investigations started quite innocently. I had been invited to explain the techniques of diamond mining to Aboriginal elders in a small settlement called Oombulgurri in northwest Australia. They told me of their alarm at the many prospectors in helicopters and four-wheel drives invading their lands. The elders and I sat in fine red dust in the shade of a fat-trunked boab tree. It was sultry, pre-monsoonal. As we talked, apart from the distant shouts of playing children, the only other sounds were the occasional buzz of flies or a parrot's staccato screech.

Australian boab tree.

I did not need to introduce these elders to diamonds. Whites first found diamonds in this region some decades ago when they examined the sacred stones carried in a pouch by a murdered Aborigine. What Aborigines now wanted from me, a sociologist with strong friendships within their community, was factual information on the consequences of a major diamond find by a major diamond company.

Six months or so earlier the Oombulgurri community had bravely denied an entry permit to Stockdale, De Beers' diamond exploration company, because they feared it might trespass in sacred areas. They had heard that mining companies had even plundered burial caves.

Their refusal had so angered the state government that it had removed from all Aboriginal communities in Western Australia the right to issue permits to visitors. Thus, the Oombulgurri community could not give an official permit when it invited me to visit them.

I had come to see them nonetheless, for they had invited me and I could see no good reason to refuse. The local legal service advised that taking away their right to invite guests was a denial of civil rights. There was seemingly little risk. The local police had never arrested anyone for accepting an Aboriginal invitation.

But perhaps I was being somewhat naïve. My conversation with the elders was soon interrupted by a schoolteacher with a radio message from Melbourne, over 3,500 miles away. The Federal Authorities had ordered the police to fly in by helicopter to arrest me! I was open-mouthed with astonishment. This seemed so over the top, so extraordinary that I could scarcely believe it. It was then that I realized that I had fallen by chance into the midst of a quiet war between diamond prospectors, the government and the tribes.

I did not wait for the police to arrive, but hired the community's boat to travel back to the slaughterhouse town of Wyndham. I hoped this would protect my hosts from being harassed by the police. The mission boat was small – apparently larger crocodiles frolicked just up stream from us. But we made it away, through the tangled mangrove roots, across the shark infested estuary, over sediments now believed by some to be rich in diamonds, safely to Wyndham. The quayside was quiet when we arrived, the dust-blown streets deserted before the oncoming monsoonal storm. We made our way back to the home of the local district nurse where we were staying. After dinner the police came around to arrest us.

The ridge in which the Argyle diamonds were found.

Some of the Aborigines on whose land lies Argyle.

I found out later that the police had been unwilling to arrest us but had been ordered into action. I wondered why, then discovered that CRA Limited was concealing a massive diamond find nearby. It had secured over one hundred square miles, surrounding its find behind high fences, security guards and closed circuit television. I was then smuggled inside it by an Aboriginal group that had been given permission to hunt their tribal lands included within the lease. My face was dirty, my hair concealed beneath a scarf. The security guards ignored me, probably thinking me a half-caste. They did not see the camera on which I sat as we drove into the heart of a secret diamond find within the red and mauve slopes of an extinct volcano. It contained, according to secret geological reports later leaked to me, more diamonds than South Africa officially had.

In Melbourne a small Australian company later showed me a highly confidential three-dimensional model revealing the drill results from this diamond deposit. It told me that it contained over 20 times the diamond concentration per tonne than there were in De Beers' South African mines. I also learned that over half of its diamonds were of gem quality. My articles about this discovery ran full page in major newspapers and were nationally syndicated.

By now, small Australian mining firms were cheering me on – but not because of my work for Aborigines. They did not want to see Australian resources going into foreign hands. Their executives and geologists fed me information.

My articles may have educated, even entertained, but politically they failed. De Beers mounted Ernest Oppenheimer's "spring offensive." He has since boasted of this. Australian mining investors were feted. It did not take long for him to secure control over the marketing of these Australian diamonds.

I then discovered that the US Justice Department had pursued De Beers' diamond cartel for half a century, accusing it of greatly exploiting the American consumer. I obtained Justice Department files under the US Freedom of Information Act. Thousands of pages came to Australia. I now had FBI and American spy reports, intercepted letters and a hundred leads.

This investigation eventually took me around the world. I made a feature-length film called *The Diamond Empire* shown on American and British television and took it to South Africa, where I found the diamond mineworkers hungry for information about their employer, De Beers. They secretly showed our film inside its mines. I was invited to speak to up to 700 miners at a time, for up to three hours a session, and I found shameful and dangerous conditions still existed inside these mines, despite apartheid having ended. Yet, they were producing the most lucrative of stones worth many times more than gold; stones that today are sold as "clean."

Everywhere I found blood on the diamond crystal. Its shame was not just on the margins of the diamond empire but in its very heart.

THE CROWN OF SHAME

The figures appeared shadowy; children darting from the darkness to vanish from the flickering light of my headlights as I

Mineworkers gathered to watch *The Diamond Empire*.

hesitatingly drove over unmade roads through the dust storm enveloping the seemingly endless shantytown. The dust had a peculiar gritty feel. It crusted my lips, irritating them. I was in Kimberley, the town that gave birth to De Beers and the modern diamond trade. The dust on my lips was kimberlite, the ore from which diamonds are extracted.

It swirled unhindered through razor wire from acres of gray waste tips, from mines dug into Kimberley's heart, clouding the air as it had for a century. But I hoped there would be a change, elation in the step of the black Africans the dust enshrouded.

Children in Kimberley dust-storm.

De Beers headquarters.

It was then 1994. South Africa was free. For the first time they were living in a democracy. When I asked for the diamond mineworkers on my arrival in Kimberley, I was misdirected to a two-storied iron roofed and iron laced building. It was the De Beers headquarters. The amused security guard pointed out the way to the nearby union office. Here diamond miners were awaiting me. Much had now changed. A former diamond mineworker was now the Premier in Kimberley.

I was taken to speak with miners in a De Beers hostel by a diamond mine in barbed wire encased wastelands. Afterwards they took me to the home of a mineworker in a Township where I was to stay, across the road from a diamond mine's

Kimberley graveyard for blacks.

Women walking to work.

waste treatment plant. On the way my host showed me the squatter camps where thousands lived in tiny shanties of corrugated iron. I thus met the people who had won De Beers its fortune.

Nothing I had read prepared me for this sea of squatter camps that stretched to the horizon. The city of diamonds on which the De Beers fortune was founded, the mines that gave Cecil Rhodes the funds needed to expand the British Empire throughout East Africa, was still surrounded by dire poverty.

Near the diamond waste reprocessing plant I came across a vast graveyard evidently reserved for blacks only. Many graves were marked only by heaps of rough rocks. Many were freshly dug. Sometimes the rock heaps were covered by the signs of grief of the extremely poor: a cracked jug, an old teapot, broken cups. From the graves' size, many were of children. Some had black tombstones. Others had the name of the dead scratched on pieces of metal. Many were nameless. The wall around the graveyard was cheaply erected out of rough rocks without municipal help. Not far away, on the city side of the blacks' township, was the large white graveyard, with neat graves spaced out in wide lawns. The fence around it was high and robust. Apartheid affected even the dead.

I had come to see how De Beers was doing in post-apartheid Africa. When I arrived in Johannesburg from London, the National Union of Mineworkers by a fortunate coincidence was about to hold a conference for shop stewards from De Beers' diamond mines. They planned to show my film, *The Diamond Empire*. They were surprised and delighted when I turned up just at the right moment and offered to talk about what we had learned while making this film. After my address I was enthusiastically invited to all the diamond mines.

KIMBERLEY – DE BEERS' HEARTLAND

Three days later I hired a car and set out to Kimberley, some five hours drive from Johannesburg. Every town I passed had a sister town of hovels. A constant stream of black servants walked along dirt paths from one to the other, some in cleanly pressed uniforms, some in gardening or garage overalls.

I found the townships around Kimberley to be separated by overgrown heaps of blue rock, the remains of diamond mines. Excavators and bulldozers moved through the haze busily reprocessing the waste to check for any diamonds missed earlier. De Beers had sold this waste to licensed contractors at so much a truckload. They had to

Women and children.

Woman cleaning Kimberley home.

sell any diamonds found back to De Beers – the only permitted buyer. I stopped by a gate to talk to some black women. They were waiting to make sure their men did not waste their pay. One De Beers' truck driver told me his take home pay for a 50 hour week was R96 – about $28.

A senior government official told how they had asked De Beers to contract unemployed black workers to search these waste tips. The answer was no, it would encourage "illicit diamond buying" (IDB) and that blacks would gather like "vultures" (De Beers' word) to search for diamonds. Instead De Beers had sold these waste tips to Canadian diamond enthusiasts.

In South Africa the law prohibiting IDB stipulated that any rough uncut diamond found on public land must be sold to the government who then resold it to De Beers. Africans gasped with amazement when I told them how I had seen diamonds openly traded on the street in Mumbai (formerly known as Bombay) and New York. For them to do so would mean jail. Despite this, I learned there was a highly secretive local black diamond market in Kimberley run by men who hated De Beers for its mean wages and treatment of workers.

Over the next days the miners drove me along countless miles of potholed and rock-strewn dirt roads lined with shacks, showing me inside the more substantial homes and not showing me the poorer ones for fear of shaming their owners. Despite their poverty, these residents were house-proud. The owners of the poorest homes took time every day to remove the dust from steps and windowsills.

Street sign.

The bare earth surrounding the hovels was raked daily and attempts were made at gardens. In the evening, their windows were lit by weak electric lights or by flickering flames, as many could not afford electricity. Power bills could easily amount to $90 a month, the entire income of a worker on the diamond dumps.

In the Kimberley Mines Division of De Beers there were between 1,200 and 1,400 workers of which 1,100 were black. Most lived in the townships and squatter camps. A senior government official in Kimberley told me they had approached De Beers for financial help to rebuild these homes in the name of the

The standard of housing in white suburbs.

Reconstruction and Development Program (RDP) of the new ANC government of National Reconciliation. De Beers replied they had given their annual 120,000 Rand ($30,000) from their Chairman's Fund and could give no more. I also visited the suburbs constructed for white miners and managers. These had names such as

The Big Hole.

"De Beers" and "Ernestville" and streets named after Ernest Oppenheimer. The homes were spacious and green with lawns; the only inadequacy were in the "maid's quarters." These were not large enough to house the numbers of servants employed. Thus early every morning I saw crowds of black women servants walking in over dusty paths from the townships and taxi stands.

The major tourist attraction in Kimberley was the "Big Hole," a vast crater of terraced sides descending to cliffs above an extremely deep lake – a diamond mine abandoned not because it had run out of diamonds but because it was endangering the stability of the town center. The dusty tips it creates are scattered throughout the town. The miners took me to another big hole on the outskirts of the city, disused and dangerously ill-protected, and showed me how the debris of diamond mining surrounded Kimberley. The museum at the Big Hole told of the exploits of the white prospectors, of the first miners, of Cecil Rhodes and the siege of Kimberley when guns, ammunition and an armored train were manufactured in De Beers' workshops as Boers and English fought for the diamond mines. But I saw no mention of the thousands of black miners whose labor built the mines or of the important role played by Kimberley's diamond bosses in developing apartheid.

The role of De Beers in the creation of apartheid

Up until the discovery of diamonds in South Africa in the 1870s, most Southern African nations or "tribes" were economically independent of the white settlers. They supplied the first miners with meat from their cattle herds and with farming products. These black nations at first controlled the alluvial diamond fields by the Orange River, traded in diamonds and restricted the white prospectors' use of mining equipment. When the large diamond deposits of Kimberley were found on the dry plateau to the east of the river, the Africans worked these deposits for white prospectors to acquire such goods as guns. When they had the funds required they would quit and return to their farms.

As the diamond diggings got deeper, the small mine companies became more and more dependent on black labor to remove the ore, break it up and to remake the roads that were always collapsing into the diggings. The wages paid to the black miners made up three quarters of the costs of the white owners. In July 1876 the owners tried to slash wages in half. The result was devastating. 4,000 black miners stopped work and went home. They did not return until wages were restored to their former level. As the Africans traditionally lived by barter, they did not require cash to survive. This gave the mine bosses little control over them.

Then taxes were imposed on the Africans in order to make them dependent on a cash income that could only be obtained by working for whites. This forced the Africans to leave their farms for the mines. Soon touts were auctioning black workers in the Market Square in Kimberley as if they were slaves. The touts took a fee equal to four months' miner's wages. The employers did not like this system for it increased their costs.

The mine owners were also concerned about the numbers of employees who supplemented their wages by retaining diamonds. Many workers, both white and black, saw little wrong in keeping a proportion of their finds. Some owners estimated that 30 to 40 percent of the stones found were going into this illegal distribution system. In 1883 a new law was passed allowing the mine owners to search all employees daily, white and black. Black employees (but not whites) had to wear mealie flour sacks at work so they had no pockets in which they could hide diamonds. In April 1884 white workers who refused to be searched were sacked by the Kimberley mines. Black workers then came out on strike in sympathy. The strike was put down by force, killing six white miners. Shortly after this the daily searching of white employees was dropped.[1]

In 1879 a Cornish mine engineer, T. C. Kitto, advocated adopting the methods used with black slaves in Brazilian diamond mines. He wrote: "The blacks are housed in barracks built in the form of a square,… an overseer locks them in every night… I believe the natives of South Africa, under European supervision, are capable of being made almost – if not quite – as good as the blacks of Brazil, providing they are dealt with in the same manner."[2] The mine owners thought this an excellent suggestion that would keep down wages and stop theft. In 1882 Cecil Rhodes advocated that all De Beers' black workers (but not white) should be confined to barracks when not at work. He calculated that selling food to the captive workers would pay half his labor costs. In July 1886 De Beers confined its 1,500-strong black work force in a barracks. By 1889 all 10,000 black miners in Kimberley were in these prison-like compounds.

This system allowed De Beers to mix convicts with blacks to further minimize labor costs. From 1884 to 1932 De Beers used hundreds of convicts in its mines, paying a minimal fee to the government instead of paying wages. Ironically, or perhaps deliberately, many of these were only imprisoned because they went to the diamond mines to seek paid work despite the government not giving them travel passes. The workers could not bring their wives or children with them into the compounds. When they wanted to leave the compound, they were dosed with mild laxatives and locked naked into cells for five to ten days with their hands fastened into leather bags. Every part of their body and excrement was inspected for diamonds. Eventually a machine was invented to inspect human stool for excreted diamonds.

Many of these diamond mine practices became enshrined in South African legislation. In 1889 it was decreed that: "No native shall work or be allowed to work in any mine, whether in open or underground mining, excepting under the responsible charge of some particular white man as his master or 'baas.'" Apartheid was now effectively established.

De Beers, apartheid and Namibia

The richest of all the diamond mines, the Oppenheimer-controlled Consolidated Diamond Mines (CDM) mine in South West Africa (now Namibia), initially imported cheap black labor from Botswana. The author Colin Newberry reported: "By 1923 over half the labor force of 5,000 consisted of outside recruits from northern Botswana who suffered a high mortality rate… with scurvy or tuberculosis."[3] Some also died from dehydration and exhaustion while searching the desert sands for diamonds. Laurie Flynn, who has extensively written on southern Africa and was a researcher on The Diamond Empire, reported seeing one of the houses provided. It was like "a telephone box set on its side."[4] Strict company regulations governed the miners' lives. In practice these had the force of law as the company paid the local police wages and expenses.

Soon the Oppenheimers were running their Namibian mine under the same apartheid system De Beers had helped develop in South Africa. Their company town, Oranjemund, had married quarters for the white workers and single sex hostels for black workers. The workforce became Ovambo tribesmen recruited en masse in northern Namibia. They were only allowed to travel to the mine if they had a contract and could not bring their wives or families. They were not allowed into retail stores, cinemas or clubs, all of which were owned by the company. Everything was segregated. There were separate counters even in the post office. At the supermarket blacks had to wait to be served at the back of the store. An internal 1972 CDM report said they were paying African workers on average 61 Rand a month while paying White workers 767 Rand.[5]

In 1969 the United Nations revoked South Africa's authority over Namibia and in 1971 the World Court upheld this decision. In 1971 and 1972 the Ovambo contract workers withdrew their labor en masse from the diamond mine, protesting that their contracts were unjust and, risking arrest, returned home. On January 10th, 1972 after a large protest meeting at Oluno, Ondongwa, a De Beers agent reported that the workers were furious about the "kontrak" and the "Draad" (the latter meant the fence or prison, meaning their quarters at the mine.)[6] They complained that they were not allowed to change jobs and could be rounded up, jailed or forcibly returned if they left their workplace. They could not go home for family sickness or family emergencies. They were frequently humiliated by being publicly stripped naked for medical examinations. It was a form of slavery.

Early mine dormitory.

One speaker said: "The contract system has changed the so-called homelands into a slave labor market... This slavery has resulted in Ovambo compounds in the form of a prison, with one entrance and sharp pieces of glass cemented on the top of walls, and hard beds made out of concrete which cripples the people."[7]

Such concrete beds were also until very recently the rule in Kimberley hostels near to the De Beers headquarters.

An internal De Beers managers' report of October 1972 reported that the miners complained of poor pay and food and the lack of privacy in hostels where ten men shared a prison-like room with closed windows at ceiling height. They could not stay up at night for the lights were switched on and off at fixed times from the administration block. There were no dining halls. There were no partitions, cubicles or doors in the lavatories so people had to defecate in public. (In 1994 I found similar conditions in De Beers' mines in South Africa.)

These conditions were not just in the diamond mines, but also in the Oppenheimers' gold mines. An internal March 1976 report by Anglo American staff at the Western Holdings mine reported the black miners were saying: "We live like animals in the compounds without our wives... The life we lead here is worse than slavery or the life of a beast of burden." When Anglo asked the Chamber of Mines' Human Resources Laboratory to analyze working conditions, they found, "poor pay, inferior living conditions, severe food shortages, dirt." It was calculated that bringing black accommodation up to full white worker standards would cost a quarter of a year's profits. This deterred change.

Oppenheimer argued that it would not be proper for his companies to use their strength and dominance of South African industry to pressurize the South African government in favor of more liberal policies. "We have to cooperate with the government on many occasions. It would be quite wrong to use Anglo to pressure the government." But former South African Prime Minister Verwoerd disagreed. He said Oppenheimer "...can pull strings. With all that monetary power and with his powerful machine, which is spread over the whole of the country, he can, if he so chooses, exercise an enormous influence against the Government and the State."

The National Union of Mineworkers was only set up in Kimberley in the 1980s although there were many earlier attempts to organize workers. Their 1987 strike involved 340,000 workers in 44 mines and was the largest in South African history. During the strike, the police raided union offices and arrested the entire regional leadership. The mine compounds were forcibly entered with armored vehicles. Fifty thousand workers were dismissed and union organization forced underground. In early 1994 bomb blasts shattered union offices. But after the ANC election victory that year the threat sharply diminished. By late 1994 NUM was one of the strongest of the South African unions, although somewhat weakened by losing many officials who had been elected to Parliament.

INVESTIGATING THE KOFFIEFONTEIN AND FINSCH DIAMOND MINES

In Kimberley in 1994, NUM asked De Beers' permission for me to go into two diamond mines, Koffiefontein and Finsch. The union branch secretary, Joseph Leburu, told me such requests were always granted and indeed the signs were good.

De Beers diamond mine described on a board erected in Kimberley.

Finsch replied that I could come and suggested arrangements. But a few days later Leburu called me into his office and said, "The branch officers of the union were called in by De Beers yesterday for what it called an 'urgent divisional meeting.' We were simply told the General Manager, John Vassey, wanted to see us. When we entered we were told they had instructions from Head Office that you were not to be allowed in because of your association with *The Diamond Empire* film. It was a two minute meeting." Leburu said he could not remember anyone else getting banned – at least since the 1985-6 State of Emergency.

This ban made De Beers mineworkers even more interested in my film and in talking to me. They quietly arranged to watch it on De Beers' premises and afterwards told me that they thought it very accurate. If the company had organized my trip to the mines, no doubt I would have had a sanitized and bowdlerized tour of all the

Terraced mine sides.

cleanest areas of the mines. Instead, I now learned about conditions in the more dangerous parts of the mines from the viewpoint of the miners.

At Koffiefontein, a 90-minute drive south from Kimberley in the Orange Free State, a shop steward took me to view the mine pit; a vast circle of cliffs encircling what looked like rotting gray cheese. This center was the diamond-rich core, made up of a blue gray kimberlite that decays when exposed, powdering into fine dust. The mine was now too deep for the use of the terraced roads that still spiraled down into the pit. Instead, shafts had been sunk alongside the pit, elevators installed, and tunnels driven horizontally into the pipe. The holes I saw in the decaying kimberlite were tunnels through which diamond ore was now extracted and the pits ventilated. Rock falls and dust storms were frequent inside the mine. Sometimes mudflows closed a mine down as at Wesselton in 1992. By 1992 the Kimberley mine was 995 meters deep, the Finsch 680 meters and Koffiefontein 370 meters deep.

The Koffiefontein diamond mine was surrounded by razor wire. The entrance gate was more appropriate to that of a prison, a fortress constructed to stop diamonds escaping. The mine was about to start reprocessing the vast waste hills nearby to seek any diamonds it had missed earlier. These hills were secluded behind more barbed wire fences patrolled by trail bikes and four-wheel drives driven by people from outside Koffiefontein, since the mine allegedly did not trust local people.

THE ASBESTOS DUST HAZARD IN DIAMOND MINES

I spoke at a mass meeting of the miners of Koffiefontein about my research and the effort by De Beers to ban me. They told me what life was like underground. Explosive methane gas was a constant danger. Dust blew in thick clouds from holes in the crater floor to obscure vision throughout the mine's levels and shafts. Sometimes they could not see more than three yards. One miner explained, "Dust is thick everywhere, on every level. It blocks our noses with black stuff despite our flimsy nosebags [dust masks]. It is especially bad when mixed with the fumes from blasting." Ventilation and dust control measures were appallingly bad on all levels. A worker told me that when

Exits from mine shafts onto mine pit floor.

they had showers after work, "we even have to bring our own soap."

I asked about health problems from the dust.

"Yes, many of us have lung and breathing problems. When the mine inspector comes, he just visits what the mine manager shows him."

"What about medical records?"

"De Beers controls all health matters. Medical certificates from doctors that do not work for De Beers may not be accepted. We are told we must get a certificate from one of the two De Beers doctors. These doctors do not listen to us. If the doctor sees you can't breathe properly, they retrench you certifying you are healthy then, when you are offered work, perhaps two months later, they then discover you are too sick to be employed! The mine chases you out so it won't have to pay [sick pay or compensation]."

I asked, "Are many miners laid off as sick?"

"De Beers hires workers as temporary in the first place – and if they fall sick they say the 'lungs are wet' and so cannot make them permanent. It is hard for us to get compensation even if permanent. White workers with damaged lungs get 49,000 to 51,000 Rand. Colored workers get over 30,000 Rand. But 2,800 Rand is the maximum for black workers."

When I gained entry into Finsch, despite being banned from it, I soon found out how very dangerous the dust in diamond mines could be. I learned that the rock within the diamond pipe sometimes contains a dangerous form of serpentine more commonly called asbestos. The union's Health and Safety Officer told me: "Sometimes the diamonds lie in asbestos." Mine staff had informed him privately that asbestos made up 30 percent of the dust contaminating most levels of the Finsch mine – although the management had denied this, admitting to only 1.5 percent asbestos. Since asbestos is considered so dangerous that a building in which it is found in the US or UK would be immediately sealed until fully protected workers could remove all traces of

The Finsch Mine.

it, even the level admitted by management was a cause for much alarm. At Finsch, remote-controlled trucks extract dangerously decayed diamond rich rocks directly from the bottom of the 423 meter deep open pit, thus creating more dense dust clouds.

The Health and Safety Officer told me, "The dust is often so thick one can only see a meter ahead. We sometimes get nosebags to wear, but we are told the mine hasn't that many and we must make one nosebag last at least a year. In 20 minutes a new mask gets filled with dust and stops working properly. Our noses are always getting plugged up, filled with black muck. The smell of the chemicals used in explosions also gives us heavy headaches, affects our sinuses." The nosebags were nothing much more than strips of cloth. The hills near Finsch are officially called the Asbestos Hills because they are full of this dangerous mineral. The Finsch diamond deposit was first discovered by prospectors looking for asbestos, not diamonds.

Kimberlite, the principal diamond-bearing ore, is made up largely of serpentine, and this often takes the form of fibrous serpentine asbestos. Samples of this fibrous form can be kept safely only inside closed glass containers, since they are known to be a major cancer risk.[8]

As for mine ventilation at Finsch, "many of the fans in the underground mine have not been working for over two years," alleged a miner. The union safety officer added, "They say electricity is so expensive that they have to turn off the fans and dust extractors for whole days at a time. The whole mine is full of dust." If these accounts of dangerous cost-saving measures are true, it is no wonder that the mining superintendent at Finsch, Mark Button, could boast in 1994: "Our costs compare with the best in the De Beers group."[9] I noted that dust blew from the mines over the nearby townships and the children's playing grounds.

I researched the asbestos allegations. A doctor in Kimberley told me he never saw the miners most affected by the dust. Only miners paid at C band or higher had health insurance. "The A and B band miners [the black miners] who are the most exposed have no health insurance. De Beers' doctors instead give them free medical aid – and keep their health records secret. Only these doctors have the relevant health records." These doctors had asked De Beers for a modern x-ray machine but they were still using a much older model. I checked with a senior nurse at a Kimberley hospital. She said that she had many patients with inflamed lung disorders that were similar to asbestosis. She did not know of any relevant independent research.

At the suggestion of a Kimberley doctor I asked staff at the De Beers geology department if they knew of any studies of asbestos content in mine dust. They did not. But I discovered reports by Russians saying that asbestos dust was a grave problem in Russian diamond mines – so the lack of published information on this in South Africa was remarkable. De Beers must have known of this danger.

UNRECORDED X-RAYING OF DIAMOND MINEWORKERS

Another health danger for mineworkers is the x-rays used in diamond mines to detect diamond theft. I was told at Koffiefontein that, "the washing plant and sorting house workers go every day to the x-ray." At the Kleinzee mine on the coast, a De Beers security guard who operated the x-rays explained:

> Many black miners are x-rayed daily as they leave the premises but they do not know it. My boss sets the rates for x-raying. It can vary but I am told it should not be done generally more than three to four times a week. But I have a manual override and when I am suspicious I can do it more often. I have to do it more often to protect myself if a miner is suspected, as I am responsible if a miner is found to have smuggled out a diamond. On the forms we only mark up three x-rays per person a week. If there are more x-rays a week for any miner, these are recorded on the forms under "S" for "Search" or "O" for "Other." Management knows what is happening.

The "General Rules for X-Raying," signed by Judy Alexander, the Senior Security Officer at the De Beers mine at Kleinzee, on November 19th, 1992, state: "The maximum permissible dose may not be exceeded i.e. 350 mr per year (about 3-4 shots per week, 12-15 per month or 150 per year)." When I showed this document to the

X-ray sign in diamond mine.

x-ray operator, he said, "There is no way the health authorities can discover how often a man is x-rayed. He can be x-rayed several times a day. De Beers is using a new pelvic area x-ray. It is supposed to be safe but pregnant women are barred from working in the mine's security areas as they are not to be x-rayed." He added that the operators have a film badge for their own protection, but no protective clothing.

At the Kimberley mines, the x-rays for the "red" high security area are not pelvic-sensitive but head to toe – and can mistake a swallowed peanut for a diamond. One such unfortunate man was rushed to the hospital for a high-powered x-ray before they discovered their error.

Homes built by De Beers for mineworkers.

Painted shack named after liberation hero.

At Koffiefontein I was taken to inspect the accommodation provided for miners. De Beers had provided some black families with round metal homes that look like water tanks with roofs. They were bitingly cold in winter and blisteringly hot in summer. Prior to the 1994 elections the National Party decided it could not leave the provision of housing for blacks solely to De Beers or the ANC. They obtained land by the mine and put one water tap in each street block. That was that. These were called "serviced blocks" but had no sewerage or electricity. These blocks were then offered to poor families to put up shanties on them, some trying to live on De Beers' wages, some unemployed. All they could afford were tin shacks. But they were allowed to name each block – so they called their apartheid housing after the heroes of the anti-apartheid movement.

But even these shacks were threatened when their children found a diamond nearby. De Beers, like a miser who wanted no one else to be rich, surrounded the area of the children's discovery with barbed wire and covered it deeply with heavy waste so that no one else might find a diamond there. Shop Steward Joseph Botile took me there and told me, "It was very beautiful here. Our children used to play here under the trees."

The area by the bushes was where the diamond was found. The township lies in the background.

Nearby more land had been locked up behind high razor wire fences solely because three white children found a diamond there. This locked down land was previously used to graze the donkeys that pulled the carts that served the black community as taxis into town. Behind the new fences, I saw strips of bare earth raked so footprints could be detected. De Beers seemed to have ultimate control over all land used by blacks.

I was also taken to the town dump. The refuse was thrown into a disused diamond digging where blue kimberlite rock could still be seen. As I drove up to it I

Tip near Koffiefontein diamond mine.

passed children walking back to the slums carrying boxes containing their scanty finds on their heads. When I arrived at the dump I found mothers gathering food scraps into plastic bags while four year-old children played in the refuse. Old people tottering on walking sticks were looking for food. One shouted at the children, telling them not to take some firewood, as he needed it. The children dropped the wood and gathered more. One child inspected soft drink bottles for any remaining liquid. A little girl in a brown dress, hair neatly braided, left the tip carrying a plastic bag and dragging a large piece of firewood. A ten-year-old followed her with an old Tupperware box and firewood. The children were not playing as I first thought, but working.

CREATING MISERY THROUGH SUB-CONTRACTING

It took me some time to discover the subcontracted or "migrant" labor hidden inside De Beers' property. Without announcing my presence to management, I went to meet the miners living on De Beers' mining leases, driving somewhat nervously up roads that bypassed the main gate. They took me first to see the accommodation provided by De Beers. There were no longer concrete beds as were provided earlier at Bultfontein mine. They were now living either in school-like dormitories or in small rooms about eight feet wide that just managed to contain two beds. Some rooms had no doors. The toilets were dilapidated. Cooking equipment was of the camping sort and minimal.

Two miners in De Beers hostel.   Cooking facility in De Beers mine.   Subcontracted camp.

But I was astonished to be told by these miners that most of them were no longer officially working for De Beers – although they lived on De Beers' land in De Beers' buildings and were working underground in a De Beers mine. They were formally working for contractors, former white employees of De Beers who were paid by De Beers to recruit and run teams of black workers.

There were approximately ten such teams of between eight and 50 members at Koffiefontein. Some members were paid only 180 Rand ($53) a month. The average was between R300 and R400 a month. If directly employed by De Beers, their minimum union-negotiated pay would have been R1,070 ($295) a month. They were not allowed to join the union. The highest paid sub-contractor I met told me he made R600 – but this was for working seven days a week, nine hours a day. Wages had not improved in international terms by 2002, when the mineworkers' union, NUM, agreed to a minimum monthly wage equivalent to $250 or about $60 a week. The subcontracted workers were accommodated in much worse conditions than were the regular De Beers workers. They also worked in much more dangerous conditions. A shop steward alleged that, as these workers were not working directly for De Beers, De Beers said it had no responsibility for their safety: "Some sub-contracted teams have no safety gear. They have no protection. No medical or unemployment provision protects them." The subcontracted workers told me they wanted to find a way to join the union. "But if our boss should find out we would be sacked. The boss would throw us out and drive to Lesotho to get replacements."

When I gained entry to Finsch, I found it was a more modern mine than Koffiefontein with newer facilities, even with its own church, so I presumed conditions for the workers might be better than in the older mines. But it was far worse. The hostels for subcontracted labor were hidden deep inside De Beers' property, accessed by private roads and invisible to the public. Again the hostels were single sex. Those for workers directly employed by De Beers were fine outside, surrounded with lawns with neat edges, but inside, there was no privacy. The miners shared small rooms with enough space for a single bedside table between their beds. The showers had no curtains or doors, were dirty and ill-maintained. The floors inside and outside the toilets were cracked, filthy and stank.

Down the side of a hill below the mine, still on De Beers' property, I found the hostels for subcontracted labor. Here about 500 men were accommodated, one half of the subcontracted labor force at Finsch, according to an ANC Member of Parliament, Godfrey Oliphant, a former mineworker. (He told me half the 2,000-strong workforce at Finsch was subcontracted.) The union took me on a tour. In one building

Housing in subcontracted camp, Finsch.

Beds on floor in subcontracted camp.

Bare-shelved shop for diamond mineworkers.

the floor had rotted away, leaving large holes covered with dustbin and saucepan lids. In one building they could not use bedsteads because the bed legs went through the rotten floor timbers – so they slept on the floor. Some rooms slept up to 14 on crowded bunks. Cooking facilities were primitive. The shower had no roof and doubled up as a refuse dump. Their tiny store had the barest essentials like white sugar

Miner cooking in hostel.

and tea. Rubble and waste covered the ground around the hostels. As for the wages, a worker in this camp told me he received only R310 a month. This was one quarter of union minimum rates. Another reported he received far less, R165 ($48) for a whole month's work. There were nine contractor gangs at Finsch, all white-controlled. A union organizer told me that when members were laid off temporarily because De Beers' requirements for diamonds had dropped (500 were thus laid off in August 1992), when production rose again, they were replaced by cheaper non-unionized contract labor. The black workers bitterly told me that the "white contractors are living in splendor on the basis of slave labor."

I was also smuggled in to meet the miners in the sparsely furnished older hostels in the Dutoitspan mine, close to Kimberley's town center. They told me De Beers had also introduced contract labor into their mine, that these workers stayed in the same hostel as them – but received less than a third of union rates and were sacked if they joined the union. They feared this practice was spreading. They told me, "We cannot help a contractee if they are wounded. They have no health protection. De Beers says it is not us, it is the contractor who is responsible." While I was there, this system was being expanded with new contractor teams.

De Beers allegedly denied any responsibility for these low paid workers – despite a provision in the Mines legislation making a mining company responsible for the well-being of all on their mine's land. De Beers took responsibility only for the workers it directly employed, but even then paid them at a minimal rate – R1,060 to R1,500 a month, scarcely enough to support a family. When the unionized mineworkers of Kimberley in 1994 asked De Beers for more pay, a shop steward told me the De Beers General Manager complained: "Ordinary people were keeping diamonds in Angola. We have no control over these people. They are giving diamonds into the wrong hands. We have to pay them market prices so we cannot afford to pay you more." (This was seemingly an admission that De Beers was buying the diamonds

Entrance to Dutoitspan mine.   Signs at Dutoitspan mine entrance.

produced by the terrorist organization UNITA.)

Apartheid is now officially abolished in South Africa but literate and intelligent black miners told me how De Beers still appointed "unqualified illiterate whites over us, even when we are much more qualified. They are stupid. Some cannot even write reports. One could not even spell 'weekend.' De Beers bends over backwards to help them but it is very hard for us to get promotion or further training." No white gets employed below the C2 wage band – while nearly all blacks are in the low-paid A and B bands.

At the Dutoitspan hostel a major complaint was that "they do not give us time off to study, just a day off before exams. We have no time to improve ourselves." They start work at dawn, knock off at 4:30 PM and must be back in the compound by 6:30 PM. As the hostel sign shows, no visitors are allowed after normal working hours. "If you go to town for a class, De Beers will not help you with transport. If you get back after 7:30 PM the canteen is closed. They would not let us bring teachers to the hostels. De Beers said, 'you don't need education. You are more educated than the educators.'" The miners complained about overcrowding: "There are six people to a room. We have been asking for two persons maximum a room but they will not give it." There were 154 workers in this hostel. Outside De Beers had put up a sign, "No visitors between 5 PM and 6 AM." This effectively stopped them having any visitors, including teachers. I had to be smuggled in.

The mineworkers were treated with scant regard. When Koffiefontein was temporarily shut on June 12th, 1982 because of a downturn in the diamond market, they were given no warning. "We were at work and about 12 o'clock we were called together and told that the mine is closed. We had to tell those who came for the afternoon shift. It was a great shock. We were not given the chance to negotiate how the close down should happen. About ten days beforehand, people wrote on the walls underground that the mine would be closing in June. De Beers then handed out letters offering a reward for information on who wrote this message. No one was found – but what they wrote was the truth."

When "in 1988 there was a flood in the mine, most of us worked 12 hour shifts to pump it out. Afterwards the white workers were given a braai [barbecue] with their families to thank them for helping. The black workers were thanked by being disciplined for being tired. If one sat down, that one was sacked."

A shop steward told me at Koffiefontein: "At every divisional (De Beers) meeting I reported abuses to management but was told I must stop 'crying' or action would be taken against me. I was told I must not speak to the press without the approval of the manager. The union office was on the mine's switchboard and one of the switchboard staff told me all union calls were taped."

The workers tried to get De Beers to contribute to improved community facilities. "It took many months' work to get De Beers to agree to put up a couple of asbestos-sheet constructed schoolrooms." They showed me the very unsafe structures provided to serve as schools for the children. They already had holes in an end wall and would have been condemned in England.

In October 2002 the National Union of Mineworkers organized a major protest at Finsch against both De Beers and the subcontracting company TNC. The mineworkers were complaining of the assaults and the racism prevalent not just at Finsch but at all De Beers mines.

THE SMALLER DIAMOND MINES NEAR KIMBERLEY

Of the smaller mines near Kimberley, the first I visited was the Bellsbank Mine. To reach it I had to travel deep into the bush down gravel tracks frequently crossed by monkeys and meerkats. On arrival, I was let through high security fences. Once inside we drove past a mine police station to the manager's office. Then, after a brief word with the manager, we drove over rubble to the migrant labor hostel. It felt as if we had traveled in a time machine back to the worst days of 19th century industrial life. Here the miners lived in three dilapidated barracklike buildings set around a compound. In its center there was a communal kitchen where many were then cooking porridge or gruel. We talked and they alleged that the mine management used beatings and intimidation – and even a pistol to threaten a miner.

Accommodation was ten to a room. They slept on bunks, often without mattresses. They covered the wires of beds with sheets of cardboard or folded blankets. The showers were accessed over a stinking drain and had no privacy. There was only cold water. It had dirt in it and tasted odd.

One miner told me, "If our wives come to visit, they must stay off the mine's premises, out of the compound. They could be arrested for trespass if smuggled in.

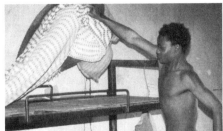

Bellsbank dormitory.   Miner revealing lack of mattress – a common complaint.

This is regarded as a criminal charge and, as such, not a matter for the union. Only white families are allowed to come to visit their husbands." The workers had no safety boots, just soft-toed rubber boots, even though they worked underground and with explosives. A methane explosion had recently seriously injured a miner.

The management had learned a lesson from Cecil Rhodes. He said the compound system would create a controlled market to which management could profitably sell food. At the shop run by management at Bellsbank prices and profits were high. Bread that cost R2 a loaf in town here cost R2.80. Chicken that cost R2.60 in town here cost R6. Twenty cigarettes went up from R2.80 to R3.60. The shop made R17,000 a week profit – despite the abysmally low wages of its customers.

One worker received, prior to deductions, R96 plus R10 food allowance a week. Another told me he received R94 a week. After their food purchases on credit had been deducted, they would receive in hand often no more than 40 Rand ($12) a week or even less. Some received nothing. These wages made the workers dread going home for weekends. "The fare home is R10. We have nothing to give our families. Our wives fight us. Our marriages break up."

Bellsbank contained, they told me, large fine diamonds, many over ten carats. It was negotiating to expand by taking over a nearby and unused De Beers diamond deposit. I asked the workers what would happen if they asked for higher wages. They told me that the management would simply close down the mine for a few months then restart on the same wage terms. Western Deep Level Mine was closed for three months that year after workers asked for higher wages.

The conditions at Bellsbank were duplicated at another mine nearby, owned by Canadians and managed from a former

Miner in dormitory.

school house, closed as a school because of a shortage of white children (black miners here as elsewhere were not allowed to have their families with them). From behind a massive desk, the manager told me the only sensible policy was to mine the diamonds as fast as possible as no one knew what would happen in the future. He thought that if Angola came on stream as a major diamond mining country after its civil war ended, the diamond market might collapse.

At Loxton, the workers lived in a compound with a disused watchtower and massive gate. In the shabby dormitories, as at Bellsbank, workers had to use sheets of cardboard to cover the wire frames of their bunk beds in the absence of mattresses. Electric lights could not be switched off because light switches were not provided.

Loxton showers.

Mineworker's bunk.

Broken high-up windows let in wind and dust. The showers had no privacy. Their diet was poverty-stricken. A small shop by the gate sold very basic rations: sugar, flour, coffee, potatoes, and some meat. Not much else. Meat was a luxury. Green vegetables were unheard of.

Yet, despite all this, the miners' spirits were high when I arrived. They had succeeded in having a manager removed. They asked me here, and at Bellsbank, to address the miners in the compound and to tell them about how the diamond industry worked internationally. I felt honored and small before these men who suffered so much just to survive. Afterwards they performed a defiant Toi Toi dance, starting in the courtyard and going down towards the manager's office. They chanted, in remarkably good spirits, "We work under ground/ we work under ground/ for no money."

From here I was taken through a security gate to yet another isolated compound – this at the Frank Smith diamond mine. By now it was getting dark. Dim lights lit the courtyard in the compound. Each room again slept many miners. Again the conditions were totally primitive. In England or America it would have been illegal to keep animals in such conditions.

An investment advisor, Doug Casey, was then recommending investment in Diamond Field Resources, the Canadian company that purchased the Frank Smith Mine and Bellsbank. It reported that Frank Smith was producing fine gem quality stones, worth some $220 per carat, and this gave the mine a "free cash flow" of some $3.3 million a year. Bellsbank's diamonds were reportedly not as good on average as Frank Smith's, but more in number. It was making a declared profit of $5 million a year. On my second trip

Mineworker cooking in dormitory.

to these mines I was invited to the home of a black miner at Loxton who had been fortunate enough to find accommodation where he could live with his wife. It was a garage beside a white-owned home. He said they were very privileged to have so much space. It was roughly furnished. A blanket curtain gave privacy to their sleeping quarters. Their hospitality was generous – they shared whatever they had with us.

Their floor was made of gravel from the mine's kimberlite waste. All the local roads were coated with this. But he told me it would be dangerous for him to put in his pocket a piece of kimberlite picked up from his floor. Even if it had no diamond in it, it's very presence in his pocket could lead to him being arrested and losing his job on suspicion of IDB – illicit diamond buying. He picked up a piece from his floor and showed it to me. It had a very tiny sparkle in it.

Stories abounded of big diamonds mined at Loxton, of the large cloth bags of diamonds seen in the management offices, although the manager told me that profits were "borderline." There was a great deal of secrecy in these appalling mines. Loxton mined rich fissures within the volcanic lava spilled by an ancient diamond-rich volcanic pipe. The pipe was not mined – for it was on a lease held securely and unmined by De Beers. I was told that when Loxton found its diamond-rich fissure, De Beers grabbed all the surrounding land and locked it up so no one else could mine it.

The main fissure was 2-3 feet wide and went very deep. When I visited, no water was used to control the dust in the unventilated tunnels and fissures. The manager said the mine would soon have ventilation – as he was now in the course of trying to get fans. This suggested to me that it must be dangerously dusty.

The management informed the union while I was there that the mine was about to introduce a mining method called the "Underhand," asking the union to agree to this while telling them it would be introduced in a week's time. This new mining system involved mineworkers some 1,200 to 1,700 feet below the surface digging into the fissure while keeping its sides braced apart – not as before by first removing the surrounding rock. The union feared the increased danger entailed by this new method. They thought the surrounding rock could be dangerously weakened by the blasting and by nearby narrow parallel fissures, but the union could not prevent this happening.

The Canadian company Diamond Field Resources took control of the Loxton and Frank Smith mines in 1994. This company was founded and headed up by Jean Boulle, whom we will also meet in Arkansas and the Congo. In 1995 Loxton passed to another Canadian company, Rex Diamonds, which was developing a diamond-rich fissure mine in Sierra Leone, where it reported good relations with both Government and RUF – before the 1997 coup forced it to suspend operations. In 2002 it reported Bellsbank's fine large rough diamonds were fetching a good price, around $300 per carat, and that it was expanding production.

In 2002 it was reported that six mineworkers had died at Loxton, four of them when they fell 180 meters to the bottom of a shaft when the cable of the elevator, or "cage," broke.

THE DIAMOND MINES OF THE FORBIDDEN COAST

I then traveled south to the richest South African diamond mines of them all, on the coast of Namaqualand. Every farmhouse I passed seemed to have a set of huts or barracks for its workers. Countless black families were walking from town to town or trying to hitchhike. With their income, cars were an impossible luxury. Often the tarmacked road had rough dirt tracks alongside it. These were for those blacks fortunate enough to have a donkey or horse drawn cart. Apartheid might have ended but grim conditions continued on many of the white-owned farms.

It was spring in Namaqualand; the hills were carpeted with flowers, purple, yellow and white. I saw

A local taxi.

"Quiver" tree.

a few ancient "quiver" trees with bark resembling silver armor and branches like heraldic drawings crowned with tufts of cacti-like leaves. The dispossessed Bushmen made quivers for their arrows from these branches. I had to stop to help a tortoise cross the road. I then descended a long dirt road, twisting and uninviting, with signs forbidding access, to a vast De Beers lease stretching along most of the western coast of South Africa – an enormous forbidden zone. I had been invited by mineworkers in the private De Beers mining town of Kleinzee to show and speak about our film *The Diamond Empire*.

The mineworkers' union applied a week in advance for me to be admitted and seemingly no alarm bells had been rung. The security guard at the gate was expecting me and called my hosts to collect me.

The union had found accommo-dation for me in a "colored" security guard's home. I could not stay with a black as they were only provided with beds in single sex hostels where they were not allowed guests. Only the coloreds and whites were provided with family homes. They were also given a black or colored servant and servant's quarters. As apartheid had been officially abolished, the reason De Beers now gave for not giving blacks married quarters was that the black workers did not belong to the correct wage band. They were nearly all in the lowest paid A and B bands which gave them rights only to single sex accommodation in a hostel. A union organizer told me, "One or two blacks are C band – but they are only window-dressing. Most are A band."

Sign on road to Kleinzee.

Mineworkers' mess at Kleinzee.

The colored family I stayed with introduced me to their black servant (to me of a scarcely distinguishable hue from the coloreds). I learned from her that she had a husband in the mine's single quarters with whom she could not stay and an eight year-old daughter whom she was not allowed to keep with her. Abe LaRouse, my host, told me, "It's a De Beers' rule." His wife added, "If my husband got a job outside the mine, even though I have a job here, I would have to move into single quarters and my children would have to leave. If a white worker gets married, he instantly gets married quarters. The administration is all white. Apartheid is really alive at Kleinzee. It is a major issue here." A black miner told me, "They are breaking up families for diamonds."

If a wife of a black miner obtained work at the mine, she was put in female single sex hostels. If she should sleep with her husband in either of their rooms, they were to be punished. A notice posted inside Villa Rosa, the female hostel, read, "Complaints have been received that men are sleeping over in Villa Rosa. Management regards

Family waiting by Kleinzee mine gate.

these offences as very serious and will act in future severely towards those that are guilty." If a woman should get pregnant she must leave for three months and not return with her child – if she wished to keep her job.

A black husband could make a booking for one of the few houses made available for conjugal visits – but the waiting list was very long as there were between 2,000 and 3,000 black workers at Kleinzee. I noted on arrival the girlfriends and wives of the miners waiting patiently outside the security gate for a brief conversation with their husbands at the gate. Black women could not enter the town if not employed by De Beers. The company might promote engagement rings but the black miners told me bitterly that for them, "this company promotes divorce."

As apartheid was officially abolished, the former primary school for coloreds at Kleinzee was now the Junior Primary for both colored and white children, the former primary school for whites now the Senior Primary for all – but not the blacks. The black workers of A and B Band did not need a school since their children were banned from the township. If black miners should bring a child to the school, it would not be allowed in.

The black workers were given no permanent status. "They are not allowed to stay here if they do not have jobs," I was told. The mining town was some 50 miles from any other town – and 80 percent of the workers were Xhosa with families in the far distant Ciskei and Transkei. Many of the wives waiting by the mine gate had traveled a long way for their brief and difficult meeting.

In 1995 three black miners' wives with young children were sent to prison for "trespassing" onto the De Beers mine site. The women were demanding the right to live with their husbands. They wanted the use of empty houses at Kleinzee but were refused by the company.[10]

Wives doing washing in shantytown.

All this seemed quite at odds with the De Beers advertising of diamonds as the symbol of love. I could not find a single black diamond miner who had bought his fiancée a diamond engagement ring.

From Kleinzee down the Forbidden Coast

It's told that when Harry Oppenheimer said he was coming to Kleinzee, four Mercedes Benz cars were brought hundreds of kilometers from Cape Town. The whole town was repainted – even the pavements were painted black and white – and everything was heavily guarded. But his plane did not land. When I asked the miners if they had ever seen an Oppenheimer, one replied, "I have been here for

19 years and I have never seen one. However if I make it to 25 years employment I may be presented to one."

Namaqualand is a continuation of the Skeleton Coast of legend, blasted by wind, where sailors dreaded shipwreck with little shelter or sources of fresh water. For hundreds of kilometers the coast is lined with sand dunes, covered with heathland and grazed by ostriches. For 275 kilometers this South African coast is also owned by De Beers; giving it a long narrow coastal empire 15 to 29 kilometers wide.

De Beers guarded the local diamonds so jealously that I was told that whenever an ostrich is killed or injured by a car, "We must call security. They call the abattoir. They have to come and slaughter it and cut out its crop. Ostriches eat small stones to help with digestion so their crop might contain diamonds. The crop is delivered to the 'DPU' or 'Diamond Protection Unit.' The ostrich meat goes to the bosses."

Ostrich on De Beers coastal mining lease.

There are several De Beers mines along this private forbidden coast, apart from the one at Kleinzee. Some 30-40 kilometers north from Kleinzee I visited the large diamond separation plants known as the Buffels Marine complex. Inland of Kleinzee, up the Buffels River, are the Buffelsbank mines. About 80 kilometers south of Kleinzee, I found a major mining center called Koingnaas, another private De Beers mining town. South still further is the De Beers mining area of Michells Bay. Much further south, on more De Beers land, is Namakwa, a major mineral sands mine. De Beers owns nearly the entire Atlantic coast of South Africa.

The town of Kleinzee was separated from the mine proper by a security fence that was floodlit and patrolled all night. I could see the lights from the house where I stayed. The mine had posted a warning: "Due to increase in diamond theft, from the 23rd March 1992, no cigarettes, pipes and tobacco, food, lip-ice, jars of cream, lighters etc. will

Car dump at Kleinzee.

be allowed to leave the mining area without being cleared through the industrial belt." This was a conveyor belt supervised by x-rays and security guards.

I was given an official De Beers tour of the Kleinzee mine, escorted by the wife of the chief geologist and by union officials. After passing through the cream painted corridors of the security division, we came out in a car park inside the security gates. Nearby was a yard for abandoned cars. No cars could leave once they have entered the mine so these were to be buried in the diggings. This was to prevent them from being used to smuggle out diamonds.

A union official pointed out to me the disused migrant labor compound. It was surrounded by two lines of barbed wire fences set far enough apart to keep workers from throwing a diamond out. At one end stood a guard tower resembling that of a concentration camp. A worker told me, "It closed in 1977. I remember how it was in 1969. It was exactly like a prison camp. About 1,000 workers stayed there, eight to a room. No women were allowed in." He added, "If an employee died here, his body must be buried here as De Beers feared thieves might hide diamonds in his corpse. The family never saw him again."

The first stop on the official tour was at a plant where we watched giant trucks dumping diamond rich conglomerate into crushing jaws. Nearby, in a small, well-

Former workers' camp at Kleinzee.   Kleinzee crusher.   Kleinzee diamond ore containers.

fortified enclosure, I saw what looked like metal gas bottles. When I asked what these were, I learned they were high security containers for the diamond rich concentrate. From the platform at the crushing works, I saw the mine stretched over the far horizon.

We traveled on to where sand was being scraped from the ancient shorelines, exposing flat eroded seashore rocks – but these were no longer on the shoreline. Kleinzee diamond mine is made up of at least six separate ancient shorelines formed when the land and sea was from 15 to 95 meters above current sea level. The richest is the deepest buried. Giant bucket draglines dig down 35 meters to expose the precious ancient shoreline – teams of "bedrock sweepers" then clean the crevices in the exposed rock. The sweepers were all blacks. Their backs were bent double while they raked through crevices with metal spikes or swept with hand brushes. Some others were using giant vacuum cleaners, poking the hoses into the potholes and deep fissures, seeking any diamonds they had trapped. These vacuum cleaners, or "transvacs," pumped the diamond-rich gravel into yellow safes on wheels. I learned that mine workers were commonly sacked whenever "on balance of probability," the mine management decides that they might have stolen diamonds. One worker told me that when he bought a car the mine administration called him in to find out how he got the money. Such checks were not unusual. The union told me that between 1993 and 1994 at least 50 workers, all bedrock cleaners, were "either dismissed, suspended or intimidated into resigning on suspicion of diamond theft."

At the De Beers controlled CDM mine north of Kleinzee they calculated they could "cleanse" some 125,000 square meters every month with some 1,000 bedrock cleaners, working in "gangs" of 20. The ancient diamond-rich fossil beaches they cleansed were on average some 760 meters wide – and up to 80 kilometers long. De Beers calculated its total extraction costs at about R4 (40 cents US) for every meter cleansed of diamonds, including the cost of removing the sand dunes from over the bedrock. Most diamonds were found in the sand immediately over the rocks or in cracks within the rocks. Sixteen meters might need to be swept on average to find

The ancient beach rocks are exposed and vacuumed.

Miner vacuuming up diamond ore.

one diamond, giving an average cost of about $6.40 per diamond – but, as the average size found was 0.8 of a carat, and they were all gem-quality, this made the whole operation highly profitable.[11]

Abe LaRouse, the former regional chairman of NUM, bravely wrote an account of his life with De Beers and gave it to me, telling me to use his name:

My friends… were all hostel dwellers, married, with an average of four children. I worked for the company as a security officer for 10 years… At the time I started we had one weekend off a month. It cost about R14 to get home… It was then an accepted fact that all of us were poor people. But this acceptance of our circumstances and living conditions was accepted with an air of desperation. We would often talk about our condition but mostly about the racist law of De Beers, the white minority's privileges… It was seen as a sin to be both a security officer and a member of the union.

The talk of Kleinzee when I arrived was of De Beers' plans to privatize town services. Many feared the loss of their jobs or severe pay cuts. It seemed De Beers planned to introduce in this richest of all South African mines a similar system to that already employed in the Kimberley mines. In future many workers would be not directly employed but subcontracted. They would consequently have their pay slashed. Already De Beers had outsourced the teams of workers that searched coastal beaches for diamonds. These now worked for around 400 Rand a month ($112) – about a third of the minimum union rates. They lived in shacks by the beach and sucked diamonds from rich diamond deposits on the nearby seabed with shore-based equipment. They also believed they would lose their jobs if they joined the mineworkers' union.

Some of these worked for Benguella Concessions, a company that operated as a partner of Australia's largest mining company, BHP. Their base was accessed from the De Beers private road from Kleinzee to Koingnaa. They worked offshore, sucking diamonds from the seabed with vacuum equipment installed on ships. I was told their divers earned 980 Rand a month. This was below De Beers' lowest rates for directly employed manual unskilled workers. From this 980 Rand food had to be deducted. This cost them 150 Rand a month when on board the ships. There were no overtime payments.

As I left the mine through the gates at Kleinzee, I gave a lift to one of the black women who had come to meet her husband at the gate. She wanted to go to

Township near Kleinzee.

the shack in which she lived in the nearest squatter camp, behind Port Nolloth, about 40 kilometers away. I noted that Port Nolloth's harbor was awash with fishing boats with hoses, lying by them on the mud like vast umbilical cords. These were connected to giant vacuum cleaners for diamonds on the ships.

DE BEERS AND THE ALEXKOR DIAMOND MINE

North of Port Nolloth lies the enormous mining lease of Alexkor. This was the only state-owned diamond mine in Southern Africa. By the time I reached its office I had driven for hours alongside it on a road that until recently was of restricted access. Its mining lease is nearly 200 km long and some seven to 12 km wide.

Here, as in Kleinzee, the union had invited me to visit. They tried to find me accommodation in the mine's guesthouse. At first the mine management agreed but then phoned to say it was full. The union checked. It had many rooms free – but the union decided to accommodate me, to my pleasure, in a home in a township set up for colored workers.

Some 800 miners came to a hall within the mine to watch our film *The Diamond Empire* – but what was meant to be a brief introductory talk became instead a marathon session as they questioned me for some three hours about the international practices of De Beers. They said they could watch the film when I was not there, as I was leaving them a copy. They were impatient for change. Pay rates for the mineworkers started at about 1,200 Rand a month, slightly above De Beers' official rates – but still scarcely a living wage.

As elsewhere, the hostel system at this mine destroyed all family life. They joked they did not have the conjugal rights possessed by the seals that were plentiful along the coast. Women were not allowed to stay overnight. If a wife found accommodation near enough, the miners could go home on Wednesday nights and weekends. Half of the 1,600 workers lived in the hostels. Some of the higher graded coloreds stayed in the coloreds' township where houses were reasonably attractive, and where I was also staying. Many of the colored workers had domestic black servants who were paid minimal rates. These were not allowed to wash themselves in the houses where they worked. They had to go to a common ablution block – despite the official end of apartheid.

On a tempestuously windy day I secured permission to tour the mine workings with a union guide, despite protests from management that it was not a good day to go out, as the workers would be in shelters. The entire mine was shrouded in dust clouds. We drove nearly blind along tracks to the widely scattered mine operations – and discovered that these dust storms had not excused the miners from working. We came across a group of bedrock cleaners on the coastline where a dike had been constructed to keep out the waves. I was told it was a particularly diamond-rich area.

Leaving the car, I was blasted with wind-blown grit and had to walk backwards to where they were working. They wore balaclavas and some had goggles. The wind

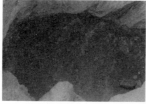

Men cleaning out crevices for diamonds.   Hole cleaned of diamond ore.

howled around them but this did not stop the gang from trying to clean the bedrock up to a white-painted stone. When they reached this, they would be entitled to a tiny bonus. They scraped the rocks beneath their feet with shovels then, bending right over, scratched the crevices empty with metal prongs and hand brushes. The management had told me that generous awards were sometimes available for a worker who picked up a good diamond. But, in reality, the workers told me diamonds are hard to see in the muddy water running around their feet. I asked many bedrock cleaners, but not one I met had received such a reward.

Occasionally they found a pothole. I climbed into one ten feet deep. A foreman told me the gravel deposits trapped in such potholes were more likely to be diamond rich when the shingle was large and rounded. They had sucked the one I climbed into empty of gravel with a transvac – the same type of vacuum cleaner that I saw at Kleinzee. Those who worked with the transvac got even fewer pickup rewards for it sucked up gravel before it could be checked for diamonds. This machine was thus highly unpopular among the workers.

The CDM mine in Namibia

The next mine north from Alexkor was larger but similar in its mining practices. On the other side of the Orange River in Namibia was the famous "Forbidden Zone" of CDM where the Oppenheimers had established their diamond fortune after taking it over from a previous German management. It is accessed via the Oppenheimer Bridge and has been under the tightest of security for a hundred years.

The chairman of the Namibian Mineworkers Union, John Shaetonhodi, told me he would have to come to meet me at Alexkor as it would take two months to get me a permit to enter CDM. But then he phoned back to ask, "Could you come

Crossing the Oppenheimer Bridge into the "Forbidden Zone" of Namibia.

this afternoon?" He had discovered if I came in immediately and did not stay later than 10 PM then my visit would not need the same security clearance. It took me only about half an hour to reach the border. I crossed the Oppenheimer Bridge with tribulation but had no problems at Namibian customs or the CDM security gate. They clearly did not know of me. I thus entered into the Forbidden Zone, driving along a road covered in sand swirling from nearby dunes. I soon reached the mining township of Oranjemund after passing through another set of high fences.

In 1979 the General Manager of CDM, J. O. Richards, telexed Anglo American and De Beers saying, "It is discriminatory, highly emotive and political dynamite… to refuse them [the black workers] the right to have their own children with them on the grounds that the houses we have provided, and are going to continue to provide, are too small for their families. The Anglo American Corporation housing standards presumably are for segregated townships in South Africa. In Oranjemund we must be careful not to lay ourselves open to accusations of establishing in 1980 segregated housing in Namibia." His protest fell on deaf ears at De Beers' headquarters.

CDM road sign.

In 1994, the living conditions of the black miners had changed little. Members of the union executive committee angrily told me, "Most miners are still in the migrant labor system. 3,000 out of the 5,000 employed are on six-month contracts. The company does not want to build us proper houses. We don't know when they will stop housing us in single sex hostels – or allow us to live here with our families."

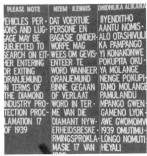

CDM vehicle sign.

They told me: "There are three hostels inside the CDM mine: Mittag houses 460 people, Uubvley 880, and North 700 – and outside there are 1,500 living in a town hostel. Accommodation is free but food is segregated. The 'B' menu is for blacks. It costs 46 Rand a month. C bands and above [i.e. whites and "coloreds"] pay 81 Rand and eat the 'A' menu in the company mess in town. C2 grade is the lowest pay for whites. It is for white women employed as typists." The mine also had ten subcontracted teams of blacks mining the inshore waters.

"If any of us are accused of diamond theft, they are dismissed even if the courts find them innocent. CDM will not let them back. The union is going to the Labor Court on this. All heads of department are white. There is only one black manager. Independence has made no difference," the union official said.

I would be remiss to describe the De Beers mines as if they were uniquely racist in practice. They existed within a whole climate of racism. As the miners again and again

Cleaning diamond beaches in the 1930s.

Cleaning diamond beaches in the same way in the 1990s.

insisted to me in 1994, apartheid had not ended in South Africa. It survived as "economic apartheid." As I traveled along the Orange River I passed many rich and meticulously kept farmland properties. But I found the farm workers still living in groups of brick huts with flat tin roofs held down with rocks, some in what looked like derelict barracks. Wages, if that is the word, were about 120 Rand a month or $55.

Some farmers made sure that even this came back to them by selling the blacks food. These wages were only enough to keep the people from starving. The lack of work elsewhere kept them from leaving. But despite these slave-like conditions, international sanctions on South Africa had ended and the wines from local vineyards were now widely available in the West.

Many whites and coloreds paid their servants wages of about only 30 Rand a week, about $9. This was for full-time work. Servants were usually not allowed to have their children live with them in the quarters provided in the yards of the white houses. The children had to stay with relatives who often lived in distant towns.

The greatest fear of many of the privileged whites was that their domestic servants and farm workers would demand wages and conditions comparable with those of white people. Most white South Africans have had it very easy. It is such wages that generated the appalling housing conditions for blacks. It is totally impossible for them on such wages to build anything other than a shack made of sheets of secondhand corrugated iron and, if they are lucky, an outside toilet.

Yet, despite the exploitation of black labor in the Oppenheimer mines, the Stellenbosch University, the top Afrikaner institution in the Cape, astonishingly saw fit to create a new chair

Agricultural housing.

called – The Harry Oppenheimer Chair for the Study of Human Rights.

Walter Sisulu, the Deputy Head of the African National Congress and a former underground mine worker, who survived years of imprisonment on Robbins Island with Nelson Mandela, told us:

The system they [the Africans] had before was broken for the mine owners. They became mere laborers in the hands of the mine owners. I crushed stones under ground in the mines. The mine owners… connived with the colonial regimes, their profits conveniently helped. The pass system directed the labor force. I had discussions with Anglo American. They sent people to talk to us. We demanded the abolition of the pass system. Our people will remain poor until the situation is reformed… The system of the mines is a horrible system because you all live in a compound…

This system continues today. It is this system that is killing our people. They [the mine owners] believe there must be no rights for the black man except rights that do not conflict with the power of the white man. They are prepared to make political concessions [but only] to keep their land and wealth.[12]

All this was still happening when I went to South Africa despite the rise to power of Nelson Mandela and the ANC. It was not that the ANC did not want reform. It was rather that it was not strong enough then to seriously challenge the Oppenheimers. It feared the consequence might be to totally disrupt the South African economy.

Alarmingly, some six years later, despite the ANC treading with care economically, not panicking the mining houses and following IMF guidelines, many of these difficulties would be exasperated, with the incomes of black-led households falling by 19 percent between 1995 and 2000, while the incomes of white-led households increased by 15 percent.

In 2000, the average weekly income of a black household would be just $60, compared with $361 for a white household, and two out of three black households in Cape Town that year would have insufficient food due to having a miniscule income below $10 a week.[13]

In August 2002, the Mineworkers' Union, NUM, agreed new pay rates for diamond mineworkers. From May 2002 the minimum would be $56 a week increasing to just under $60 in 2003. The sub-contracted were presumably still on a fraction of this.

1   *NUM Mining Handbook.* Vol. 1, 122.
2   *NUM Mining Handbook.* Vol. 1, 123.
3   Colin Newbury, *The Diamond Ring: Business, Politics and Precious Stones in South Africa, 1867-1890.* Oxford; Clarendon Press. 1989, p. 243.
4   Laurie Flynn. "Studded with Diamonds and Paved with Gold." London; Bloomsbury. 1992, p. 40.
5   Included in Appendages to the 8th Interim Thirion Report; Commission of Inquiry into Alleged Irregularities and Misapplication of Property." S.W. Africa.
6   Memorandum on Ovambo meeting from Chief Security Superintendent, CDM, Oranjemund, February 28th, 1972.
7   Flynn, p. 42. From the above memorandum by the Chief Security Officer.
8   This information is available on http://brysonburke.com/ex_serpentine.html
9   *Financial Times,* September 6th, 1994.
10 *Weekly Mail and Guardian,* November 24th, 1995.
11 Appendix to Thirion Report, p. 96.
12 Interview for *The Diamond Empire* film in 1992.
13 De Swardt and Andries du Toit, *Unraveling Chronic Poverty issues in South Africa: Some food for thought.* University of Western Cape, 2003.

Chapter 2 – In Bondage – The Child and Adult Cutters of India

It costs De Beers only a few dollars to mine a diamond, so why are the prices charged for diamond jewelry so high? They say the cutting and polishing of diamonds needs great skill – and that this costs dearly. Thus when Tim Capon, a director of De Beers Centenary,[1] wrote to the BBC after watching a pre-release copy of our film *The Diamond Empire*, he justified the high prices partly by claiming their polishing, "requires skills of a very high order."[2] True, the rare top gems are expensively and skillfully cut – but, is this true of the others – such as those used for the large engagement ring market?

De Beers sells diamonds uncut – some 65 percent of the world uncut gem diamonds in 2002 – to merchants whose cutting operations and trade they supervise – and these in turn send nearly all their gems to be cut in low-waged India. Other independent diamond producers do much the same. Thus in 2001 85 percent by weight of the world's gem quality diamonds were cut and polished in India. It imported that year some 120 million carats of uncut diamonds worth a declared $3.8 billion and sold 29 million carats of cut diamonds worth $5.2 billion. By 2002 the Indian industry employed nearly a million people and was by far India's largest single exporter.[3]

Child diamond cutter.

But in January 2001 riots broke out in Indian cities when the wages paid for cutting and polishing a diamond were cut from the equivalent of 40 cents to just 20 cents each small diamond. This shocked me. Even though I knew much about the diamond world, I had imagined with the profits within the industry so high, they must be paying more than this for the cutting of these intricate multi-sided diamonds. But I already knew of other abuses in the Indian diamond industry. When I had visited the Indian cutting workshops in Gujarat north of Mumbai in 1992, I had found many illegally employing children. I saw eight year-olds working with dangerous cutting wheels, breathing in the black diamond dust. The Indian government listed this industry as one of its most hazardous. It got worse. A European

Union investigation in the late 1990s found six year-old Indian children cutting diamonds. Many of these children were also trapped in debt bondage – a UN defined form of slavery.

Many diamond workshop owners made their workers pay for their own welfare by contributing a large part of their tiny income to the charitable trust, Jalaram Dhuaru. The daily sum it charged was equivalent to the fee they received for cutting and polishing three diamonds. Since on average they could only cut four diamonds a day (according to the authoritative *Diamond Intelligence News*), this left them with a daily income of perhaps only 20 cents a day. (I heard some coped by working long hours, to cut up to seven diamonds a day, giving them still a minute income.)

The wage cuts created so much misery in the Indian diamond cities that street protests by thousands of diamond cutters were sustained for most of January 2001. The rioters targeted diamond cutting and polishing units with stone throwing and arson attacks. Two companies of State Reserve police had to be brought in to reinforce the local police. As for the living conditions created by low wages, in September 1994 the world's press had reported a horrific outbreak of bubonic plague in these diamond-cutting workshops. This made tens of thousands of workers flee the overcrowded streets of Surat, where half of the world's gem diamonds were cut by some half a million workers. The Indian government put up roadblocks to stop them leaving, fearing they would carry the disease India-wide.

After the first two weeks of protests in 2001 there came a new wage offer. On January 16th, the Surat Diamond Manufacturer Association agreed to an increase from 10 rupees to 18 rupees (from 20 cents to 36 cents) per diamond cut and polished – still below the 21 rupees the workers had previously received. But the owners of many diamond workshops would not go along with this new offer. They said that De Beers had left them so poor that they could not pay these wages, although the value of India's diamond exports had spiraled up by 15 percent in the year 2000. The riots continued.

Then, on January 26th, 2001, a major earthquake struck the diamond cutting cities of India. Tens of thousands died – many of them diamond workers. Many were killed trying to escape from the diamond-cutting workshops in Surat and Ahmedabad.

The Medical Superintendent of the Sharadbhen Municipal Hospital, AD Dave, reported 55 deaths in one diamond workshop stampede alone. Stampedes in other diamond workshops proved equally deadly. This was because the diamond-cutting workshops had no emergency exits. They mostly had a single small exit kept locked behind security gates in order to prevent diamond thefts. The damage from the earthquake closed three quarters of the 10,000 diamond cutting workshops in Surat, employing some 600,000 workers. In March 2001 they calculated that 30,000 had died in the earthquake – and that over 50,000 families were still homeless.

Three years before the plague outbreak I was in Surat filming these diamond-cutting sweatshops. Young boy cutters worked and slept by the spinning grinding wheels, with their bedrolls hanging from the walls and ceilings. Neville Huxham, the elegantly suited head of De Beers Public Relations, ironically had revealed the existence of these workshops to me. He was anxious that I present a balanced critique of the industry. He said, "If you are going to examine the living conditions of blacks who work in South African diamond mines, put these into their proper perspective.

Contrast them with those of Aborigines in Australia and of the diamond cutters in the Indian sweatshops."

I promised him I would do this although I privately wondered if this were not a case of the pot calling the kettle black. The diamond cutters of India mostly work in the coastal western state of Gujarat, north of Mumbai. The main center for the industry is today around the city of Surat although Mumbai is also an important diamond-cutting center. All together, there are over 900,000 workers cutting over 80 percent of the world's gem diamonds in this region.[4]

Cut diamonds have provided India with its major export for more than a decade. Low-waged India was the powerhouse that drove the profits of the diamond industry sky high in the 1990s. About 500 million diamonds were cut in India in 1992.[5] Five years later this had grown to 750 million. Ninety percent of the world's diamond workers are Indians – although some of the trade has now moved to China where wages are still lower. The major Indian diamond merchants are mercantile princes with offices in all major international diamond centers. In 1993, India exported 12.5 million carats worth officially $3.44 billion. Four years later India's diamond exports were worth a billion dollars more – with another half billion earned by diamond jewelry. By 2001 India's diamond exports were worth some $6.8 billion.

Diamond Intelligence Briefs (DIB) reported in 1997 that in Surat, "It is mind boggling that for $10 one can cut some 15 stones in these ranges!" It was referring to the average-sized Indian polished diamond size of around 2.5 points (40th of a carat) – and to the higher wages then paid. By mid 2001 $20 would pay for the cutting of over 40 stones – at less than 23 cents each for cutting and polishing. According to DIB an average diamond worker in 1997, cutting some four diamonds a day, earned around $25-35 for a 55-60 hour week or about $108 a month. With the slashed wages of January 2001 they would be very lucky to make $5 a week.

When Nicky Oppenheimer, then both Chairman of the Central Selling Organization (CSO) and deputy chairman of De Beers, came to India for the first time in February 1994, accompanied by Anthony Oppenheimer, the president of the CSO, and Gary Ralfe, the Managing Director of the CSO, he announced that India was now first in the world; both in terms of the value and of the weight of diamonds processed. It had surpassed Israel – a country that dominated the diamond cutting industry in the 1970s and early 1980s. In 1993 Israel had exported $2.5 billion dollars' worth of cut diamonds, some billion dollars less than India. This was despite Israel being sent a better class of diamond to cut than was sent to India, with its cut diamond exports worth on average $817 a carat, compared to India's $219.[6] Yet Indian workers, with their smaller stones, had to put in much more skilled work than Israel to produce a carat-weight of polished diamonds.

When we went to India, the Oppenheimer cartel or CSO directly or indirectly controlled the supply of rough diamonds to India and it still does to a great extent. Since 1997 the Australian Argyle mine has also independently supplied India with diamonds, many of these being cut in Ahmedabad for very similar wages. In recent years a fierce war has waged between the Australian mine and the CSO – with the CSO trying to undermine Argyle's profits by oversupplying the merchants at high cost.

For decades the De Beers Central Selling Organization (CSO) provided the best stones to European or American diamond cutting firms, the medium range to Israel and the rest to India. It channeled the diamonds sent to India through a few favored Indian merchants as this helped it maintain control. About ten Indian families thus came to control India's entire output in 1992, and they were scarcely taxed at all. The rise of these families was one of the more significant changes in the diamond world in recent times. By 2000 there were some 40 Indian millionaire merchants. These became powerful in the diamond markets of Antwerp, New York, and even in Tel Aviv.

In India, De Beers monitored the Indian trade through a company called Hindustan Diamonds. When I met the two Indian generals on the board of Hindustan Diamonds, I asked them what their company had done to improve the living conditions of the diamond cutters. They confessed that the living conditions were poor. They said they wanted them to improve, but, they asked, what could they do?

The diamond merchants of Mumbai usually did not cut their diamonds in their own plants, although this is changing as many start their own factories. They usually contracted with a distributor who, for a commission, subcontracted the diamond cutting on a piecework basis to owners of diamond workshops, who in turn recruited their cutters from among the Patels living in impoverished agricultural villages in the state of Gujarat.

In February 1992, we hired a local film crew in Mumbai and drove in a hired coach up to hives of diamond cutting workshops in Surat. There were ten of us in the crew, twice the normal number. This was because Indian companies that hired out camera equipment and buses provided guardians for every item since paying wages was cheaper than paying insurers. This system had some disadvantages. One day when we were filming an excited crowd scene, the guardians nervously grabbed the camera from under the nose of our director and raced off with it to protect it.

SURAT – INDIA'S PRINCIPAL DIAMOND CITY

When we arrived in Surat, an excited crowd gathered around us, for they associated our equipment with feature films and movie stars. It was thus much easier to film in the workshops than in the streets, as the staircases leading up to them were so narrow that the numbers that could crowd in were limited. When I went back to the bus to get a piece of equipment, I only escaped being mobbed through the bus driver abandoning the rest of the crew and driving off – to protect the bus, not me.

Surat was the most polluted city I have ever stayed in. It was a major center for both the diamond and textile industries. Its factories belched smoke as if there was no tomorrow. The roads in the town center were lined with flimsy shanties housing workers. These might have been impoverished but were scrupulously clean inside. Many of the diamond cutters we met in these shanties had been recruited as young children and brought to the city by traveling agents that went from village to village.

An Indian researcher had gone ahead of us into to arrange for interviews, find local experts and ask for filming permissions. One of the first places he found for us to film was the "Diamond Nagir" or "Diamond Village" outside Surat. He told us that a member of the Oppenheimer family had opened it and that we had permission to film in it – but he had been told by the management that we "must not film the children."

Child labor is illegal in India, but this law is much ignored. Sharp young eyes are much prized by Indian diamond traders who have many tiny diamonds to cut. At one factory I asked to see their smallest cut diamonds. They showed me two that were no more than specks of light. They were "half-pointers." There are 100 points to a carat. A carat is one fifth of a gram. These diamonds therefore each weighed one thousandth of a gram. Each of them had been cut with many sides. They were so light that I had to turn off the fan before taking them out to examine them to insure they would not

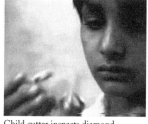
Child cutter inspects diamond.

blow away. I thought with so much skill involved in cutting them they should have had the higher prices, not the lower.

We decided to go to film in the Diamond Nagir without replying to their request that we promise not to film their childworkers in the hope that the management would not press us for a promise when we had actually arrived. It was on the outskirts of Surat, surrounded by high walls and protected by paramilitary guards. Inside we could see several apartment blocks where the workers lived, worked, ate and slept without leaving the plant compound. We entered through a military style sentry post and gate into a courtyard surrounded by single storied buildings. We parked and walked in to find a marbled reception hall that had as its centerpiece a large pool of water with plastic frogs.

From here we were ushered into the office of the brothers who ran the establishment. They were large and muscular men. Their leader sat at a vast desk with a huge light over it similar to those found over pool tables. They were keen to show off their diamond production. For our cameras they emptied out cloth bag after cloth bag, scattering thousands of diamonds onto the desk's polished surface. They clearly felt uneasy, the good humor felt false. I felt apprehensive because I knew we were intending to film the illegal child labor they employed. The decor in the room was heavy, solid – a nouveau riche style. I could not imagine the Oppenheimers in such a setting – but we were told it was Anthony Oppenheimer who had opened this place to business.

Fortunately, the brothers did not reiterate their earlier request that we not film their child labor. Perhaps they presumed we had implicitly promised. Perhaps they were too embarrassed to ask us to our face. Instead they assigned us escorts to watch us and make sure that all children were removed from the view of our camera. One of our assigned guides was a large hulk of a man who scarcely said a word; the other was a hunchback.

The factory halls to which we were taken were large but had no provision for filtering out the pervasive black dust of ground diamonds. Our assigned guides watched our video camera to see in which direction we were filming. Whenever our cameras pointed towards a child, they would drag the child away out of sight. Some of the children removed were seemingly as young as eight or nine. Most were boys. The hulk took the lead in taking away the children. This he did incredibly, directly in front of us. The hunchback meanwhile patrolled to make sure the workers did not stop work. It was like a scene from a Dickens novel. These photographs of children were taken at this time.

Child workers in factory.

As they seemingly did not understand the workings of a long focus lens, they did not realize that we were not filming the children closest to us, but those at the far sides of the workshops. We thus captured on videotape the faces of scores of under-aged workers. None of the cutters seemed to be past their twenties – and many were clearly far below the legal minimum age (15 in 1993).

After this, we returned to the diamond-cutting workshops that lay at Surat's center. The evening dusk revealed countless windows lit by long neon tubes slung low over cutting wheels. We went from workshop to workshop. They were on average not much bigger than a normal western living room. Each housed from three to five cutting tables or "ghantis." Each ghanti had four or five workers squatting around it, each cutting on his (rarely her) segment of the cutting wheel The ghanti is a "scaife," or horizontal rotating cutting wheel, driven by a motorized belt. These belts were unguarded and next to the unprotected legs of the cutters – and thus the cause of many accidents.

I watched the deft hands of the children recruited from farming villages. They had clearly learned quickly. The tiny size of the diamond they had to cut meant they could only touch the grinding wheel deftly with it for a microsecond at a time lest it be ground away. Then they would swoop the diamond up to their eye, look at it through a magnifying glass, and then lower it onto the wheel again. Each had to have 17 facets carved in it if it were to be a "single cut," 58 facets if it were a "full cut" gem.

Above the cutters were portraits of Ganesh, the Elephant God, and of other deities. Among these were slings holding the cutters' scanty belongings and sleeping mats. I met one young man who kept his toothbrush taped to his ghanti. Many lived and slept by their cutting wheels or on the flat rooftops above. Some lived in the hovels that crowded every city space. One worker took us to his home by a bus station. It was a tent with two sections, dirt floors and improvised furniture. A cloud of children enveloped him as soon as he walked in. The hovel was meticulously clean and was also inhabited by elegant sari clad women and men in tee shirts. The family made tea for us on a fire on the floor and told of how they had coped since coming to town seeking work. They counted themselves fortunate to have any income.

When I asked if they owned a diamond, they laughed at the idea of such an extravagance. They found even basic medical care very difficult to finance. They were pieceworkers – paid by the number of diamonds cut per day. They told me they had to work very long hours to survive. The average pay for polishing the top part of a diamond was then two rupees, less than eight cents in 1992. The smallest diamonds, needing the keenest eyes, were often given to the youngest child worker. If they were very lucky, they might make $15-20 a week by quickly cutting gem diamond after gem diamond for up to 12 hours a day. This was below the Indian income tax level. A few favored cutters might manage $30.

India's Factory Act did not protect the cutters. Since this Act applied only to workplaces employing more than nine workers, many owners saved costs by registering every pair of ghantis as a "workplace," no matter how many pairs there were in a workshop, thus ensuring that no "workplace" had more than nine workers. This deprived the workers of the benefits of the State Provident Scheme. Thus, if the workers fell ill or lost their job, they were put into enormous financial difficulty. The Mumbai correspondent for the diamond industry magazine, *Diamant*, starkly described their fate when laid off: "They and their families are facing virtual starvation."

There was likewise no enforcement of the Child Labor Act. During periods of diamond sales booms, or "brens" as the trade calls them, tens of thousands of children were enticed from the countryside by recruiters or even relatives, abandoning school and parents. But, whenever De Beers ordained a cutback in "Indian goods" or a recession came, they were quickly sacked. The use of child labor in the Indian diamond industry has been documented for many years. David Koskoff reported it in his 1981 work *The Diamond World.* Kantilal Chhotalal mentioned it in his authoritative study of the Indian industry, *Diamonds,* yet we found that in 1992 very little had been done to remedy the situation in these workshops.[7]

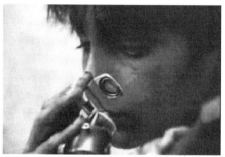

Child-worker checks the diamond he is cutting.

On the contrary, the number of children employed had been rapidly expanding. In 1989 about 11 percent of the diamond cutting workforce was below age. By 1994 the number had grown alarmingly to about 16 percent, or 64,000 children. In Surat 18 percent of the diamond workforce were under the legal minimum age, well above the national average. These children are especially vulnerable to exploitation since they live away from their families. I obtained these figures from workers in Surat and Mumbai.

An orange-robed swami, campaigning against slavery, told me that many diamond workers were in debt bondage, trapped into working for whatever an employer chose to pay. The diamond cutters interviewed in Surat confirmed this. They told me that, when they started work as children for the diamond workshops, it was very important to them that they returned at least once a year to their families for the village religious festivities. On the minimal wages paid, the only way most could do this was by borrowing the bus or train money from their employers. The terms of the loan would be that they had to work for their employer until the loan was paid off. This often turned out to be impossible on the low wages now offered – so the end result was that they were enslaved in "debt bondage."

Immediately after our film *The Diamond Empire* was shown on US and UK television, documenting among other things this child labor, there was reportedly a major campaign within the Indian diamond industry to remove the children from the industry. This campaign was assisted by two factors. First, the diamond industry started to slide into a recession. In response the industry sacked many child workers and slashed in half the wages for adults. The fierce competition from impoverished adults for work on any wages led to many children being squeezed out of work in the major centers. The other major factor was the expansion of larger factory units more suited to skilled adult labor. A survey in 1998 showed a two-thirds drop in the number of children employed. But in 2002, diamond researchers told me outside the major cutting centers many children were still used to cut the lower quality stones. By all accounts many thousands are still employed.

All the diamond cutting workshops had secure glass fronted or barred offices from which the uncut diamonds were given out as piecework. In these offices records were kept of the size of the diamond before and after cutting. Often the poorer stones lost 70 to 85 percent of their weight in cutting. The dust from them blackened the walls and floors of cutting workshops we visited. It presumably did the same to the workers' lungs. Cutters in America, Europe or Israel are less likely to be affected by dust as they were given by the CSO a better class of diamond that had much less wastage – but nonetheless even these might lose 60 percent or more of their weight in cleaving, sawing and polishing. Most of the cutters of these better stones would also be protected by dust collecting screens.

Cutting diamonds is not safe. Diamond cutting is listed in the top 10 "hazardous industries" by the Indian government. This is why it officially bans the employment of children under 15 in this industry.[8] The grinding wheels are rubbed with kerosene oil impregnated with the diamond dust needed to grind diamonds. The diamonds being cut are mounted on a small metal tool known as a tang. As diamonds are ground, fine dust sprays out. Only in one Mumbai factory did I see an attempt made to capture the diamond dust to protect the lungs of cutters.

I was told that a worker might sometimes slip out to local shops where, concealed behind groceries, jewel scales would be used in trading the diamond he or she was cutting for one of lesser quality, thus giving the worker a little better income. I did not see this happening, although I have heard there are scores of such places in Surat.[9] Rather I noted the constant supervision that made this difficult.

The Patel diamond cutters have formed an association to give themselves the healthcare that their factories would

Diamond cutting workshop in India.

not give them. They have also started a society to help fund weddings, as these are so expensive that they are a major cause of debt bondage. They save by having group weddings. The couples sit in pairs of wedding chairs while being tied together with long streamers, a symbol of the marriage bond. Not one engagement stone would be in sight. Their fierce determination to push the prospects of their children has also contributed to a drop in child labor. They want their children to have the advantages of education.

I met a doctor who tended the Patels. He spoke with controlled anger on how those that made money from the cutters' work made no effort to care for them. He said there was a heavy incidence of bootlegging, since alcohol was banned in Gujarat.

Prostitution, venereal disease and tuberculosis were all prevalent.[10] He regularly had to attend funerals of workers and found many had committed suicide, unable to cope with their life of constant attention to the angles of a billion diamonds while trying to make an income sufficient for their family's survival.

He took us to a burning ghat for corpses by the riverside. We watched the dead arrive on stretchers covered in flowers. A barn filled with wood supplied the fuel. There were eight fireplaces with grids below them for the ashes. Nearby a modern electrical crematorium sat unused and locked up.

The diamonds arrive in Surat from Mumbai carried by the "Angadias." These are messengers whose families have been in the courier trade for generations. They carry the diamonds in white cloth bags. They are cheap and efficient and operate on a basis of personal trust. In Mumbai, I witnessed a new consignment arriving from the airport to be split up and divided between the merchants. Two men dragged a very heavy chest filled with diamonds from their vehicle to a large safe room fortified with heavy bars. That was in 1992 when half a tonne of diamonds arrived a month. Five years later a normal month would see over one and a half tonnes, seven and a half million carats, of diamonds arriving in India.

THE INDIAN DIAMOND ELITE

When I heard that the families of the merchants who control the diamond trade all originated from Palanpur, a city north of Surat, I wanted to go there to see how the Indian diamond industry began. But the merchants told me not to bother, that there was nothing to see at Palanpur. It had been their city of origin purely by accident. Once one family got into diamonds, the word had spread by word of mouth. But they only introduced Palanpur families of the merchant caste to the trade. Perhaps others were deterred.

These merchants were all Jains by religion and part of a religious minority in a dominantly Muslim Palanpur. The Jains in Muslim and British Empire days served as administrators and traders. Many diamond merchants have the name Mehta, which means "accountant" and denotes an ancestral occupation. They thus did not traditionally specialize in diamonds. It is difficult to understand why they should now dominate so much of the world's diamond trade, unless it is that the Central Selling Organization (CSO) believed that a small, easily stolen and secretive commodity is best traded by family members that can preserve between themselves trust and secrecy – and thus favored these merchants with diamond supplies. It was previously mostly Jewish diamond families that dominated, perhaps for similar reasons. The Jain merchants told me they believed this to be so.

I met with leading members of these families, including the Mehta brothers who supplied the workshops where we filmed child labor, and who in their turn were supplied by the CSO. They were quiet, polite and canny. While I was in Surat, I found that warnings had gone out from the diamond cartel saying that we should not be granted interviews. Fortunately, some merchants agreed to interviews before receiving warnings and it was difficult for them now to refuse, given the Indian sense of courtesy. But they now said little and I could find in them no sense of responsibility for the working conditions of the diamond workers. It was as if they had nothing to do with the situation.

It is common knowledge that the Indian import and export figures do not reflect the true size of the trade.[11] Duty-free diamonds that are supposed to be re-exported find homes with Indian women to the tune of $ 300-400 million a year.[12] The official statistics sometimes betrayed the fixing of statistics. Thus in 1988 and 1989 the declared value for exported diamonds was lower that that recorded when they arrived overseas. A senior merchant said that although India officially exported $1.87 billion dollars worth of diamonds in 1987: "Unofficially, or de-facto, or 'for all practical purposes', or whatever way one prefers to phrase it, India's diamond production exceeded US $3.1 billion. This is a conservative estimate."[13]

I found the diamond merchants were extremely proud of their benevolence. They contributed to many charities, especially those that benefited their ancestral town, Palanpur. But much of their benevolence was normally directed towards other Jains, not towards the Patels, the workers on whose work their fortunes were based.

I had approached a merchant of considerable wealth and power in Mumbai that I thought might be inclined to give an interview. His name was Bharat S. Shah. He was somewhat more relaxed, interested in the media, not so private in his tastes. He was a former president of the Mumbai Diamond Merchants' Association and India's Exporter of the Decade for the 1980s. He sold through a company called London Star on New York's Fifth Avenue. His Indian Company was called B. Arunkumar. Shah calculated he employed about 25,000 people and admitted, "we are the biggest in India."

He had agreed to be interviewed before we went to Surat, but on my return I found it extremely difficult to contact him. I was first told he was in Delhi inspecting his stables. A little while later I was told he was at home in Mumbai and not in the office. Then I was told he was hiding lest water paints were thrown over him during an upcoming festival. Eventually, after the festival was safely over, I decided to go unannounced to his office in the hope that, face-to-face, he would not be able to refuse me. And so it turned out. My crew and I went up the elevator, across the elegant small reception area and announced ourselves. He welcomed us into his office, and showed us how he received daily hundreds of cut diamonds from Angadias couriers, weighed them and stored them away in cloth bags in a strong room that held images of Indian deities. On learning that our bank had closed before we had time to reach it, he kindly phoned it and had it re-open for us.

He told us of his daughter's wedding. He had hired a football pitch to accommodate the party guests, including diamond merchants from around the world. When we expressed interest in seeing his videos of the wedding, he took us to his home, a large mansion in a modern Indian style, with many expensive cars in its garage. He brought out a box laden with videocassettes. He had two professional cameramen shoot everything.

Clearly, the diamond-rich Jains only did things in the most magnificent of styles. We also learned of what happened when a 29 year-old diamond merchant, Arul Dalpatbhai Shah, announced he would take Diksha, meaning giving up worldly wealth and becoming a monk. There were over 40 street processions in his honor in the diamond centers in London and Antwerp as well as in his home city of Ahmedabad north of Surat, the city that now cuts Australian diamonds. Many laudatory articles appeared in the papers. One told how he designed a "khadi invitation card using vegetable colors to provide an environmentally sound alternative to the waste of expensive paper on wedding invitations."

Another pious merchant had showed us this ceremony on videotape. The monk-to-be, dressed splendidly as a turbaned prince, rode an elephant to the religious celebrations. A hundred thousand people came – eight planes were hired to bring guests from distant places. All were fed. They came to watch him become Muni Heetruchi Vijayji Maharaj. The whole occasion was a display of the wealth, power and piety of the Jain diamond merchants. His dedication was seen as ennobling the whole community.

I asked Bharat Shah if I might visit a Jain temple. He gave me an introduction to a temple in Mumbai that I found was filled with Buddhist-like statues, expressing inner peace and decorated with precious objects. An orchestra of women sat on the floor playing instruments and chanting. They invited me to join them and I did with gratitude.

DE BEERS GAINS ENTRY TO INDIA

In the early 1980s India had challenged De Beers, seeking diamond supplies to make itself independent as a cutting nation, banning De Beers-controlled operations from India. But by 1992, De Beers was entrenched in India. The rebellious Indians had seemingly been tamed. I found out by chance how this had happened. The BBC introduced me to a "fixer" for film crews who lived in the Defense Colony of New Delhi. She was a princess from Rajastan with rings on her toes, jewels in her nose and she was elegant, cultured, hard working and well connected. On my arrival she asked me would I like to meet two retired Indian generals to whom she was closely connected. She told me they did not know anything at all about diamonds but they had helped De Beers get into India. Both were on the Board of Hindustan Diamonds, the company unofficially representing De Beers in India.

The first I met was Major General D. K. Palit. He had served in the Ghurkhas and at 73 in his jodhpurs he was a spry and fit image of an Indian soldier. Every morning he practiced yoga. Every afternoon he played polo. Every evening he scaled a ladder fixed to a wall to reach his bedroom. He started the interview with a chuckle, saying he hoped I was not going to ask him anything about diamonds since he knew nothing about them, unlike polo.

I asked how then did he get on the board of Hindustan Diamonds? He smiled and said, "It was for getting them [De Beers] into India." He explained that, as he had direct access to top government officers as a senior general, he had called on government ministers to explain that De Beers' Central Selling Organization wasn't really South African. He told them it operated out of London. Why, he said, even the Russians dealt with them in London. There was therefore no reason for the Indian government to treat the cartel as South African and ban it as an apartheid-linked organization. The Indian government accepted his argument.

I then asked how De Beers paid the general for this service. He exclaimed. "Oh, I did not receive any money!" He thought for a moment and then told me that De Beers provided him with very good accommodations when he went to London. He took advantage of these trips to play polo and to meet the most prominent members of society. He loved the location of his London flat. From it he could stroll into town across Hyde Park while watching the riders exercising their horses. It was then straight along Oxford Street and on to where De Beers ran "a very decent club."

The other Indian general on the board of Hindustan Diamonds ran one of the finest elite schools in Delhi. He also served De Beers without financial reward and De Beers also helped by flying him to London. These trips helped him in his work for his charity, the Cheshire Homes.

Before Hindustan Diamonds came to be, the Indian government had sought independent diamond supplies for the Indian cutting industry by sending overseas the state owned company, Minerals and Metals Trading Corporation (MMTC) to seek contracts with miners.

India was deeply suspicious of De Beers, partly because Indians were second-class citizens in apartheid South Africa. When De Beers tried to get into India in the mid 1970s, Parliamentarian Madhu Limaye leaked, on March 26th, 1975, a confidential letter from the general manager of MMTC to the Ministry of Commerce, warning against any agreement with the Oppenheimer Diamond Trading Company, claiming that it was trying to collect intelligence on the Indian market.

But, despite this warning, De Beers had clearly found its way into India through the Hindustan Diamond Company. This company now "supervised" and "monitored" the diamond merchants of India. It was 50 percent owned by the Indian government, 30 percent by the Bank of Bermuda and 20 percent by Mumbai's Industrial Investment Trust. De Beers' own role is hidden. But, according to Kantilal Chhotalal, one of the most senior and respected diamond merchants of India, "De Beers has a large financial interest in the Bank of Bermuda."[14] This was the same bank as that used by the Oppenheimers to remove diamonds from the United States during the Second World War. It was reported by Koskoff that both the Industrial Investment Trust and the Bank of Bermuda were seen by the industry as "strawmen" for De Beers. He alleged the Trust has "a shady reputation for its past involvement in gold smuggling."[15] The two generals on Hindustan Diamonds' board both referred to their company as linked to De Beers, not to the Bank of Bermuda.[16]

De Beers had in recent years removed some of the Indian opposition to its hegemony over the diamond trade by providing India with a generous supply of rough diamonds. The Indian merchants used this to expand overseas. I witnessed an Indian merchant in his office in Israel open his regular brown cardboard box of diamonds brought by his son from the London Sight, with as much excitement as a youngster with a Christmas present. He found in it a giant diamond personally selected for him by De Beers. He had clearly been a well-behaved customer. This merchant shortly afterwards received a brusque inquiry from the CSO asking if it were true that he had helped us find accommodations. He had us write a letter saying this was not true.

In 1986 the CSO started to encourage Indian companies to set up factories in other regions with low pay rates including in Sri Lanka and in Thailand, guaranteeing them supplies of CSO rough diamonds. The Australian Argyle mining companies also helped by training diamond cutters in China where strikes were unknown. The Chinese were given better quality stones than the Indians. Chhotalal explained in 1990 that this expansion was to take advantage of countries or villages "where wages and social benefit payments are low. In Thailand social security costs are nil... The legal minimum wage was $2.89 per day in metropolitan Bangkok... In Sri Lanka... the average wage for a trained diamond worker was $75 a month."[17]

Despite the arrival of De Beers in India around 1975, MMTC, the government owned company, continued to try to get independent supplies throughout the 1980s. In September 1987 they signed agreements with Ghana, Sierra Leone, Liberia, Tanzania and Angola for joint exploration and mining rights.

This alarmed the CSO, so in 1988 it sacked 20 Indian Sightholders, including several whom had joined with the MMTC in seeking non-cartel supplies of diamonds. The CSO also increased the size of the minimum Indian Sight to force the selected "privileged" merchants to pay out $500,000 ten times a year – a fortune in anyone's terms, let alone in India. This concentrated the Indian diamond trade into even fewer hands – and soaked up all the funds at the disposal of the favored diamond merchants, thus making it very difficult for them also to buy stones on the independent market. According to Michael Grantham of the CSO, the smaller boxes of stones costing $200,000 were abolished, as "mini boxes are not a viable proposition."[18] This De Beers policy led to an increased control of the industry by the very rich.

With the help of the generals, De Beers now received favored treatment in New Delhi. The New Delhi bureaucracy instead put difficulties in the path of the independent merchants. An Indian merchant alleged to me that this had been achieved through corruption. Perhaps one example of this was what happened when the US government tried to sell off its surplus stockpile of "industrial" diamonds. Some Indian diamond merchants realized that these were really of gem quality – and wanted to buy these stones at the cheap industrial price from the US government rather than buy from the cartel.

It seems that De Beers managed to counter this by calling on friends in the Indian government. "In 1986 Indian customs stopped such parcels and imposed a heavy penalty,"[19] while still allowing in diamonds from the CSO. Why stopping diamond imports from the US stockpile was in India's interest was not explained. This enabled the CSO to buy up these thousands of diamonds at basement prices from the US.

In December 1987, the Indian government also limited non-CSO supplies of small diamonds, including some Australian, saying this action was to control the trickle of "black" diamonds into the economy. Again it was scarcely clear why this action was in India's interest. The major diamond center of Antwerp had shown no such hesitations. "Black" diamonds were welcomed there.

The De Beers Syndicate did much to foster the rise of a few Indian diamond families above the rest by giving them exclusive and very large diamond Sights. One Antwerp dealer told us that De Beers "superdealers included two major Indian concerns – Rosy Blue and Star. They received large good quality diamonds as well as poor. They cut the better diamonds outside India." De Beers provided these merchants with more diamonds than they could cut – so they unloaded a lot of their diamonds on the international Antwerp market where less fortunate merchants, not favored with a De Beers Sight, could buy them at higher prices. Some $10 billion worth of cut and uncut diamonds were sold every year in the diamond quarter of Antwerp. De Beers stringently monitored this trade from its Antwerp office to ensure the merchants did not stray too far from its pricing policies.

It is difficult to understand how De Beers could not be fully aware of conditions in the diamond-cutting sweatshops of Surat. It has inspected the factories of its Indian Sightholders, monitored the wages, and carefully vetted all new Sightholders.[20] It thus knew if they used child labor and paid minimal wages. It had within its power the improvement of these conditions. If De Beers demanded it, the merchants would have jumped to obey.

On October 23rd, 1996 the CSO told the authoritative industry newsletter *Diamond Intelligence Briefs* (DIB) that "before considering any client as a potential Sightholder, the CSO always assesses health and safety standards of the work place." DIB added, "The CSO also regularly inspects factories of Sightholders to ensure that health and safety regulations are being met, says our source." As for De Beers refusing to supply diamonds to merchants who would let them be cut by children, this simply did not correspond with what we saw in India.

The seriousness of the human rights abuse in the Indian diamond trade was recognized in 1993 by the Chairman of India's Diamond and Gem Development Corporation (GDC), S. D. Sharma. He publicly stated he expected India would eventually have to negotiate with the United States and with other countries to avert boycott threats to the purchase of diamonds from India because of the employment of children in the cutting and polishing industry.

In that same year diamond workers in Belgium, Holland and Israel took up the issue. They relaunched the old Universal Alliance of Diamond Workers (UADW) and sought to extend it throughout the world, particularly to India and Russia. Its past president, Gijs Honing, had earlier noted that they "want to see an end to perceived labor abuses in the diamond industry worldwide." These include prohibiting the employment of children under 14 years-old and improving health and safety standards, beginning with an international ban on the dangerous cobalt scaifes, which are still in use in India.

However, their pleas for the child workers met with little success with De Beers and the CSO. At first the CSO was willing to meet with them – the former CSO director Michael Grantham met with them in 1994. But, according to *Diamond Intelligence Briefs*, Grantham cast doubt on the existence of child labor in the Indian diamond workshops. He said the union had given him insufficient proof of the existence of child labor. I was most surprised by this since De Beers had told me of the child labor over ten years earlier – and it was blatantly obvious to any visitor to Surat's cutting workshops. Since Grantham's retirement, the union's efforts to negotiate on behalf of child workers with the CSO have apparently been met with no response.

But despite De Beers' denials, UADW Assistant General Secretary Yamina De Laet stated in 1997 that there was proof that children were being exploited by the diamond industry. A document circulated at its Congress charged that for certain diamond-cutting tasks the average age of the worker employed was only 12, and that these young children often worked 12 hours a day.

Unionists lobbying at the International Conference on Child Labor in the Norwegian capital of Oslo in 1997 described the diamond cutting workshops that employed child labor as the "dirty end of the diamond and precious stone business." In documentation released to journalists, the International Confederation of Trade

Unions (ICFTU) noted that while the international gem industry generated hundreds of millions of dollars in profits, "tens of thousands of children" in India worked in "cramped, filthy and dangerous conditions," for poverty wages.

De Laet of UADW told *The Namibian* newspaper in November 1997 that they had filmed children as young as six years-old working on dangerous polishing wheels. They had also filmed "people living and sleeping at their workplaces and trash, human feces and industry waste clogging the open sewers that run between the warren of gemstone shops."

Later De Beers conceded that the Union was right in saying that thousands of children were cutting diamonds. It has now admitted to some 24,000 children being employed in the Indian diamond cutting industry, but other estimates were far higher.

Debt bondage and slavery

The diamond cutting industry was not just exploiting a very young and vulnerable workforce, but was trapping these workers in debt bondage. Both practices are explicitly prohibited under the United Nations 1956 *Supplementary Convention on the Abolition of Slavery, the Slave Trade, and Institutions and Practices Similar to Slavery* as "institutions and practices similar to slavery."

Anti-Slavery International described debt bondage as "probably the least well known form of slavery today, and yet the most widely-used method of enslaving people. A person becomes a bonded laborer when their labor is demanded as a means of repayment for a loan. The person is then tricked or trapped into working for very little or no pay, often for seven days a week. The value of the work is invariably greater than the original sum of money borrowed."

The Supplementary Convention does not forbid the repayment of debts by working for the loan-giver – but forbids debt bondage in which the person making the loan can add unspecified interest or other costs to the loan or reduce the debtor's wages.

Anti-Slavery International noted: "In cases of chronic bondage, debts are inherited from one generation to the next, maintaining members of a family in permanent bondage in return for an old loan, the details of which have long been forgotten. In some cases employers who are owed money 'sell' the debt to a new employer; the difference between such transactions and the slave trade is one of semantics more than substance." It added: "In other cases, parents 'pawn' their own children, sometimes from the age of as little as four or five years of age, in return for loans which they never repay; the child consequently remains a bonded laborer for the rest of his or her childhood."

When in 1997 the South African MP Dr. Kisten Rajoo attacked De Beers for exploiting child labor in India, Garath Penny of De Beers responded, "If we find a cutter is using child labor we do not use them." Penny then tried unconvincingly to shift the blame for child labor onto the Australian mining companies by saying that many of the Indian cutters were supplied by Argyle, the Australian diamond operation that broke away in 1996 from the Central Selling Organization (CSO).

In reality, De Beers still supplied more diamonds to India than did Argyle. In 2001, it supplied Indian Sightholders with 24 percent by value of all Indian diamond imports while most of the rest came indirectly from De Beers via

Antwerp. But De Beers did not accept responsibility for workers employed by subcontractors – and the cutters employing children were themselves nearly all employed by subcontractors.

1   De Beers Centenary is a De Beers "shadow" company that was set up in Switzerland to own De Beers' South African assets when it became likely that the ANC would be elected to government in South Africa and consequently the apartheid system ended.

2   Tim Capon, of De Beers Centenary, 17 Charterhouse Street, letter to Henry Becton, the president of WGBH-TV. March 4th, 1994.

3   Statistics as quoted in the Vinod Kuriyan, "No Problems Here: Success, Complacency and Suspicion in the Indian Diamond Industry," 2002.

4   The estimate of 800,000 Indian diamond industry workers is from major Indian diamond company, Rosy Blue, 1993. By 2001 it was generally estimated that some one million were employed.

5   Kantilal Chhotalal. *Diamonds: From Mines to Markets*. Mumbai: The Gem and Jewelry Export Promotion Council. 1990, p. 91. He estimated 350 million diamonds were exported from India in 1989. In 1992 Bharat Shah estimated in an interview with the author that the figure had increased to 500 million.

6   *Business Times of India*, February 19th, 1994.

7   Koskoff, 1981. Kantilal Chhotalal, p. 62.

8   *Diamond Intelligence Briefs*. January 29th, 1988.

9   "Passage to India," *Mazal U'Bracha*. May-June 1988.

10 Koskoff, 1981.

11 *Diamond International*, March-April 1991.

12 *Mazal U'Bracha*, May-June 1988.

13 "Passage to India," in *Mazal U'Bracha*, May-June 1988.

14 Kantilal Chhotalal Mehta, "Diamonds from India." Gem and Jewelry Export Promotion Council. 1984, p. 26.

15 David Koskoff, 1981.

16 Kantilal Chhotalal Mehta, p. 15.

17 Chhotalal, p. 92.

18 Chhotalal, p. 22.

19 Ibid.

20 Roger Lappeman, a former De Beers Sightholder, provided me with papers from the dossier that De Beers kept on him. These demonstrated that De Beers monitored conditions in cutting factories.

Chapter 3 – Diamonds and Tribal Rights

Diamonds became for me a strange best friend after the Federal authorities ordered the police to fly in by helicopter to stop me discussing diamond prospecting with Aborigines in Oombulgurri. This had made me inquire further into the diamond world, for I was curious to discover why this had been seen by the authorities as so dangerous.

Oombulgurri had a turbulent 20th century history. A cross on a hill above their settlement honors Aborigines massacred by the police in 1928. Australian law was then based on the premise that Aborigines had no more land rights than had animals; that Australia was "terra nullius," no one's land, when whites arrived. When Aboriginal survivors returned to Oombulgurri in 1972, they found that in their absence a diamond prospecting camp had appeared on their Reservation called "Mumbo Jumbo" in a disparaging reference to Aboriginal spirituality. This camp was controlled by RTZ of London.

I went to Oombulgurri primarily because the local Aboriginal representative organization, the Kimberley Land Council, had asked me to provide mining information to the communities whose lands had been invaded by teams of diamond prospectors. Robert Bropho, an uncompromising and charismatic leader of his people, had driven me up to the Kimberleys from Perth. He told me he decided to work with me because I had striven to communicate without words when I first met him. The drive was some 1,500 miles long over roads that were often no more than tracks lined with high "bull-dust" ridges in which it was easy to get bogged. We slept under the stars, rising at what he called "piccaniny dawn" – the first light when the parrots began to "sing." The Aboriginal elders we met along the route told us they were not against mining as such, for their people had always mined for tool-stones and clays, but wanted miners to respect the spirit of the land and Aboriginal ancestral rights.

Their families were living under scraps of iron and canvas. Their health had been disastrously affected by the arrival of the white man. Instead of surviving into their 70s as they did before, they now died in their 40s. An Aboriginal mother in northern Australia in 1994 was 30 times more likely to die in childbirth than a white woman. Her child was three times more likely to die in the first year of life.[1] The discovery of diamonds on tribal lands should have brought the resources they desperately needed. Instead it seemed it would further endanger their survival as a people by bringing them no royalties, by depriving them of yet more land, and by swamping them with white settlers.

The wide-trunked boab trees.

Before I went to Oombulgurri, I visited the Aboriginal-run cattle station of Noonkanbah on the Fitzroy River in the southern Kimberleys. It is accessed from the one-pub town of Fitzroy Crossing by means of a narrow and humpy dirt road that crosses grassy plains broken by rocky hills similar to the "kopjes" of South Africa. Even the local boab trees were related to similar trees in southern Africa. The similarity is no coincidence. Australia was once joined to South Africa in the ancient continent of Gondwanaland. These small hills are the worn down stumps of volcanoes created by the forces that had split apart Australia and South Africa. Their eruptions brought to the surface the carbon crystals known as diamonds. One night, an Aboriginal elder sung me a millennia-old song about the eruption of volcanoes that described the correct sequence of eruptions despite them happening at least 15-20,000 years ago.

CRA Limited found small diamonds in the Noonkanbah's kopjes and on the surrounding plains and so took out mining tenements claiming over 30 square kilometers of the only cattle station then owned by Kimberley Aborigines. It needed no Aboriginal consent – not even the consent of the 240-300 Aborigines that lived in shacks on this station and ran it as a business. The state government had allegedly offered to build them houses, but only if the government builders were allowed to bring in alcohol. The community had banned alcohol and maintained their ban because it was so damaging to their people, so no houses were built. Noonkanbah was a major center for Aboriginal culture – and the place where the Kimberley Land Council was created to fight for land rights at a gathering of 1,200 Aborigines for a song and dance festival some two years before my visit.

At Noonkanbah, as I would at Oombulgurri, I sat on the sand with the elders and with the sand as my easel, drew mining plans and showed how diamonds could be scattered by erosion over large areas. The elder and spiritual leader Nipper Tabigee became my guide and teacher. He took me on a jolting drive across a dried riverbed between pools where freshwater crocodiles sometimes lived, to a rocky volcanic hill called Djada. He told me his people once gathered here for ceremonies and asked me to follow as he climbed. The hill was small, not the height of a tree. About half way up he stopped by the mouth of a cave.

"Look, Jan," he said, "can you see the bones?" I peered into the cave, momentarily blinded by the bright light outside. But when my eyes adjusted I saw long white bones inside. "These are the bones of my people shot down by a police party when I was this high." He indicated his thigh. Then, without a sign of bitterness, he quietly told me how a diamond exploration company had recently pegged and claimed the entire hill, entering the cave and taking the sacred ceremonial objects stored inside. Some were destroyed, others were taken to Melbourne and later retrieved.

This was not the only burial ground desecrated on Noonkanbah. Aboriginal elder "Friday" Mullamulla, pointing to the potentially diamond rich plains around their settlement, said, "That is all CRA… they bring bulldozer about two miles back down that way... They cut all the way around all dead bodies. All around that place where we have taken the bones of the old people."[2]

The Aboriginal people of Noonkanbah sent a petition to the state parliament written on bark and in their language, Walmajeri. In translation it read:

We are sending this letter to you important people who can speak and who are now sitting down there talking in the big house.

We, Aboriginal people of Noonkanbah Station, are sending you this letter. We truthfully beg you important people that you stop these people, namely CRA and AMAX [who were looking for oil], who are going into our land. These people have already made the place no good with their bulldozers. Our sacred places they have made no good.

They mess up our land. They expose our sacred objects. This breaks our spirit. We lose ourselves as a people. What will we as a people do if these people continue to make all our land no good?

Today we beg you that you that you truly stop them.[3]

I had many conversations with elders and others while at Noonkanbah. Their dilemma was that they had already agreed that CRA could prospect for a further three weeks if it used an Aboriginal guide to ensure no further trespass upon sacred places. Once consent was given, the elders did not want to withdraw it. But they now felt they had not been fully informed when they made their decision. No one had explained to them what would happen if diamonds were discovered. It also irked them that CRA would not concede that traditional owners had any right to royalties for the diamonds found upon their land. A spokesman for the Noonkanbah community, Dicky Skinner, said, "my law says... if CRA's name is written upon the diamond, CRA is allowed to go down and get him. If CRA's name is not on it... it is for tribal peoples."

Kimberley bush.

On reflection, the elders decided they could not trust CRA to leave after it completed its current prospecting trip. It would surely bring in many more white people if it found diamonds. They also discovered that CRA was also searching for uranium. They felt it was time for legal action to stop CRA. Once they had decided to withdraw their consent to CRA's prospecting, Nipper Tabigee and other elders took me with them to Derby in an old car with no windscreen. The inside of the car was like an endless dust storm. When we arrived, windblown and red with dust, they told their lawyer to evict CRA and made the following statement:

CRA, we have been thinking about you looking on our land. You say you only look at one part of our station then go away again after three weeks. But we say, after talking some more between ourselves, we don't want you because, if you find something up there, you may come more and more onto our land and we don't want that. Also you didn't tell us you also looking for uranium – that stuff dangerous for everyone.

Following this, the Kimberley Land Council asked me to stay longer so I could share my knowledge of diamond mining with other communities. Soon afterwards two white government lawyers came from Perth to speak to the elders at Noonkanbah about their decision to expel CRA. I was asked by the community to attend the same meeting. The lawyers spoke about the benefits that mining could bring, including a mining township populated by Aborigines, and many jobs for Aborigines. They did not mention that to date few Aborigines had been given responsible jobs in Australian mines, nor that the common experience of Aborigines living near mines, especially CRA's many mines, was of dispossession and powerlessness.

The elders then asked me to repeat what I had previously told them of diamond mining. I told them that miners normally scooped out the core of a diamond-rich extinct volcano by digging a pit at least a kilometer wide and perhaps 200 meters deep, with shafts below this for another 800 meters, and that the surrounding plains might well be bulldozed to find diamonds washed out by monsoonal rains. The discussion then continued in the Walmajeri language. Nipper Tabigee translated quietly for me. No one translated for the lawyers. I was then told the community had decided to maintain their ban on CRA. The lawyers were told to do nothing until they heard from the community.[4]

This produced a furious reaction from these government-funded lawyers. They cornered me in the woolshed and furiously questioned what right I had to give Aborigines advice. They angrily reminded me that I had no official standing with any government body. They concluded with a threat. They said they knew that I intended to visit the Aborigines at Oombulgurri and told me to watch out if I did. They did not specify what would happen to me. This perplexed me. I had told no one that I was going to Oombulgurri.

When I arrived at Wyndham, the port from which one takes a boat to Oombulgurri, I learned that the Oombulgurri Aboriginal council was concerned for my safety. They had learned that the government was trying to stop me seeing them. But, diamond prospectors were pouring onto their land. They wanted to discuss this with me, but in

Hill in the West Kimberleys with boab trees.

the circumstances, they would perfectly understand if I did not come.

I discussed all this with the elder sent to see me. He saw it as clearly a matter of civil rights. The government was denying their right to invite guests onto their tribal lands and to visit them at home. But, he wanted me to understand the risk involved in accepting their invitation.

I agreed to come. A day later I was escorted by the elder, with a woman friend of mine, on a long boat trip up crocodile infested rivers to the Aboriginal settlement of Oombulgurri where we were made very welcome.

It was not long after we arrived, while I was having a conference with the senior man and woman in the community, that we received a radio message from the other side of the country, from Melbourne saying that the Federal Government had ordered the police in by helicopter to arrest my companion and myself for not having government permission to visit this Aboriginal reservation.

Back in Wyndham after these extraordinary events I learned the police had never arrested anyone for this before. When the orders came to arrest us, they had questioned the need to fly out to get us. They asked why the fuss. They could wait until we came back to town – but the Federal government ordered them into action. I also learned that our phone calls had seemingly been intercepted.

Some months later, the Noonkanbah elders again directly challenged the State government. They wrote to it on June 9th, 1980: "You assumed we recognize the State Government's ownership of the land. Instead of this you should have recognized us, the Elders who hold the law for this country, as the real owners of the land."[5]

Premier Charles Court replied in the *West Australian* newspaper: "I do not believe that such radical and unlawful views are really theirs." He spoke of "the extremist agitation … which led the community to make absurd claims amounting to sovereignty over the Crown Land they occupy as pastoral leaseholders."[6] Fortunately, as the Noonkanbah station was leasehold and not Aboriginal reserve land, he could not ban them from having visitors.

Shortly after the Premier made this statement, the mining industry funded television advertisements showing a black hand building a wall across Australia. The accompanying voiceover claimed that Aboriginal land rights would rob other (white) Australians of their birthright. The Australian Mining Industry Council warned that Aboriginal land rights could lead to "a system of unauthorized totalitarian control by a minority within particular parts of Australia." The Aborigines had already lost nearly all the well-watered lands to white farmers. It seemed they were now about to lose the barren lands not wanted by grazers but where mineral-rich rocks were exposed for the taking.

But Charles Court and his government did not see very far into the future. In 1992 a revolutionary High Court decision, the *Mabo* case, supported by six out of the seven judges involved, stated that Aboriginal "native rights" to Crown Lands still exist in Australia. This was because the British colonial authorities had presumed to take over Aboriginal lands without making a formal order or Act of Parliament that would have had validity under "rights of conquest," or so the judges stated. Where freehold title had been granted, the judges ruled this was valid under these "rights of conquest" and so Aborigines could not reclaim these lands – but most of Australia was still Crown Land that they could reclaim.

Aborigines immediately laid claim to vast tracts of Crown Land. In 1993, a new Premier, Richard Court (the son of the previous Premier) vowed to fight this High Court ruling by all the means available. The Australian Mining Industry Council, funded by all the major mining companies, united with him in opposition. Its members feared having to pay royalties to Aboriginal nations and to protect sacred places. The Kimberley Land Council became once more locked in legal battle on behalf of the impoverished people they represented.

After my arrest in 1979 I had tried to find out why the authorities had been so jittery about my presence on Oombulgurri. I suspected that the miners had found a tantalizing deposit of diamonds on Oombulgurri, and indeed in 1993 De Beers' prospecting company Stockdale would return to Oombulgurri against Aboriginal wishes and with the explicit support of the state government. Again Aboriginal rights to ancestral lands were being swept aside.

Does Argyle have more diamonds than South Africa?

Back in 1979 I had heard a rumor that CRA was using Oombulgurri as a diversion to draw attention from a nearby enormous diamond discovery. Two days before I was arrested, I had seen excited CRA and RTZ executives in neatly pressed shorts and long white socks at the local Kununurra airport. I found they were not going to Oombulgurri but to the Argyle Cattle Station south of Oombulgurri.

I later learned from Rees Towie, Managing Director of Northern Mining, that diamonds had been found on the Argyle Station by his daughter-in law Maureen Muggeridge, the niece of the British writer Malcolm Muggeridge. She was working as a geologist for CRA on an Ashton Joint Venture project set up to look for and mine diamonds. The Joint Venture was owned 56.8 percent by CRA, 38.2 percent by Ashton Mining and 5 percent by Northern Mining. She and her prospecting party had found diamonds in phenomenal quantities in and by Smoke Creek. The soils and clays were littered with diamonds over square kilometers of the surrounding flood plains.

Maureen Muggeridge's prospecting team used a ruse to deceive the rival prospecting teams until it had pegged and claimed these diamond-rich lands. She was pregnant, so her team let it be known that they had sent her off on maternity leave – to relax on Smoke Creek. As she "relaxed," she traced the source of the diamonds to the headwaters in an ancient volcanic crater surrounded by tawny and mauve crags. She knew, on South African precedent, such a crater might be rich in diamonds down to a depth of over 3,000 feet. She soon realized that she had stumbled on the world's largest publicly known diamond deposit – a deposit worth over $10 or even $20 billion, containing as many diamonds as were then known to exist in the rest of the world.

Diamonds destroy a women's sacred site

Muggeridge might not have known that this crater was also the home of a most ancient and sacred Aboriginal woman's site, a place of enormous ritual importance to the local Aboriginal community. Her father-in-law, Rees Towie, later insisted to me that Aboriginal women did not have sacred places. His view flew in the face of everything the elders and government anthropologists told me – but it did reflect an outdated chauvinistic anthropology that held that Aboriginal men had religion and Aboriginal women had "only" magic.

CRA had management rights in the Joint Venture and it feared Aborigines would claim sacred site protection and obtain royalty rights, as they had in other parts of Australia. It thus appointed the white-haired senior Aborigine Harry Penrith (who became known as Burnam Burnam) as a consultant for public relations purposes. He was a friend of mine and subsequently leaked to the press and myself an internal CRA document dated November 1980 entitled *Public Relations Programme 1981*. This revealed that CRA saw

Local Aboriginal woman.

the campaign for the recognition of Aboriginal rights to tribal lands as CRA's prime political danger. It concluded, "if Kimberley Diamond Mines Pty. Ltd. [The Argyle operation] can resist moves to meet Aboriginal compensation/royalty claims... it's savings in the long-term will be substantially greater than the proposed expenditure on the Company's Public Relations programme next year."[7]

CRA gave its PR account to advertising company Eric White Associates, because of their "perception of our continued interaction with the Kimberley Aboriginals in accord with our own." They rejected a rival company, I.P.R., because, "I.P.R. believe that those dedicated to securing a larger share of mining revenues for Aboriginals will ultimately succeed and that our best policy is to position ourselves to conduct these negotiations… given this view, it is difficult to see how that agency could effectively work towards objectives which it does not believe are attainable."

When I interviewed Rees Towie in his elegant office in a skyscraper just off St. Kilda Road in Melbourne, he explained to me the history of this diamond discovery. He had first become interested in prospecting for diamonds in the Kimberleys when he heard that a large diamond had been found on the body of the explorer George Stansmore, who had accidentally killed himself on an 1896 expedition across the Simpson Desert to the Kimberleys. Rumors had it that he took this diamond from a dead Aborigine. It

CRA headquarters in Melbourne.

may have been among the special or shamanic stones that Aborigines sometimes carried in pouches for sacred or healing purposes. The name of the Creating God or Ancestor was sometimes given in their traditions as "The Rainbow Serpent." A stone with a rainbow in it might have had special symbolism. Towie's company thus helped start the Kimberley diamond rush, but it had to bring in CRA when he found he needed the kind of money only a large company could provide.

In the 1890s it was common for expeditions to locate water holes by capturing an Aborigine and feeding him or her salt until in desperation and pain he or she led them to a water hole. Robert Menzies, a noted explorer of Western Australia and a Fellow of the Royal Geographical Society, recounted in his autobiography how he had around 1880, when on a search for mineral deposits, set dynamite around his camp to blow up any Aborigine who tried to free the one he had captured, thus slaughtering eight Aborigines in one night.[8]

Towie described to me how his school's "old boy network" gave him entry into the diamond world. He invited a former school friend, Ewen Tyler, to join his company's board in 1972. Tyler was Managing Director of Tanganyika Holdings, a company with diamond interests that had first established the prospecting camp on Oombulgurri Aboriginal Reserve. This camp was later called "Mumbo Jumbo" and managed by CRA. Tyler in turn invited Northern Mining to join the small group of companies he was assembling to prospect for base metals in the Kimberleys. When Towie said no, Tyler revealed the object of the search was not base metals but diamonds. Remembering Stansmore's diamond, Towie jumped at the chance to join the venture. This became the "Kalumburu Joint Venture" in which Northern Mining's partners were the Belgian Sibeka Group – a member of De Beers' diamond Syndicate; London Tin – later called Malaysia Mining Corp. – also linked to the diamond Syndicate; and the Australian company Jennings Industries.

They found small diamonds within a year but could not get the prospecting funds required. In November 1975 Towie met John Collier, the head of CRA Exploration, at a cocktail party and gained his interest. In 1977 CRA became the new head of the venture, which was renamed the "Ashton Joint Venture"[9] as Tanganyika and Malaysian had spawned a new company called Ashton Mining. It was not long before they found many diamonds.

Rees Towie showed me photographs of diamonds to illustrate the colors found at Argyle. Many were rare prized colors such as red, pink and yellow. He said a large proportion would cut as gems, and indeed their shapes looked good to me even in the rough. When I asked him for further details, he introduced me to his senior geologist who took me to a room dominated by a large, plastic, three-dimensional model of the deposit. This revealed the results of the exploratory drill holes, recorded on transparent sheets within the model. He left me alone to study it.

THE SECRETS OF THE ARGYLE MINE

In the mines of South Africa, De Beers reported that 20 tonnes of diamond bearing rock was mined for every gram of diamonds recovered. But I could see from the 3-D model that at Argyle less than a tonne would produce a gram of diamonds. It showed that there were, on average, well over 1.5 grams, or 7.5 carats, of diamonds to a tonne at Argyle. One drill hole had found 26.5 carats or over 5 grams a tonne! De Beers reported that its South African mines averaged only 0.28 carats a tonne –

Rose and white Argyle diamonds.

or about a twentieth of a gram a tonne – and that their richest mine yielded only 0.76 carats a tonne. Astonished, I looked at the results of drill hole after drill hole of this Australian discovery. All were of stunning, previously unheard of, diamond richness.

It was very obvious why diamond exploration companies were funding a campaign to prevent the Aboriginal people of the Kimberleys from gaining mineral rights. They feared any possible obstacle between themselves and this bonanza. It was not so obvious why they felt a need to argue they could not afford to pay any royalties to Aborigines.

I quickly scribbled a few results from the model on my hand to help my memory. I then pulled out my notepad and wrote furiously. I had just turned a sheet to start on a fresh page when the geologist came back in. He looked over my shoulder, saw how little was on that page and said, "That's all right, you can have those results." I thanked him and left – with all the results.

I knew it was in the interests of Northern Mining for me to have these results. They owned 5 percent of the Argyle deposit and publication could increase the price of their shares. But I was puzzled to find that CRA was secretive and banned journalists from the mine site. Perhaps it feared government intervention.

Northern Mining calculated that the top 200 meters of the volcanic pipe contained about 800 million carats. The deposit at 200 meters was still as rich as it was at the higher levels and clearly kept on going deeper. From the results I had obtained I calculated that the top 200 feet of this deposit contained as many diamonds as were publicly known to exist in the rest of the world. South Africa's diamond reserves had been estimated by the US Geological Survey at 200 million carats in 1980. Argyle most probably had over a billion carats.

The implications were staggering. It seemed to me this mine could easily make the South African mines un-economic and force them to close. The only uncertainty was the quality of the Australian diamonds. But, even if they were of average quality, the Oppenheimer family who controlled South Africa's diamond mines might be extremely

Early mining works at Argyle.

worried by this discovery and certainly would not want the competition.

ABORIGINES AND ARGYLE

A year later I was again on my way back to the Kimberleys. This time I had been hired by the Religious Affairs Departments of both the British and the Australian Broadcasting Corporations, surely a powerful combination. I was researching a BBC/ABC joint *Everyman* documentary on the spiritual importance of land to Aborigines. I knew that if the West Australian authorities had any excuse I would again be excluded from Aboriginal reserves, so I decided to apply for a permit in advance. I did not want to attract attention. I wanted to go in quietly, sit down and talk – and find out what was going on.

I knew that tourists were issued permits to pass through Aboriginal Reserves over the telephone on the day they asked. So very confidently I asked the ABC Religious Affairs Department in Perth to obtain a permit for me. But two weeks passed and no permit came. By now I was on my way to the Kimberleys and could wait no longer. In Alice Springs I learned that the ABC had been told to their surprise that it would take three months to process my application. So I found a friendly civil servant and had him to phone on my behalf. I overheard his conversation. It went like "Yes, she is with the BBC. Yes, she definitely has a Pommie accent." Finally he put down the phone and grinned. "You have a permit. I persuaded them that there must be two of you. You are now the one who works for the BBC, not the one with the same name who went to the Kimberleys last year."

I went up again to see the Aborigines on whose tribal lands was the enormous Argyle diamond deposit. They mostly lived in a settlement called Warnum, near Turkey Creek. To get there I had to pass within sight of the Argyle diamond find. It was getting late as I drove up in a Toyota Landcruiser. The tree-sprinkled slopes and great cliffs of the ancient volcano glowed red and magnificent in the setting sun. The only sign that a mine lay concealed behind the range was a red scar above the cliffs, a diamond-inflicted wound that would soon destroy the entire southern end of this escarpment.

When I arrived at Turkey Creek, I found I had to dangerously ford a creek swollen with monsoonal rains to reach the house in which I was staying. As I worked my way across, holding onto a cable with one hand and balancing my bag on my head with the other, I was relieved that there was no sign of crocodiles. But next day I discovered another menace – large green frogs that lurked in toilets and leapt up when their view was overshadowed! They also sat on the sides of baths mimicking bars of bright green soap, only to hightail it up the wall on sucker pads when I reached out for the soap!

The local Aborigines told me how they had discovered CRA's secret prospecting camp. When they noted the sudden appearance of new dirt roads the community hired a plane to follow them, suspecting cattle rustlers had made them. Instead, they found the diamond camp on Smoke Creek.

The Warnum elders then told me of a sacred women's place high in the Smoke Creek valley, saying it was ancient and of high ritual importance. I found that it was within the area covered by the diamond pipe. From this sacred place, known as the Barramundi Dreaming Place, the women could look down through a gap in the crater's rim over the flat flood plains of Limestone Creek to where the barramundi in the "Dreamtime" came to rest as a hill. The barramundi is a large and delicious fish that has a symbolic role in Aboriginal culture akin to that of the salmon in ancient Celtic stories. It symbolized here one of the great creation or "dreamtime" stories and had deep spiritual significance, but the uninitiated adult could only be told of it in the simple parable form that was originally designed for uninitiated children. Some said the diamonds were the scales of the fish. It was ironic that the miners planned to destroy this sacred women's place to mine "a girl's best friend."

There was only one way Aborigines could get protection for such sacred places in Western Australian law. The West Australian Museum had the right to declare places protected – a provision originally devised in the interests of archaeology rather than Aborigines.

Aborigines in shelter at Warnum.

Museum anthropologists were now working with Aborigines to have sacred places catalogued and protected. At the request of the Kimberley Land Council, the Museum examined the site of the Argyle diamond find. On January 15th, 1980, the Museum informed CRA of a number of sacred places that required protection. However, it was relatively easy for CRA to get round this with the help of the state government. The ancient Barramundi Dreaming Place has now been totally obliterated.

The local Aborigines then sent a member, John Toby, to campaign for the recognition of their rights in Canberra, Melbourne and Sydney. I met him on May 23rd, 1980, at an International Land Rights Symposium held at the Institute for Aboriginal Studies in Canberra. The meeting, packed by representatives of all Aboriginal land councils and by most eminent anthropologists in the country, passed by an overwhelming majority a resolution "deploring the entry of CRA onto known Aboriginal sacred sites in the Smoke Creek region of the Eastern Kimberleys and requests CRA to immediately leave the area." It further called for the Noonkanbah community to be protected from pressure by mining interests.

However, CRA ignored this resolution, the destruction of the sacred sites continued, and John Toby gradually became dispirited and exhausted by the unequal fight. Eventually, CRA persuaded Toby that all he could get for his community was a small annual allowance of about $100,000 a year, which explicitly excluded any recognition of Aboriginal rights. It was specified by CRA that the sum was a hand-out that could be withdrawn at any time. Moreover it could only be spent on items approved by the company – and, as it turned out later, not on buying land. Toby obtained agreement from a few relatives to this deal – but not the consent from the elders as required under Aboriginal law, the same elders who had sent him south as their spokesman. These guardians of the land refused to endorse the CRA deal.

But CRA took advantage of this split in the community. It flew Toby and three relatives south to Perth to conclude an agreement away from his community and near to the media. CRA only needed this agreement for public relations purposes. The community telegrammed Toby to tell him not to sign. But it was too late. He had signed. On June 30th, 1980, the traditional owners responsible for this land, 40 members of the Turkey Creek Aboriginal settlement, unanimously rejected Toby's agreement as invalid under their law. Shunned by his own people, CRA then built him his own settlement at Glen Hill, close to the mine.

The leaked 1980 CRA public relations document referred to this deal with Toby. It stated that, "the public relations program will be concerned principally with: 1. Sustaining the Argyle Agreement signed with the Glen Hill Aboriginal community and isolating this agreement from the general debate on Aboriginal land rights...." CRA was concerned that its "hand-out" to Toby should not be seen as an acknowledgement of Aboriginal rights.

One of the Warnum elders, David Mowaljarlai spoke of the Argyle diamond mine on his ancestral land on May 14th, 1980:

Disturbing sacred sites and land is agony of our people. Land and mountains and spring water – the heart of the sacred sites – is really our body. Grader, bulldozer, are pressing down on our body, liver, kidney bleeding. The spirit of the landowners is sickened. Graders are scraping the skin off our flesh – a sore that will not heal up: in my language, "wilu," killing us.[10]

Diamonds thus became for them a symbol of death rather than of life. The support they had received from organizations such as the Australian Council of Churches and the Catholic Commission for Justice and Peace proved useless. This opposition could no more stop CRA than dew could stop a truck.

The local Aborigines decided to use the fund CRA had offered them to purchase back part of their traditional land from a cattle station outside the diamond mining lease. CRA refused. Instead, they were allowed to buy a garage shed. I was told the regaining of title over land was far more important to the community than was a garage – but a land title was apparently precisely what CRA did not want them to have.

CRA thus made Smoke Creek valley into a forbidden zone, and barred the public and the world's press for over a year while they deliberated over how to market its fabulous contents. It was walled off with high fences, helicopter patrols, and closed-circuit television cameras.

But in 1981 none of the guards at the sentry post by the high-barred gate questioned the dust-covered "Sheila," headscarf tied tightly, sitting in the back of a truck on a well-concealed camera with a party of Aborigines. They presumed I was

The land the Aborigines hoped to buy.   The garage shed they were permitted to buy.

either a "do-gooder" worker at the Aboriginal settlement or a half-caste, and waved us through the gate into Smoke Creek valley.

Before I went in, I had inspected the mine site from the air, accompanied by Aboriginal women elders who interpreted what I saw and what it had meant to them. They showed me how their sacred women's place had been bulldozed and turned into a truck park. The valley at the heart of the ancient volcano, a place once of stunning beauty, was now an inferno of red, scraped rock roaring with the noise of giant trucks and bulldozers. It was as if the ancient crater had come alive again.

The Aboriginal party demonstrated to me how serious they were about their hunting. They showed me that Smoke Creek, the secret diamond valley, was also rich in game and in wild plant crops. They took me through a valley densely wooded with small trees and deep water holes ringed by palms. They told me they knew the diamonds well. They appreciated their attractiveness. Their hardness had made them useful tools in former times, but not as useful as the Smoke Creek hunting grounds. There was one story about a large eggsized diamond found elsewhere in the Kimberleys through which rainbows could be seen. Elders treasured this diamond.

When I was there, sitting under the trees with them, one child picked up a small nearly transparent stone and asked, "Look Jan, is this a diamond?" I looked at its rounded edges and did not know. A short time later it had been lost. She was unconcerned.

We drove past heaps of excavated rock from the central diamond pipe which was about a mile in length. The southern half of the pipe went down to great depths and averaged over ten carats a tonne. As a carat is a fifth of a gram and there are a million grams to a tonne, these figures mean that even here diamonds are very much needles in haystacks. But in South Africa all their mines are said to operate profitably at less than one carat a tonne. South African diamond needles were therefore tiny while Australian diamond needles were suitable for darning. (I came to strongly suspect later the accuracy of De Beers' statements about the diamond content of its own mines. It could have been that they were hiding their richness in order to justify their high prices – but much more about this later.)

The Managing Director of Argyle, Michael O'Leary, said its pit would be "the same size as the two largest South African mines put together." CRA then predicted that they would mine about 22 million carats a year. World diamond production that year, 1982, was 48 million carats. In fact by 1994 the Argyle mine would be producing about 40 million carats a year. Philip Adams, writing in the Melbourne *Age*, called what the company was prepared to give Aborigines "a pitiful barter of pocket knives, mirrors, and beads for perhaps the richest piece of real estate on earth."[11]

The quality of the alluvial diamonds on the plains is higher than that of the diamonds from the pipe. Diamonds may be very hard, but they are also brittle and can shatter. Alluvial action sorts out the better from the poorer diamonds. Only the best survive. That is why in Southern Africa, the diamonds around the mouth of the Orange River and on the beaches of Namibia are practically all of the highest quality. That is why the Cambridge Gulf Exploration Company in 1993 was planning to dredge the sea bottom near Oombulgurri for diamonds washed there from Argyle and other deposits. Their executive chairman, Brian Conway, estimated they could dredge $1.5 billion dollars worth of diamonds a year. The Dutch Professor Anton Gans, who discovered diamonds off the coast of South Africa 30 years ago, said the Australian

seabed diamonds are "very high quality" gems. Conway said they are at least as good as South African diamonds.

As I drove back to Kununurra airport, past the long dramatic sandstone escarpment that led to the Argyle mine, I had the strangest of encounters. The roadside was lined with owls, in two lines, one each side of the road, silently watching me as if my passing had interrupted a secret conclave, with faces like those drawn by Kimberley Aborigines of their spirit ancestors.

When I arrived back in Melbourne, I found an intensive international commercial war raging over who would get the rights to sell the diamonds from these hills

Sorting table with rough Australian diamonds.

and plains. Not just companies, but governments were vying for them, competing against the Oppenheimer family empire and its diamond Syndicate. Harry Oppenheimer himself would eventually resolve this debate by coming to Australia for what his staff called a "spring offensive." His staff referred to him as the Godfather, marshalling the troops of his empire.

As I dug deeper I found what was happening in the Australian Kimberleys was part of a worldwide pattern.

DE BEERS, DIAMONDS AND THE BUSHMEN OF THE KALAHARI

It was not uniquely hard for Australian Aborigines.

There are a people in southern Africa with a very similar inheritance. They are the San, the group that inhabits lands now occupied by Botswana, Namibia, South Africa and other countries in southern Africa for at least 30,000 years, the hunter-gatherer people we also know of as the Bushmen. They are a people whose ancient culture is centered on their bonding with their lands, who see the face of sacredness or deity in the territory they inhabit.

The bush near Argyle.

About two hundred years ago, practically the only inhabitants of southern Africa were the many Bushman tribes or nations. Then came the Bantu tribes from the north and the White colonialists from the Cape. Stephen Corry, Director of Survival International, explains that what then happened was "genocide on a scale comparable to that of Australia or the Americas." Hundreds of thousands were killed. Still today their history is scarcely acknowledged in southern Africa where many still regard them as little more than serfs and chattels, and at the worst see them as following a way of life that is barely human.[12]

Nothing could be worse for them than to be forced off their remaining lands. In order to prevent this happening, in order to enable them to retain their economy and independence, the Central Kalahari Game Reserve was created in the heart of what is now known as Botswana.

But, as the conflict diamond campaign was getting underway, as Botswana received kudos from Global Witness and other conflict diamond campaigns, the Botswana government was cruelly forcing the last of the San off their tribal lands while leasing out their lands for exploration by diamond mining companies.

But it was not simply an eviction to facilitate diamond mining. As John Simpson, the veteran and highly respected BBC correspondent reported, "Six weeks ago, in the Kalahari Desert, I saw the brutal evidence of something I had been told about, yet could scarcely credit: that the Botswana government was trying to drive out the last remaining Bushmen of the Central Kalahari Game Reserve

Bushmen of the Kalahari. Photo: Survival International.

…There is a powerful seam of racism running through much of southern Africa towards the Bushmen; and this, rather than the fact that there are diamonds under the Central Kalahari, may explain the terrible and cruel treatment which the last Bushmen in the area have been suffering."[13]

Botswana has a black government – but the degree of racism in their treatment of Bushmen is equal to anything white Australians direct today at Aborigines. The President of Botswana, Festus Mogae, when Minister of Finance had said of the Bushmen, "How can you have a Stone Age creature continuing to exist in the Age of the Computers?" If they do not change, "like the Dodo they will perish."

The Foreign Minister of Botswana told Survival International, "We all would be concerned if any tribe should remain in the bush communing with flora and fauna."[14]

Botswana is today a country with widespread literacy and a free press. Its wealth derives 80 percent from diamonds mined in a partnership with De Beers. But most of the wealth is in the hands of government officials and their families, with the gap between the rich and the poor comparable with Brazil.

Survival International has campaigned for years on behalf of the Bushmen. The two tribes of the Reserve are the Gana and Gwi people. They speak related languages, of the Khwe family type. By the 1990s, many Bushmen had already been dispossessed by mines and cattle stations, forced into living as fringe dwellers, as beggars and as cattle hands. I had met some who were now working in the diamond mines in neighboring South Africa.

But the Gana and Gwi Bushmen had one last stronghold where they could maintain their hunter-gatherer economy and a certain amount of independence if they so wished. This was the Central Kalahari Game Reserve, set up both to protect wildlife and to protect the last great hunting range for the Bushmen. In 1989 a "Diamonds for Death" campaign fought to protect the remaining desert rivers, for these were in danger of going dry due to their water being taken for diamond mining. I had been told the campaign succeeded.

But life got increasingly difficult for these Bushmen during the 1990s. I should have guessed how hard it would be for them, for in 1981, at the Commonwealth Heads of Government Meeting in Melbourne, I was told by Maphalynane, a spokesman for Botswana's Ministry of Economic Planning, of their government's hard attitude towards the Bushmen. He said, "All the mines are on tribal traditional lands. If minerals are found, they are asked to leave. Theoretically, they can refuse but rational interest dominates. There is no financial return to the tribes." This was despite international conventions protecting the rights of indigenous minorities.

When the earlier De Beers mines were set up in Botswana, the indigenous people and others were removed. A former government minister described in parliament how people were relocated in order to make room for the De Beers' Jwaneng diamond mine.

Among the early diamond prospectors was a talented Canadian team who decided to survey much of Botswana by plane. They persuaded the American company Falconbridge to back their efforts. They surveyed several thousand square miles, including, it seems, the whole of the Kalahari Desert Reserve where some 3,000 Bushmen were living at that time. When the prospectors examined the results from some 60 locations, one site really stood out, and they knew they had at last found a commercial deposit. Falconbridge, much excited, contacted De Beers and the Oppenheimers made immediate arrangements to discuss the find. They looked at the results and immediately agreed to manage the project. Then nothing happened. No mine started up. With much disgust the Canadian geologists decided that De Beers was deliberately locking up the deposit. It had no current need for these diamonds, but would instead keep them against the day when it did need them. The Canadians went back home.[15]

Bushmen children in Kalahari.
Photo: Survival International.

The place where they had found the diamond deposit in the Kalahari was called Gope, which lay at the heart of the local Bushmen's territory. Not long after this the government, one of the wealthiest in Africa due to its diamond income, decided that they would not pay a small sum for water to be pumped from an old De Beers borehole and distributed among the Bushmen communities at Gope and other sites within the Reserve.

By the late 1990s, water was running very short even by the standards of the Kalahari Desert. The traditional water soaks were often dry for the water table was being lowered by bore holes put in to supply cattle ranches set up near to the Park.

The government started to truck water from one Bushmen settlement to the others, a temporary expedient.

But, when I obtained an environmental statement produced by Anglo American on the Gope diamond prospect, I discovered to my surprise that the miners had discovered at Gope much more than diamonds. They had established that at a depth of 90 meters the Kalahari Desert was underlain by a vast underground water reservoir. This lake was so vast that Anglo American estimated it could satisfy the gargantuan thirst of a diamond mine. The planned Gope mine would need some 12,000 cubic meters of water every single day of the decades the mine lasted. Anglo estimated that the local supply could very nearly meet this need.

Anglo estimated that over 9,000 cubic meters of water a day could be supplied by bores at the mine site without lowering the water table – but 12,000 cubic meters, the amount it actually required, would lower the water table considerably. The Botswana government noted they would have to provide compensation for the cattle ranches some 50 miles away when their bores ran dry. There was no mention of compensating the Bushmen, who had lost nearly their entire water supply.

Gope diamond exploration works.
Photo: Survival International.

The mining company knew the mine's vast wet slime ponds would attract herds of wildebeest. It noted with concern that these might be crushed against the fences needed to keep them from the water used at the mine. The company announced that it would provide a water outlet for the animals to use in the game reserve away from the fence. These animals thus received more consideration than had the Bushmen, no matter that this mine was to be in their tribal territories, in lands that in terms of international agreements were already owned by the Bushmen. The Government likewise showed more concern for the animals than the Bushmen. It decided to sink new boreholes – to water the wildlife.

After the discovery of diamonds at Gope matters got much worse for the Bushmen. The government maintained that it cost too much to truck water into their settlements. This was odd, for the government was continuing to truck water to remote settlements not inhabited by Bushmen. It was still odder when government officials came into the Bushmen settlements and wrecked their existing water supply, smashing up their water tanks and wrecking a borehole.[16]

The government would provide water for these Bushmen – but not on the Gana and Gwi tribal lands in the Central Kalahari Game Reserve where the people had always lived. It would provide it on new settlements built far from their traditional hunting grounds, ritual sites and graves – and from the Gope diamond site. This they said would help to "assimilate" the Bushmen into civilized ways.

The children who were moved found they were not allowed to speak their language in school. The adults found they needed government permits to return to hunt on their tribal lands, permits that were extraordinarily hard to obtain. They could not even visit their ancestral graves. They feared exile would kill them. They named one of their new settlements the "place of death." One of the local women said: "I'm on my way back! I'm crying. Since I dismantled my huts, I haven't built new ones, because I'm crying for my land. Even if I try to eat food, I can't taste it because I'm always thinking of my land. Thinking of the food I ate, that was hunted for me there."

The lack of water provision for Bushmen disturbed Gunnar Ring, the European Union representative in Botswana. He decided that if the government could not afford to maintain water supplies for the Bushmen, the European Union would. He would make sure EU funds were available. It was already funding the development of the Game Reserve for tourists. He announced that these EU funds could also be used to provide water for Bushmen. This offer enraged two Government Ministers, Margaret Nasha and Mompati Merafhe. They called this unwarranted interference in their affairs – and said if any foreign body offered to help the Bushmen remain in the Game Reserve, its funding would be refused.[17]

The government forced over 2,000 Bushmen from their lands. The few that refused to go found themselves ill-treated. Some were threatened with being locked up in their homes while they were set afire, burning them alive, according to documentation published by Survival International. The government even confiscated seven radio transmitters given by Survival to help communities keep in touch with each other. By May 2002 there were fewer than 30 Bushmen remaining in the Central Kalahari Game Reserve, despite the Reserve being originally set up for them. The Government even told the Bushmen that they had to be evicted from their land in order to protect the wildlife. It preferred others to care for the Reserve.

A Bushman explained: "The very big question is, 'Do Bushmen have a right to the land?' We were the land's first inhabitants, but we don't have a right to it now. We're always moving, always being relocated. We do with all our hearts want our ancestral land. We want to go back to our ancestral land. I never sleep. I'm always dreaming of my land, every day, thinking of corners I used to go to, in the morning in Molapo, gathering the foods there. If I think about them, I never sleep... I don't see life in this land. But in my land, I know all the life, I am used to it. I can eat things below and on the land."

But not everyone was being forced out of the Kalahari Game Park. The government had quietly authorized mining exploration leases and, as the Bushmen were forced out, mining companies were moving in, surveying and claiming more and more of the land.

Survival International concluded that the Botswana government clearly preferred diamonds to Bushmen – so placed advertisements in newspapers whenever it learned of the Botswana government's presence at a public event. It particularly targeted the meetings of the Kimberley Process called to plan the banning of conflict diamonds. It organized protest vigils in London, Paris, Madrid and Milan. Survival International finally labeled the Botswana diamonds "blood diamonds," for the industry was devastating the Bushmen of the Kalahari.

This dismayed the Botswana government – and De Beers. They had taken great pains to try to keep their own diamonds free from any suspicion of links with human rights violations. The Survival International campaign undercut this strategy. De Beers could not afford to have its own diamonds tainted, as that would make it harder to marginalize and taint the diamond production of Angola, Sierra Leone and the Congo – and make it harder to market De Beers diamonds as symbols of human love.

In 1996, Baroness Chalker, Britain's overseas development minister, assured the House of Lords that, if stories of forced removals of Bushmen were substantiated, then the EU would "stop its help to Botswana."[18] But later it seemed this pledge was forgotten – and this ancient culture would be totally destroyed in the interest of profits from diamonds.

Survival International protest in London. Photo: Survival International.

A most extraordinary correspondence then took place between De Beers, Anglo American, and the charity Survival International. It started with friendly notes. On April 3rd, 1998, De Beers issued a press statement to say that it was involved in the Gope diamond project, that some San families were taking advantage of the water supplies "supplied by De Beers from boreholes drilled to support prospecting activities," and that any question of "relocating" the San "is a matter entirely between the Botswana government and the benefiting communities."

An appeal came from a Bushman: "We are saying to those people who can help with campaigning not to stop campaigning, talk to the government, make a hell of a noise, and maybe it will change its policies. Organizations like Survival have to carry on making campaigns, and making noise, and informing the whole world what is happening with the Bushmen. The government is not telling the truth, when it says that people have voluntarily relocated... Even the government officials, some of them tell us that they move us only because of the diamonds. The District Commissioner said that if diamonds are found somewhere, the people have to be chased away."

On June 14th, 2000 Stephen Corry, the Director General of Survival International, wrote to Nicky Oppenheimer, the Chairman of De Beers, noting that the "government of Botswana has evicted over 1,000 'Bushmen' from the reserve and placed them in bleak resettlement camps, where they are dependent on government handouts for their survival," and that Survival believed that their removal was "largely motivated by the potential for diamond mining ... Our position is that Botswana must recognize Bushman land ownership rights over their ancestral lands or be in breach of relevant international conventions as well as natural justice."

Soon the actions of the Botswana government made the pleas of Survival International more urgent. On February 27th, 2002, Corry wrote to the directors of De Beers and Anglo American, telling them that they were about to start an international campaign to show that "Botswana's diamonds are 'conflict' diamonds and not clean as the government claimed." He concluded by saying that De Beers had influence with the government (70 percent of the government's revenues came from joint ventures with De Beers) and surely could help the Bushmen. But Nicky Oppenheimer replied denying any link between diamonds, De Beers and the eviction of the Bushmen. He made no offer to help. He instead suggested that there was no traditional Bushman settlement at Gope, and that the Bushmen had only come there because water pumped by De Beers had attracted Bushmen to the area. On March 26th, Survival International wrote to Oppenheimer again, saying "it is obviously more expedient for the government to remove the Bushmen now and so avoid both bad publicity at the time of mining, and any risk that Bushman claims over the area might inhibit or complicate extraction. We believe that, notwithstanding your response, there really is no other plausible explanation for its actions." Diamond exploration leases now covered the sites of several former Bushmen settlements in the Kalahari. "It may be pertinent to point out that, in the 33 years since we have been studying these matters, we have never come across a case anywhere in the world where tribes have been moved against their will merely to 'develop' them. In every single case, it has been because others have wanted their land or its resources." Again Survival appealed for De Beers to support the Bushmen.

On June 7th Corry again wrote to Oppenheimer asking if De Beers had told the Botswana government that the Bushmen should not be evicted. This time Ms. Fleur de Villiers replied in Oppenheimer's stead – and it seemed De Beers had not told the government this. She said the campaign would bring Survival into "disrepute" despite it being "a hitherto respected spokesman for indigenous people." She did not explain why De Beers was paying fees to hold onto mining interests at Gope that she maintained were not worth exploiting.

Corry replied to say that the Bushmen stated the Gope diamond prospect was on their traditional land and contained burial sites. A letter from Corry to Dr. Tombale, the Permanent Secretary of the Department of Minerals of the Botswana government, said, "Your assertion that there never has been a Basarwa (Bushman) community at Gope is an astonishing claim. Our own staff has visited people there over many years." Corry said he was dismayed that Dr. Tombale could write: "We are actually not aware of any site in the CKGR which is recognizable as a burial site." He asked what did he think the people had done with their dead? There were hundreds of known burial sites.

The correspondence began to heat up. Rory More O'Ferrall, Director of Public and Corporate Affairs for the De Beers group, wrote on July 12th, 2002: "When the drilling started there were no Bushmen in the vicinity of the Gope prospect. Eventually a few families were attracted to the area by the water produced." He insisted that De Beers never asked for the Bushmen to be removed. But in a later letter on October 15th he at last explained De Beers' policy. "In your letter you ask if De Beers has a policy to cover indigenous rights. We have given much thought to this matter." He then explained that they supported the abolition of apartheid but not the rights of indigenous peoples: "The new constitution made it quite clear that never again would the people of South Africa be classified by ethnicity. A policy to cover indigenous rights would head straight down that path once again, which is something that no one in southern Africa could, or should, contemplate." He quoted academics who maintained "the indigenous rights ideology is indeed based on the same discredited social theorizing that justified apartheid and separate development." He concluded: "It is, moreover, virtually impossible to assess who is indigenous. Genetic measures are meaningless given levels of hybridity in southern Africa."

Such reasoning was long ago rejected as a kind of inverted racism in Canada, Australia and other countries. De Beers should have known better as it had already been forced to recognize Aboriginal rights in its negotiations in Canada.

Back in the 1970s I had heard this same argument advanced in Australia by mining interests opposed to Aboriginal land rights. It said that Aborigines, like white people, could only hold land they had obtained by purchase or gift. But this argument had been overthrown. The law now recognized that the Aborigines already possessed the land, holding it with a communal title, and to deny their rights would be a violation of natural justice. It was no excuse to say that someone else had robbed the Bushmen. It would still be receiving stolen property. But Survival International did not push this argument with the government, fearing it would never let the Bushmen back if it thought the Bushmen might claim land or mineral rights. Survival instead wrote to Oppenheimer pointing out the inaccuracy of De Beers' statement that "few animals and no people lived permanently in the area before prospecting started." It noted: "Bushmen had lived throughout the CKGR, including the Gope area, for thousands of years."

Survival International then organized a very public protest. De Beers was about to open a high profile jewelry store in the West End of London and had

recruited the supermodel Iman to promote their diamonds. Survival announced it would picket the opening on November 21st. De Beers had a giant advertisement featuring Iman on a hoarding outside its new shop. Survival activists replaced it with a picture of a Bushman woman and the slogan "The Bushmen Aren't Forever." Iman did not to come to the store's opening.

De Beers now attacked Survival International. Lawyers acting for De Beers wrote the Charity Commission on November 18th to question

Top: The sign outside the De Beers store. Below: The same sign after Survival International activists had modified it. Photos: Survival International.

the charitable status of Survival International. Lawyers acting for Survival replied on November 20th. "[Your] letter was designed to intimidate. Our clients have not been intimidated," it read in part. "The available evidence indicates that your client has been complicit in an assault on the rights of the Gana and Gwi Bushmen, one so oppressive and extreme that their very existence as a people is now in jeopardy."

Survival believes that the Bushmen are having such a hard time because the Government knows that the "current of opinion internationally is increasingly moving in favor of recognizing indigenous communal land ownership rights." It is this that makes the Bushmen a threat. Survival suspects that the Botswana government, which includes within its ranks De Beers directors, wants the Bushmen removed before the possibility arises that the Bushmen may be able to enforce their rights to their lands within the Kalahari under international human rights law.

This is not a remote threat. Within the last year, a related people, the Khoi Khoi, have won an unprecedented victory under South African law. A South African court has recognized for the very first time their indigenous rights to their ancestral and diamond-rich lands at Alexkor.

And while Survival International continued to campaign, in 2003 the Australian mining giant, BHP-Billiton, came from the diamond fields of Canada to survey the Kalahari for diamonds from the air. They took out prospecting leases over more than 78,000 square kilometers in Botswana, with about one third of this within the Central Kalahari Game Reserve. This meant that between BHP and De Beers, virtually the entire Reserve was covered in prospecting leases. They set up a company called Kalahari Diamonds Ltd. to explore these leases. The World Bank gave it $2 million to help towards the survey costs. An investment assessment of this new company, made for the International Finance Corporation, noted the opposition of "international advocacy" groups but added, no doubt with some relief, "To date NGOs have not raised issues associated with mineral rights."[19] A spokesman for the company said, "Billiton was not involved in the removal of these people and we do not want to comment on something that does not involve us."[20]

In mid-2003 many of the Bushmen remained trapped and despondent in grim "resettlement" camps, not allowed back into the Central Kalahari Game Reserve, not allowed into their traditional land, not allowed to care for it. But an increasing number are overcoming all obstacles and making their way back onto the Reserve, where, as this book goes to press, they are staying, determined to retain the use of their land, determined not to be forced off it again. They face powerful enemies. The campaign to help the Bushmen continued as this book went to press.

1   *The Australian*, February 11th, 1995.
2   As told to Steven Hawke, unpublished document. 1978.
3   Provided to me in 1979 by the Kimberley Land Council.
4   The Ellendale diamond mine on two diamond pipes and nearby alluvials would commence operation near to the Noonkanbah community in 2002. This was to process around 700,000 tonnes of ore to produce around 335,000 carats of diamonds that would sell in 2003 for over $160 a carat in Antwerp. The mine estimated its production cost at $67 per carat.
5   Document provided by the Kimberley Land Council in 1979.
6   *West Australian*, August 8th, 1980.
7   Greg Walker, "Public Relations programme 1981." Internal CRA document dated November 1980, written by Walker, a public relations manager.
8   The full details of this incident are in the film *Munda Nyuringu*, produced by Impact Media in 1986 and available from the Australian Film Institute, or the author, who coproduced it with Robert Bropho.
9   The Ashton Joint Venture set up Kimberley Diamond Mines Ltd. to manage their diamond mines.
10 Jan Roberts. *Massacres to Mining*, p. 148.
11 *The Age*, October 11th, 1980.
12 Steven Corry, Letter to Author, April 18th, 2003.
13 John Simpson, "Simpson on Sunday," June 10th, 2002.
14 *Memorandum from Survival International to The Foreign Affairs Committee of the House of Commons*. January 2002.
15 Matthew Hart. *Diamond: A Journey to the Heart of an Obsession*. Walker & Co., 2001, pp. 67-68.
16 "Botswana Government cuts off water to last Bushman families." *One World*, February 25th, 2002.
17 *Mmegi Monitor*. February 19-25, 2002.
18 *The Sunday Telegraph*. London. February 24th, 2002.
19 *International Finance Corporation: Report to Board on a Proposed Investment in Kalahari Diamonds Ltd*. January 30th, 2003.
20 *The Guardian*. London. February 22nd, 2003.

Chapter 4 – How Diamonds Were Made Rare

The history of De Beers is woven with myths. It claims these as "facts" that justify it charging high prices for diamonds – and gets most upset if they are challenged. After I made the film *The Diamond Empire* for US, Australian, and UK television, De Beers had its London lawyers, Fasken, Campbell, Godfrey, write to the BBC because the film had "falsely" claimed that diamonds were only highly priced because, "the production of diamonds has been suppressed on the false premise that the supply of diamonds is plentiful."

My investigation of these well-spun claims was not based on rare documents but on a careful reading of dusty tomes of diamond history written by people close to the Oppenheimer family that has long controlled De Beers. Extraordinarily, these told me that De Beers' history was the very opposite of its myths.

I found that Ernest Oppenheimer, the Oppenheimer who first gained control over De Beers, repeatedly tried to keep diamonds rare by buying up deposits, hiding deposits and limiting production. I will quote his words and those of his associates – admitting that this was what they were doing. His own words are smoking guns. His actions still serve to limit the prosperity of Africa.

The Oppenheimers have also long argued against a free market in diamonds. Their stance did not damage their relations with such free trade advocates as the former UK Prime Minister Margaret Thatcher. She spent the ninth anniversary of her rise to power as Prime Minister celebrating in the London office of the Oppenheimers. They had much to thank her for. Her Office of Fair Trading had ruled that their companies had no case to answer because their price-fixing mostly affected foreigners.

The Oppenheimers maintained that price competition damaged the diamond trade. But in the 1920s, when Ernest Oppenheimer did not own De Beers, he had sold diamonds in great numbers in strenuous competition against De Beers. He only became opposed to competition when he gained control over De Beers.

CECIL RHODES AND DE BEERS

De Beers was from the first the ultimate "imperial company." It was founded by Cecil Rhodes to fund the extension of the British Empire. He set up De Beers Consolidated Mines in 1888 by exploiting the fears of European diamond merchants. They worried that newly discovered diamond deposits in South Africa would drive down the value of their expensively purchased Indian diamond stocks, and thus agreed to fund De Beers' purchase of all South Africa's diamond mines in return for a guarantee that their London "Syndicate" would have exclusive rights to its entire diamond output. But Rhodes clandestinely and illicitly sold diamonds elsewhere when he thought he was getting too little from the Syndicate.[1]

Rhodes saw creating artificial scarcity in diamonds, and therefore high prices, as a tool for paying for troops to extend the British Empire. He believed England was destined to rule Africa: "I contend that we [the English] are the first race in the world and the more of the world we inhabit, the better it is for the human race." An early version of his will left funds to regain North America for the British Empire.[2]

De Beers thus from the first traded in "conflict diamonds," using them to finance illicit wars. These helped finance his attack on the Transvaal's Boer government in 1895. De Beers' oil wagons smuggled guns past the Boer police on an ill-fated raid on gold-rich Johannesburg. His "Charter Company," also known as "The British South Africa Company," had a charter allowing it to maintain a standing army and administer conquered

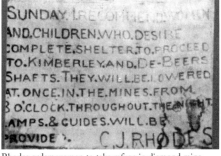

Rhodes orders women to take refuge in diamond mine.

territory. De Beers financed it with diamonds and held a quarter of its stock. His companies soon controlled half of South Africa's exports.

THE OPPENHEIMER BROTHERS JOIN THE DIAMOND TRADE

When Rhodes was at the peak of his power in May 1896, Ernest Oppenheimer was only just commencing work as a 16 year-old junior clerk in Dunkelsbuhler and Company, a member of the London Diamond Syndicate that purchased De Beers' diamonds. It already employed his brothers Louis and Bernard and was owned by a relative by marriage. Ernest stayed with Louis in the inner London suburb of Camden Town. They were to work together for the rest of their lives and even to marry sisters. Family connections were all important. Their company also employed their cousin Gustav Imroth (who later became the Managing Director of Johannesburg Consolidated Investment, one of South Africa's leading finance houses). Two more brothers, Gustav and Otto, were to follow Ernest into the diamond trade.

Ernest had been born in Friedberg near Frankfurt as the eighth child and the fifth son of the cigar merchant, Eduard Oppenheimer and his wife Nanette. It was a time of unrest. There was much resentment in Germany over the million Jewish refugees given refuge by Emperor Franz Joseph in the 1880s when they fled racial intolerance in Russia and Eastern Europe. Ernest in his turn escaped the anti-Semitism spreading in Germany by coming to London.

Louis soon became office manager and coordinator of the operations of the Diamond Syndicate. Their company expanded from diamonds to trade in other South African minerals such as coal and gold with money raised in Germany – and formed other companies including Consolidated Mines Selection (CMS). The brothers had clearly fallen on their feet.

Soon after Cecil Rhodes' death, Ernest Oppenheimer left for South Africa where he was to set up his permanent home. He went to replace a non-relative, Leon Soutro, as the local head of their diamond purchasing operation. Soutro, a very experienced diamond trader, seethed at being replaced by a 22 year-old whose main asset seemed to be family connections. His temper was not helped by Ernest's brusque and arrogant telegram: "Meet me at the station to look after luggage."

Other Oppenheimer relatives were already well established in southern Africa. His cousin, Fritz Hirschhorn, was a director of De Beers and the senior representative of the Syndicate in South Africa as well as the representative of Wernher, Beit and Company, one of the wealthiest and most powerful of the diamond trading houses. De Beers' diamonds were sorted in Hirschhorn's company's office before they were shipped to Dunkelsbuhler in London to be distributed under Otto Oppenheimer's supervision to the other Syndicate members. By virtue of his family links, Ernest Oppenheimer was now at the very center of the diamond trade.

DE BEERS AND THE PREMIER MINE

The Oppenheimers then took advantage of a serious error by De Beers. Thomas Cullinan, a local prospector, claimed to have found a major new diamond deposit but the Chairman of De Beers, Francis Oats, declared it a "salted" fraud. When Ernest's brother Bernard checked it out, he found it was authentic. He quickly claimed marketing rights to what became the Premier Mine. Bernard then directly challenged the De Beers monopoly by setting up an independent diamond marketing operation in the US. Ernest helped fund this by purchasing part of its production on behalf of Dunkelsbuhler.

De Beers remained dangerously complacent. Francis Oats addressed its 20th annual general meeting in December 1908: "Really, if one could believe all the stories which have been circulating about the discovery of new mines and methods for the artificial making of diamonds, it would be a marvel that

DE BEERS DIRECTORS PULLMAN COACH

USED BY DIRECTORS OF DE BEERS COMPANY FOR TRAVELLING ON THE MAIN LINES OF THE SOUTH AFRICAN RAILWAYS AND THE RHODESIAN RAILWAYS MANUFACTURED BY THE PULLMAN COMPANY CHICAGO U. S. A. ASSEMBLED IN THE DE BEERS WORKSHOP 1898 TAKEN FROM SERVICE 1937 MOVED TO PRESENT POSITION 1954

Pullman railway coach built for De Beers.

people are willing to buy diamonds at all." He continued: "There have been numerous discoveries of alleged mines in all parts of the world, but none of them have come to the serious production stage except German S.W. Africa where a discovery has been made of some superficial deposits of diamonds, but fortunately for our prices, these, singularly enough, are all small in size." This was a far greater error. The German discoveries were of magnificent diamonds. Oats then compounded these errors by rejecting a marketing deal with Premier. By 1907, Premier was producing 1.9 million carats a year, nearly as much as De Beers' two million carats.[3] De Beers and its Syndicate could not compete with these new producers. By 1908 it had to stockpile 18 months' unsold production. It then tried to negotiate a settlement with Premier, offering to "lock up the whole of their accumulated stock," all 18 months' worth, to keep

Diamond sorting in the field.

the prices of diamonds high[4] and by offering to purchase 30 percent of its future needs from Premier.

Premier thought little of this offer. A bitter war of words broke out between Premier and De Beers, the latter allied with the Syndicate-contracted mines Jagersfontein and Kimberley. In 1910 the Chairman of Premier spoke of "these attacks... made on us by the high priests of the diamond religion, the Taschi Lama of Jagersfontein [Sir David Harris] and the Dalai Lama of Kimberley [Sir Francis Oats]... All I can say is neither the remarks of the chairman of De Beers nor the remarks to the chairman of the Jagersfontein Company will reduce the production of [our] company by one single carat."[5] By 1908 Premier held 57 percent of the world market, forcing De Beers to close its Dutoitspan mine and to cut production at five other mines. Its diamond cartel nearly collapsed.

The Prime Minister of Cape Colony (now part of South Africa), J. X. Merriman issued a grim warning to the House of Assembly: "A discovery of a new diamond field would be a hideous calamity for us all." Then in 1908 came the news that the Germans in South West Africa were producing high-class diamonds from easily mined sand dunes.

GERMANY BECOMES A DIAMOND RIVAL

Workers crawling to retrieve diamonds.

In South West Africa the Germans had claimed rights over thousands of diamonds that were literally lying sparkling in the moonlight. The Germans employed local blacks to crawl all night in a line over the dunes putting diamonds into tins hung from their necks. Their mouths were gagged lest they try to keep a diamond by swallowing it. In 1909 the Germans set up the German Colonial Company to mine its diamonds. De Beers' share of the world market slipped down to 40 percent.

The German Colonial Company established a forbidden zone or "Sperrgebiet" along the diamond-rich coast of South West Africa, excluding the local people from their own land. In Germany the Diamond Régie of South West Africa was exclusively marketing these fine large diamonds. Fritz Hirschhorn, Ernest's cousin, was sent by De Beers to Berlin around 1909 to try to negotiate a place for De Beers in the German system – and failed.

Ernest Oppenheimer bust in Kimberley.

In 1910 Ernest Oppenheimer declared: *"Common sense tells us that the only way to increase the value of diamonds is to make them scarce, that is to reduce the production."*[6] But he did not try to cut the production of Premier, the mine his company partly owned. He would instead use it to force De Beers to heel.

Louis Oppenheimer took over Dunkelsbuhler and associated companies when their founder died in 1911. It held rights to 12.5 per cent of De Beers' diamond production. Ernest headed their operations in southern Africa.

That same year Ernest became both an alternate director of the Jagersfontein diamond mine and mayor of Kimberley.

The German operation was now destroying the Syndicate. Its major customers in Germany, Belgium and The Netherlands preferred to buy the high-class diamonds coming from the German mines. The Belgians also became rivals. They set up in Antwerp a new Syndicate to bid for the German production.

By 1913 the German Colonial Company was producing over 1.5 million carats a year from its African mines. Although De Beers and Premier together put out twice as many diamonds by weight, the German production was vastly superior in quality. The Diamond Syndicate made great efforts to regain marketing control, bidding for half of the German production but was outbid by the newly established Antwerp syndicate.[7] The London Syndicate claimed in 1914 to have a German agreement to cut production to one million carats a year – but this did not tally with German moves to expand production.

The gathering clouds of war did not interrupt the urgent efforts to save De Beers and the London Syndicate. Only five days before the outbreak of World War I, a treaty was signed in London that united the German and British diamond producers under a common system. The Germans agreed to sell their diamonds through the Syndicate and to give it a 4 percent commission and 5 percent of the profits. In return, the Germans would be guaranteed 22 percent of the world market. All the diamond producers of southern Africa signed – and the German government witnessed the agreement. For a very brief period it seemed that the Diamond Syndicate could get back to its former practice of fixing the world's diamond prices.

But within weeks this pact proved a grave mistake. Not only was it made redundant when General Louis Botha conquered the German diamond fields of S.W. Africa in 1915; as an agreement with the enemy it was a public relations disaster. After the sinking of the passenger liner Lusitania that same year, anti-German riots broke out in Kimberley. Ernest Oppenheimer was a very obvious target as a mayor of Kimberley known to be German. An angry mob stoned his car, chased him through the streets, and tore down the brass plates of E. Oppenheimer and of other German merchants. Ernest took refuge next day in a nunnery. He soon fled to London with his family.

In London, his German connections still gave him many problems. Half of the directors of CMS were based in Germany. The company A. Goerz, part owned by Oppenheimers, found it opportune to change its directors to men with Anglo-Saxon names. It even changed its name to the Union Corporation, but the Custodian of Enemy Property was not fooled and confiscated shares owned in Goerz and CMS. The British press demanded also the forfeiture of CMS interests, which now included investments in the US, Canada, Australia, and New Zealand, as well as in South Africa.

In 1916, less than a year after he had vowed never to return to South Africa, Ernest Oppenheimer returned with a scheme that should protect German investors from having their shares forfeited as enemy property. He had learned from the mining engineer, William Honnold, that there might be much gold in deep reefs around Johannesburg. Oppenheimer used this information to attract investment from the US to dilute his German base. In 1917 CMS gave him in return half ownership of its gold prospects as well as an interest in other southern African businesses.

But Oppenheimer wanted a company without any evident German history, based in South Africa rather than London so he could the more easily control it. He decided to set up this new company by enticing investors with his 50 percent interest in CMS's gold mining properties. This brought from America W. B. Thompson of the Newmont Mining Corporation and the powerful finance house of J. P. Morgan.

All that remained now was to name his new company. Oppenheimer suggested to Honnold that they call it "African American." Honnold cabled him on July 6th, 1917: "African American would suggest on this side our dark-skinned fellow countrymen and possibly result in ridicule." Oppenheimer cabled Honnold back with another suggestion, "Anglo American." This name was accepted and the company officially registered on September 25th, 1917. Oppenheimer put his interest in CMS into the new firm in return for the post of permanent Chairman and Managing Director. Honnold became a permanent director. The other US directors were W. B. Thompson and Charles Sabin, who represented the interests of J. P. Morgan.

It was not a vast amount of money that the Americans brought in – just one million pounds sterling – less than a quarter of the capital. But the German investments in Southern Africa could now be hidden from sight and protected from forfeiture. Thus were "the German interests of his principals … diffused with that of other investors."[8]

The next stage of Oppenheimer's plan came into effect after the Versailles Peace Conference of 1919. The German diamond mines in S.W. Africa were the most lucrative gem in the German colonial crown. Half of their profits went to the German government – so they were nearly certain to be forfeited to the British Crown. That is, if no strings were pulled. Quite remarkably, the Germans were allowed to retain their title – and to sell this to Ernest Oppenheimer's disguised German company, Anglo American. Prime Minister General Botha then agreed to sign over to this new company the diamond profits forfeited by the German Government to South Africa.[9] It was now clear that a deal had been done to protect German investors from the consequences of Germany's defeat.

The Oppenheimers had again stolen a march on De Beers and its Diamond Syndicate. When the Syndicate's representatives (Ernest's cousin Fritz Hirschhorn and Ross Frames of De Beers) went to Botha to seek rights to the German diamonds, they discovered they were too late. They sent an urgent message to the London directors of De Beers, warning them of the danger. But the London directors were not concerned. They replied, "German holders under belief they will remain in possession of their property and from our inquiries in Germany these holders are not disposed to sell at present."[10]

But they had been deceived. Ernest Oppenheimer had already secured the most precious possession of the former German empire, a diamond mine three times the size of Wales containing a vast number of the highest quality diamonds. To administer this treasure trove he set up Consolidated Diamond Mines of South West Africa (CDM) with a board comprised of his nominees.

Oppenheimer's German connections might have been a problem earlier – but now they proved to be his greatest asset for he had succeeded in laundering most of Germany's African assets.

The South African government stipulated in return that the government retained the right to supervise the marketing of the formerly German diamonds, thus becoming a business partner of Oppenheimer's Anglo American. His company now had easy access to financing with support from Dunkelsbuhler, from J. P. Morgan of New York, as well as from the Germans. The Morgans soon brought in another major financier, Morgan Grenfell of London.

But Oppenheimer needed more allies if he were to conquer De Beers in South Africa. He thus sought the support of the head of Barnato Brothers, S. B. "Solly" Joel, who had reminded De Beers' directors and shareholders of his power at their 1916 Annual General Meeting. "I am now speaking as the largest individual shareholder in this company: I am the largest holder in Jagersfontein and likewise in Premier. Through my having joined the board of the Premier, I have brought those gentlemen into line with us to know, and to say, that there is only one thing, and that one thing is reduced production and … higher prices."

Oppenheimer threatens De Beers

Oppenheimer now threatened to create a new Syndicate to give him the power to ration out rough diamonds to the merchants he himself chose. Oppenheimer wrote to J. P. Morgan in 1921, "From the very start I expressed the hope that besides gold we might create step by step, a leading position in the diamond world, thus concentrating by degrees in the Corporation's hands the position that the pioneers of the diamond industry formerly occupied."

Between 1919 and 1920 vast new diamond deposits were found in the Belgian Congo and Angola, covering hundreds of square miles. Diamond extraction in these lands only required a pan and brush. Ernest warned the Diamond Producers Association that Angola's diamond producers "were the principal and most dangerous competitors of all the foreign producers. They produced very cheaply and they would have no difficulty in increasing their production; in fact they could double it. Their diamonds were also of a much better quality than the Congo diamonds and, if uncontrolled, would be a very serious menace to the market."[11]

But Oppenheimer contained this threat by obtaining support from the colonial masters of Angola and the Congo, Portugal and Belgium, persuading them to give him marketing control over their diamonds. He then strengthened his relationship with Barnato Bros. by offering them a share in the profits from these new mines. His personal status was boosted when he was knighted in 1921. On April 21st, 1922 he reported to the Anglo American Board: "Further transactions have been entered into, jointly with Messrs. Barnato Brothers, with Société Internationale Forestière et Minière du Congo. Arrangements have been made… for the purchase of their future outputs with the result that there is no diamond production worthy of note that is not now controlled by either the Syndicate or by the [Anglo American] corporation and Messrs. Barnato Bros. jointly."

In 1924 Oppenheimer extended into the West African diamond fields. Here he made a deal with A. Chester Beatty, Managing Director of African Selection Trust, to market his diamonds for him – on condition that he restricted his diamond production. When diamonds were found in Sierra Leone. De Beers consulting engineer H. T. Dickenson reported after a trip to Sierra Leone in August 1935, "In my view this field as a whole will produce more diamonds in value than Angola and the Congo… I feel rather depressed, as these fields are a real menace to De Beers."[12] These words should be borne in mind today when De Beers is actively "demonizing" the diamond production of these countries as possible "blood diamonds" – even refusing stones certified by the legitimate local governments as "conflict" free.

But Oppenheimer's plans were going well. He had succeeded in excluding De Beers from all finds outside South Africa. It was time to take over De Beers and its struggling Diamond Syndicate. The first move was for Anglo American to apply for Syndicate membership. According to precedent, this would give Anglo American a diamond-marketing quota equivalent to its total diamond production. Ernest now for the first time spoke of the importance of having only one outlet for rough diamond sales in order to control prices. Naturally, the members of the Syndicate saw through this hypocritical ploy. They fought to prevent Oppenheimer getting anything but a very small quota. They had no wish to be swallowed up.

The Oppenheimer strategy developed apace. He had set his sights on acquiring such a major part of the world diamond production that De Beers would be forced to sue for peace and to yield him the place he thought he deserved. He was not plotting to overthrow the system but to take it over. His ambition was fueled by the incredible difference between the production cost of rough diamonds and the retail price they could attract.

In 1923 Oppenheimer tried to trade his way into the Syndicate. He offered it his contracts for the Angolan and Congolese diamond production, the two biggest producers outside South Africa. In return he wanted entry to the Syndicate and a guaranteed ten percent of the world diamond market for Anglo American. On May 27th, 1923 he said he had "arranged to hand over the contract for the purchase of the Angolan diamonds… to the London Diamond Syndicate, acquiring in return a participation in the general Syndicate business."[13]

But his cousin Friedrich Hirschhorn objected at sharing with an upstart he had introduced to South Africa and taught about the industry. His company, Breitmeyer, had rights to 35 percent of Syndicate diamonds and was the South African "clearing house" for all Syndicate business. He was fiercely opposed to Oppenheimer obtaining any of his company's quota. Nevertheless a compromise was grudgingly agreed. Anglo American would be offered an 8 percent share in the Syndicate's market.

Oppenheimer thought this totally inadequate. It rankled. He again plotted to set up his own Syndicate, arguing that "it would succeed because it can offer better terms than the old syndicate since it will have no old stock or commitments." He planned to totally exclude Breitmeyer. That, he said, would end their "imperious talk." His political career advanced that same year when he became a Member of Parliament for Kimberley.

Ernest Oppenheimer played the nationalist card superbly. He argued his plans would give South Africa a powerful commercial empire. He pointed out that it would allow him to manipulate the diamond production of other nations in order to protect South Africa. He asked in return that the South African government sell the ex-German diamonds via Anglo American.

He explained:

In order to protect the South African diamond industry and assure that all control diamonds shall be from Union of South Africa, Anglo American being purely South African company have, after lengthy patient negotiations:

1. Acquire considerable interest [in] Angola and entered into lengthy contract to purchase [Angolan] diamonds with limitation of output.

2. Have made contract with Congo, limiting output.

3. Have induced Belgians [to] engage Dickinson as consulting engineer for Angola and watch Congo developments.

4. Limited and purchased West African diamonds.

5. All these benefits to South African diamond industry will be lost if South West diamonds now sold [by the South African government] to Antwerp [Instead of to the Syndicate or Anglo American.][14]

The South African government then gave Oppenheimer a pretext for bidding against the Syndicate for marketing rights for the former German diamonds. On January 6th, 1925 it threatened to sell the South West Africa diamonds elsewhere if the Syndicate and Anglo American did not come to an agreement. Louis Oppenheimer reported that it had said it "had an offer for all South West Africa diamonds" that came from another party, not from Anglo American or the Syndicate. The Oppenheimers now announced that they had been forced to bid to forestall the government from selling them elsewhere. When the Oppenheimer bid was successful, they went further. They put in a bid for the marketing rights for De Beers' own production, offering more than was paid by the Syndicate. They declared the old Syndicate dead.

The Syndicate and De Beers responded in fury. A new bid came in from the Syndicate and De Beers promptly contracted with it again. Ernest Oppenheimer then accused De Beers of improperly helping the Syndicate. A stormy meeting on January 21st, 1925 ended with the Syndicate expelling both Anglo American and Dunkelsbuhler from its ranks.[15] The Oppenheimer brothers moved to set up their own Syndicate that would exclude the hitherto leading diamond trader Breitmeyer, belonging to their cousin Hirschhorn, giving its 35 percent share of the diamond trade to Anglo American.

The government expressed its pleasure at Oppenheimer's tactics. It accepted Ernest's nationalistic argument that it had replaced London-based Syndicate companies with a South African combine (ignoring perhaps its German investors). The Minister of Mines told the House on March 2nd, 1925 that he "was glad to be able to tell the House that a wedge had been driven into the Syndicate, and that no less a person than an Hon. Member sitting on the opposite side of the House [Ernest Oppenheimer], who is connected with the Anglo American corporation... was materially a participant in driving this wedge into the Syndicate."

The government had no intention of allowing Ernest Oppenheimer to rule alone. It intended to force him to accept the government as a business partner. It introduced that year the Diamond Control Act "to provide for the control of the sale and export of diamonds and for the establishment of a diamond control board in the Union." It took the power to fix diamond quotas and minimum prices, to demand and receive diamonds from producers, and to create a monopoly for both diamond sales and exports.[16] The Minister for Mines said "the whole object of this bill is not to carry out everything that is stated in it," but rather "to have a sword of Damocles hanging over combinations and combines like the Syndicate... the main object... is to protect producers [in South Africa]."

Oppenheimer, outraged, now attacked the South African government for not allowing him a monopoly. How, he asked, could the government afford to buy diamond stocks to stockpile them to keep prices high? The inference was that he had more funds available for this purpose than had the government. He said the new legislation was "nothing but confiscation."

But the government promptly used the new Act to get a diamond cutting industry established in South Africa. Until then all diamonds were exported uncut for the benefit of European diamond cutting and trading firms. Under protest, the diamond Syndicate and De Beers yielded on this. When the government made the concession of not reserving all large diamonds for cutting in South Africa, Oppenheimer protested that not many South African diamonds were large anyway. He stated, "there would hardly be a single stone [when cleaved] weighing over one carat."[17]

But Ernest Oppenheimer could not but approve of a South African government amendment that he had drafted himself. It gave preference to South African tenders. "Considering I mean to live permanently in South Africa, this very provision will be of very great assistance in future negotiations."[18]

When it was suggested to Ernest in July 1925 that he should give the Syndicate his diamond marketing contracts and rejoin them in the interests of a healthy diamond industry, he said, "You can be quite sure that I will not rejoin the Syndicate except on our own terms."[19] He continued, "I do not see how the Syndicate can make acceptable proposals to us. They have nothing to offer while we have long contracts... In my opinion, if you remain firm, you will force Joel's hand." Solly Joel was still the head of Barnato Brothers, a leading member of the Syndicate, and the major De Beers shareholder.

Anglo American now controlled over 24 percent of the world's diamond production, but Oppenheimer demanded at least a third of the world diamond market. The Syndicate would not concede this. But this impasse did not last long. Joel now decided to break the deadlock by backing the Oppenheimer's new Syndicate. The Oppenheimers were victorious. By October 22nd, 1925, all the major producers, including De Beers, were signed up with the new Syndicate.

On July 12th, 1926 Ernest Oppenheimer finally won a seat on the board of De Beers. He brought with him contracts with African diamond producers as well as for the Anglo American and Barnato production. But he was still only a board member of De Beers, not its chairman.

PANIC OVER MORE DIAMOND DISCOVERIES IN SOUTH AFRICA

But then came the unexpected discovery in 1926 and 1927 of vast new alluvial diamond fields in the Western Transvaal, in Lichtenburg, and along the Atlantic coastline of South Africa. Africa seemed to be made of diamonds. Hundreds of small-time diamond miners rushed to the scene. It was easy and cheap to mine these diamonds as they were on or near the surface. A flood of cheap diamonds hit the market. The Syndicate was in trouble with its high priced diamonds.

The Syndicate companies tried to buy up all the cheap diamonds to take them off the market. Ernest Oppenheimer told the Anglo American annual general meeting in May 1927, "The confidence of the diamond trade has been thoroughly shaken, not so much by the discovery of the rich Lichtenburg fields or the reported rich finds in Port Nollath, but by the uncontrolled exploitation of these fields." So, to protect the diamond Syndicate, Anglo American and De Beers, the South African government prepared new legislation. The Precious Stones Act of 1927 made it illegal for anyone to be found in possession of diamonds not registered with the police. All diamonds confiscated were to go to the Syndicate. This effectively made it impossible for any black to keep even a bit of kimberlite that might contain a diamond – even if his floor was made of kimberlite, as in the homes of black South Africans I visited in 1996.

In May 1927 a "combine" was created in London and Antwerp of "all direct importers of South African alluvial diamonds (by which) they agreed to sell the whole of same or part thereof through the medium of the London Diamond Syndicate."

Other steps were taken. Ernest Oppenheimer wrote to his brother, Louis, in December 1927: "The De Beers company should from time to time buy up farms in likely areas in order to prevent as far as possible a recurrence of the Lichtenburg finds. As Anglo American Corporation has the proper organization, we would do the work for the time being for De Beers, or anyhow keep them fully informed." He had in fact already taken action, as revealed by a letter he sent Louis eleven months earlier on January 19th, 1927:

> I sent you a confidential cable with reference to our purchasing certain farms … we have acquired, with the exception of one or two farms, the ground lying eastwards of Treasure Trove. We bought the farms with the mineral rights, so that we can either work them or keep them locked up. It is a most valuable purchase, which in the long run must show huge profits… Solly [of Barnato Brothers] was not inclined, nor was I, simply to hand them over to De Beers. We both felt that it was a very useful thing, for bargaining in the future, to have properties of that kind under our control… I may tell you that the total outlay is very much less than 100,000 pounds [$160,000].[20]

Oppenheimer meant to keep these diamond-concealing deals secret. He continued, "It will of course leak out in due course that we have bought this ground but Joel and I felt that it was better not to publish the fact, and for that reason we are forming a company called the 'H.L.G. Limited'… the director of the company will be one of our auditors, and the registered address will also be in his office."[21]

Oppenheimer then turned his attention to "the enormous enrichment in the oldest shingle deposits of Alexander Bay at the Orange River mouth discovered by Hans Merensky along a tidal line marked by oyster shells."[22] Oppenheimer described this as an "Aladdin's cave… a fabulously rich accumulation of large diamonds in a very small space." But he had to move quickly. He paid the then colossal sum of a million pounds ($1.6 million) for the million carats that Merensky had mined by hand in one year, and then quickly dug up the richest parts of Alexander Bay so the diamonds could be put away securely.

PROVIDING FOR WHITE DIAMOND DIGGERS

In 1927 a new producer appeared on the scene that Oppenheimer could not so easily control, the South African government. On February 25th, it took control over a large region rich in alluvial diamonds with two proclamations, Nos. 50 and 51, issued by virtue of the powers it had under the Precious Stones Amendment Act of 1907. It outlawed prospecting for precious stones on all crown and private land without a government license in both South West Africa and the adjacent South African province of Namaqualand. It thus took control over a 500-mile strip along the Atlantic coast including diamond-rich farms and the Merensky deposit – excepting one farm, Kleinzee, where there was a legal exemption, and excepting the Oppenheimer's "Forbidden Zone" in Southwest Africa (now Namibia).

The government had decided it would release the Namaqualand coastal lands to the growing numbers of small-scale white miners or white diggers who saw these rich lands as the key to their own fortune and who were thus hostile to the efforts of De Beers to exclude them. The Precious Stones Act of 1927 was designed to make these deposits "the reserve and preserve of the small man,"[23] but 60 percent of all diamonds found were to go to the government, which would market them itself.

Blacks were not to be allowed to own diamond leases or to mine their own stones. The government restricted the number of black mineworkers a white man could employ in order to ensure even competition between the white diggers. It organized races to peg claims when new land was released for diamond mining. On August 20th, 1926 the 10,000 white people lining up for one of these races included several women and a man on crutches.

The Kleinzee farm on the bleak Atlantic coast of Namaqualand was extremely rich in diamonds and owned by Chester Beatty of Selection Trust. The story of what happened next was told by Edward Wharton-Tigar, a former Managing Director of Selection Trust's West African diamond mines: "Here [at Kleinzee] there were diamonds galore, and Beatty's engineers set about recovering them, much to the consternation of the South African moguls, who had already been thrown into near panic by Hans Merensky's discovery of the famous 'oyster line' of

Diamond rush in Namaqualand.

diamonds in Alexander Bay and by the simultaneous development of new rich diamond fields at Lichtenburg."

When Oppenheimer discovered how rich Kleinzee was, he offered to invest in Beatty's company in exchange for curtailing its diamond production. Oppenheimer told Anglo American shareholders: "We arranged to acquire an interest in the company [Selection Trust] and to purchase the diamonds, always with a provision that the annual output be limited." Oppenheimer also offered to split the world between them. If Beatty agreed, "that he would not make any further incursions into South Africa," Oppenheimer would leave Selection Trust with "a free hand on the

West Coast" of central Africa, including in Sierra Leone. Beatty would eventually sell Kleinzee to Oppenheimer under this "gentleman's agreement."[24]

Oppenheimer, now with another major coastal mine under his control, told De Beers he could not disadvantage Anglo American by allowing De Beers to have Anglo American's diamond mining rights – unless Anglo and De Beers could somehow be united. He now lobbied the London branch of the Rothschild family and Joel of Barnato Bros., asking them to support his bid for the chairmanship of De Beers, making this the price of his uniting the diamond operations of both companies. Oppenheimer's cousin and rival, Hirschhorn, organized a counter lobby with the support of the French Rothschilds. He argued that it was inappropriate for the same man to head both De Beers and the Syndicate, as mining and marketing should be kept separate.

OPPENHEIMER AND THE GREAT DEPRESSION

Ernest Oppenheimer was triumphant on October 20th, 1929 when he learned he had been appointed chairman of De Beers. He now had the power to reshape the diamond trade. De Beers agreed to a new enlarged Syndicate in which South African diamond miners were joined with London marketing operations of the Syndicate. For the first time De Beers controlled both diamond mining and diamond marketing. This new, more powerful, Syndicate was now to be called the Diamond Corporation and to be wholly owned by De Beers, with De Beers having the right to appoint its directors and chairman. Ernest Oppenheimer moved quickly to solidify his family's control by placing its London operations under the control of his brother Otto. From now on the Diamond Syndicate, De Beers, and Anglo American would be simply different aspects of his personal family empire.

Nine days after Ernest Oppenheimer's appointment he faced his first and totally unexpected test. On October 29th, the crash of the New York Stock Exchange heralded the beginning of the Great Depression. It was soon evident that the diamond market was in great trouble. Oppenheimer moved swiftly to cut production to stop the prices of diamonds from tumbling, but there was a major gap in his control system. He did not control the South African government's diamond mines. It was allowing production to increase in the alluvial diamond fields of South Africa in order to placate the diggers and to increase its own revenues.

Ernest Oppenheimer warned at a De Beers board meeting on October 8th, 1930:
Do not let us shut our eyes to the fact that there are now producers in the world whose production is now limited under our agreements [who] are capable of producing diamonds much more cheaply than the De Beers Company or any other mines. For instance, you have the government and the Cape Coast Exploration Company [operating on South Africa's Atlantic coast]. We know that on Kleinzee there are 600,000 carats of diamonds and we know the adjoining farms are rich. Then you have the north bank of the Orange River, West Africa and Angola all producing diamonds cheaply.[25]

Oppenheimer summed up what was to become the principal aim of De Beers' contracts with non-South African mines – the protection of their South African mines from competition.

Oppenheimer reduced the number of diamonds in the market. "We arranged to eliminate... for two years... all inferior diamonds – from our deliveries... the company locks these temporarily undesirable diamonds away in its safes."[26]

He also ensured his companies paid minimal tax. De Beers had to pay UK tax after an appeal to the House of Lords failed in 1907. The new arrangements avoided this by setting up a Diamond Trading Company in London as a wholly owned subsidiary of the De Beers-controlled Diamond Corporation. The chairman of the Diamond Board of South West Africa, Ross Frames, condemned this as the creation of a "bogus" company, and subsequently Oppenheimer had to work hard to persuade the South African government to allow this arrangement.

He started to charge the contracted diamond mines for sorting and selling their diamonds, although in practice their diamonds would be mixed in with everyone else's and not sold separately. The Diamond Board of S.W. Africa was extremely critical of this new arrangement and of the Diamond Trading Company (still colloquially called the Syndicate). They attacked it for charging excessive sorting and marketing fees, for giving S.W. Africa only a small market quota, and for mixing their fine diamonds with poorer diamonds from De Beers' own mines – thus diminishing their return in favor of De Beers.

The South African government grew concerned at the vast power Oppenheimer had gathered to himself. The Minister of Mines told Parliament on March 2nd, 1932:

We have had the spectacle in South Africa that there is one man who is chairman of all the producing companies in South Africa, that the same man is chairman of the Diamond Corporation. He alone is the center of the whole diamond industry, and, moreover, he advocates his own case in this House. The fact is that the Hon. Member for Kimberley [Oppenheimer] can juggle, manipulate and deal with all the diamonds as he pleases, and all the men whom he brings over from overseas amount to nothing, because he turns them all round his thumb. It is necessary for the Government to take this great industry under its protection.

The South African government's unease led in 1934 to the creation of a Diamond Producer's Association under the government's chairmanship, with it having the power of veto, since all the Association's decisions had to be unanimous. The Association was to set production quotas for the unrepresented Syndicate-contracted foreign mines, and thus protect South African mines from competition.

To give the South African government its due, it suggested this arrangement should be discussed with overseas producers at an international congress in order to obtain a more democratic decision. De Beers did not agree. The government also suggested throwing out all price controls "to get a bigger share of the trade for the Union [of South Africa] by throwing open the whole of Namaqualand and trying to produce diamonds even cheaper than the Belgians and Portuguese." They realized such a strategy would make the deep De Beers mines uncompetitive, "such an action would mean the end, anyhow for a number of years, of the present big Union producers" but the government believed the potential of the 200 mile Namaqualand coastal sand dune strip was so enormous that it could easily replace the inland mines.

Ernest Oppenheimer did not cast doubts on the potential of the coastal mines but replied that "this would be suicidal, and that a big new production at this juncture would cause such a panic that the diamond trade will come to an end and no one will sell diamonds." He in turn suggested precisely the opposite measure, to end production in Namaqualand and turn the diggers off the fields.

Another governmental suggestion was that the Diamond Corporation "should refuse to sell outside [non-South African] diamonds and force its customers to buy [southern African] conference producers' diamonds instead." This would not work, Oppenheimer pointed out, for the excluded producers would set up rival marketing operations.

The final result of this debate was that Oppenheimer retained control over the marketing of southern African diamonds. During the Depression he stopped production at all the major South African diamond mines in order to prevent a fall in the price of diamonds. He persuaded the Portuguese to limit their production for three years, the Belgians for a year, and Selection Trust for two years.

By 1934 Ernest Oppenheimer was Chairman of De Beers and Anglo American, Member of Parliament, and a Knight. On December 26th, 1934 his son Harry became a director of De Beers, and would move on to become Chairman. In 1999 Harry's son Nicky became Chairman of De Beers. Ernest Oppenheimer had founded a dynasty. The Oppenheimer family would continue for decades to ration the world to keep diamonds rare and expensive. The danger from cheaper producers seemingly had been eliminated. De Beers had successfully locked away a vast stockpile of diamonds.

So, what of the claim made by De Beers' lawyers in its attack on the film *The Diamond Empire* that the Oppenheimers and De Beers never limited production to keep diamonds rare and therefore expensive? The evidence is clear. The Oppenheimers did it again and again and again, and frequently admitted to doing it. Today they are still resisting the South African government's attempts to open up these hidden resources for the benefit of smaller mining companies.

But in the 1930s there were other worrying developments for the Oppenheimers. In the United States, the major market for diamonds, there were rumors that the US had its own major diamond deposit. If this came into production, then De Beers would lose its major market in America, would not be able to keep prices high and its cartel would again be in deep trouble.

The Declining Importance of South African Diamond Production

Year	World Production in millions of carats	S.Africa's Share
1911	5.9	98 %
1916	2.7	94 %
1921	1.5	66 %
1926	5.7	69 %
1931	7.1	31 %
1936	8.2	10 %
1941	9.2	2 %
1946	10.2	15 %
1951	16.9	16 %
1956	23.7	15 %

1   Theodore Gregory Ernest. *Oppenheimer and the Economic Development of Southern Africa*. Oxford; Oxford University Press, 1962, p. 56.
2   Stefan Kanfer. *The Last Empire*. New York; Farrar Straus Giroux, 1993, p. 65.
3   Jessop, p. 45.
4   Gregory, p. 61.
5   Chairman's speech. Premier Mines AGM, 1910.
6   Jessup, p. 59.
7   Gregory, p. 69.
8   Wharton-Tigar, p. 181.
9   Ibid, p. 142. Also Flynn, p. 39.
10 Jessup, p. 112.
11 Ernest Oppenheimer to Board of Management of the Diamond Producers Association. December 7th, 1934.
12 Gregory, p. 308.
13 Ibid, p. 130.
14 Ibid, p. 145.
15 Ibid, p. 157.
16 Diamond Control Act, 1925 section 16:1.
17 Gregory, p. 127.
18 Ibid, p. 162.
19 Ernest Oppenheimer to Walter Dunkes in London. July 6th, 1925.
20 Gregory, p. 177.
21 Ibid, p.178.
22 Ernest Oppenheimer cable to Louis Oppenheimer, March 29th, 1927.
23 Minister of Mines, April 25th, 1927.
24 Wharton-Tigar, p. 183.
25 Gregory, p. 230.
26 Ibid, p. 195.

Chapter 5 – How The Only US Diamond Mine Was Sabotaged

At the beginning of the 21st century all the books on the diamond trade reported that the United States, the world's largest diamond consumer, was nearly unique among large countries in not having a diamond mine of its own. Yet Hillary Clinton wore a fine four-carat diamond from Arkansas at her husband's Presidential Ball – with a very odd story behind it.

When I started my trawl through US Justice Department records, looking for legal actions relating to De Beers, I was surprised to find reports by eminent geologists saying that a diamond deposit in Arkansas was so rich that it would have created a major diamond mine – if it had been in South Africa. Why was it then not developed?

Secret Justice Department reports suggested that sabotage stopped the development of the Murfreesboro, Pike County, field – only a few hours from Little Rock – into a major diamond mine. Geological reports indicate that it was a commercial deposit able to supply America with millions of diamonds. The reports allege that Ernest Oppenheimer had worked to stop Murfreesboro being mined. The lawyers thought the evidence warranted further investigation and the consideration of legal action – but this did not happen. The lack of a diamond mine in the US had given the Oppenheimers a lucrative captive market for their African diamonds.

Diamonds were first found in Arkansas in 1906 when a local farmer, John Huddestone, found gems while cleaning out his pigs' swill. These were sent to Tiffany's in New York where they were verified to be diamonds – although Tiffany's would have been most cautious. In 1872 its founder, Charles Tiffany, was taken in by a diamond hoax involving the "seeding" of a Colorado "find" with a sprinkling of diamonds.

TIFFANY SAYS ARKANSAS DIAMONDS EQUAL TO SOUTH AFRICAN

Tiffany was sufficiently impressed to send their chief mineralogist and Vice President, George Kunz, to Arkansas. He reported that it was a real diamond deposit – and a definite mine prospect – saying that the major problem in developing it would be the reluctance of Americans to submit to the humiliating body cavity searches and purges imposed on black miners in South Africa.[1] Thousands more diamonds were then found. The Justice Department reported over 100,000 diamonds were discovered in the top 40 feet of the field next to this pig sty, that 50,000 of these were sold to a diamond firm on Fifth Avenue, and many were cut as expensive gems.

The geologists reported that this was a volcanic deposit similar to those mined to great depths for diamonds in South Africa. In over 80 years no one had professionally drilled or otherwise examined the deposit below its top 40 feet. The 100,000 diamonds found were, in mining terms, taken from mere surface scratchings. This indicates a fortune at greater depths – at least that is what the Justice Department documents reported. They said it was most likely that this was only a surface concentration. South African diamond mines reportedly only averaged a quarter of a carat of diamonds in every a tonne of rock and yet were extremely profitable and were mined to great depths. In comparison, this Arkansas pig-run should have been an Eldorado.

THE TOURIST DIAMOND MINE

But I found this diamond deposit had been turned into a public park where amateur diggers could hire a bucket, spade and rubber boots and dig their own diamonds for $3.50 a day – as long as they did not dig a hole deeper than four feet or use any motorized equipment! The hopeful prospectors even had to fill in their holes every evening! Yet despite these restrictions, one in 200 of the many visitors found a diamond, an extraordinarily high ratio. This made

Welcoming visitors to the Arkansas diamond mine.

me extremely curious to know why, in a country that consumed more diamonds than any other on earth, was this major diamond deposit not being mined commercially?

Before going to Murfreesboro I had spoken with a top expert in New York's diamond district. He worked in a small diamond cutting workshop just off Fifth Avenue, overlooking the jewelry stores of 47th Street. Its walls were neatly hung with cutting and grinding tools, with every ledge black with dust torn from gems by grinding wheels. He was a master cutter whose nickname on the street was "The Professor" because of his knowledge of the cutting trade. He was currently repairing diamonds for Tiffany's. He told me he had cut many Arkansas diamonds and had found they made excellent gems.

I went next to the office of the US Geological Survey in Washington to discover if they knew of a diamond deposit on a former pig farm in Murfreesboro. They did. They told they held reports from several geologists, all of whom maintained it was a diamond deposit similar to those that supported major mines in South Africa.

Murfreesboro sign.

Increasingly perplexed, I asked why was it not then being mined? The senior spokesman for the Geological Survey replied they did not know for sure but he had seen reports alleging that sabotage had wrecked early efforts to establish a diamond mine. He referred me to a US Justice Department report by Thomas H. Daly of its Antitrust division.

Murfreesboro may not have a major diamond mine but it still makes a living from its diamond deposit.

When I arrived, I could not mistake it. A large sign by the road proclaimed "Welcome to Murfreesboro, the Diamond Town." The shops and the restaurants proclaimed the diamond connection. The local paper is *The Murfreesboro Diamond*. I booked a room at a hotel called The Crater of Diamonds. It seemed the discovery of the diamond deposit was the greatest thing that ever happened to Murfreesboro.

SABOTAGE IN ARKANSAS

I had arranged to interview Margaret Millar, whose late father, Howard A. Millar, set up a diamond mine here many years ago. She met me by the ploughed field in the park known as "The Crater of Diamonds," where her father once commercially mined diamonds. Tourists were now crawling over the field with plastic containers as if they were looking for strawberries. She pointed out the two buildings from her father's mine that still stood, one in the center of the field, the other a house in the woods by the open field. This had been the home of Margaret and her father. Sitting outside this house, Margaret Millar told me what happened to the mine her father started.

Howard Millar came here about 1914 to investigate farmer Huddestone's discovery. Preliminary investigation established the diamonds came from the surface of an ancient volcanic crater with a surface area of 73 acres, second only in size to the world's then foremost diamond-bearing pipe, the Premier mine in South Africa. Local investors took mining rights to 60 percent of the surface of the crater and Millar secured rights to the remaining 40 percent. The area he held was

The Arkansas diamond field.

larger than the size of many South African diamond mines so he thought his fortune made. He did not have easy access to capital but planned to fund the deeper mine works by first exploiting the diamonds in the softer upper layers of the deposit. According to Margaret, "during the 4 to 5 years they had the mine in operation it was a commercially successful venture."

But on January 13th, 1919, disaster struck. "My father's diamond plant consisted of two buildings set far apart. They were torched or burnt simultaneously. It was an arsonist type of fire. They did not catch fire from each other. It was very strange, the night watchman… was not there that particular night. Nothing was saved and there was not enough insurance or capital to start it up again since the depression was just starting in America." Some years later, a pilot told them he was paid to take aerial photographs of their mine "at the same time the plants were burnt." The pilot suspected that the people who paid for the photographs were responsible for the arson. Her parents blamed the Diamond Syndicate but they had no proof.

Her father thus was unable to find funds to drill deeper than about 70 feet. Below that depth, the rock was too hard for his equipment to penetrate. In diamond deposits in similar volcanic pipes, this softer rock is called "yellow ground," the harder "blue ground," and both contain diamonds. Millar was sure that diamonds would be present in the "blue ground" to a considerable depth, as at Premier. All the geological reports made the same prediction.

Millar found many diamonds in the "yellow ground," including a rose diamond weighing 8.43 carats. Others found larger. The largest weighed in at 40.23 carats and was named the Uncle Sam Diamond. Another, the Star of Murfreesboro Diamond weighed 34.25 carats, and the Star of Arkansas was 15.3 carats. The Uncle Sam Diamond, now owned by a Fifth Avenue merchant, was cut into an emerald shape.

The 60 percent of the diamond pipe that Millar did not own was held by the Arkansas Diamond Company. Its president, S. W. Rayburn, consulted the eminent geologist Doctor Henry S. Washington, who reported that the field was a diamond bearing volcanic pipe comparable to those of the great South African mines. In a report published jointly with Kunz, Washington stated that many of the white diamonds found here were flawless, as fine as any from South Africa, and that some yellow diamonds found were of exceptional color and clarity.[2] Kunz separately reported he had examined samples that "are absolutely perfect and are equal to the finest stones found at the Jagersfontein (South African) mine or that were ever found in India."[3]

The Arkansas Diamond Company sought confirmation of this from a highly skilled diamond mine manager and geologist, T. Fuller, a former manager of De Beers' Dutoitspan mine in Kimberley, South Africa. He sunk drill holes 25 to 50 feet into the Arkansas deposit and reported there was sufficient diamond content to make the mine commercial. He wanted to drill deeper into the blue ground to further assess the deposit but could not because, "the company was constantly hampered because of lack of funds."

Fuller found the top three to four feet of the deposit to be a black soil enriched by erosion with diamonds. Below this, he found soft decomposed kimberlitic diamond-bearing yellow ground to a depth of up to 50 feet. Under this, he found the harder, unweathered diamond-bearing rock, known as kimberlite or blue ground. He reported this mixture of decomposed weathered rock and hard rock was absolutely typical of diamond pipes in South Africa and that the rock was chemically identical with South African diamond bearing rocks.

Despite obtaining such authoritative reports, Rayburn and his directors found it remarkably difficult to raise the funds required to establish a diamond mine – perhaps because of the earlier fraudulent claim by others in Colorado. So Rayburn decided to go to England where many of the most powerful diamond merchants resided and where there was expertise in diamond mining and selling. In London, he quickly gained serious interest from Ernest Oppenheimer, who at that time, 1910, was a representative of the major firm in the Diamond Syndicate, Dunkelsbuhler and Company.

ERNEST OPPENHEIMER AND ARKANSAS

Ernest Oppenheimer was then very concerned about the rapid expansion of diamond production from vast diamond deposits found in 1908 in German South West Africa. He feared that this would swamp the world diamond market, forcing prices down. So, when two men from a remote district of Arkansas came to his door with a report from a former De Beers mine manager that they had found still more diamonds in America, his first instinct would have been to make sure they did not join the German miners as a rival producer.

Fuller's report would have easily convinced him that this was a serious prospect. He immediately commenced negotiating with Rayburn both in the US and in

London. Other Syndicate investors became involved. Rayburn offered them 49 percent of the mine for $250,000. The Syndicate rejected this, saying it wanted the entire mine. It offered to pay $450,000.[4] Rayburn hesitated at first but as the US Justice Department later reported, "these conferences, arranged with the intention of British participation... went so far as to the signing of contracts for that purpose."

But, at the last moment, Rayburn decided that he wanted to keep a piece of the action. The Justice Department report continued: "negotiations ultimately fell through, the point of control... proving to be the stumbling block." The Syndicate wanted all or nothing. If it could not buy it, then presumably it was not wanted as a rival.

A few months later, in 1911, Thomas Cochran, a partner in J. P. Morgan, a company that six years later would become a major investor in Anglo American, contacted Cochran and purchased a minority interest in the Arkansas mine. Cochran quickly expanded his interest to acquire effective management control. But this did not mean the mine was about to go ahead. Development then proceeded at a snail's pace until impatient shareholders insisted in 1919 that the mine go into production.

Cochran then appointed as mine manager S. H. Zimmerman, of whom a US Justice Department report alleged, "his function appears to have been to sabotage the mine."[5] Zimmerman first went to South Africa where he said he "happened" to meet Ernest Oppenheimer.[6] Then, as the mine commenced production, the number of diamonds found in every ton mined dropped to a hundredth of the figure achieved before he took over. Zimmerman took no responsibility for this but condemned the mine as "hopeless."

But the extremely suspicious local miners secretly investigated the diamond separation plant Zimmerman had installed. They put easily distinguished diamonds into the ore and it did not recover a single one of them. It was clearly highly defective. Zimmerman also said he had lost records of diamond sales. The lost records included sales of diamonds to the top jewelry firm, Tiffany's, as well as to companies in Detroit and Chicago. Apparently the mine's 3,000 carat stockpile of larger diamonds was spirited off to Thomas Cochran, who now held a mortgage on the mine's assets.[7] Later Cochran "auctioned these to himself for $19,000." Just one of these, the Uncle Sam diamond, was later valued at $75,000.

Local investors and miners continued to try to get the mine going. But, in 1921, according to a Justice Department report, "Ernest Oppenheimer again got interested in the property," and a meeting was held at the Morgan Company's offices in New York, attended by Rayburn, Zimmerman, Cochran and a Colonel William B. Thompson and "as a result of this meeting the (mine) plant was finally completely shut down very suddenly and for no apparent reason."[8]

Zimmerman wrote to Perry, left in charge of the mine in his absence, telling him that at this meeting, "Several strange things occurred which I will relate personally to you on return... I am sure you will be surprised and interested to hear Sir E O's views which I feel are extraordinary and unique." Perry was instructed: "Have Scotty put things in best shape for long shut down. Don't mention anything to anyone as to time of closure or conjectured reasons. I will verbally state them to you... Get all records and other data in good shape so I can quickly go over them."

THE JUSTICE DEPARTMENT INVESTIGATES

The suspicions of the investors reached Washington, triggering a Justice Department investigation. An engineer employed at the mine, George H. Vitt, told US Justice Department investigators in 1942 that the employee ordered to destroy the mine's papers had suspected sabotage, so did not destroy them. Instead, he hid them under a building. He took Vitt to where they were concealed and recovered them. Vitt also checked the "waste" rejected by Zimmerman's separation plant and found it rich in diamonds, thus strengthening suspicions that the plant had been rigged.[9]

The recovered documents convinced the Justice department that the Arkansas mine had been sabotaged. Thomas Daly's report for the Justice Department made it clear that the evidence indicated a secret sabotage deal with Oppenheimer. He noted as highly suspicious the secrecy surrounding the mine's closure, and the fact that at a time when it was closed, it was successfully selling its output to major Fifth Avenue diamond merchants.

HENRY FORD DENIED ARKANSAS DIAMONDS

The mine had indeed been closed down in the face of very strong investor and market interest – including from Henry Ford who had tested the Arkansas industrial diamonds, found them of excellent quality, had ordered many, and wanted many more to tip the tools for his Ford assembly lines. Ford was thus amazed when he heard that the mine was to be closed, so he offered to buy it. If his offer had been accepted, the mine would have been assured of a very prosperous future and an important place in American history. But Cochlin inexplicably refused to sell it, despite Ford's lucrative offer. Cochlin instead closed down the Arkansas Diamond Company in 1927 because it had supposedly defaulted on money he lent it. After this, Ford had no alternative but to buy the diamonds he needed from merchants who were supplied from overseas by the Diamond Syndicate and De Beers.

Yet, before the mine closed, Ford had agreed to pay considerably more per carat for the Arkansas diamonds than he paid for South African, because they were harder and of excellent shapes. Dr. Hugh Miser, the principal geologist of the US Geological Survey, reported that Ford "paid a premium of 28 percent because the efficiency of the Arkansas diamonds was 28 percent greater than other stones."[10] Cochlin evidently could have sold Ford all the diamonds he could produce – and could have received from Ford all the investment funds needed.

As further proof of the quality of Arkansas diamonds, Daly reported a meeting with a diamond merchant who showed him Arkansas diamonds. "Even to my inexperienced eye, it was obvious that the Arkansas diamonds were of far superior quality." The merchant told Daly… "he would be willing to buy all the diamonds he could possibly get if and when the Arkansas properties were put into operation. He said he would be willing to pay a 10 percent increase over the syndicate price in order to be sure of a domestic source of supply."[11]

The subsequent career moves of Zimmerman strengthened the Justice Department's thesis. It reported that Zimmerman took up a position with J. P. Morgan.

A Justice Department lawyer alleged: "I recently heard why the Arkansas mine shut down. Just when it was in full swing and doing nicely the manager and largest shareholder was invited to take a job with De Beers company at $15,000 salary per annum. From London he went back to New York as a partner in the firm of Morgan and Co. who are large shareholders in De Beers. It looks like a clear case of bribery and corruption."[12]

Justice Department attorney Edward Stimson concluded that the closure of the mine was due to bribery. He sought to find out if the US had jurisdiction over the actions of foreign-based companies and concluded that it might have jurisdiction in this case as the foreign company's actions had an effect in the US. He alleged: "The effect theory... is greatly strengthened by the fact that a corporation which was producing diamonds in Arkansas some years ago was closed out through the activities of the cartel by bribing the president and chief engineer with lucrative employment with other companies in the US."[13]

The Arkansas mine came briefly back to life in 1928 when Arkansas stockholders redeemed the property and began small-scale production at a level that was not a threat to anyone in the Diamond Syndicate. This operation only lasted for three years. It was shut down for lack of investment in 1931.

ARKANSAS DIAMONDS AND WORLD WAR II

In 1940, the Arkansas mine once more gained a chance of life. This time it was due to the needs of war. On February 21st, 1940, diamonds were one of the first raw materials designated by the Munitions Board as vital to national defense. The assembly line revolution introduced by Henry Ford was being applied to war industries. Thus, quality diamond-tipped tools were in great demand. With this in mind, Arkansan Ray Blick took an option on the idle and derelict Arkansas diamond mine, founded the North American Diamond Corporation, and approached Washington. He confidently asked for mining equipment as required under wartime regulations so he could commence diamond production. The government asked the United States Geological Survey to verify that there were commercial quantities of diamonds in Arkansas – and it so verified. The subsequent reports by Dr. Hugh Miller in 1940 and by Clarence Ross in 1942 were very positive.

The Director of the US Bureau of Mining, Dr. Sayers, concluded that the mine should be opened. He reported to the government: "For years this property has been unjustly talked down and it should be placed in operation." Initial testing had indicated some 40 percent of the diamonds were white, 22 percent yellow, and 37 percent brown. A mere 1 percent was of the poor quality used for diamond grinding powder or "boart." Practically all were of value as good tool stones or gems. The average size was quarter of a carat although one large section of the pipe had reported an average size of 0.4 carats with over 53 percent white, with 6 percent of these being of the highest quality gems, and 23 percent of "commercial" gem quality. All this was excellent news.

Blick went to Washington in October 1940 to press for mining equipment. But Dr. Leith of the War Production Board (WPB) told him, "The man you should see is not me but Sidney Ball... I will make an appointment for you." Ball worked for Forminiere, the company running the Congo mines that supplied the diamonds De Beers was selling to the US. De Beers was paying Ball $1-2,000 a year – and had authorized him to draw on a De Beers bank account.[14] Ball thus represented a rival company. Blick was rightly puzzled at being asked to see him and asked, "Suppose Ball does not look with favor on the proposition?" Leith replied, "In that case, you will probably have difficulty in interesting the government at all.

Blick was astonished, but he would have been even more alarmed if he had known that the US Justice Department was then investigating Ball with a view to indict him for conspiring with De Beers to restrict diamond supplies to the United States.

Then Blick was asked to meet with a committee of diamond experts at New York's Port Authority. The Justice Department reported on what happened:

Blick brought to the meeting 7,000 Arkansas diamonds and a diamond merchant expert of his own, an Ernest Schenck of Schenck and Van Haelen. The government committee comprised of the President of the diamond firm of J. K. Smit & Sons, Van Italie, and a Mr. Wagner.

Van Italie, who was marketing diamonds supplied by De Beers, took one look at the Arkansas diamonds, turned to Wagner and said, "You know what they are. They are Venezuelan diamonds. We have been buying them as Venezuelan diamonds." Blick was horrified at being accused of fraud.

But Schenck replied, "They did not come from Venezuela but from Arkansas. I have a complete record of every one." The Committee could not gainsay this and Van Italie then admitted, wherever they came from, they were "certainly all right."[15]

Van Italie was later asked to resign from the Procurement Division of the Treasury because "his partner in Holland had helped Hitler build his industrial diamond stockpile."

Blick was summoned to another meeting on January 19th, 1942. At this were R. J. Lund, the man in charge of the Government's mining procurement program; Dr. Miser, the Principal Geologist of the US Geological Survey Officer; Paul Biermont of the Army Procurement Board; Blakistone of the Naval Procurement Board; and the Director of the Bureau of Mines, Dr. Sayers. It looked at last as if the Arkansas diamond mine was receiving the serious consideration it deserved.

This time the debate centered on the depth of the diamond deposit. Lund maintained it was only "a surface concentration," but Dr. Miser pointed out that he could not say this because no one had so far tested the deposit at depth. Miser added that it was definitely a "commercial venture if properly developed." Lund wrote a memo afterwards noting. "It is an established fact... that diamonds are present in the periodtite [pipe] and that these stones, so necessary for the war effort, may be recoverable in sufficient quantities to relieve materially the present stringency and might prove of inestimable value if this emergency became acute...."[16] But, after Blick returned to Arkansas nothing happened.

PRESIDENT ROOSEVELT PROMISES ACTION

Frustrated, Blick tried to break the deadlock by going to the top. He returned to Washington with the Governor of Arkansas, Homer M. Adkins, and with Arkansas Senator Caraway, and went directly to the White House, asking to see the President on a matter of urgency. They met President Franklin D. Roosevelt in his bedroom. Roosevelt was most impressed by the quality of diamonds they poured out in front of him and said he was delighted that they were American. He promised to do his best to get the mine into production.[17]

Shortly after this Lund approved the spending of $50,000 to get mining operations started. But Blick also needed top "priority" rating if he was to get the equipment needed. Lund promised to help but instead sabotaged him. Two months later, Lund told the men supervising mining equipment that, since America was getting diamonds from Africa and Brazil, there was no need to mine diamonds in America. Yet US diplomats were in London at that time protesting that De Beers was not supplying the US with the industrial diamonds it desperately needed.

Blick persevered. Eventually he got to see Herbert Kohler, a man known as "the priority hustler in the Miscellaneous Minerals Branch."[18] Kohler said "he understood the British Syndicate was opposed to it and that he, Kohler, would take personal pride in helping North American Diamonds get over the hump and get priority." Shortly after this, Blick learned he had at last been given a priority rating. It seemed time for champagne – but then on August 6th, 1942, Lund wrote turning down their request. Their request for two Caterpillar tractors had been seen as greedy. When Blick tried to get in touch with Kohler again, he was told he had been sent to Detroit or Cleveland to work as a clerk. In fact Kohler had not left Washington, but he never again got in touch with the would-be Arkansas diamond miners.

On a subsequent trip to Washington Blick heard Lund say, in front of witnesses, "I am not at all interested in seeing any diamond mine developed in this country."[19] The US Justice Department's subsequent investigation concluded that the brick wall that stopped Blick was erected by an alliance of Washington bureaucrats, British diplomats, the Diamond Syndicate, and the US War Production Board staffed by men connected to the Diamond Syndicate.

The Justice Department reported that the chairman of the Facilities committee of the War Production Board, Fred Searls Junior, had "connections with the diamond Syndicate." Also on the committee was H. DeWitt Smith, Vice President of Newmont Mining who claimed, "Sir Ernest Oppenheimer will spend a million pounds sterling to keep these properties from going into [diamond] production." Another man connected with this committee was George E. Schafe, with interests "in companies associated with the Syndicate." Daly concluded, "these then are the men who apparently will pass upon whether or not this country is to have a domestic source of supply of industrial diamonds."[20]

Another test did get ordered, but it caused concern even before it was completed. It was a geological assessment of the Arkansas deposit by the Bureau of Mines carried out in March 1944. It was not properly funded so its geologists were limited to testing the deposit with a hand-powered bucket drill. Ray E. Blick confided to Thomas Daly:

> Word has come to other members of his organization from outside sources that the Bureau of Mines… do not intend to go further … It will be another case of sabotaging the mine properties as was done by the previous owners. He fears there may be some truth in this insofar as Sidney Ball, an employee of the Diamond Syndicate for many years, is also [at the same time] on the [Bureau of Mines] staff as a consultant for the Bureau of Mines.[21]

This financially strapped survey covered only quarter of the diamond pipe's surface and was only equipped to drill down to an average depth of 38 feet. Despite this, they found over 30 diamonds and calculated there were 27,000 carats of diamonds in the top 27 feet. They admitted not searching for small diamonds. They guessed that those they found were worth only $6 a carat. They calculated this meant the mine would produce only half the revenue needed to make it profitable. Thus in March 1944 they recommended against mining.

Yet the diamond concentration they reported was identical with that found by Doctor Miser of the US Geological Survey in 1940 and 1942, when he had concluded that the deposit was commercial. He came to his very different conclusion because he calculated the mine's potential financial return by using the prices actually achieved by Arkansas diamonds. He noted that Henry Ford paid for its industrial diamonds an average of $35 a carat in 1924 and 1925. The gem quality would attract much higher prices. But the Bureau of Mines had amateurishly guessed that only 10 percent were gems and had valued the other 90 percent by simply looking up in the Minerals Year Book to find the average price paid by the US for imported industrial diamonds. It did not notice that this was the price paid for the poorest of diamonds and at $1.98 per carat was vastly below the price Ford had actually paid for Arkansas diamonds. But this official survey ended Blick's hopes. No mining equipment was sent to Arkansas – although much equipment went to mines in the Congo that US intelligence reported were also sending diamonds to the Nazis.

However there was another assessment made of these diamonds by the Bureau of Mines at the same time. This was classified "Strictly Confidential. Not to be Released under Any Circumstances." The Bureau had secretly given a small sample of eight carats of Arkansas diamonds to three experts, instructing them explicitly and inexplicably to ignore the much higher prices that could be attracted if any were of the quality to be cut as gems. The average result from this was vastly above the $1.98 given in the Bureau's public report. J. K. Smit & Sons of New York gave an average valuation as $7.25 a carat, valuing the best at $40.50 a carat. They added, "This valuation is strictly in line with the value of industrial use and no attention has been given to the possible value of one or more of these stones for gem purposes." The other two valuers gave the widely different estimates of $11 a carat and $1.25 a carat.

Blick's experts, Schenck & Van Haelen had records for over 14,000 stones from Arkansas although they had handled many more. They found Arkansas diamonds were so hard they could only be cut with diamond powder from other Arkansas diamonds. The shape of the stones was particularly good for tools. They reported:

> some of the... users came back to us a number of times after their first purchase insisting on industrial diamonds of the same quality, even though they were not aware they were Arkansas stones.... In conclusion we can state from our practical and business experience that the property under question speaks favorably for itself, and that about 80 per cent of its production can be classified as industrial stones, the balance being largely gems. We regard these Arkansas diamonds as particularly promising for use as the cutting edges of various diamond tools.

Vitt strongly attacked "the biased and baseless statements made by War Production Board officials in what, apparently, constituted an effort to run the property down." He issued a report containing a flood of statistics to show these Arkansas diamonds were as good as South African. He noted that the 1933 average price paid by the Syndicate for gem quality diamonds from South Africa was $18 while Fuller had reported an average price for Arkansas gem diamonds of $25.16 a carat paid by Schenck.

The Bureau of Mines reported Arkansas "only" contained 0.1 carats a cubic yard. This translates to 0.19 carats a ton. They did not note that this is above the 0.17 found at the very profitable Dutoitspan mine in South Africa. W. D. McMillan, the District Engineer, wrote on May 27th, 1943: "From the available production records, it would appear that the average unit recovery of diamonds has amounted to about 0.25 carats a cubic yard" – better than the values reported for any South African mine.

Dr. Miser estimated there was 0.135 carats a cubic yard at Murfreesboro in the rock below the enriched topsoil. The average size was much the same as in South Africa and the shapes found were reported as excellent. Only the 40 percent white diamond content was relatively low. Argyle in Australia would be 50 percent white and some South African mines are said to be 75 percent white.

Was Lund of the War Production Board right when he said the Arkansas diamonds were concentrated by erosion at the surface and progressively poorer lower down?[22] His theory was contradicted even by the ultra-conservative estimates of the Bureau of Mines. They reported 43 percent of the carats found came from below 20 feet. But despite this, Lund's theory was used to discredit the mine.

The US War Production Board decision not to reopen the Arkansas diamond mine had serious consequences for America. The Justice Department spelled this out in their final report on Arkansas. "We are having a great difficulty in getting an adequate supply [of diamonds] for war uses. … We had a diamond mine in Arkansas that is not being worked because we say that we cannot afford the machinery. The importance of this domestic mine is indicated not only by Bureau of Mines tests but by the fact that the evidence shows that the Syndicate has in the past apparently paid money to keep it closed."[23]

Eventually Blick gave up and sold out.

This was not a unique story. Much the same may have happened in South America. A letter intercepted by British Intelligence and passed on to the US was from the well-known American diamond merchant Van Moppes and was sent to a relative in England. It asked him "to warn Oppenheimer about South American competition [in diamonds]" and advised him "to be ruthless in stamping it out."[24]

A PEOPLE'S DIAMOND MINE

The new post-World War II owners of the Arkansas diamond deposit did not want a repeat of these troubles so decided to develop it as a tourist venture. From 1951 until today it has operated as a toy mine, "The Crater of Diamonds Tourist Diamond Park." It became a state park in 1972 and since then the state government has continued to operate it as a tourist venture, attracting over 150,000 visitors a year.

Tourists looking for diamonds.

The people of Murfreesboro are proud of their diamond mine and promote it as the world's only truly democratic diamond mine. The park ranger told me in 1992, "The most unique thing about this is that the individual person can come and search for real genuine diamonds and, should they find one, then its theirs to keep, no matter how valuable it is… There is no other place in the world where the general public can go to search for and keep genuine rough diamonds."

A park promotional leaflet estimated that one diamond is found for every 202 visitors; that the average size is over a third of a carat; and about half are white diamonds. These numbers are extraordinary given that the visitors are only repeatedly picking over the top four feet of the deposit.

Only about half of the surface of the diamond pipe was open for the public to mine diamonds at the time of my visit. The ranger explained that the rest was closed because "it's covered in gigantic rocks, heavily wooded; it's just not a safe environment." Some of the more experienced diggers alleged they were excluded from areas into which the rainwater could wash diamonds. When I walked into the closed area it was evidently no more dangerous than any English wood. I was completely baffled at why it was considered too dangerous to mine so went back to discuss it with the ranger. This time he gave another reason: "If you had many people out in the woods digging holes, you would quickly see that it would destroy the natural beauty." This is certainly true. But, while pleasant, this was not a place of unusual beauty. Still, this was a very natural objection from a ranger whose job is to preserve the environment.

I walked over the plowed diamond-rich land, past the two shelters where water was provided for visitors to wash dirt to find diamonds. Two old-timers wore diamond pendants made from stones they had found. One woman had a ring mounted with a sizeable Arkansas stone. Past them an obviously experienced African American prospector named James Archer stood in a hole dug to the regulation depth of four feet. I stopped to talk to him. He did not stop digging as we talked. Suddenly he yelped with excitement, "There's another

James Archer mining diamonds.

Archer discovers a diamond.

one. I found another one. Sure did. Right here. Oh boy! Wow! Woo!" He picked a diamond out of a spade of earth. He said he had found eleven in three months of digging. Six were very small, under five points or a twentieth of a carat. One was over a carat, another a quarter carat yellow triangle. Later that same day he found a white quarter carat diamond. He said I had brought him luck.

What I had seen just did not make sense. There was clear incontrovertible evidence that Arkansas had produced many fine diamonds, including some worn by Hillary Clinton. In the 1990s in Canada the discovery of a few micro diamonds led to a diamond-led boom on its stock exchange. In Australia similar discoveries drew scores of companies thousands of miles out into the deserts. But in Murfreesboro thousands of gem diamonds had been discovered at a site that had transport, power and all necessary facilities near at hand.

Just where were the investors? Where were the mining companies? I just could not believe that major mining companies had not noticed the Arkansas diamond field. The US Geological Survey offices were one of their favorite ports of call. Someone must have seen the geological reports from Murfreesboro.

I was not surprised when the park ranger at Murfreesboro told me that major mining houses had indeed noted the geological reports from Murfreesboro – and that its status as a state park had initially deterred them. One company commissioned a poll that found four-fifths of the locals were against commercial mining. When around 1990 a company sought permission to do the needed wide core exploration drilling, a powerful environmental group, the Sierra Club, protested against their plans since it meant mining a federally funded state park. The Oppenheimers would have been delighted.

But the Sierra Club lost its legal action. So what now stopped Murfreesboro from becoming a major diamond mine? The answer seemed to be the Arkansas state government. In 1978, it turned down a formal proposal for serious bulk testing made by the Canadian company Cominco. In 1979, it rejected another formal proposal, this time from Superior Oil. In 1981, an approach from Anaconda was rejected. In 1983 came a flood of applications – from Anaconda, Superior Oil, Exmin (owned by Sibeka in Belgium via Luxembourg company, Sibinter), Amselco and Cominco. They were all rejected by the state. It seemed it was determined to make sure there was no diamond mine in its territory. This was extremely strange. I could understand why De Beers might not want a new diamond mine, but not why the Arkansas state authorities were so reluctant.

BILL CLINTON AND ARKANSAS DIAMONDS

A famous former Arkansas governor was also involved in the Arkansas diamond story. In January 1987, Bill Clinton appointed a special task force to assess if a commercial mine could coexist with the state park. Clinton could not have been unaware of the quality of the local diamonds since his wife was wearing them. A campaign was organized by mining companies to gain the support of public opinion for a diamond mine. Brochures titled "Mining and Tourism... They'd work together," and "Diamond Mining and Tourism: a good combination for Pike County," were distributed.

But despite all this, the State remained strangely reticent. The special task force did little. You would have thought they would have jumped at the chance to have a diamond mine. In other countries the discovery of a scattering of good diamonds would have resulted in companies racing to install the large bore drilling rigs considered essential for determining diamond content. This did not happen at Murfreesboro because the State did not permit it.

In 1992, the state decided only to allow narrow bore drilling at Murfreesboro. The park ranger told me on my 1992 visit, "Four mining companies have joined together and entered a contract with the Department of Parks and Tourism to some [narrow] core drilling… what they want to do is to determine how is the circumference and depth [of the diamond pipe]." He explained this drilling would only show the borders of the diamond deposit, not its diamond content. This was very strange. Wide bore drilling is the industry standard method of testing diamond content – but it was not permitted here. It meant one of the largest diamond bearing pipes ever discovered would still remain not properly evaluated. Only those who owned competing mines, or valued the peace and quiet of the Arkansas diamond diggings, would have found comfort in this ruling.

Clinton's State Task Force also made the unusual decision that the drill holes should be put in by the state, not by the mining companies, saying it would not trust the companies to fairly report their findings. Given the history of the industry, there was some logic to this – but the new rules would also allow the state to suppress its findings. It told mining companies that if they agreed to finance this narrow bore drilling, they would be given sole rights to tender, but only if the state decided to authorize a mine.

Then former employees of De Beers appeared in Arkansas. Surprisingly, some seemed to be trying to get the mine restarted. Raymond Boulle, who had previously worked for Oppenheimer's Diamond Corporation in Zaire, Sierra Leone and Liberia – and in London as a director for a property company attached to Oppenheimer's Diamond Trading Corporation, set up the Arkansas Diamond Development Company to do just this. His local partners in Arkansas were Sunshine Mining and Stephens Inc. The latter was a huge investment-banking firm, one of the largest outside New York.

In Murfreesboro, a local family gave me a copy of a report left with them by Kroll International, the world's largest detective agency. Their agent, Chuck Lewis, a former *60 Minutes* producer, came to discover if De Beers had been active there in recent years. Lewis' report stated, "Jean-Raymond Boulle, by his public words and his actions, has done NOTHING [his emphasis] to indicate disloyalty to or any kind of estrangement from De Beers. Quite the contrary. In addition it appears that the modus operandi of Jean-Raymond Boulle and his company, the Arkansas Diamond Development Company, fits the De Beers cartel approach and techniques."

Lewis noted that in 1980 Boulle had established, with two brothers, a diamond company in Dallas called European Diamond Importers and Cutters. He told the Dallas newspaper, *Downtown News,* in November: "We are probably the only company in the United States with a De Beers background." A year before this his company revealed at a Dallas news conference a 79 carat flawless diamond, the largest "fancy yellow" diamond in the world and the largest diamond ever offered for sale in Texas. It came "from a De Beers mine in South Africa."

De Beers is very careful with distributing such diamonds. If it came directly from De Beers, it was a mark of considerable favor. Lewis also found that Boulle's brother Bertrand was reportedly working for De Beers in Angola. His other brother, Denis, ran a diamond retail shop in Dallas.

Another Kroll agent, Nancy Bauvwald, investigated Sunshine, Boulle's partner company in Arkansas. She established that "a senior executive of Sunshine, Joseph H. Denahan, was Vice President of Finance for Engelhard Corporation from 1972 to 1984." I knew Engelhard to be closely linked to the Oppenheimers. This was established by the US Justice Department investigation.

Lewis concluded his report by saying: "it frankly denies credulity to ignore the extensive connections of, not only Jean-Raymond Boulle but all five brothers, to De Beers. To suggest that, despite these connections, in Arkansas Jean-Raymond Boulle is his own man, acting independently, is to suggest that something that walks like a duck and talks like a duck, is actually a zebra. Simply stated, it is frankly naive and illogical." Lewis also noted that Boulle had a link to Clinton through his company's lawyer, Bruce Lindsey of Wright, Lindsey and Jennings. Lindsey was a member of Bill Clinton's "inner circle" when he was Governor of Arkansas[25] and was later appointed to President Clinton's White House Staff as "Assistant to the President" and "Senior Advisor on Personnel."

But, overall, the Kroll report concluded, "since the chief aim of any cartel is to control supply, if the… Government says yes or no to diamond mining, either way De Beers wins." If the state blocks development, it was locked out of serious production. If it went ahead, friendly companies were positioned to take it over. "If somehow the US decides to allow commercial mining… then De Beers is extraordinarily well positioned to take advantage."

The park ranger had told me in passing: "When De Beers came down to visit the Crater of Diamonds at about the time the state purchased it, they were appalled at the open gate and the people coming and going." I have also learned that the state geologist gave a guided tour to a De Beers representative in the 1950s, although US law precluded De Beers from taking an active interest. The Sherman Act made the US the one place in the world where De Beers could not operate a diamond mine. Could this explain why there was no mine in Arkansas?

In South Africa, at the Main Street office of E. Oppenheimer and Son, I am sure they hope that tourists with plastic containers may long roam over the United States' major diamond field. In 1998 a 3.03 carat white flawless Arkansas diamond was cut in New York by Lazare Kaplan and authoritatively valued at $34,000. I believe, as the diamond cartel eventually and inevitably starts to lose its grip, the growing strength of the independent diamond producers will not let this Arkansas diamond deposit rest in oblivion.

1   George Kunz. "Diamonds in Arkansas." *American Institute Mining Engineers Bulletin*. Vol. 20, pp. 191-192, 1908.
2   American Institute of Mining Engineers. Vol. 39, p. 173.
3   G. F. Kunz. "Precious Stones: The mineral industry during 1918." Vol. 27, pp. 621-622.
4   Krajick claimed that Reyburn was also offered a $50,000 job for life and $500,000 by De Beers allies in New York. *Barren Lands*, p. 124.
5   Daly Report, p. 23.
6   Krajick, p. 125.
7   Ibid.
8   Daly Report, p. 23.
9   Daly Report, Appendix 7.
10 Daly Report, p. 24.
11 Justice Department archive. Daly Report. Department of Justice Antitrust Div. Memo from Edward Stimson re. conference with Donald Bliss May 13th, 1944 – a joint meeting of the State and Justice Departments.
12 Justice Department archive. Letter of April 9th, 1939.
13 Justice Department archives. See memo of conference with George W. Vitt and the Daly Report. Department of Justice, June 19th, 1943 Memo for Mr. Herbert Berman "Progress Report on Industrial Diamonds," by Edward Stimson.

14 E. Stimson to Robert Nitschke, Department of Justice, June 28th, 1946.

15 Daly Report, p. 26.

16 Justice Department archive. Memo from Office of Production Management March 9th, 1942 from R. J. Lund to W. L. Batt re. "Meeting in your office on 19 Jan. 1942 between owners of the North American Diamond Corp. and various depts."

17 Daly Report, p. 28.

18 Daly Report, p. 30.

19 Daly Report, p. 31.

20 Daly Report, p. 32.

21 Justice Department Archives, June 12th, 1943 Memo for Mr. Britt by Thomas H. Daly on meeting with Ray E. Blick of the North American Diamond Corp.

22 A theory that again surfaced in Krajick's 2001 book, *Barren Lands*, with no evidence given to sustain it.

23 Justice Department Archives. January 1950 report.

24 E. S. Stimson, Department of Justice, Memo for files, January 29th,1944, re. conference with C. Mason Farnham held on 28th January 1944.

25 *Murfreesboro Diamond*, June 28th, 1989.

Chapter 6 – Rationing the United States

In 1988, De Beers' directors reacted with indignation when it was suggested that De Beers was less than full-hearted in its support for America during World War II. They insisted that De Beers had done all it could during the war to supply the US with the diamonds it then urgently required to cut steel and draw wire for its weapons, ships and planes.

The allegations that De Beers damaged the Allied war effort came from a former head of the CIA, Admiral Stansford Turner. He stated, in an article published in the *Washington Post* on October 18th, 1988, "We should not forget that during World War Two the De Beers diamond mining company that is part of the Oppenheimer empire refused to sell the US a large quantity of industrial diamonds for war production."

This enraged the Oppenheimers. An angry retort came from Sir Philip Oppenheimer, Ernest Oppenheimer's brother and a director of De Beers. He stated, in a letter to the editor published on November 2nd, 1988:

> Our records show that strenuous efforts were in fact made by De Beers to ensure the availability of war supplies. Notwithstanding the inevitable increase in demand, our prices were maintained at the levels that had applied during the prewar period. Furthermore, sales of industrial diamonds during the war years were carried out through London under the supervision of the British government and it defies belief that the British government would have permitted a company under its jurisdiction to act in a manner that would have hampered war production in any way.
>
> The insinuation by Mr. Turner that De Beers acted in such a way is not only totally unsubstantiated, but also deeply offensive to a family that was profoundly affected by the War... The family also suffered the disappearance of relations who were living in Germany at the time...
>
> I wish to counterbalance the implication that people vitally involved in the defeat of Hitler would have taken commercial decisions that might have impeded this overriding objective.[1]

In South Africa the *Financial Mail* attacked the "ludicrous assertions that De Beers hampered the war effort 40 years ago."[2] The South African *Sunday Times* stated, "De Beers did not refuse to sell, it merely objected to the US creating a stockpile so great that it might be used to undercut the market after the war." The paper called Stansford Turner "the cretinous admiral..."3

This controversy occurred just as I was reading declassified American government documents acquired from Washington under the Freedom of Information Act. The disputed events were meticulously documented in Justice Department files sent to me that were compiled by lawyers who had investigated the diamond industry between 1942 and 1945. They fully supported the allegations made by Admiral Stansford Turner. The Justice Department staff concluded that De Beers had seriously curtailed supplies of diamonds to the US needed to make weapons and had thus damaged the US war effort. On later research trips to Washington I met the lawyers who had spent years investigating De Beers for the US government. They all told me the same story.

NO WARPLANES FOR THE UK – IF YOU WILL NOT GIVE US DIAMONDS
De Beers' withholding of industrial diamonds had so undermined the American war effort that the US threatened to withhold the supply of warplanes from Britain in 1942 if the British government did not compel the Syndicate to supply the diamonds it needed for its factories. If this threat had been carried out, it could have been catastrophic for the UK.

The evidence for this threat lay in a memorandum written on April 16th, 1942 for the US Assistant Attorney General, Thurman Arnold. It stated: "The 14 percent of the [needed diamond] stockpile we have was not obtained until it was said unofficially that we would not give planes to England if the Syndicate would not sell us the diamonds with which to make them."

Yet when the war broke out, De Beers' warehouses had contained tons of "industrial diamonds" that were too flawed, too small or too poor a shape to be cut as gems, but which would have provided the stones that US industry needed. They had been locked away in De Beers' vaults during the Depression lest they be used to create cheaper diamond jewelry and their acquisition cost had been written off against gem quality stones. But now De Beers discovered that the burgeoning war industries had created such a great demand for even these poor diamonds that they could be sold at more per gram than gold.

At the end of the Great Depression, De Beers was started to sell these poorer diamonds in great numbers to the assembly lines of the industrialized world for a few dollars each – on the condition that it could supervise their use to ensure that they were used as tools and not cut as jewels, for fear they might undercut the price of De Beers' expensive gems.

As war approached and the arms race between Germany and the Allies intensified, Otto Oppenheimer, Ernest's brother, was supervising the supply of diamonds to both sides. The mines contracted to their Syndicate in the Belgian Congo were bursting into production. Their diamond output "nearly doubled between 1936 and 1939 to supply both the Axis and United Nations war machines."4 By 1939 these mines were producing ten million carats a year of diamonds. De Beers labeled and priced these as "industrial" although some were of gem quality. Roughly half of the production went to the US and the UK and the other half to Germany and its allies.

But despite the expanded production from the Congo, it seemed that De Beers was still providing insufficient diamonds for the American war industries. At the start of the war, the United States had found itself critically short of the diamonds needed to arm itself and its allies. The Arkansas deposit was not being mined, but it still should have been easy for the United States to get the diamonds needed, given the enormous number held in the vaults of the De Beers Syndicate. The US Justice Department estimated De Beers had in 1939 in its vaults and safe-rooms 40 million carats, eight tonnes of diamonds. Other estimates were still higher. A British Government memo estimated that in December 1941 the Syndicate held 49 million carats; 29 million of these in its London vaults and the rest "elsewhere" – probably in safe-rooms at its mines in Africa.

DE BEERS CUTS INDUSTRIAL DIAMOND PRODUCTION

In 1940, the US asked De Beers to send it the diamonds needed to expand and maintain the war industries. It wanted every diamond it could get. But US officials were astonished when they discovered that De Beers had seemingly cut the production from the Congo mines by half on the outbreak of war; and had kept shuttered its diamond mines in South Africa that produced the best quality tool diamonds.

Soon, United States government officials were bitterly complaining that it was easier for Nazi Germany to get diamonds from Syndicate mines than it was for the US. They suspected that the missing half of the Congo production was still going to Germany.

THE WARTIME IMPORTANCE OF DIAMONDS

The urgent need for diamonds was described in a report written by the Special Assistant to the Attorney General, Thomas Daly, and completed on March 3rd, 1943:

All the fine filaments used in radio tubes and sound recording devices in aeroplanes, tanks, submarines, and aeroplane detectors are drawn through these diamond dies. If our supply of them is exhausted, it is obvious what will happen to our radio sets and our sound recording devices...

Diamonds are the most effective tools for cutting thousands of parts to be micrometrically identical. The cutting wear on a diamond is so infinitesimal that a diamond's cut on the last of 10,000 parts can be identical with its cut on the first part... there is no substitute for diamonds in manufacturing and sharpening carbide tools or for use as small wire dies.[5]

In another report, he noted: "A single diamond die is good for drawing 20,000 miles of wire without repolishing; the next best substitute material... can only... draw 200 miles of wire."[6]

The United States' frustration was the more acute because De Beers had held a large collection of diamonds in the United States when the war started for exhibition at the World's Fair. It also knew that the Oppenheimers' Diamond Trading Company had moved a stockpile of diamonds worth a million pounds sterling ($1.6 million) from its London headquarters to the United States for safe keeping prior to the war.

The US Army and Navy Munitions Board asked for this stockpile to be increased, saying it was essential to maintain a "full diamond stockpile in the United

States."[7] Initially the Oppenheimers thought this a good idea. If London fell, New York would be an ideal alternative base for their operations. But there was one major snag in their eyes – the Sherman Antitrust Act banned price-fixing in the US – and price-fixing was central to the Oppenheimer business practices. US law regarded price-fixing as a conspiracy to rob consumers of the benefits of the lower prices that could be brought about by competition when supplies are potentially plentiful.

US authorities were keen to get this stockpile established quickly, for the African diamond mines supplying 90 percent of Allied needs were under threat of capture by the Axis. The Germans and Italians were well on the way to controlling the northern half of Africa, Vichy France was in control in Madagascar; the Portuguese authorities in Angola and Mozambique were sympathetic to the Nazis. Belgian and French colonial officials were also susceptible to blackmail since their relatives lived in countries under Nazi occupation – and German submarines were proving a hazard to shipping across the Atlantic.

OPPENHEIMER OFFERS A DEAL

Ernest Oppenheimer thought this situation might help him overcome the Sherman Act. In early 1940, he proposed a deal for which he had already secured British and South African government approval.[8] Under this he would set up in the US "a subsidiary agency of the London Syndicate."[9] He would then guarantee to supply the United States with all the diamonds its war industries needed, and would even move a small stockpile of gem diamonds to the United States if, and only if, the US Justice Department guaranteed De Beers immunity from prosecution under the Sherman Antitrust Act.

His master plan was explained in a De Beers memo to the US government. De Beers would register in New York a company called Diamond Syndicate Incorporated that would be totally owned by his South African companies. De Beers stressed that since the Syndicate already controlled by ownership or contracts 90 percent of the world's diamond production, its proposed American company would have almost unlimited access to diamond supplies. "The De Beers group feel it is a matter of supreme importance that they be established" in the United States as the US was "about 70 percent of the world's total" diamond market. It felt that a US diamond Syndicate office would provide a "focal point for the industry in view of the unsettled conditions prevailing elsewhere."

The memo also warned the United States against other companies trying to emulate De Beers. "Care must be exercised to protect the ultimate purchaser from dealers who in isolated instances have attempted to corner the market. The South African Companies are firmly opposed to such attempts."

When they read the De Beers offer, American authorities discovered to their surprise that if they allowed De Beers immunity from prosecution, it would in return only keep in America the diamonds needed to supply the romantic jewelry trade. The De Beers proposal continued: "Industrial diamonds will continue to be sold by the Diamond Trading Company in London and American buyers of industrials will order them from London."[10] This meant the United States would gain no strategic benefit. The London headquarters of De Beers would retain a tight grip on the US war factories.

If the US refused the De Beers offer, it was feared that the supply of diamonds to the US might dry up. US officials wrote, "Taking the long view, it is conceivable that in the event De Beers not forming a company, the difficulties confronting traders here in obtaining requirements would be such that the trade… might recede further and dwindle to negligible amount." Such a development would have been disastrous for the Allied war effort.

But the US Justice Department rejected De Beers' terms. It said De Beers could not be permitted to exploit American consumers by using price fixing methods not allowed to American companies. Its assessment of the proposal finished with the words "the American consumer would continue to be at the mercy of the monopoly."[11]

As soon as De Beers heard its deal had been rejected, it moved swiftly to strip the United States of the diamond stocks it had already placed there.[12] These were immediately sent to Bermuda. De Beers ordered its American advertising agents, N. W. Ayer, to organize secure vault space in Bermuda for these diamonds, to hire office space at the Bank of Bermuda and organize special Bermudan legislation to facilitate the establishment of this new offshore diamond Syndicate facility.[13]

De Beers has since tried to shift the blame to the British government for hindering wartime diamond supplies to the United States. The British government might not have liked the idea of British diamond resources being moved to the United States, but it had nonetheless approved an American diamond stockpile.

THE BRITISH CONSULATE

De Beers then consulted the British government to see if another way could be found to control diamond supplies remitted to American industry without violating the letter of the Sherman Antitrust Act. Ernest Oppenheimer had already "arranged for two representatives of the De Beers Group, Charles Boise and E. Tappen, to be stationed in New York… to collect information and maintain a close watch on the situation." The legal situation allowed them to do no more.

The British government then helped De Beers circumvent the Sherman Act. Boise and Tappen were transformed into British diplomats. American manufacturers were duly notified that if they wanted diamonds they had to come to the British Consulate in New York where Tappen and Boise held office and could do deals from British territory. They told the American merchants that they could have no diamonds unless they agreed to being policed by them. De Beers said it wanted to be sure no American company could acquire a diamond stockpile.

De Beers laid down the law: "No American importers will be allowed more than a six months supply."[14] American customers had to agree that: "We at any time when required by the British Consulate General will make a full disclosure to him or to independent accountants appointed by him of our records and permit inspection of our stocks in order to give full evidence as to our compliance with this undertaking."[15]

All diamond imports into the US had to be approved by Boise or Tappen as well as by the Ministry of Economic Warfare in London, where Syndicate representatives dominated the relevant committee. The US Justice department noted: "final approval – including physical examination of the actual packages to be exported – rests with the Board of Trade Committee and its Sub-Committee made up exclusively of Syndicate representatives."[16]

A secret report by the Office of Strategic Services (a precursor of the CIA) confirmed that the British Government required: "American industrial diamond consumers to obtain permission from the British Consulate-General in New York for all imports." It added, "All attempts to build up an American stockpile were thwarted by the Syndicate… At present the Syndicate's monopolistic controls are defended by Sir Cecil Rodwell (the British Controller of Diamonds) and the British Government on the ground they are necessary to prevent the smuggling of diamonds to the Axis."[17] The inference was that the British suspected American diamond merchants might re-export to Germany. I could not find any evidence of such smuggling. It was a lame excuse.

The Diamond Syndicate also maintained control over US industry through its bank, Banque Diamantaire The Justice Department reported: "It is said that purchasers in the United States desiring credit [to buy diamonds] must obtain it through Banque Diamantaire," which seemingly only funded diamond purchases from the Syndicate, not from any other source.[18] All its loans had to be cleared with the Syndicate, according to a director. Two of its directors, Sir John Du Cane and William Chapple, were Diamond Cartel representatives. The US Justice Department reported the bank was suspected of being used to restrict diamond supplies to the United States. The cartel's Diamond Trading Corporation (DTC) instructed the bank on one occasion to return to it all diamonds purchased by Americans, rather than send them via "New York or other delivery points."

The Banque Diamantaire opened a branch in New York at 630 Fifth Avenue in 1941. The Justice Department wondered about this: "A question frequently raised has been how this bank managed to secure a license to do business in New York in the spring of 1941. Here was a foreign banking institution with its parent house located in enemy territory."[19] Licenses for foreign banks were hard to obtain at the best of times.

Oppenheimer was aware that the US had an alternative source of high quality tool diamonds – on the fingers of many thousands of American women. Gem quality diamonds make fine tool diamonds. But, as I will recount in a later chapter, with the help of a massive advertising campaign, De Beers would ensure that diamonds stayed firmly in the rings of America's women.

DID DE BEERS LIMIT DIAMOND SUPPLIES TO THE US?

What then of Philip Oppenheimer's recent statement that "strenuous efforts were in fact made by De Beers to ensure the availability of war supplies"? The US Justice Department came to a very different conclusion:

Agencies of the US government have been prevented from obtaining industrial diamonds and boart and establishing a stockpile in the United States, which they desired for military reasons.[20]

While the Syndicate has not completely succeeded in stopping our stockpile activities, it has placed every conceivable obstacle in our way and our current procurement program must anticipate even more intense opposition by the Syndicate. In its negotiations with the Procurement Division, the Syndicate gave one excuse after another for failing to supply our requirements. At first the Syndicate refused to sell diamonds for our stockpile, or delayed doing so because "they needed an inventory of United States domestic stocks." When that was furnished, they then stated that the "bombing of London had damaged its vaults and prevented the movement of the stocks contained therein."

When that excuse wore out, because sufficient time had elapsed for them to open their vaults, they stated that "inventory of their own stocks was necessary." After sufficient time had elapsed to make that inventory, their next excuse was that "the number of expert sorters of industrial diamonds was limited." After that excuse had served as a delaying move, the next excuse was that "the desired good quality industrial stones were not available, owing to previous sales to England and Russia and to the closing of the mines richest in good quality stones."

After that had caused another delay, the next excuse was "the demand of the United States Treasury Procurement Division for only good quality stones was contrary to the Diamond Trading Co. rule that each buyer must purchase large amounts of inferior stones with each good stone, in the same proportion that good and bad stones occur in nature and, further, that the Diamond Trading Co. believed the United States should pay a premium of at least 25 percent for the privilege of taking superior stones only."

The next excuse was that the "Procurement Division program of the United States had depleted its stocks drastically." Although this latter complaint was made as far back as last February, and although continuous insistence has been conveyed through the State Department since then, the Syndicate has refused to open a single one of its pipe mines in South Africa, all of which are closed and have been for some time.[21]

It was not that De Beers had refused to meet all of America's needs. The diamond consumption of the United States, by far the Syndicate's biggest customer, leapt in the first years of the war. In 1940 it consumed 3.5 million carats, in 1941 7.8 million carats and in 1942 9.5 million carats.[22] American frustration arose from De Beers not making available the tool diamonds needed despite having large stockpiles, because without an adequate stockpile, the US remained vulnerable, especially because it was not receiving the top quality tool-stones most needed.

The US strongly suspected that De Beers' policy was to sell all the diamonds in its stockpile, no matter how flawed, rather than to mine the quality stones desperately needed by the defense industries. There seemed no reason why the Syndicate mines in South Africa could not be re-opened. These could supply excellent tool-stones but "The [South African] Union Government declined to permit other Kimberley mines to revive operations despite American official pressure to open up…" The reason given by the South African Government [in 1943] was that "additional activity at Kimberley would hamper the South African war effort."[23]

Did De Beers keep its pledge to freeze wartime prices?

Another point made by Sir Philip Oppenheimer in his defense of his family's actions was that, "Notwithstanding the inevitable increase in demand, our prices were maintained at the levels that had applied during the pre-war period." A Justice

Department report had verified that Sir Ernest Oppenheimer had promised to do just this in 1941 as a patriotic gesture. But did he keep his word?

The US Justice Department found Oppenheimer's promise was not matched by his deeds:

> When GB declared war on Germany on September 3, 1939… prices rose about 50 percent due to exchange differential and to the fact that the (Diamond) Trading Co. added about another ten percent to cover additional taxes, increased insurance, and other incidentals. Prices of rough diamonds rose 5 percent in November 1939 and another 5 percent in January 1940. In 1941 the prices of industrial diamonds… increased 30 to 60 percent over pre-war levels, with the exception of those for crushing boart [poor quality diamonds] which declined about 50 percent.[24]

During the Depression, De Beers had stockpiled an enormous number of poor quality diamonds. The company thought they might never be able to sell these so they buried them in vaults under high security and covered their production cost in the price of the gems it sold. This was verified by a prominent US diamond merchant: "Van Italie has stated that the Syndicate has at least 25 million carats of crushing boart in stock which it has long ago written off its books and thus a sale at any price would be profitable."[25]

But by May 1944, the Oppenheimers had sold 28 million carats of the very poorest diamonds, known as "boart," for a massive profit. The Syndicate had purchased most of this from the Congo at between five and ten cents a carat. It resold them to the United States for around 50 cents a carat – a profit of 500 to 1,000 percent.[26] The Justice Department noted: "De Beers' net profits were 44 percent in 1939, 60 percent in 1940 and 114 percent in 1943."[27] "1945 was a highly prosperous year in the diamond industry… Jewelry sales reached a peak in 1945… They had by now sold all their pre-war gem diamond stocks."[28]

Ernest Oppenheimer kept some prices the same –

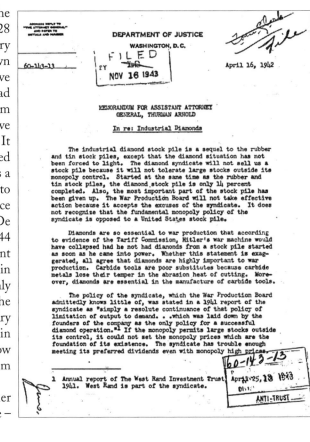

but not the quality of the goods. He had sold low quality diamonds for the price of better diamonds. His behavior was akin to a fishmonger saying he would not increase prices – and then relabeling his sardines as salmon and selling them for salmon prices.

De Beers' strategy during the war was laid out in its 1941 company report: "What is the policy of the De Beers Company? It was nothing new it was simply a resolute continuance of that policy of limitation of output to demand and sales through one channel, which had been laid down by the founders of the company as the only policy for a successful diamond trade."[29]

WAS THE US SUPPLIED WITH AN INFERIOR PRODUCT?

Government reports indicate that De Beers sold the US shipments of useless rubbish. One US government report spoke of the Diamond Trading Company's (DTC's) alleged "practice of requiring them [US dealers] to pay and take industrial diamonds… which they have not had an opportunity of examining… although the material is in many cases worthless or selected by DTC arbitrarily in series unfitted to the purchaser's needs."[30]

A report from Foreign Economic Administration said of a particular shipment of diamonds from De Beers, "not over 20 percent of the material is usable industrially…"[31]

The Syndicate's provision of diamonds of a much lower quality than specified by industry had very serious consequences for the Allied war effort. A 1943 Justice Department report told of the complaints of a tool company executive. He said that the diamonds supplied by the Syndicate "will fragment out or powder out

In its dealings with purchasers in this country both the Government and private companies the Diamond Trading Company, Ltd., as the sole selling agency for the monopoly group, has callously exploited its monopoly power. It has met the request of our Government for the establishment in this country of a large stock pile of industrial diamonds with excuses and postponements and alternative proposals.

It has publicly announced on more than one occasion that the price of industrial diamonds is being held at prewar levels. Because it has complete control of selecting the diamonds to be furnished American buyers it has deliberately foisted upon them inferior stones at prices which purported to be fair for much better merchandise. To the repeated and vehement complaints of American buyers it has thus far turned a deaf ear. This form of profiteering is the more obnoxious because it involves a most vital war material and because it has been accompanied by pious public professions of sacrifice and patriotic foregoing of profit. As a matter of fact the large amounts of money realized from the sale of industrial diamonds represent almost clear profit. Over a long period of years these stones have been found in great quantities in the process of getting the gem diamonds which were the chief objects sought after in the mines. Thus an enormous stock has accumulated, reported to be 36,000,000 carats in 1942. The gem stones have been sold, under the monopoly system, at prices which have yielded large profits after all costs have been covered. Therefore the present demand for industrial stones makes it possible for the monopoly group to withdraw them from its accumulated stock and the receipts amount to nearly pure velvet.

4. A suit against the members of the monopoly group may be instituted in the District Court for the Southern District of New York.

Robert Hunter of the US Department of Justice to Herbert Berman, report entitled: "Anti-trust violation by Diamond Monopoly, September 8, 1943." Page 5.

and the diamond cutting tools are no longer dependable or reliable, which causes tremendous shut-downs in industrial production."[32] "The industrial diamonds formerly bought for $2 a carat were now put by De Beers into the category of stones that he must pay $12 for."[33]

In 1943 the War Production Board (WPB) sent Stephen Hoffman to London to try to negotiate with De Beers to restore supplies of high quality gems for stable prices. But he reported that his meeting on September 1943 with Otto Oppenheimer and the Acting Commercial Attaché at the London Embassy Don Bliss, "produced no results worth recording." A further meeting with British Ministry of Supply staff on October 5th proved the British Government was no more amenable to helping the Americans than was De Beers.

Hoffman returned to London on October 4th, 1944 for further negotiations since the quality of industrial diamonds shipped to the US from the UK was continuing to deteriorate. De Beers' profits continued to grow. The London correspondent for the *Wall Street Journal* reported on April 19th, "The diamond boom continued unabated here as well as in the US… Sales by the Diamond Syndicate totaled $100 million last year. Rough stones have doubled in price since 1939 and are likely to rise again at the next London auction due shortly, but it is polished stones which have really rocketed in price, some by 800 percent."[34]

De Beers was very aware of the US protests. According to the Justice Department, "The most recent visit of high De Beers officials [to the United States] is in connection with the clamor which buyers are raising as a result of poor quality and high prices of the merchandise received in the last few months."[35]

It is thus difficult to find any factual basis for Philip Oppenheimer's statement that De Beers maintained during the war the price of diamonds at pre-war levels.

De Beers' operations protected by UK

The role of the British government in assisting De Beers had amazed American officials. They noted how government officials seemed to be deeply involved in De Beers' restriction of supplies to America. Hoffman reported how, on each of his trips to Britain to negotiate a better deal for the United States, the British Government defended De Beers as if it were De Beers. Hoffman concluded that "the diamond section of the Government and the Syndicate seem to be the same."[36]

One result of all this was, as we have seen, that the United States would in 1942 threaten to withhold the supply of warplanes to Britain. The Justice Department pointed out: "Dicorp [the Diamond Corporation – owned by De Beers] has utilized the sanction of government to consolidate its control and protect its interests… The fact that the techniques of control have been applied to the United States – the greatest user – in a degree all out of proportion to the basic needs of conservation and security lends to the belief that the British Government considers the interest of the Syndicate, in the long run, to be identical with the interests of the government."

De Beers blames the British Government

Tim Capon, director of De Beers Centenary, a wholly owned De Beers subsidiary, wrote in response to allegations in our documentary *The Diamond Empire*: "De Beers was operating at the time under wartime governmental supervision and it was the British Government which dictated how and where the diamond stocks should be held."[37]

To prove this, he produced a letter from Donald C. Bliss, acting commercial attaché at the US Embassy in London in 1942, to the State Department in Washington. Bliss wrote that De Beers "is completely helpless in this matter, being under the control of the Ministry of Supply."[38] Bliss also claimed: "transactions with the [US] Treasury were actually disadvantageous to the [Diamond] Trading Company, but the Directors regard it as their duty to contribute in every way possible to the war effort and they have never contemplated any course other than a substantial and adequate coverage of American stockpile requirements."[39] De Beers must have searched long and hard to uncover Bliss's testimony for Tim Capon to use. Documents favorable to De Beers in the US Justice Department's archives are extremely rare.

At that time Bliss's pro-cartel comments had perplexed US government negotiators. They asked him to justify his comments. After interviewing him on May 12th, 1944, Edward Stimson of the US Justice Department reported:

Mr. Bliss [asserted]... that De Beers and its subsidiaries, Diamond Corporation and the Diamond Trading Company,... only took a small service charge and did not derive large profits because the diamonds passed through their hands... This sharply conflicts with the information we have from other sources that Diamond Corporation paid 10c a carat for crushing boart and sold it for 50c a carat.

Bliss also said "there were now no complaints from dealers [over De Beers' pricing and quality]." This is contrary to information we have from other sources. Also contrary to Bliss's own report on quality and value... Bliss seems to have absorbed the philosophy of those who operate the cartel, perhaps because all of his contacts have been with employees of companies in the cartel.[40]

Mr. Van Berg of Rough Diamond Company, a major figure in the US industry, reported that when Bliss claimed at a War Production Board meeting that the Diamond Trading Company made a profit of only 5 percent, "they laughed at him... [Van Berg] states the shares of De Beers have gone up from £4 to £19 since the war."[41]

In 1942 the US sought a stockpile of 13 million carats for war production; by 1943 its needs had almost doubled to 22.2 million carats. But when the US Government asked De Beers to assist with this – having been privately advised that De Beers held enough diamonds to meet this request – De Beers would only agree to supply 100,000 carats a week – including the gem diamonds supplied to meet the private orders of American merchants. At this rate it would have taken decades to fulfill the US wartime requirement. By March 1944 only 6.5 million carats had been supplied to the US.[42]

In his letter to WGBH, one of the broadcasters of our film, De Beers Centenary director Tim Capon stressed that: "the diamond companies associated with De Beers were the principal suppliers of industrial diamonds to the United States during the Second World War. They supplied over 85 percent of US consumption between 1940-45." This was indeed true. De Beers had a stranglehold on US consumers and they had nowhere else to go. However Capon also claimed that the Syndicate had supplied: "86 percent of US stockpile requirements to September 1942."[43] This is contrary to the evidence I saw. The US Assistant Attorney General Arnold reported on April 16th, 1942 that only 14 percent of the stockpile diamonds had arrived.[44] Therefore 86 percent was missing, not supplied. Capon had his statistics reversed.

The US government also requested that De Beers include a reasonable proportion of good tool diamonds among the diamonds it supplied. This was reluctantly agreed by De Beers – but apparently at the cost of American diamond merchants. Leading merchants claimed the cartel simply took these stones out of their orders and sent them instead to the US government, replacing them with poorer stones.

THE CONGO MINES AND WARTIME AMERICA

Despairing of reasonable help from De Beers, the US government thought to bypass London by getting diamonds directly from De Beers' own source, the mines of the Belgian Congo. This was suggested in a Justice Department discussion paper, *The Cartel Problem in Industrial Diamonds*. It reasoned that the Congo, ruled by the Belgian government-in-exile, might find direct deals with the United States for higher prices more attractive than deals with De Beers. As De Beers was only paying six cents per carat for Congo diamonds, it seemed likely that the Belgians would be only too happy to oblige.

But, the United States had to admit defeat after spending the best part of 1944 negotiating to buy industrial diamonds from the Congo. The Belgian government-in-exile insisted on selling only to De Beers. The British government then warned the United States that any attempt to gain direct access to the Congo mines might result in the US losing all its diamond supplies. The British explained, bizarrely, that it was necessary for all diamonds to pass through London, as only this would guarantee that no diamonds reached Germany or Japan.

Another mystery surrounds the drastic drop in production levels at the Congo mines that, before the war, were working overtime to meet war production needs. The arms race had led to a vast expansion in the Congo diamond production. It was providing diamonds to both sides. But when war broke out, the Congo production suddenly officially halved from 10.9 million carats in 1940 to five million carats in 1942.

The American Government sent secret agents into the Congo to investigate if diamonds were being diverted to the Axis powers. Agent Wilbur Hoag of the Office of Strategic Services (OSS) reported from the Congo on January 22nd, 1944: "Forminiere [production] will be increased to 8,500,000 carats in 1944" as ordered. Mail was intercepted to make sure the Congo authorities complied. One such intercept was of a letter from the Managing Director of Société Générale Belgique.[45] It stated that 7,021,000 carats of crushing boart were delivered.[46]

Hoag reported in 1944 that the Congo miners were unhappy at having to increase diamond production for the Allies. "The Forminiere officials feel that the order is an attempt by De Beers to secure the exhaustion of the Congo alluvial deposits so that De Beers will have complete control of the market."[47] US diamond merchants went further: "Forminiere is unwilling to open new deposits and is supplying the needs of the Allied nations only under great pressure."[48]

The Americans were trying to acquire stockpiles of all strategic minerals, not just of diamonds. Like Britain, it could not risk becoming hostage to German U-boats for all its supplies. But they found the acquisition of other strategic materials such as tin and rubber was far easier than diamonds.

This was the more frustrating as the Syndicate and UK Government had negotiated a compromise deal over setting up a diamond stockpile to meet US needs in 1942, for which the US made many concessions. A United States Mission went to London in the fall of 1942 for the purpose of establishing a United States stockpile. Actually, the Mission returned with a United States Stockpile located in Canada. Though the US government pays half of the transportation and maintenance costs for this stockpile, it cannot, under the agreement, even attempt to acquire supplies from the stockpile until stocks in this country fall below 90 percent of those in this country in June 1942. It was supposed to be operational within six months but it was not until two years later that the necessary consent was obtained from the Belgian government-in-exile and from the Belgian companies in the Congo. "As late as January 1944 neither the Belgian Congo nor the Angola company had yet signed the agreement with the British Ministry of Supply for supplying their share of the stockpile. [Only] in February 1944, following requests from the US Embassy in London... did the Belgian Congo agree to supply its seven million carats and Angola its 700,000 carats so the Canadian stockpile could go ahead."

But then the US authorities found the diamonds it had contracted were not even in Canada. The Canadian stockpile appeared to contain far fewer diamonds than agreed on, with most of the stones remaining in London, having simply been earmarked for Canada. Also, "The US was denied permission to inspect the stockpile despite the fact that it paid half the maintenance costs."[49]

Thomas Daly, Special Assistant to the Attorney General, suggested it was time for legal action, noting, "under present syndicate regulations, our stockpile of diamonds can never be more than 50 percent complete. This shortage is a dangerous threat to a successful war effort... In its efforts to maintain its control over all diamonds, it appears that the syndicate has had more regard for maintaining market conditions and for selfish market dominance than it had for furthering the United Nations' war effort."

His proposed legal action would have a strategic objective. "The object of a suit would be to

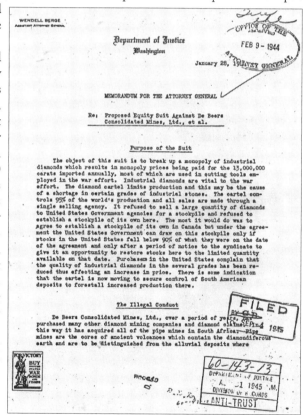

Wendell Berge, the assistant US Attorney, writes to recommend legal action against De Beers.

separate Forminiere from the cartel and to force it to terminate its contract relations with the Diamond Corporation and to deal directly with firms in the United States."[50] But when the Justice Department sought the opinion of the State Department it found: "Proposals for action against the Syndicate are usually opposed on the ground that they will be construed as unfriendly acts by the British Government... The British government looked on the trade as an indispensable source of dollars."[51]

Tension grew between American Government departments. The Justice Department decided that it should indict, not just the Congo companies, but also De Beers, as it was the principal culprit. The State Department hesitated to take on a company so closely identified with a US ally. The US War Production Board, with many former diamond industry executives holding key positions on it, seemed reluctant to blame De Beers for US shortages.

The Justice Department worried about its ability to sue companies based outside the United States but decided to proceed on the basis that De Beers did business in the US through agents. It noted that De Beers, Forminiere and other Syndicate companies, all used American agents, such as N. W. Ayer, and all held American bank accounts.

DE BEERS CHARGED WITH CONSPIRACY

On January 25th, 1945, the US Justice Department's Antitrust Division filed suit in the US District Court in New York against De Beers, four British or South African companies, three Belgian companies, and one Portuguese company, charging them with conspiring to violate the Sherman Antitrust and the Wilson Tariff Acts. Combined, these companies controlled 95 percent of the world diamond market. Also named as defendants were seven American stockholders of these companies.[52]

It charged that: "The monopoly power... exercised by the defendants through Diamond Trading Company has been asserted in arbitrary and unfair treatment of prospective purchasers and customers and by enhancement of diamond prices in the US to arbitrary and exorbitant levels."[53]

On January 29th, 1945, Federal Judge Vincent L. Leibell took steps to freeze diamond cartel assets in the US by forbidding nine foreign Syndicate diamond corporations and seven of their American stockholders from removing millions of dollars in diamonds and cash on deposit in New York City banks.[54]

A Justice Department report summarized the action:

According to the complaint filed by the Antitrust Division the illegal conspiracy consists of a continuing agreement between the defendants to:

(1) Limit the production and supply of diamonds,

(2) Restrict the quantity of diamonds imported into the United States,

(3) Fix, stabilize and enhance the prices at which diamonds are sold in the United States,

(4) Prevent dealers and consumers in the United States from purchasing diamonds from producers,

(5) Prevent all sale or purchase of diamonds for export to the United States except through the Diamond Trading Co. Ltd., and,

(6) Prevent all persons in the United States, except certain favored brokers, dealers and cutters, from purchasing diamonds from the Diamond Trading Co. Ltd.

In addition it is alleged that De Beers and its subsidiaries have further limited diamond production and enhanced prices by shutting down all mines owned and controlled by them.

It is to be hoped that successful conclusion to this suit which is presently pending will eliminate the monopolistic practices thereby insuring a free competitive market for this commodity.[55]

De Beers' reaction was swift. On February 2nd, 1945, De Beers told Associated Press that this restraining order had effectively stopped the buying of industrial diamonds for the United States in London. An Attorney for De Beers, Robert T. Swaine, declared "this order... a serious hampering of the war effort." American fears that the United States might be held to ransom by the cartel had seemingly been justified.

Fortunately for the US war-effort, the war against Germany ended a few weeks later. The legal case, however, proceeded for a time. A judge initially ruled that the US did not have the needed jurisdiction, but the Justice Department was advised that it would succeed on appeal. But then the Belgian Government intervened, through its Washington embassy, to stop the legal action proceeding. "The Belgian Congo State owns 55.47 percent of the stocks of Forminiere... The Minister of Colonies names the President and the Board of Directors and therefore the US should drop the charges, for it should not be suing an allied Government."

1   Sir Philip Oppenheimer, letter to *Washington Post*, published November 2nd, 1988.
2   *Financial Mail*, South Africa. October 28th, 1988.
3   *Sunday Times*, South Africa. October 23rd, 1988.
4   Classified draft report in US Justice Department files dated April 24, 1966. "The cartel problem in industrial diamonds." No author given.
5   Preliminary Investigation: Industrial Diamonds. Justice Department Report of April 15th, 1942.
6   Thomas Daly report. Op cit. page 10.
7   Memo Dept of Justice "Memorandum for Assistant Attorney General, Thurman Arnold. In re: Industrial diamonds," April 16th, 1942.
8   Dickenson to Lauck at N. W. Ayer, April 19th, 1940.
9   Samuel S. Isseks, Special Assistant to the Attorney General to Fowler Hamilton. March 28th, 1942.
10 This was also documented in a letter from Leon Henderson, Commissioner, to the Attorney General, October 14th, 1940. "They will not however maintain a stock of industrial diamonds in this country for sale to American consumers."
11 Memorandum for Mr. Cox, Department of Justice, November 9th, 1940.
12 Memorandum, United States Government. To the files from Herbert A. Berman re. Diamond Case, March 9th, 1945 re. Sol Van Berg of the Rough Diamond Corporation, in an interview with Herbert A. Berman of the Justice Department. In another document, a leading diamond merchant, Van Berg, confirmed these diamonds were shipped to Bermuda in 1940 and sold there.
13 Correspondence De Beers to N. W. Ayer July 22nd to October 16th, 1941, referred to by Edward S. Stimson of the US Justice Department in his June 14th, 1946 "Summary of Material from the files of N. W. Ayer and Sons."
14 Daly Report, p. 16.
15 Daly Report, p. 26.
16 Daly Report, p. 26.
17 Daly Report, p. 9.
18 Letter to Edward S. Stimson from Patrick A. Gibson. November 21st, 1944.
19 Daly Report, p. 13.
20 Daly Report, p. 23.
21 Daly Report appendix 9.
22 War Production Board estimate.
23 Ibid. p. 31.
24 Daly Report, p. 23.
25 Ibid. p. 14.
26 Dept of Justice Antitrust Division, May 13th, 1944.

27 Ibid. Complaint 2.
28 Ibid. Stimson. Op cit. 98. GDS to Shelly of Ayer, January 20th, 1944.
29 West Rand Trust Annual Report, April 25th, 1941, quoted in "Industrial Diamonds – Preliminary Investigation," Dept. of Justice. April 15th, 1942, p. 6.
30 DTC, p. 12.
31 July 15th, 1944 activities report from Foreign Economic Administration files in the National (US) Archives, p. 8.
32 Justice Department memo filed on March 3rd, 1943.
33 Ibid.
34 *Wall Street Journal*, April 17th, 1944.
35 Berman/Hunter, Department of Justice, September 8th, 1943.
36 Livingston/Haas, April 16th, 1942.
37 Tim. W. H. Capon of De Beers Centenary writing from 17 Charterhouse Street, London EC1N 6RA. March 4th, 1994, to Henry Becton, the President of WGBH-TV.
38 Capon, 1994.
39 Dispatch to the US Secretary of State from the US Embassy in London dated February 20th, 1942.
40 Edward A. Stimson. Note to Files on Conference with Mr. Donald Bliss. May 13th, 1944. Antitrust Division, Department of Justice.
41 Edward A Stimson, Special Assistant to the Attorney General, to Hon. Wendell Berge, Asst. Attorney General Department of Justice. May 18th, 1944.
42 Daly Report, pages 14 and 19.
43 Tim. W. H. Capon of De Beers Centenary writing from 17 Charterhouse Street, London EC1N 6RA. March 4th, 1994, to Henry Becton, the President of WGBH-TV.
44 Memo for Asst. Attorney General Thurman Arnold, April 16th, 1942.
45 F. Van Bree to Edgar Soggier. August 21st, 1943.
46 Edward Stimson to Mr. Berman, US Justice Department files. June 7th, 1944.
47 Edward E. Stimson to Mr. Berman; Diamond Case: "Prices and Production of Crushing Boart." Washington. June, 7th, 1944.
48 This view was confirmed by C. Mason Prnham [sic – spelling obscured in original document] in a statement he gave the Justice Department. (Given in Room 3238, Justice Building.)
49 Draft of "The Cartel Problem in Industrial Diamonds" April 24th, 1944, p. 39.
50 Daly Report, p. 8.
51 William Wassermann, in charge of US 1942 diamond mission to London, letter to Arthur Paul, December 23rd, 1942.
52 Letter from Victor H. Kramer to H. Maletz, May 23rd, 1947, Antitrust Division, Department of Justice.
53 Wendell Berge, Department of Justice, January 28th, 1944.
54 *Daily Worker*, January 30th, 1945.

Chapter 7 – Diamonds for Hitler

According to American and British intelligence, the diamond trade was guilty of much more than war profiteering and conspiracy. They were convinced that companies in the Diamond Syndicate were helping Nazi Germany obtain the industrial diamonds it needed to cut steel – and thus prolonging the war.

A Justice Department memorandum stated: "Hitler's war machine would have collapsed had he not had diamonds from a stockpile started as soon as he came to power."[1] Hitler had enough diamonds to start the war, but not enough to continue it after 1944. None of the territory Germany occupied had a diamond mine.

Senior Intelligence officers alleged that Allied measures to stop diamonds reaching Germany "were sabotaged ... by the representatives of the Diamond Trading Corporation in London through their domination of the Diamond Committee of the [British government's] Ministry of Economic Warfare."[2] The Diamond Trading Corporation was wholly owned by the Oppenheimer-controlled Syndicate and responsible for distributing diamonds to the diamond trade.

The Intelligence Officer managing the US agents in this investigation was  a Henry Lee Staples. In 1992 John Kelly, an investigative journalist working with me on *The Diamond Empire*, tracked down Henry Staples' son at the jazz club he owned in New Orleans. It turned out that Henry Staples Jr. personally knew the agents his father had worked with on this investigation and gave me a copy of his father's official secret report. Staples Sr. had died in 1989 but his son had spent the last two years of his father's life recording the story of his intelligence work. He had recorded with particular care the intelligence operation that led his father to accuse British officials of failing to stop the flow of diamonds to Germany as it "was too lucrative."[3]

Henry Staples Jr. in 1992.

When war broke out, De Beers had immediately closed all the major diamond mines in Southern Africa, paying them not to produce.[4] This left as the only major sources of wartime diamonds the De Beers stockpile in London, and the Congo mines.

The Congo mines were under the authority of the Belgian government-in-exile in London. All the diamonds they produced were exclusively contracted to the Oppenheimer and De Beers-controlled Syndicate in London.

It should not be presumed that all of Africa was hostile to the Axis powers. Sympathies and alliances teetered as the fortunes of war swayed. A pro-German government ruled in Spain, and Portugal was somewhat sympathetic to the Nazis. Some colonial officials were openly pro-Nazi. Officials in French and Belgian colonies could also be blackmailed because of their family connections in occupied Europe.

Germany stole many diamonds from Jewish and non-Jewish individuals and firms both in Germany and across occupied Europe. Many employees of Jewish diamond firms based in Antwerp unfortunately took refuge in Vichy France rather than in England, and thus many were later captured, robbed of their diamonds, and killed.

In November 1942, Allied intelligence learned Germany was short of diamonds when it intercepted German cables to consulates in Mozambique and Angola that gave urgent instructions for the purchase of 700,000 carats of diamonds. The OSS suspected that Germany then made immediate "plans to obtain them directly from the Congo."[5] The Congo mines were now the only source outside the De Beers stockpile in London that could provide the numbers of diamonds Germany required.

THE LOOTING OF ANTWERP'S DIAMOND FIRMS

A US Army report described how "immediately after the occupation of Belgium, the Commander in Chief of the Wehrmacht appointed as custodian and liquidator of Jewish firms a Herr Frensel."[6] In March 1942, Frensel said: "Our goal is to eliminate the Jew, but before we do so, we will have to tolerate them some more."

The rise of Hitler in the 1930s made many German Jewish diamond traders flee to Antwerp. When Germany invaded Belgium, some merchants then fled with their diamonds into Vichy France. Germany then decided to use a "charm offensive" to entice them back and to gain the willing cooperation of the remaining merchants. Nazi Germany's problem was that diamonds were easy to conceal and smuggle out – so it needed to win the merchants' trust. So successful were these tactics that the Nazis succeeded in persuading some to return with their diamonds to set up their businesses again.[7]

The German military at first administered the Belgian diamond trade through a "Referat Diamant" department under a Karl Holstein. He in turn appointed an Ulrich Lemburg to supervise the Antwerp diamond business. On January 30th, 1941, the German administration created a Centrale du Diamant to manage the Belgian diamond industry. Laureys reported that Flemish collaborationists, Forminière, and the Antwerp Diamond Bank dominated the industry, all watched over by the German trustee William Frensel.

Eric Laureys writes of the time, "Belgian industry dreaded a wholesale dismantling of factories [as had happened during WWI] ...During the war, Société Générale de Belgique (SG) was headed by governor Alexandre Galopin who was mandated by the Belgian government-in-exile in London to implement what was later to be called the 'policy of lesser evil' or 'Galopin doctrine.'"

Under this policy Belgian industry was to cooperate sufficiently to avoid total German control and/or destruction as well as the massive deportation of the Belgian workers to Germany. The Belgian civil servants came to a tacit agreement with the Germans, but their cooperation was limited. Laureys found they systematically slowed down and hampered German initiatives. He also found that Forminière "enraged the Germans during the whole war because of general manager Dewyspelaere's systematic administrative, legal and ethical obstructions."

I was not sure that Laureys was completely right in saying that SG hindered rather than cooperated. Perhaps they did so on occasion, but the documents I saw from other sources indicated a more willing relationship existed, at least later in the war.

In 1940-41 the Germans persuaded many mostly non-Jewish merchants to sell them diamonds at 20 percent off the normal price. They particularly found useful the merchants who had business relations with Americans – for, until the US entered the war in December 1941, Germany earned much useful foreign exchange through these merchants quite legally selling diamonds to New York.

But in February 1941 a clamp down on diamond merchants began in Belgium with the confiscation of diamonds from all merchants who had been in Antwerp for less than ten years (i.e. mostly the refugees from Germany). German diamond dealers came to Antwerp to buy "looted properties" from the Diamond Control office. Adult male Jews were forced to provide the Germans with a carat of industrial diamonds every day. But this plundering still did not meet the needs of German industry. The Germans estimated Belgium had provided them with 930,000 carats by the end of 1943 (more than twice as much as Belgium had provided by the end of 1941) perhaps enough for two years' war production. They had hoped for even more.

Part of the reason for this was a daring mission by the British destroyer Walpole to the Low Countries on May 13th, 1940, the very day of the German invasion. The Walpole landed a small group at Ymuiden who raced by car to the Diamond Bourse in Amsterdam to collect a kitbag full of diamonds of the highest quality only hours before German troops arrived. These were taken to London and stored for the war's duration with Oppenheimer's Diamond Trading Company. However this mission failed to impress the diamond merchants who would have preferred to have their families rescued. It also only secured a tiny fraction of the Low Countries' diamond stock.

Chaim Even-Zohar, the editor of the leading diamond industry magazine, *Mazal U'Bracha*, has heard a different account. He wrote to me in 2000 and said, "I have eyewitness reports on the submarine picking up the diamonds from Amsterdam. Very few people actually were willing to trust the British/De Beers with the diamonds and there was 'no room' for individuals to escape with the submarine. I only know one person who actually got diamonds back [after the war]."

The Germans tried to stop merchants from taking diamonds out of Belgium. From November 1941 all polished diamonds had to be deposited in a German-supervised bank. Rough diamonds also had to be deposited in it, starting from March 1942. Laureys recorded that after the war, government officials were astonished to discover just how docile had been the diamond merchants. They had mostly quietly handed in their diamonds even though this effectively took away the very thing that was protecting them from the gas chambers. The German authorities reported paying $274,000 for diamonds worth $1,245,700 – and that they had made a special financial provision for the rewarding of informers equal to 10 percent of the value of the diamonds seized. The money paid to the merchants had to go into the Westbank to be later transferred to the Société Françoise de Banque et de Dépôt, an "enemy" bank under German control where most of the loot was concentrated. Extraordinarily, most of these funds were still in this bank at Liberation.

Even-Zohar also explained, "At some time during the war (1942 or 1943), the Germans offered the Amsterdam Jewish diamantaires a deal: 'you and your families get safe exit from Nazi occupied territory and we get all your diamonds.' Quite a few believed the Nazis and provided detailed lists of family members, etc. These lists were used to send all these families to concentration camps after the Nazis got the diamonds."[8]

The Belgians were susceptible to pressure from the Germans. An OSS top secret report, stamped "Secret – Copy 2 of 5 Copies," expanded on the possibility of blackmail. "Since the majority of the officials and workers in the Congo had left their families in Belgium, it was likely that the Nazi threat of reprisals against these families was used to force compliance with German wishes."[9]

Eventually many Jewish and non-Jewish diamond merchants were arrested and their belongings seized. A Dr. Kurt Kadgiehn was made responsible for selling the best of the looted gem diamonds on the international market to help fund Germany's purchase of raw materials. Kadgiehn was, according to another report: "A personal financial adviser to Nazi leader Hermann Goering."[10]

While researching *The Diamond Empire* John Kelly and I met Ken Alford, who had translated German documents to track down the fortunes stolen by Nazis. He gave us documents that showed Germany had obtained 400,000 carats of diamonds from the Low Countries by 1941. Allied intelligence estimated that German industry required 500,000 carats a year. During the war the Germans must have obtained and used at least 2.5 million carats.

Germany secured a large number of diamonds from Belgian ships in Vichy harbors with the help, according to Laureys, of a German-led team of Belgians including Dewyspelaere of Forminière and of Charles Van Antwerpen, the president of the Federation of Belgian Diamond Exchanges. These were diamonds previously intended by Forminière for the De Beers marketing offices in London. The Nazis also extended special congratulations to a J. W. Urbanek for "his seizures of Belgian Congo diamonds on board of Belgian ships in 1940. This seizure amounted to 290,000 carats." There may have been more. A US diplomatic telegram sent on a report that the Germans acquired "approximately 400,000 carats outside Casablanca," that originated in the Congo or Angola.[11]

The Japanese, it should be noted, were also offering very high prices for diamonds. They had no local sources apart from some small Borneo mines. Japan covertly bought African diamonds in the Middle East. However there is a mystery here. A British Special Operations Executive (SOE) report said: "It is doubtful if Germany would have allowed Japan to capture practically the entire South American supply in the early years of the war had her own supply not been assured."[12] If this were so, it had been done right under the nose of the United States.

When the OSS and SOE intercepted further cables from the German Consulates in Angola and Mozambique, reporting that they could not find enough diamonds on the black market, the Allied intelligence officers concluded that Germany would increase efforts to get the diamonds it urgently needed from the only other source, the Diamond Syndicate's Congo mines, the same ones that supplied the Allies.

DIAMOND SYNDICATE MINES IN THE CONGO AND NAZI GERMANY

In 1940, the Diamond Syndicate reported that the Belgian Congo was producing 10,900,000 carats of diamonds a year, Angola 730,000, the Gold Coast 900,000, and Sierra Leone 850,000. Allied intelligence discounted the Gold Coast or Sierra Leone as major sources for Germany because they were under tight British administration and produced far less diamonds than the Congo. Allied intelligence from the first believed the Belgian Congo and Angola had to be Germany's major sources.

As soon as WWII began, the Congo's official production figures had dropped sharply. No such decline happened in Sierra Leone or the Gold Coast. By 1942, Congo production had officially halved to 5,000,000 carats. Oddly, the missing production exactly matched that part of the Congo's diamond production that had gone to pre-war Germany – five million carats a year.

Société Générale de Belgique (SG) owned these Congo mines. It was an important member of the Diamond Syndicate and a business partner of De Beers. Its major shareholder was the Belgian government. It controlled the security arrangements at its diamond mines. SG also controlled and exploited Congo diamonds, tin, gold, plantation and cattle interests through a company it managed, Forminière.

Early panning for diamonds in the Congo.

SG controlled the Angolan diamond fields through Diamang, a company that operated as a southern extension of Forminière. Allied Intelligence thought Angola was the second major source of diamonds for Germany. Oppenheimer interests held a direct 19 percent share in Diamang – which in turn owned the diamond company Beseka. Sir Ernest Oppenheimer said of Beseka that it "owns and operates the richest known diamond deposits in the world so far as carat content is concerned."

In mid-1943, the OSS "began to receive reports indicating... extensive activity in the smuggling of industrial diamonds to the Axis from the mining areas in the Belgian Congo and Angola ... Up until then the British officials and the Syndicate member companies in charge of security at the diamond mines insisted that security was tight at the mines whenever American intelligence had questioned it."[13] Under American pressure the British Government then agreed to investigate the security at the mines.

GERMANY GRAVELY SHORT OF VITAL INDUSTRIAL DIAMONDS

At a meeting of the Diamond Committee of the Ministry of Economic Warfare (MEW), held on November 3rd, 1943, the Chairman stated: "They [the Germans] must be dangerously short of industrial diamonds. It is unlikely that they have more than six months supply in hand at the moment. It is therefore now more necessary than ever to exercise the utmost vigilance in order to prevent smuggling even on the smallest scale."[14]

Germany had no diamond mines within its conquered or national territories. If it ran out of diamonds, its weapons and bombs factories would be very gravely handicapped. Major Schmidt of the OSS reported: "MEW studies have indicated that the German stockpile of industrial diamonds will be exhausted by April 1944. It is believed that if this clandestine flow of industrial diamonds to the enemy could be minimized during the first six months of 1944, it might have an appreciable effect on shortening the war because of the absolutely essential nature of this product to many operations of the German war machine."[15]

German documents seized at the end of the war tell us that Allied Intelligence was correct. By 1944 the Germans were gravely short of the better quality diamonds required for war production, including for the notorious V2 rockets, and were also gravely short of the foreign exchanged needed to purchase them. When they attempted to purchase them on the black market, they found them too expensive. The minutes of a German Ministerial Meeting in January 1944 said that they would have to suspend mass purchasing of diamonds in order that "the prices on foreign markets will go down."[16]

The minutes also recorded that Germany was confiscating or purchasing high-class gem quality diamonds from non-Jewish diamond businesses in Belgium, then selling them abroad to get the foreign currencies required to purchase industrial stones on the black market. "Sixty seven thousand carats of cut diamonds are still held by Belgium Aryan firms... the Four Year Plan last summer demanded the purchase of certain portions of these jewelry diamonds. They were to be resold to procure foreign exchange."[17] "Herr Ministerrat Kadgien... had to provide the German economy with foreign currency and raw material in exchange for looted diamonds."[18]

Despite the Allied blockade, he succeeded in exporting these gems to the United States through Switzerland, Sweden and Spain. "Herr Kramer had to contact firms of the USA, also Swiss, Spanish and Swedish firms,... and export polished diamonds to these destinations." Between 1942-44 Switzerland and Spain provided the main channels for German diamond exports.

Ken Alford learned from the Nuremberg records how "the finest jewelry from the Jewish concentration camp victims was sold abroad, flown in Italian planes to Rio de Janeiro, postmarked from Rio and dispatched to Japan and the USA... Proceedings were credited to the Reich's Finance Ministry."[19]

It was a dangerous time for businessmen. Alexandre Galopin, the Chairman of the Board of Governors of Société Générale, was assassinated in Brussels in April 1944.[20] The Oppenheimers were vulnerable as Jews, despite Ernest Oppenheimer converting to the Church of England in the mid 1930s. I know of no attempt to blackmail the Oppenheimers, but Allied Intelligence was so concerned that they might be compromised or blackmailed that they monitored all their movements.

Nicky Oppenheimer, the current Chairman of De Beers and former head of Syndicate operations in London, has denied outright any suggestion that De Beers helped supply Germany with diamonds. His statement did not go into any detail. He simply argued that they would not have supplied Germany when members of their family were dying at the hands of the Nazis.[21]

Even-Zohar told me Ernest Oppenheimer had a brother called Emil:
He was the only one that didn't go into diamonds and he remained in
Germany. Some of his family were killed in concentration camps. One of
Emil's sons, Karl Heinz, immigrated to Palestine in the late thirties.
I have interviewed all the children of Karl Heinz, still in Israel. Ernest did
support the family financially. Harry refused to do so. During World War II
Ernest did try to get some of his relatives out of Germany. One
Oppenheimer kin was married to a Dutch girl, who informed the Nazis
about her Jewish husband. Those who succeeded in escaping from Germany
ended up in Kenya.[22]

DID A MAJOR CORPORATION SUPPLY NAZI GERMANY WITH VITAL DIAMONDS?
During the war Allied intelligence came to the conclusion that a major international
corporation must be involved in the smuggling of diamonds to Germany. An
American OSS wartime intelligence analyst, W. Beecher, pointed the finger at the
Syndicate member company Société Générale de Belgique (SG):
It is thought by some investigators that natives or underpaid small fry
employees are responsible for the illicit diamond trade. Such a thing is
perhaps possible – but there are so many strong reasons against it that the
possibility can be all but disregarded.
Congo authorities and SG officials are above all else interested in making a
good profit from the Congo; their control of profits is absolute and no real
opposition survives there. They would be turning heaven and earth to find
diamond smugglers – if they thought large profits were being made by
unknown individuals or natives "at their expense or loss." But on the contrary,
no emotion is shown at these "staggering losses" from their mines and
passive, veiled resistance is shown if any outside investigation is attempted.
Knowing how differently the Congo officials and SG react to the genuine
loss, it seems safe to assume that diamonds are being sold to the enemy.
In October 1943 Allied intelligence finally succeeded in linking major Syndicate
names to illicit diamond trafficking in the Congo. Two British agents reported to the
Special Operations Executive office in Accra, "there was reason to suspect that high
Forminiere officials, including Firmin Van Bree, were implicated in the traffic. It was
their opinion that the Congo mines were the major source of leakage to the enemy."[23]
Another OSS report from the Congo said: "Firmin Van Bree is considered... the
most powerful single individual in the colony. He is known to have made several trips
to Lisbon where it is believed he met with representatives of the Société Générale who
were permitted [by the Germans] to leave Belgium to meet him."[24]
Van Bree's role in the Congo was unique in that he served on the boards of all the
Congo and Angolan diamond mining companies, Forminiere, Beceka, Lueta, Kasai,
Luebo and Diamang – either as President or administrator. All these companies were
members of the Oppenheimer-led Diamond Syndicate. Lueta, Kasai and Luebo were
subsidiary branches of Société Générale – which also had links to the others mentioned.
The British agent, Lt. Pearson, reported his team's security inspection of the
Congo mines: "Adequate security measures did not exist... the sinister atmosphere

which was present during the investigators' visit led them to believe that the Forminiere and B.C.A. [Beceka] companies had something serious to hide. They considered therefore that it would be easy for large quantities [of diamonds] to be sent out of the Congo clandestinely."[25]

The ease with which the Germans were seemingly obtaining diamonds infuriated the Americans, who had to fight tooth and nail to get the supplies needed for the United States. "The Syndicate is itself in the peculiar position of maintaining a much tighter system of regulation of diamond distribution in the USA than in the producing areas where there existed considerable evidence of leakage to the enemy."[26]

An OSS report said high officials of the diamond Syndicate were traveling from the Congo via Lisbon right into occupied Belgium.[27] The OSS noted that Van Bree, with the blessing of the Germans, had met in Lisbon with Cattier, the Belgian Vice Governor of Société Générale. The South African Director of Censorship regarded this as suspicious. He asked why would the Germans allow these meetings if Van Bree were not pro-German?[28] Van Bree also sat with Sir Ernest Oppenheimer on the board of Companhia de Diamantes de Angola, a major Angolan diamond producer.[29]

A translated document revealed that the Germans were extraordinarily pleased with the willing co-operation of the Syndicate's major diamond producer and supplier to the Allies, Société Générale, for it had sold Germany large numbers of diamonds.

German officials reported to Berlin that Société Générale had willingly cooperated after an initial hesitation. They added that the company "feared reactions on their large estates in the Congo if England should get to know they had been in close connection with the German Military Administration... but after consulting with the Secretary-General of the Belgian Ministry of Economy, a Mr. Leemans, the certified authorization of the five Congo companies was procured."

The Germans regarded the negotiations "as a special success... owing to the co-operation with the authorities of the Belgium diamond economy, the whole lot could be bought at normal prices on voluntary grounds... this means the covering of the whole German armament industry's needs for 3 years to 1944."[30]

It was of course also entirely possible that Société Générale's Belgian directors had hidden their true feelings from the Germans in order to protect themselves and their company. But, according to the Germans, Société Générale made considerable profits from selling these diamonds. Germany paid Société Générale $10,500,000 for diamonds in 1943, a vast sum in those days.[31] This must have been for the delivery of a vast number of diamonds. It must have made even more large deliveries, for Germany owed Société Générale a further $25 million by the time the war ended.

The post-war Belgian Government seemingly accepted the price given when it billed Germany for the $25 million owed to Société Générale, writing that it was for "a total of 576,676 carats of raw diamonds from the Congo, which on account of their characteristics can be easily identified by experts."[32]

The value given for this deal is equivalent to four times the value of the entire world's production in 1940.[33] This seems clear evidence that massive numbers of diamonds flowed from the Syndicate's mines to Germany with the active assistance of Société Générale and that the Germans paid for them generously.

The Germans also recorded successful negotiations with Forminiere, a company headed by Van Bree. "The negotiations with Forminiere were conducted on the German side by the following: a man named Schon from the Military Government of Belgium and Northern France; Dr. Wahnar from the Reichstelle fur Technische Erzeugnisse; Joh Urbanek, a diamond dealer... the payment was by bank transfer in Belgian francs. They were (for) large diamonds from the Congo."

The British Consul-General in Leopoldville, C. G. Hope Gill, wrote to London on December 29th, 1941 that:

Van Bree is so big a noise out here that the biggest local bosses, governmental as well as business, tremble and bow at his coming... I find the Congo government holds the view that sums of money, e.g. balances of wages, can be paid into their company by employees in the Congo and paid out by the Company's Brussels office to relatives in Belgium. This seems to circumvent our blockage...

I mention this because it indicates the influence of a man like Van Bree and the ease with which unscrupulous or hostile men can correspond and even transact business with enemy-occupied territory.

Referring to Van Bree's so-called friendship with England, the Consul-General said, "Van Bree is, I am told, very well 'protected' by an English peer," adding, "I have the lowest opinion of Van Bree's straightforwardness and reliability... he expressed the view that Belgians should let Britain do the fighting and see that the Congo got the profits."[34]

The hostility of British and American diplomats to Van Bree was partly a reaction to the suspicion shown towards them by the Belgian colonial government. They found it difficult to understand why they would be seen as representatives of a rival commercial empire rather than as allies. These diplomats also could not understand how Van Bree could deal with occupied Europe and still retain high status among the Allies. They suspected him of treason.

The Belgian government, the major shareholder in Societé Générale, had difficulties when patriotism and economic interests clashed. If Germany lost the war, Belgian officials foresaw that the United States could become a threat to Belgium's continued colonial rule in the Congo. Thus, some may have preferred to cooperate with Germany. This sentiment was thought so strong that the British Ministry of Economic Warfare warned the US that, if it tried to tighten security at the Congo mines to make it tougher for Germany to secure Congo diamonds, the Belgians might well make it harder in return for the Americans to secure vital diamond supplies.

The Allied intelligence reports never quite resolved the motives of the Belgian officials who supplied the Germans. Some said it must be profits. Others plausibly argued that it was because they feared for the safety of their relatives in Belgium. But what most perplexed Allied Intelligence was why Syndicate officials in London were seemingly facilitating supplies to Germany while making it difficult for the US to get the diamonds it needed to fight Germany. They feared this meant that the diamond cartel was throwing its weight behind Germany – but this seemed utterly incomprehensible when so many Jews were dying at German hands. Yet, the facts spoke for themselves. It seemed that major diamond companies, peacetime partners in the De Beers dominated Diamond Syndicate, were helping Germany fight its war.

THE AMERICAN SPIES

The US Office of Strategic Services (OSS) sent four American spies into the Congo in 1943 to discover how diamonds were flowing so easily from the Congo to Germany. This operation was organized by Henry Staples and coordinated with the British Special Operations Executive (SOE) via their Accra office in West Africa. The first agent sent was codenamed "Crisp." He was "flattered by the Belgians and incapable of suspecting them." He was replaced with an agent codenamed "Crumb" who was not given sufficient time in the Congo to discover anything.

Finally, in the summer of 1943, the OSS sent a well-trained and efficient agent codenamed "Teton." In real life his name was Dr. Wilbur Hoag.[35] His cover story was that he was looking for Americans to draft into the armed services. He soon found some of the evidence wanted. One of his first cables read:

NOW HAVE STRONG EVIDENCE THAT BIG DIAMOND SMUGGLING RING EXISTS IN CAST FOX COVE [a penciled-in notation indicated this meant CFL a major Congo railway company] IN EASTERN CONGO. THIS IS AN EMPAIN [a major Belgium finance house] ORGANIZATION... CAMUS OF CFL HAD DELIVERED 7,000,000 FRANCS WORTH OF DIAMOND TO THE ENEMY 3 YEARS AGO. DETAILS FOLLOW BY [diplomatic] POUCH.[36]

A subsequent report on August 5th, 1944 identified as a suspect Celestin Camus: "In 1941 Camus, Director General of Des Chemin de Feu du Congo [CFL] Superieur supplied Italy and Germany with 7,500,000 francs worth of industrial diamonds (about 450,000 carats)."[37]

Teton reported that a Belgian citizen of Italian origin named Zambaldi flew these into Ethiopia. "This man is at present the head of TRANSKAT, a supply organization that is a subsidiary of CFL... During 1943 Zambaldi acquired a new aeroplane and appears to have unlimited petrol. It is assumed that CFL obtained the plane for him."

His report continued, "I have no way of knowing... whether this IDB [illicit diamond buying] activity on the part of Camus was voluntary or whether he was ordered to do it by the Empain powers in Belgium. I must assume however, that the smuggling was carried out at least with the knowledge of high officials of the Empain group since M. Tricet, African director of CFL knows of Camus' activity... and Brassier head of the Bank du Congo Belge."[38] The president and vice-president of Camus' company, Chemin de Congo Superior, were Baron Jean Empain and Firmin Van Bree, respectively.

British armed forces were also monitoring the movements of the Diamond Syndicate members. In April 1944, the Royal Navy searched at sea the Portuguese ship "Quansa" which was carrying to Lisbon Firmin Van Bree and Ernesto Vlhena, Managing Director of Diamang. Later that year Harry Oppenheimer himself was targeted. British Censorship discovered in December 1944, according to a secret US Government intelligence report, that he had on him a document referring to a business group of which "British intelligence had strong suspicions ... was engaged in diamond smuggling to Germany." Also, "According to the papers obtained by Censorship from H. F. Oppenheimer, the company apparently behind this undertaking was the Compaigne Miniere do L'Oubanghi Oriental." It continued: "It was subsequently learned that this group was backed by Sir Ernest Oppenheimer to the extent of £100 a month."39

The intelligence report alleged that the leaders of this company were two Vichy France sympathizers. These men "claimed to have escaped from German occupied territory but the circumstances of their so-called escape gave strong grounds for suspecting that it was arranged in accordance with a plan of which the authorities in occupied France were not unaware." This was the only report I saw that linked Vichy French interests and the Oppenheimers.

Allied intelligence discovered that submarines, planes and ships were all used to smuggle diamonds. "It was discovered that a package, probably including diamonds, had been delivered to a submarine... in a remote spot in

-3-   SEC...

Jose Maria ARAOZ -- a Spanish resident of Rio Muni who had taken over German property early in the war.

BASTID -- a French mining engineer of Paris and Madrid, who was appointed President and Director Delege of Soguinex as a result of reorganisation carried out by Vichy under German pressure.

British intelligence had strong suspicions that the groups was engaged in diamond smuggling to Germany.

It was subsequently learned that the group was backed by Sir Ernest Oppenheimer to the extent of 100 pounds a month.

According to papers obtained by Censorship from H.F. Oppenheimer, the company which appears to have been behind this undertaking was the COMPAGNIE MINIERE DE L'OUBANGHI ORIENTAL. The company has headquarters at 21, Avenue George V, Paris. Its stockholders are given as:

	Shares
Banque de L'Indo Chine & C.N.C. Group	50,000
Jolis	24,000
J. Monteil	15,000
Compagnie General des Mines, Bruxelles	14,000
Plouin (Estrella Mining)	10,000
Gaston Hausser	6,000
Mario Pinci	5,000
E. Benedio	3,000
Small Holders	71,000
TOTAL	**200,000**

An undated wartime report by British intelligence on monitoring Ernest Oppenheimer.

South Angola." Trains were also used to take diamonds to Bulawaya in South Rhodesia [today's Zimbabwe], which was a "major collecting center for speculative smuggling."

Diamonds were also moved by plane. "Early in 1944 several parcels which had been smuggled into Cairo, apparently by fliers of Polish, Australian and perhaps other nationalities, were picked up by the British. Analysis by the Diamond Corporation in London showed they had originated in the Gold Coast, Angola, the Congo and Tanganyika."40

Another route to Germany originated in the former German colony of South West Africa (now Namibia), despite it now being occupied by South Africa. An OSS report read: "The goods are carried by pilots of the South African Air Force who operate on the shuttle service between the Union and the Middle East. It is definitely known that two members of the South African Air Force have transported diamonds to Cairo and there are nine others who are highly suspected. Efforts to round up the members of the ring have been hampered greatly by bungling on the part of the South African authorities."41

At a meeting of British and American Intelligence officers in Accra in February 1944, it was concluded that the Congo mines were the major source of diamond supplies to Germany and that it was time to introduce preventive measures. The meeting recommended that a "Commission on Diamond Security" be sent to the Congo to tighten security and that Lord Swindon should meet with Van Bree in Accra. They believed that without Van Bree's support there would be little chance of stopping the flow of diamonds to Germany.

But at this vital juncture, when the flow of vital industrial diamonds to Nazi Germany might have been stemmed, London vetoed these preventive measures. After consulting

De Beers and its Diamond Syndicate, the Ministry of Economic Warfare on June 7th, 1944 "flatly banned" the setting up of a Commission on Diamond Security to the astonishment of the intelligence services.

The British Government told the US that a meeting of Van Bree and Swindon would be inappropriate "due to the delicacy of the subject." The Belgian Government would dislike the idea and this could "have an unfavorable effect upon the increase in the production of industrial diamonds destined for the United States."[42]

The Ministry of Economic Warfare instead proposed that security at the Congo mines be put into the hands of Ernest Oppenheimer who would appoint two security advisors for the Board of Forminiere. The Diamond Syndicate thus would police itself. The US Justice Department revealed, in a document examining the case for indicting De Beers, how a management company controlled by the Oppenheimers was then told to "stop" the flow of diamonds from the Congo diamond mines to Germany.[43] But Intelligence reports indicated that diamonds kept on flowing to Germany.

The next suggestion from the Ministry was that the American OSS agents in the Congo purchase diamonds on the black market in order to prove a black market existed. The Americans were furious, for they saw this as a delaying tactic. They had already established that the Germans were not depending on random purchases on a black market, but had a well-established supply line.

The American agent "Teton" was particularly annoyed because he had previously discovered and reported a similar British cover-up "at request of Diamond Cartel." The British government had allegedly aborted two years earlier, in 1942, a British Intelligence investigation planned to stop the illicit movement of diamonds from the Congo to Germany. Teton cabled his OSS superiors on 22 July 1944:

BRITISH RPT BRITISH DISCONTINUED SERIOUS IDB [illicit diamond buying] RPT IDB INVESTIGATION IN BELGIAN CONGO TWO YEARS AGO AT REQUEST OF DIAMOND CARTEL MADE THROUGH BELGIAN GOVERNMENT. TETON CANNOT PROVE THIS BUT GOT INFO FROM A BRITISH OFFICIAL. HE RATED IT B RPT B THREE [B3 was code for "highly reliable"].

Over Teton's protests, the OSS then ordered him to try to satisfy the British request concerning the black market. The OSS nevertheless feared that this would expose him to arrest and compromise. They thus put their orders into code. Diamonds became "SAKS car." An OSS cable of May 25th, 1944 read:

SHORT PANTS FF INTERESTED IN SAKS CAR. CABLE PRICE, YEAR MODEL, MILEAGE WRITE ALL ANGLES ON RUMORS AND POSSIBLE DISSATISFACTION WITH DICORP. IT WAVING PALMS.[44] [DICORP was a marketing arm of De Beers.]

Eventually OSS tried to call off the deal. But it was too late. Their worst fears were realized when an assistant of Teton's was arrested. A cable from Teton said his assistant was:

UNDER PRESSURE PROBABLY THIRD DEGREE. HE ADMITTED WORKING FOR TETON STOP THIS UNCOVERED AMERICAN INTEREST IN IDB.

Teton himself was arrested shortly afterwards and deported from the Congo. His superiors suspected that the British Ministry of Economic Warfare (MEW) had been instrumental in having him framed and deported. On July 19th, 1944 a secret telex went from Hanley of the British OSS office in Accra to the Director of the Office of Strategic Services in Washington.

UNFORTUNATE RESULT OF IDB RPT IDB FIASCO MIGHT BE UNCHARITABLE AMERICAN MISINTERPRETATION OF MEW RPT MEW ACTIONS IN THE CASE.

The American agent Locust replaced Teton but, according to Staples, he was not nearly as efficient. He alleged he was "overconfident and indiscreet."

Then, suddenly, the Ministry of Economic Warfare decided to cancel the whole exercise. There was to be no further investigation of how Germany got its diamonds. No steps were to be taken to tighten security at the Congo mines. Yet, the Ministry had just received a most worrying report from Lord Reading, who had surveyed the security situation at the Congo mines. It said that "the quantity of African illicit diamonds… reaching Germany via the Middle East might reach as high as 100,000 carats a year."

Under the terms agreed for the joint investigation, the Americans had to follow the British lead and also shut down their investigation, but they were furious. The final Staples report stated: "OSS Accra was now convinced that the De Beers Syndicate and the Diamond Corporation were determined to prevent anyone, including the British and American Government, from prying into their affairs or those of the constituent members of the diamond cartel."

They believed "the Diamond Corporation, through its control over MEW, after hampering the investigation at many points, had finally blocked the proposed commission [to stop German supplies from the] Congo."

On September 5th, 1944 the Office of Strategic Services in Washington instructed Locust, its agent in the Congo:

A follow up telex added, "DO NOT DISCUSS ANY PHASE OF IDB OR TETON'S ACTIVITIES WITH ANYONE ESPECIALLY BRITISH."

But what did the Ministry of Economic Warfare fear would be discovered if the investigation proceeded? Why would anyone in Britain want to protect the smuggling of diamonds to the Axis powers? The investigation had established that Germany was being supplied with diamonds from the Congo. Allied Intelligence had come to the conclusion that stopping this trade could shorten the war by six months. So how could the Ministry refuse to act? The US Office of Strategic Services found these developments incredible.

Meanwhile the British were still advocating letting De Beers assist with the security for the Congo mines rather than using the intelligence services. Lord Selbourne, the British Minister for Economic Warfare, wrote to Monsieur de Vlesseohouwer, the Belgian Minister for Colonies (based in London) saying that Governor Moeller of Forminiere had "offered to lend us assistance" and that they might well be willing to accept assistance from "De Beers Company and other South African experts."

But, unbeknownst to the British, the American OSS had now turned its attention to investigating the Ministry of Economic Warfare in London. It discovered that the

Ministry's vital Diamond Committee was in the power of the Diamond Syndicate. The OSS found that "3 out of 5 representatives [on the Committee] are directly representative of the Syndicate's interests." A fourth member represented the Union of South Africa, which was also sympathetic to the Syndicate and was represented on key committees inside the Syndicate.

The OSS also claimed, "Dicorp [the Syndicate's Diamond Trading Corporation] experts had practically taken over the functions of the Diamond Committee of MEW. Reading, as a matter of fact, rarely made a move without consulting Otto Oppenheimer (the London-based brother of Sir Ernest Oppenheimer). As a result, it seemed obvious that the secret intelligence and plans of OSS and SOE were turned over to Dicorp almost as soon as they reached London."

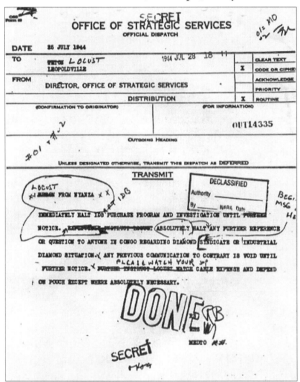

A final report by the Chief of OSS in Accra reached a much more cynical – and serious – determination, "We have come to the conclusion… that our assistance was requested in this program primarily so that the Diamond Trading Corporation [DTC] could discover how much we actually knew of the ramifications of the De Beers world monopoly."

A secret cable to the American spy Teton ordering him to halt his diamond investigation, not to mention the Diamond Syndicate and, in code advising him "please watch your step." The deciphering is hand-written on the cable. The date was July 28, 1944.

In the aftermath of World War II, there was considerable public anger in Belgium against the men who had enriched themselves by dealing with the enemy. Despite this, the post-war government of Premier Hubert Pierlot was generous towards collaborators. This was not surprising, given its intimate links with the diamond people who had managed the Belgian diamond industry under German direction. Belgium's Finance Minister served as Deputy Administrator on the Societé Générale board. A Belgian newspaper headline on November 22nd, 1954 read, "Pierlot Fronts for Cartel that Deals with Reich." It charged, "The government is the front for one of the most powerful cartels in Europe, Societé Générale de Belgique… [its] industrial machine in Belgium was orientated during the war to suit German needs."

But the anger of the American and British intelligence establishments was focused on British Government officials, not Belgian, The US Office of Strategic

Services and the British Special Executive investigators were convinced that it was primarily British Government officials, working in consultation with the Diamond Cartel, who had protected the wartime flow of diamonds going to Germany, thus possibly extending the war. They saw this as possibly involving treason.

They prepared papers for possible legal action against those responsible. The US Justice Department considered adding this charge to those they were preparing against De Beers for limiting diamond supplies to the United States. A Justice Department memo wondered: "I suppose we could not possibly make any allegation that the defendants themselves have prevented effective control of the leakage of industrial diamonds to Germany."[45] But it was decided that, since this case implicated the UK government, an American ally, it was too controversial and so was dropped.

In the 1990s, the campaign for justice for Holocaust victims resulted in President Clinton authorizing the release of all US-held records on the Nazi plunder. A preliminary report was released by the US Department of State on May 7th, 1997. A similar British report was commissioned and released by Defense Secretary Malcolm Rifkind after he and Michael Portillo were forced to withdraw an earlier statement that the UK had no relevant records.

The main focus of these reports was the stolen gold. No one had seriously examined diamonds. The American report was a grim indictment. It revealed, "It was the Reichsbank that assisted in converting victim gold coins, jewelry and gold fillings into assets – with their origins often disguised. ...$276 million in gold was sold by Germany to the Swiss National Bank and an additional $138 million was 'washed' through the Swiss National Bank and eventually re-exported to Portugal and Spain."

The State Department particularly indicted the "neutral" nations:

Switzerland was Nazi Germany's banker and financial facilitator, taking and transferring German gold – most of it looted – and providing Germany with Swiss francs to purchase needed products. Switzerland ended World War II as one of the wealthiest nations in Europe. Sweden was a critical trading partner of Nazi Germany. Its wartime exports of ball bearings to Germany were vitally important. The neutrals continued to profit from their trading links with Germany and thus contributed to prolonging one of the bloodiest conflicts in history.

No one has yet examined what price should be paid by currently-existing companies that dealt in diamonds plundered from Jewish merchants, and/or supplied or protected Germany's diamond imports, a trade more vital than that of ball bearings, thus possibly extending the death and destruction caused by the Second World War.

1 Memorandum for Assistant Attorney General, Thurman Arnold, April 16th, 1942.
2 Major A. W. Schmidt – Final Summary of OSS Report for Foreign Economic Administration and for the State Department. September 14th, 1944, p. 3.
3 Transcript of interview with Henry Staples Jr. for *The Diamond Empire*. May 1992, p. 5.
4 Report of Sir Ernest Oppenheimer to Stockholders in 1842. Also *The Times*, London. May 30th, 1942.
5 OSS undated report entitled Investigation of Diamond Smuggling in Africa. US National Archives. The author was probably Staples.
6 Feldkommandantur 525, Devisenschutz Kommando, Chief Dr. Mockel.
7 An account of these events based on Belgian archives has recently been published and is the major source for my next two pages: Eric Laureys. *De beroving van de joodse diamantairs 1940-1944. Belangen van de Duitse oorlogsindustrie versus ontjoodsingspolitiek?* Bijdragen tot de Eigentijdse Geschiedenis Nr. 7, Brussels, 2001. Also, by the same author Récupérations et indemnisations dans le secteur du diamant (§ 3.11.). In Commission d'étude sur le

sort des biens des membres de la Communauté juive de Belgique spoliés ou délaissés pendant la guerre 1940-1945, Les biens des victimes des persecutions anti-juives en Belgique – Spoliations – Rétablissement des droits, (Rapport final), Bruxelles, 2001, p. 467.

8   Even-Zohar also told me "There is a group in Belgium that calls itself 'Diamantaires of the Looted Diamonds,' or something like that, which are actively searching for evidence of what happened to those diamonds which, after the war, were collected by the Allied governments. Are you aware that some of the German diamond companies named in the Safehaven reports are still operating today?"

9   OSS "The Intelligence Problem in the Congo – Copy 2 of 5." Also see "Investigation of Diamond Smuggling in Africa." OSS. The author was probably Staples.

10   Safehaven Reports No. 179 (of June 29th, 1945) and No. 197 (of July 6th, 1945).

11   Telegram to Secretary of State, September 25th, 1944.

12   Report of Special Operations Executive (SOE), Accra, February 26th, 1944.

13   OSS Investigation of Diamond Smuggling in Africa. Undated.

14   Minutes of the Diamond Committee, Ministry of Economic Warfare, November 3rd, 1943. Sent to American authorities on December 10th, 1943.

15   OSS Report by Colonel Schmidt.

16   Minutes dated February 9th, 1944 of German Ministry Meeting on Four Year Plan held on January 17th, 1944. "Report re. Delivery of Industrial and Jewelry Diamonds to the Reich." US Forces translation.

17   Germany Ministry Meeting, January 17th, 1944.

18   Doc. No. 469, dated May 10th, 1940, from Berlin's Reichswirthschaftsminister.

19   Nuremburg trial records Interrogation of Oswald Pohl, June 7th, 1946.

20   "Summary and Analysis of Industrial Diamond Intelligence." OSS. October 1944, p. 18.

21   *World in Action*, broadcast by Granada Television in UK in 1979.

22   Personal correspondence from Chaim Even-Zohar to author, July 28th, 2000.

23   Reported in OSS Report "Investigation of Diamond Smuggling in Africa." US National Archives, 1944.

24   Secret OSS Report from Leopoldville, July 8th, 1943.

25   Ministry of Economic Warfare. Minutes of meeting of Diamond Committee, March 26th, 1944.

26   OSS "Investigation of Diamond Smuggling in Africa," p. 13.

27   Ibid.

28   Controller of Censorship in South Africa to Linsola McVeigh. November 12th, 1942 (Censorship Ref. No. 18335).

29   Edward Stimson, Department of Justice. Memorandum for the Files. July 21st, 1943.

30   Controller of Censorship op. cit.

31   Stimson Memorandum, p. 4.

32   Mission Belgie a Berlin, November 19th, 1948.

33   Calculated using production figures from *Diamond Intelligence Briefs*.

34   C. G. Hope Gill, British Consul General in Leopoldville, communication to London authorities, December 29th, 1941.

35   Communication from Henry Staples Jr. to author, May 1992.

36   Telegram to Office of Strategic Services (OSS) from Hanley in Accra, July 31st, 1944.

37   Report from Wilbur Hoag (Teton).

38   OSS Report, perhaps by Wilbur Hoag (Teton) "Outline of Industrial Diamond Smuggling as carried out by employees of C.F.L. in the Belgian Congo."

39   A secret report in US files entitled "Additional Industrial Diamond Intelligence."

40   OSS "Investigation of Diamond Smuggling in Africa," p. 7.

41   Ibid. p. 9.

42   Ibid. p. 19.

43   US Department of Justice, Antitrust Division. Memo to Files re. Conference with Mr. Donald Bliss, May 13th.1944. Also see its draft report, "The Cartel Problem in Industrial Diamonds." April 24th, 1944.

44   From Director of Strategic Services to Teton, Leopoldville. May 25th, 1944.

45   Letter from Edward S. Stimson of the US Justice Department to Patrick A. Gibson. November 21st, 1944 *Re. Prosecution Draft.*

Chapter 8 – Selling the Diamond Myth

GEM DIAMONDS AND THE SECOND WORLD WAR

The price of diamonds nearly fell in the late 1930s and 1940s. The Depression meant that few could afford their price. They cost only pennies to produce so their price could have been reduced, but Ernest Oppenheimer opted instead to close down diamond mines in South Africa. This move seemed to have been made too late. He could not afford to maintain his vast diamond stockpiles.

Then the Second World War broke out. This provided him with a dilemma. He needed to sell more gem diamonds to the US – but how could he sell more of a luxury item in wartime? It seemed inappropriate. The American advertising agency N. W. Ayer (since subsumed into the agency conglomerate BCom3) then advised him that they also had difficulties in expanding the market for their diamonds. The first was that American women would feel obliged for patriotic reasons to give their diamonds for war use, thus weakening the market for De Beers' industrial diamonds. The second was that people would feel guilty if they bought expensive luxury gems in wartime.[1] So in order to absolve American women from any trace of guilt, Ayer ran for De Beers a series of "patriotic advertisements." The box above shows the text of one of them.[2]

> **EMBLEM OF LOVE – OR WEAPON OF WAR?**
>
> 'A Jap would say it was a weapon.
> His eyes would glisten
> As he pictured the diamond
> Cracked into minute drill-head teeth
> Biting through the earth.
> In Germany today diamonds similar
> To those in your treasured sweetheart symbol
> Are being pried from women's jewelry,
> Pierced by electric-sparking platinum needles.
> 'IF IT IS NEEDED, I'LL GLADLY SACRIFICE
> MINE TOO FOR I MUST HELP HIM IN EVERY
> WAY I CAN.'
> It will help him more there over your heart.
> Fortunately we possess almost the entire world's
> supply
> Of another kind of diamond to do the hard
> work.
> The jewel diamonds are helping the war effort in
> another way.
> They are found in the same mines.
> Sales of the occasional
> Jewel stones discovered among industrials
> Help keep down the cost of industrial diamonds.

This advertisement deceived. De Beers had little need to mine more diamonds. Its vaults were full. It had closed the mines that produced both gem diamonds and the diamonds most needed for the war effort, keeping open only the Congo mines that produced at the cheapest cost the poorest quality industrial diamonds.

Other advertisements appeared with titles like "Diamonds in Overalls," "Diamonds Go to the Front," "Diamonds Break a Bottleneck," "Diamonds and the Call to Arms," "Fighting Diamonds," and "Jewelry Jeeps." De Beers poured a fortune into advertising during WWII – and made a fortune in return. It reported it was spending at an annual rate of $500,000 on advertising and sales promotion in the United States. It declared a 100 percent increase in dividends in both 1940 and 1941.

De Beers was at the same time in a bitter dispute with the Justice Department in Washington, with its "profiteering" called "obnoxious" because of its "pious public professions of sacrifice," as described in the previous chapters, and it had to keep this from the public. The Justice Department reported, "The advertising firm of N. W. Ayer and Son, Inc. and its Vice President perform many services for De Beers and its associated companies… one such service is that of heading off any unfavorable publicity which might affect the diamond monopoly."

Ayer suggested that, "the problem is to convince the American public that the diamond industry, though an admitted monopoly, operates fairly and in a manner that accords with American interests… This must be done in a way that will stand up under direct attack even from a government source."[3]

America's schoolgirls were the focus of its new campaign. As Hitler's tanks launched the Second World War, Oppenheimer's men launched a campaign in leading girls' high schools throughout the United States. They addressed school assemblies, spreading the message that a girl is not truly engaged until she wears a diamond. They justified this by quoting an invented "ancient history" for the diamond engagement ring.

It seemed De Beers was intent on inventing a new sacrament for a secular age. It wanted to make its diamonds into a national symbol of human love. But the US Justice Department saw its advertising campaign quite differently. It investigated, for it suspected that this advertising campaign was part of an illegal price-fixing exercise aimed at exploiting American consumers.

In the war's early years the government had imposed a price ceiling on the retail prices for diamond jewelry, but in 1943 jewelers succeeded in having this abolished. The money De Beers spent on advertising went up to $750,000.[4] The wartime profits of both jewelers and De Beers skyrocketed.

De Beers advertising claimed that giving women diamonds was a truly ancient tradition. But the most ancient of these traditions was entirely different. In India, diamonds were traditionally worn by men and were said to be symbols of virility since they were uniquely hard. Indian men believed the hardness of a diamond was magically transferred to its wearer, making him invulnerable in battle or manly hard in love.

Pliny the Elder, the Roman naturalist, associated diamonds with arcane rites. He reported in 77 AD in his encyclopedic *Natural History*: "The diamond… resistant to any other form of violence…is broken by the he-goat's blood, but only when the diamond has been dipped in the fresh, warm blood of the animal and struck with many blows; for even then it breaks everything except the most solid anvils and iron hammers."

But Harry Oppenheimer would wax quite differently about their gems. He wrote: "Before primitive people really want good housing, they want beads, they want decorations, they want romance and this is absolutely fundamental to the human being."

HARRY OPPENHEIMER IN THE US

To find the images needed to promote diamonds, Ernest sent his son, Harry Oppenheimer, on an exploratory mission to New York in 1938. He went first to J. P. Morgan, the financiers that helped his father set up Anglo American. They sent him to N. W. Ayer, then the largest advertising firm in the US.[5]

Harry had a serious practical problem to put before them. De Beers could not open a company office in America because its methods were illegal under the Sherman Antitrust Act that banned price-fixing. Yet, they desperately needed to gain greater access to the US market. They had over 40 million carats of unsold diamonds and, if war broke out in Europe, there was no place else to sell them.

Somehow they had to circumvent the Sherman Act. They reorganized De Beers. Harry Oppenheimer's son Nicky told my colleague Gavin McFadyen in 1992 while we were making our film *The Diamond Empire*, that the Sherman Act was a fundamental influence on the organization of De Beers.

The negotiations to gain De Beers the use of an US office were highly discreet. N. W. Ayer first received a letter that came not from De Beers or the Oppenheimers, but from an unknown Raymond R. Byrne in South Africa. Byrne subsequently told them that he was acting for De Beers, that it was considering "opening a selling office in New York" and was considering offering N. W. Ayer a contract as its advertising agent.[6] He said that he would be coming to New York to discuss this further.

But it was not Byrne who arrived on the Queen Mary shortly afterwards. It was Dickenson, the Assistant General Manager of De Beers.[7] N. W. Ayer immediately provided Dickenson with space in its own office, thus effectively giving De Beers the US office it was not able to lease in its own name. On June 22nd, 1939, De Beers signed a contract with N. W. Ayer giving it responsibility for all "newspaper, radio, outdoor and streetcar advertising for De Beers." In 1941, N. W. Ayer rented more space for Dickenson on the 11th Floor of the RCA Building at 30 Rockefeller Plaza in New York. "The lease was in Ayer's name because De Beers did not want to appear as a lessee. It reimbursed Ayer for the rent."[8] Ayer also answered letters addressed to De Beers,[9] arranged Ernest Oppenheimer's 1940 visit to New York and kept related publicity on a "dignified plane" as instructed by Dickenson.[10]

The Oppenheimers wanted to gain a much larger market for their diamonds than the rich who bought them before the Depression. They hired Ayer to persuade Mr. and Mrs. Average American to buy diamonds because they were expensive. Keeping prices high was central to the De Beers marketing strategy. The reasoning was that high prices would both enhance the popular perception that diamonds were rare and therefore precious and thus maximize De Beers' profits.

The diamond engagement ring became the central theme. An Ayer report of August 1940 stated that it had placed 3,500 diamond movie stories and 16,500 diamond news stories in the media over the past nine months,[11] of them in the high circulation magazines, including in *Readers Digest, New York Evening News, Brides Magazine*, and teenage periodicals.

DIAMONDS AND HOLLYWOOD

Ayer targeted the dream factory of Hollywood, the creator of popular myths. Ayer noted that "motion pictures seldom include scenes showing the selection or purchase of an engagement ring for a girl – it will be our plan to contact scenario writers and directors and arrange for such scenes in suitable productions." They lent diamonds to any actress who would display them to good advantage, a De Beers policy that continues today.

In 1939, Ayer took on Miss Margaret Ettinger as its Hollywood publicity representative for the De Beers account, paying her $425 a month for securing publicity for diamonds in connection with "prominent movie stars, Hollywood fashion and social events."

According to a US Justice Department report, Ettinger represented sixteen Hollywood stars including Merle Oberon, Joan Bennet and Mickey Rooney. She said she got free advertising for diamonds by persuading producers to introduce diamonds into film scenes. "Miss Ettinger stated that recently Merle Oberon appeared in a movie wearing a diamond necklace and thereafter publicized the fact… by inserting the picture in approximately 24 magazines. She is constantly on the lookout for an attempt to publicize the wearing of diamonds by Hollywood stars."[12] As part of its campaign to win over Hollywood, De Beers gave diamond jewelry to society editors and movie actresses, diamond Christmas gifts to studio fashion girls[13] and threw engagement parties for actresses.

Ayer and the Oppenheimers concentrated their efforts on Paramount, the most powerful of Hollywood studios. They convinced it to add scenes promoting the romantic allure of diamonds and even to change the names of films. Ayer reported to De Beers in 1940, "A long series of conferences with Paramount officials, capped by your own efforts, succeeded in getting the title of *Diamonds are Dangerous* changed to *Adventures in Diamonds*." Ayer prepared cards to be put in local jewelers' windows. "We are sending fifteen photographs of models decorated with diamond jewelry for distribution in advertising and publicity program of Paramount pictures in regard to *Adventures in Diamonds* motion picture." In the 1941 film *Skylark*, a scene was inserted in which diamonds were purchased for the star Claudette Coubert. In *That Uncertain Feeling* (1941) Merle Oberon dripped with $40,000 worth of De Beers' diamonds.

While De Beers was wooing Hollywood, it was not neglecting Paris, the center of the fashion world. In the last half of 1939 and in early 1940 Ayer "employed a Miss Dora Miller as its Paris representative for the De Beers account," despite the war in France. In 1941 Ayer commissioned a Miss Sarah Strauss to design 200 dolls suitable for the wartime promotion of De Beers diamonds. The boys were dressed in draftee uniform, the girls wore "simple evening dress" and tiny sparkling diamond engagement rings.[14] In 1943 De Beers shared half the cost with Macy's Department store for a gala bridal show at the Waldorf Astoria.[15] Another bridal show at the Waldorf featured 30 dolls in wedding gowns wearing Tiffany Diamonds.

De Beers has always done its best to ensure that young couples "think big" when choosing a diamond. This was achieved by appealing to male pride. One of its advertisements showed a couple looking at a diamond ring in a shop window. The caption underneath explains the woman is hesitating because "she's too shy to tell you to 'think big.'" The punch line aims straight at the male reader. "Since you are the one who makes the final financial decision, you should know why 'thinking big' is important." But this 'thinking big' is useless for investment purposes. De Beers concedes diamonds are not for investment as a cut diamond depreciates by nearly 50 percent on purchase. Jewelers normally sell diamonds at twice the price they pay to buy them. "Thinking big" was about romance and status – and being generous to De Beers.

The campaign encouraged the public to measure the worth of love by the price of the diamond. "How much should one pay for a diamond?" one advertisement asks. The De Beers advice for lovelorn American men was that: "A month's salary is a good guide." The industry today has escalated the stakes by suggesting that anything less than two months' salary is unacceptable.

Diamond adornments for men were not neglected in the advertising push. The male market was seen as a good place for the disposal of De Beers' stocks of brown diamonds. A Cartier brown diamond advertisement was included in an extensive advertising campaign launched in 1940.[16]

THE JUSTICE DEPARTMENT INVESTIGATION

These wartime activities of De Beers are well documented in the records of the US Justice Department. It suspected that N. W. Ayer & Sons was conspiring with De Beers to help it act illegally in the US. It raided Ayer's offices for incriminating documents. De Beers had anticipated this and urged Ayer to take precautions. An Ayer executive wrote: "as I have told you, Sir Ernest Oppenheimer says for us at present to have no contact with customers of the Diamond Trading Company [DTC was De Beers' marketing arm]. This includes such people as Baumgold, Van Moltes, Van Berg. His main reason is that he does not want anyone to get the idea that we represent the DTC in any sort of a sales capacity in the US."[17]

All sales of diamonds to American merchants were to take place on British territory as they might be construed as illegal acts if they took place in America. This did not mean that the US merchants had to face a hazardous Atlantic wartime crossing. The UK government helped De Beers out by allowing these otherwise illegal transactions to take place on British diplomatic territory inside the British consulate in New York.

In 1945, the Justice Department raided the office of N. W. Ayer and Son at 1680 North Vine, Hollywood. The staff pleaded ignorance, saying they had nothing to do with the De Beers account, that it was all administered by Margaret Ettinger Inc., a few doors away at 1626 North Vine. The investigators then went to see her. She told them she received instructions from the New York office of N. W. Ayer.

Meanwhile De Beers expanded its wartime advertising campaign to other countries. At a July 1944 meeting between Warner S. Shelly of Ayer and Ernest Oppenheimer in South Africa, Oppenheimer expressed interest in "promoting the diamond business in other countries... he mentioned particularly England, Canada and Argentina."[18]

In 1945, when the Justice Department finally indicted De Beers for exploiting the American consumer, its indictment made specific reference to the role played by N. W. Ayer, saying the advertising agency had assisted De Beers in illegal price-fixing. A Justice Department Memorandum for the Solicitor General prepared later read, "The defendants have employed the advertising agency N. W. Ayer since July 1st, 1939. During the 7 year period ending Aug. 30th, 1946, they have budgeted $3,586,822 [for advertising]."[19]

The official US Government Complaint against De Beers stated, "One object of this [advertising] campaign is to induce the consuming public in the United States to believe that diamonds are naturally rare and valuable and that they are inherently worth the retail prices quoted in the advertisements, prices which are several times those which would prevail under competitive conditions."[20]

De Beers was so well organized that it did not even have to pay for its advertisements. De Beers described itself as legally the agent of the diamond miners, not the owner of the diamonds. Thus, it charged the producers for sorting their diamonds, for selling their diamonds, and for advertising their diamonds. The fees for all these services were payable by the mining companies. This also meant that De Beers made its profits no matter what the advertising cost, and no matter what were the profit margins allowed to the miners.

DIAMONDS ARE FOREVER

The slogan "Diamonds are Forever" was coined by an Ayer copywriter in 1948. It was later adopted as the title and theme song of the 1971 James Bond movie starring Sean Connery. Ayer explained to De Beers the message it was designed to convey was, "Once you've bought it, never sell it." The slogan was designed to curtail the growth of a secondhand market in diamonds, thus creating for De Beers a larger market in "new" diamonds.

Apart from orchestrating its advertising campaigns, De Beers used Ayer to ensure that their London Sights system operated efficiently. This was and is the essential mechanism of the Syndicate. As mentioned earlier, De Beers named between 150 and 200 diamond merchants worldwide as Sightholders, including a number of US diamond merchants. After paying, the Sightholders were allowed to "sight" their five-weekly boxes inside De Beers' Central Selling Organization office in London. This was not only a way of controlling merchants; it was a sophisticated tool for market manipulation.

If De Beers had too many of a certain type of diamond, it could unload them in the boxes even if there were little market for them. This would force the merchants to increase the prices of the diamonds they could sell. This mechanism also helped keep De Beers and its American customers safe from prosecution under the Sherman Act as these deals were and are done outside the US.

By the 1960s, De Beers advertising had achieved its aim. The proportion of young Americans sealing their engagement with a diamond ring had risen from 50 percent in 1950 to around 80 percent in the 1960s.

Younger girls then became a new target for De Beers. A leading Indian merchant reported that "jewelry for young girls (aged 12-17) is their new thrust area... 10.4 percent of girls in this age group receive some diamond jewelry. The average retail price is $151 per piece and 33 percent of girls acquire the same piece."[21]

While the Cold War was at its height, De Beers used Ayer to sell diamonds from new Russian mines into the US. De Beers "had" to buy these diamonds so they would not compete against its own diamonds. It had Ayer expand the market by promoting "eternity rings" mounted with many small diamonds. A slogan used was: "You know you will marry her all over again. But does she? The Diamond Eternity Ring." In 1980 De Beers spent over $1.5 million promoting the eternity tradition. It was portrayed as a beautiful way that aging couples could relive the moment of their engagement. Few if any of the Russian gems imported were reported to US customs. They were imported as British, thus avoiding the duties levied on Soviet goods.

De Beers' advertising was based on creating many new myths. Diamonds actually may not last "forever." Although hard, they are brittle. A leading Fifth Avenue diamond merchant, William Goldberg, told me that when he and others dealt diamonds in the street, they stood with one foot on the road so that if they accidentally dropped one, it would land on relatively soft asphalt rather than the concrete sidewalk. Diamonds can also be destroyed by fire. A prized ingredient of traditional Indian medicine was a diamond burnt to ash.

Another message was concealed in new De Beers' advertisements that used wild and spectacular landscapes to project an image of diamond as "nature's most precious gift."[22] The subtext was simple: do not buy the cheap, synthetic diamonds, even if they are indistinguishable from "real" stones.

As De Beers spread its message around the world, it had to create diamond myths appropriate for other cultural settings. The advertising agency J. Walter Thompson did this brilliantly in Japan. At the end of the WWII, diamond jewelry was practically unheard of in Japan. Thompson then campaigned to make the gift of a diamond ring part of the Japanese tradition known as "yuino," the exchange of gifts between the families of marrying couples. Reporting the coup, the International Diamond Annual said the Thompson campaign avoided "any suggestion that traditional customs in Japan should be changed or abandoned; what it does suggest is that the diamond ring is something that extends or embellishes the age-old customs and is in full harmony with the spirit of 'yuino.'"

De Beers' campaign coincided with moves by Japanese women to "modernize" (or Americanize), so its advertising images were designed to portray diamonds as a symbol of modernity. Japanese women were pictured wearing diamonds while engaged in pursuits no traditional Japanese woman had ever done before, such as skiing or playing golf. The campaign was an unqualified success. According to the Diamond Information Center in Tokyo, by 1978 54 percent of Japanese brides-to-be received diamond rings compared to only 5 percent in 1966. By 1993, Japan was consuming more diamonds than the United States.

Germans likewise had a custom that De Beers "modernized." For centuries two gold rings symbolized eternal love for German couples. De Beers rewrote the tradition, turning the symbol into a "triset" by adding a diamond ring. Germany became the third largest consumer of diamonds in the world.

De Beers maintained the precious image of diamonds by getting them onto the ears and throats of celebrities. Elizabeth Taylor was hardly ever seen at a public function without major diamond glitter. Elton John was renowned for showing off his diamond rings and earring. In 1983 De Beers launched a dazzling photographic exhibit called "The Women of Quality." It toured the United States and featured Joan Sutherland, Liza Minelli, Carolina Herrera, Paloma Picasso and Lee Annenberg wearing "important diamond jewelry." The exhibit appeared in gala events, ballet and opera. Another successful De Beers' promotion was "Connoisseurs of Quality – fine diamonds and fine wine."

When I left Australia in 1989 to begin my investigation of the diamond trade, one of my very first stops in New York was at N. W. Ayer. When I asked who the key women used for diamond promotion were, Ayer's representative named Joan Collins, Liz Taylor and Jane Pauley, then anchor woman of the top-rated *Today* show. She told me how Ayer had seized the opportunity of Chris Evert dropping a diamond bracelet on a tennis court to launch a best selling line of "tennis bracelets."

Although the Oppenheimers are not known for wearing diamonds, De Beers has long promoted diamonds as also a symbol of male success, whether worn by a man or by "his" woman. A 1942 Ayer memo noted: "Male gift givers, always a prime advertising target, will receive increased attention."[23] In the 1980s such slogans as, "She shows you have arrived at the top," encouraged men to display "their" women as trophies. Diamonds were for men symbols of status and of conspicuous consumption. One ad explained, "No matter how you travel, you have a way of making it all look first class."

But, despite all its advertising coups, the path for De Beers and Ayer was not always easy. For example, two British royal engagements caused dismay among diamond merchants around the world. Prince Charles presented Princess Diana with a sapphire and Prince Andrew gave a 12 carat ruby engagement ring to Sarah Ferguson. These choices caused an immediate international downturn in sales of diamond engagement rings. This was so severe that an American diamond merchant recommended the trade publicly donate diamonds to the royal family to repair the slight that the royal princesses had suffered at the hands of their intended spouses.

Apart from royal engagements, the House of Windsor has greatly helped the diamond trade. At a stock taking, the Queen was found to have, apart from the Crown Jewels, 14 tiaras, 46 necklaces, 98 broaches and 37 bracelets, all mostly featuring diamonds, and a diamond engagement ring with a three carat and five smaller diamonds. In 1940, in the middle of the war, Ayer suggested the Queen had a patriotic duty to wear diamonds. It wrote, "Since Great Britain has such an important interest in the diamond business, the royal couple could be of tremendous assistance to this British industry by wearing diamonds rather than other jewels."

On "Diamond Day" at Ascot, De Beers sponsored a women's race called: "The Orloff Diamond Stakes," providing a diamond necklace as first price. They also sponsored the richest endowed horse race in the British calendar, The King George VI and Queen Elizabeth Diamond Race. To update their image, De Beers has also established an annual Diamond Rock Award, although they met a snag when they offered one of these to Bob Geldoff in 1986. He refused to accept it until he was guaranteed that the diamond had not come from apartheid South Africa.

KYLIE MINOGUE AND HARRY POTTER

These same campaign methods continued into the 21st century. The London *Daily Mail* reported that De Beers "just loves Kylie Minogue," for "the company gave her a fabulous solitaire pendant, seen in several of her videos." De Beers Marketing Manager Fiona Spence also noted with satisfaction: "J. K. Rowling wore some wonderful long drop earrings at the Harry Potter premiere."[24]

A DIFFERENT REALITY

But under all this glitter there is a very different reality. When we were filming *The Diamond Empire* in New York, a diamond merchant on 47th Street showed me a ring seemingly studded with many diamonds. "See this ring?" he asked. "It only has one genuine diamond in it and that is worth only a dollar. But it is enough to allow us to sell it for a good price as a diamond ring." He told me this was a common practice.

In 1993, a television investigation by *Prime Time* exposed a web of chicanery in diamond retailing when it sent a producer, posing as a customer, to a shop on 47th Street in New York. The staff told him the stones they sold were all high quality white diamonds. He bought a diamond for $3,700 from a merchant who told him it was worth $5,800. In another 47th Street shop he bought a diamond for $3,300 that was described to him as a "near colorless" G-H diamond. The grade was certified in writing. But when he had the stones tested at the Gemological Institute (GIA) laboratories, he was told the first was brown, the next a poor grade yellow. Both were practically worthless.

Several weeks latter another *Prime Time* producer took the first stone back to the shop from which it came. The man who had sold it to the other producer inspected it and said it was not a white diamond. He pointed out: "See – it's a little brown in color." The producer replied, "The guy who sold it to me said it was white." The diamond merchant replied with mock scorn, "How old are you? Because you are naïve... Do not believe everything that people tell you from now on, okay?" When the other diamond was taken back to the store that sold it, they offered only $800, denying it was of the standard they had previously certified. The salesman said, "Like I said, whoever got you, they got you very good."

Despite their superficiality, the De Beers advertising campaigns had achieved their initial aim of making the diamond engagement ring into a universal sacred symbol for human love. In the 1990s it expanded its semi-religious ambitions by naming as the four key diamond-themed rites of passage: a girl's sixteenth birthday, her engagement, and a couple's tenth and 25th anniversaries. These new "rites" in the De Beers liturgy enshrined as the symbol of human love the expensive carbon crystals that so richly endowed De Beers. The marketing men thus created a religion in which De Beers took the collections. This would last into the 21st century.

1   Memorandum by George Roeese Jr., January 26th, 1942. He noted, "the advisability of putting some mention of industrial diamonds in the new De Beers advertising [for gems] on the ground that industrial diamonds would not have been available in the quantities which are being received today were it not for the gem diamond operations."

2   US Justice Department files. Undated.

3   Edward S. Stimson of the US Justice Department, "Summary of Material from the files of N. W. Ayer & Sons," June 1946. p. 25.

4   Ephraim Jacobs to Robert Nitschke, Office Memorandum US government, December 9th, 1946.

5   Memo by Lauck of N. W. Ayer, August 16th, 1938.

6   Byrne, Raymond R. Letter to Ayer, May 7th, 1938.

7   R. Stimson to Robert Nitschke, Department of Justice. June 28th, 1946. This account also calls him De Beers' "Technical Director."

8   Ibid.

9   Ibid.

10 Dickenson to Lauck, April, 1940.

11 Stimson, 1946.

12 Department of Justice, Antitrust Division. Letter from Raymond D. Hunter to Samuel Flatow, February 21st, 1945.

13 Stimson, 1946.

14 Hogan to Miss Sarah Strauss, May 16th, 1941.

15 Ayer to Macys, January 13th, 1943.

16 Hogan to Paul Flato, June 10th, 1941.

17 Justice Department Report, p. 56.

18 Shelly memo of conference, February 5th, 1944.

19 Justice Department Memorandum for the Solicitor General, June 29th, 1948.

20 Memorandum for the Solicitor General, p. 19.

21 Chhotalal, *Diamonds* 1990.

22 *Diamond Registry Bulletin*, January 1992.

23 Ibid.

24 *Daily Mail*, London. December 27th, 2001.

Chapter 9 – The Forging of Diamonds

Oxyacetylene torch "growing" a flawless diamond in Washington laboratory in 1992.

Today it is relatively simple and inexpensive to synthesize the purest and most expensive types of flawless gem diamonds. This is not a theory – it is happening today in secretive De Beers factories. No expensive equipment is required. I have watched in Washington, DC as an American government scientist routinely made a flawless gem diamond with simply an oxyacetylene torch and some bottles of gas.

There are two common forms of crystallized carbon in nature. The molecules of one have layers of carbon atoms that slide apart easily. This is graphite, the lead of pencils. The other's molecules have a dense array of carbon atoms that are locked together securely. This is diamond, the hardest natural substance. Diamonds brew naturally deep underground when carbon crystallizes out of methane gas, or another ancient carbon source.

A Scottish scientist, James Ballantyne Hannay, was the first to make diamonds in 1880. He heated hydrocarbons and other chemicals in sealed iron tubes. When he sent samples of his product to the British Museum, the Keeper of Minerals certified they were real diamonds. Later, General Electric scientists would wrongly accuse him of cheating. They said he could not possibly have made diamonds, because his iron tubes could not hold the enormous pressures they believed necessary.

For several decades it was thought the heat and pressure of deep underground must be duplicated if diamonds were to be made artificially. This was the path followed by the Swedish company ASEA in 1953. In 1955 two Clarendon Laboratory scientists, Sir Francis Simon and Dr. R. Berman, made diamonds in Oxford using a catalyst as well as enormous heat and pressure.

In 1957, General Electric started to make diamonds wholesale using similar methods. The diamond trade started to panic, even though the initial stones were poor quality and only destined for diamond powder. It was widely reported that it was only a matter of time before gem quality stones would be rolling off the line. De Beers decided it must try to secure the technology, possibly so it could be locked up by patents – and so threw itself into a frantic research program. Soon ASEA in Sweden was also manufacturing diamonds. The price of synthetic low-quality boart diamonds fell below the price of mined boart.

In the 1970s Swedish and Russian researchers discovered how to make gem quality stones by this high pressure technique – and that, if they added boron, they could make expensive fine blue diamonds or, by adding nitrogen, fine yellow or fine green – all very expensive when found naturally. These stones were high quality and nearly impossible to distinguish from mined gems when cut.

Diamonds were even found in the soot produced after a TNT explosion. Dr. J. D. Johnson of the Los Alamos Weapons Laboratory found that 20 percent of the soot turned into very small diamonds. Subsequently a diamond specialist, Bruce Dunnington, went into business making diamonds. He told me he could produce 100,000 carats of tiny diamonds per explosion.

I learned that the Russians had seriously proposed to create diamonds by exploding the SS-20 rockets they were scrapping under disarmament treaties. The Russian Novosti Press Agency said, "If slight changes in the technology of the destruction of the SS-20 missiles by explosive demolition were introduced, it would be possible to obtain diamonds." The US Defense Department asked the Soviets to provide additional information before they proceeded.

But the real threat was to come. Hannay was found to be right after all. Diamonds could be made without high pressures and explosions, by a method that was much easier.

DIAMONDS FROM METHANE

It was in 1992 that I saw a scientist in a US naval laboratory in Washington growing a large gem diamond in the flame of an ordinary oxyacetylene torch. She did so by injecting common gases into the flame of the torch. She laughed, embarrassed, when I asked her if diamonds had any special meaning for her.

In the same Washington laboratories I met another scientist, James Butler, who with a small machine, the size of a food processor, was turning Washington sewage gas, collected from the adjacent Blue Plains Waste Water Treatment Plant, into diamonds. With boyish delight he informed me that sewage, "makes fine white diamonds because of the oxygen in the gases." These diamonds are all "flawless" – of the highest value if sold as gems. Instead of being a rare quality, flawlessness is practically the distinguishing characteristic of such manufactured diamonds.

Butler was researching diamonds because the US armed forces needed thousands for a particular task. He showed me diamonds that no one would like as an unexpected gift. They had been made into a superhard missile cone. He told me they are "radiation hard" – that is, they survive nuclear explosions well – and that they are a superb heat conductor with many other military and computing uses.

De Beers quietly adopted this new technology. In 1994, it opened a plant at its base in the Isle of Man to use this "vapor deposition" method to make fine gem-quality diamonds. De Beers' name did not appear on the plant and, when questioned, De Beers insisted that it was only going to use these flawless diamonds for industrial purposes.

The Russians have used this same method to forge diamonds since 1977. They had developed refinements that allowed them to make fine diamonds from alcohol or almost any other substance containing carbon. Dr. Boris Berjaguin and colleagues at the Institute of Physical Chemistry in Moscow reported that, when any such common material is mixed with atomic hydrogen and passed over a hot object, it is coated with diamonds. Dr. Russell Messier of the University of Pennsylvania later discovered that passing microwaves through a mixture of methane and hydrogen also created diamonds. Some scientists now think that the diamonds found in nature were created in a similar way – from methane gas heated by the natural blowtorch of volcanoes.

Extraordinarily, a British television journalist said that the diamonds made at the De Beers' plant on the Isle of Man were "too pure for jewels," for it is the "impurities that give diamonds their beauty."[1] Jewelers would be astonished to hear this. They sell pure flawless diamonds for astronomical prices as the rarest of beautiful gems. It seemed that De Beers had to invent a new myth on the spur of the moment to explain why flawless synthetic diamonds were not suitable to be sold as gems. They had become "too pure."

De Beers is now also growing diamonds in its Diamond Research Laboratory, a multi-million dollar plant with over 500 staff in South Africa. A 38.4 carat yellow diamond reportedly made at this plant was displayed at a Japanese exhibition, where it was explained that it was cost effective to manufacture them up to four carats in size and that they were "very clean" (i.e. did not have visible flaws). It was also again explained that De Beers was only making these gem quality diamonds for industrial purposes.

General Electric has now adopted the same technology under agreement with De Beers, and it too says it is making large gem quality diamonds solely for "high tech" purposes. The other possible competitor, Sweden's ASEA, was eliminated by being taken over by De Beers. After this ASEA stopped selling synthetic diamonds in the US. GE and De Beers are reportedly keeping their diamond synthesizing plants under as much security as a biological warfare laboratory would keep its viruses.

Russia has at least five factories capable of manufacturing gems. In the chaos after the fall of the USSR, rumors abounded that Russia was exporting synthetic gems without distinguishing them from mined gems, and wanted western partners to join them in this. They had some initial success. In 1993 an American, Thomas Chatham, announced he was working in partnership with Siberian Synthetic to manufacture and market 100 carats of gem quality diamonds a month at a tenth of the price charged by De Beers for natural stones of the same quality.

Joseph Schlussel, in his diamond company's office on Fifth Avenue in New York, showed me diamonds synthesized by Sumitomo that he had cut as gems. They were dazzling and of fine rare colors. He had previously shown them to diamond experts at New York's Diamond Exchange and reported in his trade newsletter *Diamond Registry* that "None of the experts who were shown them could identify the difference between the synthetic product and the natural stones of the same size… the experts included cutters, importers, gemologists and even some De Beers executives."

Sumitomo's sales representative in the United States, Richard Ladd, felt a need to emphasize, "Not a large number are being sold… nothing that should concern De Beers." He then contradictorily said that a "large number" had been sold in 100 piece parcels. It seems most were of a good size – four-tenths of a carat. He insisted Sumitomo would not sell the two carat stones it had made, for the firm had an "understanding" with De Beers concerning industrial diamonds that they feared to disturb. The definitive diamond testing laboratory in the US, the Gemological

Institute of America (GIA), "has warned that natural diamond cannot be distinguished from polished [diamonds]... using loupe or microscope."[2]

These diamonds can be grown to great size. The Russians had grown a first class gem diamond weighing three kilograms. This was cut as super-hard optical glass for use in spacecraft instruments.

Some extremely unusual carbon sources have been used. I was amazed when I came across an advertisement in 1988 in a Phoenix, Arizona, newspaper, the *Sun City Daily News*, exhorting customers to: "turn the ashes of your beloved into a diamond"! We can apparently reduce a dead husband or wife to an ornament in order to reproduce the sparkle in their eyes.

FIXING DIAMONDS

There are other technologies available to make or enhance diamonds. Sumitomo Electric Industries can coat natural diamonds with a transparent and invisible fine layer of synthetic diamond to make a diamond more valuable by increasing its weight past the magic one-carat mark.

In a Fifth Avenue building I met the son of Yahuda, a man who knew how to mend diamonds – and who had set up a company to do just this. He told me the technique invented by his father made flawed diamonds look nearly flawless, and thus much more valuable. He cautiously added that they always inject a tiny amount of blue die into the diamonds they treat to make sure jewelers are not deceived. I stared through the loupe and could hardly see the wisp of blue. The industry newsletter *Rapaport Report* reported in December 1987 that a $250 per carat diamond could be made into a $1,200 diamond by thus filling its "gletzes" (cracks), and that this was very hard to detect. A quarter of all gem diamonds can be thus improved. Many tens of thousands have been.

Russian scientists have also proposed a way of "fixing" brown Australian diamonds to make them white and thus much pricier. Evgeny Polyansky, the Deputy Science Director of the Russian Research Institute for Synthesis of Materials, said, "It takes just one hour to convert an Australian brown to a fine blue or to a perfect colorlessness." In 1994, this Research Institute was specializing in the synthesis of diamond, garnet, emerald, sapphire and other gems for overseas hard currency markets. The GIA warns that some diamonds are also being "adjusted" in color by the techniques used to coat camera lenses.

Then there are the hundreds of diamonds that are enhanced in specially licensed atomic reactors in the US. The radiation improves their color and is scarcely detectable – except with a Geiger counter. The diamonds treated can be dangerously radioactive afterwards, according to authoritative diamond industry sources. The Nuclear Regulatory Commission insists that diamond customers be told if their diamond has been irradiated. When did you last check your diamond with a Geiger counter?

THE WORLD DIVIDED BETWEEN GENERAL ELECTRIC AND DE BEERS

Diamonds are now openly manufactured, but supposedly only for industrial purposes. In the 1980s, De Beers and General Electric held 45 percent each of the world's market for synthetic industrial diamonds. Out of the 200 million carats of diamonds used for industrial purposes in the West in 1980, 180 million carats of them were manufactured. The US Justice Department reported in 1967 that they had heard the new diamonds were in some cases better than the natural.[3]

When De Beers first manufactured synthetic diamonds, General Electric took action against it in South African courts, accusing it of stealing their patented high-pressure technology for fabricating diamonds. The US Justice Department reported, "A fight between G.E. and De Beers over the South African patent rights went almost to the Supreme Court there before G.E. sold its South African patent to the Syndicate for US$8 million." The settlement included a GE license allowing De Beers "to market and produce diamonds in a number of European countries for an unspecified royalty." The GE technique can make gem quality stones, but the public talk was only of industrial stones.

The US Department of Justice suspected that General Electric and De Beers had, after settling, conspired to divide up the world's market, to keep others out, and fix prices. It was also alleged that General Electric and De Beers made an agreement not to cut their manufactured diamonds as gems. The initial panic in the diamond trade was quelled when it was announced that the manufacturing of gem quality stones would be "uneconomic."

Dr. Arthur Bueche, General Electric's Vice President for Research and Development, came to Lazare Kaplan, a Fifth Avenue diamond company now managed by Maurice Tempelsman, to show the new synthetics and say publicly, "We come to assure you that we are not competing. We have no reason to harm the diamond industry."

In 1989, General Electric invented a form of diamonds that only contained Carbon-12; natural diamonds also have a little of Carbon-13 with a slightly different molecular structure. It reported that these "are equal or better than most natural gemstone diamonds in quality, are virtually indistinguishable from natural gemstone diamonds and conduct heat more efficiently."

DE BEERS AGAIN INDICTED BY A US COURT

But legal dangers loomed for De Beers and General Electric from the beginning of this relationship. Any plan to divide up the world market could be illegal. The American Justice Department still believed De Beers was exploiting American consumers. When it indicted De Beers after World War II, the action did not succeed since the judge ruled that De Beers was not legally present in the US and then the Belgian Government intervened to prevent an appeal by the US. But it did not go all De Beers' way. It allegedly had to sign a consent decree agreeing not to do business in the US.[4] The Justice Department soon came to suspect that De Beers was breaking its pledge.

De Beers sold gem diamonds to American merchants in London to keep these deals outside the reach of the US Sherman Act. But De Beers was selling industrial diamonds in the US – and in the 1960s the Justice Department thought this made De Beers vulnerable to US law. An uncensored section of a heavily censored Justice Department report stated:

After De Beers succeeded in duplicating GE's synthetic boart and began marketing it in this country, it did not use the cash-and-carry system [the "Sight" system] which previously had kept it out of the reach of the Antitrust Division, but appointed an exclusive distributor in the US, Engelhard Industries. They probably felt that in synthetics they were not monopolists and thus didn't have to worry about antitrust... [but] the financial ties between Engelhard and the Syndicate are significant. The Oppenheimers' Anglo American had directors on Engelhard's board.

The Justice Department also thought De Beers was trying to gain monopoly control over the US market for synthetic diamond grit by buying up its major American customers – and General Electric's customers as well. They reported, "We have heard from at least four separate and independent sources that the Syndicate has purchased control of one or more diamond tool making companies in the United States (including the Number One firm in the field)." Mr. Rudd, former director of De Beers in South Africa, was reported as, "now active in the management of Michael Werdiger Inc., the syndicate's principal US distributor."

A grand jury was sworn in by the Justice Department in 1972 to investigate if there were a case against De Beers. A watch began at the airports for De Beers' directors. Blank arrest warrants were signed. Any director who dared to step onto US soil would be compelled to give evidence.

This upset De Beers enormously. The Justice Department files record that, "Mrs. Oppenheimer was in New York several weeks ago, but that H O [Harry Oppenheimer] had not come with her as originally presumed. [Name censored] stated H O is extremely upset at not being able to go come to the US. The Rothschild on the De Beers board, who had been very upset at being told that he could not come to the US because of the diamond investigation, has now resigned from the board. [Name censored] told us he would inform us if Rothschild ever came to the US."

Rothschild was very angry. He liked to shop in New York City. His resignation from the De Beers board caused a major internal crisis, more upsetting for De Beers than the grand jury's appointment. His family's vast wealth some 90 years earlier had played a vital role in the creation of De Beers.

The Justice Department memo continued: "[Name censored] said the standing instructions for the De Beers-Anglo American organization is that, during the time of the investigation, there would be no contact with the US except through brokers. It is generally believed in the De Beers organization that this rule can be relaxed when in October (in their opinion) the investigation will be over and all will be clear."[5]

Engelhard allegedly moved its board's meetings to London so Anglo American directors could attend them, and Anglo shifted its US office to Toronto in Canada. Fifth Avenue diamond merchant Maurice Tempelsman was allegedly "in constant contact with Harry Oppenheimer relaying to him information on the progress of this antitrust investigation."[6]

But despite all these precautions by De Beers, the Justice Department in 1974 recommended indicting De Beers on criminal charges, not just for its deals on synthetic diamonds, but for:

monopolizing... gem diamonds... This unlawful activity has deprived the American consumer of unrestricted supplies of gemstones and required them to pay artificially high prices resulting in monopoly profits to De Beers. The nature of the conduct and the intent of the parties is such that a strong case can be made out for returning criminal indictments against the company and its Chairman Harry F. Oppenheimer... [It would] label the parties as illegal monopolists exploiting the diamond producing and consuming nations of the world.

They noted it should be relatively easy to serve the indictment on Harry Oppenheimer as he "maintains an apartment at the Waldorf Astoria in New York."[7]

But the plea from Justice Department staff failed to overcome the Department's jurisdiction worries. There was little doubt that De Beers' practices forced American consumers to pay exorbitant prices for gems, but De Beers had done these deals in London. The Department's previous efforts to sue De Beers had failed partly because of this. Perhaps this time it could persuade a judge that such dodges should not be allowed to protect De Beers. But the Department of Justice decided to go for the softer and safer target. It would indict De Beers over industrial diamonds, since these deals were done in the US.

But the Justice Department found it hard to find a South African attorney willing to serve its indictment on De Beers. The attorney who eventually served it on De Beers in South Africa recorded in an affidavit that the De Beers official he gave it to tore up the court papers in front of him, dropped the fragments and trampled on them.

The Justice Department also decided to proceed against two Diamond Syndicate-linked American companies, ANCO Diamond Abrasives Corporation, and Diamond Abrasives Corporation. When the attorneys raided their offices they found records of price fixing meetings they had attended in South Africa. Both companies pled no contest.

De Beers at first maintained it would not attend an American court, claiming it did not do business in the US. But one day, unexpectedly, a lawyer from a prestigious legal firm arrived at the Justice Department to say De Beers was now willing to effectively plead guilty, but only on one condition; that the name of their diamond subsidiary in Ireland was substituted for their own on the indictment. He explained this was because the South African government would strongly object to a South African company accepting the jurisdiction of an American court. This deal was accepted. Instead of De Beers, they indicted De Beers Industrial Diamond Division (Ireland) Ltd.

Once this deal was concluded, the De Beers lawyer divulged why De Beers had settled. The company wanted Emile Rothschild back on the board. It had offered him a seat on the board of their sister company Anglo American but he had said he would not accept it if it meant he could not go shopping in America. He had demanded the Oppenheimers first settle their quarrel with the Justice Department.

THE VERDICT

The court found De Beers' subsidiary and the two American companies guilty. They were fined and bound not to act as a cartel. They paid a $125,000 bond to guarantee their good behavior for the next five years. They were fortunate that the Justice Department had acted against them when they did. At that time, a violation of the antitrust legislation was only a misdemeanor with a maximum fine of $50,000. The following year the law changed, making the same offense a criminal felony attracting a million dollar fine.[8]

The Consent Decree read, "The consenting defendant is enjoined and restrained [from any action that would] fix, maintain or stabilize the price to be charged... to any third person...[or] allocate, limit or divide territories, markets or customers for the sale of diamond grit, submit non-competitive, collusive or rigged bids or quotations for any sale of diamond grit... for 5 years. They must report regularly to the court."

The Justice Department also looked at allegations that De Beers was conspiring to run a price fixing conspiracy in synthetics jointly with General Electric. In an earlier investigation they had noted that Harry Oppenheimer reportedly "had a meeting with General Electric in New York in October of 1966 and... several subsequent meetings in London with G.E."[9] In the 1990s the Justice Department picked up this earlier investigation and carried it forward. This happened partly because they found a top executive ready to talk, Edward Russell, former head of GE's synthetic diamond division. He made wide-ranging allegations, but the case was eventually lost. To the chagrin of the Justice Department, Russell accepted a settlement offer from General Electric. After this, the Justice Department found they could not obtain the documents needed to support his allegations.

Because of these difficulties, US Attorney General Janet Reno proposed new legislation on June 13th, 1994, to allow the Justice Department to conduct joint investigations into international cartels alongside foreign governments. US law already allows such joint investigations in criminal and securities cases.

Blue gem diamonds and General Electric

Before Russell accepted the settlement offer, I had him interviewed for *The Diamond Empire*. He explained that splitting up the world market for diamond-tipped saw blades was worth nearly $300 million a year to both De Beers and General Electric.[10] He also told us about blue gem diamonds.

Russell claimed that General Electric had known for years how to make blue diamonds identical to the ones that De Beers sold as rare and costly. The only reason it had not done so was because it wished to keep De Beers happy.

Russell told us:

You hear a lot that it is costly to grow gem diamonds. What isn't said is that... say it takes you four days to grow a one carat stone, a two carat stone takes six days and a three carat takes seven days. What happens is the cost per carat is coming down while the profits go up exponentially...After a very short period of development, we [GE] were making three to four carat gem stones, flawless E's, a very high grade of diamond. As we were growing them synthetically, we had a number of advantages. We could grow them all to the same size and a cutter could cut them all uniformly. We could include certain impurities such as boron and make different colors such as (rare) blues... It was very easy to grow a three to four carat blue diamond.

Once we had established our technical ability to do this, we started to look at the four billion-dollar gem market. We got in touch with Zoroski's... the 50 percent owner of Zales. They became very interested... we were looking at a joint venture with Zoroski's to make gemstones. We had everything set up. Zoroski's had actually hired the Boston Consulting Group to do a study. We initially targeted large stones, as in nature anything over two carats is rare. We laid out a strategy... We would put out the stones slowly, not affecting the natural stone market, aiming for a $50-100 million business a year... It would have been very hard to distinguish our stones from mined stones. Maybe a laboratory with the right equipment but it is not an easy task.

He concluded that although General Electric ended this project, "the technology is there. I think someone will do it eventually."

Selling "natural" diamonds

With all these developments, the story that "gem" diamonds were harder to manufacture than "industrial" diamonds was no longer sustainable. De Beers had to work out a new story that would enable it to sell an invisible physical property for high prices – for the difference between a flawless synthetic diamond and a flawless natural diamond is microscopic. De Beers wanted to persuade customers to pay vastly more for a natural diamond than they would for a synthetic – despite not being able to see a difference between them.

The situation grew worse for De Beers in the late 1990s. Other new synthetic gems were introduced such as the moissanite colorless gem then known as C3. It was hard like a diamond, with a score of 9.25 on the Mohs scale, and had many other similarities to diamonds. It was, and is, a competitive threat to diamonds since it could be graded on the same color and clarity scale. It also passed the standard diamond tests so could easily be taken for a "real" diamond.

De Beers denied reports of Russian progress in manufacturing colorless or white synthetic diamonds, despite admitting they were discussing these with the Russians. The well-known industry newsletter *Diamond Intelligence Briefs* noted that that the Russians might not be the first to introduce synthetic diamonds commercially – perhaps a reference to De Beers' own synthetic.

But De Beers was nursing another secret. It had for decades maintained a price list that set a much higher price for a white diamond than for a brown. It claimed that white were rarer and more beautiful and used this to drive down the value of the Australian Argyle diamonds, claiming that they were mostly of a cheap brown color, unlike the whiter stones from its own mines. But De Beers had known and kept secret for over 20 years that diamonds only turned brown in the last stages of their volcanic forging, and that this brown tint could be easily removed. De Beers had accumulated a vast stockpile of brown "B2" diamonds bought at cheap prices to keep them off the market. It knew that if it had let out this secret, it would have had to pay much more for these diamonds.

It was not until 1998, after De Beers lost control over Australian diamond production, that General Electric announced it was going to "color enhance" brown diamonds by turning them into whites. It would do this through a partnership with

Pegasus Overseas Limited (POL). This was a subsidiary of Lazare Kaplan International, owned by De Beers' favorite diamond merchant, Maurice Tempelsman. It was hard to imagine that Tempelsman would do this without De Beers' prior agreement.

The New York diamond dealers had thought the problem of synthetically improved diamonds solved when the Federal Trade Commission (FTC) listed the most common diamond enhancements as treatments that must be revealed to customers – even if they were permanent and invisible. But this new GE-Pegasus treatment was not listed and Lazare Kaplan insisted it would be undetectable. Immediately the Australian diamond miners announced they were investing in a GIA investigation into just how undetectable was this treatment.

After an urgent meeting with the Federal Trade Commission, Eli Haas of the Diamond Dealers Club of New York reported, "Everybody is up in arms about the Lazare Kaplan situation, I believe that De Beers is spending 24 hours a day trying to find a way to recognize [the process]." The Club wanted the FTC to add the GE process to the list of diamond treatments that must be disclosed. When asked what's so bad about the GE-Pegasus process, Haas responded, "What if people could make $100 bills that look and act just like the real thing and nobody would be able to tell the difference until a year or five years from now?"

General Electric and Lazare Kaplan said there was no need to panic for they would use a laser to inscribe the treated diamonds with the words "GE POL," so that dealers could tell that they were treated. But this inscription would be in extremely small letters and placed on the girdle, a part of the diamond that is normally hidden in the jewelry setting. It was also scarcely permanent. Within weeks of this safeguard's introduction, diamonds were found with the POL inscription partially polished off. If it had been polished off completely, no one would have known that these stones were treated.

It was thus becoming harder and harder for De Beers to maintain their myths. The company needed to convince the public that its diamonds were all natural, not synthetic and mass produced. In 1998-1999 De Beers tested a method of doing this. It inscribed a tiny De Beers logo and security number on the face of their diamonds, so small that customers had to be told that it was there, since a microscope would be needed to see it. Again the public was being sold an invisible quality for much money.

The first trial of this system was in England in 1999-2000. De Beers was delighted to discover that customers would pay more for these microscopically inscribed official "De Beers" stones, in complete trust that a company so close to the English aristocracy would not dream of inscribing synthetic diamonds. The system was then introduced worldwide. In the millennium year, De Beers made even more money from the diamonds it had invisibly marked as "Millennium Diamonds."

Stephen Lussier of De Beers was reassuring: "With our brand mark, the consumer does not need to fear that there are any hidden, unknown or undeclared treatments, or that the stone is a synthetic." He however did not explain why De Beers should be blindly trusted – or how De Beers could guarantee a stone was not enhanced artificially after it had been inscribed.

De Beers said it would only inscribe the stones sold through its Central Selling Organization. It would sell uncut unmarked stones to merchants who would get them cut and polished before returning them for inscription. Lussier did not explain how the company would know that a stone returned to them for inscription was the same one that they had sold – and not swapped for a conflict diamond. It would in fact be impossible for De Beers to tell if this had happened. It had also patented the devices needed to see their inscription and would be selling these expensive tools to the retail trade. It would also charge a separate fee for the inscribing service. Their scheme thus promised to be highly profitable.

But their branding scheme was immediately investigated by the European Union as an abuse of De Beers' monopoly position. De Beers won a tentative approval for its scheme yet, in 2001, it would come again under legal attack in New York for alleged illegal price-fixing, but more about this later.[11]

1   News item on ITV television, UK, January 12th, 1994.
2   *Diamond Intelligence Newsletter*. December 22nd, 1987.
3   Carl W. Schwarz: July 7th, 1967 to Wilbur L. Fulgate, US Justice Department 1.
4   US Department of Justice memorandum, January 22nd, 1945, quoted in Kroll Report, 1989.
5   Memo from Richard L. Daerr, Jr., June 10th, 1974.
6   Richard L. Daerr, Jr. US Justice Department Memorandum. "Diamond Investigation. Telephone conversation," September 12th, 1974.
7   Richard Daerr and Stephen Kilgriff, "Re. Indictments in Gem Diamonds," November 22nd, 1974.
8   This judgment was in Trade Regulation Reports, case 62,056 US v DE BEERS Industrial Diamond Division (Ireland) Ltd., ANCO Diamond Abrasives Corp. and Diamond Abrasives Corp. in US District Court, Southern District of New York entered December 8th, 1976.
9   Richard L. Daerr, Jr. Memorandum. "Diamonds Grand Jury: Telephone conversation." June 7th, 1974. Filed June 10th, 1974.
10 Also confirmed by the *Columbus Dispatch* April 24th, 1992.
11 *Rapaport News* August 2002.

Chapter 10 – Selling Conflict Diamonds to the White House

One spring day in 1992, I found myself deep under Manhattan's streets inside a massive bank vault surrounded by tables piled high with small boxes wrapped in red paper. I opened one of these and found it filled with folded white papers. I unfolded some of the papers. They were filled with clear white diamonds. I picked out another box at random. It too was full of diamonds. There were bucket-sized containers on the floor by my feet, also filled with diamonds. Many were of good shape and color with no obvious flaws. As I played with them, two security guards and a government official watched me. They had agreed to take me to this vault so I could film the US strategic diamond reserve. These diamonds were acquired by the US to make sure American industry would never again be at the mercy of the diamond cartel or of a military blockade.

Each box was labeled with either the diamond Syndicate's address at De Beers' headquarters in London or that of a Leon Tempelsman and Son in New York. The diamond-laden tables also were clear evidence that the US, despite not being allowed its own diamond stockpile during WWII, had acquired one postwar. It seemed clear that a deal had been struck with De Beers, in spite of the ban on the cartel doing business in the US.

I first came across the other name on the labels, Leon Tempelsman and Son, in the evidence gathered by the US Justice Department's diamond cartel investigation. Although many names in the documents were censored, and thus blotted out with thick lines, the name Leon Tempelsman and Son survived in documents that described this American company's close association with the Oppenheimers.

Leon Tempelsman and Son was founded by a Leon Tempelsman and was now run by his son Maurice Tempelsman and his grandson, another Leon, from a Fifth Avenue New York office. It marketed the diamonds it cut through the well-known jewelers, Lazare Kaplan, a company Tempelsman purchased in 1984. They were supplied with uncut diamonds by the cartel every five weeks at the regular London Sights and had them cut in workshops on an American Indian reservation and in Puerto Rico.

When I called at their office in 1989, I met the younger Leon. He told me with pride that his father sold the US its diamond stockpile. Leon told me he was managing the business while his father concentrated on wider "strategic" matters as well as escorting Jackie Onassis about town.

According to letters I found in Justice and State Department files, Maurice had become Mr. Oppenheimer's unofficial US representative in the 1950s, when Maurice was still in his twenties. He still visits Congress and the White House and has long been a powerful advocate for diamond cartel interests. In recent years he has proposed multi-billion dollar diamond deals to President Yeltsin, met with President Mandela, and helped smooth the course of the cartel in democratic southern Africa. He has moved for decades in the most powerful of political circles, counting the Roosevelts, Kennedys, and Clintons as friends.[1] He arranged a meeting for Harry Oppenheimer with President-elect John F. Kennedy and has long helped shape US foreign policy in Africa in De Beers' favor.

Maurice Tempelsman's links to the Oppenheimers date back to 1947 when, the legend says, despite being only 18, he boldly approached Ernest Oppenheimer on a visit to South Africa. As it happened, the ambitious young man had arrived at a very opportune moment when the Oppenheimers were looking for a middleman who might conceal their role in politically difficult diamond deals.

De Beers, as described above, had just escaped from facing charges in an American court for exploiting American consumers, charges that were ruled inadmissible on the grounds that De Beers was "not doing business" in the United States. They had instead used American agents, such as N. W. Ayer. But De Beers still faced legal problems in the US. A 1951 US government memorandum indicated that De Beers was still being watched with a view to possible future legal action. It noted that De Beers was still restricting supplies to US diamond companies: "The restriction is enforced by Diamond Syndicate's refusing to supply United States firms that do not stay in line with the Syndicate instructions."[2]

WHY DE BEERS RECRUITED MAURICE TEMPELSMAN

The US wanted to never again be at the mercy of a foreign diamond company. In 1946, the White House had decided to mandate the establishment of a strategic American diamond stockpile. The US then exerted heavy pressure on the Belgians, the colonial masters of the Congo, asking them to drop their exclusive marketing contract with the Oppenheimers and instead sell Congolese diamonds directly into the US stockpile. The US Department of State began negotiations with Jas Jolis, one of the largest importers of rough diamonds in the US, and the owner of a 250,000 sq. kilometer prospecting lease in the Congo basin, to expand his mine to supply the US stockpile. The State Department noted: "In view of the pending case by the Department of Justice against the international diamond cartel, the proposed development of a source of supply outside the cartel might be considered a salutary development."[3]

These steps finally forced the Oppenheimers to concede that they could no longer prevent the US from acquiring its own diamond stockpile. Their principal concern now became both to keep control over the Belgian diamonds and to persuade the US to stockpile only diamonds that could not be resold except on De Beers' terms. This was not so easy when De Beers was banned from the United States as an illegal cartel.

The Syndicate lit upon a strategy similar to the one employed to market their diamonds inside the US by using N. W. Ayer as an agent. They sought a US diamond merchant who could handle the US government, and who was ostensibly independent of them – preferably one with strong family links to Belgium and thus to the Belgian Congo. A declassified State Department memo reported it was then that Moens de Fernig, a leading director of the principal Belgian company in the Syndicate, Société Générale, took on the responsibility of finding a suitable Belgian diamond agent resident in New York. Among the many Belgians who fled Antwerp was Leon Tempelsman, an Orthodox Jew. He had arrived in New York in 1940, accompanied by his 11 year-old son Maurice. By 1945, Maurice had left school to start work in his father's New York diamond brokerage.

De Fernig thought the young Tempelsman might be ideal for their purpose. A State Department memo stated. "Moens de Fernig had himself taken the initiative of bringing Templesman [sic] into the picture and urging the latter to investigate the possibilities of a… barter deal with the US."[4] Tempelsman readily agreed to play this role. Fernig's suggestion of an American middleman would bypass America's reluctance to do a deal with De Beers. His suggestion of a barter deal also helped bypass the US post-war cash crisis. By swapping other goods for diamonds, the US would be able to pay for diamonds without using dollars – and it would thus be much less obvious that the diamonds came from the cartel.

Maurice did so well that within three years the Belgians and the Oppenheimers were using him, and him alone, to sell millions of diamonds to the United States government, despite the fact that the US was at the same time trying to sue De Beers as an illegal price-fixing cartel. One of his deals would involve a secret three-way swap of tobacco, diamonds and uranium.

THE FIRST DIAMOND BARTER DEALS

Tempelsman's first deal, at the age of 21, utilized the European currency obtained by the US for sales made under the Marshall Plan. Tempelsman successfully proposed to supply diamonds to the US stockpile in return for payments in European currencies. This deal set up a pattern that Maurice would exploit for the rest of his life. For the next 50 years or more, he would be the "independent" American diamond merchant who could secretly front for De Beers and the Oppenheimers.

Thus, the Belgians, the Oppenheimers, and the Syndicate found their way to the US Government's purse. They sold Maurice diamonds in bulk, the only "outsider" ever to be so favored. The Syndicate's diamonds flooded into the US by the million and were stored at Fort Knox, West Point, and other secure repositories – including the vaults under Manhattan where I had inspected them.

The next Tempelsman deal was more elaborate. In 1952, he devised a barter deal using American agricultural surplus as a form of currency. He would barter the Syndicate's diamonds to the US Agricultural Department for wheat or other agricultural goods. The Agricultural Department would then sell these diamonds to the US government for its stockpile – so the only cash paid out would be from one federal department to another. Tempelsman would then sell the US agricultural surplus overseas, and presumably also be rewarded by the Syndicate.

But these deals were modest compared with Tempelsman's later achievements. His greatest feat was when he persuaded the White House to buy more millions of diamonds for the US stockpile when the officials managing the stockpile were protesting that they already had many more than needed. They had in fact overspent their budget and were consequently trying to sell diamonds, not buy them.

Maurice achieved this despite an initial rebuff. In 1954, the Executive Office of the President reported, "A current offer of industrial diamonds for wheat has been declined because the Corporation could not be reimbursed in stockpile dollars, the stockpile goal for industrial diamonds having been reached."[5] But ingeniously, Tempelsman then made the government an offer it felt it could not refuse.

Tempelsman discovered that US Customs had seized large numbers of fine gem quality diamonds from smugglers and put these in the national stockpile, since it was not legally permitted to sell them. Tempelsman knew he could make excellent profits if he could buy them at industrial diamond prices, then cut and sell them for jewelry. So, he proposed to swap them for a greater number of industrial diamonds.[6] The Administration was impressed by a deal by which it gained more diamonds by weight – no matter if the stones it received were not worth a fraction of those it gave away – and no matter that its stockpile was bloated with diamonds. This deal needed special legislation but Tempelsman persuaded Congress.

Thus, the diamond cartel acquired the United States government as its major customer. The Belgian government, the major shareholder in the Congo diamond companies, also reaped the benefits, as did Tempelsman. By his mid-20s, he was an extremely wealthy man.

Tempelsman's boldness in deal making had clearly paid off. His subsequent barter deals were made directly with the White House and the State Department. He also cultivated a large network of American political, diplomatic and commercial contacts, making him still more valuable to the diamond cartel.

As an "independent" American merchant, he could observe and deal in Central and West Africa without being seen by Africans as a representative of either the old colonial order or of the Oppenheimers. When he learned in 1957 that Ghana under President Nkrumah planned to sell diamonds independently of De Beers since De Beers was based in apartheid South Africa, Tempelsman immediately presented himself to the Ghanaians as an independent non-South African merchant and set up an office there. This allowed him both to monitor developments and buy up diamonds, with the effect that fewer strayed from hands sympathetic to the Oppenheimers.

He was also particularly well placed to similarly intercede in the Congo, where he was well known both as an independent American merchant, and as one who could complete lucrative barter deals. When the Congo moved towards independence, he monitored the Belgian control over the Congo's diamond mines – knowing that, if it became shaky, Oppenheimer and De Beers would need to act quickly to ensure they did not lose marketing control over the vast diamond resources of the Congo basin.

TEMPELSMAN AND THE KENNEDYS
Maurice felt he needed more political clout for his deals, so he convinced his father Leon to make hefty donations to the presidential campaign of Democrat candidate

Adlai Stevenson who, in return, agreed to take Tempelsman on as a client of his private law firm. In his 25th year Maurice set out with Stevenson to Africa to impress the local politicians. Stevenson admitted to working for Tempelsman: "in certain matters, mostly relating to South Africa and Ghana, from 1955 to 1960."[7] Tempelsman was said to be Stevenson's major account, paying him over $50,000 a year. In 1960, Stevenson expressed to Tempelsman his "everlasting thanks for all you have done for me – and for so long."[8]

Although Tempelsman had secured himself friends on both sides of the political divide with generous donations, it was eventually his Democratic contacts that proved the more useful, as can be seen from the prominence given in his office to the signed portraits of Presidents John F. Kennedy and Lyndon B. Johnson.

His introduction to the Kennedys may have come through Theodore Sorensen, a lawyer who practiced in the same office as Stevenson. When John F. Kennedy was preparing to run for president in 1959, Sorensen became his speechwriter. That same year, when Oppenheimer expressed a wish to meet John F. Kennedy, Tempelsman was able to bring them together. A confidential diamond industry source told the US Justice Department, "Tempelsman was the man who arranged the meeting for Harry Oppenheimer with John Kennedy when Kennedy was president-elect. The meeting was held at the Carlyle Hotel" – a prestigious establishment in Manhattan.[9]

THE DIAMOND SIGHTS

It was easy for the Oppenheimers to discreetly reward Tempelsman – they could put the finest diamonds into his supplies while charging him only moderate prices. When he became a London Sightholder, it became even easier for De Beers to reward him confidentially. The London Sight was designed in part to enable the Syndicate to reward or fine in total secrecy the world's top diamond merchants. As the boxes were sold at prefixed prices, the prices paid did not need to match the contents. Those punished with poor stones rarely refuse to accept their boxes, for doing so could put at jeopardy their entire supply of diamonds. Punishments were thus meted out for such crimes as buying diamonds from other sources. Tempelsman's high standing with the Oppenheimers was confirmed by reports that he had the largest diamond Sight of any American diamond merchant.

Maurice Tempelsman made many trips to Africa after 1957, often accompanied by Adlai Stevenson. He visited political leaders in the rich diamond mining regions of West Africa and the Congo basin, paying particular attention to those who might be inclined to market diamonds outside the cartel. He even purchased diamonds from them as an ostensible rival to De Beers. The Oppenheimer reaction to this gave a vital clue to the real role played by Tempelsman. He continued to be in their good books, he continued to receive his diamond Sight. Yet De Beers punished harshly other merchants who had committed the "sin" of buying diamonds from outside sources. New York-based diamond merchant Harry Winston was punished so severely for doing this that he described the CSO as a "most vicious system."[10]

The late 1950s, when African states were starting to break free from colonial bonds, were a critical time for the Syndicate. The British, Belgian, and Portuguese Colonial Offices could no longer be relied on to deliver diamonds from their former colonies. When Ghana became one of the first to achieve independence in 1957, Tempelsman and Stevenson promptly came to visit.

Vice President Nixon toured Africa that same year to try to gain commercial influence for the US in the emerging nations. But American policy makers, accustomed to thinking in Cold War terms, did not appreciate that Africans, freed from Europe's yoke, might like the freedom of talking to the Russians to evaluate them for themselves. Kwame Nkrumah, the Prime Minister of Ghana from 1957 to 1960 and its President from 1960 to 1966, wrote long friendly letters to President Kennedy and had amiable meetings with him to explain his need to talk to all sides and to be "balanced" in foreign policy.

But the cold warriors of the State Department would not allow the Africans such freedom, nor indeed would Tempelsman, whose lobbying in Washington was filled with Cold War rhetoric. He spoke of a "vacuum, which must be filled by western commercial interests... a dangerous vacuum, very tempting to Eastern Bloc commercial activities."[11] He suggested that his diamond deals would help fill this vacuum.

Ghana was then the world's second biggest producer of diamonds after the Congo. But Nkrumah, as I briefly mentioned above, soon after taking office, took its diamonds out of the Syndicate's control and established the Free Diamond Market at Pra, near the Ghanaian capital of Accra. He hoped this would become the diamond center for black Africa, enabling black nations to market their diamonds independently of apartheid South Africa.

The Diamond Cartel, Tempelsman, and Lumumba

Another major worry for De Beers and Tempelsman was the Belgian Congo. It too was moving to independence. It contained the world's largest known diamond deposits and had in Patrice Lumumba an elected and popular Prime Minister of considerable intelligence who believed, with much justification, that Belgium had plundered his country and left it impoverished. His speech at the Congo's independence ceremonies on June 30th, 1960, made western businesses fear they were about to lose easy access to his country's natural wealth, for he said in future Congolese resources would be used primarily for the benefit of the Congolese. In 1959 the Congo's diamond fields produced 14 million carats – about a third of the world's production. In the first six months of 1960, its mines had produced over nine million carats – nearly half the world's production. This was still controlled by Société Générale, the company that Western intelligence had accused of supplying diamonds to Hitler some 16 years earlier.

The Belgians panicked. They feared they would lose their lucrative trade in Congolese resources, so immediately took action. Belgian troops invited themselves back into the Congo. The Belgians claimed this was to protect both the Syndicate diamond mining companies and the majority interest in their mines held by the Belgian Government. Lumumba promptly denounced this invasion as a gross violation of his country's sovereignty, but on July 11th, 1960 when he saw the danger the European diamond mine staff really were in from locals bent on vengeance for the years of colonization, he pragmatically agreed to Belgian troops staying on to protect them.

But he had a shock the very next day when his plane was prevented from landing in Katanga by troops led by Belgian officers. The day before, the Congolese province of Katanga had declared its independence – so the action of these troops prevented him from quickly intervening to negotiate an end to this secession.

Société Générale then gave the rebels vital financial support. Katanga was producing a quarter of the world's copper and three-quarters of the world's cobalt. The company immediately paid the royalties due to the Congo, 1.25 billion Belgian Francs, to Katanga instead.

Powerful businessmen also planned for the diamond rich Kasai province to join Katanga in secession. When, on the August 9th, 1960, Albert Kalonji declared South Kasai independent, it was dubbed the "Republique de la Forminière"[12] – Forminière being the diamond mining subsidiary of Société Générale. Thus, within a month of independence, the Congo was torn apart, with its richest parts detached and under the control of Belgian companies.

Moïse Tshombe, heading the revolt in Katanga, was also the local figurehead for Belgian interests. The attitude of those behind his political party, Conakat, could be judged by the contribution made by the local Catholic bishop, Msgr. Jean-Felix de Hemptinne, to Tshombe's 1959 manifesto: "The black race has nothing behind it. It is a people without writing, without history, without philosophy, without any consistency ... no civilization, no energy, no ideas, no interests to defend."[13]

This could be contrasted with what Lumumba had said in his speech at his country's independence celebrations, "We have known sarcasm and insults, endured blows morning, noon and night, because we were 'niggers.'"[14]

Lumumba immediately broke off diplomatic relations with Belgium. He announced that if all Belgian troops did not leave the Congo within two days he would seek support from the only overseas power that seemed willing to help – the Soviet Union. But this threat was his undoing. President Nkrumah had warned him that such a step would alienate the US. It convinced Washington that Lumumba was, in the words of the head of the CIA, Allen Dulles, "a Castro or worse." On July 19th, the American Ambassador in the Congo, Clare Timberlake, cabled Washington to say that, "Lumumba's government must be destroyed." CIA agent Larry Devlin cabled CIA headquarters from the Congo on August 18th: "Embassy and Station believe Congo experiencing classic Communist take-over Government."[15]

We know that Lumumba's threat to seek Soviet help was either a bluff or a plan that was quickly dropped, for he simultaneously appealed for UN military aid[16] and, when the Belgians ignored his ultimatum, he did not go to Russia but instead flew to New York to appeal for US and UN help to stop the dismemberment of his country. When he arrived there, waiting for him at the Barclay Hotel was a letter from Adlai Stevenson, welcoming him to the United States and asking if he would meet "a young friend of mine," Maurice Tempelsman.[17] Tempelsman wanted to meet to discuss the marketing of the Congo's diamonds.

Lumumba's trip was successful. He obtained United Nations troops to replace the Belgian troops. The UN Secretary-General, Dag Hammarskjold, was so impressed by Lumumba and his exposition on the Congo's problems that he exclaimed: "Now no one can tell me that man is irrational."

Lumumba's personal security officer in New York was a Joseph Mobutu – later known as Mobutu Sese Seko. I learned of this from a former Ghanaian diplomat, Paul Baddo, whom I met in his elegant Upper West Side apartment. He knew Tempelsman well, having given him introductions when he first went to Ghana – and knew Lumumba and Mobutu. He showed me the statue Lumumba gave him when he came to visit. He told me that Mobutu accompanied him. It could not have been long after this that Mobutu started to plan his betrayal of Lumumba.

It was clear that the Belgians might fail to maintain control over the Congo's diamonds, and a new strategy was needed if the cartel were to retain its hold over the marketing of these stones. In August 1960 Stevenson sought a meeting for Tempelsman with the Secretary-General of the United Nations, Dag Hammarskjold.

As Hammarskjold was away, Stevenson instead met Hammarskjold's deputy, Andrew Cordier. Stevenson was frank with him about Tempelsman's relationship with Oppenheimer:

> Tempelsman is closely connected in business with the Anglo American companies of South Africa and Harry Oppenheimer, whom you will recognize as the largest industrialist in that country… I don't know if the exodus of the Belgians [from the Congo] is arrested or not… [but] if needed, in the Katanga copper mines or in the Congo diamond mines, Oppenheimer has indicated to Tempelsman that he would make some of his personnel available… to keep the mines operating.

He suggested Hammarskjold meet with Tempelsman before the latter left for South Africa, "where he will see Harry Oppenheimer."

Stevenson later cabled Tempelsman at the luxurious Carlton Hotel in Johannesburg: "Harsh suppression [of] Lumumba supporters may cause violence and [is] dangerous. Do not expect Belgian technical exodus yet. Anticipate Lumumba would quickly fill vacuum with [Soviet] Bloc technicians. South Africans probably unwelcome. Anticipate early Soviet Loan [to Lumumba]."[18]

This added urgency to the discussions between Tempelsman and Oppenheimer. If Lumumba installed Russian diamond technicians, he might also choose to jointly market the output of his mines with the Russians. Both countries had massive diamond reserves capable of breaking the Oppenheimer cartel.

Tempelsman felt it was time to send his own permanent representative to the Congo to monitor developments and to try to get Oppenheimer's men into the Congo's mines. He appointed a George Wittman, allegedly a former CIA operative. Tempelsman had "strong links with the CIA," according to Paul Baddo.[19] Adlai Stevenson also sent a telegram to the UN Secretary-General, asking for a briefing for "my friend Maurice Tempelsman and his associate George Wittman…" His telegram went on to say: "You will recall that Tempelsman has large interests in Africa. Wittman is leaving for the Congo in a few days to develop plans for aiding the continuity of operation of the copper and diamond mines." He also introduced Wittman to Sture Linner, the UN Head of Civil Operations in the Congo, and to General R. Dayal of the UN military force in the Congo.[20] By September 1960 Wittman was firmly installed as an observer of Congo politics for the diamond overlords and was close to many of the leading players.

DIAMOND PROVINCE SECESSION

The diamond-rich Kasai province had seceded while Lumumba was in New York in 1960. It was now illegally exporting its diamonds to Congo-Brazzaville, an adjacent state to the north, which almost overnight became the world's largest exporter of diamonds, despite having no diamond mine of its own. This loss of revenue was another disaster for the Congo and for Lumumba. But it was not a disaster for the Syndicate. Its diamond buyers had shifted to Congo-Brazzaville. This state now became a center for the men plotting to overthrow Lumumba.

Lumumba quickly moved to recover Kasai. It was his home state and he was confident of victory. He sent troops into Kasai, ostensibly to stop warfare between the Lulau and Baluba tribes, but in reality to end the secessionist rebellion led by Albert Kalonji. The Tempelsman plan to bring in Oppenheimer's men became impractical when Lumumba recovered the diamond mines. He was doing alarmingly well. The Belgian staff in the diamond mines continued to work and production continued without any need for Oppenheimer's help. Lumumba then moved to re-conquer Katanga, sending his troops on August 28th, 1960 to within 32 kilometers of the Katanga border. The Congolese Parliament rallied behind Lumumba. It looked as if he would succeed in re-establishing the authority of his elected government.

But behind the scenes, the CIA and the Belgians were working hard to ensure that Lumumba did not succeed. The CIA had moved its agent Larry Devlin from Brussels to the Congo in July 1990 – just days after the Congo gained its independence. Devlin was strategically placed. A year earlier in Brussels, he had formed a friendship with the Congolese soldier Joseph Mobutu who had then become Lumumba's personal security chief. Reportedly, Mobutu first met with Tempelsman around this time – although Tempelsman has since denied this.[21]

THE CIA, THE BELGIANS, AND LUMUMBA

The CIA was concerned about Lumumba's friendliness to Russia, so it planned a drastic solution: His murder. This was revealed by a US Senate Committee, chaired by Senator Frank Church, which in 1975 had investigated CIA attempts to assassinate foreign leaders.[22] One of the witnesses it called was Larry Devlin, the CIA agent. He gave his evidence using the pseudonym of station officer Hedgeman.

This disclosed that on August 18th, 1960, the US National Security Council, the body that oversees the CIA for the White House, had met in Washington to discuss the Congo. Next day the CIA had authorized its Congo Station to proceed to replace Lumumba's government with a "pro-Western group." This directive went to Larry Devlin as Head of (the CIA) Station in the Congo. Seven days later, a direct order went from President Dwight Eisenhower to the "Special Group" of the National Security Council. It was to dispose of Lumumba by any means.[23] This instruction was given also to Devlin.

The CIA and the Belgians joined forces and tried to get the support of the President of the Congo, Joseph Kasa Vubu, for their moves against the elected Prime Minister, Lumumba, but failed. Larry Devlin reported this to Langley, the CIA headquarters, on August 24th, 1960.

The CIA drugs expert, Dr. Sidney Gottlieb, was then instructed to seek advice from the Army Chemical Corps at Fort Detrick about a poison that could kill Lumumba without being traced back to the US, preferably a poison indigenous to Africa.[24]

The Americans and Belgians now backed Devlin's choice of the 29-year-old Colonel Mobutu to replace Lumumba. The CIA, in order to make sure of Mobutu's loyalty, persuaded him that Lumumba was planning to kill him and only the CIA could guarantee his survival. On September 14th, ignoring a vote by the Congolese Senate endorsing Lumumba by a 41 to 2 majority, Mobutu tried to stage a coup and to close the Soviet Embassy but was unsuccessful. Lumumba was prevented from immediately punishing Mobutu for this treachery by the troops the US had armed and equipped for Mobutu.

Lumumba's public support had to be undermined. A propaganda war was launched against Lumumba. One slogan read, "For Lumumba, thousands of diamonds. For our women, millions of tears." It seemingly had little effect. He retained much popular support.

In the meantime, the UN, invited into the Congo by Lumumba, proceeded to betray him. On September 7th, 1960 a Belgian Sabena aircraft filled with nine tons of weapons landed in Katanga[25] while at the same time the UN did everything it could to prevent Lumumba getting arms or fuel for his planes.

In the same month, CIA poisons expert Dr. Gottlieb arrived from the US with the virus chosen to kill Lumumba without creating any suspicion of foul play. Wittman, Tempelsman's Congo representative, also arrived in the Congo about this time, for it was a few days after Wittman's arrival that Devlin met with Dr. Gottlieb to discuss how the virus could be administered. When Justin O'Donnell, a Senior CIA Case Officer, also arrived to join Devlin in the assassination attempt, he was shown the "virus" in the station refrigerator and later commented, "I knew it was not for someone to get his polio shot up to date."

But Devlin could find no one on Lumumba's staff willing to put the virus into Lumumba's food or toothpaste so, in frustration, it was eventually dumped into the Congo River. Devlin then requested by cable a "HIGH POWER FOREIGN MADE RIFLE WITH TELESCOPIC SCOPE AND SILENCER" be sent to him via the diplomatic bag from the US.[26] He also located a suitable place to ambush Lumumba. O'Donnell rented "an observation post overlooking Lumumba's palace," but no opportunity presented itself that would not have betrayed the hand of the CIA.

There is no evidence among the declassified papers available to me that Tempelsman's office played a part in planning Lumumba's murder. However, there was no doubt about whom it supported in the Congo. Marc Garsin, who represented Tempelsman's diamond business in the Congo in 1963 and from 1965 to 1972, told my associate producer John Kelly in an interview, "We were pro-Mobutu from the beginning. Lumumba and the others were jokers. Mobutu was the only solution at the time."[27] A "leading US diplomat" allegedly told historian Richard Mahoney that Tempelsman was working "hand-in-glove" with the CIA station in the Congo and that Wittman was "an unfrocked agent."[28] Tempelsman's later recruitment of Devlin to be his principal local representative indicated at the very least that Tempelsman did not strongly disapprove of Devlin's role in planning the assassination of Lumumba.

Instead Tempelsman used the relationship between Mobutu and Devlin to strengthen his Congo business.[29]

But while the CIA and Belgians were conspiring, crowds in Leopoldville were cheering Lumumba, fighting to touch him, calling him their "savior." This was in October 1960 – a month after Wittman arrived in the Congo. This was the same month when UN Secretary-General Dag Hammarskjold asked all the Belgian nationals to withdraw from the Congo. At that moment it seemed publicly as if both the Belgians and Mobutu were on the way out. The British government now officially recognized that Lumumba remained the legitimate elected authority.

This was not however a situation the British and Americans had wanted. When the British Foreign Secretary Lord Home met with the US President, Dwight Eisenhower, on September 19th, 1960, Eisenhower "expressed his wish that Lumumba would fall into a river full of crocodiles." A week later, when the British Prime Minister Harold Macmillan and Lord Home met the US President, the minutes record that Lord Home, "raised the question why we had not got rid of Lumumba at the present time. If he came back into power there would be immediate stress on the Katangan issue, which would get us into all sorts of legalistic difficulties. He stressed now was the time to get rid of Lumumba."[30]

A month later, the US selected Cyrille Adoula as its choice for a replacement prime minister since he was "favorably known to the US embassy staff." It did not matter to the US that Lumumba was the elected Prime Minister recognized by the British.

A coup was soon underway. Mobutu gave his military forces directions to support Adoula. President Joseph Kasa Vubu, allegedly after receiving payment from the CIA,[31] declared on the radio that he was replacing Lumumba with Adoula as Prime Minister. But the Congo Parliament refused to endorse the President's action, making invalid Adoula's appointment as Prime Minister since the Congo's constitution stipulated that new Prime Ministers must be ratified by parliament. It instead demanded that Lumumba be restored to his elected position. But Mobutu then used his troops and the parliament was suspended.

On November 9th, Wittman's advice to Tempelsman seemingly had little to do with their diamond business. "The main and ultimate strength of Adoula has been the position maintained by General Mobutu [but]… Mobutu's control over the army is now being severely questioned… The decisive element in this will be a determination whether (1) Mobutu still maintains adequate control over the army units… and (2) if he does, will he act to prevent the assumption of Government leadership by parliamentary or non-parliamentary means by leftists such as Gbenye."[32]

THE US AND BELGIAN ROLE IN THE MURDER OF LUMUMBA
Why was the United States so determined to kill Lumumba? A State Department report shed some light:

The Mobutu soldiers seemed to have no fight in them… The anti-Lumumba forces were opposed to the idea of reconvening Parliament, and our best-qualified observers confirmed that they had good reason to be afraid. The idea of new elections was thought unthinkable for the same reason: and that reason was, essentially, Lumumba. Even in jail in Katanga, that charismatic leader was the largest single factor in Congolese politics. Everyone agreed that even if his enemies were to unite, Lumumba would probably sway over Parliament again if he were allowed to address that body. So Parliament, whose approval was required to give any government legitimacy, was to remain closed. This was a highly embarrassing position for the US, as a democratic country, to be supporting. But it was felt that we had no other choice… the murder of Lumumba was… a perfectly logical distasteful political event.[33]

This document was of course classified "Secret." It was dated the same month, November 1960, in which Larry Devlin was made Head of the CIA in the Congo.[34] Some thirty years later Devlin would confide that he did not think Lumumba was a communist but that "he naively thought he could use the Commies."[35]

Other CIA agents were recruited into the Devlin assassination team. One was code-named QJ/WIN "a foreign citizen with a criminal background." According to Richard Moloney, his real name was Mozes Maschkivitzan and he was a Belgian. It is possible that his appointment was a joint Belgian-American initiative[36] since Belgium was conspiring with the US to assassinate Lumumba. The Belgians named this "Operation Barracuda."[37]

Another CIA agent was WI/Rogue, "a forger and a former bank robber" who planned an "execution squad." The CIA provided WI/Rogue with plastic surgery and a toupee to hide his identity. CIA's Africa division recommended him as a man who "can rationalize all actions." His particular job was to neutralize Lumumba supporters in the north of the Congo.

It was not long after this that Lumumba was seized and thrown into prison by the plotters. He was brutally tortured. The final act came on January 17th, 1961 when

the Leopoldville authorities placed, "Lumumba and two of his leading supporters aboard an aeroplane bound officially for Bakwana." Other supporters of Lumumba had been "killed there in horrible circumstances… the place was known as the 'slaughterhouse.' "[38]

Lumumba left a final testimony in a letter to his wife, Pauline Opango, written just before he was put onto the plane. "Neither brutal assaults, nor cruel mistreatment, nor torture have ever led me to beg for mercy, for I prefer to die with my head held high, unshakeable faith and the greatest confidence in

Lumumba under arrest.

the destiny of my country rather than live in slavery and contempt for sacred principles … Africa will write its own history, and both north and south of the Sahara it will be a history full of glory and dignity."[39]

But the people planning his death tried to demonize Lumumba, referring to him as "Satan." The plane took him to Katanga and, after further torture, Lumumba was killed on January 17th, 1961 with the complicity of Belgian officials, of the President of Katanga, Moïse Tshombe, and of the CIA. A CIA officer drove around with Lumumba's body in his car's trunk until a way was found to dispose of it, according to the report of the Senate Intelligence Committee and John Stockwell, a former CIA chief in Angola.[40] According to Belgian records,

Lumumba's corpse was finally put on a truck and taken to a place where it could be cut up and dissolved in acid.

Paul Sakwa, a former CIA agent, told me he later heard Devlin boasting of his role in Lumumba's death.[41] Other reports said "Congolese working for the CIA" carried out the murder.[42] Devlin's former colleague, John Stockwell, reported that Larry Devlin was responsible for the subsequent rise of Mobutu. Devlin "shuffled new governments like cards but finally settled on Mobutu."[43]

This claim that Americans selected the replacement government for the Congo needs to be placed alongside valuable research by Ludo De Witte, published in 2001 in *The Assassination of Lumumba*. He claimed that Belgium bore the prime responsibility for the murder of Lumumba. He particularly documented the role played by the Belgian advisors to Mobutu and others in his faction. His claim caused a sensation in Belgium and brought about a Parliamentary Inquiry.

But this was because he drew on unpublished Belgian documents rather than American. He added a preface to the later English edition of his book that acknowledged: "Other parties were equally guilty. True, the Belgians and the Congolese actually killed Lumumba, but without the steps taken by Washington and the UN during the preceding months, the assassination could not have taken place."

My own sources were mostly American government papers. They revealed there was a far more active American role than previously recorded.

The Belgian parliamentary inquiry into the circumstances of Lumumba's death reported, on November 16th, 2001 that Belgian officers had watched while Katangan police officers killed Lumumba. It further noted that the plane that took Lumumba to his death belonged to the Belgian Sabena Airline and that the Belgian King Baudouin knew of his murder. The inquiry concluded that Belgian government ministers bore "moral responsibility" for Lumumba's murder.[44]

Lumumba's murder occurred three days before President John F. Kennedy's inauguration. This timing suggests that the CIA feared Kennedy might withdraw the Presidential authorization for the murder, and become instead a champion of African freedom. His first Foreign Relations speech in the Senate in 1957 called for the independence of Algeria. On December 12th, 1960, while he was president-elect, his brother Edward, and two leading Democrats, Al Gore and Frank Church, met with President Nkrumah and gave strong public support to "the freedom of political prisoners in the Congo" – which notably included Lumumba. Kennedy's newly appointed Assistant Secretary of State, Governor G. Mennen Williams, warned a Belgian diplomat only two days before Kennedy's inauguration that no harm must come to Lumumba. He was too late. Lumumba had been murdered the day before.

THE DIAMOND DEAL AND THE CONGO COUP

While the assassins were plotting, Tempelsman had been carefully preparing a new diamond barter deal that would quietly finance those who would seize power. It was clearly organized in advance, for once Lumumba's death was confirmed, Governor A. Moeller de Ladersous, a director of the Diamond Syndicate Company Beceka, wasted no time in announcing Belgian support for Tempelsman's diamond deal. (I could find no evidence that this deal was ever offered to Lumumba.)

Adoula quickly and energetically also endorsed the Tempelsman deal as "Prime Minister," although he was still not endorsed by Parliament as the Constitution required. He personally cabled President Kennedy to announce his support for the Tempelsman scheme. His sudden enthusiasm caught the White House off-guard. Tempelsman had only just lodged this barter proposal for approval by the US Department of Agriculture. The American historian Richard Mahoney investigated the reason for this sudden enthusiasm for Tempelsman's deal and alleged that the "diplomats and observers he had interviewed stated that Tempelsman was paying off Adoula's ministers and certain parliamentarians" as well as "working hand-in-glove with the CIA station."[45]

The Belgians, who first picked Tempelsman to be their unofficial representative in diamond barter deals, were still very supportive of him. He wrote, "Governor Moeller de Ladersous has frequently offered to assist us in carrying out the expenses of the operation... but I have consistently refused to let him do this as I felt this would possibly expose us to criticism by the Congolese as being the 'stooges' of the Belgians."[46]

But Tempelsman found he had a major problem in Washington. The custodians of the US diamond stockpile still maintained that they had too many diamonds and did not want any more.[47]

So Adlai Stevenson came to his assistance. He was now US ambassador to the UN, a Cabinet rank. He wrote to Tempelsman on August 7th, 1961, saying "I spoke to George Ball [Under Secretary of State] about your proposed barter... I reminded him that anything that would help the Congo economy might in the long run be a saving for us. The attitude in the Department about barter deals is, I suspect, rather negative in view of the fact that they disrupt markets of our friends and cause endless troubles with them. The Canadians on wheat are a good example."

Tempelsman lobbied, saying his diamond barter deal would be a discreet way of funding a pro-Western faction in the Congo that was supported by the CIA, namely Adoula and Mobutu. Eventually he won support from the US State Department, most likely with support from people in the CIA; "The State Department has concluded that it is in the political interest of the US to implement this project."[48]

Yet Cyrille Adoula was not yet securely in power, despite backing from Mobutu's armed forces. He had no electoral mandate – and his administration remained illegal. The Kennedy Administration then decided the "best" solution was for Adoula to head a government of reconciliation that included former supporters of Lumumba and was endorsed by Parliament. But the party Lumumba had headed would have none of this. Despite his death, it was still the only legitimate elected government in the Congo. It now looked likely to reestablish its authority by military means. Adoula remained unendorsed by Parliament and too unpopular to win any election.

Tempelsman continued to campaign for Adoula. He warned Governor Williams that, if the "Lumumbists" took over the diamond areas of Kasai, "the opportunity for the Soviet Union to entrench itself in these areas would be acute... [Soviet] control of both the mines and their output would become an established fact." Tempelsman suggested to the Kennedy administration that his barter deal could be viewed as "a tool of American diplomacy in the Congo" that "could not be said to be direct intervention by the US." He said the deal would give Adoula $54 million of American government money without this appearing to outsiders to be an American political intervention. He knew that Adoula would give him his diamond deal – and that the diamond cartel would be in severe trouble if Russia gained marketing rights to Congo's diamonds.

TEMPELSMAN AND A COUP ATTEMPT IN GHANA

As these events unfolded, the US sought to overthrow another elected African government that happened to dislike De Beers and like Lumumba – and Tempelsman's local office was clearly involved. The target was Kwame Nkrumah, the popular and renowned President of Ghana who had taken the marketing of his country's diamonds out of the control of apartheid South Africa and De Beers.

On August 8th, 1960, around the time of Lumumba's UN visit, Nkrumah made a secret formal agreement with Lumumba to form a joint federal state of Ghana and the Congo. It was to have a common currency and joint foreign affairs and defense departments. It was to be called the African Union Government and other African states were to be invited to join it "with a view to liberate the whole continent of Africa from colonialism and imperialism."[49]

Nkrumah, in the interest of evenhandedness, had sought development aid from both the West and the Soviet Union. This was enough to damn him in the eyes of the CIA. It picked a replacement for him, the former Finance Minister, Gbedemah. Plans were laid for a coup. George Ball, the Undersecretary of State, told President Kennedy there was a chance that Nkrumah would soon be overthrown and a "really solid government installed." Tempelsman's office in Accra, the capital of Ghana, would play an important role.

I discovered Tempelsman's role through declassified letters released to me by the US State Department. Among them were angry letters from George Ball of the State Department to Tempelsman, castigating him for the careless leak of the coup plans. It seems that Gbedemah was using Tempelsman's office in Accra as a means of covertly communicating with the US government, rather than using the US Embassy. Tempelsman's representative in Ghana, a Mr. Grosse, had felt able to promise him US help. When the coup was exposed, Grosse phoned Tempelsman's New York office and "spilled everything" – including the names of local CIA operatives. But the phone line was tapped by Ghanaian counter-intelligence. They thus learned the identity of the local CIA Head of Station and the role of the US – and of Maurice Tempelsman's company – in the planning of the coup.

George Ball phoned Tempelsman to coldly tell him that Grosse had been "quite indiscreet" and to ask Tempelsman to recall him.[50] Gbedemah had to flee Ghana. The head of the Africa Division at the CIA, Bronson Tweedy, reportedly slaved at his desk all that weekend trying to repair the damage.

When President Nkrumah learned of this plot, he had it investigated by the highly respected British lawyer, Godfrey Bing Q.C., who told the historian Mahoney that his report pointed the finger "at certain foreign companies," and at Tempelsman's company in particular. He confirmed: "Ghanaian security agents had Grosse's line tapped, exactly as Bundy [in the State Department] feared."[51]

But President Kennedy remained "more appreciative" of Tempelsman's role than was Ball. He said Tempelsman should not be "downgraded" – an odd thing to say about a man not officially employed by the government – for carelessly exposing a plot to overthrow a foreign government. Shortly afterwards, Kennedy approved legislation to allow diamond barter deals to be done for reasons of political advantage rather than US stockpile requirements. This was effectively a permit for Tempelsman to arrange deals intended to covertly support pro-American African politicians such as Mobutu.

I believe this was the beginning of what we now know of as "conflict diamonds" in the Congo. From now on diamonds would be extensively used to discreetly fund wars, coups, repression, and dictatorships in Africa. The result can be seen today in the Congo, Angola, Liberia and Sierra Leone.

But Maurice Tempelsman's work was not always popular in Washington. Sometimes he used his connections to initiate political deals before Washington approved of them. In November 1961 McGeorge Bundy of the White House, who monitored covert actions for President Kennedy, phoned George Ball to ask him about "this fellow Tempelsman who keeps slipping things through the back door." He was referring to Gbedemah's coup attempt. His comment suggests that Tempelsman had a larger role in this plot than has hitherto been revealed. Ball described Tempelsman as "a rather dubious fellow... smooth, softspoken... a manipulator." He added cynically that, although Tempelsman used to fund the Republican Party and was a close friend of Sherman Adams, he now "emerges as a Democrat and a great friend of the New Frontier."[52]

I asked Paul Baddo, the former Ghanaian diplomat, why would Tempelsman's staff be involved in a coup against Nkrumah? Baddo thought it was to punish him "for favoring state enterprises," such as the state's diamond marketing enterprise set up in Pra that locally replaced De Beers.

Nkrumah was eventually overthrown in a CIA sponsored coup in 1964.[53] The new government predictably gave back to De Beers the exclusive marketing contract for their diamond production.

Although Tempelsman was of a Belgian family and recruited by Belgians, his efforts in the 1960s began eventually to be regarded with deep suspicion in Belgium. Some thought he had evolved to become the stalking horse of South African and US business. It could have been Tempelsman's efforts to have Belgian diamond mine staff replaced by Oppenheimer's men in the Congo that made the Belgians see him differently.

The Belgians suspected that the latest Tempelsman deal in the Congo had received covert US support when the US simultaneously gave Mobutu the military air transport he needed to defeat the legal "Lumumbist" government. Stevenson defended Tempelsman, protesting that the timing was purely a coincidence, saying that the planes could not have been an influence as they were given when the barter deal was not yet closed. This argument was misleading. It was not for lack of Adoula's and Mobutu's approval that the barter deal was not sealed, but rather because of divisions in the US administration over whether they should buy unwanted diamonds in support of Adoula and Mobutu.

Tempelsman's deals started to come under public attack in Belgium. He wrote to Stevenson, "under the existing emotional climate, I doubt we can count solely on ... the Belgian and French papers... respect for accuracy or sense of fair play."[54] More seriously, Count Moens de Fernig of Beceka, the man who had recruited Tempelsman for the barter deals, had decided to dump him. The State Department reported in

March 1963 that Belgian diamond companies were moving away from supporting Tempelsman's diamond schemes. Moens de Fernig now said that they no longer needed Tempelsman, for they had no diamonds "which they could not sell through their regular commercial channels."

Tempelsman protested to the State Department that this "was simply not true" but the Belgians pointed out that the barter deals had been their idea, not his. They had thought they needed him. They no longer did.[55]

But it no longer mattered to the Americans if the Belgians approved or not. The White House had decided it would use diamond barter deals with the Congo to "further the economic or foreign policy interests of the United States." With Tempelsman's assistance, the US had decided to use diamonds to give covert long-term support for the corrupt regime of Mobutu, a disastrous course that would impoverish Central Africa for many decades. On February 13th, 1963, the Department of Agriculture announced that it was prepared to consider new diamond barter deals.[56] Tempelsman again submitted his proposal, backing it with heavy lobbying. "[He is] a heavy contributor in Democratic politics... [His deal] is under discussion between Orville Freeman and George Ball... Tempelsman has also interested a number of Congressmen..."[57]

But the custodians of the strategic industrial diamond stockpile did not realize what was happening. They maintained that buying more diamonds was ridiculous – whatever the President or State Department said. The US did not need more diamonds. It had too many.

DIAMONDS FOR ENRICHED URANIUM

The stockpile custodians fought a rearguard battle to stop Tempelsman and the diamond Syndicate selling them a flood of unwanted diamonds. On February 14th, 1964, G. Griffith Johnson replied to Adlai Stevenson:

The Department has... arrived at the conclusion that it would not be desirable to proceed [with the Tempelsman deal]... for a number of reasons. Perhaps most important is that at the present time it did not appear that the current monetary situation in the Congo would permit such a deal to have constructive results... Finally it should be noted that we have a very large surplus of industrial diamonds in the stockpile area, so that the diamonds we would obtain from the barter deal would be of no use to us at all. In fact it appears quite possible that we shall be pressed into engaging in a surplus disposal program in industrial diamonds in the not too distant future.

Tempelsman thus was still fighting an uphill battle trying to sell an unwilling customer something it did not want, despite the White House decision to allow diamond sales for strategic reasons. The deal was still unsigned when President John F. Kennedy was assassinated on November 22nd, 1963, so he had to renegotiate it with the office of President Lyndon B. Johnson at a time when there was increasing pressure from the anti-apartheid movement for sanctions on South Africa.

President Johnson then received a telegram from President Joseph Kasa Vubu of the Congo begging him to support Tempelsman's proposal. It was assessed by the highest intelligence body in the US, the Executive Office of the President in the National Security Council. Its report stated: "This telegram has nothing to do with

US policy in the Congo. It is simply renewed pressure by Kasa Vubu for a Tempelsman-sponsored barter deal on surplus commodities, which has been sporadically promoted over the past four years. My guess is that Kasa Vubu expects to make a little private profit on the deal: he has for a long time supported the Tempelsman proposal… I do not believe the President should get involved."

Tempelsman now modified his proposal so that it better suited current US strategic concerns, wedding these with those of the Oppenheimers. He knew the government was having difficulties organizing imports of uranium from South Africa without it appearing to the public as if it were violating the sanctions it had itself imposed on South Africa's apartheid regime. In South Africa, the mining industry was likewise hurt by these sanctions and seeking a way around them. The sanctions also caused grave concern to the South African government. It wanted to purchase enriched uranium for a nuclear reactor and for nuclear weapons.

The Executive Office of the President reported: "Tempelsman has recently revived this proposal, possibly as part of a packaged deal with a South African uranium barter." Barter would avoid using traceable funds. The controversial enriched uranium deal could be concealed if it were part of a deal for Congolese diamonds.

It was now revealed that Tempelsman did not only represent American interests. He had officially represented the South African mining industry since 1961. In December 1963, the American embassy in Pretoria sent a telegram to the Secretary of State stating that the South African government had worked "with Tempelsman as agent of the Transvaal Chamber of Mines for two years."[58]

The embassy told the State Department that, since the South African Government knew Tempelsman, it was "willing in principle to accept concept of barter and willing to negotiate at once."[59] The South Africans had prepared a pricey "shopping list." In exchange for what was evidently a large quantity of their uranium ore, they wanted civilian aircraft, perhaps Boeing 707s, "military equipment if acceptable to us," and a considerable sum in hard currency. This currency requirement posed a problem. The agricultural surpluses in the deal had to be valuable enough to be sold to a major Western country. So part of this deal became a sale of a US "surplus" of tobacco to the United Kingdom. Tobacco was thus used to quietly purchase both Mobutu's diamonds and South African uranium.

All sides recognized the need to keep these details highly secret. The cable from the American embassy said that the South African Government would complete the negotiations by means of "separate letters to us with no reference to uranium."[60] All this was being done with the knowledge of the White House. A footnote typed onto the bottom of this cable, classified "Secret," read: "Passed to White House at 12.10 p.m., 6th December 1963." Another secret State Department cable, dated December 23rd, 1964, warned about the need for secrecy over the bartered shipment of enriched uranium to South Africa because "it could outrage the moderate Africans we're trying to calm down." It said that the South African Foreign Minister Muller would probably agree to "no publicity." This cable threw light on the secret alliance behind the barter deal. It said Muller would probably understand their need for secrecy because "we are in the same boat in the Congo" and the US was "doing a job" in the Congo that South Africa couldn't do.[61] This could only have been supporting the Mobutu dictatorship.

Tempelsman's influence in the White House was so remarkable that it engendered considerable concern at the highest levels of the US State Department. Dean Rusk, the Secretary of State, could not understand how Tempelsman was so well informed. He cabled the Pretoria embassy in December 1963 warning:

Re. Tempelsman. We unaware how he informed [sic] about Washington meetings and wish emphasize again discussions are confidential and should not be discussed, even with him... We do not understand how his role in discussing deferral arrangements could be helpful since his earlier suggestions re barter alone recommended the US accept some $50m worth of uranium in addition [to the] present contract as incentive. As you know, we cannot accept any additional uranium oxide or other S.A. materials.

Finally, his close association with the gold producers committee in South Africa, in addition to the fact that he will almost certainly be one of the barter dealers in the US involved in implementing the transaction, raises questions regarding the suitability of his active participation in the negotiations. We believe it precludes his acting in an advisory capacity to the US team and should rule out his presence during negotiations with SAG. [South African Government] (Signed) RUSK

The US was still highly involved in the Congo. Alongside Belgium, it helped to arm a military operation against the Lumumba government, which in 1964 still controlled nearly 40 percent of the Congo. The operation involved some 300 Belgian officers and many mercenaries. Its victory was very savage – some 200,000 lives were lost.[62] After this further US funds were needed to support Adoula.

Tempelsman now won his battle. President Johnson gave his approval to the barter deal and the US Department of Agriculture approved it on April 13th, 1965. It officially included $27.5 million worth of diamonds, $84 million worth of agricultural surplus and the earlier contracted uranium. The quantity of uranium ore involved was not specified, and there was no mention of the enriched uranium. The Department stipulated, "no one firm [i.e. Tempelsman] can have more than half the deal." But the Department imposed an extraordinary condition: The companies involved had to be approved by the Diamond Syndicate companies in Belgium and the Congo and by the South African authorities. It should be noted that Oppenheimer's companies also mined uranium.[63]

The primary political beneficiary in the Congo was Mobutu. Six months later, he seized full power and suspended Parliament. He would remain in power for many decades, plundering his country's resources, while continuing to be financed by deals with diamond companies.

The immediate result of Tempelsman's 1965 diamond deal was that Tempelsman swapped a vast amount of American farm products, including tobacco, for hard currency, enriched uranium and cartel diamonds, to the dismay of friendly countries whose agricultural exports consequently suffered. American government vaults overflowed with the Syndicate's diamonds. South Africa got the enriched uranium it needed for nuclear weapons, despite the anti-apartheid sanctions. Tempelsman's influence over African and US politics was now established.

Was the US Government cheated?

There were serious doubts about the quality of the diamonds purchased in the barter deals. The staff supervising the sorting of the millions of diamonds in the Government's vaults suspected that many of the diamonds purchased for drills and cutting tools were actually low-grade boart, useless for these purposes and worth a third of what the Government paid.

When I researched the semi-sacrosanct archives of the *New York Times*, known affectionately as the "Morgue," looking for information on the diamond industry, I found on the final day of my search a deeply buried bundle of reports entitled "The Diamond Stockpile Swindle." These were from a security officer working in the Federal diamond stockpile in 1964.

His name was Special Agent Paul R. Gordon. He had been working for a year in the Industrial Diamond Stockpile Inventory Site leased from the First City National Bank – probably the same vaults that I had visited in 1991. His job entailed, among other things, watching the team of diamond sorters employed to check and classify the contents of all the newly arrived boxes of diamonds before they were stored.

Gordon reported: "In the course of my assignment as security officer at the project, I observed the opening of the sealed packages for the purpose of re-sorting. I discovered that a number of packages did not contain the grade or kind of diamonds as specified on the label attached to the package, and some packages did not contain diamond stones but boart." The sorters confirmed his observation. Many were indeed boart – the cheapest diamonds, so flawed that they were only useful if crushed into diamond powder. He inquired as to the price paid for this material. The captain of the sorting team, F. T. Engelhart, consulted the records and found that these cost the government $6.50 a carat. Their market value at the most was only $2.20. He concluded: "I suppose we can conjecture that they did not anticipate an examination of the stockpile until an emergency had arisen, such as a shooting war."

Following the leaking of Morgan's report, the *New York Times* noted that the FBI had investigated the charges and had verified Morgan's discovery, confirming that "there was considerable laxity in the diamond buying program and the Government probably lost some money. How much, no one could say definitely." No legal action ever resulted.[64]

US Congress protects the diamond cartel

Just one year after the uranium, tobacco and diamond deal was concluded, in 1966 Congress was asked to authorize the disposal of "the entire [diamond] stockpile excess." As part of its investigation into the influence of the diamond cartel in the United States, the US Justice Department calculated, "By the end of this year [1967] we will have about 28 million carats of industrial diamonds in our stockpiles, some eight to ten million carats more than our stockpile objectives." The stockpile also contained "well over 40 million carats of boart… about half … in excess." In short, the US stockpile had an excess of 28-30 million carats, about six tonnes of diamonds. Tempelsman had been superb as a salesman. The US now had to sell what he had sold it.

But this disposal proposal caused uproar in the American diamond industry – and great consternation in the Syndicate's office in London. De Beers had prevented the

US acquiring a diamond stockpile during the Second World War precisely because it feared the US government would do this – sell its diamonds in bulk onto the world market, thus depressing prices. These protests forced a Congressional investigation. The ensuing report stated: "Industry testimony during the hearings… opposed any such grant of authority on the basis that [the stockpile administrators]… had not yet consulted with industry on a disposal program that would not disrupt the market." So, the government agreed to form an industry task force to discuss the diamond disposal program.

According to a Justice Department attorney, Carl W. Schwarz, "This group (which included at least one man who we understand is connected with the Syndicate) decided that the US market could absorb only about 90,000 carats a year without 'disruption' [of De Beers' operations], and in view of the fact that at this rate it would take more than 90 years to sell the stockpile excess domestically, recommended that GSA [stockpile administrators] sell the diamonds back to the Syndicate." But this recommendation was unrealistic. The Syndicate had no intention of helping out the US by buying back the surplus. It has always had more diamonds than it needed. But the US government could have forced the Syndicate to buy them. The Russians had done just this when it threatened to flood the diamond market.

Schwarz noted that the Syndicate might be at some legal risk if it did buy back the diamonds: "GSA's only reason to believe that the syndicate may be interested in buying the stockpile is an 'informal' contact with Charles W. Engelhard of Engelhard-Hanover who is a substantial shareholder and director of De Beers' parent company, the Anglo American Corporation of South Africa. If GSA ultimately does sell to the syndicate and if Engelhard acts as an agent for the syndicate, we might use him as a source of jurisdiction over the syndicate for another antitrust suit."

But the diamond lobby was successful. Congress blocked the bulk sale of the diamond surplus and stipulated instead a rate of sale that wouldn't upset the diamond Syndicate's price controlling mechanism – despite this mechanism being illegal in the US. The government agreed not to release more than 90,000 carats a year onto the diamond market for the next 20 years. In 1997, after 20 years at this rate, the US would still have a surplus of 6-7 million diamonds.

Schwarz reported in 1967: "GSA recently took bids (for the second time) on the first 90,000 carats of the stockpile excess. Only 4 companies submitted bids at all, and on most of the 78 lots there was only one bid… All bids were rejected (for not offering enough)." He also noted, "the tool making industry is … scared stiff that the syndicate or dealers would summarily cut off their supplies for buying outside of channels… If the GSA did sell to De Beers I would be surprised to see the Syndicate pay anywhere near $13 a carat."[65]

He was proven correct. When De Beers decided to bid for all the better stones, the seven million carats of the "tool" stones that could be cut as gems, it offered not the $106 to $130 million that the administration expected, but only $15 million – about $2 a carat, less than the price paid on the open market for the lowest quality boart.

This proposed deal outraged the Justice Department so in 1968 it went to the White House. Wilbur L. Fulgate explained why: "The result is that De Beers, for the sum of $15 million dollars, will be able to neutralize the effect of the stockpile for five years and establish a pattern for obtaining the remainder. The commitment by the

United States not to sell any more of the stockpile would be for the very purpose of protecting the monopoly of the diamond syndicate. This commitment, together with the involvement of Engelhard Industries, might make it more difficult for us to bring an antitrust suit against the syndicate."

In the 1980s, the US continued to sell off its surplus stockpiled diamonds gradually, at around 1.5 million diamonds a year for between $3.62 and $14.89 a carat. In 1997, when I last checked, the US government was still selling off this legacy from Maurice Tempelsman slowly, so as not to upset De Beers.

While I was in the diamond vaults there were also two Indian merchants present. They were examining the "industrial diamonds" the government had to sell. They were interested principally in those with few flaws that could be easily cut as gems. If sold as tool stones, they could supply the world's needs for eight years. But if resold as gems, the Indians knew they would attract far higher prices than the average government price of $13 a carat. However, this potential bonanza was not to be. Someone soon persuaded the Indian government to ban the imports of these diamonds on the grounds that they would disturb the market. They were to be left for De Beers.

Tempelsman's operations in Africa and his American deals were clearly unusual for a diamond merchant, but this was how America's most formidable diamond merchant established his family's fortune, swamping the American diamond stockpile. For over 40 years he would continue as a discreet diamond dealer for the Oppenheimers, serving their interests even in Nelson Mandela's post-apartheid South Africa, and with UNITA in Angola.

1   Department of Justice Memo to files, Richard L. Daerr, Jr., September 12th, 1974.
2   William T. Jeter to Marcus Hollabaugh. US Government Office Memorandum, May 24th, 1951.
3   Department of State *Proposed Exploitation of Diamond Deposits in the Congo Basin.* March 25th, 1947.
4   State Department cable, March 6th, 1963 – author unknown.
5   Executive Office of the President, Office of Defense Mobilization, paper on "Barter of Agricultural Surpluses for Industrial Diamonds," March 12th, 1954.
6   Ibid.
7   Adlai Stevenson, letter to Tempelsman, January 4th, 1962. State Department Files.
8   Adlai Stevenson, letter to Tempelsman, August 12th, 1960. State Department Files.
9   Richard L. Daerr, Jr. Memo to Files September 12th, 1974, Dept. of Justice. The name of the informant is redacted.
10 Koskoff, p. 143.
11 Richard D. Mahoney. *The Kennedy Policy in the Congo. 1961-1963*, Dissertation; John Hopkins University School of Advanced International Studies, 1979, p 261.
12 Ludo De Witte. *The Assassination of Lumumba*, New York; Verso Books, 2001, p. 12.
13 De Witte, p. 32.
14 De Witte, p. 2.
15 Steven Weissman "The CIA and US Policy in Zaire and Angola" in *Dirty Work 2. The CIA in Africa*. Publ. Lyle Stuart, Secaucus, New Jersey. 1979, p. 185.
16 Congolese Government cable to UN, quoted in De Witte p. 8.
17 Adlai Stevenson, letter to Patrice Lumumba, Prime Minister, Republic of Congo, July 1960.
18 Adlai Stevenson, letter to Tempelsman at the Carlton Hotel, Johannesburg, August 25th, 1960.
19 Interview with author, 1991.
20 Adlai E. Stevenson to Sture Linner, September 15th, 1960. State Department.
21 Crawford Young and Thomas Turner. *The Rise and Fall of the Zairian State*. Madison, WI: Univ. Wis. Press, 1985, p. 176.
22 "Alleged Assassination Plots Involving Foreign Leaders." An Interim Report of the Select Committee to Study Governmental Operations with respect to Intelligence Activities, United States Senate 1975. (Hereafter called Senate Intelligence Committee Report.)

23 Senate Select Intelligence Committee Report (Church Committee), Assassination Plots pp. 60, 15.
24 Dr. Sydney Gottlieb headed the CIA Chemical Department. For further details see Wayne Madsen's *Genocide and Covert Operations in Africa 1993-99.* pp. 163-4
25 De Witte, p. 21.
26 Senate Intelligence Committee Report, p. 32.
27 Interview with Marc Garsin March 13th, 1992 by John Kelly for *The Diamond Empire.*
28 The historian, Richard D. Mahoney was reported to be the son of a US diplomat stationed in Ghana in the 1960s. His book was entitled *Sons and Brothers.*
29 Church Commission Report.
30 De Witte, p. xvi.
31 Stephen Weissman, "The CIA and US Policy in Zaire and Angola" p. 186.
32 Memo. from George H. Wittman to Maurice Tempelsman, November 9th, 1960. A typing error by Wittman or his secretary misdated this letter as written in 1961, not 1960.
33 Church Commission, p. 5.
34 Ellen Ray, William Schaap, Karl van Meter and Louis Wolf. *Dirty Work 2. The CIA in Africa.* Publ. Lyle Stuart, Secaucus, New Jersey. 1979, p. 349.
35 Shoumatoff, "Lumumba: Not for want of trying." *Newsweek* December 1st, 1973, p. 31
36 De Witte, p. 186.
37 De Witte, p. 24.
38 UN Report, November 11th, 1961, p 109.
39 The entire letter is quoted De Witte, pp. 184-5.
40 John Stockwell, head of CIA Angolan Mission, learned of this from the driver of this car. He knew the driver as a CIA officer who had trained him. See his *In Search Of Enemies*, New York: WW Norton, 1978. De Witte made no reference to this evidence of CIA involvement.
41 Personal communication to author, November 1995.
42 Ellen Ray, William Schaap, Karl Van Meter, Louis Wolf, p. 350.
43 Stockwell, p. 136.
44 Ian Black, "Belgium Blamed For Icon's Murder." *The Guardian.* November 17th, 2001.
45 Mahoney, p. 264.
46 Letter from Maurice Tempelsman to Governor Adlai Stevenson, November 15th, 1961.
47 The Supplementary Advisory Committee on Barter reported in its minutes: "After several meetings during October-November 1961, it was the 'consensus of opinion' that the proposal should not be accepted at that time."
48 State Department memo headed "Congo Diamond Deal 2 August 1961."
49 Kwame Nkrumah *Challenge of the Congo: A Case Study of Foreign Pressures in an Independent State.* London: Panaf Books, 1967, pp. 30-31.
50 Telephone conversation, Ball to Tempelsman, September 29th, 1961.
51 Mahoney's sources for this were Memorandum for the President. W. W. Rostow, September 24th, 1961. Weekend reading papers to Hyannis Port. Telephone conversations Ball to Bundy, Ball to Fredericks, Ball to Tempelsman September 24th, 1961, letter Geoffrey Bing to Mahoney, March 4th, 1977.
52 Telephone conversation: Ball to Bundy. November 4th, 1961.
53 Seymour Hersh, "CIA said to have aided plotters who overthrew Nkrumah in Ghana" in *Dirty Work 2*, 1979. Also John Stockwell's *In Search of Enemies.*
54 Memo Tempelsman to Stevenson, January 9th, 1963.
55 The evidence for this was in a State Department cable. "Moens de Fernig had himself taken the initiative of bringing Tempelsman into the picture and urging the latter to investigate the possibilities of a . . . barter deal with the US." State Department Memo, March 6th, 1963 – author unknown.
56 Mahoney, footnote 53.
57 Bill Brubeck to Mr. Valenti, Executive Office of the President, National Security Council, December 5th, 1964.
58 Satterthwaite to Secretary of State, December 6th, 1963, Incoming Telegram. State Department files.
59 Ibid.
60 Ibid.
61 RWK to Mac, cc Chuck Johnson, State Department, Lyndon Johnson Library. December 23rd, 1964.
62 De Witte, p. 164.
63 State cable to American embassy in Pretoria, December 23rd, 1963, State Department files.
64 Note by the "City Desk" of the *New York Times* dated April 28th,1964.
65 Report on Stockpile Disposal. By Carl W. Schwarz, Justice Department, to Wilbur L. Fulgate on September 12th, 1967. Justice Department files.

Chapter 11 – The most powerful of diamond merchants

Maurice Tempelsman's barter deals, swapping surplus farm products for diamonds, explained how he became a millionaire and a supporter of Mobutu, but not how he also became a valued friend of the White House under the Kennedys and Presidents Johnson and Clinton as well as a companion of Jackie Onassis. This was a story that might seem appropriate for a James Bond movie – although it had consequences that were not at all happy.

Secret US government memos, cables and letters, and my interviews in Africa and the US, revealed Maurice Tempelsman to be much more than a trader of crystals. This somewhat stout, balding diamond merchant headed a small private diamond company that was so staffed with former American spies that it could be mistaken for an intelligence network. Why had he picked men with such talents? Did he need them in order to help protect the diamond cartel and the Oppenheimers who controlled it?

I first suspected what lay behind his cloak when State Department documents revealed that his diamond company's office in Ghana had contact with the plotters of the coup attempt against Ghana's first elected leader.[1] Tempelsman's role as a diamond merchant did not explain why this should be so nor why President John F. Kennedy said he would not "downgrade" him when that plot misfired.

Tempelsman has long had great influence in matters affecting America's foreign policy. For example: in 1994, nearly 40 years later, Tempelsman's private diamond business was able to offer the Russian government $4 billion of US government funds – coincidentally or not, just a few weeks after he had hosted President Clinton on his yacht.

Tempelsman's ready access to the White House was put to use by Oppenheimer back in 1966 when he feared that his companies might lose access to electricity generated by the Kariba dam after Ian Smith refused to yield Rhodesia (now Zimbabwe) to black majority rule. Tempelsman wrote to President Johnson on March 8th, 1966, "I have had occasion to discuss the Rhodesian situation with Mr. Harry Oppenheimer whom you met last year (1965) when he was in the United States." Tempelsman suggested that "this hostage [the dam]" be removed "from control of this or a successor Rhodesian government" by means of a British or UN military take-over of the dam to ensure it continued to serve South African interests. "This could be achieved either through direct British control of the installation or possibly through UN participation."

But the Congo remained the major focus of Tempelsman's African operations during the 1960s. He supported Adoula and Mobutu with diamond barter deals despite US Ambassador Edmund Gullion called the Adoula-Mobutu clique "obscurantist, arbitrary, primitive, totalitarian, willful and irresponsible."[2]

In October 1965, when President Kasa Vubu sought to appoint a more neutral government than that of Adoula, the CIA backed a successful coup by Mobutu who then named himself President. Mobutu consequently expressed his gratitude to Devlin[3] for helping him win this prize.

Marc Garsin, who was Tempelsman's Congo representative from 1963 to 1972, told us, "There was me, Larry Devlin, Hank Cohen [State Department diplomat] and it was a fantastic time… I met regularly with Larry Devlin in Zaire [the Congo] and knew he was CIA."[4] Mobutu was delighted with his American support team. His subsequent actions showed he believed the Americans were so committed to supporting him that they would not oppose him enriching himself by expropriating Belgian mining interests.

Tempelsman and Mobutu

Pierre Davister, an influential Belgian journalist and consultant, alleged: "Tempelsman was involved in the United States' political manipulations in the Congo."[5] Garsin confirmed this. He told us that he and Tempelsman sought "to prove to Mobutu that the Belgians were screwing him and that the Americans offered the best deal… For instance, [we let him know that] the copper the Belgians took out of the Congo also contained gold and silver which the Belgians extracted in Belgium where they refined the copper – and they never told the Congolese."

Soon after Mobutu seized power, Tempelsman went for marketing control over the Congo's copper, proposing a deal that encouraged Mobutu to seize the Belgian interests. "Tempelsman gave Mobutu a proposal for government control of copper marketing and offered himself as manager of the new enterprise [in 1966] … shortly before Mobutu seized Union Miniere of Haut Katanga [UMHK]."[6] Mobutu then seized Belgian owned assets worth some $800 million and gave the revenues from these to his friends, associates and relatives.[7]

Immediately after this, Tempelsman flew into Kinshasa (the new name assigned by Mobutu to Leopoldville), met with Mobutu and offered to give him the staff to run the seized mines. He told him they would be provided by Oppenheimer. He then flew to Johannesburg, discussed these plans with Harry Oppenheimer, and returned to Kinshasa.

These moves made the Belgians gasp. The US State Department also felt very uncomfortable. It feared Mobutu's action might encourage others to nationalize Western holdings. It thus asked Tempelsman to try to bring about a compromise. Tempelsman responded by instead trying to gain support for Mobutu's seizure. The US Embassy reported that "Tempelsman raised suggestion that UMHK [Union Miniere's mining group in Katanga] might have provoked Mobutu into the seizure" by encouraging the secession of Katanga.

Since Mobutu had not offered any compensation, the directors of Union Miniere, UMHK's parent company, said they would seize Katanga's previous year's mineral revenues and confiscate the 15 percent equity the Congo state owned in its Belgian operations. Tempelsman immediately advised Mobutu to take the Belgians to court for stealing this equity and revenue. Mobutu agreed. But Tempelsman was being somewhat devious, according to the US embassy. It reported that, "the gist of the approach is to convince Mobutu that he now has a legal case against the Belgians, not to have the Belgians taken to court, but to provide a way of putting Tempelsman's lawyers in control of the dispute."

Tempelsman's plan succeeded. Mobutu agreed to hire Tempelsman's own lawyer, Theodore Sorensen, to act for him against Union Miniere. From now on the Belgians were negotiating with Tempelsman rather than with Mobutu. The State Department was delighted with the success of this strategy, dubbing it the "Tempelsman Plan." Mobutu now had three Americans as his key advisors: Devlin, Sorensen and Tempelsman – with a fourth, Garsin, acting as a backup for Tempelsman.

Mobutu was very grateful to Tempelsman for helping him enrich his family with the vast assets formerly owned by Belgium. On Christmas Day 1966 he phoned Tempelsman to tell him that he was being given as a "Christmas present" the rights to one of the world's richest copper deposits. Tempelsman immediately put together a consortium to exploit this that included Oppenheimer's Anglo American, Standard Oil of Indiana, Mitsui Industries and an unnamed French government corporation, but eventually this venture was abandoned.

The State Department reported on January 15th, 1967, that, "Tempelsman is playing an increasingly central role as GDRC [Government of the Democratic Republic of the Congo] technical advisor and mediator [the rest of this paragraph was censored]." Tempelsman also considered offering Robert MacNamara, the president of the World Bank, as a mediator to Mobutu, but dropped this plan when it was not needed. But MacNamara still informally joined the Tempelsman team. Garsin told us that, "during the struggle with the Belgians, Robert MacNamara assisted Tempelsman's lawyer, Ted Sorensen, because they were close friends. MacNamara did not do this in his official capacity." The American State Department did its best to stop the Belgians countering the Tempelsman strategy. A US diplomat reported how he had calmed the fears of Mayer, the Washington representative of Société Générale: "I was disturbed to learn that some circles in Belgium seemed to think the US Government was now busily helping the Congolese set up separate marketing arrangements and I could assure him that this was not so." He smoothly assured the Belgians that Tempelsman was trying to protect Belgian interests: "It was my understanding that [Tempelsman] was trying hard to heal the breach [between the Belgians and Mobutu]. Privately I could tell him that I understood he had been talking so sternly to the [Congolese] leaders that they even suspected him of being a UMHK (Union Miniere) agent."

These soothing words were intended to prevent Société Générale from making problems for the "Tempelsman plan" before it was finalized. "I cautioned… that damage could be done to Tempelsman's efforts at conciliation if there were publicity about his visit. Mr. Mayer assured me that he would not be talking to the press about the problem in general or about Tempelsman." Tempelsman now had free rein. He moved quickly to bring in Harry Oppenheimer as an advisor to Mobutu.

Tempelsman wired his employee in New York, Pendleton, in code – his office had learned its lesson after the Nkrumah coup fiasco – ordering him to tell Oppenheimer to expect Mobutu to invite him to Kinshasa. Tempelsman also instructed him to tell the US State Department that Mobutu would be inviting "Harry O" to Kinshasa. In all these developments, the White House was kept fully informed. Tempelsman copied all telexes to them.[8]

Ted Sorensen then worked out the "text of the draft [Mobutu] ordinance on compensation."[9] Blake, a US diplomat in the Congo, enthused about this to Washington, saying Tempelsman had "unselfishly" negotiated a package that gave the Belgians an even better return from Congo copper and other metals than they had before, even keeping them in place as mine managers. He said Tempelsman had acted entirely without thinking of his own and Oppenheimer's financial interests.

At first sight this seemed true. Under his plan, the Congo kept the ownership of its minerals and the mineral concessions but Union Miniere retained management. The Congolese government would pay Union Miniere a management fee of 6.5 percent of total mine revenues – more than the Belgians' previous official profit margin. The Belgians were guaranteed this return – even if the mines made no profits. On the face of it, this was a good deal for the Belgians and a poor deal for the Congo, so it was surprising that Mobutu agreed.

But, off the record, there was allegedly a private kick-back arrangement for Mobutu that kept him very happy. Pierre Davister, who later became a top Mobutu consultant, alleged the private arrangement was that Union Miniere would "give him [Mobutu] part of their royalties and these were to go into Mobutu's personal fortune." Mobutu also would receive his choice in gems from his country's diamond production.

The US diplomat Blake had been completely fooled into saying that the Oppenheimers would receive no benefit from Tempelsman's deal. The small print said Oppenheimer's company Britmond was to market all the Congo's diamond output and be paid for this 25 percent of the gross revenues of the diamond mines – more than current total net profits! The Belgians had been charging a "mine management fee" that was only a quarter of this.

Marc Garsin, Tempelsman representative in Kinshasa, boasted in a 1991 interview for *The Diamond Empire* that he and Tempelsman "assisted Harry Oppenheimer in getting back into the Congo." He proudly claimed, "I was instrumental in the return of Oppenheimer to the Congo and took care of Britmond [Oppenheimer's company]. I'm sure Tempelsman got something for that. Since that time, Tempelsman, and now his representative Jerry Funk, represented Britmond before Mobutu." Jerry Funk became Tempelsman's representative in Zaire about 1988. He was a former member of the US National Security Council, the body that supervises the CIA.

Tempelsman did more for the Oppenheimers. He agreed to police the diamond mining operations in the Congo and to check the government's production reports. The settlement terms included: "A Tempelsman sponsored control organization will make sample checks of MIBA exports to insure the company's compliance and accuracy of state declarations. Further control will be carried out on a spot basis at London [by the Oppenheimer companies]." He would naturally take a fee for this.

Tempelsman also took on the extra responsibility of buying diamonds in the field to combat the "illegal" sale of diamonds. This enabled him to gather intelligence in the remoter diamond fields. According to a US State Department memo of June 7th, 1967, "Tempelsman will establish buying offices in Kinshasa, Takikapa and Bakvanga. Since it is highly dangerous for the diggers to transport their diamonds even short distances, the purchasing offices may well need helicopters and other transportation equipment to go to digging sites."[10]

Mobutu also rewarded Tempelsman by giving him valuable diamond prospecting rights in the diamond-rich Kasai province. Mobutu also showed his appreciation for the US government's help when Vice President Humphrey visited Zaire in 1968. Mobutu gave Humphrey's wife a diamond estimated to be worth $100,000. Six years later, embarrassed by adverse publicity, Humphrey handed this over to the White House Protocol Office. It is now enshrined in the Smithsonian Institute in Washington.

Mobutu's rise from a salaried army officer in 1965 to becoming one of the world's richest men by the 1980s was largely attributed by the *Washington Post* to his personal control over his country's diamonds.[11] He had his staff select the finest diamonds from the mine's daily production for his personal benefit. It is difficult to believe that he could have done this without the diamond Syndicate's knowledge and tacit concurrence, especially with Tempelsman officially monitoring the production, with the mines still managed by Belgian members of the Syndicate, and with Oppenheimer's men checking the diamonds as they arrived in Europe.

Mobutu spent decades enriching himself with his country's resources. A 1980 Zairian National Assembly report stated Mobutu had transferred nearly $4 billion to overseas bank accounts belonging to himself and his family between 1977 and 1979. This was on top of whatever was paid by Belgian companies into his overseas accounts and in addition to the cobalt and diamonds Mobutu secretly exported and sold for his private gain.

The same report listed two transfers of 36.9 million Belgian Francs and nine transfers of 18.8 million Belgian Francs into Mobutu's own accounts and an "au porteur" account of a million US dollars. (An "au porteur" account can be drawn on by anyone holding the deposit certificate without any other identification.) His family members also received 15 million Swiss Francs and 14.1 million Belgian Francs in 1978. This was impoverishing his country, which had the lowest wages in independent Africa. It was practically impossible for any ordinary family to survive on an official income. Government officials received so little pay (it had declined by 1980 to less than 10 percent of the 1960 rate in real terms[12]) that they had, in effect, to impose their own taxes by unofficially imposing fees or "bribes."

CIA CHIEF JOINS DIAMOND TRADE

Tempelsman lost the help of Larry Devlin between 1968 and 1972 while Devlin was in Laos supervising controversial CIA paramilitary operations. But in 1972 Devlin was promoted to be the Head of the African Division of the CIA[13] and returned to what was now "Zaire" – the new name given to the Congo by Mobutu in 1971.

After two years in this job, Devlin quit to take up a four-year contract as Tempelsman's new representative in Zaire, although he had never been trained in the diamond industry. Garsin told us: "In 1974 I was kicked out of Zaire and I hired Devlin to replace me. He's done a great job and knows everyone." Devlin was quite a catch. The *New York Times* reported that "Larry Devlin had better access to Mobutu than the American government."[14]

In practice, the nature of Devlin's work had not entirely changed when he joined Tempelsman's staff. John Stockwell, a CIA colleague who worked in Zaire in 1975, reported, "Devlin continued to do work for the CIA while working for Tempelsman." Allegedly, he retained a "key operational role in the CIA's station."[15]

Stephen Cohen, Deputy Assistant Secretary of State, told us in an 1991 interview for *The Diamond Empire* that State Department officials believed that Devlin, even while employed by Tempelsman, "functioned as the true representative of the US Government in President Mobutu's eyes" and had retained an official covert role. "It was commonly believed by the State Department officers in Zaire that Devlin had complete access to classified [US] government files after he left the government." Another State Department official said Devlin was extremely influential: "Devlin's strategic relationship with the President helped on occasion to undercut US foreign policy directives."

While contracted to Tempelsman, Devlin allegedly also worked for a company called "Cainves-Zaire," headquartered in the same Kinshasa Texaco office building that housed Tempelsman's office and the local offices of the CIA – then also managing US support for UNITA in Angola. Whether Cainves-Zaire was a Tempelsman company or a CIA front is not known – but Devlin was allegedly still with them in 1979.[16] Devlin stayed in Tempelsman's service from 1974 until 1988, retaining throughout this period a close relationship with Mobutu.

This relationship survived a major rupture between the Americans and Mobutu Sese Seko; Mobutu expelled the US Ambassador and arrested most of the CIA's Zairian agents in 1975, charging that they were trying to overthrow his government. John Stockwell, a CIA officer in Zaire, claimed that Mobutu was seeking a scapegoat he could blame for his country's economic woes.[17]

Tempelsman also tried to recruit John Stockwell when he resigned as the head of the CIA Angolan Task Force. Stockwell turned his offer down – but Tempelsman succeeded in recruiting Colonel John Gerassi, the former head of the American Military Mission to Zaire, as an assistant for Devlin. Tempelsman was clearly gathering to himself considerable intelligence and military expertise.

President Mobutu came to Washington about the time Devlin and Gerassi joined Tempelsman's staff. He was the first black African leader to be entertained by President Nixon. Tempelsman reportedly acted as an unofficial "greeter'" for the US government, lavishly entertaining Mobutu on his yacht in Washington.[18] Tempelsman then became New York's Honorary Consul for Zaire.

Tempelsman also increased his influence by employing a company with close contacts with the Belgian government. On April 12, 1979, he wrote to Mme. Simonet-Angenent, the wife of Belgium's Foreign Minister Henri Simonet, at her company, S.A. Sivanco, saying it was a "great pleasure seeing you again during your visit to New York last week. I wish to confirm that we will retain the consulting services of Sivanco at a fee of $20,000 per annum." He said further fees would come later.

ZAIRE BREAKS WITH DIAMOND CARTEL

By the late 1970s, the relationship between De Beers and the Mobutu government was in severe trouble. In 1979 Citoyen Kakusa, the Director General of Sozacom, the government's mineral marketing agency, accused De Beers' marketing arm, the CSO, of skimming off most of the profits from Zaire's diamond mines. He alleged that the CSO that year had made a $19 million profit from selling Zaire's industrial diamonds while only paying Zaire $2 million. To add insult to injury, the CSO had also charged Zaire for its expenses in buying diamonds illegally smuggled from Zaire.[19]

In the light of these revelations, Mobutu decided to cancel the provision that Zaire pay 25 percent of its diamond income to the Syndicate, presumably as a marketing fee. He rejected Tempelsman's advice, ended the Oppenheimer marketing contract, and instead sold his diamonds to two Belgian companies headquartered in Antwerp, called Caddi and Glasol, as well as to the Industrial Diamond Corporation headed by Jack Lunzer in London. The three firms agreed to pay more than De Beers' going rate. Their success in landing this deal encouraged Caddi and Glasol to bid against De Beers for marketing control over the newly discovered Australian diamonds.

De Beers decided that it was vital for it to regain full control over the marketing of Zaire's diamonds. If Zaire were to make a success of life outside the cartel, other producers would be sorely tempted to break away. Harry Oppenheimer said in September 1981: "I can't pretend that we are pleased that anyone breaks away. It's a bad example."

Once more Tempelsman rode to the rescue. In 1981 he flew to Kinshasa with Anthony Oppenheimer, the son of Ernest's nephew Sir Philip Oppenheimer, and again returned in 1983. The CSO at the same time showed its teeth. The diamond market was flooded with Zaire-type diamonds from its stockpile, lowering the world price. This cut by a third the diamond revenues of Zaire. Production in Zaire's mines fell. Security became lax and smuggling increased. Harry Oppenheimer said, "The Zaire experience should be looked upon as a warning rather than as an example."[20]

Suddenly Zaire found it was much harder to get the money needed for a new diamond dredger ($40 million), for a new mine on a large unexploited volcanic pipe ($120 million), and for new alluvial mines in a vast practically unexploited field called Tchikapa, near the Angolan border. In Frankfurt, Sir Philip Oppenheimer said Zaire would now have trouble securing vitally needed IMF loans.

The Ashton Joint Venture in Australia learned its lesson.[21] When it announced in 1982 that it would give the cartel marketing rights over Australian diamonds, Mobutu's men conceded defeat and rejoined the cartel. The Australian capitulation doomed Zaire's bid for diamond independence, for it had given the CSO a bulk supply of diamonds that it could use to again flood the market for Zaire's diamonds.

When the time came for the Australian Argyle Mine to renegotiate their five-year contract with the Syndicate, De Beers applied pressure just as it had done with Zaire, dumping its stockpile of Australian stones onto the market, lowering prices for Australian diamonds, making it harder for Australia to negotiate a better price. Australia consequently accepted a price of around $12 a carat, far less than that offered to Zaire.

Perhaps Mobutu was more skilful in his negotiations than the naive Australians. He had achieved a higher price despite it being generally agreed that the Australian diamonds were of a better quality.

The Mobutu Cut?

Mobutu's most lucrative operation happened at the end of each working day at the MIBA diamond plant in Mbuji-Mayi, when that day's diamond production was displayed before three officials: a son of Mobutu, a director representing the European stockholders, and the Zairian director of the company. Each took a share of that day's finds. Mobutu's share was nearly half. What was left, after being stripped of most of its better gems, was then evaluated and declared as the official production of Zaire. Thus, Zaire's diamonds were officially only 5 percent gems instead of the more likely 33 percent to 50 percent. Mobutu was also able to "double dip" by plundering the funds received for the "official" production in MIBA's Belgian bank accounts. Tax was paid only on the revenue from the leftover poorer diamonds, further diminishing government income.

In June 1983, a woman was stopped by customs officials at Brussels airport as she tried to use the special VIP route reserved for a head of state. She was carrying $6 million worth of jewels and uncut diamonds. She explained she was the secretary of Mobutu's second wife, Bobi Ladawa, and that the diamonds were dowry gems for which Ladawa was seeking a talented jeweler.

This plunder did not endanger the cartel. It could buy the plundered gems when they arrived in Europe. The Belgian authorities uniquely allowed a De Beers company to buy smuggled diamonds in Antwerp with a dollar cash account.

According to a 1993 report in *African Business*, Mobutu and his associates smuggled abroad diamonds to the value of $300 million a year. Zaire declared its 1992 official diamond production as 13 million carats – but other industry sources reported the real production to be 30 million carats. The missing 17 million carats represented in volume nearly twice the production of all South African diamond mines.

Mobutu acquired a palace in Switzerland, villas and chateaux in France, Belgium, Italy and Portugal. He built a "new Versailles," complete with illuminated fountains, at his birthplace of Ghadolite, 700 kilometers north of Kinshasa. But when any Zairians outside the privileged elite tried to acquire a diamond for themselves, the government did all in its power to prevent them. On one occasion, Mobutu's troops, policing the diamond fields in a helicopter gunship, massacred a party of picnicking school children mistaken for unlicensed diamond prospectors.

Mobutu loses US support

Mobutu's impoverishment of Zaire and displays of plundered wealth eventually embarrassed the US government. Tempelsman publicly distanced himself from Mobutu in 1980 – but this was not easy. Tempelsman reacted angrily when a headline appeared in the *Washington Post* proclaiming: US BUSINESSMAN PLAYS A KEY ROLE AS AIDE TO MOBUTU. In articles appearing on December 30th and 31st, 1980, it alleged that Tempelsman was "close to President Mobutu Sese Seko of Zaire" and continued to "help Mobutu in many ways" despite the human rights violations occurring under Mobutu. It continued: "The exact nature of Tempelsman's involvement with Mobutu is not known and [his] New York office was not forthcoming with information. But a diplomatic source who knows both men describes their relationship as 'very personal' and said that both are reaping substantial earnings from the gem diamond trade."

Tempelsman angrily wrote to the *Washington Post* on January 14th, 1981 protesting: I have had no business relationship with President Mobutu directly or indirectly... We share no business interests in MIBA, Britmond, the Tenke Fungurume Mining Society or any other concern. President Mobutu and other Zaire officials do not personally own any shares or other interests in these companies... I have never represented President Mobutu's interest in Washington, lobbied on his or his Government's behalf, or involved myself in political matters on his behalf... or (now) involve myself in any other way in US-Zaire relations beyond the usual cooperation when possible with US officials and the making of such representations as may from time to time be necessary and appropriate to protect this company's legitimate business interests.

In March 1981, Tempelsman was again forced to defend himself. On March 5th the House Subcommittee on Africa called Professor Lemarchand to give evidence on human rights violations in Zaire. His testimony referred to an "indecently close relationship" between a former CIA station chief and a "leading US financier."

Tempelsman's letter of March 8th, 1980 to the Chairman of the House Subcommittee on Africa Subcommittee, Stephen J. Solarz, said, "My business in no way depends on Zaire receiving more or less financial assistance from the United States, or in the rise or fall of this country's standing and influence in Zaire, or even on the rise of fall of any particular leader in Zaire... I know of no reason why those who have severed all ties with [the CIA], as I am satisfied Mr. Devlin has, should not be at least as eligible for employment in those areas of the world they know best, as any ex-Congressman who chooses to remain in Washington as a lawyer or lobbyist."

Solarz replied on March 26th: "Thank you for your recent telephone inquiry and letter expressing your concern about the way in which your name came up at the Subcommittee on Africa's March 5th hearing on Zaire ... in all honesty, I cannot agree that the above questions and answers support your complaint that, as Chairman of the Subcommittee on Africa, I permitted 'false and scurrilous innuendo' concerning [Tempelsman] to be injected into the hearing." Solarz said the *Washington Post* was highly respected and its articles were properly included in the Hearing's record. He advised Tempelsman to sue the *Washington Post*, if he felt he had been maligned.

Ten years later, when another article critical of Tempelsman was published, in *Vanity Fair* in November 1990, Robert Kasmire of Adams & Rinehart Inc., Tempelsman's public relations consultants, declared: "Robert Klien's article... was clearly off the mark in suggesting Maurice Tempelsman and his company, Lazare Kaplan International Inc., represent De Beers in Africa or anywhere else. On the contrary, Mr. Tempelsman's success in independently obtaining from Angola a direct supply of uncut gem diamonds for his own company obviously conflicts with the cartel's traditional reach for exclusive market control." But Tempelsman gave up this supply without protest when Angola contracted to give all its diamonds directly to De Beers.

US State and Justice Department records are rich in information about the relationship between Tempelsman and De Beers. For example; an informant described as well connected in the diamond industry (identity censored by the US Justice Department) alleged to a Justice Department attorney, Richard L. Daerr Jr., in August 1974: "Tempelsman is a key man in the US as far as contacts with Harry Oppenheimer," and had acted as "an agent" for De Beers in several instances.[22] For example, "Tempelsman acted for De Beers [in a deal that] involved contracts for purchase in the Belgian Congo. He negotiated for De Beers on industrial diamonds… Tempelsman is in constant contact with Harry Oppenheimer, relaying to him information on the progress of this antitrust investigation. Amongst those in the know he is looked to as Harry Oppenheimer's representative in the US."[23]

Perhaps the reason why Tempelsman defended his "independent" status so vehemently was because his work in Africa required him to be seen as an independent American diamond merchant not linked to apartheid South Africa – and as a friend able to advise as a "neutral" in negotiations with De Beers?

Although Tempelsman stated that Mobutu and he "share no business interest" in such concerns as "MIBA and Britmond," both he and Mobutu were involved in these companies' operations. Much of Mobutu's wealth reportedly came from his access to diamonds mined by the state-controlled MIBA. Britmond purchased for the Oppenheimers the diamonds not taken by Mobutu. Tempelsman's people policed the MIBA diamond production, verifying its records. He represented Britmond in negotiations with Mobutu.

Tempelsman also expanded into Sierra Leone and formed a close relationship with its President, Siaka Stevens, trying to raise for him the funds needed for a new diamond mine with the aid of Theodore Sorensen,[24] Tempelsman's lawyer who had also acted as legal adviser to Mobutu. Tempelsman instructed Sorensen to work out a diamond contract for Sierra Leone as he had done for Mobutu. Under this Tempelsman received rights to 27 percent of Sierra Leone's diamonds. He set up an "independent" cutting factory – and De Beers bought a share in it.

POWERFUL CONNECTIONS

Tempelsman boosted his reputation in Africa by associating with prominent and powerful Americans. In 1957 he traveled in Africa with the presidential hopeful Adlai Stevenson. In 1980, his Vice President William Ullman traveled with the younger Kennedys in a trip organized with Oppenheimer's Anglo American. According to the *Soweto Post* of Friday, July 11th, 1980, Ullman turned up at the OAU (Organization of African Unity) annual conference of Heads of State in Freetown, at receptions given by and for presidents, accompanied by John F. Kennedy Jr., the son of the assassinated US President who was said to be working temporarily for Tempelsman in Zaire and Africa. The *Soweto Post* published a photograph of John F. Kennedy Jr. with African children in Soweto. The caption said he "was a guest of Anglo American who took him into Soweto." The article pointed out: "The baldish man next to him is Bill Ullman, an employee of Leon Tempelsman and Company, a New York firm dealing in diamonds and metals."25 Tempelsman also took President Kennedy's daughter, Caroline Kennedy, to Africa. She was treated to a tour of Oppenheimer's diamond mine in Namibia.

I queried this connection between Tempelsman and President Kennedy's children when I visited Senator Ted Kennedy's Washington office in 1988. A staffer told me how, after the assassination of President Kennedy, Tempelsman had practically "brought up" the Kennedy children. He had formed a close personal bond with Jacqueline Onassis and frequently escorted her. She had even modeled his diamond jewelry for him. He was beside her when she died in 1994.

I made a further discovery when working in the Australian Broadcasting Corporation's New York office by Rockefeller Center. A brochure from a conservative think tank called National Endowment for Democracy landed on my desk. "Give us a call," it said, "and we can provide you with the experts you need for your programs."

Connected with the Endowment was a man named Jerry Funk, the African expert on the National Security Council. The National Security Council advised the President. It helped to control the CIA. Oliver North had been a member of it. So, I asked to be put in touch with him. Fortunately, he was also visiting New York. I phoned him at his hotel.

"Would you be able to give me some time?"

"I am sorry, I cannot. I am leaving tomorrow for Zaire. Maurice Tempelsman has hired me."

I was astonished. I had not mentioned Tempelsman to him. Garsin later told me that Funk's work for Tempelsman in Zaire included representing Harry Oppenheimer's Britmond diamond company before Mobutu. When I looked into Jerry Funk's background I found that he was involved in US attempts to influence black African trade unions in the 1970s. He worked on the staff of the International Federation of Petroleum and Chemical Workers which "in the mid-1970s was dissolved when it was revealed to be a front for the CIA."26 He then worked as the Deputy Director of the African American Labor Center (AALC) set up in 1964 allegedly with help from the CIA. The AALC refused in 1976 to take part in the international boycott against South Africa on the grounds that similar actions were not planned against the Communist bloc. He left the AALC in 1979 when he was appointed as an expert on Africa to the National Security Council.

More evidence on Maurice Tempelsman's links with the CIA emerged when I interviewed Paul Baddo in 1991. Baddo was the head of the African Services Institute, a New York college that educated several thousand African civil servants and diplomats, funded in part by the Ford Foundation.

Baddo had also acted as a consultant for several West African countries. He told me he believed Maurice Tempelsman to be clearly linked to intelligence "because he chairs the Board of the African American Institute and this has strong CIA links." He added that the president of the Institute was Frank Ferrari, the former CIA official in charge of Youth Programs. The State Department funded the Institute. In 1991, a Cold War mentality still prevailed there and staff without this mentality "got short shift," according to Baddo. Nevertheless, Baddo's college and the Institute held joint summer programs and joint discussions of policy. He said, "I spent time to try to impress on the CIA there that they shouldn't try to use Cold War tactics in Africa."

Baddo explained that Tempelsman presented himself as an expert on Africa to the government and they had used him as such. I asked Baddo why intelligence connections were so seemingly important in the diamond business. He explained that secrecy is key to the diamond trade, since it operated by concealing production and diamond resources. He told me of a major diamond enterprise in Sierra Leone run by Israeli intelligence – he had warned Sierra Leone's government about this to little effect. "Diamonds," he told me, "were very useful as payments for intelligence." He then warned me: "The trade is dangerous to tangle with."

Tempelsman's work for the Oppenheimers in Africa was founded on his careful footwork in Washington. His knowledge of that city was never more needed than when sanctions on South African diamonds were proposed as part of US anti-apartheid legislation.

When I visited Senator Edward Kennedy's office in 1988, the Senator was working to secure the passage of a bill to impose sanctions because, he said, he had been to South Africa and had seen for himself the abhorrent nature of apartheid. He was collaborating on the bill with the Congressional Black Caucus and the House Foreign Affairs Committee.[27] At that time it looked as if the bill would include sanctions on South African diamonds, despite, according to Congressional aides, the constant visits to Kennedy's office by Tempelsman or his representatives lobbying against sanctions.

By 1988, Tempelsman had moved past the Cold War ethos of the 1960s. He was now part of the liberal establishment and anti-apartheid. His campaign against diamond sanctions was thus described as pro-black Africa rather than pro-South Africa. He argued these sanctions would hurt an innocent party, Botswana, as De Beers mixed its diamonds with the South African. He maintained they could not be told apart. There was no suggestion that Botswana be invited to directly send its diamonds to the US instead of allowing De Beers to sell them to America.

This Tempelsman campaign left his liberal associates nervous. Sorensen, a long-term Tempelsman associate, was now counsel at the law firm representing Tempelsman's Lazare Kaplan, but he "flatly denied he lobbied for Tempelsman"[28] in an interview given to Sheila Kaplan, a writer with the influential Washington journal, *Legal Times*. But Kaplan was told by Jewelers of America representative, John Sategaj that Sorensen was "in the thick of the diamond sanctions debate." Kaplan's article further alleged that Sorensen was "doing the bidding" of the diamond cartel. This was surprising. Sorenson, as the Vice Chairman of the Democratic Party National Platform Committee, had overseen the inclusion of a strongly worded anti-apartheid/pro-sanctions plank into the Democratic platform. This was despite an $85,000 donation given that year by Tempelsman to the Democratic National Committee.

According to the *Legal Times*, Donald McHenry, a former US Ambassador to the United Nations, was working as a partner for a company that worked for De Beers, IRC Group Inc. He refused to discuss De Beers but when told an IRC associate had confirmed the firm did work for De Beers, snapped the associate "is in hot water." He said IRC did economic reports and that he would "not be happy with advancing the cause." IRC's William Banden Heuvel, a former special assistant to Attorney General Robert Kennedy, was "apparently working on the De Beers account [and] Tempelsman has tapped Howard Marlowe of Marlowe and Company, who was the president of the American League of Lobbyists and lobbyist Milton Gwirzman of Van Dyke Associates." It was alleged that De Beers had asked 20 of its customers to contribute $10,000 each to a special fighting fund to pay for this campaign while contributing itself at least $200,000.

Meanwhile international diamond merchant organizations were debating whether they should have congresses in South Africa, fearing to taint their industry with an association with apartheid. They considered moving the venue for the 1988 World Diamond Congress away from South Africa. The President of the World Federation of Diamond Bourses, Ed Goldstein, stated, "If it's bad for the image of the diamond industry, we will not go there." De Beers itself did not attend an important World Diamond Congress in the US. Doing so might have exposed it to legal action by the US Justice Department over price-fixing.

Tempelsman's efforts to protect De Beers and South African diamond imports into the US were unremitting. He flew to Chicago to meet with Senator Paul Simon, the sponsor of the Senate version of the sanctions bill, and flew with Sorensen to Washington to meet with Wolpe, the chairman of the House Subcommittee on Africa, shortly before the House was to vote on the bill in August 1988.

Tempelsman also targeted Congressman Dymally, a principal proponent of the sanctions bill. When a Dymally aide mentioned to Tempelsman that the Congressman's favorite charity, the Dymally Scholarship Fund, was in need of a donation of $34,000, Tempelsman reportedly immediately sent it this sum. He also sent the Congressman a personal honorarium of $2,000, the legal maximum possible.[29] The House of Representatives was to outlaw this practice in December 1989.

A staff member of the House Subcommittee on Africa gave me a copy of a Tempelsman office memo that argued against sanctions on South African diamonds. It said that since diamonds were only one twentieth of the imports from South Africa in 1987, diamond sanctions would not work as they "would not noticeably injure or influence the Government of South Africa." This ignored the vast revenues De Beers made by selling diamonds mined by other countries.

Evading US Customs

Tempelsman's memo gave the impression that few South African diamonds entered the US. On investigation, I found that there had been a dramatic drop in the numbers reported to Customs – and found out the reason why. A spokesman for the US International Trade Commission's Diamond Section, Stanley Garil, had advised diamond merchants that they could minimize their exposure to sanctions if they labeled the South African diamonds that passed through London on their way to the US as British. His words wrought statistical magic. In 1987, the numbers of diamonds declared to US Customs as South African fell to an eighth of the previous level while US diamond imports from Britain went up by 12 times.

Another argument was that it was impractical to impose sanctions on South African diamonds, as rough diamonds could not be distinguished by origin. US Customs would have had to employ experts – but I know from visiting diamond-cutting factories around the world that merchants can tell at a glance the origin of most diamonds. Nonetheless, this was a serious difficulty. In 1988, US Customs had only one diamond expert on its staff in New York, despite this city being the center of the US diamond trade. (In 1999 De Beers admitted it could tell the origin of uncut diamonds when it faced an UN embargo on diamonds sold by UNITA.)

Perhaps the most significant opposition to diamond sanctions came from the Pentagon. I was in Senator Kennedy's office talking with his Foreign Policy advisor when suddenly he asked me, "Do you know anything about B2 diamonds?"

I was mystified. All I could think of was a bomber aircraft called a B52. I probed him for further information. "Why are you interested in them?"

He refused to elaborate further but said, "We would be very grateful for anything you can find out about these diamonds." He paused. "Apparently they only came from one place in the world, the South African Premier mine."

A few weeks later, I discovered why Kennedy's office needed this information. I was flipping through a specialist industrial diamond magazine in a diamond merchant's office in London when I came across a mention of a blue diamond considered by the Pentagon to be its best friend. This was the 2B. It was sought for the "Star Wars" program because of its peculiar electrical and heat-conducting qualities.

I was reading this magazine while waiting for an interview with Jack Lunzer, a diamond merchant who dealt worldwide from Hatton Garden. When I was ushered into his inner office, I asked him which mines produce 2B diamonds. He replied, "They came from all over the place. Why, even your Australian Argyle mine produces them."

When I returned to Washington, I made more enquiries. It seemed the Pentagon had only wanted a few of these diamonds but since it had been incorrectly told they only came from South Africa, the Pentagon had opposed sanctions on South African diamonds.

The end result of this campaign was complete victory for Tempelsman. Sorensen, the attorney who had previously drafted diamond agreements for Mobutu, now drafted clauses for the House of Representatives Bill, which were duly passed into law. These were "to exempt from economic sanctions uncut diamonds in instances where the importer could argue he did not know the source." First the Pentagon, then Congress, had been duped into a decision that was critical to the survival of the diamond cartel.

1   *Memorandum for the President*, From W.W. Rostow, 24 September 1961. Weekend Reading Papers to Hyannis Port. Telephone conversations Ball to Bundy, Ball to Fredericks, Ball to Tempelsman September 24th, 1961, letter Geoffrey Bing to Mahoney, March 4th, 1977.

2   Madeleine Kalb. *The Congo Cables: The Cold War in Africa – from Eisenhower to Kennedy*. New York: Macmillan Publishing Co. Inc., 1982, p. 377.

3   Weissman, pp. 190-191.

4   Interview with Marc Garsin, 1991 in Manhattan by John Kelly, associate producer of *The Diamond Empire*.

5   Jonathan Kwitney. *Endless Enemies*. New York: Penguin, 1984.

6   Author's interview with Steve Askin, Zaire specialist, in New York for *The Diamond Empire*, May 1992.

7   Kalb, p. 380.

8   Memo February 6th, 1967 Confidential. US Government. From AFCM Armistead M. Lee to AFC Mr. L. Dean Brown. Subject Union Miniere: Telephone conversations with Sorensen and Pendleton.

9   January 11th, 1967 Memo US Govt. Confidential Excise. To files from Armistead M. Lee, Summary of Tempelsman's telex of January 11th, 1967.
10 State Department Memorandum of Conversation. June 8th, 1967. The participants included Maurice Tempelsman.
11 Leon Dash, *Washington Post.* December 31st, 1979.
12 Kalb, p. 387.
13 Stockwell, p. 136.
14 *New York Times.* December 6th, 1981.
15 *Dirty Work 2*, p. 350.
16 Ibid.
17 Stockwell, p. 44.
18 Mahoney dissertation.
19 "CSO Denies Zaire Rip Off Charge," *Rand Daily Mail.* August 10th, 1981.
20 *Financial Times.* March 9th, 1983. See also *Wall Street Journal.* July 7th, 1983.
21 CRA marketing report: Internal company document.
22 Richard L. Daerr, Jr. Memo to Files, September 12th, 1974, Dept. of Justice.
23 Ibid.
24 *Washington Post.* July 14th, 1980.
25 *Business Day's* editor Ken Owen alleged Ullman was a "CIA sleeper." See later reference to Ullman in this book.
26 Barry Cohen "The CIA and African Trade Unions," p. 76.
27 Bill HR 1051 to ban South African diamonds was subsumed into the embargo on all South African products, excepting strategic minerals, drafted by Wolpe and by the Congressional Black Caucus and passed by full Foreign Affairs Committee. It also called on the President to conduct an anti-monopoly investigation of the cartel.
28 *Legal Times.* October 30th, 1989. The law firm was Paul, Weiss, Rifkind, Wharton and Garrison.
29 Ibid.

Chapter 12 – The Secret Movement of Diamonds

It was not only in the Congo that the diamond cartel employed former spies and embedded itself in secrecy. Ian Fleming had studied his diamond merchants at close hand in Africa. He reported that Harry Oppenheimer had recruited Sir Percy Sillitoe, the former head of MI5, to update and strengthen De Beers' security and intelligence systems throughout Africa.[1] Good intelligence was seen as vital for the protection of the diamond Syndicate.

De Beers had to hide a fortune in diamond production in the 1980s. The United Nations tried to protect Namibia prior to independence by forbidding foreign corporations from exporting its resources. Throughout this period, De Beers continued to export vast numbers of fine Namibian diamonds in defiance of United Nation decrees – and had to hide these exports lest they be forfeited. Justice Pieter Thirion of the Natal Supreme Court revealed how this was done. He discovered that Namibian diamonds were secretly sold to a company called Diamond Sales Ltd. that operated out of Bermuda, but was owned by the Oppenheimers via Liberia. In the first half of 1983 this trade was worth $717 million.

Justice Thirion received minimal cooperation from De Beers in his legal inquiries. He reported that the evidence given by the resident CDM director in Namibia, Douglas Hoofe, was, "not very interesting… an insult to even the lowliest form of intelligence."[2] Thirion also noted that large sums, amounting to billions of Rand a year, were allotted to "Head Office Expenditure" and commented that this was a "favorite item whereby multinational companies effect a distribution of income among its subsidiaries so as to reduce the liability for the payment of taxes."[3]

CDM refused to answer the charge that it had engaged in transfer pricing. The allegation was that it had sold South West Africa's diamonds for little or no profit to a De Beers company registered in Bermuda , which resold them at a much higher price to De Beers' operations in London, thus creating for De Beers a very good profit that was virtually tax free – given how low were Bermuda taxes. It also meant the country whose resources were being mined received only a minimal return. This remains a widely used tactic in the mining industry.

CONCEALING THE ORIGINS OF DIAMONDS

There are many ways to conceal the origin of diamonds. The freeport trick is probably the best. De Beers had three European operations at inland freeports, next to airports and serviced by their private airline. One was at the Zurich airport's freeport in Switzerland, another at Shannon airport's freeport in Ireland, and the third at the freeport on the Isle of Man. De Beers' planes could taxi directly from the runway into the De Beers compound. De Beers thus could unload a cargo of diamonds, gold, or any other commodity with minimal exposure.

Diamonds received new identity papers at the Zurich Freeport. A Swiss customs official told me that if De Beers' local freeport office received by air a diamond from Russia and wanted to hide its origin, all it had to do was to fill in the paperwork needed to export that diamond to London then, before putting it on the London plane, to "change its mind," and import it instead into Switzerland. Under Swiss law it would now be recorded as a British diamond. It would not retain a trace of its Russian origin. Thus Russian diamonds could be brought into the US as if mined in Britain and not attract the duty levied on Russian gems. Millions of dollars in duty otherwise payable to the US could thus be evaded.

Switzerland became a base for the diamond cartel after the British government imposed sanctions on South Africa and began planning to bring its anti-cartel laws into line with those of (what was then) the European Economic Community. Under these laws, the fine for price-fixing went to over a million pounds sterling, and individual directors were liable to fines of up to £100,000 ($160,000). These laws did not apply in Switzerland as it stood outside the Community. The cartel thus moved the paperwork of many operations to Switzerland.

On August 12th, 1988, the *Neue Zuercher Zeitung*, a Zurich based newspaper, reported that "fear of further sanctions against the apartheid regime in South Africa," had led to diamonds being diverted to Switzerland. In 1986 the imports of precious stones into Switzerland was worth 1.7 million Swiss Francs. One year later it had become a flood worth 189 million Swiss Francs.

In the following year, imports of diamonds into Switzerland doubled. The increase was so remarkable that it was discussed in the Swiss Federal Cabinet. The Swiss Bundesrat, or Upper House, cautiously declared it would act to stop Switzerland serving as a haven for South African companies – but only if other countries imposed effective sanctions on South Africa. No other country did. Thus the Swiss action was only symbolic and no more effective than the Catholic priest who in 1988 led his congregation in a torch lit procession around De Beers' Swiss headquarters in Lucerne as a protest against a business that profited from apartheid.

But the Swiss government soon had less reason to feel nervous about its role as a haven for South African diamonds. The flow from southern Africa stopped as abruptly as it had started. Instead, a new flood of diamonds came into Switzerland from Bermuda, a country with coconuts and no diamond mines. De Beers had done their accustomed alchemy. In 1991, Bermuda dispatched $583 million of diamonds to Switzerland.

De Beers' relations with Margaret Thatcher's government were exceptionally friendly, despite De Beers moving the ownership of its London offices to a shadowy Swiss-based company. Sir Gordon Borrie, director general of the UK Office of Fair Trading, stated, "As De Beers sells most of its stones overseas, the ill-effects which might flow from the operation of that monopoly would be negligible as far as the United Kingdom is concerned."

The Oppenheimers wished to conceal the flood of Russian diamonds arriving in the UK in the 1980s. They feared that, if the numbers were known, it would drive the price of diamonds down. The UK agreed to cooperate. The Johannesburg *Star* reported on January 23rd, 1982 that De Beers had persuaded the British government to stop publishing the "sensitive figures" that gave the origins of the UK's uncut diamond imports. 1980 was the last year with published figures. That year uncut diamond imports from the Soviet Union were valued at £367 million – half the total value of all UK imports from the Soviets. The British Board of Trade in November 1988 confirmed that these statistics were still "classified" and added the order suspending publication was also "classified."[4] Such a secret classification for a non-strategic, non-military import was unique. The UK authorities concealed the uncut diamond import statistics from 1980 onwards by including diamonds together with bricks and glassware, commodities it described as "similar," and publishing only the combined figure.

The two centers for Oppenheimer diamond cartel operations in Europe, Britain and Switzerland, possessed, according to statistics, giant invisible diamond mines. This was evident if one compared the official British and Swiss diamond import and export statistics. According to the British government, the UK was mostly supplied by Switzerland with uncut diamonds, but according to the Swiss authorities, it was Britain that supplied the Swiss.

This became even stranger when the official records were further examined. UK customs recorded in 1987 only $70 million worth of diamond exports to Switzerland. Clearly on the way to Switzerland De Beers had waved the magic wand and multiplied them tenfold because Switzerland that same year recorded over $700 million worth of diamonds arriving from Britain. De Beers also wove a similar magic over Swiss exports. British customs that same year recorded three times more diamonds arriving from Switzerland than Switzerland recorded sending to Britain.

There was still more powerful sorcery in other years. Swiss records said they exported in 1982 just $33 million worth of diamonds to the United Kingdom but British records recorded over a billion dollars worth of diamonds arriving from Switzerland that same year. More diamond magic sparkled in 1991 when $29 million worth of British diamond exports was transmuted into diamonds worth in Switzerland some $652 million.[5] As for the countries that thought they mined the world's diamonds, Namibia, South Africa, Botswana, Zaire, Russia and Australia – most of their diamonds seemed to vanish before they reached Europe. On the face of it, these countries exported their diamonds into a vacuum.

One possible explanation for some of this magic could have been that the cartel wished to minimize the profits made in Britain by exaggerating the value of the diamonds on arrival in Britain. This would have minimized their tax liability in the United Kingdom. Since it purchased its uncut diamonds for only a few dollars each, the profit margins in the UK would be enormous – and the tax paid on profits would be correspondingly great – unless countermeasures were taken.

DE BEERS INVESTIGATED BY KROLL

De Beers' tax payment strategies came under close scrutiny in 1988-89 from the world's biggest detective agency, Kroll Associates of New York. The Oppenheimers were trying to complete a hostile takeover of another mining giant, Consolidated Gold Fields of the UK. In response, Gold Fields hired Kroll to investigate De Beers. I met the principal UK officers of Kroll in their Curzon Street, London office, the former office of MI6 and the only office I have visited where a combination lock protected the ladies' toilet! Supposedly retired spies heavily staffed Kroll. Since I met with them, Kroll had been hired to search for wealth taken by Iraq from Kuwait and to find the diamonds and gold that vanished from Kremlin vaults during the coup against Gorbachev.

Kroll discovered that De Beers played a version of hopscotch to minimize taxes. They were constantly moving their registered office address to countries with lower taxes or greater secrecy. In practice, these moves were only on paper. The operating offices physically stayed at the same location. But the company registered as owning the office constantly shifted to another brass plate on a wall in yet another tax haven. If all UK, US and Australian citizens were able to do the same, the registered population of, say, the tiny British Virgin Islands, would be in the hundreds of millions while the United States, British and Australian governments would be effectively tax-less, officially unpopulated and unequivocally broke.

Thus, when the Irish government decided to impose a small 10 percent tax on the twelve Oppenheimer diamond companies registered as resident in Ireland, all of them suddenly changed their registered owner's address to a holding company in the British Virgin Islands. When it became illegal in Sweden to trade with apartheid South Africa, the cartel's Swedish assets in the industrial diamond company Scandiamant were immediately transferred to HPT Ltd., also in the British Virgin Islands.

De Beers controlled two companies in Bermuda, where the cartel had been accused of running a "transfer pricing" operation. One was Diamond Sales Ltd., and the other Saffron Services Ltd. The first had a registered place of business in the UK but said it was owned in Liberia, a country without diamond mines (but with a lot of diamond smugglers). The second registered itself in 1987 as owned in tax haven Panama.

The cartel's private airline, Dravidan Air Services Ltd., formerly Smithfield Diamonds Ltd. or International Air Services Ltd., flew aircraft out of Heathrow and into the freeports. It was owned, not in Britain, certainly not in South Africa, but in the Cayman Islands. When De Beers took control after the death of Williamson of his diamond mine in Tanzania (formerly Tanganyika), and the leading local newspaper denounced this as a "partnership with the South African corporation openly supporting apartheid," De Beers promptly went invisible in Tanzania. The Oppenheimers simply renamed their local operation Willcroft Co. and gave it a brass plate address in the Bahamas.[6]

There was something familiar for me in these registered addresses. When I had previously researched the international arms trade, I found its operations were often laundered through the same countries that quietly hosted the cartel's companies. These countries were the registered addresses of a thousand extremely nasty operations. Some of these permitted the use of bearer shares – making it impossible to trace ownership or corporate responsibility – a device allegedly used by President Mobutu.

The cartel showed no particular loyalty to the UK despite all the help it received from its government. All but one of the eight Oppenheimer diamond companies on the Isle of Man, manufacturing synthetic diamonds and related products, were officially owned not in the UK but in Panama. Its industrial diamond operation in Reading, PCP, was owned in Luxembourg. The cartel's main office in London's Charterhouse Street also housed many phantom operations registered elsewhere.

One of their companies trading in black Africa was called Chichester Diamond Services (UK) Ltd. It was registered in Panama although it traded from an office adjacent to the cartel's (CSO's) offices in London. Another company operating out of these same offices had a nearly identical name: Chichester Diamond Services Ltd. This company, unlike its namesake, was not owned by the cartel directly but was a subsidiary of the merchant banker Hambros.

Hambros was part of another quiet network interlocked with that of the Oppenheimers, allegedly with links to MI6, part of British Intelligence.[7] Members of the Hambro family were on the boards of Anglo American, Chichester Diamond Services Ltd., Charterhouse Gem Company, I. Hennig and Co. as well as City & East-West. The latter company traded Russian diamonds; in July 1983, Hambros owned it, then, in October 1985, it passed to CWE Ltd. Anstalt, a company in low-tax Liechtenstein. A director of this company, Norman Cassleton-Elliot, was also on the board of the De Beers' Diamond Trading Co. Ltd. and on the board of its CSO Valuations operation in Lucerne.

DE BEERS' SHADOW COMPANIES

The UK's Midland Bank (now HSBC) helped restructure the diamond empire through a little known Zurich bank it controlled called Guyerzeller. Midland owned two-thirds of Guyerzeller; the Oppenheimers' companies owned the other third. The Guyerzeller Bank helped duplicate in Zurich the major elements of the cartel's operations in London by using nominal Swiss companies as holding companies for De Beers' London operations. This gave the Oppenheimer companies a bolthole if the UK implemented European anti-cartel law. Another advantage was the minimal tax paid in Switzerland on income earned abroad. While seven of the eight Oppenheimer companies on the Isle of Man were officially owned in Panama, Guyerzeller in Zurich owned the other. The Panama seven were at the same time "domiciled" (given a home) with Montebello AG, a Swiss company operating from the same premises as Guyerzeller Bank.

CSO Valuations (Proprietary) Ltd. performs the key task in the London operation of valuing diamonds. It was once an offshoot of a similarly named South African company. It too officially became a Swiss operation, owned by CSO Valuations AG. The Swiss had seemingly taken over totally. The principal address of the Diamond Trading Co., a central cartel company, became officially Langensandstrasse 27, Lucerne. Its president in 1991 was not an Oppenheimer but Camillo Andina of the Guyerzeller Bank.

Even the Central Selling Organization (CSO) Ltd., another key diamond cartel operation, was given a Swiss shadow called Central Diamond Selling Organization (CSO) Ltd. This was set up in November 1983. The London operations of the

"Diamond Trading Company Ltd." were put into the legal custody of a nearly identically named Swiss operation. Its owners seemingly became not the Oppenheimers but the Swiss-registered CSO operation, as well as Rolf Santschi, director of the Guyerzeller Bank. Likewise the Oppenheimer diamond property company, Dicorprop Ltd. – once wholly owned by Diamond Corporation (Pty.) Ltd. of South Africa – had since 1987 been owned by Dicorp Holding Ltd. in Vaduz, Switzerland, and, again, Rolf Santschi.

An observer might be pardoned for thinking that Rolf Santschi was the secret man behind the Oppenheimers, the Swiss banker behind the throne. But he was rather the administrator of a stack of brass plates, managing De Beers' shadow refuge in Switzerland under the direction of Midland Bank and the Oppenheimers.

De Beers would set up De Beers Centenary in Switzerland as soon as democracy came to South Africa, an operation that cut the tax base of the ANC government. In 2002 yet another Swiss entity would appear – "De Beers Societé Anonym" to hold De Beers' assets and debts, again well away from the South Africa.[8]

The Kroll study proved an invaluable help to Gold Fields Ltd. in its last ditch courtroom battle against the Oppenheimer takeover. Judge Michael Mukasey in New York District Court in 1989 noted it was "significant that De Beers, as one of the protagonists in this take-over, has apparently sought to monopolize the world supply of diamonds." He concluded that, if he allowed the takeover to go ahead, the Oppenheimers might be able to manipulate the world price of gold. He was in no doubt as to the role of Harry Oppenheimer in both Anglo American and De Beers. "The plaintiffs have presented substantial affidavits and other evidence demonstrating that the entire group is controlled by Harry Oppenheimer through Central Holdings," he said. He ultimately ruled against the takeover.

DE BEERS' SECRET BASE IN LIBERIA

The use of "flags of convenience" goes to the very top of the Oppenheimer operation. The financial chief and director of Gold Fields, Anthony Hitchens, during the hostile take-over attempt by De Beers, told me in an interview on the 29th of July 1988 that E. Oppenheimer & Son, the central instrument of Oppenheimer family control over their diamond empire, was not registered in South Africa, although operating out of Johannesburg. Instead it was registered in Liberia. This was still true in 2002, despite the association of Liberia with conflict diamonds, arms smuggling and dodgy ships.

Hitchens had asked me: "Do you know that the very top executives of De Beers and Anglo are paid directly by E. Oppenheimer and Son, a Liberian registered company?" He alleged that E. Oppenheimer and Son was trying to smooth the path of its take-over by offering Gold Fields' chief executive officer Rudolph Agnew a richly paying directorship with nominal duties in probably a Liechtenstein company. Hitchens further asked: "What did it do for shareholders' rights when officials are paid secretly?" The principal shareholders in E. Oppenheimer and Son were Harry Oppenheimer and his son and daughter, Nicholas (Nicky) and Mary.

Hitchens alleged that Julian Ogilvie Thompson, the Chairman of De Beers and the deputy chairman of Anglo American, had been given shares in an Oppenheimer holding company registered in Luxembourg. These functioned as "golden handcuffs" as the recipient only retained them at the pleasure of the Oppenheimers. This supposedly was a common Oppenheimer practice. Edward Wharton-Tigar, former Managing Director of Selection Trust's Sierra Leone diamond mines, described in his autobiography how these gift directorships might involve lucrative fees and minimal work. He told me in an interview in London in 1989 that De Beers paid below market rate prices for the diamonds his company produced after giving lucrative directorships to directors of his company.

Hitchens showed me several tomes he had stored behind his desk, and told me these were the results of the Kroll investigation into De Beers. He then asked: "Do you know that De Beers finance some MI6 operations?" I pressed him for proof but he said his source was confidential. I suspected that it was Kroll since it had links to former intelligence personnel. Some three years later I learned from an experienced diamond industry researcher and colleague, Laurie Flynn, that De Beers allegedly used a security firm headed by a former member of BOSS, the South African intelligence service, to monitor the movements of its own diamond sorting staff in London.

The De Beers Secret Security Force

But there is another reason why Harry Oppenheimer would need a security operation, another reason why he retained the services of people like Sir Percy Sillitoe, the former head of MI5. Despite all Oppenheimer's deals, some diamonds were escaping his cartel's grip and were being traded independently, especially in West Africa. In southern Africa where De Beers has sway, he did not have the same problem. There such trade is labeled IDB, or Illicit Diamond Buying, and is illegal. De Beers had to find other ways to stop this trade in other parts of Africa.

In the 1950s smugglers outside the cartel traded about 20 percent of all uncut diamond gems. In the 1980s, according to the internal cartel figures, this proportion was between 10 and 20 percent. Nearly as many were smuggled worldwide as South Africa produced. Sir Percy Sillitoe reported, after an investigation conducted for Harry Oppenheimer, "Since the end of the war, smuggled diamonds had become a sort of international crooks' currency."[9] Sillitoe discovered that major Belgian diamond merchants were so anxious to get an independent source to escape rationing by the Syndicate that they were secretly funding many a smuggling operation.[10]

Sillitoe set up the International Diamond Security Organization for the Oppenheimers in order to find and seize illicit diamonds. Among those he recruited was Lebanese mercenary Fred Kamil, who in turn recruited and organized more armed agents. Kamil, when interviewed for *The Diamond Empire* in South America, alleged that he and his recruits set up ambushes in Sierra Leone to kill diamond traders not authorized by De Beers and the local government. He also said he laid minefields to kill the smugglers and independent traders – and these in practice killed indiscriminately many innocent people.[11]

Fouad "Fred" Kamil in 1992.

Kamil explained how he had imprisoned suspected diamond smugglers in a secret private prison outside Johannesburg. He openly admitted to working as a "terrorist" within the diamond trade. Today he says he hates diamonds for all the misery they cause.

In 1995, the diamond fields of Sierra Leone were secured by Executive Outcome (now Northbridge Services), a firm of UK/South African mercenaries hired by the government, while a civil war raged for control over the diamond fields. The young men working in the diamond mines then earned around 50 cents a day.[12]

Many Africans thought it unjust that colonial governments had contracted their countries' entire diamond output to foreign corporations. In West Africa, they thought it even more unjust that mercenaries should now lay in ambush, allegedly on De Beers' orders, in order to stop them from taking diamonds to higher paying diamond merchants in neighboring countries, especially when De Beers had encouraged "illicit diamonds" elsewhere by setting up buying offices to purchase directly from smugglers. When Zaire decided in 1981 to sell its diamonds outside the cartel, De Beers' diamond buyers had immediately appeared on its borders to buy from smugglers. This was seen as a punishment for Zaire.

The UK government, in a Green Paper on "Private Military Companies," dated August 30th, 2002, named De Beers as employing such military companies for "covert reconnaissance" in Botswana, Namibia, and Angola. It listed De Beers as having done this on five occasions. No other company was listed more than once.

Diamonds lend themselves to being traded secretly as they are an easily carried and highly priced commodity, During World War II, refugees from the Nazis found them to be an ideal form of portable wealth. Kamil alleged that the cartel sold diamonds on the black market to raise untraceable funds that they could then use to bribe high government officials.[13] The Syndicate's success in keeping diamonds expensive, despite their low production costs and plentifulness, made them ideal for both smuggling and financing illegal operations.

MOBUTU'S ILLICIT EXPORTS

Zairian export statistics betrayed the numbers of diamonds illegally leaving Zaire under President Mobutu. In 1992 for example, Zaire officially estimated its total diamond production as 13.2 million carats – all exported to the Syndicate via offices in Belgium. The Syndicate paid $10 a carat or less for these diamonds, minus its marketing expenses and other fees, amounting normally to around 15-18 percent of the price paid. Belgium should thus have recorded the arrival of no more than $132 million worth of Zairian diamonds. But magically Belgian import figures recorded twice as many diamonds, a healthy $271 million, as arriving from Zaire. Much of the missing production was taken illicitly by shareholder representatives and by Mobutu's family, as described previously.

But these figures do not reveal the full extent of Zairian production. The Zairian National Conference and *New African* magazine estimated in November 1993 that Mobutu smuggled out $300 million worth of diamonds every year.

Zaire, now again known as the Congo, was rendered destitute by this pillaging, despite being a country rich with natural resources. The diamond center of Mbuji-Mayi in 1994 had a population of one million but no state hospitals, practically no electricity, and very few phones.[14] Yet Mbuji-Mayi's gaudily painted diamond trading houses and the open-air diamond market were handling an estimated $5 million worth of diamonds every week. Mobutu had a South African trained Mining Brigade protect the diamond mines that were the basis of his power. A Zairian court in Mbuji-Mayi reported that this brigade had tortured to death seven independent miners by administering electrical shocks.[15]

There were, and still are, secretive diamond buying networks throughout Central and West Africa. The Israeli secret services and Lebanese nationals ran and still run networks with reputations for ruthlessness. Lebanese, Israelis, Belgians, Armenians, and the PLO are all represented in the diamond markets of Sierra Leone. During the Beirut war, this trade helped support the various warring factions.

In Zaire, the Lebanese firm Sozadis and the Israeli firm Overseas Diamonds were allegedly "comptoirs," the name given to diamond dealers who buy from illegal diggers and smugglers. Mobutu's family reportedly had interests in both companies.[16] Sibeka noted that the profits Mobutu made from deals with "illicit" smaller dealers had protected Zaire's diamond mines from being completed stripped – as had happened to Zaire's lucrative cobalt mine.[17]

In 1992, President Mobutu was challenged by Tshisekedi, a newly elected Prime Minister with a mandate to end corruption. In September 1992, Tshisekedi sent gendarmes and civil servants to Central Bank Governor Nyemba, asking him to shut down Mobutu's illegal diamond operation. But Nyemba refused, for Mobutu's elite guard "protected" him. In late 1993 a bill before the Belgian Parliament called for a UN embargo on "Zairian illicit diamonds and cobalt exports" to force Mobutu to stop "the systematic sabotage of the democratization process in Zaire." But no serious action resulted.

De Beers' diamond buyers in Zaire and West Africa were fresh-faced youths from elite English schools. The more adventurous of the unscholarly well-bred students often saw themselves as having two choices, the army or De Beers. The youths choosing De Beers were told they could buy diamonds in Central Africa with no questions asked. They came on six-month stints with ample supplies and boxes of cash and were given houses with steel gates. They had a wild social life with De Beers supplying even a speedboat for water skiing. When one buyer was murdered in 1993, De Beers flew in two Scotland Yard detectives who, within about 24 hours, had found a possible culprit. A London city solicitor, who witnessed these events, alleged in a conversation with the author that he then witnessed a cool and matter of fact discussion between some of those involved on whether or not the suspect would survive.

It was estimated by *New African* magazine in 1991 that De Beers had spent $500-800 million that year buying smuggled diamonds. This was a vast sum even for them. In February 1993 they spent at least $6 million on a 777 carat stone thought to have come from Angola.

THE EARLY RELATIONSHIP BETWEEN DE BEERS AND UNITA
Angola was a major source of smuggled diamonds. It remains enormously rich in diamonds, with diamond-rich extinct volcanoes situated along major fault lines across the country. Erosion meant that much of their diamond content was spread across the

country and into the Congo. It was one country that De Beers definitely did not want as a rival producer. If the left-wing government in Luanda had marketed their diamonds in an alliance with the Russians, it could have threatened the very survival of the Syndicate.

It therefore may have suited De Beers that South Africa and the CIA were funding and arming the rebel movement of UNITA, and helping it seize Angola's diamond fields. De Beers' buyers were positioned to buy diamonds from UNITA, giving it all the funds needed for weapons. The CIA promised UNITA that America would give them complete support. UNITA thus felt it had no need to negotiate and instead could pursue military action with every hope of a victory. Some saw their cause as that of Christians against a Socialist government. The end result was that hundreds of thousands died, and over a million people became refugees. This was the start of one of the worst of what we now call the blood diamond wars.

John Stockwell, who oversaw this operation for the CIA, told how the UNITA foreign minister Jorges Sangumba picked him up at the house of Stuart Methven, Devlin's successor as the CIA Chief of Station in Kinshasa, and took him into Angola to meet the UNITA chief, Jonas Savimbi, in 1975.[18] Tempelsman later tried to capitalize on Stockwell's link with Savimbi as he had with Devlin's link with Mobutu and offered Stockwell a job. Stockwell, as mentioned earlier, had refused him. Much later on, in 1997, Tempelsman would offer Savimbi a deal by which UNITA could be officially established in the diamond business with the cartel's blessing and with US government funding.

Richard Dowden, the first white reporter for five years to reach the Angolan diamond mines, found in 1983 that UNITA was heavily engaged in the diamond trade. Its diamond operation was well organized and professionally advised. It was smuggling them out overland to Zaire and Zambia, or flying them out from its many airstrips. Some were sold via Mobutu, some went directly to Antwerp, and some went by helicopter to South Africa.

Dowden discovered that De Beers had at the same time formed a relationship with the Angolan government – and secured secret contracts for the output of the diamond mines UNITA was attacking – so it seemed that whatever happened in Angola, De Beers would get its diamonds. A company called the British Mine Police was hired to protect the diamond mines with helicopter gunships. Another British company called Defence Systems International also claimed to be defending the mines. Dowden saw the remains of a Hercules transport plane shot down while ferrying supplies into the mines and possibly diamonds out. Its owner was Air America, a company exposed as a CIA operation during the Vietnam War.[19] The CIA and De Beers clearly had unparalleled access at that time to the Angolan diamond trade.

The De Beers connection with the Angolan government was so concealed that it seemed both sides found it embarrassing. The Angolan government sold its diamonds to Mining and Technical Services – a company ostensibly not connected to any South African company but incorporated in Liechtenstein. But in reality, its main office was adjacent to the De Beers' London office.

Maurice Tempelsman agreed in February 1989 to purchase about $20 million worth of diamonds from the Angolan government. He also offered advice on how to restrain the diamond rush. In December 1990, the government decided to give De Beers the exclusive right to market Angolan diamonds, in the hope that this would stop De Beers buying from UNITA.[20] De Beers' contract was in conflict with Tempelsman's but this apparently was not a problem. He accepted losing his Angolan diamonds, for his main supply was guaranteed thanks to his status as a Sightholder. If he helped De Beers, it could put very good diamonds into his boxes.

But the Angolan ceasefire of 1992 could have meant a near-disastrous flood of diamonds that might have forced prices down if De Beers' buyers had failed to remove them from the market. De Beers filmed tens of thousands of demobbed troops digging diamonds over a landscape denuded from horizon to horizon. (An excerpt from this was shown over De Beers' protests in our documentary *The Diamond Empire*.) Helicopters were landing every few days in the bush with people from Zaire, Lebanon, and South Africa seeking to buy the precious stones, sometimes using counterfeit money or drug proceeds. A mining director in Lucapa, Kiame Matadidi described it as, "very violent, very violent indeed. It is wild prospecting."[21] Freelance diggers, known as "garimpeiros," swarmed across the hillsides. UNITA's forces were deeply involved.

De Beers was hard pressed to buy the enormous numbers of good quality diamonds being mined in Angola. The Australian diamond miners were told their diamonds would have to be stockpiled rather than sold, due to the flood of Angolan stones. De Beers also used its "need" to buy Angolan diamonds as a justification for keeping black wages down in South Africa.[22]

In 1992, UNITA again became De Beers' main Angolan partner. UNITA had refused to abide by the election results, restarted the war, and captured the major diamond fields around Cafunfo. In 1993, UNITA seized considerable diamond stocks from the Angolan government. In late 1994 I was told by senior government sources in Namibia and in South Africa that helicopters were flying into UNITA-held territory at night from Botswana, Namibia, and South Africa to trade arms and other goods for diamonds.

UNITA channeled a large part of its smuggling through Mobutu, making him even wealthier. "Angolan diamonds are reported to account for at least 50 percent of the stones appearing in Zaire's (official) export total. Diamond experts can identify the Angolan diamonds as they are of higher quality."[23] A new diamond province, centered on Tembo, appeared in Zaire, next to that part of Angola controlled by UNITA. The Kinshasa weekly, *Soft de Finance*, in September 1993 described the wild diamond market in Tembo where merchants flying in from Kinshasa traded weapons, radios, beer and other goods for diamonds.[24]

In late 1993 a bill in the Belgian parliament called for an embargo on "UNITA's diamond trade used to finance the armed rebellion in Angola." Belgians were embarrassed at the brazen UNITA sales operation in Antwerp, and at the involvement of their diamond industry in helping to finance this extremely bloody war.

Smuggled Angolan diamonds, rhino horn, and ivory

In 1994 I was given a copy of an affidavit accusing De Beers' Namibian subsidiary, CDM, of illegally buying elephant tusks and rhino horn as well as diamonds. It was signed by a diamond buyer named Thomas George Pearson.

Pearson alleged in his affidavit: "I was employed by CDM Pty. Ltd. in Namibia as a Diamond Buyer from June 30th to November 1992. [I was given] a detailed briefing by Roger Burchill, Head of CDM Security Department. My appointment was that of an undercover unlicensed diamond buyer in Namibia and Angola. My flat was equipped with a hidden video camera as well as a voice recorder provided by CDM and each transaction was recorded on tape for delivery to Roger Burchill."

He was told the buying operations would be recorded so the people selling diamonds to him could be arrested – but "as a result of these transactions no one was ever arrested despite CDM and Nampols [Namibian police] knowledge that all business deals conducted with smugglers were illegal.... Approximately 35 illegal transactions took place in the flat and at other locations during this 6-month period... My remuneration from CDM amounted to one third of the... price paid."

Sworn statements from others involved supported his statement. Since Pearson did not have a diamond-buying license, every aspect of this operation was illegal. He further alleged: "On a few occasions smugglers brought in rhino horns and elephant tusks, which I was instructed to buy on behalf of Roger Burchill and Chief Inspector Brink. Both gentlemen provided cash for the purchase of these articles, which was subsequently delivered to either Roger Burchill in person or to Chief Inspector Brink at the CDM Center or at the garage at his private residence. On one occasion Roger Burchill gave me R250,000 in cash with the instruction to go into Angola to purchase diamonds from UNITA."[25]

CASH TRANSACTIONS IN ANTWERP

Most smuggled diamonds not bought by De Beers in Africa would eventually arrive in Antwerp, where they could be openly sold with no questions asked. In Antwerp shop window signs announced: "Rough Diamonds Bought." But De Beers in Antwerp had quietly set up a secretive cash-based diamond buying operation run through Napol Diamonds. This was regularly receiving American dollar notes from the Diamond Trading Company (DTC), via a Swiss Bank.

Napol Diamonds needed to conceal the dollar cash transactions so they wrote to Mr. Bowery of the London office of the Diamond Trading Company on February 24th, 1982:

We refer to our invoice no. 23/82 of Feb. 24th containing carats 4,740 for US$816,395. The actual amount of this shipment is only US$665,717. As I told you on the telephone last week, I always keep a float of US$ notes to pay for the purchases made at the Kroon building. On December 31st, I had in my cash US$149,186. In the diamond trade here no one deals in cash US$ and it would have provoked questions if the aforementioned amount appeared on my end of year balance sheet.

The only way to make them disappear was to ask Mr. Godwin to issue a "bordereau" for that amount as if it were in payment of a purchase but which actually never took place. When we submit the purchase chits to customs we obviously had to add the B 452 for US$149,186.

This last sentence was ticked and "OK" had been written in by hand – presumably by a DTC official.

In 1993 the above letter was leaked to outsiders, so Godwin of Napol wrote to Mr. C. P. R. Wyndham in Johannesburg on June 18th, 1993 explaining that the Belgian authorities had sanctioned their unique secret cash operation to buy up "undeclared" or illicit diamonds for De Beers:

Paragraphs 2, 3 and 4 of our letter refer to Belgium Customs authorization no. A/6083 of 17/11/80 permitting us to buy undeclared diamonds on the Antwerp markets on condition that these purchases would be exported in their entirety to DTC London. These transactions were paid in cash dollars... imported from the Swiss Bank Corporation in Zurich... Our company was then and still is today in a unique position and in order to keep it as discreet as possible... we considered our letter to be for internal use... As stated, we were the only firm with that authorization and therefore the only one to be allowed to transact in cash dollars."

False diamond invoicing is an established practice in the diamond trade, according to a textbook on diamond insurance written by the Israeli authority, Alexander Rechter: "The insurers have recognized the fact that the declared value of any specific shipment of diamonds may well be different from its true value... they thus allow every diamond shipment to be insured for a sum different from its declared value, as long as the insured receives the prior agreement of the insurers for this."

He continued:

[for] the purposes of declaring to the airlines, the following arrangements have been made.

A. Shipments with a value of up to $25,000 will be declared to the airlines at their true value.

B. For Shipments above $25,000 (there are two alternatives.)

1. $25,000 to $33,000. Declared to the airlines at 20 percent of their true value and an additional premium paid on the full value.

2. The shipments declared to the airlines at 75 percent of their value or $25,000, whichever is the higher.[26]

In 1998, the tax authorities in Belgium made an effort to overcome the secrecy of the multibillion-dollar Antwerp diamond market so they could check if the correct amounts were paid in income tax. A letter sent by a senior tax officer, A. Best, on January 5th to the Antwerp diamond companies read, "For income tax purposes ... the hitherto used notation on the invoices in regard to the description of the goods traded (solely noting the number of carats and [if it is] rough or polished) is clearly insufficient for us to consider the books as provable."

Best went on to say that they also needed to know the numbers, color, cut, proportions, and clarity of the diamonds sold, if they were to be able to independently check the declared profits. At the moment, they did not even know if the diamonds declared were natural or synthetic.

This request met with cries of outrage. Some merchants said that such demands would end the diamond trade in Antwerp. The editor of *Diamond Intelligence Briefs* wrote, "The privacy, secrecy and efficiency of the open market brings many African, Russian and South American rough sellers to Antwerp. These rough sellers know very well that most or all of this rough is not going to be processed in Antwerp, but they still prefer the Antwerp market because the confidentiality is guaranteed. Israel, for example, tries to attract rough buying offices to Israel, but requires the rough seller to register and open bank accounts, and these are all conditions that many open market rough sellers try to avoid."

The former Budget Minister Hugo Schiltz (VU party) stated, "The diamond sector [has] established a facade behind which a worldwide net of transactions was conducted." But the editor of DIB thought the Belgian authorities should perhaps allow this and forgo normal income taxes: "In India, the government has exempted diamond exporters from paying any tax on profits. In Israel, diamantaires pay a nominal tax based on turnover. In these countries, the two major competitors of Belgium, the government has accommodated the needs of the diamond industries." This suggested he thought paying income tax an inappropriate imposition for his industry.

The diamond trade evidently has a history of deception – it is in the nature of their game. If they are to keep their profits and prices high, they must conceal the fact that the commodity they trade as rare and precious can be mined and cut in great numbers at very low cost. This has always been an essential part of their strategy.

1   "Sir Percy, They Presume": Ian Fleming, *The Diamond Smugglers*, New York, 1957, p. 6.
2   Supplement to *Windhoek Observer*. July 7th, 1984.
3   Thirion Commission Eighth Interim Report, p. 327.
4   Pallister, p. 104. Kroll telephone conversation with the Department of Trade, (Russia Desk) November 10th, 1988.
5   *Diamond International Magazine*. May-June 1992.
6   Stefan Kanfer. *The Last Empire: De Beers, Diamonds and the World.* New York: Farrar Straus Giroux, 1993, p. 292.
7   Sir Charles Hambro was allegedly involved with MI6 operations into Eastern Europe according to a documentary on Robert Maxwell broadcast on Channel 4, UK, on January 26th, 1995.
8   As noted on the website of the Ombudsman for Diamonds of the Republic of South Africa, March 2002.
9   Percy Sillitoe, *Cloak Without Dagger.* Abelard Schuman Co.; New York, 1955, p. 196.
10 Edward Epstein. *Sunday Times*, London. June 6th, 1982.
11 Kanfer, p. 248.
12 BBC *Assignment*, broadcast February 24th, 1996.
13 London *Sunday Telegraph.* March 3rd, 1976.
14 *Washington Post*. March 21st, 1994.
15 *African Business*, December 1993.
16 *African Confidential*, April 16th, 1993.
17 Confidential source in Belgian diamond industry, 1993.
18 *Covert Action*. January 1980.
19 *The Times*, London. October 14th, 1983.
20 *Diamond International*, May-June 1992, p. 54.
21 Reuters report, 1993.
23 *New African*, 1993.
24 *African Business*, December 1993.
25 Sworn Statement by Thomas George Pearson made before John Justin Henry, Commissioner of Oaths. July 15th, 1993.
26 Alexander Richter, *Diamonds: A Legal Perspective.* Shacham Publications; Tel Aviv, Israel, 1987.

Chapter 13 – Conflict diamonds and the diamond wars

The "conflict diamond" campaign tainted diamonds and thus was not welcomed by the jewelry merchants. They would have liked diamonds to be seen as simply symbols of love – but surprisingly, this stigma suited a new De Beers strategy.

The change came about, at least on the face of it, due to international pressure to stop the purchase of "conflict" diamonds. The campaign targeted insurgents in Angola and Sierra Leone who had funded their weapon purchases with locally mined diamonds. According to the UN, between 1992 and 1998 the rebel army of UNITA in Angola made $3-4 billion from diamond sales. When Princess Diana met with Angolan land mine victims, she met victims of the proceeds of diamond sales.

The UN Fowler Report alleged and documented how a former De Beers Sightholder, Joe De Decker, supplied some of UNITA's military needs between 1993 and 1994, carrying on this trade alongside Mobutu's government officials until 1997. He allegedly flew with his brother Ronnie into UNITA-controlled territory in a private Lear jet from South Africa. His brother's job was to organize the flow of former Cold War weapons from Eastern Europe, while he bought the UNITA diamonds in parcels worth up to $6 million each and sent them to the diamond merchants of Antwerp – where De Beers also had its buying office. De Beers at that time was purchasing many diamonds mined by UNITA.

De Beers' purchases helped fund a murderous war against an internationally recognized Angolan government. In 1996 and 1997 these purchases provided much of De Beers' profits. Even when there were more UNITA diamonds than De Beers needed, it continued to purchase them. De Beers' buyers bought from uniformed UNITA troops at offices just inside Zaire. UNITA used the funds thus raised to purchase MiG fighters and thousands of tons of armaments.

De Beers might well have argued that it was helping resist "communism" by buying these diamonds – and helping an undercover US policy. The CIA had supplied UNITA from the 1960s. It had maintained this support for decades and sent in US military advisors and agents. Maurice Tempelsman, Harry Oppenheimer's close associate, recruited some of his diamond office staff from these men.

De Beers' decision in 1999 to stop buying from UNITA did not happen purely for humanitarian reasons. It happened after American companies found large oil fields in territory controlled by the Angolan government. Angola was soon supplying 10 percent of US needs. It had not proved as hostile towards Western businesses as the CIA had predicted.

When the Clinton Administration decided it could no longer treat the oil-rich Angolan government as a pariah state, it unsuccessfully put pressure on UNITA to stop fighting. UNITA had been given a radio frequency by the *Voice of America* for its radio station. Clinton took this away and issued Executive Order 12865 on September 23rd, 1993, declaring UNITA "a continuing threat to the foreign policy objectives of the US."

De Beers now became publicly critical of UNITA – but mostly for the "crime" of selling diamonds onto the open market rather than through the Angolan government. De Beers also allegedly hired the UK/South African-based mercenary group Executive Outcome to protect the government's diamond mines and put pressure on UNITA.

While these events were unfolding, De Beers was still buying the diamonds produced by miners working under the supervision of UNITA militia. But De Beers knew that this system would lose its usefulness as, without US support, UNITA was starting to lose its war.

De Beers feared it would not be able to make as good an arrangement with the Angolan government as it had with UNITA. The Russians were in Luanda actively seeking diamond marketing rights. Already a diamond mine had been put under Russian management. This presented a real danger to the cartel. It was therefore not surprising that there soon arrived on the scene De Beers' favored American diamond merchant, Maurice Tempelsman, with a plan to give De Beers sole rights to all Angolan diamonds, whether produced by the government or by UNITA.

Once more he was reported to be an "independent," rather than a man closely linked to the diamond cartel. Press reports described him as a man solely concerned with helping the Angolan government market its diamonds, not particularly interested in taking any equity in its mining concerns. But he was focused on the key preoccupation of the cartel. It estimated that the diamonds remaining in Angola were worth between $50 and $60 billion – and De Beers very much wanted sole marketing rights to them.

Tempelsman was surely kept well informed of the changes in US policy, since he was a frequent visitor to the Clinton White House. The Angolan government was also changing its policies in order to undercut UNITA's support. It started to sell some of its diamonds to De Beers – and Tempelsman was given permission to open a cutting factory there. He also entered into a diamond marketing partnership with Jean Boulle, whom we last met in Arkansas, apparently planning to re-open the Crater of Diamonds mine.

Boulle operated in Africa in a fashion similar to Tempelsman – but seemingly with a closer connection to mercenary groups than to the CIA. He was a former De Beers manager in Zaire with diamond interests in Sierra Leone and Angola. He had moved his corporate headquarters to Hope, Arkansas, President Clinton's hometown, a move that had gained him a meeting with Clinton.

Tempelsman had by now finely honed his ability to influence a Democratic Administration. He was a guest at the Clinton White House nearly a dozen times and the Clintons were his guests on his 70-foot yacht, *Relemar.* His companies gave $145,000 to Democratic Party committees.[1] He soon used these contacts to devise a way for De Beers to gain sole rights to Angolan diamonds.

TEMPELSMAN PLANS FOR UNITA

Tempelsman devised a plan between 1996 and 1997, not to remove diamond revenues from UNITA, but to protect UNITA's diamond income and its trade with De Beers. It was designed to guarantee the continued peaceful existence of UNITA. The Clinton Administration backed it.

He proposed a joint diamond mining and marketing operation for UNITA and the Angolan government, that would contract to sell to De Beers all the diamonds produced. De Beers loved the plan. He had US support at the highest of levels – and the likelihood of US funding. This was no easy thing to achieve. For over 20 years the Federal Export-Import Bank (Ex-Im) had refused to sponsor any projects in Angola under an explicit statutory ban on lending to Angola until a free and fair election has been held in that country.

Tempelsman could not have achieved this if he were not close to the US Intelligence community and White House. The National Security Council, the body advising the White House on intelligence matters, was persuaded to extraordinarily declare that it was in the United States' strategic interest to have just one company control and market Angolan diamonds – thus once more dovetailing US interests with those of De Beers.

In the summer of 1996, Tempelsman obtained from Assistant Secretary of State George E. Moose a public letter suggesting that the US might fund Tempelsman's plan. Moose wrote that this plan would help UNITA settle down by giving it a steady income, and would also help stabilize the Angolan government. "I believe the proposal, as you've outlined it, is a constructive proposal on an important issue, which must be resolved if the peace process is to move forward."

Tempelsman was to use this letter to try to persuade the Angolans to back his scheme. A State Department spokesperson said that the Moose letter was "a vehicle for Tempelsman to get his feet in the door." A US Africa division official commented under conditions of anonymity: "This is commercial diplomacy taken to a new place. He's using the US government... Tempelsman wanted us to tell Ex-Im: 'This is a foreign policy imperative. We would like you to do it even if it is risky.'"

Tempelsman argued for his plan on political lines rather than for its commercial wisdom and profitability. On October 10th, 1996, accompanied by his attorney Sorenson, he met with Anthony Lake, the National Security Advisor, and with Lake's deputy, Shawn McCormick, Advisor to the National Security Council, the White House's elite intelligence people. The agenda was the US strategy for Angola. All agreed to back Tempelsman's plan. Lake instructed McCormick to tell OPIC and the Ex-Im Bank that their funds would be needed and that "from a foreign policy perspective, the proposal has merit." Other State Department officials then "were told to support Tempelsman."[2]

In May 1997, the US Ambassador Donald Steinbeck and National Security Council Advisor Shawn McCormick praised his plan in meetings with the Angolan

Government and with Savimbi of UNITA. Classified cables record that McCormick told the Angolan President dos Santos on May 2nd that UNITA must have its diamond business regularized and that UNITA needed resources to make the transition towards peace. McCormick suggested that the government should cease trying to take back the diamond resources held by UNITA. At a separate meeting that same day with Savimbi, Steinbeck mentioned the "Lazare Kaplan project" (Tempelsman's company) and his hope that the Government would respect UNITA's diamond income since US agencies were involved in the Tempelsman deal.

Tempelsman met both with Savimbi of UNITA and with the Angolan government. He proposed that the government yield diamond fields to UNITA – thus keeping UNITA in the business of supplying De Beers – and perhaps supplying a new cutting factory wanted by Tempelsman. He even offered American government money to UNITA in order to help it mine diamonds more efficiently.

But eventually his plan failed, perhaps because UNITA still hoped for military victory, perhaps because the Angolan government had no wish to yield diamond mines to a murderous rebel group that had killed thousands after refusing to accept it had lost a national election – and perhaps because the relationship between De Beers and UNITA had deteriorated. Savimbi was now selling many of UNITA's diamonds on the open market rather than to De Beers.

CLINTON, DE BEERS, AND CONFLICT DIAMONDS

The failure of Tempelsman's plan led to a revision of US government policy. The US decided that if there could be no deal with Savimbi, then a way must be found to stop UNITA having a diamond income. Unsurprisingly, De Beers had come to much the same conclusion, but it felt it could only stop buying UNITA's diamonds if UNITA was stopped from marketing them, or they were kept off the market by other means and so were not a threat to its market-control. De Beers would now welcome any scheme that prevented UNITA from selling diamonds onto the open market. Up until now De Beers had been spending a fortune on UNITA's diamonds. If these were removed from the market, then it might have the funds to buy control over rival mines elsewhere. Perhaps it could buy a Canadian mine, perhaps an Australian?

Suddenly the US, De Beers and the UK all discovered the international campaign against the sale of diamonds used to fund wars and seemingly adopted it with zest. No matter what the humanitarian arguments for it, it would give them another way to remove UNITA's diamonds from the open market. This was a major change of policy. The US for one would never have agreed to it during the decades that they had funded UNITA.

But the new US policy towards Angola had a military underside that bypassed the official US concern about conflict diamonds. The Clinton Administration allegedly made it a covert condition of US aid to Angola that Angola cease hiring mercenaries supplied by Executive Outcome – and instead use mercenaries supplied by an American company close to US Intelligence. It was also decided that diamonds secured by these American mercenaries would be exempted from the conflict diamond embargo.

As a result of Clinton's pressure, Angola's army stopped being trained by Executive Outcome and instead was tutored by Military Professional Resources Inc. (MPRI) of Virginia. MPRI had been created as part of a new privatized and covert model for US military intervention. It was not as independent as it looked. A host of Pentagon generals were involved with it.

The Angolan government's diamond business was itself decidedly murky. It used mercenary companies to recover diamond mines from UNITA and then seemingly rewarded these mercenaries with diamonds. The United States was now seemingly also hoping to profit from having its mercenaries in Angola.

The US wanted the Executive Outcome private army to play a diminished role. It was associated with Diamond Works, a company registered originally in the Isle of Man in which Boulle was involved. This was another company with a diamond link. It specialized in sending paramilitary security teams to secure diamond leases. One of its principal security operators was a J. C. Erasmus. The South African *Mail and Guardian* had alleged of him: "Like many of Branch Energy's South African staff, he is a former member of apartheid South Africa's notorious Civil Co-operation Bureau death squad." He was also a shareholder in Diamond Works.

In Sierra Leone diamonds were financing another bloody war and mercenaries were again involved. Executive Outcome held a 40 percent share in Branch Energy/Diamond Works' Sierra Leone operation. Independent observers noted that these mostly white mercenaries seemed to have scant concern about killing black Africans.

Despite the US intervention, Executive Outcome continued fighting inside Angola until mercenaries from another outfit, the Belgium-linked IDAS, replaced it. IDAS had close links to MPRI – and with Boulle who had landed the output of the Angolan Cuango diamond mine when it was won back from UNITA. Diamond Works then won the rights to the diamonds from the recovered Lunda Norte mine. This confusion would only be partially sorted out when the government set up Ascorp as a national diamond monopoly.

But north of Angola, along Zaire's eastern frontier with Rwanda and Uganda, dramatic and horrific events then occurred that would create a much larger diamond-financed war.

THE CONGO DIAMOND WARS

In the Congo, chaos and war was about to replace the long rule of the despot Mobutu, and in this chaos would also be the covert teams of the US military. This would become the murkiest of the diamond wars, one that would kill over two million people, an under-reported horrific catastrophe.

It began on the eastern borders of the Congo, in the little-known countries of Rwanda and Burundi It was originally a local issue. Here the Tutsi nation had long ruled over the Hutu nation. It had been so from before the arrival of Europeans and continued during the colonial era. When democracy arrived in Rwanda in 1962, the Hutu majority gained power over their previous masters. Many Tutsis then fled to Uganda or into Zaire. A negotiated power-sharing agreement then kept the peace for three years.

But the Hutus feared the Tutsi were plotting to regain power. When a surface-to-air missile shot down the plane of the Hutu President Habyrimana on April 6th, 1994, a Tutsi plot was immediately suspected. (A UN investigation would justify their fears. It concluded that Kabila, a Tutsi general trained in the United States, had authorized this attack. Other independent investigators saw the hand of the United States in the provision of the missiles.)[3] This assassination triggered a most horrific massacre of some 700,000 Rwandan Tutsi by the Hutus – and the murder of thousands of moderate Hutus who had opposed this massacre. This terrible disaster led to another civil war in Rwanda in which Tutsis killed some 50,000 Hutus. In Burundi another 100,000 died. The only effective Western effort to save lives was by the French, according to Herman Cohn, the head of the US State Department's Africa bureau under President Bush (senior); "At least the French sent people in here to stop the killing… that's more than we did."[4] He said this saved "the lives of between 20,000 and 40,000 Tutsis."[5] An official of the British-based charity Oxfam told the Congressional House International Relations Committee in 1996, "During the past months of slaughter, the United States has been the key player in halting action on Rwanda [to prevent the massacres]."[6]

The US was now forming close military connections with the Tutsis, and with their leader, Paul Kakame, the general whom the UN would name as responsible for assassinating the Hutu President. A US diplomat wrote to Amnesty International, to say that three months before the assassination, American Special Forces, "Green Berets," had begun to train Kakame's Tutsi troops "to professionalize what started as a guerrilla army, and to expose their officers to management of a multiethnic force."[7] This may have been motivated by sympathy for the Tutsi as victims of a genocidal massacre, or perhaps as part of a long-term US strategy to remove the commercial influence of the French, whose Foreign Legionnaires had trained the Hutu troops.[8]

Paul Kakame also formed an alliance with the Ugandan President Museveni, whom he had helped seize power in a 1986 coup and whom he had served as Head of Military Intelligence.

The military support given by the Pentagon to the Tutsi General was highly secret and not even reported to the US Congress. US military "training missions" were exempt from Congressional Oversight. The Pentagon took full advantage of this by setting up a "Special Operations Command" with some 47,000 troops. These it had sent out in small teams quietly to some 45 African countries, and elsewhere in the world, on over 2,000 armed missions, all virtually unnoticed by the Western media, and all in the interest of furthering American influence and business penetration.[9]

The US was now ready to drop its support for Mobutu in neighboring Zaire, despite having given his government over $1.5 billion in aid since 1965. He had enriched himself by plundering his country's resources and this had brought him into ill repute. But, perhaps more importantly for US policymakers, he had been found unreliable as a business partner. Mining deals with US companies had collapsed. He had canceled his contracts with De Beers several times in order to try to negotiate a better personal take.

The US now had useful regional military alliances. The Tutsi alliance on Zaire's eastern border was prepared for the task of overthrowing Mobutu. The Congolese hero Kabila, who in the 1960s led a military revolt against Mobutu, was recruited as a figurehead for a liberation movement. He was given an army of Rwandan and Ugandan troops. They were poor countries, but found they had no great difficulty in raising dollars to pay their troops for this task.

When the US mercenary outfit MPRI contemplated offering Mobutu aid against the army being raised against him, the US State Department sharply told them not to even think of it. They were asked instead to train the Tutsi. CIA agents were then secretly sent into Zaire to prepare for the soon-to-come invasion force.

Kagame had his own reason to want to invade Zaire. Mobutu had given refuge to over one million Hutus from Rwanda who had fled fearing Tutsi revenge killings. Museveni of Uganda also wanted a pretext to invade Zaire. He wanted to attack the Ugandan rebel groups who had set up bases there.

Clinton's Ambassador to Rwanda, Robert Gribbin, met with Kabila some 30 to 40 times over the next eighteen months. US military aid allegedly was sent to Kabila through the innocuous-sounding International Rescue Committee.[10]

In 1996, Kagame of Rwanda made a quick visit to Washington. On his return the joint Ugandan-Rwandan invasion of Zaire was launched. Western backers expected the invasion force to quickly wrest from Mobutu his rich copper and diamond mines and to return them to Western interests. US Air Force C-130 Hercules aircraft delivered tanks and other arms for the invasion army. They first landed at Entebbe airport in Uganda but soon were flying directly to captured airstrips inside Zaire. This American involvement in a major invasion went virtually unnoticed by the rest of the world.

The troops had swift success. Kabila set up his headquarters in the former palace of President Mobutu in Goma. By early 1997 the US State Department also had a diplomat stationed in Goma, although Mobutu was still in power. Kabila announced that Zaire would once again be known under its old name of the Congo – or, to be precise, as the Democratic Republic of the Congo (DRC).

But Kabila did not regard De Beers with friendly eyes. It had only just stopped trading with Mobutu. De Beers thus needed to find another way to secure control over the Congo's diamonds.

Then, just as Kabila's forces were capturing the Congo diamond mines, there stepped in a certain Jean Boulle. He offered Kabila the loan of a private Lear executive jet, financial support, and, just as Maurice Tempelsman had originally boosted his standing in Africa by lending the leader of SWAPO an executive jet and by traveling with prestigious Americans, Boulle brought the independently-minded African American US Congressional Representative Cynthia McKinney to see Kabila. Kabila responded as Boulle had hoped. Boulle's company landed a contract for the marketing of the Congo's diamonds. Kabila evidently did not know then of the Kroll report that concluded that Boulle appeared as an independent but was closely associated with De Beers.

Within seven months Mobutu had fallen and Kabila was the head of the Congo's government. Kabila had promised much to the corporations that gave support to his invasion – but he was determined not to be their servant. In the 1960s he had admired Lumumba, a leader who had tried to put the interests of the Congo first. Kabila likewise was determined not to be the servant of the Ugandans, the Rwandan Tutsi or of the Americans, who had made his ascent possible. He may have been appointed as a figurehead, but that was not how he saw his job. He was determined to be independent.

But his army was under a Tutsi Chief of Staff. He had very little control over the Ugandan and Rwandan invasion troops that were officially his allies. His Rwandan Tutsi allies started to seek out the Hutu refugees, torturing and killing them. The Ugandans sought out the Congo camps of the Ugandan rebels – and both the Tutsi and the Ugandans started to pillage the natural resources of the Congo. Kabila feared to intercede. He knew that the Tutsi would seek to replace him if he tried to stop them.

At this point President Mandela of South Africa offered his advice – and strongly recommended bringing in two major South African enterprises, De Beers and Anglo American. He told him they had the strength to help develop his country. It seems Kabila listened to Mandela. He was persuaded to cancel the contract he had given to Boulle and to instead consider a contract with De Beers – which immediately set up diamond buying offices in the Congo.

Boulle was furious – for a short while. He filed an action in a US court for a billion dollars against De Beers and Anglo American, but in March 1998 dropped this action allegedly in return for a partnership with De Beers in a diamond venture. This apparently made Kabila suspicious of Boulle – and that same month, President Clinton toured Africa accompanied by Maurice Tempelsman.

Kabila did not go ahead with a deal with De Beers, and moreover decided that he was not prepared to give exclusive deals for the Congo's diamonds to Boulle or to anyone else associated with De Beers. Kabila was not proving amenable to Western manipulation – and not even to the persuasive words of Mandela.

Kabila soon found himself blamed for the atrocities committed by the Rwandan troops, despite them not being under his command. He suspected his reputation was being blackened as part of a plot to justify a coup against him. He decided to fire Kabare, his Tutsi Head of the Armed Forces. On June 27th, 1998, he ordered all Tutsi forces to leave the Congo, giving as the reason their atrocities against the Hutu refugees – and their plot against him.

He was right to fear a plot. In Brussels a group calling itself Council for the Democratic Federal Republic of the Congo, CRFDC, was allegedly ready to replace him. It declared itself in favor of the "globalization" of the Congo's economy – meaning the opening of its resources to multinational corporations. The Tutsi with their allies were now prepared to overthrow him. Ample funds had seemingly been found and detailed military plans prepared.

Thus, within days of being sacked, Kabare was leading a second Ugandan and Rwandan invasion of the Congo. Two airborne waves of Ugandan paratroopers flew across the Congo to seize the ports and the key hydroelectric dam supplying both water and power to the capital, Kinshasa. They hoped overthrowing Kabila would be as easy as overthrowing Mobutu. But although Kabila did not recover control over the capital's main water supply for weeks, he succeeded in rallying his people against the now very unpopular foreign troops.

At first it seemed that Rwanda and Uganda would succeed. American newspapers now reported that the Tutsi invaders had with them US Special Operations troops. The Rwandan and Ugandan military had by now received over five years of US training. Wayne A. Downing, the former commander of the Pentagon's Special Operations, told the *Washington Post* that in Special Operations missions "there is definitely a political card played... They are a direct instrument of US foreign policy."[11] The US continued to be secretly and directly involved in the chaos and fighting now engulfing the Congo.

It seemed that US Special Forces were being used to covertly extend US power and commerce over Africa, and in so doing replace the influence of Europe. The Clinton Administration was particularly determined to replace the influence of the French and Belgians. The US Secretary of State, Madeleine Albright, vetoed the re-appointment of the UN Secretary-General Boutros-Ghali because she thought him pro-French.

Kabila appealed for support to the United Nations and to the Organization for African Unity (OAU). In mid-August the OAU ordered the invading forces to lay down their arms. They ignored this order. They instead set up headquarters in Mobutu's old palace in Goma and invited Mobutu's former generals to visit and help them. They retained from Mobutu's days many links with the US Republican Party as well as with De Beers. Dick Cheney had met with these generals prior to his election as Vice President. Military help for the invaders came from South Africa. Soon the invaders were laying siege to the Congolese diamond mines at Mbuji-Mayi.

This pointed to the key objective of this new invasion. It was now obvious the key issue at its heart was who would control the Congo's resources, and in particular, its diamond mines. Kabila resolved to hold the diamond mines at all cost. Without them he would not have the revenues needed to resist the invasion.

De Beers' actions were seemingly designed to help these invaders. In the midst of this crisis, it suddenly shut its buying offices at the diamond mines and in Kinshasa. It adamantly refused every request from Kabila to reopen them – thus making it much harder for Kabila to raise the funds needed to resist the invasion. This made it look as if the rebels, with US military assistance, would succeed in overthrowing Kabila.

At this point, something happened that the US simply had not anticipated. Many African countries rallied to support Kabila. Troops arrived to help him from Angola, Zimbabwe, Sudan, Chad and Namibia – and this enabled him to slow down and halt the advance of the invasion. When two Rwandan battalions found themselves trapped, they sought and gained permission to take refuge in the UNITA-controlled areas of Northern Angola. UNITA had previously regarded the Rwandans with suspicion because of their role in overthrowing Savimbi's friend Mobutu – but Savimbi now found he shared common interests with the Rwandans. UNITA's troops were airlifted to fight alongside the Rwandan invaders in the siege of the Mbuji-Mayi diamond mines. In return, Rwanda became a new route out for UNITA's diamonds.

It would take months of fierce fighting, but Kabila managed to hold onto the vital diamond mines, thus securing an income for his government. He helped his allies in Namibia and Zimbabwe pay for the armies they had sent him by giving them rights to the production from some of the Congo diamond mines. In return, Zimbabwe garrisoned the diamond town of Mbuji-Mayi to make it safe for the Kabila government.

UNITA troops then invaded a part of Namibia, to "punish" it for helping the Congo. This was now growing into a very major war – far bigger than its foreign backers had intended. The chaos was threatening their economic interests. They had hoped that the invasion would help them secure access to the Congo's resources.

Instead their allies were helping themselves within the occupied territories, and Kabila had retained the diamonds.

At this stage, a diplomatic offensive succeeded in getting representatives of the invading forces to the negotiating table with Kabila. Maurice Tempelsman was also there. He reportedly tried to ease the path of the negotiations by inviting the heads of African governments to a white-glove dinner at the prestigious Metropolitan Club in New York City.[12]

The deal struck in 1999 was that the invasion forces would leave the Congo, as Kabila had demanded, and be replaced by a peacekeeping force. But unfortunately the invaders were given six months to leave. They used this time to organize a massive theft of Congolese resources. Uganda and Rwanda used the 40 percent of the Congo that they had captured as if it had been given to them to strip naked. They went for rare minerals that were more valuable than gold such as coltan, used for computer chips. They took timber from the rain forests with no regard for good husbandry. This was documented in a report from the UN's Secretary-General to its Security Council on April 12th, 2000.

It started to look as if the invaders would never leave. Human Rights Watch spokesman Des Forges noted, "In August 2000 Uganda airlifted 163,000 Congolese children to Kampala for military training...."

But although Uganda and Rwanda stole and sold over a million dollars worth of Congo's diamonds, the major diamond mines remained in Congolese hands. When Laurent Kabila was assassinated in a suspected coup, his son Joseph Kabila continued his father's strategy, but perhaps was more sympathetic to the peace attempts.

De Beers still refused support to the Kabila government. It instead said it would not buy any diamonds from war zones even if sold by Kabila's internationally recognized government. But fortunately Israeli merchants came to the aid of Kabila, helping him by setting up an alternative diamond marketing system through a company called IDI. Kabila in return gave this company for a limited period exclusive diamond marketing rights to Congolese diamonds.

THE CIVIL WAR IN SIERRA LEONE

The Sierra Leonean government had become dependent on mercenaries provided by the UK/South African company Executive Outcome, paying for them with $1.5 million per month from the Kono diamond mine. It was a chaotic situation. The government had no popular mandate, for it was not elected, and depended on these foreign mercenaries. Lord Avebury suspected a major part of the output of its diamond mines was still being traded illicitly by local officials or mercenaries, without paying government taxes.[13]

In 1991 civilian rule was restored in Sierra Leone, but under the unpopular President Momah. Within a year he was overthrown by military coup but this was only partially successful. Strasser, the leader of the coup, failed to win control over the whole country and faced armed opposition from a group called the Revolutionary United Front (RUF). The RUF purportedly was opposed to government corruption but eventually came to fund its army with diamonds from Kono extracted with considerable cruelty. It was widely reported that they mined with the help of slave labor and cut off limbs to punish disobedient miners. Even children lost limbs to the thugs it employed.

Strasser was overthrown in an army coup in 1996. The army replaced him with an elected leader, Kabbah. He failed to make peace with the RUF rebels but came under IMF pressure to get rid of the Executive Outcome mercenaries. Without their aid, he was swiftly overthrown by a coup organized by Kormah who formed an alliance with the RUF rebels. This alliance brought peace for a while but was highly unpopular with the UK Government since it saw the RUF as a terrorist organization. Although Sierra Leone had been wrecked by continual civil war for years, with elected leaders constantly overthrown by the military, the UK now swung its weight behind Kabbah as the last elected leader.

Kabbah was soon restored to power with UK and Nigerian military support. In the subsequent Peace Treaty of Lome, Kabbah agreed to share power with RUF ministers appointed to his Cabinet. They took up their offices – but tensions continued. Suddenly Kabbah ambushed the RUF, removing them from power, arresting many while they were still carrying out their ministerial duties.

But the RUF militia still retained their control over the diamond mines. The UK knew this could not continue if the position of the new anti-RUF government was to be secured. The atrocities carried out by some within the RUF now received a great deal of long-overdue media attention. Little media attention was given to atrocities committed by Government allies although these were also documented by Human Rights Watch.[14] The UK soon afterwards announced it would impose sanctions on the "conflict" diamonds produced by RUF.

THE CONFLICT DIAMOND CAMPAIGN BEGINS.

It was into this context that a little known but determined campaigning group, Global Witness, in 1998 issued a 14-page indictment of the role of diamonds in the war in Angola entitled *A Rough Trade*, following this up some months later with a further report *Fatal Transactions*, distributing this to editors worldwide. These documents succeeded in bring the role of diamonds in supporting war to the public's attention.

De Beers' reaction to this was at first confused but many other organizations seized on the publicity to push for restrictions on this trade. Within a year, in 1999, the UN Security Council had banned the purchase of Angolan diamonds from UNITA and from other unlicensed sources. It then sent out the members of Expert Panels to investigate across Africa how best to prevent conflict diamonds being traded around the world.

The De Beers decision to join the campaign to ban blood diamonds was welcomed by Global Witness and by the UK government, which in earlier years had been very protective towards De Beers. British Foreign Office Minister Peter Hain said the decision was "excellent news." The British Foreign Secretary, Robin Cook, called on a meeting in Berlin of foreign ministers from the G8 to take steps to curtail the worldwide trade in illegal diamonds. It announced that it would be asking Global Witness to research the possibility of a certification scheme for diamonds.

Robin Cook secured agreement at the G8 meeting for a scheme to curtail the sale of "stolen" diamonds that had helped finance violent conflicts, such as those in Angola, and Sierra Leone. Such a scheme could have far reaching effects on the diamond marketing industry, for it seemed likely to include all diamonds moving through irregular channels, whether from conflict zones or not. Some estimated that a third of the world's diamonds moved through irregular channels.[15]

The UK government proceeded to fund a diamond certification scheme under which government diamonds were to be exported in certified bags. This was meant officially to stop "conflict diamonds" reaching the market – but surprisingly De Beers initially declined to participate, as "they don't want to get into any funny business."[16] It instead said it would not buy any Sierra Leonean diamonds, no matter who sold them, whether it was the legitimate government or not. This was perhaps because it knew officials on both sides had been selling diamonds on the open market – but its impact was to tarnish by implication all of Sierra Leone's diamonds and thus to diminish the number of diamonds in the "legitimate" market.

In Angola, De Beers also did not simply ban "conflict diamonds" produced by UNITA. It instead announced on October 5th, 1999 that it would no longer buy Angolan diamonds even if they were warranted "conflict free" and issued with the Angolan government's internationally recognized certificates of origin. It was likewise continuing its policy of not buying any of the diamonds produced in the Congo by the Kabila government, despite these being legitimate.

By so acting, De Beers had revealed its priorities apparently lay, not just in trying to stop conflict diamonds, but rather in using this campaign to embargo diamond production by rivals. It seemingly did not matter to it that by not buying legitimate Sierra Leonean, Congolese and Angolan diamonds, it was effectively damaging the legitimate incomes of these poverty-stricken nations.

The De Beers decision to ban so many diamonds was predictably met with cynicism in the diamond trade. Merchants in Antwerp said De Beers would never be able to put this into effect. They agreed that Angolan stones could be recognized by an expert – but noted that De Beers did not say it would stop selling the many diamonds from the Congo, from Angola, and from Sierra Leone, that it already held in its stockpiles. These were identical to the stones supposedly forbidden as conflict diamonds.

But when De Beers found its blanket ban on Angolan and Sierra Leonean diamonds had not been followed by other merchants or governments, it acknowledged that it would not be able to continue with its broad ban, once these states had set in place a system of certificates guaranteeing stones were conflict-free. This must have been seen as a risky strategy by some at De Beers. They would have known that if the certification system was not handled right, De Beers could lose control. It was playing a dangerous game in allowing some diamonds to be officially tainted and had to restrict the meaning of "conflict diamonds" to include only stones produced outside De Beers' control.

These moves were to develop into what we know today as "the Kimberley Process," designed to ban conflict diamonds through a system of government certification. As noted in the Introduction, this scheme would ban mostly "illicit stones" sold outside government monopolies and outside De Beers' marketing system, stones that mostly had no association with conflict.

Fortunately, before the system was even tested, the civil wars in Angola and Sierra Leone died down, but vicious killings were continuing in the Congo, despite the presence of UN troops, at the time this book went to press in 2003.

1   *Washington Post.* August 2nd, 1997.
2   Ibid.
3   Testimony to this effect was given by Wayne Madsen and others at the "Smoking Gun" US Congressional Hearing in March 2001.Also see Wayne Madsen's well-informed book, *Genocide and Covert Operations in Africa 1993-1999,* The Edwin Mellen Press, Lewiston-Queenston-Lampeter. 1999/2000. This quotes evidence surrounding the assassination of the Rwanda President Habyarima, including testimony from a Rwandan ambassador alleging that Belgians fired the Sam missiles used, pp. 109-111.
4   *New York Times.* July 8th, 1998. A10.
5   "Former US official denies role in killer missile attack," Agence Frence Presse, July 7th, 1998.
6   Prepared Statement of Jeff Drumtra, African Policy Analyst, US Committee of Refugeees, before the House International Relations Committee, International Operations and Human Rights Subcommittee, Federal News Service, May 5th, 1998.
7   *Rwanda: Ending the Silence"* Amnesty International, quoting its correspondence with a US diplomatic official. AFR 47/32/96, September 23rd, 1997. 44.
8   AAP Newsfeed: "French Forces trained former Rwandan Regime." April 14, 1998, quoting a 1998 French parliamentary inquiry. This is also cited in Madsen, pp. 125 and 118-9.
9   Evidence presented at above-cited Congressional Hearing, March 2001.
10 William Eagle, "Zaire/Allegations." Voice of America Background Report, March 21st, 1997.
11 Lynne Duke, "Africans Use Training In Unexpected Ways." *Washington Post,* July 14th, 1998, p. A1.
12 Nicole Wifeld, Associated Press, January 25th, 2000.
14 These crimes are described in some more detail in this book's Introduction.
15 Global Witness, 2001.
16 *The Guardian.* London. September 16th, 2000 quoting Ndola-Myers and the Sierra Leone diamond office.

Chapter 14 – The Secrets of the World's Most Prolific Diamond Mine; and Lessons From Fraud in Sierra Leone

At the time of the enormous Argyle diamond discovery in 1979, the Oppenheimer family had ruled the world of diamonds for over 50 years, rationing out diamonds little by little. But, when the news of the oncoming tidal wave of Australian diamonds reached them in 1980, their empire's foundations were already undermined.

Early excavations on ridge at Argyle.

Their rule was based on having rights to the production of nearly all the world's diamonds. It was widely held that they controlled 80 percent of the world's diamonds, but documents leaked to me from within the diamond cartel in 1981 revealed that in fact they then controlled the production of only 39 percent of the world's rough diamonds. The discovery in Australia of a diamond deposit greater than the official diamond reserves of South Africa thus seemed likely to spell disaster for their diamond empire. If they failed to get control over the Australian diamonds, their share of the world production would drop to less than 25 percent, making their monopoly impossible to maintain.

The scale of the threat to De Beers was undeniable. In its 1981 reports, CRA, the manager of Ashton Joint Venture, estimated that the Argyle diamond deposit would produce 20 million carats annually, expanding the world's diamond production from 48 to 68 million carats. This would prove a gross underestimate. By 1987, the Argyle mine was producing a flood of 34.4 million carats a year. By the 1990s, its production had gone up to a sparkling 40 million carats, or eight tonnes of diamonds, a year – five times the production of South Africa.

THREE DOLLARS A CARAT OF DIAMONDS

The Argyle cattle station deep in the Australian outback was so rich in diamonds that a highly paid work force could rip diamonds from its cold volcanic rocks for less than

$2.90 a carat, according to internal reports. A secret CRA report, produced with help from De Beers, contrasted this with the production costs at mines in southern Africa. Although De Beers paid its black miners a wage that was less than an eighth of an Australian miner's, it cost $33 to mine a carat at Kimberley, $19 at Premier, and $9 at Orapa in Botswana. It even cost three times more than in Australia to mine a diamond in Zaire, despite its mineworkers' wages being less than one twentieth of those paid in Australia. These production costs startled me. I had then presumed they would be much higher given the extremely high prices per carat charged in a jewelry store. If Australia was producing so cheaply, then clearly the price of diamonds could tumble down a very long way.[1]

It seemed there was only one conclusion possible for De Beers. Australian diamonds must not compete. Harry Oppenheimer, then Chairman of De Beers, fervently expressed a hope that Australia would market its gems "in a way that doesn't invite a great deal of competition with other people."[2] The Australian Prime Minister, Malcolm Fraser, had a very different view, declaring in 1981 that Australian diamonds should not "only serve to strengthen a South African monopoly."[3]

The signs of trouble were then everywhere. De Beers' diamond sales in 1981 were

half those of 1980 and profits were down 34 percent. It had to cut its dividend for the first time since World War II. It couldn't sell the diamonds in its warehouses. The journalist Edward Jay Epstein in his 1982 best seller *The Diamond Invention* predicted the immanent end to the diamond empire.[4]

Processing plant at Argyle.

Terraces excavated at Argyle on flank of extinct volcano.

De Beers was then stockpiling 60 percent of its diamond production rather than let the price of diamonds drop.[5] The Australian discovery could not have come at a worse time for De Beers.

Harry Oppenheimer felt compelled to come out of semi-retirement to take personal control over De Beers' vital negotiations in Australia. He still had access to massive financial reserves created by very high profit margins, in 1981 garnering $1.1 billion in declared profits from diamond sales of $2.8 billion. These marvelous profit margins depended on his companies maintaining control over the world's diamond supply. But despite their vast riches, they could not afford to buy the enormous numbers of diamonds Australia could produce if they had to pay for them the values given to their South African diamond production. At South African prices, it would have cost them over $4 billion a year to buy up the Australian production.

The average value De Beers' valuers assigned to De Beers' own production was $110 a carat. The lowest was $31 a carat for diamonds from their Finsch mine – nearly three times its production cost of $12 a carat. Alan Jones, Managing Director of Ashton Mining, wistfully said to me when I interviewed him in 1981, "If we were the

Syndicate and we could set our price at the 'South African Fixed Price,' the Argyle deposit would be worth at least a hundred billion dollars."

But valuers trained by the Central Selling Organization (CSO), the De Beers marketing operation, gave the Australian stones an average value of only $11 dollars a carat. The independent valuers employed to check this figure were not allowed to use independent criteria. All they could do was to check that the diamonds were classified into the correct types. They then had to use CSO-provided tables to assign dollar values to each type. On the few large stones, they were allowed to take educated guesses at what a CSO-dominated market would pay. They were thus not truly independent. They had to follow CSO guidelines.

This was not surprising – since the value of diamonds was artificially set. The diamond market was so dominated by De Beers that the industry generally accepted that De Beers had the right to make up its own prices.

But at that time I did not understand quite how all this worked – so I went for an explanation to Albert Joris, one of the first valuers to look at the Argyle diamonds. We met at his bayside home on Sydney Harbor facing the Opera House. He was now in semi-retirement but was still one of the most experienced men in the Australian diamond industry. He came from an old Belgian diamond family and had spent his entire life valuing diamonds and running a successful diamond trading company. He was an advisor of Dr. John Williamson, the owner of a vast diamond deposit in Tanganyika (now Tanzania), who had forced the Oppenheimers in 1952 to grant their mine an unprecedented 10 percent share of the world market in exchange for the right to market its diamonds.

Workers' accommodation at Argyle with swimming pool as central feature.

Joris told me that when Northern Mining discovered the Argyle diamond deposit it saw him as an obvious choice for valuing its diamonds. He was contracted to value sample parcels of thousands of Argyle diamonds chosen at random. The first samples he received had the normal mix of high and low quality stones and he gave these values pitched, he admitted, "conservatively low." One sample he valued at $21.76 a carat and another at $15.70 a carat. But surprisingly CRA, Northern Mining's much richer partner, protested that he had set the value far too high. This Joris found most perplexing.

Northern Mining brought in an international team of valuers to check Joris' valuations. But CRA was project manager and denied them access to the diamonds. Northern Mining circumvented this by putting the valuers on its staff for a dollar a week. CRA could no longer deny them access since Northern Mining was part of the Ashton Joint Venture – but it could still select the diamonds that they saw.

FRAUD ALLEGATIONS AT ARGYLE

Joris then made a very serious allegation. He publicly stated that the sample of Argyle's diamonds sent to international valuers in July 1981 was fraudulent. He was certain that it had been stripped of many of its best stones. It was not like the lots he saw earlier. It contained no high quality stones below three quarters of a carat. There were no good quality drill diamonds or good quality colored stones and this, he said, was geologically impossible. The sample "had all the appearance of being stripped." If true, this meant that someone was trying to ensure that Argyle's diamonds were undervalued.

The samples Joris saw earlier in January 1981 had been "14.7 percent magnificent gems." But this new sample was only "4.2 percent gems." He alleged that CRA must have worked hand in glove with De Beers' people to produce this fraudulent sample. While Joris valued further samples at between $20 and $25 a carat, the CSO valuers valued them from $7.50 to $10.80 a carat.

Joris made his allegations public in a letter to one of Australia's leading current affairs magazines, *The Bulletin,* in October 1981, but nothing happened. There was no government inquiry – and no libel action. Yet his allegations were extremely serious. He was one of the foremost experts in Australia and these allegedly fraudulent valuations were crucial in establishing both the price paid by the CSO for Argyle's diamonds and Australia's revenue from its diamonds.

CRA reacted to these varying estimates with a press release in February 1982: "It has become apparent that there are misconceptions that the valuations placed on the Argyle diamonds by the AJV [Ashton Joint Venture] are too low, and that the Argyle diamonds will be sold at less than their true value." It then simply quoted the low values given to the sample Joris called fraudulent, as if those values were undisputed and authoritative. I asked Joris why a company might want to conceal the richness of its diamond find. He replied, "Because the CSO is dictating that the price must be low."

It made sense that the CSO would want the price low. But CRA's role as the Argyle mine manager was becoming more and more curious. If Joris were to be believed, it was allowing its customer to set its prices – surely a unique arrangement in any industry. But why would CRA allow this? Did it really believe that the Argyle diamonds were only worth $10 a carat on the international market? Why would it want to cut its own profits? Alternatively, could it be that Northern Mining was simply trying to drive up the value of its shares by securing the highest possible evaluation?

I went back to Northern Mining and asked for evidence that the Argyle diamond deposit was as wonderful as Joris had maintained. I was then shown the top-secret valuations provided by Argyle's own geologists and gemologists.

Diamond ore on way to x-ray separating plant.

The reports I saw assessed in detail the value of Argyle's diamonds according to the four key factors used by the diamond industry of weight, color, shape and clarity.

THE SECRET ASSESSMENT OF AUSTRALIAN DIAMONDS

I first looked to see if Argyle's diamonds were much smaller than South Africa's diamonds. The reports told me that 22.4 percent of the diamonds at Argyle were a very respectable three quarters of a carat or larger, and that 9.3 percent were above one carat in weight. This would be respectable even in South Africa. If Argyle produced 40 million carats a year (as it did in 1994), two million carats a year would be over one carat in weight. This would be double South Africa's production of this expensively sized diamond. Moreover, about 200,000 of Argyle's diamonds every year would be above two carats in weight.

As for still larger stones, the Argyle mine's separation plant was not designed to produce such large stones, but to break them up. Argyle in 1982 produced a 41.7 carat gem diamond but its survival was reported as a fluke. Greg Walker, a public relations spokesman for CRA, told me any stone of this size would normally be shattered by the plant's crusher. "This is why we don't put much emphasis on the size of diamonds discovered at Argyle." This was a most extraordinary admission. Argyle's plant was designed in a manner that would smash large diamonds – these were simply presumed not to exist. It was also convenient for De Beers, as it already had more large diamonds than it could sell at the prices it charged.

Later I acquired reports from the Indian diamond merchants that cut Australian diamonds. These revealed that the above figures were conservative for, "20 percent or more of Argyle's gems were one carat or more."[6] This was a high ratio. Stones of such size usually attracted premium prices – but Argyle was selling them to De Beers at just $7 to $12 a carat.

A reason given later by CRA, to justify it accepting a still lower price from the CSO than the $12 originally quoted by the CSO, was that it was now mining the previously unreported tiny diamonds in the ore, thus bringing down the average value to $9 a carat. But this would mean CRA was extracting even more diamonds per tonne than the high figures I saw originally.

CRA evidently was determined to talk down the value of its diamonds. In 1981 when I asked about the color of its diamonds, a CRA spokesman said they were "just beer-bottle browns" – the lowest valued of the diamond colors. At the time I cynically thought this a good color for beer swilling Aussies. I had visions of brown diamond studded beer bottles. But the CRA internal reports revealed Argyle had more of the prized white diamonds than of brown. Half of the diamonds in the main part of the pipe were whites ranging between the very highly prized "exceptional white" or top "D" color and the "top crystal" or "J" color, a slightly tinted white. Argyle today produces 20 million carats of white diamonds against a total South African production of six to seven million carats of white diamonds. (In 2002, De Beers admitted that it was easy to change brown diamonds into white, and that it had known how to do this for 20 years.)

Alan Jones, the Managing Director of Ashton Mining, told me white diamonds were higher priced simply because De Beers had more whites than any other color and thus advertised them more. He commented, "If we joined the CSO, we'd expect part of the advertising budget to be spent on advertising the browns." A confidential Ashton Joint Venture marketing report I saw said the brown diamonds were marketed in South East Asia to "darker skin races [but]… unfortunately diamond imports into most of these countries are either prohibited or very highly taxed… encouraging the trade to be illicit."

Argyle: Land stripped for its diamonds.

Not all Argyle's diamonds were white or brown. They came in other colors too. The rare colors are far more prized than whites. A pink colored diamond is one of the rarest in the world. A small well-cut flawless pink could sell for hundreds of thousands of dollars. These internal reports told me that one percent of Argyle's diamonds were pinks, an extremely high proportion by international standards. I also learned from the internal reports that about two percent of the Argyle stones were yellow; a less rare but highly valued color.

When I visited Antwerp, I was able to see thousands of Argyle diamonds and even to run my hands through large plastic containers of them. The pink diamonds were obvious and many. Argyle would produce some 400,000 carats a year of pink diamonds, 10,000 times the "one in a million" mentioned in advertisements. Argyle is now the world's principal source of pink diamonds.

CRA must have known it was unfairly belittling its own diamonds. Eight years after saying they were mostly "beer bottle browns," it marketed its brown diamonds with great verve as "champagne" and "cognac." It commissioned the Queen's own jeweler, Australian Stewart Devlin, to cut Argyle brown diamonds into exquisite jewelry. When I first met Devlin he was surrounded by pieces of clockwork machinery, all heavily encrusted with brown diamonds. These he was assembling into clockwork eggs that would open to display rotating fairground carousels. They would delight royalty and exhibition-goers worldwide. The Queen's jeweler was enthusiastic about Australia's brown diamonds. He maintained that Argyle should be able to make a fortune from its brown stones for they were so much "warmer" than the ice-cold whites.

As for the third key criteria, clarity; the Ashton Joint Venture internal reports stated that one in ten thousand of the Argyle diamonds were "loupe clean" or "flawless" which means that a jeweler using the standard jeweler's magnifying glass could not detect a flaw in them. Such stones are equally rare in other deep mines. However, Argyle has more diamonds than usual that are "twinned," in which two crystals are interlocked. These are harder to cut than normal and thus would attract a lower price if sold for jewelry. They could however make fine tool stones.

If diamonds have many flaws, they cannot be cut as gems. Sir Rod Carnegie, Chairman of CRA said in June 1982 that only 10 percent of Argyle's output was of gem quality, although a spokesman for his company had earlier told me only 5 percent were of gem quality. The figures varied. A different CRA spokesman told me 7 percent of Argyle's diamonds were "clean enough for gems" so to clear up the confusion I asked him what they defined as gems. He said diamonds "cutable in New York." I was much surprised. No diamond merchant I knew defined "gem-quality" so narrowly. I knew only the very best gems were cut in New York. Over 90 percent of the gem-quality diamonds produced worldwide were cut in Israel and India. If this was CRA's definition of "gem-quality," then it was no surprise that only 5-10 percent of Argyle's diamond production would be of gem-quality. This is what I would also expect of the production of the major De Beers mines in Kimberley.

I then asked him how many of their stones were "industrial" in quality – a term used for diamonds not suitable for cutting as gems. CRA's spokesman replied, "Fifty percent." I then put to him the obvious question, "What then are the other 43 percent?" He firmly replied, "Near-gems."

I was very puzzled by this response. There was no category of *near-gems* in my then current (1981) diamond industry reference books. So I asked him what were "near-gems?" He replied, "Stones that can be cut as gems if the market demands it." Such a definition seemed something of a charade. I thought, surely any diamond capable of being cut as a gem would be cut as a gem – given how much more it would be worth? I later learned that the "near-gem" classification had just been invented – and that most of the sparklers on the world's engagement rings are made from stones now defined as "near-gems." The buyers of jewelry are not told of this degradation. It certainly has not lowered retail prices.

IS ARGYLE A GEM DIAMOND MINE?

The Australian public and government were warned by CRA not to expect a great return from the giant Argyle diamond mine, since its diamonds were of low quality; but in private Mr. E. Tyler of Ashton told a Joint Venture meeting on July 3rd, 1982: "Argyle was a gem mine since it would be obtaining 85 percent of its sale revenues from its gems and near-gems." But publicly, Ashton kept in line with CRA. They issued a statement in March 1983 that only 5 percent of Argyle's diamonds were gems. But Tyler's private words have since proved correct. When Argyle went into production not five but 50 percent of Argyle's diamonds by weight were to be cut as gems.

The CSO seemingly can vary at will its classifications of stones into industrials, near-gems and gems. In November 1981 the CSO downgraded Argyle still further, and paid even less for Argyle's brown gems "because of the low retail demand for brown diamonds." In a similar fashion, many diamonds from the American and Russian industrial stockpiles have recently been purchased by De Beers and diamond merchants, redefined and cut as gems.

The classification of diamonds into gems, near-gems, and industrials is more a matter of marketing than of intrinsic value or geology. The Managing Director of Northern Mining, Rees Towie, told his Board in 1981 that 15 percent of Argyle's diamonds were of top gem quality. Their chief geologist told me 10 percent of the mine's gems were "first rate gems of New York market standard," thus confirming the words of the CRA spokesman. The Indians who cut the stones later reported that the overall top-class gem count from Argyle came to 14 percent, even if one excluded the "near-gems." This was in line with Northern Mining and Albert Joris' earlier estimates.

It should be noted that, even if only 10 percent of Argyle's diamonds were gems, given the numbers that Argyle would produce, this would give Argyle a gem production equivalent in quantity to De Beers' official total gem production from all its South African, Namibian, and Botswanan mines combined.[7]

Above all else, the factor that made the Argyle mine superior to all the South African diamond mines was simply the vast numbers of diamonds it contained. When CRA drilled the Argyle diamond deposit to establish its diamond content, putting in large core drill holes on a 50-meter grid pattern, they had discovered a diamond treasure trove beyond imagination.

According to De Beers, the richest diamond mine in Kimberley, South Africa, contains only quarter of a carat (0.05 grams) of diamond a metric tonne. Bear this in mind as you read the figures below. It will help you understand why these seemingly boring lists of numbers created so much excitement in the Ashton Joint Venture boardrooms – and were kept so highly confidential.

Secret drill results at Argyle

The following are the secret results from two typical drill holes in the southern half of the volcanic pipe up which diamond-rich lava flowed some millions of years ago. These drill holes were code numbered LDC6 and LDC3. The first had 10.39, 14.85, 24.14 and 8.48 carats of diamonds per tonne, in samples taken every 20 meters. LDC6 had 2.96, 8.77, 26.47, 18.48, 15.45, 5.02, 10.86 and 14.46 carats of diamonds per tonne. Argyle averaged near the surface about 6.75 carats to a tonne.

These figures are incredibly richer than those found in De Beers' own diamond-pipe mines – according to the figures they shared with the Argyle consortium. They said the South African average was only 0.28 carats per tonne, and that its Dutoitspan mine has 0.17 carats a tonne, the De Beers mine 0.21 carats a tonne, the Wesselton mine 0.23 carats a tonne, and the Premier 0.37 carats a tonne.

The geological model of the Argyle deposit revealed its diamond-rich volcanic pipe is shaped like an upside down human leg and foot. At the surface the deposit is foot shaped, with the toes at the northern end where the deposit is relatively shallow and averaging ten carats a tonne. The southern end is the ankle and leg – going down to great depths with an average of 13 carats a tonne. The drill cores in this southern end showed it was as rich at depth as it was at the surface. Looking at the detailed drilling results, it was very difficult for me to understand how CRA had obtained their announced average figure of about five carats a tonne, unless they were including the more barren ground outside the pipe that would need to be removed to construct the mining pit.

In April 1981, Northern Mining estimated in a private paper for its Board, that there would be 800 million to 2 billion carats at Argyle at a very cautious five carats a tonne. Its Managing Director Towie told me that they were more likely to achieve a minimum of 7.7 carats a tonne, giving the deposit a minimum reserve figure of 1.2 billion carats contained within 200 meters of the surface. They had so far only drilled to 200 meters. He felt Argyle must contain diamonds at commercial concentrations down to 700 meters at least, since this is what happened at other pipe mines. This would more than double its diamond content to well over 2.4 billion carats – twice the known diamond reserves of the rest of the world. In 1980 the US Bureau of Mines said the world's total diamond reserve was 1.259 billion carats and that South Africa had a total reserve of just 200 million carats. (A spokesman for the Bureau told me in 1992 that its figures were based on estimates from De Beers.)

The incredible richness of the Argyle pipe was reaffirmed in 1982 by a report revealing concentrations in further drilling of 16.3 carats a tonne.[8] It said the average was 12.4 carats a tonne, many times the figures reported in South Africa. This confirmed my earlier estimate of about 13 carats a tonne based on the first drilling surveys.

But I must issue a caveat. I was to learn in 1994 that the Canadian and Russian diamond deposits also held diamonds at concentrations well over those reported by De Beers for South Africa. This led me to consider the possibility that De Beers might be deliberately vastly underreporting the diamond content of its South African mines in order to help maintain the myth that diamonds are rare and therefore expensive.

But if CRA knew that the concentrations and quality of Argyle diamonds were much higher than it admitted publicly, why was it selling the diamonds to the CSO at such low prices? Was it simply being realistic? Did CRA believe there was only one customer out there capable of buying the Argyle diamonds and selling them internationally – a customer that could not afford higher prices – or would not pay them?

On further investigation, I found the diamond world had more surprises for me. It was not as monolithic as I thought. The CSO had to compete against rivals for the marketing rights to the Argyle diamonds and, astonishingly, CRA's staff had recommended many of the rival bids as much more profitable to CRA than the CSO bid that would soon be accepted by CRA.

RIVALS TO THE CARTEL

Initially CRA did not want to put the marketing rights out to competitive tender. It intended simply to offer Harry Oppenheimer's CSO the marketing contract. In early 1981 CRA recommended the CSO as the only appropriate buyer for the Australian diamonds.[9] (It may be relevant that the Oppenheimers' financial interests were represented on the board of CRA's parent company, RTZ of London.) But, after the Australian Prime Minister Malcolm Fraser attacked CRA's proposed deal as strengthening apartheid South Africa, it became politically necessary for CRA to at least appear to look for alternatives.[10]

CRA then found it surprisingly easy to find diamond merchants willing to bid against De Beers. Zaire, then the world's biggest diamond producer, had just broken away from De Beers and contracted the marketing rights for its diamonds to the influential Belgian diamond firms of Caddi and Glasol. These firms soon realized that if they could also acquire the Australian rights they would control more diamond production than did De Beers. The Indian government was also very interested in obtaining independent diamond supplies for its low-cost cutting workshops in order to end their dependency on supplies from the De Beers cartel.

CRA's staff reported that Glasol was willing to buy the Australian diamonds "at market prices," offering "offer bank guarantees" of its credit-worthiness, and that David Caddi had offered to buy the entire output of Argyle without deducting the CSO's 10 percent sorting and marketing fee. As he had offered to pay prices 3 percent below the CSO prices, this made his offer 7 percent better than Oppenheimer's.

There was also an offer from diamond merchant Jack Lunzer of Industrial Diamond in London's Hatton Garden, made in association with the Belgians. He offered a price of $18 a carat – over 50 percent above De Beers' first offer, and over twice as much as De Beers was later to pay for the Australian diamonds.

The Indian government wanted to break free from the Oppenheimer system whereby Indians got the poorest stones to cut and the better quality stones went to whites to cut – to Americans, Europeans or to Israelis. An Indian merchant told me they were second-class citizens in De Beers' diamond world, just as Indians were in South Africa.

The Indians offered the Ashton Joint Venture $18 a carat for the entire Australian production. This offer came from the Minerals and Mining Trading Corporation (MMTC), a state owned company that CRA described as under "charter by the Indian government to increase supplies of diamonds from non-De Beers sources." MMTC had already secured the diamond production of Ghana and the Central African Republic and were seeking to secure the Botswanan. A senior official of the Indian High Commission in Canberra told me at that time that Australia and India should "line up together" to market Argyle's entire output, as it would be mutually profitable "to oust the middle-man of South Africa."

CRA noted that the Indians were remarkably unafraid of De Beers: "The Indian industry generally was not as concerned as the other cutting centers about possible De Beers reaction to their purchases from the AJV [Ashton Joint Venture]." Star Diamonds and Vijalykumar, the two largest diamond firms in India, had offered to purchase all of the Australian diamonds, despite both firms having close association with De Beers. CRA was impressed, noting that "the management of both firms is young, aggressive and well organized,"[11] and that they each purchased over $100 million worth of rough diamonds annually.

There was also a prospective bid from a coalition of the Indian firms of Rosy Blue and B. Arunkumar, with the Israeli firm of Steinmetz. They suggested to CRA a fixed volume contract with a minimum floor price just below that of the CSO. Again CRA was impressed, noting this was a "far better deal than that offered in any other meeting. Even De Beers proposed no price or revenue guarantees."[12]

The CSO thus was outbid by the Belgians and the Indians. It was not just that it was offering less than any other bidder for the Australian diamonds. It also demanded that it be given the right to limit Argyle's production whenever it suited it. The others did not. It would also charge a 7.5 to 10 percent marketing fee plus a 5 percent advertising fee calculated against the mine's gross income. The Indians and Belgians would not charge any fee – this last factor alone made their offers vastly more attractive than that of Oppenheimer.

The Indian government did not give up hope that Australia would eventually strike a deal to export diamonds directly to India. It could not believe the Australians would not eventually recognize the superiority of their offer. When the Australian Trade Minister, John Dawkins, visited India in October 1985, the Indian Commerce Minister Khused Alam Khan asked him if a deal could still be done. Nothing happened. The Federal Labor government was unwilling to interfere. The Indian Prime Minister, Rajiv Ghandi, came to Australia that same year to argue the case but again seemingly to no avail. For the next decade, Australian diamonds went to India via the De Beers cartel and on cartel terms.

I then started to look for evidence from other diamond mines to see if similar allegations of fraudulent pricing had been made elsewhere. I did not expect to be able to find such evidence too easily. It is not every day that one gets such an insight into the running of a diamond mine as I had received in Australia.

How De Beers defrauded Sierra Leone

Then, in London, I met Edward Wharton-Tigar, the Managing Director of the Selection Trust diamond mines of Sierra Leone between 1952 and 1964, and Managing Director of Selection Trust from 1964 to 1975. He told me in great detail how De Beers, through the CSO, had fraudulently undervalued the diamonds in his diamond mines – and how he had forced them to compensate his company for doing so. He was the only man I interviewed who had bested De Beers. He had even published this story and not been sued. The book in which he told the story, *Burning Bright: The Autobiography of Edward Wharton-Tigar*, was reviewed positively by the diamond press. Allegedly, De Beers bought up most of the copies of his book rather than have them widely sold.

I interviewed him at his elegant West Kensington home where he was spending his retirement mounting his collection of cigarette cards for their eventual home in the British Museum. He had credit in the *Guinness Book of Records* for holding the world's largest collection of cigarette cards.

He told me that when Selection Trust appointed him manager of the Sierra Leone diamond mines, he had no experience of diamonds but had worked in conventional lead and zinc mines. He was therefore surprised to find that the CSO, his one and only customer, set the prices they paid for the diamonds. Under the circumstances, he thought it only prudent to check if his company was receiving a reasonable price. But when he asked an employee to check the price that would be paid for some of their diamonds on the open market, the employee refused to do so because "De Beers had forbidden it." Wharton-Tigar then ordered him to do as he was told – and he came back with better prices than the CSO's. He then sought a second opinion from leading New York diamond company, Lazare Kaplan (pre-Tempelsman takeover). They confirmed he was being underpaid.

When Wharton-Tigar challenged De Beers with this evidence, "the moguls of De Beers reacted as if I had suggested the crown jewels were fakes." He could not get them to agree to negotiations until "I gave instructions to stop our monthly deliveries to the CSO until the matter was resolved." The CSO tried to get the British Colonial Office to put pressure on him, as they had on Dr. Williamson, Joris' Tanganyika friend. When Williamson refused to accept low prices for his diamonds, the British Colonial Office had threatened him with nationalization. Wharton-Tigar says he "received a phone call from a senior civil servant who said that the Department strongly disapproved of our quarrel with the Diamond Corporation." (The Diamond Corporation was part of the CSO in London – and part of De Beers.) But Wharton-Tigar treated this phone call as a bluff and did not hear from them again.

Soon afterwards, he received a telegram from "Harry Oppenheimer inviting me to stay with him for a few days in Johannesburg." After a week of tough negotiations, Oppenheimer agreed to lift the price.

The following month, Wharton-Tigar sent off his diamonds as usual to the CSO in London but was amazed to find that he received the same payment as before. He discovered on investigation that "somewhat mysteriously, the proportion of gems to industrial grades had dropped by the exact amount needed for the average price of the overall delivery to remain unchanged."

He looked at the returns telling him how the CSO had classified his diamonds. He found that when he added together all the gem quality categories, 17.8 percent had been classified as gems, a sharp drop from the previous shipment when 23.6 percent were said to be gem quality. He noted this was precisely the fall in quality that was needed to stop his company's income rising after the negotiated increase in prices.

This prompted him to check the percentage of gems in previous shipments. Much to his amazement he found that, when he added together the gem sub-categories of the previous 48 shipments, each had been certified as being precisely 23.6 percent gem-quality. He knew this was geologically impossible. The diamond content of deposits mined always varied at least a little. He looked back still further. He found a price increase granted by the CSO some nine years earlier had been similarly neutralized by a decline in certified quality.

He reflected that "one did not have to be an expert to realize that this meant the sorting… was being carried out to a pre-arranged plan with no regard to the actual contents of the shipments. Moreover we, the shippers, were paying handsomely for this (sorting) operation…This seemed to be a most reprehensible act and I was determined that it must be exposed."

He then decided to take out some of the gems before sending them to the CSO in London. The CSO certified the gem content of this consignment at precisely the same as before. It had not noticed the missing stones. He did this for three shipments. The CSO still did not notice. Clearly it was not even looking at consignments before issuing its valuation. This revealed just how little the diamond prices set by the CSO had to do with the real value of stones. He concluded that this was, "a clear indication that the sorting [by the CSO] was being carried out to pre-determined percentages without reference to what was on the table."

Wharton-Tigar said, "I decided to gamble on a complete exposé. From the next shipment we removed *all* the recognizable gemstones which we figured would reduce the cutable content to eight percent at the most." He instead brought the removed gems to London in a suitcase. "When we made delivery [of the diamonds with the gems removed] to the Diamond Development Corporation, I sought out its chairman, Herman David, who, incidentally, was also chairman of the All England Tennis Club and a prominent figure at Wimbledon each year, and asked him to have his sorters pay particular attention to the cutable proportion as I had noticed that the percentage had been dropping over the years. He patted me on the back as if pacifying an unruly child and assured me that he would do so."

When Wharton-Tigar received the CSO valuation, it said that he now had 18.5 percent gems in the shipment – a 0.7 percent increase on the previous month's level –

and more than twice this shipment's real gem content. He then confronted Herman David by opening his suitcase and showing him the removed gem diamonds. He also sent a strong telegram of protest to Harry Oppenheimer, telling him that Selection Trust would sort and sell its own diamonds as soon as the CSO contract expired. Oppenheimer replied urging Wharton-Tigar to do nothing until he got to London.

Oppenheimer eventually agreed to pay Selection Trust compensation for all the undervalued shipments. It was unclear if the Sierra Leone authorities were ever compensated or even told of the serious loss of revenue to their impoverished country that this had presumably entailed.

From Wharton-Tigar's account, it seemed De Beers invented diamond valuations with little regard to the diamonds valued. The fact that he had published this extremely serious allegation in his autobiography without any legal repercussions from De Beers made me think it possible that De Beers was capable of similar maneuvers in Australia.[13]

Ashton Mining's chief, Alan Jones, confessed to me that it was "very difficult to know the real value of the stones" at Argyle although "Oppenheimer was enthusiastic about the Australian diamonds." He said information within the cartel was hard to come by for "neither party can speak openly once you've joined the club."

It now was evident that the Argyle diamond deposit was absolutely fabulous and unlike any seen before in the world – and the Argyle deal was unlike any normal contract. Normally the seller talks up his product. Here the seller was talking down his product. As in Sierra Leone, it looked strangely as if the customer set the prices for the goods it bought.

At the 1981 Conference of Commonwealth Heads of Government in Melbourne, I was told by delegates from Commonwealth diamond producing nations, Botswana, Sierra Leone, and Ghana, of their experiences with De Beers, of their fears that Australia might strengthen its cartel with her diamonds, and of their hope that Australia might one day join with them and strengthen their ability to stand against De Beers.

Mr. Maphalynane, of Botswana's Ministry of Economic Planning, told me, "We secured a half share [in all profits] in exchange for mineral rights and 20 percent of the capital" – this was a much better deal than secured by the Australians. He was cautious about any move to economic independence. "We cannot afford to rock the boat unless in collusion with a major producer like Australia." He suggested that what was needed was "an association of diamond-producing nations that could share among themselves their expertise and experience."

Their deal with De Beers made them a junior partner, not much better than a client since they had no policy role despite their place on De Beers' board. He confided, "We are not happy with the CSO. They have all the information, we have none. We always have the feeling that we may not have a fair deal." He did not like their major industry having production quotas set by South Africans. He advised me that De Beers would "make Australian diamonds subsidize South African diamonds."[14] The Botswana government also, as I have noted, had in turn a hard policy towards the Bushman tribes that lived in their deserts, moving them on whenever mineral deposits were found.

The secret Argyle marketing documents made it clear that the offer the CSO made for the Argyle diamonds was the lowest received. Yet Oppenheimer knew the CSO offer was likely to be successful. He had his own ways of doing things. He had offered the Ashton Joint Venture a junior partnership much as he had done with Botswana. He asked the Australians in return to agree to cut their planned diamond output.[15]

But CRA feared putting its US operations, or those of its parent company, RTZ, at risk by so openly joining the diamond cartel. The company had to settle out of court that year, 1981, for joining a uranium cartel.[16] Ogilvie Thompson, the Chief Executive of Anglo American, noted, "the [Ashton Joint Venture] negotiations were protracted and complex primarily because of the nature of the product and an antitrust problem peculiar to the leading Australian shareholder."

Harry Oppenheimer was besieged on all sides in 1981. He knew he had to regain control over Zaire's diamonds to preserve his empire. So he decided to reduce Zaire's income by flooding the world diamond market with Zairian diamonds from his stockpile. The merchants holding contracts with the Zairian government were targeted in a most gentlemanly way. Jack Lunzer was not boycotted but instead found a De Beers salesman at his office offering him consignments of identical diamonds at a lower price than he was paying the Zairians. The message was clear. He had to stop buying directly from Zaire. Otherwise he would find De Beers using its commercial muscle against him. Oppenheimer shortly afterwards said with quiet satisfaction that Zaire's fate "should be looked on as a warning."

This message was clearly received in Australia. Northern Mining's Chief Executive, Rees Towie, animatedly showed me just how dramatically Oppenheimer's tactics had reduced the price of Zaire's diamonds by drawing charts and giving statistics. He also told me he suspected his independent stance against the CSO deal was being undermined by people close to Oppenheimer buying shares in his company. He felt he would not be able to resist much longer. He believed that Oppenheimer would soon win the Australian diamonds marketing contract for the very low price he had offered. The price offered would prove irrelevant. So also would be the comparative value of the diamonds. The deal would be decided purely on the basis of financial muscle.

AUSTRALIA SIGNS UP WITH THE CARTEL

Towie's prediction was correct. On February 19th, 1982 CRA announced the first details of its deal with Oppenheimer. Extraordinarily it had accepted the lowest bid. Within a year, Northern Mining was no longer a problem for De Beers or CRA for it had been taken over by an Australian investor, Alan Bond – internationally known for winning yachting's major trophy, the America's Cup. Bond then offered to sell Northern Mining's interest in the Argyle Mine to the Oppenheimer companies, or so William Nagel told me. Nagel was one of De Beers' leading brokers. He told me he had discussed this deal with Bond.

Allegedly, the Oppenheimers also had the banks put pressure on the Ashton Joint Venture. Kantilal Chhotalal, a much-respected Indian diamond merchant and historian of the industry, reported, "MMTC's efforts to enter the Australian venture in collaboration with five Indian firms failed. Significantly De Beers was successful, since pressure was brought to bear by De Beers on the Australian Argyle Diamond's banks. The Argyle mines raised $175 million through a project finance facility, A$100 million through a leveraged lease agreement, and a US $50 million Eurobond issue from international institutions, on condition its output was only sold through De Beers."[17]

The international consequences were immediate. The Zaire independent marketing operation collapsed and their government immediately had to sign back on with the CSO. They could not stand against De Beers, not now that it had bulk supplies of Australian diamonds.

CRA won a few concessions from Oppenheimer to help appease Australian politicians. He would permit a tiny proportion of Argyle's high-class gems, just 10,000 carats out of millions, to be cut in Australia. All others would be cut overseas. CRA said this concession was due to "De Beers' concern to preserve their image." Yet Paul Keating, a future Prime Minister, had called in Parliament for the establishment of a massive new diamond industry with "huge potential benefit."[18] He was right about the potential. If the 10 percent of top class Argyle gems had been cut in Australia, they would have been worth something akin to the $618 a carat Russia received in 1986 for its cut diamonds.[19] This meant that 10 percent of Argyle's output would have given Australia over seven times the value of the total Oppenheimer offer. Joris went over these conclusions with me and scornfully concluded: "They could have thrown all the rest of the output into Sydney Harbor and still been vastly better off." Instead, Australia timidly accepted Oppenheimer's concession of a few diamonds for a relatively tiny Australian cutting factory.

The agreement with De Beers gave it 75 percent of the cheaper gems and industrials. CRA would be allowed to sell the remaining 25 percent on the Antwerp and Mumbai markets. All the top class gems, apart from the very few to be cut in Australia, would go to De Beers. As mentioned, it paid initially just $12 a carat From this it took about 15 percent as marketing fees, bringing the price it initially paid down to about $10 a carat.

In return for the marketing contract, the CSO gave no price or revenue guarantees. Inevitably, as soon as the deal was done, it cut the price it paid Argyle, lowering it from $12 to $10.80 in October 1981. No open protest came from CRA. Further reductions inevitably followed. In January 1982 it went down to between $7.75 and $8.40 a carat, far less than the $10 a carat then paid to Zaire, a country supposed to have the world's poorest diamonds. CRA made no public protest but explained the market was depressed. In February 1982 CRA told the government they now expected to get slightly more, $9 a carat. But a CRA internal report of that time said they really expected to get even less, about $7 a carat, giving them, they estimated, a tiny per carat profit of A$0.90, or about US$0.75.

These prices are incredibly low when one considers the high retail value of diamonds. The CSO's profits from the Australian diamonds must have been astronomical. But this could not be checked. Despite acting as Argyle's agent in reselling its diamonds, the CSO said it could not tell how much it got for selling Argyle's diamonds – since it mixed together diamonds from all sources before selling them. The CSO simply said: "Trust me" – and the Australians helplessly agreed.

Argyle also agreed to pay the CSO a sorting, valuing, and marketing fee of about 10 percent, calculated on the value the CSO gave the diamonds, without deducting any mining costs. Rees Towie told me that this equaled 25 to 33 percent of the expected profits of the mine. The CSO would also get on top of this an advertising fee that Ashton Mining's Alan Jones estimated at another five percent of Argyle's gross income. These fees combined to equal nearly 50 percent of Argyle's net profits. This the CSO would receive without having to invest a cent in the mine and irrespective of the profitability of the mine. If the mine made no profits – the CSO would still receive its fees. This system also allowed the CSO to adjust where they took profits. If they set a lower price for Argyle stones, their fee would fall, but their profits on reselling the diamonds would increase. For Oppenheimer, this was a brilliant deal. But for the Australians it was a most strange deal. They could have escaped all these fees if they had accepted any of the rival marketing bids.

The deal did provide for "independent assessors" to check the prices the CSO set. But CRA ceded to the CSO one final power that effectively undermined any independent assessment. The CSO were given "the right of refusal on the selection of the check valuers." The CSO thus not only set the prices it paid, but had the power to ensure that the "independent valuers" were people that they liked.

Excavating diamond ore at Bow River near Argyle.

And, to make absolutely sure that Argyle's competition would not hurt De Beers' mines, CRA agreed that it would not produce more than 25 million carats a year without the consent of the CSO. CRA also agreed that the CSO could impose further production restrictions on the mine at any time, forcing it to stockpile or cut production. These quotas would be set by a De Beers-dominated South African committee chaired by a representative of the South African government with veto rights. This meant that the South African mines owned by De Beers were protected from competition from other diamond mines contracted to the cartel. Finally, even if De Beers ran short of cash to pay for the Australian diamonds, CRA would still be barred from selling its diamonds elsewhere.

Through signing this deal, CRA had given the South African government more control over this Australian mine than had the Australian government.[20] The Australian government's power to control the diamond industry had been sharply diminished by its surprising abolition of diamond export licenses the very year Argyle was discovered. After this abolition, the best Argyle diamonds could legally be simply put in a briefcase and exported, as I was told by one of the company executives involved – as long as the South Africans allowed it.

Paul Keating for the Labor Opposition issued a press statement attacking the agreement between the CSO and CRA: "The deal negotiated between CRA and De Beers for the marketing of the Argyle diamonds will effectively shift the profit center of Argyle from Australia to South Africa."[21] In Parliament, he deplored the "very low" price of $9 a carat agreed to by CRA.[22]

It seemed incomprehensible to me that CRA could accept these terms when both the Belgians and Indians had offered higher prices, no production limits, and no fees. It still seems hard to believe that they could not find a bank to back these better offers with mine development funds.

But I still had not solved the key enigma. Why was CRA willing to sell the diamonds so cheaply? Why was it seemingly trying to hide what it had found in the Kimberleys?

DE BEERS AND DIRECTORS' PAYMENTS.

Similar questions were asked earlier by the Managing Director of Selection Trust's diamond mines in Sierra Leone, Wharton-Tigar. He wondered why the directors of Selection Trust had allowed their one and only customer, De Beers, to set the prices it paid for their diamonds without any effective check. His curiosity was particularly aroused when one of his directors, Charles Boise, severely reprimanded him for daring to question the prices paid by the diamond Syndicate. Boise suggested he apologize to the Oppenheimers or resign.

> Next day I made a study of some of the company's confidential files. They revealed that Boise had a large personal shareholding in one of the Diamond Corporation [Oppenheimer] companies… the shares were currently paying a 100 per cent dividend, which meant that he was getting a return of many thousands of pounds – five times more, in fact, than his fees and dividends from our Selection Trust group which in themselves added up to a not inconsiderable total. No wonder De Beers could rely on him for support in getting rid of the young troublemaker who wanted to upset their established way of doing business.[23]

Other discrepancies now started to make sense to Wharton-Tigar. He had wondered, when he became Managing Director of Central African Selection Trust (CAST), why:

> my new position seemed to carry with it an appointment to the boards of several companies in the De Beers group concerned with the sorting and selling of diamonds. The combined directors' fees more than doubled my net income since some of the companies were registered in South Africa and payments were not taxed in the United Kingdom. It struck me as curious that the chief executive of a diamond-mining company, which was not even in the De Beers group, should receive more financial reward from companies that bought the product than from those that produced it. When I asked what services I could perform for the diamond companies, I was told that nothing was required apart from an occasional appearance at board meetings.[24]

He believed that De Beers also used invitations to use their private club facilities, including regular formal meals, as a form of bribery. His invitation was withdrawn when he started to question De Beers. But when he adopted a still tougher stand, things quickly changed. He contacted Philip Oppenheimer, the cousin of Harry Oppenheimer who controlled diamond cartel operations in London, "I hinted that if he did not wish to cooperate, I would have no alternative but to suspend deliveries to the Diamond Corporation of all our West African production [of diamonds]... this approach seemed to have the desired effect. I was invited to the Monday luncheons at St. Andrews."[25]

This sort of favor is reminiscent of the reports from two Indian generals who helped the cartel by persuading the Indian government that the CSO was not South African and therefore not to be boycotted under anti-apartheid provisions. The generals told me, when we met in India, how grateful they were that De Beers had generously made available to them its club's facilities when all they had done was to help De Beers get into India.

When Wharton-Tigar tried to talk to Charles Boise about these puzzling "perks" and asked him why the De Beers companies paid such relatively high fees to "outside" directors who did nothing to earn them: "He evaded my questions and seemed irritated I should be asking them. Instead, he said I should get to know the De Beers people in London better and he started taking me round each Monday for lunch at their headquarters at St. Andrew's House... here we were entertained most royally with Scotch salmon and other delicacies which were then... very expensive. I got to know the senior staff quite well, including Philip Oppenheimer, son of Sir Ernest's brother Otto, whom Boise had shrewdly invited to join the CAST board as long ago as the 1930s when his reputation was at low ebb... following a much publicized court case in which he bore the brunt of the blame for some highly irregular actions by De Beers which forced diamond producers in British Guinea into bankruptcy."[26]

Thus Wharton-Tigar found out how the Oppenheimer business worked and how they seemingly persuaded outside directors to accept deals that disadvantaged their own companies. I had no evidence that the same deals had been made in Australia, but this precedent made me want to query just how Oppenheimer had persuaded CRA to agree to such poor terms.

One night in Sydney, amid a wild thunderstorm, I heard fresh stories of how De Beers allegedly used gifts of directorships and the fees paid in tax haven countries to their advantage. Representatives of Kroll, the powerful American private detective agency, had taken me to dinner at the Opera House. They had been hired by Gold Fields to fight off a takeover attempt by Minorco, a company used by Oppenheimer to hold much of his vast international empire from a non-South African base. These Kroll operatives told me, to the dramatic accompaniment of lightning and thunder, that Gold Fields' key directors had been offered cushy directorships paid from tax haven accounts if they allowed the takeover of their company.

De Beers did not neglect public relations in its campaign to get the Argyle contract, appointing Neville Huxham, one of their top South African public relations officers, to the case. It also gave some of the Australian journalists reporting the diamond industry a De Beers-hosted tour of South Africa. I was instead offered and accepted a free dinner and interview with Huxham at one of Melbourne's more expensive restaurants half way up a skyscraper next to CRA's Australian headquarters.

I discovered later that Rupert Clark, the father-in-law to CRA's Chairman Sir Rod Carnegie, had stayed with Harry Oppenheimer in South Africa in February 1982 – the year that the Oppenheimers came to control almost the entire production of high class gems in Australia – excepting the ones produced by the small Bow River mine near to Argyle.

But this gap was soon closed after Harry Oppenheimer came to Australia in September 1988. He introduced Robert de Crespigny, an Australian who had visited him in South Africa, to the diamond business. Oppenheimer put into de Crespigny's newly set up mining company his own (Anglo American) interests in Australia in return for shares,[27] even though de Crespigny was inexperienced in mining matters.

Not long afterwards de Crespigny took over the Bow River diamond mine. Soon afterwards it was contracted to the CSO – even though it had been selling its diamonds on the free market at around $25-30 a carat, over twice the price the CSO was paying to Argyle. It perhaps was not surprising that the Bow River mine was closed down some seven years later.

Paul Keating, when Shadow Minister for Minerals and Energy, attacked the CRA deal with De Beers as disadvantaging Australia. He said, "I regard the CRA deal as a poorly negotiated one from Australia's point of view. The Ashton Joint Venture should really be negotiating from a position of strength... Australia could really split the CSO monopoly and achieve an arrangement where it was shared 50-50 with Australia. I'm disappointed that CRA seems to underrate the strength of its negotiating position."[28]

But the marketing contract with the CSO was signed soon after the election of

Diamond separation plant at Bow River.

a Labor federal government in which Keating was prominent. In April 1983 the Labor government approved the deal with the cartel. A strangely muted Keating said, "there was no real commercial alternative... at least in the short term." And when Keating became Prime Minister, the contract between Argyle and the CSO was renewed again without any significant revision or protest.

AUSTRALIA GROWS UNHAPPY WITH DE BEERS

But life within the De Beers cartel predictably proved uncomfortable. Argyle gradually began to see the contract with the CSO as a major marketing mistake – although it could be argued that it was a necessary learning exercise. The CSO imposed further price cuts – and then stockpiled more than a year's production of the Australian stones they had agreed to sell as agents, thus slashing Argyle's revenues. They even forced Argyle to build a further diamond stockpile in Australia.

John Robinson of Ashton Mining explained, "At the time the contract was initially signed, some five-odd years ago, we were really under the understanding that it would provide us with some insurance and some certainty and for that we were obviously prepared to pay the premium to the CSO for managing the market. The way things turned out proved that we were wrong." He said they expected the CSO to make sure they sold the maximum number of Argyle diamonds and to keep up the prices. "Neither of these things transpired," he said.

In 1992, the CSO instructed Argyle to stockpile about a fifth of its output to help keep up the price of diamonds internationally because, "Angola [meaning SWAPO] was releasing a lot of goods into the market." The Australians went along with this. John Robinson continued, "We believed that it was only fair that we should play our role in the overall market. It was a price defensive mechanism." He said Argyle believed De Beers when it said it was limiting supplies to protect the market for Argyle's stones. "Then Russia started releasing fairly good quality rough out of its stocks that prolonged the deferred purchases arrangement." But Argyle still believed that the diamond cartel was protecting its interests – although it fretted at having to pay tax to the West Australian government on diamonds mined that had been stockpiled rather than sold.

But then Russia "started to release more Indian type goods and then suddenly … our prices fell [i.e. De Beers cut the price it paid the Australians.]" Robinson protested about this. "I remember that they got very annoyed with me." Then in "February 1993 the CSO dumped large quantities of smalls on the market. A number of special multimillion carat deals were given to certain people." The CSO was using its stockpile of Australian diamonds as a weapon against the Russians.

The Australians did not appreciate this. They were interested in making money, not in altruistically supporting the CSO. Robinson said they told the CSO, "Look you are not managing the market correctly. One minute you are starving the market of the goods that they want and the next, there is a feast. You are dumping. There is no way you can get proper prices. There is no confidence [created] in the product [by dumping]."

Argyle also found De Beers' attitude towards the marketing of its brown, or "champagne," diamonds very irritating. Robinson continued: "To go back a bit, when we first started the champagne promotion De Beers was very negative about it. They saw this as cannibalizing the white end of the market" – in other words as hurting the market for the diamonds coming out of De Beers' own mines.

The Australians wanted to sell their stockpile before prices dropped too far and so told the CSO, "If the prices are

Explosion at Argyle.

going to fall then we should not be deferring any of our sales." But the CSO did not agree to this. "For us that was the last straw – we did not have price certainty and yet we were still carrying the burden of deferred purchases … Reduced purchasing was in the rules… But we didn't buy into seeing ourselves penalized on price … It was no good just protecting the top end of the market to allow price increases, while allowing our end of the market to fall."

In 1996 the CSO again said that they regretfully had to continue to restrict the sale of Australian diamonds because there were too many Angolan diamonds (from UNITA) on the open market that De Beers simply had to buy up to keep the prices high. Robinson commented, "I thought that this statement was somewhat at odds with their argument that the top end of the market was moving along very nicely and that there was strong demand there… I really never got a sensible response to this."

ARGYLE BREAKS WITH DIAMOND CARTEL – AND UPSETS ISRAEL

In July 1996, Argyle decided it had had enough. It would not renew its marketing contract with the Central Selling Organization (CSO). Argyle now did what it should have done much earlier. It set up an alliance with the Indian merchants and founded the Indo-Argyle Diamond Council to promote Australian diamonds.

But this alarmed the powerful Israeli diamond-cutting firms that had long been supported by the diamond cartel. The CSO selected for Israel a better class of diamonds to cut than it sent to India. The Israelis feared India would now obtain the better quality Australian diamonds.

Chaim Even-Zohar, the editor of a leading Israeli diamond magazine, asked Gilchrist of Argyle, "By value, about 65 percent of Argyle's output is comprised of diamonds of plus 11 points and up. If India is the ideal cutting center for Argyle's smaller goods, Argyle's bigger sizes appear to be perfect for manufacturing in Israel. Why is it that we don't see more of these larger goods in Tel Aviv?" Israel or Antwerp would cut the stones better. Gilchrist responded, "We don't underestimate the Indians. I believe, honestly, that the Indians are currently capable of manufacturing almost the whole range of product. And one of the only reasons that they haven't got a bigger market share is that the CSO is standing between them and expansion."

"Strategically, the CSO does not want the Indians to get too big," he continued. "The Indians, however, have shown an ability to adapt to some of the latest technology pretty readily, though they haven't got the sophistication of technology that you have in Israel ... Israel puts a lot into process control rather than into people control, so Israel de-skills the operation, and allows it to be done by people who have only three or four years of experience, not ten or twenty years." Argyle was also subcontracting the cutting of its pink diamonds to China, Sri Lanka and Mauritius – all countries with vastly lower wages than Israel.

The Australian diamond industry was now set to expand. Ashton Mining brought into production the Merlin diamond mine that Robinson said was "part of a much larger diamond province" to produce around a million carats of good quality diamonds a year. These also would be marketed outside the cartel.[29] Ashton also hoped to expand production into Finland and into Indonesia where it had interests in a Kalamantan dredging prospect where the diamonds were worth around $200 a carat uncut.

But first Argyle had to survive the counterattack from the CSO. It launched against Argyle the same kind of savage market attack that it had previously used against both Zaire and Russia to deter them from selling independently – but with one difference. It had used its control over Argyle's diamonds to threaten the sales of Zaire and Russian stones. Now it used Argyle's own diamonds against Argyle. It sold large lots of the Australian stones from its stockpiles to Indian Sightholders to bring Argyle's revenues down. This made Mike Mitchell of Argyle ask, "If they had Argyle material that they could have sold into that market before, then why didn't they? Why were they not selling all that they could of the Argyle goods before?" This made life uncomfortable for the Indian Sightholders who had to buy more diamonds from De Beers than they needed or could afford.

Nicky Oppenheimer, Chairman of De Beers, noted, "The situation in India is of concern … the industry there is confused by what is happening and worried about it. Our hope is that this confusion and worry will not last too long." De Beers' Managing Director Ralfe hopefully noted that this flood of diamonds into India and lower prices would force Argyle back into the CSO. He added, "The Indian industry collectively believes that … in the normal rational course of events it was only to be expected that Argyle would sign up again with the CSO."

De Beers' communications manager Tom Tweedy promised in December 1996 that Argyle's diamond production would be back under De Beers' control before too long, alleging that Argyle had neither the production nor the quality to go it alone. His image of the industry was that traditional within De Beers, of a patriarchal family ruled by the Oppenheimer clan. He concluded: "We are all one family. We may be an unhappy one at times. This is just a family rift." Argyle executives were astonished when CSO officials charged that they had behaved in a "selfish" manner, in not renewing their contract. One executive demanded, "Since when is it a crime for a company to act in its own best interests?"

But the pressure on Argyle did not succeed. In the summer of 1998 Argyle's diamond production enjoyed 10 percent price increases on the free market. The Indian merchants allied to Argyle grew in strength, and Zales, a major US marketing company, contracted to promote and sell Australian diamonds. Thus finally, after nearly 20 years of production, the Argyle diamonds became the threat to the diamond cartel that Harry Oppenheimer perceived and tried to prevent. With one stroke, De Beers lost control over a vast number of diamonds and, more importantly, when its stockpiles ran down, it would no longer have vast numbers of Australian diamonds to use as a weapon to keep other producers in order. It was now evident that De Beers' strategy had always been to keep Australian diamonds low priced, off the market, and stockpiled as a weapon against other miners.

1   The comparative figures on diamond prices, cost of production, and qualities and sizes of rough diamonds in this chapter are all from Argyle's internal reports, produced with the assistance of De Beers, and made available to me by members of the Argyle consortium. Most of these figures have never been published before. They reveal a state of affairs in the diamond industry surprisingly different from common public perceptions.

2   *Financial Times*, London. September 1981 (Day unknown).

3   Hansard. H. Of R., October 20th, 1981, at 2066. 125.

4   This was its name in the UK. In the US this book was called *The Rise And Fall Of Diamonds*.

5   1982 De Beers Annual Report.

6   Chhotalal, p. 24.

7   Internal CSO table of reserves per mine, 1980.

8   *Australian Financial Review*, January 28th, 1982.

9   Northern Mining gave me a private viewing of the marketing documents for the Ashton Joint Venture. This included details of the rival bids.

10 Hansard, H. of R., October 20th, 1981, at 2066.

11 Ibid.

12 Ibid.

13 De Beers allegedly bought many copies of his book so as to remove it from the market. – Private email from well-known diamond industry figure close to the Oppenheimers.

14 Interviews conducted by author at Commonwealth Heads of Government meeting, Melbourne, 1981.

15 A. Deans. "Argyle carats may be cut back." *Australian Business*, November 5th, 1981, p. 18.

16 Roger Moody. *The Gulliver File*. London: Zed Books, 1992, p. 502.

17 Chhotalal gave as his source an undated article in the *Sunday Times* of London.

18 125 Hansard. H. Of R. Australia. October 15th, 1981, at 2066.

19 Chhotalal, p. 42.

20 The South African government later gave up this right, fearing it would lead to sanctions. But the replacement South African committee effectively retained South African control over Australia's diamond production.

21 Private communication to author from Australian writer/researcher, 1994.

22 Ibid.

23 Wharton-Tigar, p. 193.

24 Wharton-Tigar, p. 179.

25 Wharton-Tigar, p. 194.

26 Wharton-Tigar, p. 179.

27 S. Bagwell. "How Robert Struck Gold." *The Australian Financial Review*, September 29th, 1989.

28 G. Kitney. "South Africans Gain Vital Grip on Australian Diamonds." *National Times*. February 21-27, 1982.

29 The Merlin diamond mine would soon be taken over by CRA, with other Ashton mining diamond interests in Australia, and controversially shut down.

Chapter 15 – The Diamonds of the Frozen North

By the time my diamond film was completed I had researched the diamond trade for 14 years and I was, I must confess, sick of diamonds. But within a month of the film appearing on the BBC, I was in the Arctic, on De Beers' mining prospects, staying with the Dene, a native people of far north Canada, going out with dog teams, watching a magnificent herd of 350,000 caribou and marveling at the vibrant Northern Lights scouring the night sky – all because of De Beers' paranoia. It had threatened local people to try to stop a showing of my film – so the Canadians had invited me to visit them. I felt I owed De Beers a bouquet for inadvertently bringing me back to working in a wonderful wilderness and with indigenous people.

Canada's central northern province of the Northwest Territory has proved so rich in diamonds that De Beers fought to gain marketing control over the prospective mines as they had in Australia. This time they had first to negotiate with Australia's giant Broken Hill Proprietary Ltd. (BHP), one of the world's largest mining companies, for it had gained control over diamond deposits in the Canadian tundra that rivaled or exceeded those of Kimberley, South Africa.

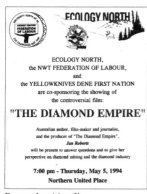

ECOLOGY NORTH,
the NWT FEDERATION OF LABOUR,
and
the YELLOWKNIVES DENE FIRST NATION
are co-sponsoring the showing of
the controversial film:

"THE DIAMOND EMPIRE"

Australian author, film-maker and journalist,
and the producer of "The Diamond Empire",
Jan Roberts
will be present to answer questions and to give her
perspective on diamond mining and the diamond industry

7:00 pm - Thursday, May 5, 1994
Northern United Place

Poster advertising film.

De Beers sent CSO executive committee secretary George Burne to the Arctic in May 1994. He took with him a De Beers promotional film to show the locals. Then in Yellowknife, the capital of the Northwest Territory, he came across a poster advertising a public showing of my film *The Diamond Empire*. He acted immediately to try to stop this – although it had already been on Canadian cable television. Within days Ecology North, the local community group that planned to put on the film, received a letter from one of Canada's most prominent law firms, Toronto's Fasken, Campbell, Godfrey.

The letter read, "We have been retained by De Beers Centenary A.G. ('De Beers'). Our client has advised us that it is the intention of Ecology North to show a film known as *The Diamond Empire* on Tuesday, March 15th, 1994 in

Yellowknife. We have reviewed a newspaper article indicating that the broadcast will be open to the public at no charge. On behalf of De Beers, we hereby inform you that the film contains statements defamatory of De Beers and the Oppenheimer family."

The first "defamatory statement" the letter mentioned was that my film "wrongly suggests the production of diamonds has been suppressed on the false premise that the supply of diamonds is plentiful." It continued, "we are advised by De Beers that this film has not been shown by broadcasters in Britain and Australia as a consequence to its defamatory content." The lawyers threatened Ecology North with dire consequences if they showed the film. (In fact it was shown a few weeks later in Britain by the BBC, albeit in edited form.)

These threats really provoked the ire of Yellowknife residents. The director of Ecology North, Chris O'Brien, responded, "They don't want this information to be seen in the North, and this is one of the ways they're trying to prevent it."

Gagged!

The local paper, the *Yellowknifer*, ran a single-word headline: GAGGED! Its editorial was headed, "My, What Strong Arms You Have." The piece read in part: "De Beers

 pulled off a disastrous piece of public relations this week when it muzzled public debate on the diamond industry... If De Beers is trying to undo its popular image of a manipulative monopoly, it could hardly have chosen a rougher road. Public interest in *The Diamond Empire* has been piqued. And De Beers appears to be living up to the allegation – deserved or undeserved – that it is a powerful, money-hungry and cynical conglomerate... Falling back on threats against little guys is no way to combat an image problem."

When Burne wrote to the Ministry of Energy, Mines and Petroleum Resources of the Northwest Territories to thank him for "your kind arrangements made for my visit to Yellowknife," he continued, "The only blight on my visit was to read the attached article in the *Yellowknifer* on the plane.... The production of the film *The Diamond Empire* by the BBC and the Australians has been the subject of considerable controversy for some time." He concluded, "it is most unfortunate that Ecology North... seeks to damage the value of diamonds even before mining has commenced in the NWT. If you think it appropriate, I would be most grateful if the various important people I spoke to in Yellowknife could be shown a copy of our letter to Henry Becton (WGBH)."

The WGBH he referred to was the American television station that had transmitted *The Diamond Empire* throughout North America as a feature-length special in the documentary series *Frontline*. De Beers did not threaten it with legal action. Perhaps they could not take such action in the US, since their major defense against being indicted under US anti-price rigging laws was that De Beers did not have a legal presence in the US.

In the Northwest Territories Legislative Assembly, Mr. Antoine, on March 18th, spoke of this "David and Goliath" struggle. He noted: "last week in Yellowknife, a De Beers representative, Mr. George Burne, showed a promotional video about the industry" but there were "other points of view about the industry." De Beers was "depriving northerners of the opportunity to make up their own minds…. We don't need big international mining companies making up our minds for us by telling us what sorts of information we can or cannot see. If that sort of conduct is typical of the diamond industry, the people of the NWT should think very carefully indeed before giving approval to any diamond mining on our lands."

Of course De Beers' efforts to have the film banned kindled a great deal of interest. The NW Territories' Federation of Labor announced they would show the film. Ecology North contacted me, offering to bring me to Canada to speak to the film. They commented that: "If they had left us alone we would have shown the film to about 60 people and that would have been that."

By now De Beers realized that its threats had seriously backfired. Bill J. Lear, De Beers' director of Corporate Communications in London (incorporated in Switzerland) wrote to Ecology North withdrawing their threat of legal action. "The papers in this matter," he wrote, "have now been referred for my personal attention. I regret that it appears, from the inquiries I have carried out, that, due to no fault on the part of Mr. Campion [their Toronto lawyer], his letter may have been a product of a misunderstanding." He stated that they had made the mistake of thinking Ecology North was exhibiting the British version of the film rather than the American, a flimsy excuse given that Burne had expressly referred to the version aired on American public television.[1]

Lear added:

I now understand… it is your wish to screen a programme which has already been broadcast in the US by WGBH as part of its 'Frontline' series. That programme, we suspect as a result of the inadequacies of the BBC's research, is deeply flawed. It is based on the premise that diamonds of whatever quality, whether industrial or gem stones, are so plentiful that production has been suppressed. That premise is false, as anyone with any knowledge of the diamond industry must know. De Beers invests a great deal of money in prospecting for new, commercially viable, mines – as do other major mining companies… Despite the reservations concerning the WGBH broadcast, no legal action has been taken or is contemplated against WGBH.

If, as I have been given to understand, your intention is to show to a limited audience the same programme that has already been broadcast in the US, you have my assurance that legal proceedings will not be brought against you nor against other groups – for example the NWT Federation of Labor. I recognise that the most appropriate forum where the truth or otherwise of the allegations may be determined is in an action against the BBC… As you no doubt know, De Beers is investing large sums of money in prospecting in the Northwest Territories and would like to establish a relationship with the community, based on candour and openness to criticism.[2]

This distinction he made between the versions of my film, one broadcast by the BBC (in two 50 minute parts in prime time on successive Sundays) and the other a feature-length version broadcast by WGBH, seemed fictitious. The American version was stronger and closer to my original script. The version made for the BBC had been partly censored and weakened in the final stages of production – although De Beers still hated it.

The powerful Sierra Legal Defense Fund responded on behalf of Ecology North: "Ecology North wishes to extend to De Beers/Centenary an invitation to participate in a public information forum." A press release said the public screening of *The Diamond Empire* would be at this public forum. But De Beers replied to say that it preferred not to attend the showing of the film.

These were the events that preceded my arrival in Yellowknife. To reach the town I had to fly across the Atlantic, then north from a spring green Canada until I was crossing a land of countless frozen lakes and granite outcrops. I first saw Yellowknife when my eyes followed pale ice roads crossing a frozen lake to find it on the northern shore, obvious and incongruous with several multi-story buildings. Yellowknife then had about 30,000 inhabitants and was a true frontier town. The tarmac road from the south ended there. The railroad didn't reach this far.

The film was put on in the largest hall in town and it was standing room only. Local people, government people, and members of the native Dene people, came and invited me to visit them. De Beers had been invited but they did not turn up until immediately after I left town some weeks later. They then seemingly tried to counter my words by flying in experts from South Africa to tour the Dene settlements, distributing t-shirts with the slogan "Diamonds are forever."

What De Beers clearly found most upsetting about the film was that it presented evidence to show that diamonds were not rare enough to justify the prices it charged. They obviously felt this could do economic damage to them in the Northwest Territories. Yet if we were right, and diamonds were not rare, why was De Beers seemingly backing the establishment of new diamond mines in Canada? Why was De Beers offering to help sell Canadian diamonds? I was sure from all that I had learned that world diamond supplies were ample, so I felt there could only be one answer. De Beers was hoist with its own petard. It could not publicly say Canadian diamonds was superfluous to requirements and at the same time maintain that diamonds were rare. They wanted to persuade the local miners to let them have marketing control – then the myth of scarcity could be protected by their traditional means of restricting distribution and imposing production quotas.

There was an alternative. They might be able to maintain high prices without fighting for control over independent diamond mines in the same fashion as had worked with the Russians: by simply persuading the independent producers and merchants to keep to the story that diamonds were rare – and to cooperate by quietly refusing to let the gem prices drop below the prices set by De Beers. But, this was risky. It might only be working with the Russians because De Beers controlled much of the rest of the market.

De Beers in any case wanted Canadian marketing contracts since these were potentially very lucrative. As we have seen in the previous chapter, De Beers took as its standard fees at least 15 percent of a mine's gross income – perhaps half or more of its total net profit. This meant the De Beers' take in Canada would be more than seven times the government royalty.

THE DENE INDIANS AND DIAMONDS

The government told the Dene that they would receive in return for permitting the mining 1.5 percent of the Government's royalty. In total this would amount to about 0.3 percent of the total profits before De Beers took its fees. In other words, De Beers would get about 150 times as much as the Sahtu, Kuchin, Dogrib and Yellowknife tribes of Dene. No wonder they were giving out T-shirts to the Dene.

T-shirts were not the only gift. When I went to visit one remote Dogrib community, living in log cabins by a frozen lake over which the caribou passed every spring, I found the trees around it were festooned with orange plastic ribbons. Several were glued to the trunks of the trees with sap from slashes and from crudely carved code numbers. Monopros, the De Beers prospecting company, had inflicted this unbiodegradable litter over thousands of square kilometers of wilderness. No doubt other companies did the same elsewhere in the region. One successful diamond prospector lamented, "When we started this, we weren't worried about what would happen. We had this land to ourselves. In the places where I went, I thought maybe I was the first person ever there." But he could never feel like this again. "There's millions of claim posts out there. To be part of something that caused this, that really kills me. I would give up everything I have for it never to have happened."[3] I went out into the forest to tear off some ribbons to leave just one small area undisfigured.

The community told me Monopros had tried to stake the very heart of the village – but were stopped by the protests of the chief and council. I stayed for some time with the community, and discussed diamond mining with them. After I left, a mining company, believed to be Monopros, flew in Kentucky Fried Chicken and Coca Cola as a gift to the community. The staking maps revealed that Monopros was still claiming the site of this village, despite their promises to leave the people's living area alone.

The Bureau of Mines told me of what they called "the Corridor of Hope" – a 100-kilometer band in the southern part of the tundra with many diamond deposits. The central part of this band was held by the Australian company, BHP, and it had on its lease at least 16 diamond-bearing volcanic pipes – of which 11 were commercial or near commercial. A government geologist told me many other pipes had been found and were being tested. BHP had already announced plans to construct four giant diamond mines on four adjacent pipes, draining the lakes over them, moving the fish to other lakes.

Canadians call this area the "Barrenland" or "Barrens" – but this name didn't hold true for the Dene. When I stayed with them, in a wilderness that stretched from horizon to horizon, I found it incredibly rich in food, but I must admit that I was there in spring. The

Caribou in northern Canada.

snow was melting and, as I walked along the edge of snowfields, I found the land covered in thawing juniper berries, blueberries, bearberries, berries of all kinds. They had been snapfrozen the previous fall and now were appearing, well-matured and slightly alcoholic, just as the bears were waking and thousands of migrating birds returning. The Dene would laugh at me when I returned with my mouth stained with berry juice. The Dene larders were well-stocked. The lakes and rivers were rich in fine, large, unpolluted fish. Caribou meat was easy to acquire. The people (for that is what Dene means in their language) had hunted the same large herd for over 7,000 years. In 2002 their Bathurst Herd was 350,000 strong. They loved their land. They took me out by dog sleigh and skidoo to show it to me.

BHP

BHP, or Broken Hill Proprietary, is Australia's first home grown transnational mining corporation. It is now known as BHP Billiton following a takeover of Shell's metals mining arm, Billiton. Its early fortune was made in the outback mining town of Broken Hill. It had not mined diamonds until recently.

From the information BHP made public, it clearly had in Canada a world-class discovery, equivalent to the Kimberley region that gave De Beers its first fortune. The first four mines would be each half a mile wide and at least 1,000 feet deep. Similar deposits in Russia are mined down to 1,500 feet. The tallest skyscraper yet built would not reach to their rim. The waste rock would be dumped onto tips over sixteen stories tall – taller than the pyramids and extremely obvious in these open lands. Some rock would be ground up and diluted with water in search for diamonds and then dumped as slurry into nearby lakes, filling them to the brim.

All this was to be done in the tundra for the sake of fine jewelry, in an extremely fragile and unspoilt world, where it would take another ice age to erase the damage. When Chris O'Brien, the spokesman for Ecology North, took me out into the wilderness, he took care to step gently on the lichens, explaining that if they are damaged, "they will take many, many years to recover in our harsh climate."

BHP was also digging its diamond mines in the migratory path of one of the greatest herds of migratory animals left in the world, the 350,000 caribou of the Bathurst Herd. These caribou, the gray and white antlered deer of the arctic regions, give birth every June and July in the endless Arctic summer day by Bathurst Inlet on the Arctic Ocean. They then move southwest, shoulder-to-shoulder in vast numbers, sheltering each other from biting flies. By late August the flies are less plentiful, so, in the southern tundra, they break up into smaller groups, rut, and eat richly of carpets of yellow, red and green lichens. The diamonds first found by BHP are in the rutting grounds by Lac de Gras – a French translation of its Dene name meaning "fattening lake" – where caribou get fat before the winter.

On either side of the BHP discoveries lay other diamond finds. To the west lay Tanquery's, to the south RTZ's – and those of other companies allied with De Beers. If all these are developed, it will mean daily blasting, a network of truck roads, airports, vast pits, and waste tips across this herd's migration routes.

A FRAGILE LAND

A Dene woman showed me photographs of her family camping, hunting caribou, and catching giant trout on a long and beautiful lake. She told me this was by the very lake BHP planned to fill with slurry. The Dene families in summer travel throughout this land by canoe over a web of rivers. In winter the men hunt by skidoo and dog sleigh over frozen rivers. They greet every lake with a prayer, thank

God for their safe travels, and thank every caribou killed by placing water or fresh snow within its mouth.

They dry and smoke the meat they need on tepee frames to sustain them between the herd's spring and autumn migrations. The Dene have long maintained their right to hunt all their ancestral lands, refusing government efforts to confine them to reservations. They have evaded the fate of the hunters of buffalo on the prairies for their land is much too cold, sometimes as low as -65°C, even to be coveted by whites for timber trees. (The trees are so small that I felt like a giant!) Then came the discovery of diamonds and other minerals.

In one of Yellowknife's towering office blocks, built on land stiff with permafrost, I was surprised when a government official, a wildlife specialist, repeatedly told me that diamond mining was environmentally benign and would not have the slightest effect on wildlife – although he went on to explain that nothing like this diamond rush had ever been experienced in this vast region, and minimal research had been done on its impact on wildlife.

His speech sounded like a party political broadcast. I was later told that civil servants were under pressure to follow an official line and avoid controversy, for the government feared another inquiry like that into the MacKenzie Valley Pipeline that determined any pipeline would affect the unique tide of life that is the caribou. But diamond mining on this scale, with the associated roads and hydroelectric schemes, with the other mining and game hunting schemes that could piggyback on top of this development, would probably have a vastly greater impact than could any pipeline.

BHP knew how fragile this land is. Its project report warned, "Because of the severe climate, low fertility of soils and surface waters and the widespread occurrence of permafrost, the recovery of various ecosystem components from damage by development activity is usually slow. This means that exceptional care must be exercised to minimize disturbances which could persist long after the activity itself has ceased."[4]

They frankly admitted they would not be able to restore the land after they had mined it. Their report continued: "The waste rock piles, all weather roads, airstrips and industrial plant sites... will remain evident for a long time after closure." As for the lakes covering the deposits they planed to mine, BHP conceded that, "There will likely be no practical possibility of restoring the productivity of these water bodies... nutrients will sink... contributing to oxygen depletion... Attempts will not be made at revegetation since substantial growth will not likely occur."[5]

They also admitted that the millennia old migration of the great Bathurst Herd could be affected. "Noise from aircraft and vehicles could temporarily drive certain wildlife species out of the area... disturb their habitat and migration routes." "Temporary" could mean for well over a century, as diamond mines in South Africa have continued operations for a long time.

BHP acknowledged the area was home "for grizzly bears, foxes, wolverines and caribou... and wolves are regularly seen in this area" and that "wildlife denning sites in disturbed or exploited eskers may not again become usable even when operations cease." Eskers are sinuous sand and gravel ridges, covered by moss and shrubs, left by rivers that once flowed under ice sheets. In a land of granite and muskeg swamps, these are vital to bears and wolves as they often provide the only soft dry land for digging dens. The Dene for the same reason for thousands of years put their graves in these eskers, and these are held to be sacred places. They are also the natural elevated roads where the summer breeze keeps away the flies, taken by the hunters and the caribou. I walked some eskers and discovered that they are covered in rich multicolored lawns of lichen beneath scattered pine, aspen and birch – by far the easiest route to walk when the lakes are thawed. The eskers are also used by BHP for mining roads and as a source of gravel. They may have other uses. The BHP project manager waxed enthusiastic during a plane journey about the prospects of finding good class alluvial diamonds deep within them.

The diamond deposits and lakes targeted by BHP were already joined by a road and by an airstrip big enough for C-130 Hercules aircraft, all built out of gravel mined from eskers. The richest of these pipes was codenamed 93J. Early samples showed it to contain four carats a tonne. This was far richer than any pipe in South Africa, according to De Beers.

Another danger noted by the Dene is the possibility that one of the many heavy trucks that supply the mines with diesel fuel over the ice roads will fall through the ice, polluting lakes rich in fish, beaver, and muskrat. The companies create multi-lane highways so a cracked lane can refreeze while others are used. All this makes for significant risk. In 1994 one truck did break through the ice. Fortunately it was in a shallow place. The truck was sawn out of the ice and rescued. The ice road to the diamond fields passes by MacKay Lake where a Dene graveyard has already been destroyed by truckers, according to a Dene spokesman.

Why take so many risks? Why mine diamonds in such a fragile wilderness? Government geologist, Mike Beauregard explained that Canadian diamonds are of good shape – better than the South African, which tend to be twisted, and the Australian, which tend to be fused together in couples. Jaap P. Zwaon, BHP's South African Chief Mining Engineer, showed me a photo of typical Canadian diamonds. About 80 percent were white, the color most prized in De Beers advertisements. Only 65 percent are white in South Africa.

BHP cutely named the two lakes they intended to drain first "Koala" and "Panda." Dene hunter Fred Sangre told me this renaming should not have happened. "There are Dene names for these lakes. The land up there contains the graves of our ancestors… All our hunting trails are marked with graves." I asked government archaeologist Tom Andrews, the man responsible for checking mining company applications, if he had checked for graves in the eskers that BHP has mined for gravel or used for roads. He said, "Yes, I did personally – but I can only tell if there are recent Christian burials as these are marked with wooden crosses. Other burials I cannot detect." He thought no one else had checked. Dene elders later confirmed that they had not been given the opportunity to check the eskers BHP used. BHP's report acknowledged: "The project site is located within the traditional Dene (and Inuit) land use area and they may have been in the region from as far back as 7,000 years."

I was privileged to go out with the Dene to a small settlement deep among the frozen lakes. They lived in wooden houses that all had one very unusual feature. Hanging high above the stove in the living room were red clothes strung on clotheslines, or so I first thought. I soon learned that they were drying caribou meat. They offered me a traditional meal of dried caribou meat and pieces of white caribou fat. I enjoyed it. I soon learned that the meat could have different flavors, depending on the wood used to smoke it.

Then a black-haired Dene woman looked at a photo I had brought. It was of uncut Australian diamonds. "Is that what diamonds look like?" she asked. She went to a cabinet in the corner of the room and brought back a small container. In it were several small stones. She sprinkled them on the table in front of me. Her daughter reached out and picked up one. It was small, misty white, crystalline. "Is that a diamond?" she asked.

I did not know for sure. It looked like the rough diamonds I had seen. "These stones were found in the stomach of a caribou," she said. I had watched part of a herd pass her door, a long line crossing the ice on the way to their summer birthing lands on the edge of the Arctic Ocean.

Behind these mining negotiations lay major constitutional issues. Since 1973 there has been serious legal doubt about the treaties upon which rested the Canadian government's claim to mineral rights in the Northwest Territories. When gold was discovered in the region, the federal government sent officers to persuade the relevant tribes to sign a document by which mineral and land rights were given up. This was known as Treaty Eight. Then, when in the 1920s rich oil fields and more gold fields were discovered, the federal government again sent out negotiators to other Dene tribes to secure further mineral rights. This was known as Treaty Eleven. In 1973 a judge ruled that, despite these treaties, the Indians still retained their rights. The Indians claimed they had been tricked, that no mention had been made of land surrender by the federal negotiators; that they had only spoken of offering a guarantee that their hunting would not be disturbed. No one had explained that if they signed the treaty put before them, they would be signing away their mineral rights.

The Canadian government after the discovery of diamonds again sent out negotiators to try to obtain what was effectively another treaty between the Canadian government and a people who have never been conquered, again to obtain mineral rights. The Sahtu Dene further to the west and north, away from the BHP discoveries, had conceded by 1994; but I heard their chiefs afterwards denouncing this new treaty on the radio, saying that they had been tricked into giving up land. They had also settled for a tiny fraction of the return for mining received by Aborigines in Australia's Northern Territory – and BHP must have known this. In Australia, a similar mine might pay about $15 million a year to the local Aborigines. In Canada, they were offered at first about $600,000 a year. Similar offers were made to the Dogrib, Yellowknife, and other Dene bands. In Yellowknife it was expected that BHP would make around $500 million a year from diamonds.

In Australia, the Ranger uranium mine paid Aborigines 4.25 percent of its gross income, not of net profits as in Canada. If the Dene nation got the same, it would get $59 million on a net mine profit of 25 percent – vastly above the $2.5 million then on offer.

While these negotiations were going on, suspiciously low estimates were given for the value of the diamonds contained in these diamond pipes – for example the Misery pipe was said to contain diamonds only worth on average $33 a carat. When the mine got its approval, the estimate rose to $117 a carat, with four carats per tonne. Panda pipe had ten carats per tonne at a value of $132 per carat and the Fox pipe three carats per tonne valued at $126 a carat.

After leaving Yellowknife, I went to Ottawa where I requested a meeting with the Department of Indian Affairs and Northern Development. I was very surprised on arriving at their office to be told they had difficulty in finding a room big enough to accommodate all who wanted to attend. I walked into a boardroom to find myself in front of many directors of departments and senior officials, all keen to discuss the diamond industry. After some two hours of discussion, a senior official told me that serious consideration would be given to holding a full regional review on the impact of these mining plans.

DE BEERS AND ITS PROSPECTING IN CANADA

Of the major companies exploring for diamonds, there was one that seemed singularly unfortunate. De Beers owned a prospecting company called Monopros that could not find many diamonds at all, or so it seemed. This might be thought surprising. One would think that since De Beers had much more expertise than anyone else, it would be good at finding diamonds. It certainly had looked at enough land in Canada and had enough time. Local geologists reported that De Beers had been secretively surveying in Canada for nearly 30 years.

In 1982, when Monopros was called Diapros, a party of Canadian prospectors chanced upon its large well-funded prospecting camp deep in the barrens. When the Canadians learned who owned this camp, they were most intrigued. They thought De Beers must be on to something to be pouring so much money into the area. The Canadians looked harder and went on to find the large diamond deposits that BHP is now mining. Yet Monopros had staked five times more land than BHP without seemingly discovering many diamonds. It also sent its mineral samples for testing in South Africa, thus ensuring no one in Canada had access to its results. A former Monopros employee said it was "like working for the Mafia," that the firm was obsessed with secrecy.

I recognized this behavior pattern. It was just like its sister company in Australia, Stockdale Prospecting, which also searched vast regions without finding many diamonds. Stockdale was also obsessed with secrecy. Some years earlier, when I had phoned it to ask for a copy of De Beers' annual report, they behaved as if it were a classified document. It made me wonder if both companies had been instructed that their job was simply to keep De Beers informed as to the whereabouts of diamond deposits, while convincingly concealing the existence of any promising finds.

While I was in Kimberley in South Africa, a member of De Beers' staff told me that diamond ore samples would provide a means for any diamonds discovered overseas to be secretly moved to De Beers vaults in South Africa as such samples are rarely if ever inspected by government. But, since De Beers kept secret the diamond content of samples received, there was currently no way of saying this was done in the case of Canada.

When others found diamond deposits, then De Beers might seek to buy control. It had thus purchased a diamond deposit found in volcanic dykes at Snap Lake, southeast of BHP at Lac de Gras. Here, unlike at Gope in Botswana, it had been forced by national law to recognize the rights of the indigenous people and to negotiate with them. The deposit was said to be rich, but De Beers announced, once it had control, that the diamond content was less than it had thought. It blamed this, and government bureaucracy, when it announced it would have to put off developing the area for a few more years.

De Beers also purchased an interest in a diamond deposit held by a Canadian company, Rhonda Corporation, on Nunavut indigenous land. This project became frozen in conflict when De Beers admitted it had understated the diamond content in the samples it tested, thus making funding the mine more difficult.

De Beers was also in difficulties because the Canadian government had decided to follow the Russian precedent and set up a diamond cutting industry locally, using diamonds directly purchased from the mining companies. BHP Billiton had agreed to this, as had other producers. The Dene would invest in diamond cutting, hoping this would give their communities a stable income. The local cutting would focus on the better sized diamonds. But De Beers hated the idea. It had managed to stop this happening on any significant scale in Botswana, South Africa, Angola and Namibia. It had told these countries that if they wanted to cut diamonds, they would have to purchase them at commercial rates from De Beers in London rather than from the local mines. This was how it had always managed the diamond world. It was how it kept its power. This was the way it maximized its profits – and minimized income for the diamond mining states.

They feared that Canada had set a precedent that would be used in southern Africa to force similar concessions from it there, allowing full commercial diamond cutting of reasonably sized stones to be established in Africa, to the detriment particularly of Israel and Belgium, for De Beers normally sent them these sizes.

The Oppenheimers were not only interested in diamonds. In 1993 their company Minorco bought 3.03 million shares in Metall Mining from Metallgellschaft in Germany. This company controlled a major base metals deposit at Izok Lake, near BHP's development. Its plans reportedly included sending ore north to a new Arctic Ocean port at the rate of one truck with two heavy trailers every ten minutes – again across a caribou migration route.

While I was in Yellowknife there was constant speculation about how Canadian diamond production could fit into the world market. One rumor was that it was going ahead with De Beers' support solely because South African mines were starting to become uneconomical. It was speculated that, if the Oppenheimer companies were forced to pay proper rates to their quarter of a million black workers, then they might quickly close their African diamond mines as uneconomical, making more room for Canada.

But De Beers could only control Canada if BHP and RTZ gave them marketing contracts, and if Canada remained without US-style antitrust laws. The US Justice Department attorneys told me, when I visited them in Washington in June 1994, that they were watching what was happening in Canada. If De Beers got the rights to market the Canadian diamonds, then, they said, they would examine if it were legal for Canada to take part in a conspiracy to rig prices and overcharge American customers.

Another rumor was that Russia and Australia were starting to run out of diamonds and that this would give BHP an opening into the world market. This was wishful thinking, probably based on the Argyle diamond mine only declaring part of its reserves, and on Russia having problems financing its mine expansions.

BHP insisted that it had no deal with De Beers and was not negotiating with the cartel when we met in the spring of 1994, but while I was in Yellowknife, I noted that a visit by De Beers' senior executives from London had coincided with a visit by a senior BHP executive from Australia.

DIAMOND MINING STARTS IN CANADA

Not long after my visit, in December 1994, BHP announced it planned to go ahead with Ekati diamond mine. It would pay into the Dene treasury a first installment of just 1.2 million Canadian dollars and promise to employ some Dene.

In June 1995, BHP produced the eight-volume Environmental Impact Statement that I quoted from earlier. It proposed not one mine, but five – with more that could follow at a later date. They were going to drain seven lakes and excavate the lake floors. Each pit was to be half a mile wide. Over a billion tons of rock and earth would be moved. This would be tipped into heaps as high as the Arc de Triomphe in Paris, 50 meters tall, or be used to fill lakes. Several lakes would be joined into a "Long Lake" to be used for sewage and waste water.

The six-floor high processing plant would cover an area several times bigger than a soccer field. The pits it served were miles apart. At least some 40 square miles would be affected. BHP predicted that the larger wild animals would avoid the place and others would be scarcely disturbed.

Kevin Krajick described the land that was about to be destroyed for diamonds in his book *Barren Lands*. He told how bears and other predators were attracted to human settlements. They raided houses for food, given half a chance. He told the story of how a wolverine "demolished a whole kitchen to carry away some roast beef." He now feared the bear population would be devastated as they were likely to be managed through shootings.

Krajick told how the wolves created dens on the eskers with extensive views, so they could see what was coming. These dens were used for generation after generation. Some den complexes held bones dated to seven thousand years ago. Rare musk oxen still inhabited the local area. The local Dene had long woven this land with sacred stories. The nearby Yamba Lake was named for the great shaman Yamozhah. Nearby on an esker were circles of stones that some 7,000 years ago had held down the caribou skin roofs of Dene tents. There were also scatterings of stone tools.

A 94-year-old Dogrib Elder, Suri Rabesca, told Krajick about the place. "Between those two lakes there is a Wha Ti ['Long Sand' – Dene for esker] that runs down to a narrow place. There the water is flowing very fast. A lot of caribou cross. People used to wait right there in birchwood canoes to spear them. Yes, that's been a good spot for a long time…. Bears hide behind those rocks and wait for the caribou to cross. When the caribou is almost on shore, the bear comes out and kills it right there in the water. Watch out." He laughed. Then Krajick asked about the graves. "There is a lot buried out there. They are everywhere."[6]

Environmental groups put up a fierce fight to minimize the damage that could be caused by diamond-mining. BHP made some concessions, particularly by setting up an educational fund for Dene communities. In late 1996 it won government approval for its plans for what it had now named as the "Ekati" mine. That winter some 1,800 heavy trucks went up the ice roads to the BHP site, taking in equipment and supplies. Over 2,000 trucks would go up the following winter. It was a very lucrative deal. BHP estimated its profit on the first four pipes, if mined to just half their feasible depth, at $8 to $16 billion.

The first diamonds from the Ekati mine were sold on the open market in 1997. BHP's diamond marketing manager William Zimmerman said the firm was closely monitoring the performance of the Australian Argyle mine as it had just broken free of the CSO – and would be monitoring the anticipated counterattack by the CSO.

Although BHP had earlier denied it, the company had indeed been negotiating with De Beers, but it finally decided to escape the danger of US antitrust action by agreeing to sell only 35 percent of their diamonds through De Beers. The rest it would sell on the open market in Antwerp. It got an average of $124 a carat. It held back all the largest gems of above 10.8 carats for sale at some future date – as also did South Africa and Russia. The widespread nature of this practice suggests that the producers saw it as particularly important to keep their large stones off the market to preserve the incredibly high prices achieved by the few large stones released.

By mid-1999 BHP was producing around three million carats per year. In 2002 it would achieve a very high profit-ratio of $330 million out of total revenue before tax of $700 million, on a production of 3.65 million carats. When this five-year contract expired in 2003, its confidence was high, and so it decided to sell in future all its diamonds outside the cartel.

RTZ, the owners of the Argyle diamond mine in Australia, were the next to set up a Canadian diamond mine, Diavik. It was working in partnership with the local Aber Diamond Corporation. They had proved reserves of at least 107 million carats at Lac de Gras, a place of much beauty, according to the Dene. It was 200 miles by ice road from Yellowknife. This road could only support heavy trucks for six weeks a year.

RTZ would bring Diavik into production in early 2003. It planned to produce six million carats a year and would sell its share, 60 percent, outside the diamond cartel. Its partner Aber, with 40 percent of the diamonds, in a move that might well set a future pattern for diamond mines, agreed to sell directly to Tiffany's in New York. This was even more alarming for De Beers. It put it entirely out of the loop.

But the Canadian government had imposed a tough condition. It had insisted that RTZ set aside $130 million as a bond to cover the restoration of their mine site when the mine came to the end of its life. This was, I believe, the first time a diamond mining company was forced to take seriously the cost of restoring land after mining. In the context of the Canadian wilderness, this was a very necessary precaution. By 2003 some of the fears that had worried environmentalists before the mines got approval were starting to come true.

A local woman, Alice Lafferty, observed about the BHP mine, "There used to be lots of caribou. But we don't see no caribou there now … Now there's nothing, caribou don't go close because they heard all kinds of noise and they smell that smoke. They go the other way. They don't see caribou around there, only big grizzly bears. Bears, they go around there for garbage."

BHP Billiton had sounded very confident beforehand whenever the danger of water pollution was discussed. But on March 31, 2001, Canada's Environmental Monitoring Agency reported it had found very disturbing and completely unanticipated problems at the mine. Pollution had spread down the waterways and into lakes. The pit appropriately named by BHP as "Misery" contained biotite schist, from which acids were leaching. The tip from the Panda mine was leaching sulphates, a sign of acid formation. Some lakes had depressed oxygen levels – a critical problem for fish in winter, when the lakes are covered in ice. There were changed levels of phytoplankton in the lakes. The inevitable use of explosives polluted some lakes with nitrates. Other mine practices were polluting with ammonia. It was alarming that this was happening so quickly – especially since BHP had just announced that it intended to double the size and extent of its mine complex. BHP was trying to remedy these problems, but it all added to the feeling that the mines constituted a gigantic environmental experiment.

Environmentalists also warned beforehand that the practice of approving each mining development in isolation, without investigating adequately the cumulative impact of all the developments, could lead to disaster. The authorities had admitted that they did not have all the answers; that they would have to do further research, and on the promise by the mining companies of such research, had given them approval. The environmental plans approved in practice were only relevant to early stages of mine development. Before BHP had even got its mine underway, it had added mining another diamond pipe to its plans. Within two years it had added four more, the Fox, Sable, Beartooth, and Pigeon pipes, more than doubling the size of the mine. These made it the largest diamond development in the world. BHP had also only discussed mining to a depth of 300 meters. By precedent at other similar mines, it would probably mine to twice the depth. All around the BHP mine, other mine projects now were underway. The door was open to industrialize a vast tract of former wilderness, all within the range of the great Bathurst caribou herd.

The same principle of putting off decisions until they were too late had also been followed in matters of Canadian Aboriginal rights. At RTZ's Diavik mine, set up on land not covered by previous treaties with the First Nations, making a settlement with the people who legally held the mineral rights was left to be concluded at some future date, after the mine had started.

John Zoe, a Dogrib chief negotiator, said Diavik had been rushed through regulatory processes. "What Diavik wants to do with this mine has never been done before…the potential negative consequences are terrifying to us and to all downstream users of the water."

Diavik Diamonds began building a massive six-kilometer long and 30 meters wide dyke, cutting off one end of the 60-kilometer long Lac de Gras, 140 miles south of the Arctic Circle, so the water could be drained out. Some of the diamond pipes discovered under this lake were covered by over 25 meters of water. After draining the water, excavating and mining the four diamond-rich volcanic pipes found in the lake floor and on an island, to a depth of 400 meters, the miners would pile the quarried rock to create a potential toxic mountain, within a setting visited by tens of thousands of caribou annually. Diavik expected to mine at least six million carats of diamonds here when full production began in 2005. It too was expanding from its approved base before it even got into production. It had discovered another commercial pipe, Piranha, near to its borders with the BHP lease.

During construction of the dyke, it had installed plastic silt curtains to protect fish habitat in the rest of the lake, as specified in its water license. This scheme was only partially successful. During a bad storm in 2001 part of a curtain came off its anchors and blew inland, letting silt out into the rest of the lake. It could not be fixed until the weather calmed. This happened several times that summer.

The Diavik mine is on a summer grazing area for the Bathurst caribou herd and on its biannual migratory route. The Dogrib First Nation described this herd as "the lifeblood of our people." They urged the government to slow down the process to ensure that environmental and community concerns were properly addressed. Zoe asked, "The diamonds aren't going anywhere. We have been harvesting on this land and the Bathurst Caribou have been traversing it since before human memory. How can the demands of Diavik for an immediate approval be balanced against this history and these needs today?"

THE RUSSIAN CHALLENGE TO DE BEERS

In the Russian tundra, swamps rather than the small lakes of Canada covered the diamond rocks. This made the sinking of pits more difficult. The Russians had also been reckless in their mining methods. They had even used nuclear explosives to look for oil near to the diamond mines. One explosion was three kilometers from the diamond-mining town of Udachny. There were twelve such blasts in the diamond-mining Russian state of Yakutia between 1973 and 1987. Even without these explosions, the pollution from the diamond mines themselves was so acute that local authorities had threatened to close the mines.[7]

Every winter the great Mirny "Peace" pit is filled with a freezing turgid soup of noxious fumes from vehicles, explosives, and even the rocks themselves. Fumes closed their richer diamond mine, the Udachnaya, for 1,529 hours (about two months) in 1990.[8] Russian scientists have published papers on dangers that seemed to have attracted scant attention in Canada. A report on the Udachnaya diamond mine was quite sensational. It reported, "[methane rich] gases are extremely widespread… the quantity of gases liberated spontaneously was variable and locally reached hundreds of thousands of cubic meters… the initial pressure ranged from 50 to 70 atmospheres."[9] I was later to find that miners were injured by methane gas explosions in South African diamond mines. This gives weight to the theory that diamonds are formed by volcanic heat applied to methane gas.

Gas explosions might have played a key role in the very formation of diamonds. They could ensure that diamonds move rapidly up the volcanic pipes from where they form at a depth of over 150 kilometers. If they went slowly, they would be more likely to catch fire – for diamonds are made up of flammable crystallized carbon. Russian diamonds have even been found to be explosive on occasion – due to gas inclusions.

Russia sometimes imports the larger diamonds it needs for diamond tools because of the danger that its own diamonds might explode.[10]

Asbestos: a serious danger to diamond miners

Russian geologists reported another danger, long ignored in De Beers publications. The kimberlite rocks of diamond pits mostly consist of olivine, which alters to serpentine. One type of serpentine is asbestos, a mineral that can kill through lung disease. Russian research shows that weathered serpentine also exhibits dangerous fibers, or asbestos-like characteristics. "Individual globules [of serpentine] congregate into extended snakelike growths."[11] In Britain, a Health and Safety executive report estimated that some 10,000 premature annual deaths will be caused by asbestos by 2020.[12] BHP admits serpentine is present in their Canadian diamond discoveries but says it is not dangerous.

The Russian diamond fields are over 6,500 kilometers from Moscow, in part of the Russian Federation once known as Yakutia and now as Sakha. Its capital Yakutsk has 200,000 inhabitants. At three million square kilometers, Sakha is larger than India and almost as large as the Northwest Territories of Canada. The local people, the Yakuts, look Mongolian, as do the Dene of north Canada. They speak a language akin to Turkish. Over 80 percent of the population still spoke their own language in 1994. They also depend in large measure on their reindeer herds and have benefited only marginally, if that, from diamond mining.

Sakha is every bit as cold as northern Canada. The local Lena River freezes to five meters. The temperature drops to -50 or -60°C. The houses have insulated hot water heating pipes mounted on trestles to stop the pipes melting the permafrost, destroying the foundations of houses built on frozen earth. Winter is the easiest time to get around, for, as in Canada, frozen rivers can be used as roads or airstrips.

Yet despite the extreme weather, Russia produces a veritable flood of diamonds. About three times more Russian gems than South African entered the world market in 1993. The CSO purchased $1.2 billion dollars worth at $68 a carat from Russia that year. The Russian mines were then, sadly for the CSO, the only major world-class mines over which it could not impose production quotas. The CSO thus lived in perpetual fear that Russia would flood even more diamonds onto the world markets.

Russia humbles the diamond empire

The story of Russia and De Beers needs to be understood if one wishes to understand the Canadian diamond industry, for Russia had effectively created the conditions the Canadians were inheriting. In the decade before the Canadian mines came into existence, Russia had effectively humbled De Beers, forcing it to accept that diamonds could be sold onto the free market, and forcing it to agree to diamonds being cut in large numbers in a producing country.

It was not until after the end of the Cold War that the West had learned just how rich were the Russian diamond deposits. Mike Beauregard, a Canadian government geologist, told me that Russian geologists showed a very interesting slide when visiting Yellowknife in the early 1990s. "I don't know if he showed it by mistake. These figures were very secret. The slide gave a figure of over four carats a tonne for one of the Russian mines." This was well over four times the diamond concentration reported by De Beers for its South African mines. The Russians also gave him a formula by which one could calculate the diamonds that could be found per tonne in the different types of diamond mines. Beauregard applied it to the Russian mines and calculated that the Mir pipe had nearly 11 carats per tonne – around Argyle's internal figures, but apparently much richer in quality at 30 percent gem and 40 percent near-gem. He estimated the Udachny mine had nearly eight carats per tonne. The BHP Ekati mine in Canada would turn out to be just as rich. But why then had De Beers declared diamond content results from its South African mines that were so very much lower than those produced by this formula?

All together, Siberia had, he informed me, 800 clusters of volcanic pipes of which five clusters held diamonds. Seven pipes in three of these clusters were currently being mined and "thirteen more pipes [are] assessed as economically viable."[13] In addition to the deposits in Siberia, Russia had an enormously rich unmined diamond field near Archangelsk in the north of European Russia.

The total number of diamonds mined in Russia was a state secret, but only oil, and perhaps gold, brought the Russian government more foreign exchange. The US Bureau of Mines estimated the 1992 Russian production at twice as much as the South African, at nearly 18 million carats worth $1.8 billion dollars. Of this, a billion dollars worth went to the CSO. The rest the Russians retained to cut themselves. In the 1990s, Russia was unique in the diamond world as a producer that was also a major cutter. Their uncut and cut diamond exports gave Russia about 40 percent of the world natural diamond market.[14]

They also had a secret weapon that made De Beers extremely nervous, a stockpile of top class very large gem diamonds. From 1945 until early 1990, the Soviet Union did not sell any diamonds larger than ten carats – and hardly any over five carats. Instead these diamonds became part of the national treasury. The Russian State Diamond Fund thus came to hold a treasure trove estimated to be worth perhaps $7 billion – more than the CSO's 1994 stockpile of $5 billion.

In 1990 Harry Oppenheimer negotiated what he called a very generous agreement with the Soviet Union. His companies would market $5 billion worth of Russian diamonds over a five year period and also loan the Soviets a billion dollars against the security of a billion dollars worth of the Russian stockpile. The CSO said it would charge the Soviets lower marketing and advertising fees than paid by any other cartel customer, just 7 percent for marketing and 3 percent for advertising. (Of course, this still amounted to half a billion dollars for the CSO.) A billion dollar diamond stockpile was duly shipped to London as the loan's security. But De Beers discovered this was only a fraction of the total Russian stockpile and that they had thus failed to neutralize the danger from Russia.[15]

In 1992, freed from the constraints imposed by anti-apartheid sanctions, the Oppenheimers were able to openly work with the Russians. So they tried to bring the Russians under control by setting up two joint ventures with them: Polestar and Northstar. They also offered to help rehabilitate the Mir mine, to help in the commencement of underground operations, and to help with a new mine, Jubilee.

They also agreed, in order to gain the right to market Russia's diamonds, that the CSO would use Russian diamonds to supply 26 percent of world's diamond market. The deal was presumably highly profitable, for that year De Beers declared profits of $4.4 billion.

Then the Russians started to query the CSO's generosity. A parliamentary investigation found the CSO made a 200 percent profit on the Russian diamonds, nearly $10 billion. Since De Beers valued its own South African diamond production at a carat price three times higher than it paid the Russians, this was not surprising. Suddenly the deal seemed far less favorable.

Boris Yeltsin's takeover in Russia was bad news for De Beers. He had lambasted Gorbachev for signing a contract with the CSO that was unfavorable to Russia. When Harry and Nicky Oppenheimer went to Moscow in February 1993 to open De Beers' first Moscow office, Yeltsin snubbed them by canceling their appointment to see him at the last minute.

Yeltsin let the Siberian state of Sakha keep 20 percent of the profits made from their diamonds in order to keep it in the Russian Federation. The job of selling its diamonds was given to a state-owned corporation called Almazy Rossii-Sakha (ARS), owned 20 percent by Sakha, 45 percent by the Russian federation, 10 percent by a servicemen's fund and 20 percent by the workers in the mines.

Moscow did not trust ARS, despite having a substantial share in it. It suspected that ARS had succumbed to Oppenheimer's wooing and become too close to De Beers. It thus asked the Russian Precious Stones and Metals Committee (Komdragmet), under the chairmanship of a close associate of Yeltsin, Evgeny M. Bychkov, to control the Russian stockpile and check the prices negotiated by ARS for its diamonds. When Bychkov was asked about his relationship with ARS, he bluntly replied, "How can you speak of a relationship where one party is working just for De Beers and the other party is working for the state of Russia. De Beers likes ARS, but we don't like the way they do business."[16]

Moscow desperately needed more foreign exchange, so it sought to find loopholes in the deal it had signed with the CSO. The Russian armaments industry used barter to sell diamonds outside the cartel. It swapped Thai rice that it could resell for diamonds.[17] Increased numbers of diamonds were sold as "technical goods," as the contract with De Beers only covered gem diamonds. Technical goods were officially near-gems, but as Ivan Gotovtsov of Sakha Diamond, admitted, "It is practically impossible to fix a line between technicals and gems."[18]

In an interview with the editor of the Israeli diamond magazine *Mazal U'Bracha*, in January 1993, Bychkov was asked why parcels of top quality Russian diamonds, valued at $1,000 to $4,000 a carat, had appeared in the market, when Russia had promised De Beers it would independently sell only industrials or cheap gems. "How could these be explained? Surely their release violated the Russian contract with De Beers?" Bychkov replied: "These were not our stones...We have the feeling that De Beers is just looking for someone to blame. De Beers should be grateful for Russian help," for "We supply 26 percent of the total diamond sales of De Beers."

Bychkov added, "De Beers sold [in 1993] Indian goods worth some 1.6 billion dollars... When De Beers does something like this, it's OK... So if Russia had sold the same goods in the amount of 60 to 70 million dollars, how could we be said to have destabilized the market and damaged the price?... De Beers should stop pressuring us."

He continued, "Russia has probably upset the normal flow of things at De Beers. We have changed our diamond policy and, whereas before everything used to go through one channel, now there is a second channel and De Beers can't work out what is going on... I would really like to be able to sell our rough to the Israeli and Antwerp market directly. But at the present time according to the agreement with De Beers we are only allowed to sell technical goods."

"To our great misfortune, there is a vast difference in price between what appears on the De Beers price list and the sum which we get on the open market. ... We can get from between 20-30 percent more for our stones on the open market."

Bychkov said that Russia felt that De Beers "is trying to push around anyone who has joint ventures with us.... Our current relationship with De Beers is such that they want us to remain as a source of raw materials... De Beers is doing everything so that domestic polishing industries do not develop in countries that mine diamonds. At least eight nations, including Russia, Botswana, Australia and Angola, have signed agreements to export [uncut] diamonds through De Beers." But, he concluded emphatically, "None of these, except us, has a domestic industry. If they began polishing their own diamonds, there would be no need for De Beers."

Bychkov in October 1993 again attacked De Beers. "The prices of Russian diamonds are determined by the consumer [De Beers] and, as the saying goes: 'without right of appeal.' Most importantly we will never know about the real prices at which De Beers sell our diamonds.... Sooner or later we will do away with the paradoxical situations, where Russia occupies a leading place in the world in diamond extraction and yet receives only $500 million a year, while Belgium and Israel, which do not have diamonds of their own, sell diamonds worth some $2.5 to 3 billion each. We aim to follow their footsteps."[19]

De Beers tried to curb the Russian sales in many ways. They dropped two prominent Antwerp merchants from the list of Sightholders because they had bought diamonds from Russia. But Russia had enough diamonds to support any merchant dropped by De Beers. The Russians grew in confidence as they weathered the CSO attack. In December 1993 Russia sold in Antwerp nearly $80 million in large uncut stones in direct violation of its agreement with De Beers. Russia then offered merchants Moscow Sights in a rival system modeled on and parallel to the De Beers system.

The CSO attacked Russia publicly for "flooding the market." Gary Ralfe of De Beers complained to the *Financial Times* in 1993 that $40 to $50 million of uncut Russian gems had leaked out in just two weeks. In March 1995 he repeated similar accusations, but with higher figures, saying Russia had sold a billion dollars worth of diamonds outside the CSO in the previous year.

Russia continued to make inroads into the diamond world. When De Beers' Russian contract came up for renegotiation, Credit Lyonnais Securities, a major investment house, warned, "We think... potential investors in De Beers ought to be aware that the current upturn may represent the peak of the CSO's monopolistic hold on the international diamond market."

Eventually the CSO made an historical concession. They said they would share control over their cartel with the Russians. Anthony Oppenheimer, the President of the CSO, stated "There are two major production blocks in the world – namely the Russians on one hand and De Beers (plus Botswana) on the other. It is in both of our interest to work together." The Russians hoped they had forced De Beers to share control over the diamond world, by using the tactics originally employed by Ernest Oppenheimer to force De Beers into doing his will by threatening competition.

The Russian challenge was the greater because of the diamonds they chose to cut and market. They gave their cutters a better class of diamonds than they gave the CSO. Sergei Ulin, a director of ARS, said, "We sell where the profits are biggest. The gems we sell to De Beers are worth one third of those sold to our cutting industry."[20]

PRESIDENT CLINTON, TEMPELSMAN AND THE RUSSIANS

The Oppenheimers had greater problems with the Russians than they cared to admit. Buying the Angolan diamonds put on the market by UNITA had sapped the De Beers fortune. By 1993, even if the Russians had agreed to sell them their vast stockpile, the Oppenheimers no longer had the needed cash. So they turned once again to their invaluable American troubleshooter and middleman, Maurice Tempelsman, and he in turn sought the billions De Beers needed to gain control of the Russian stockpile from the American taxpayer. Ignoring the US Justice Department campaign to indict De Beers for price-fixing, Tempelsman went straight to his contacts in the White House. In the Fall of 1993 he and Jackie Onassis hosted Bill and Hillary Clinton on board Tempelsman's giant yacht, *Relemar*, in Martha's Vineyard.[21] Soon after this he offered the Russians several billion dollars of US government funds – and an intergovernmental loan backed by the US.

On December 17th, 1993 Tempelsman sent a memorandum marked "highly confidential" to Boris Fyodorav, Russian Deputy Prime Minister responsible for diamonds, offering Moscow a $3.3 billion loan at 6 percent interest. These funds would be obtained either from the American government or from the World Bank. In return for this, Russia was to allow him to select $4.5 billion of rough diamonds from the Russian stockpile to be held in escrow overseas as collateral for ten years under De Beers' supervision. Tempelsman proposed the deal would be formulated as between the two sovereign governments of Russia and the US. As part of this deal, he wanted the Russians to guarantee they would not sell any diamonds still remaining in the stockpile. He said this was to guarantee the diamonds held in escrow retained their value.

Tempelsman knew that the deal might still leave a substantial part of the Russian stockpile untouched, as some estimated it to be worth some $20 billion dollars. So he also wanted Russia to agree to an independent valuation of its entire stockpile. The proposal document, prepared by his firm, Lazare Kaplan, hinted that the very best stones in the stockpile would be selected as security for the loan, thus "neutralizing" the diamonds that most threatened De Beers' dominance of the world diamond market.

When Tempelsman visited Moscow that same month, he said his company, Lazare Kaplan, would expect a fee of 1.5 percent of the sum raised, plus expenses and consulting fees. He must have felt that he was likely to succeed. He knew Bychkov had been trying to negotiate an independent loan on the basis of a diamond collateral, without support from the CSO. Bychkov had found the banks insisted on the CSO selecting and valuing the Russian stones to be held as collateral. It seemed as if the CSO had got to the banks. This was too much for the Russians. The Tempelsman deal was put on ice.

Thus Tempelsman had once more attempted to use US money and diplomacy to secure the diamond cartel's future. In the 1960s he had proposed deals to keep the Russians at bay – in order to help the Oppenheimers get control in central Africa. In the 1970s he proposed deals that supported Mobutu as a pro-US politician, helping Oppenheimer gain the Congo's diamonds. Now he offered to support Russia, reversing his earlier Cold War rhetoric – but again in a deal that benefited the Oppenheimers by preserving the dominance of De Beers.

The Russians needed these funds to pay for the development of a major diamond find in the far north near Archangelsk. Vladimir Sukin, a geologist, told Reuters' Fiona Fleck: "There are billions of dollars right under our feet, under the birch and pine. We are not hiding what we have any more, we're proud of it. This is the Lomonosov, Europe's first diamond field – and it's not the last… it was found 15 years ago and kept secret for fear of upsetting the market. Our diamonds are of very high quality with half of them gems. We could mine this deposit for 30 years. We should mine as soon as possible."[22] There were 60 diamond bearing pipe deposits in the area around Lomonosov, with reserves estimated to be worth up to $12 billion. The CSO was very reluctant to have another major mine start up outside their cartel. But the Russians pressed on with it.

But Tempelsman was being overoptimistic. The US government funding for his deal became politically dubious, for in February 1994 the US Justice Department indicted De Beers for price-fixing. His proposed deal also met opposition from wary Russian officials, who thought it overly favored the CSO.

The CSO Managing Director Gary Ralfe then came by private jet to Sakha in September 1994 to woo ARS.[23] The ARS Vice President seemed to share the dreams of De Beers' advertisements. He said, "I have a dream. I want to see Russian couples buying diamond engagement and wedding rings as they do in the West. We have no tradition of this at present, but I hope the Russian church will help promote the idea."[24] He wanted Sakha to have a close relationship with De Beers.

But a tougher line prevailed in Moscow, where it was noted that De Beers was paying Sakha $205 per carat,[25] while paying Moscow under the Gorbachev deal only $68 a carat. This was partly because Moscow sent poorer stones to De Beers – but Moscow knew the price differential was much too great to be so justified. It verified this by selling similar diamonds to India for a higher price.

GOLDEN ADA AND DE BEERS

The Russians then tried to set up an international diamond-marketing network to rival De Beers. Their first move was to set up a distribution office in San Francisco known as the Golden ADA. Bychkov appointed Kazlenok to head it. On arrival he said his mission was to punch a giant hole in the De Beers cartel. His selling operation was to be financed with a fortune sent over from the Russian Treasury. It was not long before 5.3 tons of gold coins arrived as well as thousands of diamonds. Unfortunately Kazlenok allegedly felt that he had to establish his credentials by showing he had an unlimited checkbook, and thus squandered many millions. Despite, or maybe because of this, he attracted support from noted city figures and apparently was even introduced to Hillary Clinton.

This move was potentially a very serious threat to De Beers – and it immediately attracted its attention.

A pretext was needed to shut it down. At that time New York diamond merchants, including De Beers' Sightholders, on advice from US customs as I discussed earlier, invoiced Russian diamonds as coming from the UK. This allowed them to avoid a customs duty uniquely levied on Russian diamonds since Cold War days. No action had ever been taken to stop this practice. But if Golden ADA did much the same, then this could be a good excuse to close it down. And so it happened.

Golden ADA was raided by tax officials and closed down for invoicing Russian diamonds as coming from Zaire. The press ridiculed Golden ADA, not knowing how it was trapped. Bychkov accused De Beers of being behind this action. De Beers in turn tried to discredit Bychkov. Chaim Even-Zohar, the editor of *Mazal U'Bracha*, told Bychkov in an interview, "I cannot remember any time in recent history when De Beers made as many direct accusations against one organization and one man as they had against you and the Komdragmet." In February 1996 further action was taken to try to discredit Bychkov. He was arrested in Russia for "criminal negligence," but as soon as Yeltsin heard about this, he had the charges dropped. Bychkov became a principal in a major Russian bank – and is still a power in the Russian diamond industry.

When Bychkov temporarily lost political influence after the Golden ADA fiasco in San Francisco, the path of De Beers in Russia grew easier. The Komdragmet survived, but only as a department within the Finance Ministry. A deal was struck with De Beers. In return for partially financing the new mine, De Beers was offered a 26 percent interest in it. Tempelsman also looked like securing the biggest of prizes. He was negotiating a $450 million 10-year contract for the purchase of almost the entire Russian mining output of diamonds sized ten carats and up. This would be a joint venture with the Komdragmet.

But a few weeks later this deal was in trouble. In November 1996 the Russian government launched an investigation into the relations between ARS and the De Beers diamond monopoly. It was rough for a while, but when De Beers finally secured a new contract, they found that Russians were still independently selling rough diamonds onto the open market. It estimated that this involved some $1 billion worth of diamonds. The CSO had agreed to buy some $1.1 billion worth – but the Russians only presented them with some $600-700 million worth. The CSO were also forced by the Russians to buy "junk," while the best diamonds went onto the open market.

Tempelsman utilized his close link to the White House to favor De Beers' friends in Russia. According to a Moscow report, he introduced the ARS chief Viacheslav A. Shtyrov to President Clinton during a Washington visit in which he was given guarantees from the Federal Export-Import Bank for finance for ARS's imports of vital mining equipment. There was of course an extra price to pay for this. Tempelsman made the equipment deal part-and-parcel of his diamond purchasing contract in order to guarantee the delivery to him of top-class Russian diamonds. But his deal still was threatened by the prevailing Russian suspicion of De Beers.

In December 1996 De Beers decided to talk tougher. It sent an ultimatum to the Russians – either it got the diamonds it had contracted for or the contract would be terminated. But this backfired. CSO Chairman Nicky Oppenheimer offered to visit Moscow to resolve this "crisis," but the Minister of Finance had "no time" to see him so his trip was cancelled.

Consequently, a peeved Nicky Oppenheimer wrote a letter to the Russian Prime Minister, copying it to the Minister of Finance, to the Minister of Industry, to Yakutian President Mikhael Nikolayev, and to the ARS President Vichilov Shtyrov, among others. When this did not produce the desired response, De Beers felt it had no option but to cancel the contract. The publicity this attracted did De Beers far more harm than it did Russia. De Beers' share price plummeted. It was seen as De Beers abandoning its effort to control the world diamond mining market. Sightholders wondered if De Beers would now let them buy directly from Russia, but the CSO soon enlightened them. It instructed them to stay away from Russian diamonds so that it could keep the pressure up on Russia. The Russians meantime said that all this fuss was quite unnecessary. They were still prepared to negotiate a contract with the CSO.

De Beers got no credit in the diamond trade for its handling of this crisis. Its Sightholders noted that the merchants who bought Russian diamonds on the open market made much more money than those who remained loyal to De Beers.

In August 1997, Yeltsin issued a Diamond Decree under which the domestic cutting industry would get priority rights to Russia's diamond production. This was the final straw for De Beers. It gave in to Russian pressure.

In November, the CSO reluctantly agreed to a trade agreement under which it would only get a third of the Russian production – $550 million worth. It would also be obliged to buy any further diamonds offered by the Russians, even if they were of poor quality, up to a total of $1.25 billion. The CSO was thus reduced to becoming the buyer of last resort for the diamonds Russia had failed to sell on the open market.

President Yeltsin also authorized another government agency, Almazjuvelirexport, to sell rough diamonds. This also the CSO had to accept. The new trade agreement also provided a guarantee for the ARS so it could secure financial aid, including $500 million in credit from several of the world's major banks through NatWest Markets.

The Russians also started to expand its rival buying operations in Africa. ARS president Vyacheslav Shtyrov said in 1998, "In principle I think that De Beers is very unhappy that we are in Angola. And we're not pleased that De Beers is getting into the Russian industry in regards to development of diamond deposits in Russia." De Beers' newly formed company, Soglasiye, had an interest in the rich Lomonosov diamond deposit in Russia's Archangelsk region, and De Beers still retained a hold over Russian access to international funding for new diamond mines.

But the Arctic diamond flood continued unabated. In Finland, Ashton Mining found what was possibly an even bigger diamond discovery than that of Canada. They had located two swarms of kimberlite diamond pipes, most of which contained diamonds. One diamond pipe yielded 17 carats per 100 tons, vastly above official South African levels. RTZ, the British mining giant, took up nearby exploration leases. (The Sami people, indigenous inhabitants of northern Scandinavia, had protested at RTZ's 1994 annual general meeting that RTZ was disturbing the grazing grounds of their reindeer.)[26]

It is not surprising that the frozen north should be so rich in diamonds. It contains ancient continental rocks similar to those found in Australia and southern Africa. As the Northern Hemisphere contains much more of such rocks than does the Southern, it is likely to contain many more diamonds than the southern continents. The Arctic Ocean near to the diamond finds is also likely to be as rich in diamonds as are the seas off southern Africa.

So this is the context in which the new discoveries in Canada needed to be put. As they came into production, they entered a world in which prices would fall if the flood of diamonds available were allowed to enter the free market, where De Beers' resources were stretched to the limit in trying to prevent this free market, and where new technology meant that pure gem diamonds could be economically produced in factories.

But it should be remembered that Russia, the first country to take on De Beers, did not want the prices to fall. They wanted to join in the diamond game in partnership with De Beers, to maintain the myth, to keep the prices high. BHP and RTZ in Canada shared the same ambition. They all wanted to charge high prices and recoup vast profits for a relatively cheap commodity.

1   Bill J. Lear, De Beers' director of Corporate Communications in London (incorporated in Switzerland) in a letter in early 1994 to Ecology North withdrawing their threat of legal action.
2   Ibid.
3   Kevin Krajick, *Barren Lands: An Epic Search for Diamonds in the North American Arctic*. Owl Books, 2002, p. 372.
4   BHP Project Report, 4-11.
5   BHP Project Report, 5-17.
6   Krajick, p. 368.
7   Reuters report, "Yurakh." July 7th, 1993.
8   A. Russudov et al, "Environment protection problems in mining of Udahnaya pipe diamond deposit under severe conditions of Far North," in *Environmental Issues and Waste Management in Energy and Minerals Production*. R.K. Singhal et al (ed.), A.A. Rotterdam; Netherlands, 1992, pp. 319-327.
9   Endnote. A. I. Krastov et al, "Gases and bitumens in rocks of the Udachnaya pipe." *Doklady Akademii Nauk SSSR*, Vol. 228, No. 5, 1976, pp. 1204-1207.
10 *Financial Times*. August 13th, 1987.
11 N. N. Zinchuk et al, "Variation of the mineral composition and structural features of the kimberlites of the Yakutiya during weathering." *Geologiya i Geofizika*, Vol. 23, no. 2, 1982, pp 42-52.
12 *The Guardian*. London. November 25th, 1994.
13 Department of Energy, Mines and Petroleum Resources, Minerals Division, Government of the Northwest Territories. "Diamonds and the Northwest Territories" December 1993.
14 Koskoff, p. 318.
15 *Daily Telegraph*. London. May 19th, 1994 – all but $350 million has been repaid of the $1 billion loan.
16 *Mazal U'Bracha*. January 1993.
17 *Mazal U'Bracha* Issue 55. October 1992.
18 *Independent on Sunday*. London. November 13th, 1994.
19 *Aeroflot*, October 1993.
20 Reuters report, April 16th, 1993.
21 Wayne Madsen op. cit. 92.
22 Fiona Fleck, Reuters Report, July 7th, 1993.
23 *Independent on Sunday*. London. November 13th, 1993.
24 *The Moscow Times*. November 17th, 1992.
25 By a 1992 agreement.
26 *Financial Times*. September 9th, 1994.

Chapter 16 – The diamond heartland of De Beers

As the independent Russian, Australian, and Canadian diamond producers grew stronger, De Beers had become increasingly dependent on the output of its southern African mines. These still dominated world gem diamond supplies and gave De Beers its continuing strength. In 2002, De Beers controlled 65 percent of the world rough diamond trade, with 50 percent of the world's gem diamond supplies, by values set by De Beers, coming from its own mines. The southern African mines thus remained vital to the De Beers system. They were, and still are in 2003, the heart of the world's rough diamond industry.

If I was to complete my investigation, and put the other mines in context, I needed to know more about the De Beers' heartland. I was particularly curious to learn

The fortified entrance to the Namdeb (formerly CDM) mine.

if it could possibly be secretly as rich per tonne as the new independent diamond mines of other continents. Was it really afflicted, as De Beers had said, with the lowest carat per tonne rates in the world?

I decided I had first to go back to basics and look at how De Beers had managed its diamond production over the past few decades. I thought it would help if I could read the reports of the only judicial commission inquiry ever to gain access to De Beers' internal mine documents. It was held under Justice Thirion and examined the diamond mines of the "Forbidden Zone" that covered hundreds of square miles along the wild Atlantic coast of Namibia and the lower Orange River – but only a short synopsis of its reports had been made public. The internal mine reports included were still wrapped in secrecy. To secure them I went to Namibia.

This took me first to Orangemund, the headquarters of CDM's operation in the Forbidden Zone, where I had arranged several interviews. To get there I had to cross the Oppenheimer Bridge over the Orange River into Namibia, then go through the CDM security gates into the mining town. I was soon at the heavily fortified main gate into the diamond zone with its grim watchtower. When, soon

CDM guard returns to post.

CDM sign listing accidents.

after arrival, I took a photograph of a sign announcing that this sand dune mining operation had only 31 "disabling injuries" in the previous 12 months, a heavily built white man immediately accosted me. He stalked out from a building by this watchtower and demanded I put away my camera as this notice was in a CDM "security zone."

I soon learned that here, as at the Kleinzee and Alexkor mines to the South, miserably paid black miners were sent out to closely inspect the bedrock exposed by the removal of sand dunes, like police forensic teams. Their job was to find the fine gems stuck in crevices. This vast mining lease contained several diamond-rich ancient beaches, now exposed above the sea and stretching to the north for over 60 kilometers. The Thirion Report explains, "Grades are consistent to 60 km north" and are "slightly higher past the 60-kilometer mark."[1] The rent paid to the Namibian government by CDM for the 20,000 square kilometers was incredibly only R812.40 ($350) per year. Its lease did not expire until 2010.

This Forbidden Zone had provided the Oppenheimers with at least $10 billion of diamonds. Between 1964 and 1975 it provided 40 percent by value of De Beers' output. After 1975, when independence looked likely, De Beers stopped publishing how many diamonds it was taking out from here. Little of these profits went back into developing Namibia. De Beers instead

Coastal diamond separation plant.

used CDM to finance its mines in Botswana, lending millions of dollars to a company called De Beers Holdings, or Debhold.

I have mentioned how the United Nations ordered all exports of Namibian minerals to stop before Namibia obtained its independence in order to protect its heritage of wealth – and how this UN order had made absolutely no difference to De Beers. It had defied the United Nations – moving the diamonds out along secret routes via the Bahamas and Switzerland. I had heard that this plundering had been extensively documented by the Thirion Commission.

Overmining Namibia

I found out more when I drove north to Namibia's capital, Windhoek. On arrival there I took delivery of a very scarce set of documents labeled "Geheim. Secret." They were the CDM mine management documents tabled before the Thirion

Gazelle passed on way to Windhoek.

Commission of Inquiry. My rare copy was *Annexure Copy No. 7.* They gave to me the details on how De Beers had managed Namibia's diamonds.

Normally a mineral deposit is mined to an average grade, with poorer and richer deposits mined simultaneously. If rich deposits are stripped out first, the mine's life is shortened since it becomes uneconomic earlier. This is called "overmining" and can have devastating results. A 1994 report stated that South Africa lost gold production worth over R2 billion due to overmining at the Roodepoort Deep gold mine.[2]

A 1982 internal CDM report reproduced in this Annexure stated, "Our present strategy… is best described as a 'power dive' and unless we have a conscious change in strategy, we will power the mine into the ground." Gordon Brown, a former technical assistant to the mine's manager, told me, "they decided to go hell for leather. They moved production of the largest stones up towards two million carats a year."[3] They worked round the clock, seven days a week. "Towards the end of 1986 we were running out of the high grade." CDM had deliberately overmined.

Another reproduced CDM internal document called "Confidential Life of Mine Forecast" of May 1982 estimated that this would make the mine uneconomical by 1994, that is, soon after Namibia's independence. It estimated that diamond "reserves will be depleted at the end of 1994 and that annual carat production will decline steadily from the current level of 1.41m to 0.2m in 1994…. During this period of 14 years it is estimated that some 12 million carats will be produced." The target date for the mine's exhaustion seemed no coincidence. De Beers had clearly planned to leave independent Namibia with an exhausted mine.

This power dive would be highly profitable for De Beers. This document continued, "Based on present day prices the revenues anticipated from this production is R3,440 million while operating costs are anticipated to be R1,764 million, and capital expenditure R307 million."[4] This calculation was based on a 1991 price per carat of about 275 Rand. In fact by 1993 the price per carat was over 900 Rand ($260), so the profits were three times larger. The diamonds extracted went to De Beers' London vaults, becoming a valued part of a stockpile said in 1993 to be worth $4.12 billion. This may not have been the stockpile's real value in the marketplace, since "diamond stocks are valued at average cost of production in the case of mining companies."[5] If so, the stockpile's real value would have been many times greater, given the cost of production figures detailed earlier, and the diamonds from CDM were amongst the very finest in it. The average size of the diamonds mined at CDM shrunk by a quarter between 1966 and 1981 since the larger stones were taken first. They went down from an average 0.88 carats to a still very valuable 0.61 carats a stone. The weight of diamonds found also declined by a half in the same period, from 0.35 carats to 0.18 carats per tonne of sand and gravel.[6]

But CDM's plans changed dramatically when it realized in the late 1980s that Namibia had a fortune in diamonds lying offshore on the seabed. CDM knew it could not possibly extract all these diamonds before Namibia gained its independence. (De Beers had been slow on the uptake. Sam Collins had taken over 300,000 carats from a small area of sea floor in Hottentots Bay in the 1970s.)

CDM and De Beers realized that they would have to befriend the incoming SWAPO government if they were to benefit from these offshore riches. This meant they must not be seen to have destroyed their shore-based mine prior to independence.

Overmining ceased. They started to mine diamonds that they had earlier ignored in favor of bigger stones. They thus reactivated a mine they had closed at Elizabeth Bay in the northern part of their lease. Gordon Brown told me, "We locked it up after taking its deflated areas." Deflated areas contain diamonds exposed by the wind that could be picked up with ease. A highly confidential CDM report said that if they mined it slowly, it could be successfully mined to the year 2040 or longer, producing revenue of over a billion Rand, although the average size would drop to 0.17 of a carat.[7] This contrasted to the North Blocks of the Upper Terraces, where the average size extracted had been a vastly more valuable 1.6 carats. CDM had already wrecked these by overmining.

THE DANGER OF TOURISTS

There was another reason to reopen the Elizabeth Bay mine. Melvin Foster, a CDM mining manager, reported they needed to put in "a relatively minor production facility

at Elizabeth Bay... at the earliest opportunity... effectively countering the moves to declare certain areas open to tourists."[8] CDM's Chief Security Superintendent, J. S. T. Fletcher, wrote tourism would mean "the screen of inhospitable terrain and regulation... would be cast aside. The innocent tourist would... be inquisitive about the presence

Bus taking De Beers workers from Luderitz to Elizabeth Bay mine.

of diamonds... such a facility would permit the adherents of SWAPO... easier access into the present forbidden area, either to procure diamonds with which to swell party funds or to seek liaison links with their opposite numbers and sympathizers inside the diamond area, unmonitored and uncontrolled."[9]

Yet De Beers had known for decades that Elizabeth Bay was rich in diamonds. It had simply not wanted to mine it since its diamonds were surplus to its requirements. It had held onto it because it did not want anyone else mine it. An internal CDM report said that 1.6 million carats of diamonds were lying there exposed under the desert winds. There was also another rich storehouse of over 15 million carats in the conglomerate rock below. The company estimated these were worth over one billion Rand. No wonder they wanted to keep the public out.[10] It did not cost much for De Beers to keep it locked up. The lease for the whole region cost De Beers less than $30 a year.

Landscape in Forbidden Zone.

In 1995 I was invited to stay with a family in Luderitz. This was a nine-hour drive from Windhoek. About one hour before I reached it, I passed large CDM signs telling me I was now in the "Sperrgebiet" (Forbidden Zone) and ordering me not to leave the roadway.

I was greatly surprised at the beauty of this forbidden land. Its rocky mountains swept up dramatically from silver and green plains that were graced by scimitar curved golden dunes. From the road I could see the glassed-in CDM guard post on a distant peak overlooking CDM's private road to Oranjemund. (Many locals want this road to be opened to the public, as the only alternative route is hundreds of miles longer via South Africa.) The old German railway line nearby was covered with large sand drifts. Under the Oppenheimers it had gone to ruin. Clearly tourism was not wanted.

But things were changing. The road I drove down to Luderitz through a small part of the Forbidden Zone had only been tarred in the previous year. Two bulldozers were now clearing the railway line.

LUDERITZ AND ITS DIAMONDS

Luderitz itself was a shock. I expected a prosperous town, for I knew it was now a base for the world's largest diamond sea-floor mining fleet. The diamonds extracted

Hovels in Luderitz.

by these ships had given this town of about 4,000 inhabitants the highest per capita income in Namibia. It had long been a wealthy place. I had just passed the forts dug into mountainsides that had protected a diamond trade that once took five million carats from here to Germany.

But what I found was a town that enshrined the evil consequences of economic apartheid. The town center was a small, slowly decaying area where only a few whites lived. Next to this lay a large residential area inhabited by blacks, with by far the worst living conditions I saw in Namibia. Many lived in tin shacks cobbled together from metal waste. The water services were on the verge of total collapse. Medical facilities were poor, healthcare expensive. The town's roads were dirt tracks over and around rocks and rubble. Yet, these were the blacks who mined diamonds at Elizabeth Bay for De Beers.

I stayed amid this squalor in a clean small brick home with a view of

Luderitz harbor.

the fleet of fishing boats converted into diamond pumping boats with their long hoses floating from their sterns. Beyond the blacks' camp, out of sight in the next valley, lay the better but still poor houses of the colored township.

Diamond boats with hoses in Luderitz harbor.

Diver at work with vacuum.

On the far side of the harbor lay Shark Island with monuments commemorating the Germans that landed there. There was no sign to tell how this was also Namibia's Alcatraz, that here her freedom fighters were interned in a concentration camp in which over 2,000 died. It seemed that people of Luderitz were being robbed even of their recent history.

I set out to find out just what was happening on the diamond boats. My inquiries were greatly helped when I met a young, enthusiastic and enterprising Namibian TV producer and news reporter, Christa Oaes, who was making a documentary about them.

When she showed me her rough footage, I found she had penetrated into areas that no other outside filmmaker had ever reached. She had filmed within the Forbidden Zone on De Beers' beaches. She had filmed out on the boats – interviewing black and white divers, owners, and government officials – and she had gathered all the elements together for a first rate documentary. Her film would cause a storm when it was shown in 1995 as a two-part special on Namibian Television.

She found the converted trawlers could fill 1,200 bags in a single day, each bag containing 15 kilograms of diamond-rich gravel pumped from the ocean floor. Since there was no government policing of these boats, no regular searching of the boats or of their owners, and no independent record of the numbers of diamonds found, it may be presumed that the owners of the boats would be tempted to underdeclare their diamond catch. The owner of one vessel said he found on average one diamond in every three bags, but his divers contradicted him in separate interviews.[11]

The divers said that sometimes there might be one diamond a bag but in many places they found from five to ten, or even 30 diamonds or more to a bag. The boat owners reported the average size was around one third of a carat – but De Beers had internally reported that one seabed area it searched contained diamonds weighing on average one extremely valuable carat, and other areas were averaging a valuable half a carat in size. All the diamonds found were of fine gem quality.

One boat owner said he pumped up 400 carats of gem diamonds a day; but, if one believed instead his divers, he was finding from 1,200 to over 12,000 carats a day. If the owner was right, his production of diamonds averaging one third of a carat would be worth at least $120,000 a day. But, if the divers were right, his real income would have been on a good day between half a million and two million dollars a day. The only limit to the harvest was the weather. Over the course of a year, only one day in three was calm enough to pump.

The government put inspectors on board the fishing boats to supervise the fish catch but it did not put one inspector on the diamond boats. The Deputy Minister of Mines and Energy told a mine union conference I attended that he had noted, when visiting a boat, that its captain simply carried the day's diamond catch off in his pocket. The Minister admitted there was utterly no security – totally unlike in the land-based mines.[12]

Christa Oaes filmed a captain picking out diamonds by hand from the gravels panned onto tables in front of him while still at sea. The diamonds were then put into plastic camera film cases and dropped into the captain's pocket. I noted that there were several diamonds in every pan of gravel filmed. I also noted that the black Namibians employed on the boats were engaged in manual shipboard tasks while the white divers did the lucrative work.

Her underwater footage showed young white South African divers guiding suction hoses into gullies and potholes on the sea floor. These contained beds of diamond-rich gravels up to four meters thick. These were removed by suction – devastating to any sea life present on the sea floor. They worked underwater in depths up to 50 meters, but diamond rich deposits occurred up to 500 meters below the surface. Larger ships and submersibles owned by De Beers were exploiting these deeper deposits. All these deposits lay along ancient beach lines – just as did the onshore sand dune deposits.

De Beers Marine held by far the largest and richest area of Namibia's diamond waters. In 2000 it was operating a fleet of nine large ships on the deeper diamond beds. One vessel found in one week nearly 5,000 gems of above 0.9 carats in size. The average size reported was 0.7 to 0.8 carats – but since some onshore beaches averaged 1.8 carats, submerged beaches were likely to be richer than reported. All these vessels operated utterly unsupervised by the Namibian government and were supplied by unchecked boats and helicopters from South Africa. De Beers' boats also went unsupervised from the marine diamond fields to Cape Town for refits. It was no wonder that De Beers soon decided to concentrate its mining efforts on these offshore mining fields. By 2002 it would be declaring a diamond "catch" of over 500,000 carats a year from the Namibian seabed, and was planning a production of 800,000 carats in 2006.

The Namibian government trusted De Beers not to misbehave. Dr. Hongala, the Permanent Secretary for Minerals and Energy admitted there were no safeguards when he was interviewed by Oaes, and added, "I don't want to believe that credible companies would take diamonds out [undeclared] by helicopter."[13]

In 1995, De Beers declared 400,000 carats as the year's production for their whole fleet. This raised many questions. It was only the equivalent of one month's production for a converted trawler. These much smaller boats could pump well over 100,000 carats a week. Since De Beers' vessels have submersibles that could work 24 hours a day and use far more powerful pumps than are on the Luderitz boats, a fleet of them should have produced vastly more.

It was hard for any outsider to check just what De Beers' boats were producing. De Beers had installed on its boats machines originally designed to can fruit to can diamond concentrate. The canned diamonds were stacked up on the boats like canned peaches in a warehouse. This gave De Beers more security – and crucially more secrecy. No one else knew what was in the cans. A very skeptical former CDM manager suggested to me that these ships were the perfect way to move undeclared diamonds from country to country, or from shore to sea. De Beers has since started to can diamonds also in its Botswana mines.

All the diamond boats operating out of Luderitz were owned and controlled by foreign companies (South African, Canada's Diamond Fields or Australia's BHP), excepting two subcontracted boats owned by white Namibians. The Namibian Mining Commissioner, Walden, reported, "We have not directly licensed a single Namibian offshore company." He added that this was because nearly all undersea mining rights were given away by the South African colonial government before independence and now, "There is an agreement between the South African and Namibian governments to honor any existing rights."[14]

In an interview with the Deputy Prime Minister I learned that SWAPO, prior to independence, promised South Africa that its companies would retain their lucrative concessions. An identical agreement was also made to gain the return of Walvis Bay and the diamond-rich offshore islands. The South African regime took advantage of this concession by selling perpetual mining rights to Namibian waters. This had effectively excluded Namibians from their own diamond wealth. Thus Namibians watched from Luderitz hovels while foreign whites made an incredible fortune.

Even failed South African applications have been given precedence over Namibian. In 1995 the South African company ODM was given precedence over a Namibian application for the only remaining unalloted area of diamond-rich Namibian seabed. ODM's successful argument was that it had purchased the rights of a small South African company that had unsuccessfully asked the South African government for these waters in 1966. The citizens of Luderitz petitioned against this as ODM arranged to lucratively sell on these rights to the Australian company BHP.

The Namibian company involved was extremely disappointed. It had even secured an appropriate vessel. But when ODM's later application was given preference, it was forced to subcontract the services of its vessel to ODM. The night after it made this deal, the Namibian boat mysteriously broke loose, drifted dexterously through an anchored fleet and out of the harbor entrance onto distant rocks. Allegedly, no investigation was carried out.

All diamonds found on the ocean bed or beaches by these smaller boats were supposed to be sent to Windhoek for official valuation. The average value given officially was between about $100-150 a carat. But this might well have been only a third of their real value. Local boat operators were amazed when they learned that the same valuers gave CDM's practically identical diamonds, including the much smaller ones from Elizabeth Bay, a value three times greater, $336 per carat. Internal CDM documents that I saw revealed that CDM gave its own diamonds an average value of $377 per carat. It valued some of its larger stones at just over $1,000 per carat. CDM's successor, Namdeb, would estimate in 2000 that the average value of its stones was $324 a carat. This suggested that the government's official valuer was severely under-valuing any diamonds produced by the smaller trawling companies. This would create a temptation to smuggle out these diamonds and have them valued and sold in Antwerp to obtain its higher prices.

Fraud was easy. A woman showed me a blank official Diamond Board valuation form, already signed and stamped, onto which any figure could have been written. I was told such forms were easy to obtain. (This later made me wonder how easy it would become to obtain Kimberley Process certificates, verifying diamonds are not conflict stones.)

The Namibian government was operating very much in the dark in trying to monitor its diamond industry. It had no way of checking if the values De Beers set on diamonds corresponded to the values obtainable on the international market. De Beers refused to tell the Namibian government what price it got when it sold its diamonds in London – even though De Beers charged a marketing and valuation fee for this service, and acted as the government's agent. The government had to content itself with vague and unverifiable De Beers estimates.

The Namibian Auditor General reported: "CDM has constantly pleaded incapable of providing final selling figures, firstly because the final selling is not done by either it or Prime Trading, but by the CSO which is a totally different legal entity, acting as it does, outside the sphere of influence of CDM/Prime Trading."[15] The CSO was of course in Europe. Needless to say, CDM and Prime Trading belonged to the Oppenheimer empire – as did the CSO – so they presumably knew what each other was doing.

The second reason De Beers gave for not knowing the price the Namibian diamonds fetched was that the Namibian stones had been mixed by the CSO with diamonds from many other countries prior to being sold. The Auditor General quoted "from a reply from CDM 'once the diamonds have been sold by Prime Trading, they are sorted with large quantities of similar diamonds from other producers in what is known as the London mix' after which Namibian stones can no longer be identified." He concluded dryly: "This complicates the function of my auditors."[16]

When I spoke to De Beers' diamond sorters in Windhoek, I discovered another way in which the company could cut government revenues. The sorters said they had been instructed to sort the stones to create a category of "near-gems." Thus, after being graded at 98-100 percent gem quality for nearly a hundred years, Namibian diamonds were now being graded as five to 10 percent "near-gems" and priced accordingly. All this was being done on the basis of unilateral De Beers decisions.

In 1992, the Namibian export duty on rough diamonds was 10 percent of the "declared value," but it remained impossible for the government to check if CDM was giving the correct value to its stones. The 1991 Report of the Auditor General stated, "the Namibian Diamond Industry is so completely intermingled with the international diamond trading business that auditing in the true sense of the word of some of the books and accounts of the local industry is not possible."

In 1995 the Namibian government gave up on trying to obtain the CSO selling price for their diamonds. They decided instead to impose a 10 percent royalty on the basis of an independently checked valuation. On the face of it, this should have solved the problem for them – but the method they chose (or, more likely, were permitted under De Beers' contracts) was deeply flawed. The independent valuers appointed were not allowed to check the values the diamonds would have if marketed independently on the free market. They were instead told to check only if the diamonds were correctly sorted into the CSO fixed-price boxes. (There are over 3,000 such boxes.) There was no check on the prices that the CSO had allotted to each box. This exercise told the government little. Ultimately it had to depend on the goodwill of the CSO. It was very hard for it to check even the smaller producers. Allegedly it allowed some companies to simply give their cost of production as the value of their diamonds, much as De Beers itself did when giving a value to its stockpile.

There was yet another way that Namibia was open to being cheated. Inside South Africa the De Beers Kleinzee-Koingnaas mine was producing diamonds nearly equal in value to CDM's. But Gordon Brown, a former member of CDM's management team, alleged during an interview with me that De Beers sometimes secretly swapped the larger Namibian diamonds with smaller Kleinzee diamonds – thus declaring as South African a valuable part of their Namibian output. He alleged this involved about 30,000 to 40,000 carats annually between 1973 and 1975.

POWERING DOWN THE RICH KLEINZEE MINE

At Kleinzee in South Africa, where presumably there was no political imperative to overmine, the size of diamonds remained higher. Its staff told me in 1994 that the average size of a diamond on a nearby marine terrace was an excellent 0.85 carat. It got lower as one traveled away from Kleinzee along the De Beers-controlled coastline. Thirty kilometers north it was 0.37 carat, while at Koingnaas, 50 miles to the south, it went down to 0.3 carat. But these smaller sizes were also of gem quality and much more valuable than gold.

In 1993 nearly a 1,000 workers were laid off at Kleinzee because De Beers said it had been forced to purchase so many Russian and Angolan (UNITA)

diamonds to keep the market stable, that they had more diamonds than they needed. Production dropped from one million to 600,000 carats a year at Kleinzee. These were being mined at a grade of 18.6 gem carats a hundred tonnes – above the official rate for all other South African mines owned by De Beers. This made Kleinzee the richest De Beers mine in South Africa.

But, after the election of the ANC, De Beers' plans for Kleinzee changed. It may have been that a wary De Beers thought it was now time to secure as many

A miner cleans the cracks in the rocks, looking for diamonds.

diamonds as it could as quickly as possible, in case the ANC imposed tough new conditions. From all the evidence, it seems that De Beers then decided to overmine Kleinzee, and perhaps its other South African land-based mines. Perhaps it thought that once these mines were exhausted, it would be able to shift its production to the overshore. It would have noticed that the black-controlled and ANC-allied mining unions had little influence on the diamond boats. These relatively lightly staffed, unpoliced, and non-union vessels were far more flexible and secure – and thus the seabed looked likely to supply most of De Beers' future requirements in Namibia and South Africa.

This may have been why, in September 1994, just after the ANC victory, the De Beers *Namaqualand Mines Chronicle* told the workers at the Kleinzee-Koingass mine: "It has always been De Beers practice to look no more than ten years ahead in 'life of mine planning', for this reason many people have expressed their disbelief when we now tell them this mine is coming to an end. However the reality is that we have only 10 to 12 years to go before Namaqualand Mines ceases operations... Kleinzee is planned to cease production in 2004 and Koingnaas in 2005. This is based on current carat production throughout this period... The geology department does not expect to find any major new reserves that would significantly extend the life of mine... if we want to mine low grade ore, it is essential for us to contain our costs."

Vacuuming up diamonds at Kleinzee.

This was disastrous news for the Kleinzee community. It lived in a remote location and had no other resources to build on. It was also most surprising. This mine was legendary for the quality of its diamonds. A fortune had been produced here – and was still being produced every year. The mine was comfortably supporting two towns and other settlements – all within the De Beers coastal security zone.

The mineworkers had every reason to be perplexed. Diamond production had not dropped – as might have been expected if the mine was coming to a natural end. Nor was the management planning to run the mine down slowly over as long a period as possible to give the residents time to adjust. Rather it announced it was going to increase production dramatically from 600,000 to one million carats a year. This De Beers intended to keep up for the next twelve years so it was clear that it intended to get out as many diamonds as possible as quickly as possible. This was going to be a powerdive into oblivion – much as had once been planned for CDM.

Presumably this major increase in production would give the mine a good income, and allow De Beers to increase the very low pay given to its black miners? Perhaps it would increase the quality of the housing provided, so that the black workers would be allowed to have their wives with them, as was permitted for the colored and white workers? But De Beers' statement went on to say: "The increase in production at Tweepad (one of the local plants) is a major opportunity. We can use this to get leaner/meaner..."

This frightened the community. How could De Beers get "leaner/meaner"? De Beers explained this as if it were a government rather than a private company. It said it was about to "privatize" all town and mine services by setting up a system of sub-contractors, to cut costs. It explained: "Privatization – our first goal is for employees... to tender to take on these sections privately, as sub-contractors to the mine... Company equipment can be bought or leased... [We are also] bringing in outside contractors."

The workers had every reason to fear this. De Beers had introduced this same system earlier into other South African mines, where it sub-contracted out even the mineworkers. These sub-contracted miners were now on a third of the union-negotiated minimum pay, could not join the union, and had much less healthcare or other protection.

Yet Kleinzee was then producing diamonds conservatively valued by De Beers at an average of over R850 ($270) a carat. The mine report of January 18th, 1994 congratulated the workers for achieving a cost of production per carat of R201 ($50). This indicated a profit of $220 per carat, or of 440 percent. The 12 million carats they planned to mine over the next 12 years would be worth 12 billion Rand (over $3 billion), of which its profits would be, prior to paying the CSO fees to itself, about nine billion Rand.

It is no wonder that an armored car was provided by De Beers to move diamonds from this mine to the airport. Yet this mine was supposed to be at the tail end of its production, and very poor.

As at other De Beers mines, whenever the issue of increased pay came up, the workers were told that the mine was in its last days so that every economy was needed to extend its life. But, on the above figures, a production of one million carats a year would yield revenue for each one of the 3,000 miners employed of over $80,000 a year, many, many times more than it was paying the workers ... De Beers paid its diamond miners lower wages than did any other miner in Namaqualand. Many miners got just over R1,000 a month gross, and, after deductions, the average

Miners brushing beach rocks for diamonds.

take home pay was around R700 or $195 a month – less than 1/30th of what each one of them had earned the company. In 2002 De Beers agreed a new national minimum pay for its mineworkers. It was just $57 a week. This was for the unionized miners, the subcontracted ones might get perhaps half this.

Having seen the desperate poverty of the local Africans, I thought it an enormous shame that these diamonds were not being used to kick-start the economy. They were found in a region with one of the lowest average incomes in South Africa. It was not just that De Beers was escaping with most of the wealth. If these high-class diamonds had been cut locally, instead of being exported unprocessed, then South Africa would have more than tripled its revenue from these diamonds. If Kleinzee were to integrate mining and cutting, the township would be guaranteed a long profitable life. But I learned that when the ANC Chairman of the Parliamentary Standing Committee on Minerals and Energy, Marcel Golding, visited Kleinzee he was told by De Beers that the mine could not even contribute to the government's National Reconstruction and Development Program as it was too poor and was facing an immanent closure.

Does De Beers hide diamond deposits?
In a world where De Beers has more diamonds than it can sell, I thought it sensible to inquire if the Kleinzee mine might have diamond reserves that De Beers was concealing to make it appear less viable than it really was.

I was talking over tea to the mineworkers when I happened to mention that I had learned that De Beers had hidden diamond deposits elsewhere by turning their sites into nature preserves, where mining would be forbidden for reasons of "conservation." (This is what happened to Diamond Area 2 in Namibia, a vast area north of Luderitz.)

The miners laughed when they heard this and one told me, "We have a game park here too! De Beers has made it out of part of the mining lease. It didn't have much wildlife but De Beers trucked in some bucks [deer]! It is a prohibited area. You cannot go in there unless you are management." I decided to visit it. I drove down the De Beers private road that stretches straight from horizon to horizon along this coast. Eventually I came across a sign on a gate that read: "De Beers Cons. Mines Ltd. Private Nature Reserve. Restricted Area."

By the gate was a vacuum trailer used for sucking up diamonds. Just inside the gate I found a truck unloading a large core drill of the type used to establish diamond reserves. Several unloaded large-bore drilling pipes were lying near the vacuum trailer. The drilling gear would force these down through the sand to the underlying rocks of a former coastline. The pipes were wide enough to send down a mineworker after the

core was extracted to check on the diamond content in cavities in the rock below. I could also see the top of a drilling crane concealed behind low trees. De Beers geologists at Kleinzee later told me that an ancient buried riverbed underlay this game reserve, and that it had diamond reserves that could well "double" the life of the mine – if ever exploited. This made the planned closure of this mine even more outrageous. Presumably De Beers was "stockpiling" this diamond deposit for a possible rainy day.

Diamond exploration equipment in private De Beers game park near Kleinzee.

I learned later that this diamond reserve was but the tip of a diamond iceberg. The seas immediately adjacent to the Kleinzee and Koingnaas mines held still greater treasures. One of the marine diamond mining companies operating here, Ocean Diamond Mining, estimated it had on its lease a diamond reserve of 51 million carats of gem quality stones. This it valued at a minimum of $10.2 billion. (It calculated this using conservatively a value of $200 a carat – using De Beers' figures; they were more likely to be worth over $300 a carat, $15 billion.) Their lease only covered a small part of the offshore reserves. The total reserves must be vastly more.

De Beers had to share the waters closest to the shore with other companies, since it was slow off the mark in realizing their potential. Its way of obtaining leases was unusual, to say the least. Ogilvie Thompson, the chairman of De Beers, said he was tipped off by Air Force Brigadier Johann Blaauw about a chance to obtain marine concessions off Namaqualand. Thompson then passed relevant documents to Blaauw at a pre-arranged spot on the N1 highway. Why Blaauw played so important a role was not revealed by Thompson – nor why Thompson acted in such a furtive way. Blaauw had an interesting explanation for his own role. He said the Government gave him rights to offshore diamond concessions as a reward for obtaining Israeli radioactive tritium wanted for hydrogen bombs in a swap for South African uranium concentrate.[17]

UNDERSEA OPERATIONS AT ALEXKOR
Alexkor lay to the north of Kleinzee. It now had its own fleet of diamond pumping boats. The marine lease next to theirs was held by Benguella Concessions, in which

Australian BHP has a share. Benguella was sampling some 7,000 square kilometers of seabed with two vessels testing to six meters below the seabed.

At Alexkor, on Alexander Bay north of Kleinzee, the colored workers told me how they took delight in telling the managers, contracted by an Afrikaans company, that the ANC controlled their mine. Ironically De Beers was originally prevented from securing this mine by the apartheid regime, as it was wanted for small-time white miners. But in 2003 De Beers was trying to secure control and might well succeed.

If they do succeed, they will have complete control over diamonds along more than 700 km of coastline. Alexkor's lease is nearly 200 km long and some seven to 12 km wide. To the south it is bordered by the vast Kleinzee De Beers lease and to the north by the even larger CDM De Beers lease.

The Alexkor mine management had replaced nearly all its black labor force with colored workers before the 1994 elections, allegedly because the Afrikaans management expected coloreds to vote for the National Party. The National Party had expected to win the diamond province of Northern Cape with its capital of Kimberley. There was talk of making part of it into a homeland for whites. The hostels at the nearby Transhex mine also now housed only colored miners. If this were the plan, they miscalculated. The ANC won Northern Cape by a slender margin. (Note that the term "coloreds" does not necessarily mean having some white blood and thus fairer skin. The local indigenous nation, the Khoi Khoi or Bushmen, are labeled as "colored.")

Alexkor did not have the same air of secrecy as pervaded the De Beers mines. Tourists were given an extensive tour, especially of the seal colony and of an oyster farm, where discarded plastic Coke bottles were used as floats for lucrative oyster beds. When asked, the guide denied emphatically that there had been any overmining and said the mine had a long future. She stated, "Only 4 percent of the area has so far been mined." But given the size of the mine's lease, their target for diamond production was surprisingly low. It was only 174,000 carats in 1994, just a sixth of CDM's. This low limit was not because they had few diamonds. De Beers had enforced it. Their marketing contract with De Beers amazingly limited their output to less than 200,000 carats a year, thus stopping the mine even attempting to reach its full potential. When in 2001 they ran into financial problems, I wondered if it was because of the De Beers imposed restriction.

All of its production was contracted to the CSO. In 1993 they received 900 Rand ($260) a carat for their high quality output. The 1994 delivery to De Beers gave Alexkor an annual income of R156.6 million or nearly R100,000 ($30,000) a worker.

I found it very difficult to get the above figures. The management told me they were prohibited from giving out the mine's Annual Report without ministerial approval. It was extraordinarily secretive for a state-owned operation. They told me they had at least two million carats not yet mined. I thought this a very conservative estimate. It was only including the reserves on a small part of the lease, which was only now being systematically explored for the first time – and a good new deposit had just been found. A manager told me that the cut-off grade below which deposits were not mined was far higher than at other mines.

This meant many diamonds that would have been mined elsewhere would extraordinarily be left in the ground at Alexander Bay.

I found the mine had recently built a dyke some meters out to sea, in the fashion of the De Beers CDM mine to the north, but far smaller. They then found, as at CDM, that the near-shore seabed was rich in diamonds. The dyked area gave them 17,000 carats in one day, their richest day's picking in recent years.

I was most perplexed when I discovered the mine management had not followed up this success. Perhaps so high a production was not needed to meet the modest production targets allowed by De Beers? (I found it hard to remember that De Beers did not own this mine.) The seabed further out had also proved rich in diamonds. I saw stacked by the diamond separation plant rows of white cloth bags containing diamond gravels sucked from the seabed by its fleet. In 1994 the mine management estimated the seabed deposits would last at least 20 years, perhaps indefinitely. They were not subcontracting near-shore and offshore mining but were, unlike De Beers, paying full pay rates and a generous bonus to their divers. They had a decompression chamber, unlike Luderitz, where there were no such safety measures. It is likely these ocean diamonds are by far the greatest treasure at Alexander Bay. As the mine was by the mouth of the Orange River, next to De Beers' lucrative marine leases and to CDM, they could well contain over 100 million carats, worth in excess of $350 a carat or $35 billion in total. De Beers had hopes that the South African government would sell it this mine. If they did, then one could be sure that De Beers would remove its production restrictions as soon as it suited it.

BURYING DIAMONDS AT THE TRANSHEX MINE

The union people at Alexkor also took me to inspect Transhex's Baken Mine near lower Orange River. We drove out along a dirt road that still had on it the abandoned gates of the pass system set up to control the movements of nonwhites.

A Khoi Khoi union official told me this land had belonged to his people for more than 1,000 years, as did much of Namaqualand. Like Australia's Aborigines, they are now demanding the restitution of their land rights.

Transhex is South Africa's largest diamond producer after De Beers. It is ultimately controlled by the Ruperts, the second richest family in South Africa after the Oppenheimers. They own such international brands as Cartier and through their Rembrandt Group own 51% of Transhex. At Baken the miners were paid approximately R1,300 a month,

Road to Baken mine.

around $130. The single sex accommodation was of a better standard, but still had two to four to a room. Only a few had married quarters.

I had secured permission to visit in advance, but it was not expected that union officials would drive me to the mine. The local manager was taken back, but nevertheless drove us around the mine while anxiously telling us the excavations were safe with walls at 65 degree angles and sound; apart from that small area of high

Inside the Baken mine.

break-away that we could not help noticing. I think he thought our visit might be related to safety matters. The union had complained about dangerous cliffs.

The mine turned out to be large and very mechanized, with four separation plants and 65 earthmoving machines operated by 300 employees. They were mining gravel buried up to 65 meters deep in a 15 million year-old disused channel of the Orange River. Transhex's 1994 report cautiously said these gravels, and those on nearby river terraces, "generally yield diamonds of good quality and size." Nearby CDM deposits on the Namibian side of the Orange River contained large diamonds with an average size of from 0.85 to 1.3 carats, 85 percent of them in top categories of value – unbroken crystals of Top Silver to Cape colors, K to O on the official GIA scale – very fine diamonds.

But the local miners told me that they were amazed that Transhex seemed totally uninterested in the river bed crevices and pot holes that everywhere else had been found to trap the best diamonds. I asked the manager about this. He answered by jokingly pointing at a backhoe. "There is our bedrock cleaner." Bedrock cleaners are an essential part of diamond extraction in De Beers' mines, and at Alexkor. These men are equipped with small picks and brushes. Their job is to ensure that no diamonds are missed at the bottom of crevices and potholes. Sometimes they were also armed with powerful vacuum cleaners. The mechanical backhoe the manager pointed out was clearly incapable of reaching the diamonds in crevices. His flippant answer seemed incredible. He admitted to finding diamonds in the loose sand over the rockbeds, so geologically speaking, diamonds simply had to be present in the crevices and potholes below the sand.

The mineworkers explained to me that there was no one employed as a bedrock cleaner at Transhex's mine, because the company was deliberately keeping its workers inside machines such as excavators and backhoes, so as to minimize diamond theft. This seemed far-fetched, but what other explanation was there? I was surprised to find that the Alexkor 1993 Annual Report seemed to confirm what they had told me. It said that, if diamond theft did not subside, "Alexkor will, like other neighboring mines, be forced to resort to mechanical means."

It seemed to me that Transhex was simply working at speed, bulldozing up the diamonds found in loose gravels and leaving all others. I wondered if, like Alexkor, it was working to a De Beers-imposed production control regime.

The internal De Beers prospecting handbook instructs its staff, when exploring similar deposits, to first use a large core auger drill, up to 1.6 meters in diameter, to penetrate the overburden of sand or gravel. When it reaches the rocks below the sand, a man is to be lowered down the shaft created by the drill "to carry out the final excavations using jackhammers, spades and brushes." He may even blast aside boulders. The handbook stressed, "It is essential that the bedrock is effectively cleaned" at the bottom of the drill shaft, otherwise diamond content could not be accurately assessed. De Beers thus held that diamonds were likely to be found on the bedrock. This made sense. The diamonds were alluvial, washed here by river waters or seas many

Digging down to the buried river bed.

thousands of years ago. They were also heavy. They would sit on the rocks or get trapped in crevices (as they had done at Kleinzee, CDM and Alexkor). Transhex must have known this.

The other Transhex mining practice that perplexed its workers was its failure to search "conglomerates," river gravels concreted together by calcite and gypsum. They told me, "All conglomerates are dumped as waste as the mine has no crushing plants." I saw this for myself. Large boulders were falling uncrushed out of the separation plant.

In the nearby CDM mine, De Beers had discovered that crushing conglomerates made a great difference to their profits. It found that although only 9 percent of the ore reserves by tonnage were conglomerates, they contained 21 percent of the diamonds,[18] averaging 0.42 carats per cubic meter. In the northern part of the CDM lease, over 60 percent of the diamonds were in the conglomerates. But CDM discovered this in the 1970s.[19] Why then was Transhex not investing in a crushing plant?

I put this question to the mine manager. He answered, "We do not need a crusher. We rejected the conglomerate. We tested it and it is not economic." But the mineworkers told me quite a different story. "We tested the conglomerates for the management. We cleaned out a place and put a block of conglomerate, about 1.6 meters wide, on a grizzley (an iron table with metal bars). We broke it up with hammers. We found seven diamonds. The largest was 16 carats. The management told us we were not to talk about this."

I noted the mine was burying these untested conglomerates under waste rock dumped on the unswept riverbed – thus concealing diamond-rich crevices with diamond-rich rocks. The mineworkers said to me that, if the mine management did not want these diamonds, then they should let someone else mine them before they reburied them under 65 meters of waste rock.

I told earlier how De Beers had itself buried a beautiful area under heavy waste at Koffiefontein after an African child had found a diamond there, and how De Beers had refused permission for African workers to extract missed diamonds from the waste tips at Kimberley. The southern African rivers, coasts and seas might be rich in diamonds, but its people were poor with 60 percent of its black population having no electricity. It was sad that within the diamond empire the marketing needs of De Beers had seemingly so distorted the diamond industry's priorities that diamonds were sadly being buried rather than being used to enrich the people who mined them.

1   Thirion Commission. *Eighth Interim Report.* Annexure.
2   *South African Mining Engineering News* 1994.
3   Conglomerates are rocks naturally concreted together.
4   Thirion Commission, *Eighth Interim Report.* Annexure. Commission of Inquiry into alleged irregularities and misapplication of property in representative authorities and the central authority of South West Africa: Control by the state over the prospecting and mining for and disposing of minerals in South West Africa.

5   *Diamond Intelligence Briefs*, May 16th, 1988. "Diamond stocks are valued at the average cost of production in the case of mining companies."
6   Thirion Commission.
7   Annexure Elizabeth Bay. Estimated revenue from Elizabeth Bay was 162,000,000 Rand, over $40 million.
8   Confidential Report by Melvin Foster, CDM Mining Manager. "The prospecting and development of deposits occurring outside the current security area at CDM: a mining strategy." April 2nd, 1981.
9   Flynn p. 52.
10 Thirion Commission. *Eighth Interim Report.* – Appended documents, p. 134.
11 NBC interviews by Christa Oaes in early 1995.
12 Mineworkers' Union of Namibia regional conference, March 1995.
13 NBC interview by Christa Oaes in early 1995.
14 NBC Interview with Walden in early 1995.
15 Auditor General's 1991 Report on the Diamond Board and CDM.
16 Auditor General's 1991 Report on the Diamond Board Accounts.
17 *African Confidential*, February 4th, 1994.
18 Thirion Commission. p. 13. Annexures. Report by T. L. Pretorius. CDM Assistant General Manager.
19 Thirion Commission, p. 13.

Chapter 17 – Defending the Crown

There was no doubt about the threat to De Beers embodied in the ascension to power of the black majority in South Africa. The African National Congress (ANC) had promised to nationalize the diamond mines when it took over. The Oppenheimers and their companies prior to these elections thus did all they could to influence the ANC to try to avert total disaster for them.

The ANC knew they were taking over in a country with laws uniquely shaped by corporate mining giants. In South Africa, unlike most other countries, mineral rights were privately purchased, and could be hoarded without being used. Thus large areas were "locked up." It was a cheap and unaccountable way of stockpiling a supply that was surplus to corporate requirements. It was also a country in which the diamond mining industry paid remarkably low taxes. According to the government's Department of Finance, in 1993-4, the year before the election, the taxes it paid totaled just 1.2 percent of the value of the diamonds it sold.

It was also a country where there was a unique crime, Illicit Diamond Buying (IDB) that South Africa had also exported to her economic colonies of Botswana and Namibia. Nowhere else in the world could a person be locked up simply for trying to sell an uncut diamond. The police in South Africa used informers, rewards, and entrapment to enforce this, putting in jeopardy innocent foreigners and South Africans. Diamonds were instead exported in bulk by De Beers to be traded overseas. This was a major reason why South Africa had not developed into a major diamond-trading center like London or Antwerp. The mining companies, including De Beers and Transhex, advocated that this practice should continue, saying, if mineworkers could sell diamonds to local cutters, then they would not be able to stop diamond theft. Diamond mining and cutting simply should not be allowed to happen in the same country, or so De Beers publicly said when the ANC organized an inquiry into the local diamond trade.

South Africa was the fortress from which De Beers had ruled the diamond world for a century, and it would be appropriately defended. The ANC knew to step carefully. Careful negotiations started prior to the elections. The ANC met with Gavin O'Reilly, Chairman of Anglo American, in Lusaka back in 1985, at a time when the ANC was still outlawed in South Africa. In 1994, after winning the election, Mandela visited the Premier diamond mine, lunched with De Beers' Deputy Chairman Nicky F. Oppenheimer and talked about worldwide diamond industry.

The talk of nationalization faded. The Mandela strategy of national reconciliation focused instead on what the industry would do voluntarily – and on averting the chaos that would ensue if the barons of industry decided to quit black South Africa. It was thus agreed that the election winning ANC and the election losing National party would form a government of National Unity to rule for the first five years of democracy. Pik Botha, the former Minister of Foreign Affairs, became the Minister of Mining and Energy. This closed off the immediate path to nationalization, but the diamond industry remained wary. They knew the ANC contained many people who were still angry about the years of exploitation.

When an ANC research paper suggested mineral resources should ultimately belong to the state, the corporate fingers twitched as they hovered over panic buttons. In a few hours over a billion dollars left South Africa, sparked by a single sentence in the 80-page document. The sentence in question read: "The minerals in the ground belong to all South Africans, including future generations." Such a policy would, of course, merely put South Africa on the same footing as other major mineral producers such as Canada and Australia.

But then Mandela went on to say:

We wish to open up our minerals industry to greater participation and competition. It is not in the best interests of any economy that large corporations should exercise virtual monopoly rights over the mineral resources.

Before the advent of colonialism, there were thousands of small mining operations throughout the Southern African region. Today however mining is the preserve of the white minority with a highly concentrated ownership. We feel that small and medium scale ventures present valuable prospects for the re-entry of our people into this industry which, by becoming more competitive and efficient would benefit the community at large.

He directly mentioned Oppenheimer's Anglo American when the controversy erupted, "Obviously there are powerful vested interests. Most of our newspapers … are controlled either by companies close to the ruling National Party or by Anglo American, our biggest mining house, which feel threatened by attempts to open up the economy."

Mandela suggested ways forward that could benefit the Oppenheimers: "Measures which may be employed include reducing our substantial public sector in areas where this will enhance efficiency" – in other words, he might privatize. But he might also do what the Oppenheimers feared and increase "the public sector in strategic areas through share purchases, joint ventures, the establishment of public corporations or through nationalization. We do not preclude any economy strategy.… Our racially distorted income distribution remains one of the most unequal in the world."[1] Mandela thus still had not dropped the option of nationalization. It was there if needed.

REMOVING RESOURCES FROM BLACK SOUTH AFRICA

But the Oppenheimers had not waited until after the election to insulate their wealth from a black South Africa. They had already acted. De Beers had previously

The diamond-rich desert of Namibia.

earned 80 percent of its income from outside South Africa but, only one month after Mandela left prison, it announced that in future these vast revenues would not come to South Africa but go to a Swiss entity called "De Beers Centenary." This did not affect its shareholders. All of them automatically became shareholders of De Beers Centenary. But the move put several billion dollars out of the tax reach of Mandela's government.

These changes also meant that CDM, the prize Namibian mine whose diamonds were once controlled by the South African government, was no longer owned by a South African company. Its title deeds moved to an Oppenheimer-owned company in Switzerland. The Oppenheimers also provided still greater protection, obscurity, and secrecy through their key private family company, E. Oppenheimer and Sons, though which they controlled both De Beers and Anglo American. It was registered in the secretive African state of Liberia – where to evade regulation and inspection, many old merchant ships are also registered.

The Oppenheimers also arranged for the transfer overseas of a vast sum in untaxed funds every year from their South African diamond mines to a Swiss bank account. They organized this by having their mines pay fees for services rendered to their newly registered, and nominal, Swiss companies – as if these Swiss brass plates had sorted, advertised or sold their diamonds for them. In reality these jobs were still being done by De Beers in South Africa and London.

This removed over $1 billion annually from the taxable income of southern Africa. The De Beers-controlled Venetia mine reported it would be paying the Swiss shadow CSO fees of between $227 and $350 million a year, about twice the mine's estimated operating cost of $167 million a year.[2] This tactic dramatically lowered the profits De Beers declared in South Africa and thus also dramatically cut the revenues of the Mandela government. It is this type of legal and financial engineering and tax avoidance that has attracted so much attention of late in the United States, where companies such as scandal-ridden Tyco International have avoided domestic taxes by incorporating in Bermuda and other tax havens, while still operating principally out of the US. Shareholder and media pressure, if not proposed legislation, may soon severely curtail these practices in the US, but non-US companies such as De Beers remain free to lower the tax base of their true home countries.

The South African government's Department of Finance reported that the contribution of the diamond trade to the total tax revenue of South Africa had fallen from an already very low 0.69 percent in 1980-81 to just 0.07 percent in 1995-96.

When I learned of these tactics, I wondered if De Beers was also removing from the country the best diamonds from its stockpiles and diamond mines. I knew Judge Thirion had accused De Beers of doing just this in Namibia before it got its independence.

Miner with ANC poster.

On inquiry in Kimberley and Johannesburg, I found this was exactly what it had done. It had shipped out South Africa's fabulous stockpile of the finest gems, retained by law for cutting by whites prior to the 1994 elections. In 2002 South Africa was still trying to get these returned from London. I also discovered, as I have mentioned, that De Beers put the mines producing the best gems into overdrive before the election.

Cyril Ramaphosa, the Secretary-General of the ANC, had stated in September 1994, at the opening of the ANC's Mineral and Energy Policy Center, that the mining industry could not remain concentrated "in a few white hands" and that its structure was out of touch with the needs of the country. He hoped that blacks would soon own mines, large, medium and small.[3] But by 1999, after five years of the Government of National Unity, little had changed in the mining industry.

HIDING DEPOSITS OF SOUTHERN AFRICAN DIAMONDS

Since De Beers had controlled most of the South African diamond mines for a century, it knew much more than the government about where unmined diamonds could be found. It was quite legal in South Africa, unlike in most other countries, to warehouse mineral leases without ever mining them, while retaining as confidential all the results gained from prospecting on them.

Some of its discoveries it had deliberately hidden in newly-created game parks as earlier mentioned. Apart from the private De Beers game park on a diamond-rich part of the Kleinzee diamond lease mentioned above, allegedly rich diamond deposits were locked up in the Richtersveld Nature Reserve on the Orange River. This park has "all the top mining houses involved in its management structure," according to a union official at the nearby Alexkor mine.

The mine manager at Roxton Mine, west of Kimberley, told me eagerly how he would love to get his hands on some unused De Beers hectares nearby, which De Beers had also destined to be a game park. He thought these contained the diamond pipe from which his diamond-rich fissure originated. When his company first found its diamonds, De Beers had quickly purchased land each side of his, to stop him expanding out. It had

Roads were blocked to stop access to Diamond Area One.

then just sat on this land, making no move to mine it. De Beers also had not bothered to mine other fissure deposits found near its pipe mines.

In Namibia, De Beers had a problem with the over-abundance of diamonds in the vast region it leased extremely cheaply, previously named by the Germans as the "Forbidden Zone." This was divided into two regions, "Diamond Area One" south of Luderitz, and "Diamond Area Two," north of Luderitz. The former was the richer, so that is where the mining was concentrated. But its geologists had also had a good look at Diamond Area Two, and reported it had pockets of profitable diamonds that could be easily extracted without even having to remove sand hills.

The problem was, these diamonds were surplus to De Beers' requirements.

CDM simply sat on this approximately 9,000 square kilometer coastal lease for many years, paying just R400 ($165) rent annually. This eventually started to worry De Beers' local management. They wondered if the local authorities would complain about this lack of activity. On February 12th, 1978, CDM wrote to the Chairman of De Beers, "There are a number of questions; [one of these is] the political aspect of De Beers sitting on a large tract of territory ostensibly to no purpose."

But an elegant solution was found. Diamond Area Two was turned into a national park in 1987. Its diamonds were thus made unmineable, as mining is not allowed in national parks. In the future environmentalists would do De Beers' work for them by helping to protect this land. It is a beautiful region, and perhaps this is the best thing to happen to it. But, it is interesting to understand just how a diamond lease could become a park.

The mineworkers at Finsch told me of an unmined diamond pipe located nearby that was owned by De Beers and rumored to be rich. Other mineworkers and geologists told me of other unmined deposits held by De Beers. One was near Koffiefontein, another north of Pretoria, and another near to the Venetia mine. De Beers created next to this the Venetia Limpopo Nature Reserve. In August 2002 it announced it would provide some 89,000 acres of this to the Vhembe-Dongila National Park on South Africa's northern border, South African National Parks would administer it but De Beers would retain title.[4] Bindeman, of the South African Diamond Board, told me, "We do not say it from the rooftops, but diamonds are not rare except, maybe, for some qualities."

De Beers uniquely knows how many diamonds remain in South Africa. Unlocking this information became a key task for the ANC government.

Anglo American and De Beers meanwhile took full advantage of South Africa losing its pariah status with the end of apartheid. As soon as they thought they could expand into black Africa in their own name, they "repurchased" African investments previously moved to European companies to escape the apartheid tag. Before the conflict diamond controversy arose in 1999, they had announced new diamond ventures in Sierra Leone, Ghana and Tanzania. The last was particularly interesting. It was to reopen the famous Williamson mine closed by De Beers supposedly because it had run out of economically mineable diamonds.

But in moving into black Africa they partly misjudged. Many remained suspicious of them. Kabila in the Congo would refuse to recontract with De Beers since it had supported Mobutu's corrupt regime.

De Beers apparently encountered a different problem in Angola. Reportedly De Santos, the President of Angola, saw *The Diamond Empire*, our film on De Beers, and ordered the Director General of the Department of Mines to halt all further negotiations with De Beers. Nicky Oppenheimer was there at the time seeking marine concessions and had to leave empty handed. I have not yet verified this story.

DID DE BEERS DECLARE ITS MINES TO BE POORER THAN THEY ARE?

At the start of my investigation over 20 years ago in 1979, I believed finding a diamond in a South African diamond mine was like finding a needle in a haystack –

for this was what De Beers had told me. I was informed that the mines in Kimberley had only 0.2 of a carat, a twentieth of a gram, in a tonne of ore.

Such a figure made me believe that the content of the Argyle mine at six to 26 carats a tonne was sensational. When I wrote up the Argyle figures for the newspapers, I was published prominently and worldwide. But, years later, when I learned that Canada had four carats a tonne and Russia had over seven carats a tonne – 35 times more than the South African mines, these figures made me look more skeptically at the figures that De Beers had published for its similar South African mines. Could these really be so much poorer than similar pipes elsewhere, or had De Beers lied in order to make diamonds seem extremely rare, or perhaps to hide its mines' real wealth?

When I investigated the Argyle mine in Australia, I met a man called Graham Brier who had worked as an overseer in De Beers' mines in South Africa. He told me they occasionally found fissures containing so many diamonds that the white overseers closed down that part of the mine and, in great secrecy, literally shoveled up the diamonds that came tumbling out. He also told me of rich dykes radiating out from diamond mines. At that time I did not know what to make of this, although Brier evidently had firsthand knowledge of diamond mining and prospecting.

But in Kimberley I found De Beers employees who confirmed this story, telling me to my amazement that sometimes 4,000 carats were found in a single tonne of ore. My informants were highly experienced De Beers workers. They seemed to be speaking with authority.

Black-controlled small mining companies would soon find diamond deposits in South Africa richer than any De Beers had declared, including a smaller one with 4.5 carats a tonne, as rich as the Canadian discoveries. De Beers had previously held every one of these, and left every one unmined.

De Beers, Africans, and diamond cutting

Southern Africa has all that is needed to establish substantial diamond cutting and diamond jewelry industries. It has rich gold, platinum, and diamond mines. Why has this never happened?

I found the principal reason was that De Beers has put obstacles in the way. For decades it had given southern Africa's best production to well-paid, white cutters in America, Europe and Israel. It still rewarded its well-behaved merchants with "sweeteners," high-class uncut Namibian, Alexkor and Kleinzee diamonds, even after the rise of the Indian diamond merchants who mostly traded in poorer stones.

In recent years De Beers has argued strongly against setting up a major cutting industry in southern Africa, saying that it was best for South Africa to concentrate on mining; insisting that cutting in South Africa could never be more than a marginal industry.

But the De Beers spin-doctors had missed out a key bit of history. South Africa did once have a prosperous diamond cutting industry, but it was for whites only. The former apartheid regime had retained for local white cutters a significant number of the finest diamonds mined by De Beers.

G. Bindeman, the executive director of the South African Diamond Board told me, "We would check the layout [tables with all recently produced diamonds sorted into heaps by size and type] and tell De Beers what they could not export; these became 'South African goods.'" Abe Sher, a Johannesburg diamond authority, explained, "Diamonds of 10.8 carats upwards were not allowed to leave the country."

Roger Lappeman, a former Sightholder, confirmed this: "We had to cut big stones in South Africa because there were only white cutters and they had high salaries." The average labor cost for diamond cutters in Antwerp in 1981 was $25,000 a year, and in New York, $30,000 a year. Under apartheid, diamond cutting in South Africa was originally by law reserved for whites. As De Beers could not impose its usual marketing fees on these diamonds, the prices charged to the locals were 10 percent less than in London. The stockpile retained to support these cutters grew, according to Johannesburg diamond merchants, to over three million carats of the best stones – worth billions of US dollars.

In the late 1980s, when apartheid restrictions on diamond cutting relaxed: "The government allowed coloreds to cut [poor quality] diamonds after some pressure," according to Lappeman, a South African diamond merchant and former De Beers Sightholder. "This made it possible to cut smaller diamonds. I set up a pilot plant to train black women and soon had a factory. By 1989 I had trained thousands. By 1990 there were about 4,500 blacks employed in several factories. De Beers did not then oppose this.

"So then Botswana asked, 'If Lappeman can do it, why can't we?' They pressed for their own cutting industry. So they got a factory there too. Maurice Tempelsman also came in there [starting his own cutting factory]. Then the Namibians asked me, and then the Angolans approached me. [By now] I was employing more black diamond cutters than any other South African."

But what he did not mention was that the black cutters could be paid extremely low wages, a tiny fraction of that paid to white diamond cutters. Mrs. M. Steenkamp told me, "The wages at the cutting factory in Kimberley were 40 Rand [then about $13] a fortnight. The fares for daily travel to and from the townships were R2.60." After traveling expenses they thus made 14 Rand [$4.60] a fortnight. I also learnt that some owners kept wages still lower by employing only "apprentices."

De Beers knew how little these workers were being paid, for it kept a close watch on all Sightholders, frequently inspecting their cutting works. A confidential CSO inspection report dated September 13th, 1990 stated:

> The Pietersburg factory [of Lappeman] has been closed because of industrial action. On Monday 10th Sept., the workforce, encouraged by militant members of SACAWU who promised to obtain a minimum wage of R650 a month, staged a 'sit-in' and presented the management with a long list of grievances. Gavin Liggett, the factory manager, rejected these out of hand and, over the course of the day issued the entire workforce with 1st, 2nd and 3rd warnings, finally dismissing all the employees…
> Lappeman sees this situation as a temporary respite from his cash flow problems and an opportunity to start afresh with just the most productive of the workers.

In conclusion, R. More O'Ferrall of the CSO ruled that they would "maintain support" for Lappeman.

Another CSO note about Lappeman read: "Some workers [are] taking home R57 or $11 a month. Despite this there has been no repeat of the union disruption of 1990. Recommendation for 1993. Maintain Support. Signed N. C. R. Pleasance." The standard form that Sightholders had to complete for the CSO included data on wages and mortgages. The data he entered included: "Polisher. European 3,000 [Rand], Polisher colored 800. No apprentices." The CSO seemingly took the very low pay rates for granted. But it did take particular note of the fact that he had an "80 percent mortgage on home" and that he blamed the CSO for creating problems by overcharging for rough diamonds. Lappeman alleged that as a result, De Beers gave its confidential file on his business to his insurers, and doctored it to portray his business badly. He was particularly sad that the CSO failed to record in its notes on his business that his factory had provided cheap diamonds for De Beers to give employees for its centenary celebrations.

But De Beers moved to close down this black-staffed diamond cutting industry as the ANC moved towards power by slashing the supplies of suitable stones. Bindeman told me, "In 1989 there was an output of 1.5 million carats of polished South African goods but by 1993 it had fallen to 608,000 carats… South African production fell off because we could not get the right goods [from De Beers]." Why a black-staffed South African diamond cutting industry was seen as a threat by De Beers is a mystery.

De Beers now also ended the 10 percent "discount" it had previously given to South African cutters. Surprisingly, Bindeman approved of this, since it ended "unfair privileges for South Africans." Yet the reason for this "discount" was simply that De Beers could not charge its regular 10 percent marketing fee on stones it had not marketed. From now on, De Beers insisted, local cutters had to buy their supplies from it in London at international prices, even if the stones they wanted had been mined in South Africa.

But, when the Johannesburg cutting firms reluctantly went to London, they were shocked to find De Beers charging them so much more that it was cheaper for them to import rough diamonds from Russia. Robin Corbit of Jewel City, the principal diamond-cutting center in Johannesburg, told me, "De Beers is trying to keep producing and manufacturing countries separate. It is controlling supplies to South Africa. The Sightholders are crying. They have doubled the price. There is only 1 percent to 2 percent profit on De Beers stones – but 20 percent profit on Russian rough."

The surviving, mostly white, South African diamond cutting firms deeply resented having to get their diamonds from London. They were desperate to regain direct access to South African diamonds. Bindeman told me: "South Africa is uniquely covered by diamond mines. No one can explain why we are different! We have all aspects of the industry… Diamond equipment is manufactured here. We are bloody good all rounders." Abe Sher said: "The finish here is the best in the world. No one refuses our goods. The mineral wealth belongs to the people. Israel and Antwerp have grown out of cutting South African goods."

So in 1994, immediately after winning the election, the ANC Northern Cape provincial government in Kimberley decided to reopen a diamond cutting plant with facilities for 1,500 employees that had closed when De Beers restricted supplies to it. This initiative worried De Beers, so it invited government representatives around to Ernest Oppenheimer House, where its staff carefully explained why it was not a good idea to try to start up a diamond cutting industry. Blacks were unaccustomed to cutting diamonds. It was delicate work. It needed great skill. One slip could ruin a stone.

Oppenheimer House in Kimberley.

The richest diamond cliff in Alexcorp, now allegedly being mined out.

The Northern Cape government persisted. It tried to get the diamonds it needed from the state-owned Alexkor mine in their state, thus bypassing De Beers. This plan failed when they discovered that Alexkor was contracted to give all its diamonds to De Beers. I felt this could explain the reports that Alexkor had started over-mining. De Beers might want the best diamonds out while it still had exclusive rights to them.

Alexkor miners had shown me a low cliff within its mining lease with a thick gravel bed at its base. They told me: "This bed is so rich that the mine usually only touches it if they are running short of meeting the quota. Just three truckloads will meet the mine's [annual] production target. But it is being mined out now. We don't know why this is happening. We are very concerned." I knew this cliff was near to where Hans Merensky found 487 diamonds under a single flat rock.

But the plan to restart this cutting work was supported by the diamond merchants of Johannesburg. They wanted the ANC to adopt a national policy of encouraging diamond cutting and were confident it could be a success, if freed from De Beers-imposed restrictions.

But there was opposition to a local cutting industry within the national ANC office. An unsigned "Aide Memoire to the President of the ANC" was circulated to the ANC's senior circles. It argued against a South African diamond cutting industry with all the reasons put forward by De Beers, maintaining that South Africa could not become a diamond cutting nation because of "the high wages paid compared with other centers," and because India had "family diamond cutting and polishing traditions that date back centuries." while "South Africa does not have the advantage of a gem polishing culture." But, as I have reported, I had met the cutters of India – they were recruited from rural workers. Quality South African cut diamonds would not be competing against Indian cutters but against highly paid European, American, and Israeli cutters, as they had done successfully for decades, when cut by white South Africans.

I would hear these same arguments in Namibia. Their Deputy Minister for Mines and Energy in March 1995 told the Mineworkers conference that the low profits made by the small Botswana diamond-cutting industry revealed their inability to compete with India. He failed to consider that De Beers sold the fine Namibian diamonds to European and Israeli diamond cutters. African cutters would have to compete against them, not against low-paid Asians. But he agreed that the case for a local cutting industry should be considered, announcing that De Beers and the Namibian government were to conduct an immediate investigation into whether a diamond cutting industry could be set up in Namibia.

But a De Beers precondition for this study had effectively disemboweled it from the first. It was that any cutting industry in Namibia had to be supplied by the CSO in London, at the CSO's international prices, rather than directly from the local mines.

The Deputy Minister told how he had received a stack of applications from firms wanting to set up cutting works in Namibia, but added disdainfully, "They all said they would only come if they had direct access to Namibia's diamonds." He concluded this probably meant they only wanted to come if they could buy and cut "illegal diamonds."

His scorn seemed misplaced. In 1994 India had made $3.5 billion from cutting diamonds and Israel made $2.5 billion. Namibia, with the world's finest diamonds made practically nothing from cut diamonds.

In 1999, the South African government held a Commission of Inquiry into the diamond industry. At this De Beers added two arguments to its usual list. One was that a diamond mining country would run into trouble if it had a cutting industry, because this would lead to increased theft from the mines as these stones could be sold to local diamond cutters, and that South African mines simply were not producing enough of the right kinds of diamonds for a South African cutting industry.

A skilled cutter in New York.

The professional diamond cutters who came to this Inquiry vigorously argued against De Beers, saying they had no need to compete against India. They could compete against the countries with higher costs that cut the better diamonds. They pointed out that India, Israel, and Belgium were now making billions of dollars from cutting and polishing South African diamonds. Why did this have to be done overseas? Why were there not enough of the "right sorts" of diamonds for them to cut, when South Africa was exporting over ten million carats a year? But a powerful push to "educate" the ANC against diamond cutting then came from the other side of town, from Anglo American headquarters. It built and ran diamond mines for its sister company, De Beers, and had long experience in dealing with black governments all over Africa. They now naturally adopted the same methods to influence the new black government of South Africa. They preferred to deal discreetly with its leadership. They had friends that could help with this that they had used before, persuasive people such as Maurice Tempelsman, who could present themselves as independent advisors.

DE BEERS AND THE NEW BLACK GOVERNMENT OF SOUTH AFRICA
I had arranged to dine in Cape Town in 1994 with Marcel Golding, the Chairman of the Parliamentary Standing Committee on Minerals and Energy. I was astonished

when his first question was: "What can you tell me about Tempelsman?" Golding was curious to know why this diamond merchant would contact him to invite him to dine in New York. That same day, I visited a church group organized to "promote democracy." The priest in charge also told me he knew of Maurice Tempelsman; he played a key role in an American organization called SAFE (South African Free Elections) that had funded them before the 1994 elections.

He told me that Nelson Mandela had addressed a working lunch meeting of SAFE at the Metropolitan Club in New York on September 28th, 1993. Its lawyers were Tempelsman's lawyers. Theodore C. Sorensen, Tempelsman and Mobutu's former lawyer, was now the pro bono counsel to SAFE. Also involved with SAFE was Robert S. McNamara, who cooperated with Tempelsman when at the World Bank. The SAFE headquarters in Johannesburg was set up in October 1993 by an attorney, Loren M. Braithwaite, who was with the law firm of Paul, Weiss, Rifkind, Wharton & Garrison; again, Tempelsman's lawyers. The lobbying continued. In 1996 Tempelsman was photographed with Archbishop Tutu. I was somewhat disquieted by all this, given Tempelsman's long term links to former senior members of US Intelligence.

Perhaps De Beers needed an intermediary? As the ANC drew near to power, De Beers had freed itself of government ties. They no longer worked with the South African government to set production levels for foreign diamond mines. Bindeman explained, "About 1986, because of sanctions and because of the fears that the 'partnership' between the government and De Beers could draw fire, the Diamond Producers Association[5] was disbanded and replaced by the Producers' Committee. I am an Observer. I attend all its meetings. The Director General of Mineral and Energy Affairs attends all its meetings. It is very much a voluntary thing. It has on it representatives of De Beers and of Namibia. Ogilvie Thompson and the Oppenheimers are on the committee. It is a very high profile committee. But the decisions are taken by De Beers."

Bindeman told me a deeper partnership was on the cards, that the ANC government was considering buying shares in De Beers on the model of Botswana and Namibia. Paul Jourdan, the ANC's national mineral policy coordinator, informed me that the government "might consider" sharing in the running of the diamond cartel.

Julian Ogilvie Thompson of De Beers recommended the ANC to sell off national assets, rather than increase taxes, to fund its Reconstruction and Development Program (RDP). He suggested starting with selling forests, commercial buildings, telecommunications, oil pipelines and airports. The Oppenheimers could buy up some of these assets. Mr. Thabo Mbeki, the Deputy President, seemingly agreed.[6] There was a clear target. De Beers would later bid for Alexkor, to give itself near total control over the southern African Atlantic coastline.

As rumored, De Beers was also quietly discussing another deal with the government. It offered to sell it a share in the ownership of De Beers. In return, it wanted the Illicit Diamond Buying (IDB) law to remain, outlawing the public's possession of rough diamonds, and a guarantee that it would continue to have the sole right to market South African diamonds.

The debate raged on.

Nelson Mandela said it was unacceptable for four companies to control the Johannesburg stock exchange.[7] The Oppenheimers protested they only controlled 25 percent, not the higher figure rumored. Cyril Ramaphosa, the ANC General Secretary, had hoped change could come through cooperation; saying that legislation to force change would be a last-ditch resort. Anglo American offered for black ownership a company called Johannesburg Consolidated Investments, but said it would first strip from it the company's platinum mines and diamond interests. Ramaphosa was not impressed. He said the offer had its "crown jewels" removed.

Paul Jourdan continued to defend De Beers from within the ANC. He insisted the "Third World" needed cartels to protect themselves from the "First World." "We support the diamond cartel. The free market does not work. We just question whether or not a private company should run the cartel. We are looking at whether the government can run it jointly with private enterprise. More industries should have a cartel. We are looking at an increasing role for Anglo American throughout southern Africa, in Angola. We want jobs for our people."

When I asked what he would advise if the US sought South African support for an antitrust action against De Beers, he said he would support De Beers. *The Diamond World Review* reported Jourdan as saying, "We have no particular objection to the way in which the CSO operates and feel that it serves the interests of the diamond industry."[8]

On February 11th, 1994 the *Financial Times* quoted Paul Jourdan as saying the ANC has no intention of expropriating or nationalizing mineral rights or mining companies or of imposing mineral marketing boards. The newspaper commented, "He could have fooled those who read the original proposals."

A member of the ANC's Executive told me that Jourdan's statements did not necessarily represent ANC policy. He added, "Nelson Mandela had declined a seat on De Beers' board." The government would not go into partnership with De Beers. Instead an inquiry into the diamond industry was to be instigated in 1995.

De Beers might also be heading for trouble with the South African Competition Board for the Board backed the American anti-trust approach. In one of its decisions it cited a US Supreme Court judgment against price-fixing cartels: "Whatever economic justification particular price fixing agreements may be thought to have, the law does not permit an inquiry into their reasonableness. They are all banned because of their actual or potential threat to the nervous system of the economy."[9]

De Beers told the government that, although its Kimberley and Kleinzee mines would close in a few years time since they were mined out and uneconomic, unfortunately creating much unemployment, it would be pleased to serve by seeking out more diamonds that it could mine. It explained that no one else could do this so efficiently. It wanted the ANC to believe that it really needed De Beers, for it knew the critical time was coming.

It would start in 1999 – the year coalition government ended and the ANC began to govern on its own. That same year South Africa would freeze exports of De Beers' rough diamonds, saying that it suspected De Beers had declared too low a value for them; that De Beers should have declared the value its diamonds would have on the international market, not a lower value resembling their cost of production. It was trying to force De Beers to lift its veil of secrecy.

De Beers and Black Empowerment in southern Africa

The ANC policy of black empowerment was put into effect after 1999, as soon as it came to full power in South Africa.[10] The time for urging voluntary action had passed. It would now be legislating to force mining companies to "empower" black-run corporations, perhaps by giving them access to unmined deposits.

De Beers had anticipated it might be forced to do this and thought it best to start to do so voluntarily. It selected a few of its unmined resources and sold them to new black-run companies. These were all small leases, nothing that endangered De Beers' overall control, and, hidden in the small print of the confidential contracts underlying these De Beers "empowerments" were some strange conditions.

Woman returning to township.

One of the black-run companies it "empowered" was the New Diamond Company (NDC), which was soon expanding rapidly, taking over more and more diamond deposits, mostly ones that De Beers had not been using. It bought control from De Beers over unused mines and mining dumps in Kimberley and Jagersfontein. But, secretly, it was in thrall to De Beers. It had to agree in advance to sell all the diamonds it found to De Beers. A third clause stipulated: "NDC also agrees not to invest in any manner in any company, enterprise or partnership engaged in the mining or marketing of diamonds" without offering De Beers a partnership. Gary Ralfe enthused, "De Beers is proud of its association with NDC, a company we value as a partner in the South African diamond industry."

When South African authorities heard of these secret clauses, they were scathing, saying that this was no way to "empower" blacks. But these deals provided clear evidence for the first time that South Africa had diamond deposits with the same number of carats a tonne as found in Australia, Canada and Russia, and that De Beers had held such deposits for over 70 years without mining them.

De Beers sold to NDC a smallish diamond deposit at Kamfersdam that it had purchased in 1926 but never mined. NDC announced this had 28 carats a hundred tonnes, with diamonds valued by De Beers at $77 a carat. NDC also bought from De Beers a mine's tailings dump, and found this contained a good 12 carats a hundred tonnes. These were close to the diamond content found in De Beers' inland mines, with the average diamond content declared for them 28 carats a hundred tonnes.[11] But then NDC purchased the unmined small Marsfontein deposit from De Beers to find it contained good diamonds at 457.16 carats per hundred tonnes – far above the declared industry average in South Africa – but in line with discoveries elsewhere. De Beers explained to NDC that it had not mined this deposit itself, as it was too small!

De Beers also set up a strategic relationship with Tokyo Sexwale's Mvelaphanda (Mvela) group. It would work with Mvela, but only after it agreed in advance that De Beers would manage and control any large-scale deposits discovered. But, in general, the government's effort to use persuasion to get blacks into the world of business had failed. In 1998 there were 35 black controlled companies listed on the stock exchange. By 2003 the number had dropped to 23 companies with only 2 percent of the market. Then came a government statement that 51 percent of the mining industry should be in black hands by 2010. This caused an immediate panic in the boardrooms of De Beers and Anglo American, but it turned out to be a "negotiating statement." The final agreement was for a target of 26 percent to be in black hands by 2010, but this time the government would not rely just on persuasion.

The government pressed on with its radical Minerals Development Bill. This established that the mineral resources of South Africa belonged to the people of South Africa. In the future, mining companies would have to lease mineral rights from the government as they did in Australia and Canada. Large mining leases would be for 30 years and renewable. Prospecting leases would be limited to three years maximum, and, if the companies decided not to mine them, they had to make public the results of their prospecting. They would not be allowed to hang onto land they were not using and the government's permission had to be given to dispose of bulk samples. (De Beers had been suspected of moving diamonds as "bulk ore samples.")

De Beers argued hard against these terms, saying mining leases should remain private, and the information gathered through prospecting should also remain private, but without success.

De Beers also objected to the bill's provision that minerals be processed within South Africa if possible. It feared that this would lead to the establishment of a major South African diamond cutting industry. Clause 3/3 of the Bill stated, "any person who intends to beneficiate any mineral mined in the republic outside the republic must obtain the written permission of the minister." De Beers publicly wondered whether this was a violation of WTO rules.

De Beers had made good profits from exporting South African diamonds at near cost-of-production prices to itself in London, then selling back to the surviving South African diamond cutting businesses at international prices. In 2001 this brought it $430 million dollars.

A major change in De Beers' policies had just been brought about by its failure to contract the diamond supplies it needed from mines in Russia, Canada and Australia. It was being forced to depend more on southern Africa and to expand its own production. Thus it had announced expansion plans for Finsch and Premier.

But in June 2002 De Beers warned that the bill might force it to cancel its expansion program and close down mines, with the loss of 60,000 jobs. It had planned to invest $856 million dollars (7 billion Rand), 1.5 billion Rand at the Finsch mine and 5.5 billion at Premier. It warned: "The relevant mine will shortly be mined out and mine closure would be inevitable."

The Minerals and Energy Minister replied that the cabinet was "quite comfortable" with the bill. He explained the plan was to help pass into black hands good quality mineral reserves currently in the hands of the big mining houses.

The signs were also not good for De Beers when the government started to privatize Alexkor in 2003. The government awarded an initial management contract to the Nabera consortium, made up of several small black-controlled companies. It said it would announce in 2003 its decision on what company would be allowed to buy 51 percent, with the government retaining 49 percent.

But, a South African court then ruled that there is a valid indigenous land rights claim to all or most of the Alexkor lease. This was the first time indigenous rights had been recognized within South Africa. The Supreme Court of Appeal ruled in March 2003 that the Richtersveld community "is entitled to restitution and has a valid claim to the land" that Alexkor is mining. It was then announced that this meant a delay until June of a decision on who would be allowed to purchase control over the Alexkor mine. (The mine was still suffering from severe production limitation, and in 2002 was only extracting 10,000 to 12,000 carats a year from its very large and certainly rich mining lease, taking into account its seabed reserves.)

These indigenous claims might also affect the Transhex mine. In 1994 when I visited Alexkor and Transhex's Baken mine, I was told by a Khoi mineworker that this land once belonged to their people and was now wrecked. This hopefully meant that they would be able to negotiate compensation and regain the use of some land. They hoped it would also mean the restoration of some of the priceless natural features of their ancient land.

The Transhex mine had undergone great changes in recent years. The wealthy black South African, Sexwele, a former prisoner on Robben Island who had become the Premier of the Gauteng Province that contains Johannesburg, had since secured diamond leases over the middle reaches of the Orange River. He then traded these leases for a minority share in Transhex. This gave Transhex control over a large part of the Orange River. It has since announced that it would also study if it could extract diamonds from the cemented gravels at Baken, the same agglomerates that I had witnessed being buried untouched without any attempt to extract the diamonds from them.

TEMPELSMAN IN NAMIBIA

In 1995 Tempelsman was already entrenched in Namibia as the financial advisor of the President, Sam Nujomo, with Jerry Funk, formerly of the US National Security Council, staffing Tempelsman's Windhoek office – a strategic move as independent Namibia was attempting to renegotiate its De Beers contract. Tempelsman was in position to provide in Namibia the same excellent service to the Oppenheimers that he had given them since 1950, for he was seen locally as the independent merchant who could tell the Namibians how to negotiate with De Beers.

Tempelsman had first met Nujomo prior to Namibia's independence in the early days of his party, SWAPO. As its campaign started to succeed, Tempelsman lent Nujomo his private plane and helped him when he visited the United Nations. Tempelsman also instructed Bill Ullman, a man who had allegedly previously worked for the CIA,[12] to contact the SWAPO offices in Europe, offering them assistance.

In 1989, as the elections grew closer, Tempelsman posted Ullman to Namibia to monitor developments. SWAPO was then developing its economic policies. One of these was to support the setting up of a major local diamond cutting industry, something long opposed by De Beers. It had asked a former CDM manager, Gordon Brown, to help them with this. When I met Brown, he told me Ullman and he had met. Ullman had positioned himself well to learn what was happening, by persuading SWAPO's Head of Finance, Anton Lubowski, to accommodate him in his own home. But Ullman did not stay long in town. According to allegations published in the *Windhoek Observer*,[13] he fled back to New York after being discovered rifling through Lubowski's files. Around this time sensitive papers also went missing. The editor of

Business Day, Ken Owen, exposed Ullman's background in an article headlined "A CIA Sleeper Surfaces in Windhoek."

Brown believes Tempelsman then intervened to persuade SWAPO to drop its plans to set up a major Namibian diamond cutting industry. (Another key event was the assassination of Lubowski, the key SWAPO economics advisor, at the gate to his house on September 12th, 1989.)

After Nujomo became President of Namibia, his relationship with Tempelsman continued. Tempelsman arranged much of a State Visit by President Nujomo to the US, including for a helicopter to fly Nujomo to his yacht.

When I visited Namibia in 1995, the major Namibian trade unions persuaded me to describe at a press conference in Windhoek what I knew of Maurice Tempelsman and Jerry Funk.[14] I mentioned among other things that Funk had previously worked for the American African Labor Center, a suspected CIA front organization. My words were widely reported. That night a Dan O'Laughlin asked to meet me. He was staying at my hotel. I went to his room, as he asked, but was alarmed when he jumped up and locked the door half way through our discussion. He told me he had worked in Africa for the same American African Labor Center for 20 years. He complained that he often had "shit put on him" by allegations that it was linked to the CIA: "When Africans hear the word CIA they get negative." He assured me the Center had nothing to do with the CIA, although he admitted that the American government wholly funded it.

His questions came fast. "What is your agenda? Are you working for yourself? When are you leaving? What time is your plane tomorrow? Do you go to the USA?" He insisted I was wrong in saying the National Security Council controlled the CIA. (It advises the White House and the White House controls the CIA.) He had insisted that our conversation was "off record," yet at its end he said: "I will report having met you and this conversation to Washington."

In December 1994, the Namibian government announced the outcome of its further negotiations with De Beers. "The government was invited by De Beers to become a partner and will have its obligations like any other shareholder." In order to gain this "partnership" for "free," the Namibian government had accepted that De Beers would keep total marketing control over all the diamonds Namibia produced. CDM would also be renamed Namdeb.

The chairman of Namdeb's Management Committee, R. A. A. Gower, explained this change meant little. "It is not appropriate or necessary… to distinguish between 'the old CDM' and the 'new Namdeb.' This is one and the same company."[15] I noted the Namdeb letterhead listed as directors three members of the Oppenheimer family and no Namibian. It remained a private "proprietary company," unlisted on the stock exchange and thus without the disclosure requirements imposed upon public companies.

TEMPELSMAN: DON'T CHECK DE BEERS' PRICES.

De Beers had for years set its own prices for the Namibian rough diamonds it purchased. But in the late 1990s Namibians were starting to ask for a much greater share in their own diamond industry.

The government passed new legislation that promised to have a major impact. In 2002 it forced Namdeb to relinquish several diamond concessions it had locked up without exploring. It also allowed others to mine diamonds. Some small leases were given to local "disadvantaged" people.

A small cutting industry started. De Beers itself responded to the national mood by setting up small cutting workshops in both Namibia and Botswana. But, De Beers

insisted, with the local government's concurrence, that the diamonds they cut were bought from it in London at international prices. The diamonds purchased were also very small.

Gary Ralfe, the Managing Director of De Beers, was utterly opposed to the establishment of a significant cutting

Nambeb office.

industry in southern Africa like that of Russia. He said of plans in Botswana, "It would be national folly to prescribe that a percentage of their diamonds needed to be cut locally."

The Namibian and Botswanan governments seemingly did not protest, for they had been led to believe that De Beers knew what it was doing. But a much larger storm was about to break.

In 2001 the Namibian government was aghast when it heard that De Beers was cutting the price it would pay for Namibia's diamonds, and was seriously considering cutting Namibia's diamond production by imposing a production quota. Namibia depended on its diamond revenues for over 40 percent of its national revenues, so any cutback was extremely serious. It seemed De Beers had too many fine large Namibian stones in its stockpile and, at the high price it had set for them, they were not selling fast. The company was instead concentrating on selling the cheaper production of its other mines.

The new Diamond Act enabled the government to do something about this for it contained a clause allowing it to test the prices De Beers paid for Namibian diamonds by selling up to 10 percent of its Namibian production on the open market. In 2002 the government decided to use this provision. It hoped to discover if De Beers was undervaluing its diamonds and thus owed it more money.

The following previously unpublished correspondence then was leaked to me. I discovered the Minister of Mines and Energy, Jesaya Nyamu, wrote to Gary Ralfe, the Managing Director of De Beers, on August 28th, 2001. His letter read in part:

We have great difficulty with the price and potential quota cutbacks addressed at the meeting, not just because of the considerable immediate loss of revenues to Namibia they represent but more so

Large diamond of the kind found in Namibia.

because they are at the center of the agreement between us. One of the basic premises on which we have approved two renewals of the Namdeb-De Beers Sales Agreement since Independence is that in return for exclusivity and a substantial fee, De Beers assures both the offtake of Namdeb's full production and price stability in the market, through good and bad times. In several of the past few years, however, this assurance has in practice been absent. The fact that our diamonds occupy a unique and irreplaceable role in the marketplace compounds our concern.

As expressed to you, we hope that the current price reduction will not be followed by others. And we strongly hope that De Beers will seriously reconsider any contemplated move to impose, in addition, quota restrictions on Namdeb. Our position is not exactly the same as others from whom De Beers sources its diamonds, for a variety of reasons. There is in our mind little question that a market exists for all our goods, at solid prices, in spite of the weakened industry conditions which we acknowledge. We would thus be forced seriously to consider all options should De Beers pursue any further cutbacks.

He then went on to discuss a diamond mining boat that they had recently purchased from De Beers. "The fact remains that an enormously expensive vessel whose viability was affirmed by De Beers in the month before its transfer into Namibian ownership was within three months of that transfer destined for long-term dry-docking and large-scale overhaul." He was urgently seeking compensation.

When no satisfactory reply was received, the Cabinet invoked Section 59 of the Diamond Act of 1999. This Section read, "If the minister is satisfied that it is necessary in order to measure international market prices for unpolished diamonds, he or she may ... require ... a producer ... to sell ... on such terms and conditions customary in the diamond trade, such quantities ... of unpolished diamonds as the Minister may reasonably specify." The penalty for not obeying such instructions was a fine of up to N$100,000 or two years in jail.

The government notified De Beers, instructing it to carry out its orders on April 30th, 2002. It received no answer. In June the Minister wrote again to Gary Ralfe of De Beers.

Re. Notice to invoke section 59 of the Diamond Act of 1999.

The letter dated 30/04/2002 from myself to yourself on the above subject matter refers. Since then my office has not yet received any response from yourself on the issue. I am therefore left with no other alternative but to assume that silence on your part implies consent.

Relations were rapidly deteriorating. Then the principal troubleshooter for the Oppenheimers, Maurice Tempelsman, flew into town. He met the President, Sam Nujomo, and did all he could to dissuade him from checking the accuracy of the prices De Beers paid for Namibia's diamonds. He even warned that to threaten De Beers with an independent check on its prices had the same disadvantages as threatening a state with "nuclear war."

Tempelsman was helped by having the brother-in-law of the President, Aaron Mushimba, as his local business partner in North Bank Diamonds, a company registered in the Bahamas. At the conclusion of these discussions, Tempelsman went back to New York to prepare what he hoped would be a persuasive letter to the President. This extraordinary confidential communication was also leaked to me, and reads in part:

Maurice Tempelsman

May 27, 2002

Dear Mr. President,
Three weeks ago you honored me, not only by granting me a hearing on a matter I consider of the highest importance for Namibia and the diamond industry, but also by taking me into your confidence concerning those domestic budgetary issues bearing on that matter. I consequently undertook to assign my team, extensively experienced in devising financing solutions for our friends in the Russian Federation and for African and other governments elsewhere, to assess Namibia's circumstances, allowing me promptly to report back to you. This I now do.

After some general comments about the Namibian budget and the country's airline, he went on to say:

Mr. President, an associate of mine is one of the world's more prominent investment bankers: James Harmon, past Chairman of the US Export-Import Bank.... I would be pleased to make available Mr. Harmon or others ... for such brain-storming with your officials as may be useful....

James Harmon was the Head of the Export-Import Bank between 1997 and 2001. He took over from Tempelsman as Chairman of the Corporate Council on Africa in mid-January 2002. The letter continued:

Upon receiving your mandate to proceed, I would be in a position expeditiously to assemble the US$80 million-plus bank financing package underlying the proposal ... in the current financial year.

Then, although he was not officially acting as De Beers' agent, he set out the conditions that De Beers would impose before the government received this money. The government would have to guarantee De Beers exclusive rights to Namibia's diamonds until 2008 and never again to threaten an independent check on De Beers' prices.

Mr. President, whether we wish it or not, the proposal above cannot bear fruit without the cooperation at several levels of your partner in Namdeb, De Beers, and thus some acknowledgement of their interests. They have already every incentive to extend such cooperation, and I firmly believe they will. But both they and the bank lenders will, as part of this process, undoubtedly seek formal assurances that during the term of the financing facility there will be no legal conflicts between Government and De Beers over marketing, and no disruption of the delivery for sale through De Beers of Namdeb's entire production. To accommodate the repayment schedule that is envisioned, the Sales Agreement and arrangements that have prevailed over the past decade would predictably have to be extended through 2008 (three years beyond their currently scheduled renegotiation date).

He then went on to discuss an agreement by De Beers, negotiated with the government over the past year, to pay millions of dollars because of "the poor performance of a De Beers-built mining vessel (the 'Gariep')." De Beers evidently had frozen payment of this. He concluded, "Should the path of conflict be replaced by one of resumed cooperation, I again have little doubt that the millions of dollars previously conceded by De Beers will rapidly find their way into Government's coffers."

Mr. President, you may recall that on my last visit I drew an analogy between Section 59 and nuclear weapons. Both are worth more when threatened than when used – and the threats themselves can be made neither too lightly nor too frequently. Government has invoked the specter of Section 59 at a time of pressing national needs. All would gain if that weapon were now to be disarmed for an appropriate period, clearing the way for a substantial infusion of financial resources permitting those national needs to be met. Such strategic decisions are never easy; but you have earned the world's respect, not to mention my sustained admiration, by making them wisely many times before, in many circumstances, for the benefit of your land and people.

It was hand signed, "Maurice."

He included two pages to explain the deal. One was headed: "US$80 million Namibia Diamond Revenue Acceleration Facility." In this there was no more talk of a diamond production cutback. It instead said that diamond "production at Namdeb is projected to increase in the years following 2003 from 1.3 million carats to 1.7 million carats towards the end of the decade."

He promised Namdeb could obtain immediately US$80 million dollars, if it agreed to a "pre-sale" of some of its future output. This money would be provided through an offshore loan made not to the government but to De Beers, "the buyer of Namdeb's diamonds." De Beers would presumably keep US$30 million of this, as he went on to say this would mean "the State Revenue Fund" would receive "at least US$50 million in fresh, unrestricted money." Interest charges and costs would be passed on to Namdeb for "repayment from 2004." Tempelsman finally noted that this offer involved "no necessity for public disclosure or debate" and therefore could be kept secret.

When I first read this, I realized how explosive it would be in southern Africa if made public. Other letters were then leaked to me. It was the first time I had learned of a Tempelsman deal while it was still in the making. It clearly would have serious consequences for Namibia, so I thought it better not to hold the information for this book but to make it public immediately before Tempelsman's deal was concluded. My subsequent articles appeared in the Namibian and South African press and there was a furious reaction. Tempelsman flew back to Namibia, but his deal, once made public, had become impossible.

The Minister for Mining, Njamu, was sacked, allegedly for refusing to follow a Cabinet decision to implement Section 59. It seems that he was afraid of upsetting De Beers still further. He was quoted as saying "They [the international diamond merchants] are the law in Namibia." His replacement as Minister, Dr. Nicky Iyamba, later admitted: "The Cabinet did discuss the possibility of invoking Section 59" and after this "many people approached the Ministry saying they would give the government more than it was getting" for the Namibian diamond output. But he did not explain why the government decided to reject these higher offers and stay with the contract with De Beers.

Nor did he explain for some months why the government then gave De Beers most of what it wanted, despite the withdrawal of the Tempelsman offer. The Finance

Minister, Nangolo Mbumba tersely said, "The loan is off the table. We don't have to talk about it." Nor why the President sacked the Prime Minister, Hage Geingebs, allegedly for leaking the above correspondence.

Three months later the Minister for Mining lamely explained that the Cabinet dropped its plans to check De Beers' prices, "when the Government realized that there was no urgent need to borrow money because of increased revenue from diamonds."

But some months after this, when the government published its official statistics, I leant that Namdeb had in fact produced fewer diamonds in 2002, not more as the Minister had suggested. Production fell 8 percent in 2002 to a total of 1.27 million carats as against 1.38 million carats in 2001.

On reflection, it was strange that the government had to enact a law to give itself the power to check De Beers' prices, for it was officially a partner with De Beers in Namdeb in mining the country's diamonds. Their need to pass this legislation indicated how little information and power they really held within Namdeb.

But ironically, this feeble partnership was about to give the Namibian government a major international problem. In 2002 the anti-cartel section of the European Union announced it was investigating De Beers for having a collusive price-fixing agreement with the governments of both Namibia and Botswana. This remained in 2003 by far the most serious legal threat to the De Beers cartel.

When Namibia introduced a Competition Bill in 2003 along European Union lines to ban price-fixing, perhaps in order for Namibia to qualify for European aid, this again raised alarm at De Beers and Namdeb.

Inge Zaamwani, the Managing Director of Namdeb, wrote to the Minister of Trade and Industry asking for her company to remain shielded from competition. She requested that the diamond industry "be treated as a special case" and explicitly exempted from the Competition Bill then being discussed in the National Assembly. But this may have been a most imprudent move. If successful, it could create severe difficulties for Namibia and De Beers, its partner in Namdeb, with the European competition authority. It was said to be entirely coincidental that Maurice Tempelsman flew into town at the same time.

1   Nelson Mandela. "Monopoly in SA mines must end." *Sunday Times*. London. February 20th, 1994.
2   These figures were revealed in an Investor's Profile published by Venetia in the 1990s.
3   Cyril Ramaphosa, ANC Sec. General. *Business Day*, September 29th, 1994.
4   *Rapaport News*, August 2002.
5   The production quotas of foreign mines contracted to De Beers were set by the Diamond Producers Association (DPA).
6   *The Independent*. October 31st, 1994.
7   In a May 1993 speech.
8   *The Diamond World Review* (no 80).
9   *Engineering News*. September 23rd, 1994. The Supreme Court case cited was. *US vs. Socony-Vacuum Oil Co.*
10 The ANC had agreed to form a coalition government with the National Party for its first five years in office, 1994-1999.
11 CRA internal marketing document made available to author.
12 Confidential discussion with the author, September 1994. Also, the editor of a Namibian national paper told me that Bill Ullman was certainly once in the CIA.
13 September 9th, 2002.
14 Barry Cohen, *The CIA and African Trade Unions* in *Dirty Work 2*, ed. Ray, Schaap, Van Metre and Wolf, Lyle Stuart. 1979, page 74.
15 R. A. A. Gower, Director of Namdeb Diamond Corporation (Proprietary) Ltd. Letter to Christa Oaes, Namibian Broadcasting Corporation. March 1st, 1995.

Chapter 18 – The Future of the Diamond Trade

CERTIFYING DIAMONDS AS "PURE"

I was asked back to southern Africa to be a keynote speaker at the first post-apartheid international conference of southern African diamond mine workers. This was sponsored by all the major mining unions and held in Namibia. I was asked to speak on how apartheid had strengthened De Beers – and on possible ways forward for the diamond industry.

I spoke on how I thought the diamond trade could better serve Africa. I suggested that, if diamonds were both mined and cut in South Africa by workers employed on reasonable post-apartheid terms, if jewelry were made incorporating South African gold, platinum, precious stones and local artistic traditions, they could surely be successfully marketed to the rest of the world as African "liberation" jewels with a good pedigree, unlike the old diamonds sold by companies that had profited from apartheid.

I suggested a system of diamond certificates that could guarantee that the stone on an engagement ring was not produced by child labor or by miners working in foul conditions, saying that the mining and cutting operations had been in accordance with an internationally agreed code, with an independent authority verifying this. I thought that, if couples really wanted to buy a diamond to symbolize their love, then it had to be fit for the purpose.

A few years later, I was surprised when De Beers proposed a somewhat similar system, but without any method of verifying its ethical assertions and guarantees. They would mark diamonds they had supplied with a tiny De Beers logo and an identification number. This, they said, would guarantee that a diamond was genuinely De Beers and thus "properly produced." It was hoped that this would protect De Beers from accusations that their diamonds were associated with human rights violations. De Beers said it would also warrant that inscribed stones were not artificially made or treated.

But this scheme was greeted with skepticism. Diamond merchants asked: how could this De Beers warranty give this protection? It seemed to demand a blind and naïve acceptance of De Beers' words. It was offering to inscribe stones it had supplied as rough if they are sent back to it after polishing. How would De Beers know these were the same stones? How would they know if someone in debt bondage had cut it? De Beers had a very poor record in cutting off diamond supplies to merchants that used debt bonded and child workers. The CSO had denied it had a responsibility to police and stop this practice. What also of the diamonds produced from De Beers' asbestos-polluted mines?

Many merchants suspected this new De Beers tactic was primarily conceived to discourage the selling of diamonds outside the CSO and to enhance De Beers' revenues. They feared it would give De Beers more power. It certainly would give merchants higher costs, for they would have to pay perhaps $20 to $40 a diamond for the inscription service. Jewelry stores would also have to invest in equipment to read the inscription. Many diamond merchants were already angry with the CSO for repeatedly increasing the prices of the better diamonds while the retail market was lackluster. This was wrecking havoc with their once lucrative profits.

DIAMOND MERCHANTS ORGANIZE AGAINST DE BEERS

By 1997, the fury of the diamond trade led to what DIB called, "Its first ever challenge to the monopolistic rough diamond distribution system of De Beers." In Singapore, on August 27th, the Presidents of World Federation of Diamond Bourses and the International Diamond Manufacturers Association unanimously adopted a resolution that read in part: "The diamond industry is in a state of crisis. The pricing and marketing policies of De Beers have resulted in unacceptably low profitability, which threatens the viability of diamantaires world-wide.

"Our industry finds it difficult to continue to support the De Beers single channel marketing system and its self-appointed role as custodians of the diamond industry when it does not support trade profitability."

Another resolution read, "CSO policies with regard to allocations have not properly reflected market conditions. The industry's indebtedness to banks is at a dangerous all-time high. Manufacturers' continual lack of profitability threatens our future. Without significant and intermediate improvement in this area, the viability of the current system is endangered." This was signed by: Yigal Hausman, President, IDMA, President, The Israel Diamond Manufacturers Association; Jacques Roisen, Honorary President, IDMA; Eduard Denckens, President, Syndikaat Der Belgische Diamantnijverheid (SBD); Raymond Vets, President, Vereniging Van Kempische Diamantwerkgevers VZW; Sean Cohen, Chairman, The Master Diamond Cutters Association of South Africa; Chirakitti Tang, President, The Thai Diamond Manufacturers Association; Alan Kleinberg, President, Diamond Manufacturers & Importers Association of America. The revolt was unprecedented.

The response of De Beers was to talk tough. Gary Ralfe, Managing Director of De Beers, declared: "The CSO will absolutely not lower gem diamond prices." It suggested that the diamond merchants were being disloyal to their family head and that De Beers Chairman Nicky Oppenheimer would be personally hurt by the vote of no confidence in a system that his father and grandfather had nurtured over their lifetimes.

The vehemence of the reaction to this caught De Beers off guard. Merchants gathered in Singapore to discuss "sanctions against De Beers," including buying more from Russians, Angolans, Canadians and Australians. Some suggested reporting De Beers to the antitrust authorities or of artificially improving the inscribed De Beers diamonds to discredit De Beers in the eyes of the public, for it had promised that its diamonds would remain untreated. Having alternative supplies of rough diamonds had made a great difference to the trade. If it had remained totally dependent on De Beers, merchants could not have discussed rebellion so openly.

Until now few Sightholders would have risked the wrath of the CSO. They knew the CSO could seriously penalize them for rebellion by changing the contents of their boxes. But this time the merchants had the strength of numbers.

DE BEERS FACES A REVOLT BY DIAMOND MINERS

De Beers previously had forced errant miners into submission by using its vast stockpiles to destroy the markets for the diamond types they produced. The CSO's stockpile was said to include some 16-18 tons of Argyle's diamonds, or two years' production. They had used this to drive down prices on the free market for Argyle's diamonds whenever Argyle came to renegotiate its five-year contracts with the CSO. When the contract came up for renegotiation in 1996, De Beers had flooded the market with 60 percent more Argyle diamonds than normal. But this time the tactic misfired – Argyle refused to sign and went independent. This made life much more difficult for De Beers.

New alliances of diamond producers appeared. The Australians started to develop new diamond mines in Australia, Canada, Indonesia and Finland, in partnership with local and British capital. The Russians became part of the "M Diamond" mining project in Mongolia, a Malaysian venture and moved also into Namibia and Angola.

Angola was rich in fine diamonds and Almazy, the Russian diamond marketing company, was helping with their marketing. At the Catoca Angolan mine, with reserves of over 300 million carats, the Russians, Brazilians, and an Israeli company, LID, were jointly setting up a new cutting plant. A Namibian deal signed in Moscow between President Sam Nujomo and President Yeltsin had the potential of revolutionizing the economy of that diamond rich nation. These new alliances posed the most serious challenge ever faced by the cartel.

De Beers had however secured some minor relief when it signed a new contract with the Russians in October 1997. Unfortunately for De Beers it was on far less advantageous terms. It was initially only for a year but was later extended to the end of 2001.

NICKY OPPENHEIMER TAKES OVER DE BEERS – AND THE REVOLT CONTINUES

Nicky Oppenheimer took over the Chairmanship of De Beers on January 1st, 1998. He reminded everyone: "I will be the third generation of the Oppenheimer family to take on this role, following in the footsteps of my father, Harry, and my grandfather, Ernest, who became Chairman in 1929." Two years later Nicky appointed his son Jonathan as Director of Industrial Operations. The dynasty continued.

But by now the revolt against De Beers was so unprecedented that it helped trigger a 42 percent fall in the value of De Beers' shares. Paul Goris, general manager of Antwerp Diamond Bank, speaking at a *Financial Times* conference in London, commented, "One has to reconcile himself to the fact that the days of a predictable and stable [diamond] market, an exclusive single-channeled supply and guaranteed profit are probably over." A 41 percent drop in De Beers' sales, to $1.6 billion, accompanied this financial panic.

De Beers next was faced, for the very first time, with difficulties in exporting their own South African diamonds to Europe. The ANC government in 1998 and 1999 froze diamond exports, because it suspected that De Beers under-valued its diamonds. De Beers had also refused to honor an agreement to return the crown jewels of South Africa, the vast stockpile of diamonds of the highest quality that had been accumulated under laws passed by the previous apartheid government. De Beers admitted it took these diamonds to London the year before the ANC was elected to power. The company blandly stated, "Discussions with the relevant authorities have continued for many months, but it is still not possible to indicate when regular exports will resume."

Bulk-selling "near-gems"

De Beers' troubles were compounded by the accumulation of diamond stockpiles around the world of unprecedented size. It only had itself to blame for one of these, having forced Argyle to stockpile its output while it was under contract. It was now independent and had 12-14 tons of diamonds (60-70 million carats) stockpiled, worth perhaps over one billion dollars. Russia had stockpiles worth an estimated $3-4 billion, containing many large stones, and the Indians had a stockpile of an estimated $2 billion, of which three quarters were polished. These stockpiles might make it extremely difficult to sustain the myth that diamonds are expensive because they are rare.

Argyle, Zaire, and Russia were all now releasing smaller uncut gem diamonds. The MIBA mine in the Congo increased production from 540,000 carats a month to 700,000. It was getting around $30 a carat, much more than the $10 that De Beers had previously paid for them. Although De Beers could still buy these more expensive stones on the open market, it no longer had any control over the numbers sold.

The problems were compounded by the nature of the Russian, the Australian and its own stockpile. They were not only made up of smaller stones. All three had also been stockpiling the largest and supposedly most valuable, those over ten carats in weight. The problem with these was that, at the price De Beers had set for them, there simply was not a market for most of them. They might have to be retained for years. The international market wanted mostly cheaper smaller stones.

De Beers needed to sell its better stones. It had a giant stockpile. If merchants wanted its cheapest not its dearest, this was a major problem. It had purchased many very cheaply as "near-gems," frequently at under $3 per quarter-carat stone, but it did not have enough of these cheap stones and it had too many of the dearer. It solved this problem with a stroke, for it was emperor of the diamond world. It reclassified a vast number of its better class diamonds as "near-gems" and sold them at near-gem prices to be cut as gems!

This reverse alchemy made it vast profits. By the mid-1990s De Beers was relabelling and pricing as "near-gems" an incredible 72 percent (by weight) of all the cutable diamonds it sold, while at the same time blithely pretending it had not cut the price of "gems." Merchants finding it hard to afford the high priced "gems" found these new "near-gems" much more profitable – and they went like hot cakes.

This completely blurred the diffence between "near-gems" and "gems." A major practical distinction between them until now was the amount of the diamond that had to be ground away to turn it into a cut gem. "Near-gems" had to lose perhaps 70 percent by weight. "Gems" lost around 50 percent by weight. The distinction now became much less.

By 1998 most of the world's gem diamonds were being cut from stones labeled misleadingly by De Beers as "near-gems." That year 70 percent of the 20 million carats (four tonnes) of cut and polished diamonds produced had been manufactured out of near-gems. A diamond publication enthused: "This 'near-gem' revolution caused a redefining of world-wide consumer markets. More diamonds can be afforded by more people." Because De Beers had created the illusion that all diamonds were rare, these cheap diamonds now sold at retail as gems for very large profits.

It had slashed the price at which it sold uncut diamonds but there was no intention to cut the retail price of diamonds. The public would not be told that the average engagement ring might now contain a diamond that originally cost $3. De Beers' diamond advertising helped to ensure this. The only snag for De Beers was that these cheap rough diamonds undercut the market for De Beers' higher priced uncut gems. It thus decided to try to sell these to the luxury top-end market by building a chain of elegant De Beers retail stores.

De Beers' stockpile remained very full. It still held over $4 billion worth of diamonds – and the millions of diamonds needed to undermine independent producers. In 1998 it attacked the profits of the independent Australians by sharply reducing the prices it charged for stockpiled Australian stones. This attack was expected. John Robinson, Ashton's chief executive, jokingly said this was "a coincidence not entirely coincidental." Others called it a "slap in the face" for Argyle.

In September 1999 De Beers released the largest yet number of uncut diamonds at its monthly Sight. In a six-month period it flooded the market with 44 percent more rough diamonds than it had released in the same period of the previous year. Argyle weathered the attack well via strong links with the US market through the major retailer Zales, and partnerships with Indian merchants. It seemed that more radical tactics were called for if the cartel were to survive.

DE BEERS DUMPS HALF OF ITS DIAMOND STOCKPILE

But no one could have imagined what the Oppenheimers would do next. In November 1999 Nicky Oppenheimer announced that he was going to sell nearly half of De Beers' $4.6 billion diamond stockpile, priced apparently by cost of acquisition therefore worth far more in the market place. This caused, as planned, many difficulties for the independent miners. De Beers' spokesman explained, "It's part of our strategic plan."

The Russians knew that they were also targets. A Russian newspaper reported, "The leak from De Beers' headquarters suggested that a total of $2.5 billion worth of rough stones might be dumped by the corporation on the market." It thought De Beers had "the aim of intimidating market participants, [especially] Russian diamond producers who had repeatedly stated that they were ready to independently sell rough diamonds on the world market."

This move was absolutely revolutionary for De Beers. It was deserting its century-old strategy of limiting the supply of diamonds to keep them rare and expensive. It was instead placing its trust in the wish of its rivals to keep the retail price of diamonds as high as De Beers had traditionally set it and not to compete in pricing. A new informal diamond price-fixing cartel seemingly was coming into existence even as De Beers flooded the markets.

The new strategy also demonstrated a great confidence in the power of advertising. De Beers was confident the news of the diamond flood would not be permitted to reach the consumers. It believed that all producers would want to keep up the illusion of scarcity.

Thus the CSO continued to pour out a flood of cheaper diamonds. It sold large numbers of Argyle stones to be cut as gems in India at the April and June Sights, pricing these at between $2 and $10 a carat.

These gigantic Sight boxes would temporarily exhaust, as De Beers had planned, the funds of many merchants, reducing the market for the independent miners. (This was also why Indian merchants slashed the wages of their diamond cutters in half in January 2001.) A sated world market would absorb 25 percent less of De Beers' uncut diamonds in the first half of 2001 – and Argyle diamond mine would be forced to cancel one of its own diamond Sights.

It was a very high-risk strategy for De Beers. While trusting in the independent miners having a common interest in preserving the myth of scarcity, it hoped, once it had punished them by flooding their market, to re-contract them and welcome them back into the cartel's ranks. But what fate would then await them? Going on past performance, they would find their diamonds stockpiled or sold for low prices. Argyle had learned its lesson. It would not go back to the cartel.

In 2000 De Beers tried another tactic. They offered to buy Ashton Mining, the owner of a 40 percent stake in Argyle. They failed only because the European Union blocked the deal on anti-competitive grounds. This was particularly serious for De Beers, for at the same time it had also failed to gain marketing control over a new Canadian diamond mine. (Ashton Mining's interest in Argyle was instead to be purchased by its partner CRA, giving the latter complete control.)

De Beers was to have another serious disappointment. In 2001 it was forced to concede that the Russians could in future sell half of their massive production independently on the world market. It then learned that there was a risk it would not get even this. The deal had first to get the approval of the European Union. Article 86 of the Treaty of Rome prohibited the abusive exploitation of a position of dominance.

Nicky Oppenheimer cautioned, "There may come a time in the future when things change and not such a high proportion of diamonds are marketed though the CSO and then we would have to look to turning our advertising skills to making sure that we look after De Beers."

It was time for De Beers to build itself a private redoubt.

DE BEERS GOES PRIVATE

De Beers stunned the financial world when it announced on February 1, 2001, it was "going private," an enormously costly operation. It would change from being a public company with vast cash resources, to a private one with large debts incurred by buying out investors.

This move would also make it into a private company controlled by the Oppenheimer family through De Beers Investments (DBI). The family would directly own 45 percent. Anglo American, which the family dominated, would hold 45 percent, and the remaining 10 percent would belong to Debswana, a joint-venture part-owned by the Botswana government but effectively controlled by its partner, De Beers. De Beers had always in practice been a "family" company, controlled by the Oppenheimers, but now it would be so officially. This would enable them to operate much more secretly.

This removed all investors who might dislike De Beers' practice of locking up a fortune in its still gigantic $2.3 billion stockpile. Such practices were alien to modern investment advisors, but they were key to the cartel's very profitable survival. Privatizing the company also enabled it to close down the tax shelter operation in Switzerland, run through De Beers Centenary.

But, the principal reason given for this privatization was that De Beers had officially decided to let the "free market" look after the diamonds produced and marketed by others, while it focused on the marketing of the diamonds that came from the mines contracted to it. De Beers' Managing Director, Gary Ralfe, explained, "Prices in near-gem or cheaper qualities will be determined by free market forces. It could also mean … De Beers will … ensure that what money it feels it can afford to spend on the promotion of diamond jewelry is focused on diamonds that come out of its own mines and those of its partners in Africa or pass through the CSO, rather than giving a free ride in its promotions to those diamonds which remain outside the CSO system."

Part of this story was true. De Beers would focus on its own diamonds, but because it had no other choice. It had lost marketing control over a large part of the world's diamond production. But it also had felt happier about trusting this "free market." It had discovered that the independent producers were in practice letting it set the prices. They liked that De Beers seemingly kept the price of diamonds moving upwards. They were all now expanding rapidly, taking advantage of the high profit margins De Beers had engineered for itself, and they were finding diamonds were much more plentiful than De Beers had ever admitted. The new informal diamond cartel was rapidly taking shape.

BHP was not just involved in diamonds in Canada. It was very active in De Beers' heartland: prospecting in South Africa and Botswana, mining seabed diamonds, and it was curious about the lands De Beers had locked up. It hired aircraft to survey from the air much of Botswana and South Africa. Alrosa had moved out of Siberia to develop a major diamond mine in partnership with the Angolan government and RTZ was building on its success in Australia by opening diamond mines in Canada and Zimbabwe. Even the Indians were getting back into mining. In 1981 the Indian mining body, MMTC, had sought supplies from mines that were not controlled by the cartel. It had then failed. Now it was back looking in Namibia.

But De Beers was by no means down and out. It controlled mines in southern Africa that produced 45-50 percent of the world's diamonds by value, remaining by far the most powerful of the producers. It also held contracts for the marketing of another 15 percent of world diamond production.

If De Beers could no longer rely on controlling diamonds produced by others with exclusive marketing agreements, it had to take the more expensive option of buying or developing its own mines. It revamped its international exploration program and, after more than 20 years of "unsuccessful" exploration outside southern Africa, it started to develop mines in Canada. It also, as I have mentioned, reversed its previous plan to shut down the Finsch and Premier mines, announcing multiple billion-rand expansion programs for both. De Beers now needed their diamonds. It also announced what Namibians called a Big Hairy Audacious Goal (BHAG) to double the value of Namdeb's output by 2005.

The Oppenheimers also decided to go into Angola. They knew it was rich in diamonds. They had earlier, perhaps foolishly, refused to buy the certified diamonds marketed by its government. The Israeli merchant Lev Leviev was now lucratively doing the job that De Beers had once done, marketing Angola's diamonds, now 10 percent of world production by value. De Beers needed to get back in, so it explained to the Angolan government that it was a reformed company. It was no longer trying to control the international marketing of diamonds. It was not coming in to replace Lev Leviev. All it wanted was the chance to develop new diamond mines in Angola – over which it would naturally have exclusive marketing control. Gary Ralfe of De Beers stated, at a press conference on February 6th, 2003, that they would sell only diamonds they had mined, so would not try to replace Ascorp's monopoly control over the rest of Angola's production. But the rumors were that in fact they were planning to move in as a rival and undermine the position of Ascorp.

De Beers gets a make-over and becomes a "brand"

De Beers thought it most unjust that rival miners were making great profits by taking advantage of advertising they had not paid for. Its advertising still kept the price of diamonds high by maintaining the myth of diamonds as rare and unique. Previously these companies would have paid it marketing fees. It also needed to find a new way to market its top-class gems, a way that would persuade consumers to pay the high prices it was determined to collect.

De Beers brought in Bain & Company, an American firm of management consultants. It recommended De Beers put its faith in its "brand," saying the De Beers name was under-utilized, affirming that it was now the day of the brand. It recommended an advertising makeover to make the De Beers name so attractive that it would become "the Supplier of Choice" for everyone.

This advice was to be expected. The theme song of PR experts, and the grail of major corporations, was now the promotion of brand names, rather than advertising how they gave better value, and cared for their employees. Around the world companies were spending a fortune on promoting brand images, while economizing by having their goods made by others in the cheapest sweatshops in the lowest-cost countries. Onto these they would put their high profile labels, enabling them to be sold for prices that had much more to do with advertising fictions than production costs. The consumer's money was thus increasingly going on little more than labels.[1]

De Beers had long done just this. Its name had featured on a million billboards. But, it had let others benefit by selling the diamonds it advertised to the public. In future it would sell diamonds itself to the public, in as upmarket a way as it could. By going private, De Beers also ensured that the stock market would not be allowed to judge the value of the De Beers brand, as happened with other companies. It had long practiced the art of selling the "emperor's new clothes;"[2] it would now find new ways of selling the invisible aspects of a diamond for high cost. Its brand makeover would simply mean that it did this more effectively, or so it was hoped.

This meant that it had to stop other diamond merchants from selling De Beers' diamonds under the De Beers name. It told them in future they would have to sell their goods under the new "Forevermark" brand, or in their own name. This was a risky strategy for De Beers. It was not like other corporations. It had survived as a cartel by allowing merchants who kept its rules to use its much-advertised name. If it removed this privilege, then merchants had lost an incentive that had helped to keep them loyal.

Gary Ralfe of De Beers stated, "In five years' time we envisage an industry in which there are multiple and competitive brands. As we have learned from other industries, competing brands stimulate global demand." Naturally, there was no mention of price competition. Gareth Penny of De Beers explained that prices could go up if De Beers succeeded in changing diamonds from a product into an emotion and selling them as dreams. He also noted that a new "Thanksgiving" diamond was about to be promoted. He suggested that branding could alleviate the concern of customers over conflict diamonds, synthetic diamonds, treated diamonds and diamond simulants, since De Beers would keep its diamonds "clean."

DISQUIET AMONG DIAMOND MERCHANTS

Many of the long-term merchants lamented what they saw as a growth of mistrust in the industry. They did not like the talk of diamonds being tainted by human rights abuse, nor what they saw as the increasing competitiveness of De Beers. This was not family-like. The Jewish and Indian Jain diamond merchants had always operated on a family basis since this gave them the greater security when dealing with a small, easy to conceal, and expensive commodity.

Merchants staffed their new offices in Israel, Belgium, and New York with brothers and sons they had inducted into the trade. These offices were comfortable and relaxing, with feminine touches such as flowers; for they were wanted primarily to give an impression of "family" and reliability, or so observed Professor Sallie Westwood.[3] She described the role of male bonding in the diamond trade and noted that now, although "money had always a magical quality, providing status against caste background," many of the merchants were feeling betrayed by the lack of family values in the new dispensation.

A diamond merchant told her, "We were the pioneers in the trade, but more importantly among Jains you know which family you are dealing with and if a trader doesn't pay you, then you can contact his father or his uncle and he does not want this to happen." In practice it was a trust, backed by knowledge, surveillance, and a rough justice.

The merchants in Israel faced another problem. The Intifada kept away many international customers. Its diamond center had become much less popular. In 1991 the Israeli diamond industry had employed 9,581 production workers in 641 workshops and factories. By 2002 this had dropped to 3,500 workers in just 300 plants. This was not just because of extra automation. Some of the Israeli industry had fled, driven not only by the Intifada, but by the wish for greater profits. They were now sending their diamonds to be cut in China, Thailand, Ukraine, and Romania, anywhere that was both quieter and cheaper. The trade remained a hugely important source of revenue for Israel. In 2000 its companies sold diamonds worth $5.2 billion. Schmuel Schnitzer, President of the Israeli Diamond Exchange, in 2002 said some 45 percent of their diamonds were cut and polished outside Israel. He also predicted that automation should cut production costs in Israel to about $12-14 a carat by 2006.

Meanwhile the Belgian diamond industry came under criticism. A well-known NGO, Partnership Africa-Canada, noted the discrepancy in the figures for exports from the Central African Republic to Antwerp and thought this indicated a trade in conflict diamonds. The Africans reported they sent only half the value of diamonds to Antwerp as Antwerp reported receiving. The conclusion was that only half of the diamonds exported were registered with the African authorities; that is, half of them were illicitly traded. The Diamond High Council of Antwerp had a surprising response. They stopped releasing import statistics that identified the countries of origin.

DE BEERS OPENS ITS FIRST JEWELRY STORE

The new De Beers policy of only marketing its own diamonds went along with its new "pure" stance. It announced none of its diamonds could be blood or conflict diamonds, because it "does not buy diamonds on the open market."[4]

High profits were promised, so the next stage in the re-invention of De Beers was to organize the marketing of its branded stones in exclusive De Beers stores for very high prices. De Beers formed a joint venture with a luxury goods conglomerate, LVMH to give its branded diamonds the right image. The first store was to open in London with others following in New York and other cities. This would be the very first time that De Beers would sell its diamonds directly to the public.

De Beers took advantage of the conflict diamond campaign to distinguish its diamonds from all others. It guaranteed that no "conflict" diamond would ever be sold under the De Beers brand.

De Beers did not want to release diamonds that might drive down prices, so in 2002-3 it allegedly destroyed many of the smaller stones in its stockpile, It gave the destroyed stones a "book price" of only 50 cents a carat, while others gave them an average value of $200,[5] indicating that they were of good quality. This discrepancy was caused by De Beers' bookkeeping convention of pricing the stones in its stockpile by cost of acquisition rather than market price.

But the De Beers plan to have a celebrity launch in November 2002 of its elegant new store in London, just down the street from Tiffany's and Cartier, ran into trouble when Survival International organized a demonstration outside, protesting the eviction of thousands of Bushmen from their homelands in the Kalahari, with their lands surveyed for diamond mining. The opening rites became a public relations disaster for De Beers, as mentioned earlier. Iman, the wife of David Bowie, reportedly withdrew after meeting with Survival International's chief executive. The shop explained the supermodel's absence, saying it was for "family reasons," and instead boasted that ex-Spice Girl Mel B had attended its party afterwards.

The subsequent press reports associated De Beers' new diamond store and its newly branded diamonds with human rights violations in Botswana. The subsequent argument in the press was over whether the Bushmen were evicted due to Botswanan racism or due to diamonds. It was likely to have been both. It seemed the manifest racist attitudes of prominent politicians made it easy for the Bushmen's rights to be ignored when assigning diamond prospecting rights to their lands.[6] The question was not addressed of whether it was right for De Beers or any other mining company to accept rights allotted in such circumstances.

THE PROBLEMS OF A CARTEL

De Beers knew it was risky to market diamonds inscribed with its own name. In November 1999, Nicky Oppenheimer told the *Financial Times* that he was worried that selling inscribed diamonds would make it easier for De Beers to be sued by the European Union. It would effectively be branding its diamonds with the information that they were sold through a price-fixing scheme.

Then, when Nicky Oppenheimer sought a meeting with US Assistant Attorney General Joel Klein in early 2000 to discuss the anti-cartel laws, he was refused a meeting. De Beers' Andy Lamont said the US situation was a "serious constraint on the way that De Beers does business." He concluded, "Our effort didn't work this time, but we recognize that it will be a long time to resolve."

When in 2002, as Nicky Oppenheimer had anticipated, the EU Competition Commission objected that De Beers "might want to favor the joint venture [with LVMH] in relation to the supply of rough diamonds," De Beers found again the slippery turf of a possible anti-cartel action. This delayed the opening of its Old Bond Street store, but eventually, cautiously, the EU permitted the marketing scheme and the shop launch went ahead.

More bad news for De Beers came in 2002 when the US District Court in New York ruled that De Beers and Nicky Oppenheimer had violated antitrust laws. This action was brought by three New York diamond merchants who had purchased diamonds from De Beers Sightholders. They charged that De Beers had made them overpay for goods, saying that it had unlawfully "controlled the supply and managed the prices in the US" and had "ostensibly moved out of the US to avoid prosecution by the US Department of Justice."[7] The suit also contended: "De Beers has entered many collusive agreements and undertaken many collusive acts with its partners. This includes agreements made in acts undertaken with numerous De Beers partners that are US citizens or that do substantial business here." The defendants found guilty allegedly were Gary Ralfe, Managing Director, De Beers; Nicky Oppenheimer, Chairman, De Beers; De Beers Centenary AG and De Beers Consolidated Mines Ltd. At the time of writing, the penalty was still under consideration.

This action indicated the depth of alienation that now existed between De Beers and parts of the diamond trade. This was also indicated by a resolution passed on

February 6th, 2003 at a meeting of the New York Diamond Club. "Following discussion on the De Beers role in the diamond trade, and the potential conflict with United States antitrust and monopoly laws, Mr. Bruce Smith moved that we request that New York State Attorney General Eliot Spitzer uphold the antitrust and monopoly laws in connection with De Beers' activities in New York State and the United States. Seconded by Mr. Yaron Hahami, this was adopted by the Board in a secret ballot by a vote of 7-2 with 1 abstention. Messrs. Abraham, Cohen, and Halzami were appointed to a Committee to carry out this resolution."

The relief that De Beers felt when the European Union allowed their new marketing scheme was short lived. On January 6th, 2003, the European Commission ruled against De Beers' contract with Alrosa for supplies of Russian diamonds. It said, "By eliminating competition for Alrosa, the European Commission takes the view that by entering into this agreement De Beers has abused its dominant position in the rough diamond market." This had serious consequences for the cartel. It caused Alrosa to start to market its vast production outside the control of De Beers.

De Beers must have feared an even more serious action. It was entirely possible that the European Union would decide that its business arrangements with Botswana and Namibia were "collusive agreements," set up to manipulate world prices and restrict competition. If this happened, it could be devastating for De Beers.

The grave legal difficulties with the European Union may have been behind De Beers' decision in 2001-2 to found a new Swiss company called "De Beers Societé Anonym" to hold its assets and debts outside the EU.

By 2003, four mining groups had come to dominate the world's diamond production. By revenues De Beers mines produced 48 percent, Alrosa 20 percent, BHP Billiton 8 percent, and RTZ 5 percent. These four seemed set to increase their dominance with several new mines underway. But their "competition" had not caused a fall in the value of gem diamonds. The investors in these new mines depended on the diamond price staying high.

In practice De Beers had been allowed by the other diamond producers to continue to set the world's prices. Despite its makeover, De Beers was still engaged in the same game. It still worked to keep prices high and to prevent competition. In the 1930s it took over a Diamond Syndicate made up of major European diamond traders. Perhaps it was now part of a new Syndicate made out of production companies?

Tempelsman comes to the rescue in Canada

De Beers had another problem in Canada. The country was too close to the United States for the US Justice Department not to notice what it did. If De Beers won a contract from a Canadian diamond mine for the marketing of a large part of its diamonds, there was a serious danger that the US Justice Department would use the Sherman Act against them. The major Canadian diamond mining companies knew this and were careful. If De Beers were to reduce the danger from competitive marketing it would need to find another route.

The Canadians were not so wary of Maurice Tempelsman and his company, Lazare Kaplan International. So when the Tahera prospecting company sought to market the diamonds from its Jericho diamond deposit, just south of the Arctic Circle near the Bathurst Inlet, it was pleased to find what seemed like a safe pair of hands for its diamonds in Lazare Kaplan. It decided to give it marketing rights to 75-100 percent of all its diamonds, signing a Letter of Intent in March 2003. This letter also gave Lazare Kaplan a right to participate on the same terms in any further discovery.

DE BEERS AND HUMAN RIGHTS

There was another key element in De Beers' new "Supplier of Choice" strategy; the reform of its Sightholders system, through which it supplied its rough gem diamonds to the world market. It would first rename the Central Selling Organization (CSO) that supplied these merchants, calling it the Diamond Trading Company (DTC). It remained wholly controlled by De Beers.

The merchant chosen to be a Sightholder would come as before to London every five weeks to pick up a box of diamonds, but now would have more say over its contents. He would also have, for the first time, the security of a contract, even if only for two years. The number of Sightholders would be cut to around 125. These would be selected from merchants able to afford large and expensive boxes; probably all would be multi-millionaires.

But the new Sightholders, from July 2001, would have to submit to tighter conditions. They would have to prove to the DTC that they were ethically acceptable, agreeing not to deal in conflict diamonds, and to have nothing to do with child labor or other socially unacceptable practices.

They would be permitted to return the larger of the diamonds in their boxes, after they were cut, to be inscribed with the De Beers' logo. Thus De Beers sought to guarantee that all its stones were ethically clean. It hoped this system would help protect their diamonds against the kind of consumer backlash that had hit the fur trade at the end of the last century.

Nicky Oppenheimer said, "We believe this strategy will make our DTC marketing arm the first choice for rough diamonds."

The ethical standards were entirely laudable. But would these merchants and De Beers deliver? There were many human rights abuses in the diamond trade that would have to be eliminated.

They still had many difficulties over conflict diamonds. Alex Yearsley of Global Witness reported in November 2002, "Despite two years of repeated promises, the diamond industry has failed to deliver a detailed and credible self-regulating system that will stem the flow of conflict diamonds." How could De Beers then guarantee its stones were not from conflict zones?

De Beers has frequently engaged in unusual behavior. I was most surprised to find De Beers listed in a British government Green Paper tabled in the House Of Commons on February 12th, 2002 entitled, "Private Military Companies: Options for Regulation." This listed entities that had employed private military companies in Africa. De Beers' name came up five times. No other corporation was named more than once. According the British Government, De Beers had employed these mercenary outfits in Angola, Namibia and twice in Botswana for "Covert Reconnaissance."

On October 27th, 2002 the United Nations, in a report commissioned by the Security Council, named De Beers and Anglo American as companies that had violated ethical guidelines through their involvement in the Democratic Republic of the Congo (DRC).

This was a severe blow to De Beers since it so much depended on its good name, a name that was now its brand. Brian Roodt of De Beers said the company was puzzled by its inclusion. "We're trying to get hold of the UN to find out what the specifics are in relation to their allegations."

But De Beers knew why it was in trouble in the Congo.

A year earlier, in 2001, Amnesty International had inspected the main center for diamond mining in the Congo, the rich MIBA mines in Mbuji-Mayi that had once provided the US with its vital industrial diamond stockpile. It reported these were now a scene of daily shootings, frequent murders, maiming and illegal imprisonment, all at the hands of guards posted to protect the mines. Amnesty noted that De Beers held a minority financial interest in MIBA and requested De Beers' help in ending these abuses.

Amnesty's observers witnessed the gunfire aimed at the illegal prospectors. Bodies were found in the rivers by the diamond mines. There were atrocious conditions in the mine's jails, where prisoners were not provided with toilet facilities, showers, or even food. They were instead supposed to be fed by relatives, who had to pay the guards for the privilege. The average age of the prisoners was 15.

Amnesty reported, "Every day, blood is being spilled in the diamond fields of government-controlled Democratic Republic of Congo and nobody in the international community is taking any notice… Dozens of suspected illegal diamond miners, including children, are being shot dead every year, and many more are being seriously wounded, by security guards who are flouting the law with apparently complete impunity."

In the poverty-stricken, chaotic Congo, only just emerging from a war that had killed over two million people, where malnutrition now affected a quarter or more of the population, the lure of MIBA's diamonds was too great to resist. Many hundreds tried to make an illegal living by stealing from its diamond concessions. "In so doing, they were taking an enormous personal risk and many paid the ultimate price at the hands of armed security guards." Amnesty International called these "extrajudicial executions. … There is effectively a state of anarchy reigning in the diamond fields of Mbuji-Mayi."

The MIBA-hired guards worked alongside both government and Zimbabwean troops, and Amnesty reported that all three took part in these atrocities. The Zimbabwe forces were there at the government's invitation. They had played a vital role in protecting the mines from an invading Rwandan army but, as the Congo's government did not have the money to pay them, it had instead rewarded Zimbabwe with a share in these diamond fields.

The guards shot mostly the desperate young and very poor who did not have the money to pay them. But every night the guards would let in and take money from "over a thousand" who could afford to pay them, allowing them into the mines to mine illegally under the cover of darkness.

Amnesty reported, "Guards will often give a group of illegal miners a password which they must use to leave the concession at the end of their clandestine shift; in October 2001 the price of a password was the equivalent of about $7 US dollars.

Sometimes the miners are also charged per head, and the guards frequently also insist upon a share of the diamonds gathered. Given that on any particular night there are likely to be over a thousand illegal miners within the polygone [area of alluvial diamond mining], it is easy to see that guards working in complicity with these miners stand to add significantly to their official wages, which are understood to be around $10 a day." Sometimes the guards, after taking money, would "renege on those deals, demanding a larger share than originally agreed or simply taking everything at gunpoint. In some cases, guards have opened fire without warning on the very people they had earlier taken bribes from and allowed into the concessions."

The illegal miners allowed inside would frantically "dig holes some 20 to 30 meters deep, lower each other down by rope, and then tunnel out horizontally from the bottom of the holes in search of diamonds." Amnesty witnessed a group of some 70 illegal miners engaged in this.

MIBA says that they regularly bulldoze over these holes but that the illegal miners simply dig new holes. Amnesty International received disturbing reports, however, that MIBA officials were sometimes guilty of bulldozing over the holes without properly checking whether there were miners down the holes at the time. For example, five illegal miners, including Mandefu Tshiovo Kabeya, who was just nine years-old at the time, were reportedly buried alive in April 2000.

Amnesty found, "Local journalists and human rights activists who denounced these human rights abuses have been arbitrarily detained and subjected to other forms of intimidation. [Yet,] to Amnesty International's knowledge, not a single MIBA guard has ever been put on trial, let alone convicted, for the unlawful killing of an illegal miner."

Senior MIBA officials interviewed by Amnesty denied much of this was happening. One official conceded that there was occasionally what he described as an accident, in which illegal miners were shot. He claimed to know of only two such "accidents" having occurred since the beginning of 2001. Disturbingly, he also conceded that when illegal miners were killed within the diamond concessions, MIBA took no steps to investigate the circumstances of the death. In answer to a question on what was done by MIBA in such situations, the official simply replied, "Rien" ("Nothing").

This picture of misery was added to when a United Nations Panel of Experts reported in October 2002 on the *Illegal Exploitation of the Natural Resources and Other Forms of Wealth of the Democratic Republic of the Congo (DRC)*.

It was not just the illegal miners that stole from MIBA. The UN reported that the management of the mine probably stole far more. "The State-owned Société Minière de Bakwanga (MIBA) diamond company has been plundered by management that condones widespread theft by company insiders." It continued: "These losses are probably modest compared to the losses from a third theft ring that involves high level MIBA managers and occurs inside the cleaning, sorting and classification operation facility. The thefts include gem and near-gem production. About 50 percent of all company revenues are generated by the three to four percent of gem and near-gem production. The drop in revenues resulting from theft has been estimated at about 25 per cent of total revenue, roughly 25 million dollars per annum.

Under pressure from its creditors, MIBA was obliged to engage the services of a private security firm, Overseas Security Services, which determined that a criminal syndicate was operating inside the classification operation." It seemed to me that a system remained in place similar to that organized by Mobutu earlier for his self-enrichment.

Congo's foreign minister, Okitundu, welcomed most of the UN report, disagreeing only with its treatment of Zimbabweans. He thought the Panel was wrong to equate Zimbabwe, whose troops propped up the Kinshasa government, with Uganda and Rwanda, who had invaded his country. Zimbabwe's soldiers, he said, have "paid the price of blood in order that the Democratic Republic of the Congo shall live."

But the Congolese diamond leases used to pay for Zimbabwe's military help, in practice benefited private companies belonging to a small circle close to President Mugabe; creating what the UN described as an "inner circle of Zimbabwe Defense Forces diamond traders who have turned Harare into a significant illicit diamond-trading center."

The UN described the consequence in the Congo. Public health was so bad that "12 per cent of all children under 5 years old died every year." Very few of these "deaths resulted from violence. Deaths instead result from illness – malaria and dysentery: conditions closely linked to malnutrition and the absence of medical facilities." Four out of the five fresh water plants in the region surrounding these diamond mines had broken down. The remaining plant was operating at ten percent of capacity.

The report might give the impression that nothing was going right in the DRC. But in 2002 the value of the official diamond exports went up by 40 percent over 2001 to a total value of $396 million. Most of these diamonds were not from the major mines but from small-scale producers who had sold their production legitimately within the country. In 2002 the total production of these smaller producers was worth $321 million, or 81 percent of the total. MIBA should have had a much larger share but its production was slashed by corruption and theft.

The UN then described how the pillaged diamonds, many taken out by the invading forces of Uganda and Rwanda, had traveled to the international markets:

> Reliable sources have told the Panel that gem diamonds from Mbuji-Mayi in the Democratic Republic of the Congo account for much of the phenomenal increase in diamonds transiting through Dubai in recent years. Exports from the United Arab Emirates to Antwerp increased to $149.5 million in 2001 from $4.2 million in 1998, according to the Diamond High Council. The Panel has been told of chartered flights direct from Mbuji-Mayi to Dubai, and other routes via Dar es Salaam, on which illicit diamond exports have been carried. Likewise, Dubai has become a transit point for coltan from the Uganda-controlled area and a portion of the diamonds originating from Kisangani in the Rwanda-controlled area. The arms and diamond smuggler Victor Bout uses the United Arab Emirates as his permanent base, with nine of his aircraft stationed at Ra's al Khaimah.

Bout was of course the notorious arms smuggler we met in the Introduction. In April 2003 Global Witness brought out a report entitled: *For a Few Dollars More: How al Qaeda moved into the diamond trade.*

It had discovered by closely reading the records of al-Qaeda members on trial in the United States that diamonds were frequently mentioned as an easy source of wealth, and that diamonds were traded by al-Qaeda not only in West Africa but also in Kenya. It also noted that Hezbollah has traded diamonds in Africa for much longer than al-Qaeda. Most of the diamonds traded in Kenya and the other East African states would have come out of the Congo.

Global Witness used the danger that terrorists posed to argue that the Kimberley Process needed teeth if the use of diamonds to fund terrorism were to stop. But it seemed to me that their approach needed broadening. I was alarmed to find trading in non-conflict illicit diamonds listed as deserving to be suppressed as rigorously. In the vast majority of cases illicit stones have no connection with any militaristic operation and none with conflict diamonds. They are much more often the product of traders trying to escape taxes or to evade exclusive government marketing deals that had the effect of restricting prices.

Global Witness also focused exclusively on Arab terrorism as if it were the major problem in diamond-producing Africa. As documented in this book, this is simply not true. Its operations in the diamond fields of Africa are of minor consequence, compared with the impact of those controlled by the West. Charles Taylor in Liberia was mostly funded by an American-based operation, not by any of the listed terrorist groups. CIA and Mossad people have long operated in the African diamond trade, as have numerous European and American mercenary firms. And, above all, it is mostly European and South African mining interests that have profited in the impoverished and pillaged diamond fields of Africa over the past one hundred years.

In March 2003 De Beers and Anglo American were shocked when they heard that the Truth and Reconciliation Commission had recommended to the South African government that businesses be made to pay reparations to victims of apartheid, and had specifically singled out South Africa's mining corporations, saying that there was a particularly strong case against them because of their behavior under apartheid.

This ruling was immediately followed up by the launch of a legal action in the United States against De Beers and Anglo American. This took advantage of the "US Alien Tort Claims Act" that allowed federal courts to hold liable any entity that had violated the laws of other nations. This law enabled Holocaust survivors to successfully sue Swiss banks and German and Austrian companies that used slave labor. The lawyer who had this success, Ed Fagan, was now claiming multibillion dollar compensation from Anglo and De Beers for the victims of apartheid. The South African government said it would not intervene, but would follow the case with interest.

Did De Beers also bear any responsibility for the situation in the Congo? Both Amnesty International and the UN believed this was so. Amnesty concluded:

Although the primary responsibility for addressing the human rights violations associated with MIBA's diamond concessions lies with the DRC state authorities, MIBA itself also has a role to play in promoting respect for human rights within its sphere of influence. Considered as a state actor, MIBA is bound by the provisions of international human rights law, but as a business entity it is also expected to meet the same ethical standards of corporate practice required of all businesses. This applies equally to the minority shareholders in MIBA, De Beers and Umicore.

The Congo Government owned 80 percent of MIBA, with the remaining 20 percent owned by a group called Sibeka, made up by De Beers, with a 19.56 percent stake, and a Belgian company called Umicore (formerly Union Miniere). Both Sibeka and Union Miniere had once played a major role in the Diamond Syndicate.

De Beers lost influence in the Congo when Kabila came to power, because of its relationship with Mobutu. Since then it had kept its head down and waited for things to change. During the war in the Congo: "The DRC government exercising direct political and operational control over the company." It employed some 6,000 workers and around 1,300 security guards. Its official annual turnover [after pillaging] was "in the region of $70 million."

De Beers responded to the UN charge of October 2002 by saying it was puzzled, acting as if it had no business interest there. But a month earlier De Beers had spoken of its interest in promising new prospects in the Congo. Anglo American's Michael Spicer likewise denied any involvement in the Congo, telling Reuters the miner "had had no operations in the Congo since the 1960s." But, while the UN was completing its investigation, Anglo had been developing a project in the Congo. It had only ended its involvement three months before the publication of the UN report.[8]

The UN warned that corporations had grave duties in such situations. It noted that "Belgium and the United Kingdom had stressed the burden of ensuring transparency in commercial and financial flows or supply chains should be borne primarily by private companies and should be based on either voluntary measures or the OECD Guidelines for Multinational Enterprises."

The UN Panel then published a list of corporations that were acting the Congo "in violation of the OECD Guidelines for Multinational Enterprises."

This list included De Beers and Anglo American, as well as one American, one Swiss and six Belgian diamond-trading companies. It listed De Beers and Anglo American as legally compelled to follow these Guidelines, since their country of registration had adopted the Guidelines.

Amnesty International wondered at the limitations of the Kimberley Process, for it certified as "conflict free" the diamonds produced by MIBA. These stones were produced by a legal government-owned mine. Only stones traded by rebels could not be given a "conflict free" certificate.

Amnesty noted that, "There has so far been no international pressure on the DRC government to break the link between its diamond trade and human rights abuses. On the contrary, in April 2002 the DRC government was able to sign, unchallenged, a new international system of diamond certification agreed through the Kimberley Process. The international system is intended to stem the trade in so-called conflict diamonds by armed political groups.

"It seems hypocritical for the DRC government to flaunt its apparent commitment to respecting human rights by joining the Kimberley Process, when serious abuses linked to its own diamond trade are occurring on a daily basis."

Amnesty made a particularly strong plea for support from De Beers since it was part of MIBA. It noted:

De Beers has itself developed a series of best practice principles for the gem diamond industry, part of the objective of which is to ensure that the diamond trade is not associated with, or complicit in, abuses against local populations. For example, under the heading "Consumer confidence," De Beers' principles state that:

The injury and hardship suffered by local populations (and the potential for it) when conflicts arise in diamond producing areas are unacceptable, as is seeking to profit from such conflicts.

Under the heading "Business Practices," the De Beers text continues:

We are committed to operating our businesses in such a way that we neither engage in, nor encourage in any manner, the following practices which are regarded as unacceptable and against the public interest and that of the diamond industry: [...] [the] buying and trading of rough diamonds from areas where this would encourage or support conflict and human suffering.

Amnesty finished up asking De Beers and the other minority shareholders in MIBA to "Take every step to ensure that their involvement in the DRC's diamond trade is consistent with their obligations under international law to promote and respect human rights within their sphere of influence."

Likewise Stephen Corry of Survival International has noted other human rights areas that the diamond industry needs to address if its diamonds are to be regarded as truly "clean." He wrote:

De Beers in Botswana has done worse than merely shirk its responsibilities towards those whose lands it might want to mine. By spuriously claiming that indigenous peoples' rights could lead to apartheid – an assertion which would be comical if it were not so tragic – it is actively trying to repress the movement towards justice for southern Africa's indigenous peoples ... De Beers, by denying the rights of Africa's indigenous peoples, by exploring and mining their land with impunity, by joining with governments which are destroying them – "like Siamese twins" as Botswana's president says of his relationship with De Beers – De Beers stands shoulder to shoulder with him in the dock, guilty of the destruction of some of the world's "first people," as the Bushman of the Kalahari call themselves. Rather than simply deploring the situation, and walking away, what is simply needed is a code for prospecting and mining enshrining international human rights law, enforced by a truly effective revised Kimberley Process.

In 2003, the UN was also very concerned about human rights in the diamond mines of Sierra Leone. Reportedly rebels were not mutilating children any longer in the diamond mines, but, in March 2003, the United Nations Under-Secretary-General Olara A. Otunnu, declared one of the "tremendous challenges" still ahead for Sierra Leone was stemming the extensive use of children as labor in diamond mines. [9]

Yet, the diamonds they produced could be legitimately labeled conflict free. The Kimberley Process simply was not sensitive enough to rule this out. Thus, diamonds produced by child labor were still marketed as clean diamonds to unsuspecting consumers, and might even be graced with a De Beers logo.

The Kimberley Process, outlawing Conflict Diamonds, was by early 2003 enshrined in law in the United States with some 60 other countries also actively working to implement it. Despite all its shortcomings, this was a very important moment. For the first time a serious legally mandated effort was being made to clean up the diamond trade. The Clean Diamond Trade Act summarized why this was so:

"Congress finds the following:

(1) Funds derived from the sale of rough diamonds are being used by rebels and state actors to finance military activities, overthrow legitimate governments, subvert international efforts to promote peace and stability, and commit horrifying atrocities against unarmed civilians. During the past decade, more than 6,500,000 people from Sierra Leone, Angola, and the Democratic Republic of the Congo have been driven from their homes by wars waged in large part for control of diamond mining areas. A million of these are refugees eking out a miserable existence in neighboring countries, and tens of thousands have fled to the United States. Approximately 3,700,000 people have died during these wars."

Precautions were built into the Act to ensure its effectiveness. Not the least among these was a requirement for the General Accounting Office (GAO) to issue a report in two years on the effectiveness of the Act. Before the Act was passed, the GAO issued a most trenchant critique of the Kimberley Process as it stood, saying that it had no independent monitoring and could be ineffective.

As the Kimberley Process came to be mandated in law around the world in 2003, the pressure started to grow for a "Round Two" that would give it real teeth, with independent monitoring and verification, with it extended to cover other human rights violations within the diamond trade. Only if this happened could the intent enshrined in the very name of the Clean Diamond Trade Act be actually realized.

This move to have a Round Two alarmed the Chairman of De Beers, Nicky Oppenheimer. At a dinner on April 29th, 2003 hosted by De Beers for the delegates from 60 countries to a Kimberley Process conference, Nicky Oppenheimer said he did have, "one area of apparent concern and debate. At the Conflict Diamonds Conference held in Washington recently the agenda spoke of 'Phase Two' of the Kimberley Process. It was pointed out by one delegate that there is no 'Phase Two,' that the mandate of the Process was to tackle conflict diamonds – nothing more, nothing less …This is, of course, absolutely correct. There is no mandate to go beyond conflict."

He admitted, "we must do all we can within Kimberley, as agreed by all parties, to prevent the abuse of diamond resources – vital to the producing countries." But continued: "In order to do this, there is no need to extend or exceed the mandate or to set up Kimberley Two. The provisions you have all so skillfully crafted provide the industry with precisely the insulation it requires to ensure that any diamond that tarnishes the image of our beautiful product and threatens the integrity of our business is excluded utterly and completely."

The reason why there needs to be a "Kimberley Two" lies precisely in his final words. If there is no revision to the certificate, then human rights abuses will continue to tarnish the diamond. Currently there is utterly no guarantee that a certificated "Kimberley Process" stone will not have been cut illegally by a child working in dangerous conditions, or mined by a miner breathing asbestos dust, or come from land from which indigenous people have unjustly evicted. In other words, the intentions of the legislators will have been violated. The diamonds sold in our shops may have Kimberley Certificates, but they will not have been guaranteed clean.

This is however a time of change, and a time when, with good will, we could have a system of "Clean Diamond Certificates" that truly enforce codes of conduct for miners and for cutters, protecting the rights of all. A chance to make diamonds not just a sign of human love, but also a sign of human justice and fair play. If this book in any way contributes to this, then it was well worth writing.

It is quite astonishing that De Beers has managed to continue to fix the world diamond prices into the 21st century and to dominate the diamond market, despite so many challenges. But it seemingly has not put anywhere near the same effort into ensuring that justice and fair play were enshrined in its business practices, into ensuring that diamond cutters were not exploited and that healthy working conditions prevailed in the trade. If it had, then this book would not have needed to be written.

1   The promotion of labels rather than value had helped create a worldwide protest movement as documented by Naomi Klein in her book *No Logo*, published in 2000.
2   I am referring to the children's story in which an emperor was sold clothes that were so fine, or so said the merchant, that they could not be seen. The emperor paid generously and was very proud as he walked around clad in nothing else but his new invisible clothes.
3   Sally Westwood. "A Real Romance: Gender, Ethnicity and Risk in the Indian Diamond Trade." Lecture delivered on September 18th, 2000, at the East Indies House. Professor of Sociology, University of Leicester.
4   Press Statement by De Beers in December 2000 made in response to press reports of al-Qaeda trading in conflict diamonds. Buying on "the open market" seemingly was not the same as buying diamonds from companies like De Decker, which allegedly brokered diamonds from UNITA.
5   Report on the webpage of the Diamond Ombudsman of the Republic of South Africa. March 2002.
6   *Mail on Sunday*. London. November 17th, 2002.
7   Rapaport, *Diamonds.net* Website. August 9th, 2001. This contains the fullest description of the case that I could find.
8   Reuters, October 22nd, 2002.
9   *The Reporter*, Gaborone, Botswana. March 7th, 2003.

Epilogue – Dangers of the Hunt: The Making of *The Diamond Empire* and of this book

I have told how the hunt of the diamond cartel began for me under the fat trunked boab tree at Oombulgurri. But helicopter borne police were by no means the only danger. Between the start of this adventure and the conclusion of this book lay over 20 years. At first I thought maybe two years, perhaps three. I had no idea how long and hard a hunt it would be.

Author with Aboriginal woman, traditional owner of sacred site and anthropologist aiding in fight to protect it.

I should have been warned when one of my first funders, Film Victoria, an Australian state government body, insisted that I insure my life, naming it as the beneficiary. I was then sure that they were being utterly paranoid.

My initial newspaper article on diamonds was published in 1981 and told that the world's biggest diamond deposit had been discovered in Australia and De Beers sought control of it. The article, my first for a major paper, was of an audacious size, three broadsheet pages long. It was advertised on television and nationally syndicated.[1]

I had written it because I did not want to see ensconced in Australia a company so deeply involved in apartheid. Before it appeared, I briefed Paul Keating, a future Prime Minister who was then Opposition Leader. This led him to condemn in Parliament the "negligence of the Government" in leaving the marketing of Australia's diamonds to "the whim of individual companies and the caprice of De Beers." However when he became Prime Minister he did nothing to change this.[2]

De Beers had to fight hard to get control over Australian diamonds – and to stop it acquiring a strong cutting industry. A rival proposal from major Belgian diamond merchants proposed an alternative line up of producing states. The Indian Prime Minister came to Australia to back an alliance that would cut out De Beers.

My articles may have educated, even entertained, but politically they failed. De Beers mounted what Ernest Oppenheimer's lieutenants called his "spring offensive."

He has since boasted of how he took personal charge of this campaign. Some journalists were flown all expenses paid to South Africa.

I decided to investigate the cartel's operations worldwide. This I knew would be a costly process no paper could finance, so I wrote a proposal for a television series. I tried to secure for this an interview with Harry Oppenheimer. De Beers' senior executive in Australia gave me dinner high in a sterile office tower and politely, urbanely, agreed to try to help.

I then discovered that the US Justice Department had been hunting De Beers for half a century. I requested its files under US Freedom of Information legislation. Thousands of pages came. I received FBI and spy reports, intercepted letters, and hundreds of leads. My previous low budget film, on gold mining and Aborigines, had won an Australian Film Institute Nomination as one of the year's best documentaries.[3] This helped me now in fund raising.

In 1987 Jonathan Holmes of the Australian Broadcasting Corporation (ABC) became very enthusiastic about my film project, but he needed other broadcasters to share its costs. A month later he phoned from England to say he had interest from the BBC. "Would I be ready to start on March 17th?" But March came, April then May. The BBC hierarchy was unexpectedly slow to ratify plans but, in the meantime, not wanting to waste time, the ABC sent me on an initial research trip. I was excited, riding high. Then in New York I saw De Beers' advertising agents, N. W. Ayer. They asked me who backed the project. I told them the ABC, and added naively that I hoped for the BBC. Ayer got in touch that day with De Beers in London. Next day with a one paragraph fax, the BBC Controller declined our film.

I urgently had to find a replacement investor to keep the project alive. I searched London, and within two weeks had serious expressions of interest from both Thames Television and Channel 4. The producer at Thames had just made the controversial *Death on the Rock* documentary on the SAS killings of IRA agents in Gibraltar. He had a reputation for strong, bold films, as had Roger Bolton, its executive producer.

I went to see De Beers in London to see if they would allow us to film their mines and sorting rooms. I met them at their Central Selling Office in Westgate House near the diamond merchants of Hatton Garden; a street known in the 18th century as the hangout of highwaymen and villains. It was where Charles Dickens placed his criminal mastermind "Fagin." De Beers' people were aloof, refined perhaps, but not the gentry that rode to hounds. They seemed more to me like the Oxford graduates that planned coups and spying missions and discussed Mozart. When I went to see them, they discussed the diamond trade as if it were their fiefdom and I the lady-in-begging.

But by now I had sufficient television support to make De Beers take my project seriously. The ABC sent Jonathan Holmes to London. He met with Thames and Channel 4 and suggested I choose Thames as they had more money. He advised me to get myself ready. Once again my film seemed about to happen.

I was back in Australia when I heard by phone that Thames had decided they needed the consent of De Beers in advance before they would make this film. This was a great surprise. Getting the advance permission of corporate "targets" was not usual in investigative television. Jonathan Holmes of the ABC was astonished. He told

Thames that they would need to secure my approval before approaching De Beers as it was my project, but they went to De Beers regardless.

I abandoned Thames and went to Channel 4. It agreed and said its initial funds would be invested in two weeks. My film was still alive. But three weeks later a fax came saying Channel 4 could not invest "in the foreseeable future" since someone else by a "remarkable coincidence" had proposed to do a film on diamonds with the blessing of De Beers!

I flew back to London and sat on Channel 4's doorstep for two months, showering them with research, showing that De Beers were not so mighty. I proved I could get information from inside the cartel; that I could do this without De Beers' agreement and could probably gain the filming access needed. Channel 4 then agreed to fund my research. Two months later I began a trip around the world with a consultant film director to research the series and hopefully this book.

It was not easy. We were banned from the giant new Australian diamond mine, even though we had backing from British and Australian television – and even though they let in tourists. But we gained access to the nearby smaller but important Bow River diamond mine.

We went to Russia to talk to its cagey diamond people. From here we traveled to Israel where we met Chaim Even-Zohar, the editor of the world's leading diamond magazine *Mazal U'Bracha*. He was ensconced behind Fort Knox-like security in the twin diamond trading towers of Ramat Gan. He greeted me very affably; "So you are the lady half the diamond trade wants to talk to and the other half wants to avoid?" I laughed this off but was rather perplexed. He smiled and told me he was talking all the time to De Beers in London. He then asked: "'How did you get on in Moscow?" He surprised me again. I had not mentioned to anyone in Israel my visit to Moscow. He then said that our every movement had been monitored for three months, ever since we got Channel 4's support.

In Israel a major diamond merchant found himself in trouble for helping us find accommodation in a Tel Aviv hotel. A letter came from the cartel asking sharply why he was assisting us. This arrived just after he had proudly opened in front of us his monthly box of diamonds from the CSO, finding in it a magnificent gemstone. He displayed this to our cameras, as if it were a badge of merit. The Syndicate's letter now made him fear he would find in his next box poor quality diamonds. He had us immediately write a letter saying that he had not really helped us much at all.

I left the heavily protected Israeli diamond cutting factories and went to visit an Arab jeweler in Jerusalem. I was with him in a car when it went out of control on a straight road at low speed, hit a rock and somersaulted. I could not understand the world I saw when we stopped moving. We were upside down, hanging by seat-straps. I feared the car might catch fire. I tried to kick out a window, but my companion more sensibly wound a window up and we escaped.

We were waiting by the wrecked car for a friend to arrive from Jerusalem when a passing bus stopped. The passengers swarmed out carrying cameras and raced across to us. The leader panted, "Are you OK?" I was scarcely able to say "Yes" before he had asked out his second question. "Are you baptized?" He ignored my obviously Arab companion. I muttered, perplexed, "Yes," whereupon he turned to his companions and cried out "Alleluia. She would have been saved if she had died." They answered with more exultant "Alleluias" and "Amens." This seemed totally unreal, so like a scene from a black-humor movie that it was scarcely believable.

I blinked, shook my head. The delusion continued with prayer and a sermon. Struggling back to reality, all I could think of was the implicit insult to my companion, for his salvation was obviously of no concern to them. I called out "Who said only the baptized go to heaven?" "The Bible, sister" the leader replied. He opened the book, jammed his finger on a text and held it out to me. Our friend arrived at this time to take us back to Jerusalem and, as we drove off, I opened the window and called out: "You Pharisees!" I found next day that I was in considerable shock from the blow to my head. I suffered from concussion for the next three months as I struggled on with the project. We never found out why the car went out of control.

As I was recuperating I met an independent diamond miner by a Swiss mountain lake. His boats sucked diamonds off the seabed near Namibia with giant vacuum cleaners. He said it was quite easy money as the seabed there was littered with diamonds. He agreed to us filming his operation – but first wanted to check with his friends in London – who were also friends of De Beers. He was surprised to be told not to cooperate with us. He strode agitatedly around the room, then said, "No one is going to tell me what to do. I would like you to come and I will invite you." Other diamond merchants later reacted similarly to De Beers' big brother tactics.

At this point, I lost the funding from Channel 4. But the script was researched and written, so I took it to WGBH, the makers of the investigative North American program *Frontline*. They enthusiastically pre-purchased it immediately. They wanted it as a feature-length special. Within four days, the BBC also said they wanted the program and would take it as a three part series of one hour documentaries. I had now raised two thirds of the needed funds. The BBC was willing to guarantee in writing that this would be an Australian production controlled by my Australian company. This opened the way for me to get the rest of my budget from the Australian government.

I then approached the Australian Film Finance Corporation (FFC) for the remaining funding I needed for *The Diamond Empire*. It normally funded all Australian productions that raised a third of their budgets internationally. I had raised two thirds and thus had high expectations.

We obtained the funding but, just as we were going into production, an FFC officer phoned to tell me I must renew a government certificate of our project as Australian within four days. I protested that our certificate did not need renewal, and that such certificates were never issued in less than ten days, but he insisted, saying that if I did not obtain it in four days, our funding would be cancelled. When a perplexed Australian government department told me it could not see why I needed a new certificate and in any case could not issue another so quickly, our funding was cancelled and was not restored when the new certificate came in the usual ten days. It felt as if our film was being sabotaged.

Some months later, after much lobbying, the FFC board again decided to fund our project. The FFC officer who phoned to tell me the decision congratulated me, then chuckled. He added that there was a new condition. It was that I persuade the

BBC to cover all financial risks. I was stunned. I knew that the BBC had earlier refused the FFC this very unusual guarantee. Such a condition would abort the funding offer – as he probably knew. I asked him, "Has any other filmmaker been asked for such a guarantee?" He could not remember. On checking I found no other documentary maker had ever been asked to obtain one. I also learned the FFC board had not been told that this guarantee would be a problem. A board member told me it had slipped past practically unnoticed. He was surprised; he would have expected to be told if it presented a difficulty.

I skim over these events, but at the time it was very hard to keep the film alive. I had raised many hundreds of thousands of dollars, but needed to raise the entire budget if any funds were to arrive. We had planned an expensive project that would investigate De Beers in five continents. I was not interested in a fight against the FFC. My sights were set elsewhere. I was concerned about issues such as child labor and consumer exploitation. I knew I was planning a tough movie against men with very powerful connections in the financial world. I just did not anticipate how much such a film would scare potential funders.

I negotiated as agilely as a circus acrobat to raise the needed funds and some months later I finally succeeded. The FFC removed its impossible condition. I now had all I needed to carry out the world's most international of television investigations. But by now my personal resources were exhausted. The FFC finally stipulated that I had to personally pay the costs incurred by these delays, even though they were not of my doing. I was also instructed that I was not to have a salary equal to that of the director I hired, nor even to have a production fee or profit margin. All this did not matter to me. What was important was at last we were getting into production.

We first went to shoot in India. De Beers did not realize that we were there at first. Diamond merchants promised us interviews. Then they received phone calls telling them not to cooperate. But I gentled my way in. I turned up unexpected in their offices, smiling and open, camera crew behind me, asking powerful merchants for their assistance. They could not be impolite. They honored the pledges they had made before coming under pressure from De Beers.

William Goldberg.

After India we went to the United States. Here Tiffany's, Harry Winston, and nearly all the leading Fifth Avenue jewelers refused to take part in the film, despite my asking in the name of the BBC and WGBH.

Then William Goldberg, a leading diamond merchant on Fifth Avenue, agreed to an interview but when we turned up he suggested he was the wrong man. Alarmed, I asked him if he had received a phone call. He answered, "I was told you worked for blacks in Australia and made life difficult for diamond mining companies." I confessed this was true and told him of my work for Aborigines. I told him how they, like Jews, had land they regarded as sacred. He then agreed to be interviewed and gave us lunch.

Garsin, a former employee of Tempelsman, changed his mind about being interviewed on camera but only after he had told us about deals done with Mobutu.

We secured over 20 interviews in the US despite all threats. I was now credited by the BBC as the producer and principal journalist. The shoots came in precisely on budget, as had the Indian. The film was underway. Our interviewees told us tales of the romance and dealing, of the trickery, power and influences that shaped a fascinating trade in which men sold diamonds as an ornament of women and as an icon of human love.

I renewed contact with the Oppenheimers. When I had contacted them years earlier, their staff had told me they would consider being in our film when we had raised the needed finance. But instead the gloves came off the corporate fists.

The film director I had hired, Gavin McFadyen, wrote to Nicky Oppenheimer to discuss access to De Beers' facilities. The reply came from him personally:

Your project does sound an interesting one. The diamond industry is certainly very fascinating and with its diverse participants would make engaging television viewing, and I am sure there is much that you would wish to discuss with me and my colleagues at De Beers.

Your letter did arouse my curiosity in one particular respect. Industry gossip has, for some time, been reporting that a group of people whose past projects have been very anti-mining, were considering producing a documentary on diamonds. I assume the BBC would not be involved in production of a partisan documentary, but it does seem to be rather coincidental! I look forward to getting more details of the various areas you are planning to cover so that we will be able to see where we can be helpful to you.

Yours sincerely, Nicky Oppenheimer.

Oppenheimer then phoned our director to invite him to a butler-serviced lunch at 17 Charterhouse Street, the cartel's London headquarters. When the director saw me afterwards, he reported the "conversation over lunch was totally about you." He was told that, "We need extraordinary guarantees that Jan Roberts would not guide the whole series."

They noted that I had written the contracted script. The director told me he replied (to my astonishment) that my script "was no longer part of the architecture of the series." He told me he had pretended this was so for tactical reasons, although my script was mandated by our contracts. His reply did not satisfy Oppenheimer. He said that I was clearly central to the film as I controlled the purse strings.

McFadyen by now was becoming unnerved by the unremitting hostility of De Beers. He wrote again to De Beers, this time to say the BBC would guarantee that my views would be tempered with other views. This was of course true. He told me this was meant to be a soothing letter. My script remained the contracted script. But I began to suspect he might advise the BBC that the only way to resolve these problems would be if I were sacrificed.

A second letter came from De Beers – this time from Nicky Oppenheimer's companion at lunch, Fleur de Villiers. It conveyed the decision by De Beers not to help the film and then added:

The other matter which still causes us grave concern is the extent of Ms. Janine Roberts' involvement, given her record of fierce antagonism to mining and to the companies involved in it. You emphasized at our lunch and state in your letter that the BBC would take steps to ensure that the series did not reflect one person's view

of the industry. Nevertheless, Ms. Roberts is described in your Commissioning Editor, Singer's letters of introduction as "the producer," and "principle journalist" [sic] of the programme and as the person who has 'agreed to organize and implement the filming schedule.' I am sure you will understand, therefore, that our doubts about the impartiality of the programme remain.
Yours sincerely, Fleur de Villiers.

It was not long after this that McFadyen had a private meeting with Andre Singer of the BBC, our Commissioning Editor. When he returned, he stunned me by saying: "Singer had a very good idea. He suggested you do the book of the series and we do the film. He will try to get you a BBC book contract." In this case "we" was the director, McFadyen, and his friend of many years, Laurie Flynn, the BBC's representative on our project – both long term friends of Singer's. When I said, "No way, this is my film," Flynn and McFadyen then refused to go on the next shoot to Africa with me. They maintained their stand for weeks, wrecking our schedule and budget. They knew contractually I could not sack them without the BBC's permission. Yet I was legally responsible to the investors for bringing the film in on budget. I felt blackmailed and was shocked. They remained determined to take control over the film.

I went to Singer at the BBC to ask what I should do. He told me the BBC would not permit me to sack them, and that it was two against one. He promised to supervise the African shoot in my stead, if I let them go without me, and to ensure this shoot came in on budget. He assured me that I otherwise remained fully in charge of the script and project. These promises were noted between us in writing.

I gave way because it was my job to keep the project alive. I was afraid of it being cancelled. I had worked hard to create it in the hope that it would in some way help improve conditions in the diamond industry. I had some comfort in thinking that my script was still contractually mandated; that I had already shot a large part of it and

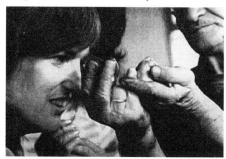

that the BBC was now policing it. I thought perhaps the director could not work with a woman. I remembered how he had been cantankerous in India, exploding when I asked a crew member to stop whispering during one of my filmed interviews. He had frostily told me that only he as director had the right to address crew members. Another time, when he was too ill to direct and so sent me out to film alone, he had become angry when I

Author inspecting a diamond.

later said how good "my" crew had been. When I reminded him that I had hired him, he had exploded; "You promised not to mention that!" But, my job as producer had been to soothe feelings, and keep things going on location as smoothly as possible. This I had done. The Indian shoot had been successful. I had hired the director after the BBC had approved him. The BBC then stipulated his hire in our contracts, so I now had to live with my mistakes and attribute them to my inexperience. But Flynn, McFadyen and Singer of the BBC were old friends and I was, in this context, the outsider. I had thought their friendship would strengthen the film, but this had proven mistaken.

I was then dismayed to be told that the crew had gone very greatly over budget while in Africa despite the BBC's supervision and guarantee, and had not got what was expected. I was legally responsible for this over-spend as the producer. All my pleas for a crisis meeting with the BBC now seemingly fell on deaf ears.

The accountant then formally advised me that I must notify the insurers and ask them for help. The shoots I controlled had come in on budget so I expected their support, but instead the insurers to my surprise warned me, saying that since I was officially the "employer" of Flynn and McFadyen, I was responsible for their over-spending and so could be removed. I was aghast! I now think I had been naïve. The insurers would have realized that their only way of getting the needed funds from the BBC would be to do its bidding.

My control over the film was rapidly slipping away. The minutes of a discussion at the BBC recorded that the BBC's Commissioning Editor, Andre Singer, said to Laurie Flynn and to others on my staff, "Jan Roberts is outgunned."

Then on November 1st, 1992 a gang obtained entry into my home. I was assaulted sexually and, when I resisted, my head was used as a punch-bag, my cheekbone fractured, my nose broken. There was no attempt to rob me. They fled when I managed to use an emergency button to contact security. The consequent pains, trauma and concussion troubled me for years. A cracked lens in my one good eye required surgery in 1997.

The day after the assault the insurers ambushed me. They asked if I could come to see them, then astonished me by demanding to my damaged face that I stop work on the film. It was to be given to my British staff. Flynn, my researcher, was to become the producer. When I asked for reasons, they refused them. But I was able to resist, for our film's Australian funding had been given on condition that the producer was a resident of Australia – and Flynn was English. I was left wondering at the coincidence of this happening immediately after the beating. I flew back to Australia to seek support. My lawyer advised me to take the BBC to arbitration to force it to meet its contracts. I did so – and the BBC lawyers tried to settle out of court.

But I found my body just could not take the trauma any longer. I had thought myself tougher than I was. I had not fully recovered from the beating. The Royal Women's Hospital in Melbourne to my surprise and shock found I was in critical danger from a deep vein thrombosis. The hospital Registrar warned me that I would be in danger of death for the next two weeks. I was given a buzzer and told to keep it in my hand at all times. I was to use it if I felt myself going unconscious. I went onto oxygen as my lungs were blocked with blood clots. I had never been ill like this before, nor ever had such a warning.

The next day I had to use the buzzer and the nurses rushed and saved me, and the following day a barrister acting for the BBC and FFC insisted that I sign immediately a contract giving up my film to the BBC and stopping my arbitration action against the BBC. If I did not, I was threatened with the film being terminated. If I agreed, I was told my script would be adhered to.

The doctors and nurses asked if they could bar the lawyers from me. But the lawyers had already told me that, if I did not agree, they would take legal action to try to seize the film in two days time while I was still critically ill. I never had conceived the BBC could so act. I had no money for a lawyer and, in any case, was much too ill to find one in the time I had. I was now seriously worried that the stress would indeed kill me. In disgust and anger I threw their contract across the ward.

I now sadly realized that the only way I had to protect my life from this pressure, to make the BBC drop their pressure on me and still to keep the film alive, was to sign the wretched thing giving them the film. I tried to protect my rights by signing a statutory declaration that I had agreed to the BBC demands only under duress. I was confident that no court would uphold a contract signed in such circumstances. I could not believe the BBC could have acted so ruthlessly. I knew if I found a scene like this in a script I would scrub it out as much too melodramatic.

My statutory declaration in a scrawling, labored handwriting said: "*I was on Wednesday 12th May 1993, told that I would not be given my right to defend myself if I choose not to sign the settlement… Because I was told that I had no chance to defend myself, I agreed to the out of court settlement. I knew that if I did not agree the film would be killed.*"

I would not have signed if the BBC had not at the same time formally promised to complete the film according to my script, and to send me within seven days any film research material they possessed so I could write a book of the investigation behind the film. Yet none of the promised research material came. They had what they wanted from me.

As I recovered, I reflected that I had given myself to this investigation perhaps to a ridiculous degree. I am not sure why I was so tenacious. For good or bad, the diamond world became part of my world. Yet, I was determined not to be silenced. I decided I would write this book even if no help came from the BBC. I was left alone by the cartel as I started to write it. I think they thought me defeated and certainly I was traumatized.

However De Beers knew they had not completely silenced me. Perhaps it knew the BBC retained a legal commitment to make the film to my script. It now hired a leading public relations company that specialized in monitoring investigative documentaries. Its Managing Director went to our interviewees to discover what they had told us. A diamond merchant received the following letter from John Stoneborough, Managing Director of Walborough Media Relations. The name of the merchant is deleted to protect him.

STRATEGIC ADVICE
PROGRAMME INFORMATION DATABASE
Dear Mr. [name deleted],
Further to my conversation with your office manager, we are a media relations consultancy currently under contract to Hill and Knowlton, Public Relations consultants to De Beers at Charterhouse Street, London.
We have been retained to advise them on a forthcoming BBC documentary on the Diamond Industry, scheduled for the spring of 1993.
In my conversations with Mr. (name deleted), I have been led to understand that you may have been asked to take part in this programme? If this is correct
I would appreciate the opportunity of discussing the interview with you.
I shall try to call you
Yours Sincerely, John Stoneborough.

Such a letter would make most diamond merchants very nervous – given their dependence on De Beers. The dossier Walborough gathered was put to immediate use. T. W. H. Capon of De Beers sent a letter to the Managing Director of the BBC saying, "Despite the lack of specific information on the programme contents we have been compiling an extensive dossier… to assist you in your obligation of accuracy, balance and impartiality… unless it is your intention to withhold information about the contents of the programme from us, we would ask you to supply us with a transcript… without delay, in order that we can provide you, where necessary, with the background material."[4]

Will Wyall, the BBC executive, replied to this on September 29th, 1993. He said: "The production process is not yet complete" and therefore a film copy was "not available."[5]

De Beers did not wait for the BBC to provide a copy. They acquired a copy of the unreleased film in a final cut version. How De Beers achieved this no one knew, as the BBC always keeps tight security on investigative documentaries. It was rumored that De Beers had acquired it indirectly from the ABC in Australia. The ABC had dropped *The Diamond Empire* from its schedule a week before it was to be transmitted, allegedly under pressure from De Beers. It would not show it in Australia even after it had been transmitted in North America and the UK.

De Beers' solicitors, Peter Carter-Ruck and Partners, wrote to the BBC on September 24th, 1993 asking the BBC to remove from the film an interview with Gordon Brown, a former De Beers employee, who described in the film the ill treatment suffered by black miners at De Beers' hands. Brown had been found to be a reliable witness by Justice Thirion during his Commission's inquiries.[6] Carter-Ruck now attacked Gordon Brown's credibility by extraordinarily alleging that he offered to stop our film if De Beers paid him to do so.

Some months later I met with Brown in Namibia. He had a very different account of what had happened. He alleged De Beers had asked him not to cooperate with the BBC and to give them his copies of sworn statements from witnesses who alleged De Beers had traded in smuggled Angolan diamonds, ivory and rhino horn.

De Beers did not succeed in stopping the film's release in the US. It aired in prime time as a special episode of *Frontline*. The *New York Times* reported in its review of the film, "If you believe that diamonds are rare, romantic or forever, you have very likely been dazzled by the international diamond cartel." When I saw the film, I was delighted. WGBH had followed my script as contracted. The film was powerful and strong. They used my interviews. I was off-camera during interviews but my voice was in the film. But I was mystified to discover at its end that I had received no credit for my work as producer and interviewer. I asked WGBH why. They wrote to say these credits were removed on instruction from the BBC.

The BBC then scheduled the documentary for broadcast in two parts in the UK on Sunday April 17th and April 24th 1994 at 9:05 PM, an excellent time slot. I had a week's notice of the broadcast – not courtesy of the BBC, but by my mother noticing it in the schedules.

The General Secretary of the Media Union, BECTU, intervened to have my credits as producer and writer restored before it was broadcast, but the BBC's

Secretary-General replied to say that, although I had worked as the producer and writer, I had given the BBC the right to change the credits when I signed away the film in hospital. When I protested that I only did so to protect myself when critically ill, he coldly replied that he did not dispute the circumstances. He had my affidavit in front of him but he still maintained what I signed for them was legal.

The first episode ran well and strong, as I had wanted in great measure. I was delighted, had champagne with friends. De Beers may have succeeded in getting rid of me but they had not stopped my film. But when I saw the second episode I was dismayed by the cuts. All mention of Australian Aborigines had been deleted as well as of any questionable deals in Australia. The contracted third hour of my film had totally vanished.

But I was still pleased that it had come out. I did not want a fight with the BBC. The object of the exercise was to make a film that illuminated the abuses in the diamond trade. The film did this. It was now out, shared with millions. But I was still perplexed why the BBC had insisted on removing my main production credit. Only when I watched it on video for the second time did I notice to my surprise that I had had a major victory. My name was featured full screen and Flynn's credit as Producer had vanished. Someone at the BBC had taken note of my protest. True, I was now credited only for the original idea and development, but as prominently as if I had the producer's credit.

I later saw an extraordinary letter sent to the BBC by the De Beers' solicitors. It indignantly complained that my name was still in the credits despite the BBC's assurance that I had been removed. They accused the BBC of reneging on its word. I thus had it confirmed that the BBC had earlier tried to placate De Beers over my removal. The solicitors said De Beers remained very unhappy that the film said the high price of diamonds was not due to their rarity but because De Beers had restricted their production. De Beers in its anger now threatened the BBC with legal action.

A BBC lawyer contacted me. He asked, "De Beers is threatening us with legal action. We understand you did all the research for the film. We need your help to defend the film. Would you be willing to help us?" He invited me to dinner to discuss this. When we met I agreed to help, on condition that the BBC restored my credit as producer whenever the film was shown in future. He agreed – much to my surprise. Why had the BBC refused me earlier? It seemed it was all right when they needed me. But a few days later the lawyer told me that they would not be able to give me credit as producer but would have to find some other similar form of words. He explained, "Apparently we promised De Beers not to credit you as producer."[7]

The BBC never agreed that a word of the film was false or libelous nor did any court find against it, but extraordinarily, under pressure from De Beers, the BBC promised it would not sell the film for broadcast in any other countries, despite having earlier contracted with my company to distribute it.

Thus, although my film was shown in North America and in the UK without being found libelous, it has not been sold to either South African or Namibian television, both of which I understand sought to buy it, or to other countries for fear of provoking De Beers. Likewise my film was never seen in Australia. I hope one day it will be.

But afterwards I found to my surprise that this was not the end of my investigation. I was to tour the film through the diamond mines of De Beers in Southern Africa and, while doing this, discover much that is in this book. I was also to travel with the film to Arctic Canada and to the lands of the Dene where De Beers' threats to stop the film's exhibition caused me to be invited to speak before the people of Yellowknife.

I then obtained from Transworld, now a division of German media giant Bertelsmann AG's Random House, one of the world's largest publishers, an international contract for a book on the diamond trade. They were so impressed with the first draft that they sent me their "Reader's Comments." She stated that "Jan Roberts' exposure of the diamond cartel is sensational, well documented and very controversial. The allegations and claims within it make it an important book, but also a marketable book... It could be a hot property correctly handled."[8] They even lent me free of charge an apartment with a servant on the slopes of Table Mountain in which to stay while I researched the diamond industry in southern Africa for this book. When the time of publication drew near, Transworld gave the book a rave write-up in their Forthcoming Titles catalog. They told me that two major newspapers were competing for serialization rights.

But then something happened. Perhaps someone from Anglo American noticed it in the catalog. They would have seen it, for they were investors in Transworld in South Africa, as the publishers had told me. Within three months of when my book was due to appear under the renowned Doubleday imprint, it was canceled. Transworld said "notable and powerful businessmen and politicians" would not want the book to appear and, although it might win any legal action, it still feared the legal cost. I was shocked, to say the least, to have the plug pulled at the very last minute, and again wondered if outside pressure had been exerted.

For the next few years after this, the major publishers I approached would not touch the book. The rejection seemed to have tainted it. Little Brown, part of AOL Time Warner, wrote when they first saw my manuscript saying clearly it would make a "superb" book, then wrote again saying that they hoped I would find a publisher that was "less cowardly."

When I put up a website on diamonds to ensure that I was not totally silenced, the editor of the leading diamond magazine *Mazal U'Bracha* wrote to me to tell me that De Beers and Maurice Tempelsman had examined my site, as had the Argyle diamond companies in Australia. He noted that the Australians were surprised how accurate it was on Argyle.

The editor advised me to take down what I had put up as it was "too valuable" to leave up for free downloads. I also received congratulations from the official valuer of diamonds for the Republic of South Africa who wrote saying that he also had many problems with De Beers, as did many others. He put up a direct link between his website and my own to help promote my book.

The website led to me being invited to testify before the United States Congress in February 2001, and it also helped find me a publisher. The book you hold in your hands is the result.

If I could speak of what I would like to see; I would like diamonds to regain their true sparkle, for them to become a symbol of nature's richness, an emblem of freedom

South African children living by a De Beers diamond mine.

rather than of avarice – and to be of much greater benefit to the African diamond-rich nations.

I am now looking forward to this book appearing. I hope it will finally get this investigation out of my hair. I hope now that I have not been so badly bitten by the diamond hound that I cannot let go, relax and spend a few years in a hot bath.

In this book diamonds have served as a window through which I have taken you, my readers, inside the glitter and greed of the most extraordinary of cartels. Thank you for traveling with me.

1   *The Age.* August 22nd, 1981.
2   124 Hansard. H. Of R., 27 August 1981, at 864, 865.
3   *Munda Nyuringu: He's taken the land, he believes it is his, he won't give it back,* co-produced and co-directed by Aboriginal Elder Robert Bropho and Janine Roberts, 1984.
4   From T. W. H. Capon of 17 Charterhouse Street, on September 10th, 1993 to the Managing Director of the BBC, Will Wyatt, occasioned by a BBC press release about our film.
5   Quoted by Peter Carter-Ruck and Partners, acting for De Beers, in a letter of February 14th, 1994 to Roy Baker, Litigation Department, BBC.
6   Thirion Commission. Eighth Interim Report, p. 317.
7   Meeting between Roy Baker of the BBC's litigation department and the author.
8   "Reader's Report for Transworld Publishers." Carol Flyod, February 1st, 1994.

Glossary

Anglo American	Anglo American plc, a publicly traded company based in the UK and owning a major share of De Beers, founded by Ernest Oppenheimer.
Argyle	The name of a major diamond mine in northwest Australia that is ultimately owned and controlled by Rio Tinto (formerly RTZ) of London.
BHP Billiton	The current identity of a much expanded Australian mining company originally known as Broken Hill Proprietary Ltd., that from 2000 has mined diamonds in Canada and extracted them offshore in South Africa.
Briefke	A small rectangular sheet of white paper folded to store cut diamonds.
Brilliant	A cut round diamond.
Brutting	The process of applying the girdle to a cut gem. (Normally covered by the mounting.)
Carat	A fifth of a gram. The weight measure of a diamond.
CAST	Consolidated African Selection Trust, a Ghana-based diamond mining company, the corporate parent of SLST in Sierra Leone.
CDM	Originally an abbreviation for Consolidated Diamond Mines, Ltd., a company founded by Ernest Oppenheimer to mine diamonds in South West Africa, now called Namibia. Namdeb has now replaced it.
CSO	The Central Selling Organisation, made up of several De Beers-owned and controlled companies, that sells uncut diamonds to selected diamond merchants. In 2003 this function was taken over by another De Beers entity, the Diamond Trading Company.
Clarity	The structural quality of a diamond.
CRA	An Australian subsidiary of Rio Tinto of London.

Crown	The upper side of a cut diamond.
Cut	Shape and quality of the cutting of a diamond.
CZ	Cubic Zirconium sold as an imitation diamond.
D	A completely colorless cut diamond.
D-Flawless	D in color, and flawless, as seen with the 10x magnifying loupe.
De Beers	The company set up originally by Cecil Rhodes to control the diamond production of South Africa and to exclusively sell these diamonds to the Syndicate in London. In 2003 it is a private corporation, 45% owned by a Liberian-registered Oppenheimer family company, 45% owned by Anglo American plc (a company in which the Oppenheimers also play a commanding role) and 10% by the Debswana Diamond Company (Pty.) Ltd., a company owned in equal shares by the government of the Republic of Botswana and De Beers Centenary AG.
DIAMANG	Companhia de Diamantes de Angola, a company set up to exploit the diamond resources of Angola.
Diamantaire	Anyone professionally involved with diamond manufacturing or marketing.
Diamond Cartel	The corporate mechanism by which De Beers controls the marketing and pricing of most of the world's rough diamonds. Also see "Syndicate."
Diamond Corporation	A De Beers-owned company, set up to purchase the production of non-De Beers-owned diamond mining companies.
Diamond High Council	The "parliament" of the Antwerp diamond industry. (Also known as DHC or HRD.)
Diamond Trading Company	A De Beers-owned company (DTC) that sells rough diamonds to diamond merchants.
Fancy Colors	Naturally colored diamonds, excluding many less intense browns since there are too many of them on the market to excite a high price.
Four Cs	The four qualities by which a cut diamond is judged, carat, color, clarity and cut.
GE	General Electric, an American company that makes artificial diamonds.
GIA	The Gemological Institute of America; has a diamond-grading laboratory.
Girdle	The thin circular mid-section or equator of a cut diamond.
HDC	Hindustan Diamond Company, a joint venture of the Indian government and the DTC.
HRD	See Diamond High Council above.

I	Imperfect. A stone in which a flaw can easily be seen.
IDB	Illicit Diamond Buying. A crime in southern Africa.
IF	Internally Flawless gem.
Kimberlite	A volcanic rock that may contain diamonds.
Kimberlite pipe	A volcanic plug-hole filled by kimberlite.
Loupe	A jeweler's 10x standard magnifying glass.
Make	The proportions and finish of a cut diamond.
Melange	A mixed parcel of diamonds of varying grades and sizes.
Melee	Smallish diamonds.
MIBA	Societe Generale de Bakwanga, the principal diamond-mining company in the Congo.
MPLA	The Popular Movement for the Liberation of Angola, Angola's governing party.
Namdeb	A company owned between De Beers and the Namibian Government, under De Beers' effective control, to mine diamonds on and offshore.
NGO	Non-Governmental Organization. Often concerned with humanitarian issues. May be independent or dependent on government funding.
NMDC	National Mineral Development Corporation Limited, an Indian Government-owned rough diamond trading company that also operated India's only diamond mine, the small Panna mine.
Pavilion	The underside of a cut diamond.
Polished	A finished cut diamond.
Rough	An uncut diamond in its natural state.
Rio Tinto	A London-based major mining company, formerly known as RTZ. Also incorporates CRA Limited of Australia.
RUF	A major armed rebel movement in Sierra Leone that financed itself from mining and selling uncut diamonds.
SI	Slightly Imperfect clarity grade in a cut diamond.
Sibeka	Societe d'Enterprise et d'Investissements du Beceka. The Belgian-owned company that once controlled MIBA and through it the major diamond mines of the Congo. In 2002 it still retained a small interest in MIBA. It was also part of the Syndicate.
Sightholder	A diamond merchant invited to buy rough diamonds on a regular basis.
Sights	Normally refers to the five-weekly inspection and delivery of rough diamonds to the invited Sightholders by the CSO or DTC. Also refers to similar occasions organized by other diamond mining

	companies.
SLST	Sierra Leone Selection Trust, the original diamond-mining corporation in Sierra Leone.
Syndicate	In-trade reference to either the CSO or DTC, the corporate mechanism by which De Beers controls the marketing and pricing of most of the world's rough diamonds. The term originally meant the London-based syndicate of diamond buyers to which De Beers sold its entire diamond production.
UNITA	National Union for the Total Independence of Angola. A major armed rebel-movement in Angola, once heavily supported by covert American aid, since then dependent on revenues from illicit diamond marketing.
VSI	Very Slightly Imperfect cut diamond. A clarity grade.
VVSI	Very Very Slightly Imperfect clarity in a cut diamond.

Selected Bibliography

Balfour, Ian. *Famous Diamonds*, London: Collins, 1987.

Bruton, Eric. *Diamonds*, 3rd ed. London: N.A.G. Press, 1976.

Chhotalal, Kantilal. *Diamonds: From Mines to Markets*. Bombay: The Gem & Jewellery Export Promotion Council. 1990.

Epstein, Edward Jay. *The Rise and Fall of Diamonds: the Shattering of a Brilliant Illusion*. New York: Simon & Schuster, 1982.

Flynn, Laurie. *Studded with Diamonds and Paved with Gold: Miners, Mining Companies and Human Rights in Southern Africa*. London: Bloomsbury Publishing Ltd., 1992.

Gregory, Theodore. *Ernest Oppenheimer and the Economic Development of Southern Africa*, London: Oxford University Press, 1962

Gooch, Charmain, and Yearsley, Alex. *A Rough Trade*. London: Global Witness Ltd., 1994.

Hart, Matthew. *Diamonds: A Journey to the Heart of an Obsession*, New York: Walker and Company, 2001.

Hocking, Anthony. *Oppenheimer and Son*. Johannesburg: McGraw-Hill, 1973.

Jessup, Edward. *Ernest Oppenheimer: A Study in Power*, London: Rex Collins Ltd., 1979.

Kalb, Madeleine, *The Congo Cables: The Cold War in Africa – from Eisenhower to Kennedy*. New York: Macmillan Publishing Co. Inc., 1982.

Kanfer, Stefan. *The Last Empire: De Beers, Diamonds and the World*. New York: Farrar Straus Giroux, 1993.

Koskoff, David E., *The Diamond World*, New York: Harper & Row, 1981.

Krajick, Kevin. *Barren Lands: An Epic Search for Diamonds in the North American Arctic*. New York: Times Books, 2001

Lanning, Greg. with Marti Mueller, *Africa Undermined: Mining Companies and the Underdevelopment of Africa*. London: Penguin Books, 1979.

Legrand, Jacques. *Diamonds: Myth, Magic and Reality*. Maillard, Robert, editor-in-chief. New York: Crown Publishers, Inc., 1980.

Nkrumah, Kwame. *Challenge of the Congo: A Case Study of Foreign Pressures in an Independent State*. London: Panaf Books, 1967.

Ray, Ellen; Schaap, William; Meter, Karl Van and Wolf, Louis, eds., *Dirty Work 2:*

The CIA in Africa. Secaucus, NJ: Lyle Stuart Inc., 1979.

Smillie, Ian; Gberie, Lansana; and Hazleton, Ralph. *The Heart of the Matter: Sierra Leone, Diamnds and Human Security,* Ottawa: Partnership Africa Canada, 2000.

Stockwell, John. *In Search of Enemies: A CIA Story.* New York: W. W. Norton & Company, 1978.

Wharton-Tigar, Edward (with Wilson, A. J.) *Burning Bright: The Autobiography of Edward Wharton-Tigar,* London: Metal Bulletin Books Ltd., 1987.

Witte, Ludo De. *The Assassination of Lumumba.* Translated by Ann Wright and Renee Fenby. London: Verso, 2001.

Appendix

Clean Diamond Trade Act H.R.1584

One Hundred Eighth Congress
of the
United States of America
AT THE FIRST SESSION

Begun and held at the City of Washington on Tuesday,
the seventh day of January, two thousand and three
An Act
To implement effective measures to stop trade in conflict diamonds, and for other purposes.
Be it enacted by the Senate and House of Representatives of the United States of America in Congress assembled,
SECTION 1. SHORT TITLE.
This Act may be cited as the 'Clean Diamond Trade Act'.
SEC. 2. FINDINGS.
Congress finds the following:
(1) Funds derived from the sale of rough diamonds are being used by rebels and state actors to finance military activities, overthrow legitimate governments, subvert international efforts to promote peace and stability, and commit horrifying atrocities against unarmed civilians. During the past decade, more than 6,500,000 people from Sierra Leone, Angola, and the Democratic Republic of the Congo have been driven from their homes by wars waged in large part for control of diamond mining areas. A million of these are refugees eking out a miserable existence in neighboring countries, and tens of thousands have fled to the United States. Approximately 3,700,000 people have died during these wars.
(2) The countries caught in this fighting are home to nearly 70,000,000 people whose societies have been torn apart not only by fighting but also by terrible human rights violations.
(3) Human rights and humanitarian advocates, the diamond trade as represented by the World Diamond Council, and the United States Government have been working to block the trade in conflict diamonds. Their efforts have helped to build a consensus that action is urgently needed to end the trade in conflict diamonds.
(4) The United Nations Security Council has acted at various times under chapter VII of the Charter of the United Nations to address threats to international peace and security posed by conflicts linked to diamonds. Through these actions, it has prohibited all states from exporting weapons to certain countries affected by such conflicts. It has further required all states to prohibit the direct and indirect import of rough diamonds from Sierra Leone unless the diamonds are controlled under specified certificate of origin regimes and to prohibit absolutely the direct and indirect import of rough diamonds from Liberia.
(5) In response, the United States implemented sanctions restricting the importation of rough diamonds from Sierra Leone to those diamonds accompanied by specified certificates of origin and fully prohibiting the importation of rough diamonds from Liberia. The United States is now taking further action against trade in conflict diamonds.
(6) Without effective action to eliminate trade in conflict diamonds, the trade in legitimate diamonds faces the threat of a consumer backlash that could damage the economies of countries not involved in the trade in conflict diamonds and penalize members of the legitimate trade and the people they employ. To prevent that, South Africa and more than 30 other countries are involved in working, through the

'Kimberley Process', toward devising a solution to this problem. As the consumer of a majority of the world's supply of diamonds, the United States has an obligation to help sever the link between diamonds and conflict and press for implementation of an effective solution.

(7) Failure to curtail the trade in conflict diamonds or to differentiate between the trade in conflict diamonds and the trade in legitimate diamonds could have a severe negative impact on the legitimate diamond trade in countries such as Botswana, Namibia, South Africa, and Tanzania.

(8) Initiatives of the United States seek to resolve the regional conflicts in sub-Saharan Africa which facilitate the trade in conflict diamonds.

(9) The Interlaken Declaration on the Kimberley Process Certification Scheme for Rough Diamonds of November 5, 2002, states that Participants will ensure that measures taken to implement the Kimberley Process Certification Scheme for Rough Diamonds will be consistent with international trade rules.

SEC. 3. DEFINITIONS.

In this Act :

(1) APPROPRIATE CONGRESSIONAL COMMITTEES- The term 'appropriate congressional committees' means the Committee on Ways and Means and the Committee on International Relations of the House of Representatives, and the Committee on Finance and the Committee on Foreign Relations of the Senate.

(2) CONTROLLED THROUGH THE KIMBERLEY PROCESS CERTIFICATION SCHEME- An importation or exportation of rough diamonds is 'controlled through the Kimberley Process Certification Scheme' if it is an importation from the territory of a Participant or exportation to the territory of a Participant of rough diamonds that is—

(A) carried out in accordance with the Kimberley Process Certification Scheme, as set forth in regulations promulgated by the President; or

(B) controlled under a system determined by the President to meet substantially the standards, practices, and procedures of the Kimberley Process Certification Scheme.

(3) EXPORTING AUTHORITY- The term 'exporting authority' means 1 or more entities designated by a Participant from whose territory a shipment of rough diamonds is being exported as having the authority to validate the Kimberley Process Certificate.

(4) IMPORTING AUTHORITY- The term 'importing authority' means 1 or more entities designated by a Participant into whose territory a shipment of rough diamonds is imported as having the authority to enforce the laws and regulations of the Participant regulating imports, including the verification of the Kimberley Process Certificate accompanying the shipment.

(5) KIMBERLEY PROCESS CERTIFICATE- The term 'Kimberley Process Certificate' means a forgery resistant document of a Participant that demonstrates that an importation or exportation of rough diamonds has been controlled through the Kimberley Process Certification Scheme and contains the minimum elements set forth in Annex I to the Kimberley Process Certification Scheme.

(6) KIMBERLEY PROCESS CERTIFICATION SCHEME- The term 'Kimberley Process Certification Scheme' means those standards, practices, and procedures of the international certification scheme for rough diamonds presented in the document entitled 'Kimberley Process Certification Scheme' referred to in the Interlaken Declaration on the Kimberley Process Certification Scheme for Rough Diamonds of November 5, 2002.

(7) PARTICIPANT- The term 'Participant' means a state, customs territory, or regional economic integration organization identified by the Secretary of State.

(8) PERSON- The term 'person' means an individual or entity.

(9) ROUGH DIAMOND – The term 'rough diamond' means any diamond that is unworked or simply sawn, cleaved, or bruted and classifiable under subheading 7102.10, 7102.21, or 7102.31 of the Harmonized Tariff Schedule of the United States.

(10) UNITED STATES- The term 'United States', when used in the geographic sense, means the several States, the District of Columbia, and any commonwealth, territory, or possession of the United States.

(11) UNITED STATES PERSON- The term 'United States person' means—

(A) any United States citizen or any alien admitted for permanent residence into the United States;

(B) any entity organized under the laws of the United States or any jurisdiction within the United States (including its foreign branches); and

(C) any person in the United States.

SEC. 4. MEASURES FOR THE IMPORTATION AND EXPORTATION OF ROUGH DIAMONDS.

(a) PROHIBITION- The President shall prohibit the importation into, or exportation from, the United States of any rough diamond , from whatever source, that has not been controlled through the Kimberley Process Certification Scheme.

(b) WAIVER- The President may waive the requirements set forth in subsection (a) with respect to a particular country for periods of not more than 1 year each, if, with respect to each such waiver—

(1) the President determines and reports to the appropriate congressional committees that such country is taking effective steps to implement the Kimberley Process Certification Scheme; or

(2) the President determines that the waiver is in the national interests of the United States, and reports such determination to the appropriate congressional committees, together with the reasons therefor.

SEC. 5. REGULATORY AND OTHER AUTHORITY.

(a) IN GENERAL- The President is authorized to and shall as necessary issue such proclamations, regulations, licenses, and orders, and conduct such investigations, as may be necessary to carry out this Act .

(b) RECORDKEEPING- Any United States person seeking to export from or import into the United States any rough diamonds shall keep a full record of, in the form of reports or otherwise, complete information relating to any act or transaction to which any prohibition imposed under section 4(a) applies. The President may require such person to furnish such information under oath, including the production of books of account, records, contracts, letters, memoranda, or other papers, in the custody or control of such person.

(c) OVERSIGHT- The President shall require the appropriate Government agency to conduct annual reviews of the standards, practices, and procedures of any entity in the United States that issues Kimberley Process Certificates for the exportation from the United States of rough diamonds to determine whether such standards, practices, and procedures are in accordance with the Kimberley Process Certification Scheme. The President shall transmit to the appropriate congressional committees a report on each annual review under this subsection.

SEC. 6. IMPORTING AND EXPORTING AUTHORITIES.

(a) IN THE UNITED STATES- For purposes of this Act -

(1) the importing authority shall be the United States Bureau of Customs and Border Protection or, in the case of a territory or possession of the United States with its own customs administration, analogous officials; and

(2) the exporting authority shall be the Bureau of the Census.

(b) OF OTHER COUNTRIES- The President shall publish in the Federal Register a list of all Participants, and all exporting authorities and importing authorities of Participants. The President shall update the list as necessary.

SEC. 7. STATEMENT OF POLICY.

The Congress supports the policy that the President shall take appropriate steps to promote and facilitate the adoption by the international community of the Kimberley Process Certification Scheme implemented under this Act.

SEC. 8. ENFORCEMENT.

(a) IN GENERAL- In addition to the enforcement provisions set forth in subsection (b)—

(1) a civil penalty of not to exceed $10,000 may be imposed on any person who violates, or attempts to violate, any license, order, or regulation issued under this Act ; and

(2) whoever willfully violates, or willfully attempts to violate, any license, order, or regulation issued under this Act shall, upon conviction, be fined not more than $50,000, or, if a natural person, may be imprisoned for not more than 10 years, or both; and any officer, director, or agent of any corporation who willfully participates in such violation may be punished by a like fine, imprisonment, or both.

(b) IMPORT VIOLATIONS- Those customs laws of the United States, both civil and criminal, including those laws relating to seizure and forfeiture, that apply to articles imported in violation of such laws shall apply with respect to rough diamonds imported in violation of this Act .

(c) AUTHORITY TO ENFORCE- The United States Bureau of Customs and Border Protection and the United States Bureau of Immigration and Customs Enforcement are authorized, as appropriate, to enforce the provisions of subsection (a) and to enforce the laws and regulations governing exports of rough diamonds, including with respect to the validation of the Kimberley Process Certificate by the exporting authority.

SEC. 9. TECHNICAL ASSISTANCE.

The President may direct the appropriate agencies of the United States Government to make available technical assistance to countries seeking to implement the Kimberley Process Certification Scheme.

SEC. 10. SENSE OF CONGRESS.

(a) ONGOING PROCESS- It is the sense of the Congress that the Kimberley Process Certification Scheme, officially launched on January 1, 2003, is an ongoing process. The President should work with Participants to strengthen the Kimberley Process Certification Scheme through the adoption of measures for the sharing of statistics on the production of and trade in rough diamonds, and for monitoring the effectiveness of the Kimberley Process Certification Scheme in stemming trade in diamonds the importation or exportation of which is not controlled through the Kimberley Process Certification Scheme.

(b) STATISTICS AND REPORTING- It is the sense of the Congress that under Annex III to the Kimberley Process Certification Scheme, Participants recognized that reliable and comparable data on the international trade in rough diamonds are an essential tool for the effective implementation of the Kimberley Process Certification Scheme. Therefore, the executive branch should continue to—

(1) keep and publish statistics on imports and exports of rough diamonds under subheadings 7102.10.00, 7102.21, and 7102.31.00 of the Harmonized Tariff Schedule of the United States;

(2) make these statistics available for analysis by interested parties and by Participants; and

(3) take a leadership role in negotiating a standardized methodology among Participants for reporting statistics on imports and exports of rough diamonds.

SEC. 11. KIMBERLEY PROCESS IMPLEMENTATION COORDINATING COMMITTEE.

The President shall establish a Kimberley Process Implementation Coordinating Committee to coordinate the implementation of this Act. The Committee shall be composed of the following individuals or their designees:

(1) The Secretary of the Treasury and the Secretary of State, who shall be co-chairpersons.

(2) The Secretary of Commerce.

(3) The United States Trade Representative.

(4) The Secretary of Homeland Security.

(5) A representative of any other agency the President deems appropriate.

SEC. 12. REPORTS.

(a) ANNUAL REPORTS- Not later than 1 year after the date of the enactment of this Act and every 12 months thereafter for such period as this Act is in effect, the President shall transmit to the Congress a report—

(1) describing actions taken by countries that have exported rough diamonds to the United States during the preceding 12-month period to control the exportation of the diamonds through the Kimberley Process Certification Scheme;

(2) describing whether there is statistical information or other evidence that would indicate efforts to circumvent the Kimberley Process Certification Scheme, including cutting rough diamonds for the purpose of circumventing the Kimberley Process Certification Scheme;

(3) identifying each country that, during the preceding 12-month period, exported rough diamonds to the United States and was exporting rough diamonds not controlled through the Kimberley Process Certification Scheme, if the failure to do so has significantly increased the likelihood that those diamonds not so controlled are being imported into the United States; and

(4) identifying any problems or obstacles encountered in the implementation of this Act or the Kimberly Process Certification Scheme.

(b) SEMIANNUAL REPORTS- For each country identified in subsection (a)(3), the President, during such period as this Act is in effect, shall, every 6 months after the initial report in which the country was identified, transmit to the Congress a report that explains what actions have been taken by the United States or such country since the previous report to ensure that diamonds the exportation of which was not controlled through the Kimberley Process Certification Scheme are not being imported from that country into the United States. The requirement to issue a semiannual report with respect to a country under this subsection shall remain in effect until such time as the country is controlling the importation and exportation of rough diamonds through the Kimberley Process Certification Scheme.

SEC. 13. GAO REPORT.

Not later than 24 months after the effective date of this Act , the Comptroller General of the United States shall transmit a report to the Congress on the effectiveness of the provisions of this Act in preventing the importation or exportation of rough diamonds that is prohibited under section 4. The Comptroller General shall include in the report any recommendations on any modifications to this Act that may be necessary.

SEC. 14. DELEGATION OF AUTHORITIES.

The President may delegate the duties and authorities under this Act to such officers, officials, departments, or agencies of the United States Government as the President deems appropriate.

SEC. 15. EFFECTIVE DATE.

This Act shall take effect on the date on which the President certifies to the Congress that—

(1) an applicable waiver that has been granted by the World Trade Organization is in effect; or

(2) an applicable decision in a resolution adopted by the United Nations Security Council pursuant to Chapter VII of the Charter of the United Nations is in effect.

This Act shall thereafter remain in effect during those periods in which, as certified by the President to the Congress, an applicable waiver or decision referred to in paragraph (1) or (2) is in effect.

Speaker of the House of Representatives.

Vice President of the United States and President of the Senate.

Index

Index